The Upper Room

DICTIONARY

of

CHRISTIAN
SPIRITUAL
FORMATION

The Upper Room

DICTIONARY

of

CHRISTIAN SPIRITUAL FORMATION

Keith Beasley-Topliffe, *Editor*

UPPER ROOM BOOKS®
NASHVILLE

Cover photo: Photodisc, Inc.
Cover design: Bruce Gore / Gore Studio, Inc.
First Printing: 2003

Library of Congress Cataloging-in-Publication Data
The Upper Room dictionary of Christian spiritual formation / Keith Beasley-Topliffe, editor.
   p. cm.
   ISBN 0-8358-0993-5
   1. Spiritual formation—Dictionaries. I. Beasley-Topliffe, Keith. II. Title: Dictionary of
Christian spiritual formation
   BV4501.3.U67   2003
   248'.03—dc21   2002010160

Printed in the United States of America

CONTENTS

INTRODUCTION

EACH CHRISTIAN GENERATION must discover for itself that experience *of* God and a living relationship *with* God are more important in our lives than knowledge *about* God. Or, to put it more briefly, Christian spiritual *formation* is more vital than Christian theological *information.* This was the great truth discovered by John Wesley in eighteenth-century England, by Jonathan Edwards in the American Great Awakening, by evangelists like Dwight L. Moody and Phoebe Palmer in the nineteenth century and by many recent writers on prayer and worship. We hunger to know God, not simply to know about God.

Each generation, therefore, produces its own books on prayer, its own accounts of Christian experience, its own guidance for those who would help others to grow spiritually. Each generation finds again the importance of small groups for spiritual nurture and accountability. And each generation rediscovers the riches produced by earlier generations of Christians, the spiritual classics.

The Upper Room, a United Methodist-related ecumenical organization dedicated to providing resources for spiritual growth and spiritual leadership, felt the time was right for a new dictionary of Christian spiritual formation, an introduction to the key people, practices, and ideas of Christian spirituality. Such a reference work could complement the volumes in *The Upper Room Spiritual Classics* and *The Spiritual Formation Bible.* It could aid pastors and others leading *Companions in Christ,* an intensive small-group experience in spiritual formation. There are, of course, many other introductions to Christian spirituality, even other dictionaries. None offers the practical help for American Protestant pastors, laity, and students that we felt was needed.

Our goal is to offer you a basic resource for exploring the history and practice of spiritual formation. While this dictionary contains articles on some of the key concepts in mystical theology, its primary emphasis is more practical: how we are formed and re-formed as Christians, and how we can be transformed by God's grace. This dictionary can help you answer practical questions:

What is spiritual formation?
Who is Teresa of Ávila and what did she teach about the spiritual life?

What are the stages of spiritual growth?
How does my personality affect the way I pray?
How could I start a covenant group for spiritual support?
What does it mean to abandon myself to God?

You will find several different types of articles in these pages. Many briefly introduce spiritual writers and models from the earliest Christians to the present. Others offer discussions of topics: African spirituality, awe, body and spirituality, community, compassion. Some offer methods of prayer or group practice such as *lectio divina*, breath prayer, or discernment. Many of these articles include a suggested individual or group process placed in a pagewide box. Finally, a few articles offer the text and history of particular prayers from the Lord's Prayer to the Serenity Prayer.

You can, of course, simply look up topics of immediate interest to you. But you might want to try browsing. Rather than starting at Abandonment and working your way through to Zinzendorf, you might begin with a major article and follow the cross-references (marked by **boldface** print) wherever they lead. Some good starting points would be the articles on Prayer, Imagery, Conformity to the Will of God, Dispositions, Discipline, and Stages of Spiritual Growth. Perhaps the most basic starting points are the articles on Spirituality and Formation, Spiritual. You might also want to look at the charts in the back of the dictionary that compare several major streams of Christian spirituality and cross-reference articles on those streams. If you desire greater depth than these articles offer, you may pursue the suggestions for further reading, which are basic next steps for your exploration of the topic, not exhaustive bibliographies.

You may wonder how to find what you want. Articles about people are alphabetized under the person's last name (Wesley, John), except when that is simply a place associated with the person (Francis of Assisi). Titles (Mother, Brother, Meister) are never used for alphabetizing. For further examples, see the special book title-to-author chart in the back of the dictionary. Articles about topics are easily found. Apart from the article on Spirituality itself, other articles with the words *spiritual* or *spirituality* in the title are under the other key word: Music and Spirituality or Reading, Spiritual.

Finally, each article ends with initials that identify the author of the article. The List of Contributors that follows this Introduction is alphabetized by those initials.

KEITH BEASLEY-TOPLIFFE, *Editor*

LIST OF CONTRIBUTORS

AHF – Albert H. Frank, assistant director of Moravian Music Foundation and adjunct Professor of Moravian Church History, Moravian Theological Seminary

ASJ – Amy Sturdivant Jennings, M.Div., Baptist, continuing education student with Stillpoint's mentorship program for spiritual direction in Nashville, Tennessee

BKB – Bernard K. Bangley, Presbyterian, retired pastor living in Lexington, Virginia; author of *Near to the Heart of God*

CIZ – Cynthia I. Zirlott, Ph.D., United Methodist, Executive Director of Souljourney-online.com; Christian educator, retreat leader, spiritual director

DDW – D. Darrell Woomer, United Methodist minister and musician; chaplain, Lebanon Valley College, Annville, Pennsylvania

EBA – E. Byron Anderson, United Methodist pastor, Assistant Professor of Worship at Christian Theological Seminary, Indianapolis, Indiana; editor of *Worship Matters*

EGH – E. Glenn Hinson, adjunct professor at Louisville Presbyterian Seminary and Lexington Theological Seminary; Senior Professor of spirituality and church history at Baptist Seminary of Kentucky; author of numerous books and articles on church history and spirituality

EJC – Elizabeth J. Canham, Episcopal priest, founder of Stillpoint Ministries; author of *Heart Whispers*; members.aol.com/hospimundi

EKM – Ellen K. McCormack, Ph.D., Soul Center Director, East Liberty Presbyterian Church, Pittsburgh, Pennsylvania

ELS – E. Lee Self, Christian Church (Disciples of Christ) ordained minister, retreat leader, and writer

EWF – Elizabeth W. Fribance, retired United Methodist pastor living in Mechanicsburg, Pennsylvania

FPS – Frederick P. Schenker, pastor of Trinity Evangelical Lutheran Church, Wexford, Pennsylvania

GAB – Grace Adolphsen Brame, Ph.D., teaches The Integration of Theology and Spirituality at LaSalle University; author of *Faith, the Yes of the Heart* and *Receptive Prayer*; lay Lutheran pastor, retreat leader, and professional singer

GSC – Gregory S. Clapper, Ph.D., United Methodist, Professor at University of Indianapolis; author of *As If the Heart Mattered: A Wesleyan Spirituality* and *When the World Breaks Your Heart: Spiritual Ways of Living with Tragedy*

HLR – Howard L. Rice, Presbyterian, Professor emeritus, San Francisco Theological Seminary; author of *The Pastor As Spiritual Guide*

HWC – Harry W. Camp, lawyer and spiritual director living in McMinnville, Tennessee

JB – James Byrne, pastor and teacher from Clackamas, Oregon

JCW – J. Cameron West, United Methodist minister; Vice President for Student Life and Dean of Students, Brevard College, Brevard, North Carolina

JEV – Jane E. Vennard, senior adjunct faculty in prayer and spirituality, Iliff School of Theology; author of *Praying with Body and Soul* and *Embracing the World*

Contributors

JHS – Julie Hilton Steele, United Methodist pastor from Cary, North Carolina

JLJ – Jan L. Johnson, writer, retreat leader, and spiritual director from Simi Valley, California; author of many books including *When the Soul Listens*

JLM – Jerry L. Mercer, professor at Asbury Theological Seminary, author, United Methodist minister (retired)

JLW – Jennifer Lynn Woodruff, librarian of the General Commission on Archives and History, Madison, New Jersey; Ph.D. candidate at Duke University, United Methodist clergy

JNE – John N. Elliott, United Methodist pastor (retired) from Franklin, Indiana

JS – Jody Seymour, Senior Minister, First United Methodist Church, Gastonia, North Carolina; author of *Finding God between the Lines* and *A Time for Healing: Overcoming the Perils of Ministry*

JWK – John W. Kloepfer, Ph.D., Presbyterian pastor in LaFayette, New York

KC – Kathy Crane, Presbyterian, teacher, writer, prayer group and spiritual formation group leader; graduate of Princeton Theological Seminary and Shalem Institute of Spiritual Formation

KHC – Kenneth H. Carter Jr., United Methodist pastor, Western North Carolina Conference; author of *The Gifted Pastor* and *The Pastor As Steward*

KIG – Kent Ira Groff, Presbyterian minister; Director of Oasis Ministries for Spiritual Development, Camp Hill, Pennsylvania; author of *What Would I Believe If I Didn't Believe Anything?: A Handbook for Spiritual Orphans*

KRB – Keith R. Beasley-Topliffe, pastor of Fifth Street United Methodist Church, Harrisburg, Pennsylvania; editor of *The Upper Room Spiritual Classics* and author of *Surrendering to God.*

KS – Kenneth Swanson, Ph.D., Dean and Rector at Christ Church Cathedral, Nashville, Tennessee; author of *Uncommon Prayer: Approaching Intimacy with God*

LJP – Larry J. Peacock, United Methodist pastor, Malibu, California; author of *Heart and Soul* and *Water Words*

LKB – L. Kline Beasley-Topliffe, research biologist with Massachusetts General Hospital, living in Wellesley, Massachusetts

LSP – Leonora S. Pruner, United Methodist, author of *Love's Secret Storm* and *Love's Silent Gift*

MB – Michael Battle, Assistant Professor of Spirituality and Black Church Studies, Duke University Divinity School; author of *Reconciliation: The Ubuntu Theology of Desmond Tutu*

MD – Michael Downey, Professor of Systematic Theology and Spirituality, Saint John's Seminary, Camarillo; Cardinal's Theologian, Archdiocese of Los Angeles

NGS – N. Graham Standish, Presbyterian Church (USA) pastor in Zelienople, Pennsylvania; author of *Discovering the Narrow Path* and *Paradoxes for Living*

NVV – Nicki Verploegen Vandergrift, Director of Spiritual and Ministerial Development at Weston Jesuit School of Theology in Cambridge, Massachusetts; author of *Organic Spirituality: A Sixfold Path for Contemplative Living*

PDB – Patricia D. Brown, Ph.D., Director of Spiritworks Center for Formation and Leadership, author of *Learning to Lead from Your Spiritual Center*

PDJ – Philip D. Jamieson, Assistant Professor of Pastoral Theology, University of Dubuque Theological Seminary

PWC – Paul Wesley Chilcote, United Methodist; Academic Dean, Asbury Theological Seminary, Orlando, Florida; author of *Praying in the Wesleyan Spirit*

RMH – Russell M. Hart, Center Director, The Center for Spiritual Formation, Carlisle, Pennsylvania; author of *The Icon through Western Eyes, Crossing the Border: An Introduction to the Practice of Christian Mysticism,* and *Communing with the Saints*

SAF – Stephanie A. Ford, Ph.D., ordained minister, Alliance of Baptists; Assistant

Professor of Christian Spirituality, Earlham School of Religion

SAW – Shelly A. Wilson, United Church of Christ pastor; director of retreats and spiritual formation at Inn of the Red Thread, a retreat center near Sparta, North Carolina

SEW – Susan E. Willhauck, United Methodist; Assistant Professor of Christian Formation and Director of Lay Education at Wesley Theological Seminary

SFP – Samuel F. (Skip) Parvin, United Methodist pastor in Orlando, Florida; author of *The Gospel according to The Simpsons: Leader's Guide for Group Study*

SH – Steve Harper, Vice President and Professor of Spiritual Formation, Asbury Theological Seminary, Orlando, Florida; author of ten books, including *John Wesley's Message for Today*

SN – Sandi Nesbit, United Church of Christ minister and spiritual director in St. Joseph, Michigan

TCW – Thomas C. Webb, retired pastor, United Methodist Church

TS – Tom Schwanda, Associate Professor of Spiritual Formation, Reformed Bible College, Grand Rapids and adjunct Associate Professor of Christian spirituality, Fuller Theological Seminary; author of *Celebrating God's Presence: The Transforming Power of Public Worship*

WBF – W. Brian Fleming, Minister of Education and Youth at Arden First Baptist Church, Arden, North Carolina

WMW – Wendy M. Wright, Ph.D., Professor of Theology (John C. Kenefick Chair in the Humanities), Creighton University, Omaha, Nebraska

WW – Walt Westbrook, United Methodist pastor and spiritual director in Clarksville, Virginia

A

ABANDONMENT. The concept of "letting go" or "giving over." In Christian spirituality, the word *abandonment* became popular in the seventeenth century.

Biblical words such as *surrender, faith, belief, trust* reflect the idea of abandonment. Jesus says, "If any want to become my followers, let them deny themselves and take up their cross and follow me" (Matt. 16:24). This deliberate turning away from self-interest, identifying fully with Jesus, and following him faithfully throughout one's life is definitive of being abandoned *to* God. It is putting God's will before anything else. The depth of this teaching becomes clearer as we progress in faith. Abandonment is a continual, God-empowered choice; a desire to please only God; a choice that shapes what we are and do.

Spiritual literature employs four uses of the word *abandonment*; two speak of abandonment *by* God and two of abandonment *to* God. First, *abandonment as judgment*: God withdraws from the person whose heart is hardened as an enticement to conversion, or perhaps God withdraws entirely as punishment for sin. Second, *abandonment as trial*: God tests the sincerity of believers by seeming to withdraw from them for a time. Third, *abandonment as surrender*: The believer cooperates with God's **will** by submitting to it in blind (unknowing) faith. Fourth, *abandonment as* **union** *with God*: The believer rests in faith and **assurance** of God's **love**, even in the greatest trials. Abandonment as trial, surrender, and union has to do with progression in faith, moving from chaos to peace, head to heart, and complication to simplicity. Abandonment to God becomes a way of life, a perpetual surrendering of the self to God in childlike trust.

Abandonment attempts to answer the question of how to relate to God with the answer: "Surrender your mind and heart to God, trust completely in God's unknown providence, and be confident that God will guide you safely through the dark maze of life to the eternal kingdom." The goal of abandonment is to be like Christ.

Abandonment as a spiritual path is identified most closely with the writings of **Jean Pierre de Caussade**, **John of the Cross**, and later with the early writings of **Thomas Merton**. In the writings of Caussade (especially *Abandonment to Divine Providence*), abandonment is a Christian response to God's call to faith. While not negative, the word does convey a renunciation or surrender of human effort in favor of dependence on God's hidden providence in the **present moment** of life. Abandonment emphasizes the nearness of God beyond the senses and beyond logic. Such faith produces joy, confidence, and a desire to help others. Abandonment accepts the trials of life, as well as peaceful times, as expressions of God's will. This is not fatalism but an attempt to cope with pain by going through it. Dependence on God is its own reward, and God is to be praised for who God is, not what God gives.

Abandonment, as understood by its advocates, seems especially fitted for times of stress. It recognizes the world as a dark place, God as a real (though hidden) presence, and spiritual life as inexplicable in conventional ways. It challenges us to give up self-promotion and self-justification and confronts us with our weaknesses and sins, pointing us to a God who is faithful in steadfast love.

The following scripture and books provide further reflective reading and prayer: Psalms 63:1-8; 131; Matthew 5:1-11; 16:13-28; Colossians 3:1-17; Jean Pierre de Caussade, *Abandonment to Divine Providence, The Fire of*

Divine Love; Thomas Merton, *The Ascent to Truth*; Keith Beasley-Topliffe, *Surrendering to God.* JLM

ACCIDIE. (Greek *akedia*, sometimes spelled *acedia*), the sin of losing heart in the middle of the struggle. Often translated as *sloth*, that term's modern connotation of laziness does not well describe accidie.

Reflecting its origins in the struggles of the desert monastic movement, accidie was associated with the "destruction that wastes at noonday"(Ps. 91:6). It was tempting in the heat of midday to give up on the work of the spirit. Accidie combined two sins (sadness and spiritual lethargy) from earlier lists of the deadly sins. The combination of the two caused this disorder to be defined as despair in the face of **grace**. Judas was often offered as an example, given his hopelessness at the possibility of redemption. Accidie can be simultaneously marked by both a listlessness of spirit and increased activity. Workaholics may often be guilty of the sin of accidie. Hyperactivity has replaced a proper dedication to the more important tasks of building relationships and leading a healthy spiritual life.

Often listed as the fourth of the **seven deadly sins**, accidie's middle position is not by accident. Standing after the "hot sins" of pride, envy, and anger, accidie marked the sin of giving up, a weariness of spiritual warfare and the ongoing necessity of cooperating with grace—surrender to the world. The life that followed would be marked by sins of possessing: avarice, gluttony, and lust.

The antidote to accidie is not merely increased activity. As stated above, such action may only serve as a cover for the problem, allowing despondency to become despair. Instead, the answer to accidie is a renewed fortitude based upon a remembrance of God's mercies and the merits of Jesus Christ. This alone can serve as a call to continued "fighting of the good fight."

The classic discussion of accidie is in Book 10 of **John Cassian**'s *Institutes.* PDJ

ADORATION. Gratitude not only for God's gifts but also for God's self, constancy, being, and goodness. Adoration as a prayer of gratitude and veneration has been and continues to be a mainstay of Christian prayer.

A prayer of adoration addresses God in joyful, unending **love**. Adoration accepts, deepens, and intensifies our relationship with God. We adore Christ for what he has done and continues to do in his personal concern for us individually and collectively. With prayer, we praise and thank God by accepting that activity and its purpose in our lives and in the world, and we give ourselves in return.

In 787 the Second Council of Nicaea, during the Iconoclastic Controversy, reserved *adoration* strictly for the worship of God alone, ruling that the term was not to be applied to earthly rulers or to **angels** and **saints** who could be venerated but not adored.

During the seventeenth century the French School, a reform movement led by **Pierre de Bérulle** and his successor Jean-Jacques Olier, developed a spirituality of adoration that essentially connected prayer and ministry. Their adoration prayer centered on a threefold spiritual synthesis: to look at Jesus, leading to acts of **holiness**; to unite in Jesus, leading to **union** with God; and to act in Jesus, leading to the power of Christ.

We do not adore God's power or goodness but God in God's self as the limit that surpasses all our ability of comprehension or understanding. The other side of adoration is our absolute self-surrender or **abandonment** before the absoluteness of God. We surrender and accept our full dependence on God. Because we need to adore and relate to that which is absolute and incomparable and no language exists to express it, the prayer of adoration may be silent. Adoration often finds expression in gestures of bowing, kneeling, prostrating, and genuflecting.

For further reading, see *Bérulle and the French School: Selected Writings*, edited by William M. Thompson and translated by Lowell M. Glendon. PDB

AELRED OF RIEVAULX (ca. 1110–67), Cistercian monk, spiritual writer. Aelred was raised in a foster home, the court of King David of Scotland. There he gained popularity and success but became restless and dissatisfied. At the age of twenty-four he left the court abruptly and offered himself at the gate of Rievaulx, a Cistercian monastery, to become a monk. He quickly rose in responsibility, first as novice master and later as leader of a group of monks that started a new monastery. Later he was recalled to become abbot at Rievaulx and supervised many daughter houses as well. He had a close relationship with **Bernard of Clairvaux**, since Clairvaux was the mother house of Rievaulx. Bernard ordered Aelred to write *The Mirror of Charity*, a treatise on love.

Aelred is best known for *Spiritual Friendship*, written over a span of years, in which he reflected on Cicero's theories of friendship and went far beyond. He advocated friendship on both the natural and the supernatural planes. He wrote from the perspective of his own experiences with friendship, through which he experienced a higher and deeper relationship with Christ and with God. Friendship was a reflection of the love of God, with God being the source.

Aelred, conscious of the dangers and pitfalls of friendship in monasteries, maintained that loving one's immediate neighbors with charity and goodwill offered a foretaste of heaven. No conflict existed between love of friends and love of God. Judgment of what was right would contribute to true friendship, which required constant attention. Aelred died as he had lived, surrounded by a crowd of monks. EWF

AFFECTIVE SPIRITUALITY. A concern with the life of the "heart," a metaphor for the center of the human being. The Hebrew Bible sometimes used a different image to describe the center of a human being, namely the kidneys (translated "reins" in the King James Version, cf. Psalm 16:7.) These varied physiological images help to make clear that when spiritual writers speak about the "heart," they are not attaching magical qualities to the physical blood pump. "Heart" language in this sense— often expressed in terms of love, joy, fear, and peace—signals the writer's intention to address what is most central to who we are spiritually, just as the heart is most central to who we are physically. Understanding who or what a person loves or what brings joy or what brings fear or peace will give a better sense of who that person is than social status, career title, or any of the other more "objective" categories or classifications that our culture often uses to describe a person.

Some assume that affective spirituality refers to sentimental forms of spirituality based on apparently haphazard and unpredictable sensations; however, this is an unjust stereotype. When looking at the spiritual writings of those who emphasize the life of the heart (from **Augustine** through **Bernard of Clairvaux**, **John Wesley**, and **Kierkegaard**), clearly their vision of a religion of the heart does not entail a life of self-absorption (or a "curving in on one's self," as **Luther** defined sinfulness). For such thinkers, the affective life of the Christian heart does not simply arise spontaneously as the German theologian Schleiermacher (1768–1834) would have it in his universally present "feeling of absolute dependence." Instead, the desired Christian "heart" is typically seen as the result of a disciplined, patterned way of life.

Contemporary understandings of the nature of emotion influenced by Kierkegaard and Austrian philosopher Wittgenstein (1889–1951) have demonstrated that affectivity involves more than mere sensation or feeling. These thinkers have shown that the affective life of the heart is not necessarily arcane and unknowable but has a discernible grammar or logic primarily in reference to the objects that generate the emotions and the behaviors toward which these emotions dispose a person.

Fixing attention on the proper object is crucial for the Christian formation of the heart (Heb. 12:2; Col. 3:1-2). Hearts are most typically fixed on the proper objects through the means of **grace** (e.g., scripture reading, liturgy, prayer, attendance at the **sacraments**, etc.). When called to confess our sins in a worship service, our hearts become marked by **humility** and sorrow for **sin**. Hearing the word of **forgiveness** and taking the bread and wine invites us to experience the joy of salvation and a deep gratitude. When we hear that we are loved, our hearts develop an answering love of God and neighbor.

Just as the Christian heart is formed by attention to the word of the gospel, so the affective life must express itself beyond mere felt sensation in concrete action to be truly worthy of the name "Christian." As Matthew 25:31-46 indicates, our relationship of love and worship of God must show itself in concrete practice to be real. Like a battery charged with power only to spend it, our hearts are properly discharged when they lead us to self-giving acts of service in the world.

In addition to the classic *Treatise on Religious Affections* by **Jonathan Edwards**, you might read *The Soul in Paraphrase: Prayer and the Religious Affections* by Don E. Saliers and *As If the Heart Mattered: A Wesleyan Spirituality* by Gregory S. Clapper. GSC

AFRICAN-AMERICAN SPIRITUALITY. The word *spirituality* derives from *spiritus*, the breath of God that transforms life more than can be imagined. From this understanding of spirituality African-American spirituality is displayed through the practices of social transformation. African-American spirituality is not practiced exclusively through the clarity of cognitive function (e.g., *lectio divina*) but through what is often seen as the obscure spiritual practices of shouting, call-and-response worship, and holy dance. Therefore, African-American spirituality begins not with cognitive function but with a communal sense of devotion and mystery. Devotion is readily seen through spiritual practices of the Negro spiritual, black preaching, gospel music, and the testimonial, all of which aim at the social transformation of race relations in the United States. This trajectory from inner devotion to a rich display of practices defines African-American spirituality.

African-American spirituality must be defined through its practices because, while considered a part of mainline churches, it is an alternative vision of pentecostalism or evangelicalism. However, the call for social transformation takes precedence over the emphasis on personal **conversion**. Because of this insight into social transformation, African-American spirituality exhibits more of a public and "**positive way**" type of spirituality in which *communities*, not just the individual, practice God's presence. The spiritual practices of the black church in the civil rights movement display African-American spirituality as a social force to be reckoned with, even within the political world. In light of the relevance of this spirituality to social transformation, African-American spirituality is vital to understanding spirituality in general for several reasons.

First, African-American spirituality addresses the loss of **community** in North American life. Western cultures need a way to grow spiritually with a vibrant Christian identity, yet in a manner that does not oppress other spiritualities. Second, the emphasis upon social transformation has made African-American spirituality crucial to the discussion of maintaining spiritual practices that do not oppress but transform. For example, in destroyed urban neighborhoods and deserted rural ones, practices within African-American spirituality are often the only remnants in which all people can learn the satisfactions of social transformation, even though these same people may be obliged to practice being human beyond the confines of oppressive systems. Social transformation requires an imagination not only developed through cognitive spirituality but also through visceral forms that lead outside of self into community.

Lastly, African-American spirituality offers a different vision of the *mysterium tremendum*. **Mysticism** is the claim of immediacy of contemplative intuition. Through African-American practices not only do individuals seek such immediacy but whole communities do as well, bringing about social transformation. The concept that a community can be mystical seems strange to Western notions of self-contained spirituality. Even as we attempt to describe something we call spirituality and even more particularly African-American spirituality, we come with our cognitive, categorizing faculty of knowing as opposed to ways of knowing through communal practices. The sense that African-American spirituality has "soul" is valuable here in that the soul is defined as the core of one's being, where one is most truly one's self. African-American spirituality teaches that one is most truly one's self in community. From such community one can then understand the African proverb: Two antelope walk together so that one might blow the dust from the other's eyes.

For further reading, see the works of **Howard Thurman**. MB

AFRICAN SPIRITUALITY. In much of Western culture, spirituality has been understood as a distinctively personal journey. Although Western influences of various kinds profoundly affect African society, the African experience of the self in **community** remains the foundation of African self-understanding. In contrast to Western spirituality, African spirituality affirms that the individual does not exist apart from the community. The classic phrasing of this intrinsic relationship was stated by John Mbiti and carried on by Archbishop **Desmond Tutu** as an *ubuntu* sensibility, namely, "I am, because we are; and since we are, therefore I am." For the African person all of life is one continuous movement of community from birth to death and beyond. In essence, therefore, African spirituality is a spirituality of community.

A sensibility of interdependence is one characteristic of African spirituality. The African person is part of the whole, and the spiritual life flows from the corporate experience and never in isolation from it. African communal practices of God's presence define

who an African person is and who an African person can become. African individuality and freedom are always balanced by the destiny of the community; therefore, recognizing the presence of the community of saints or ancestors is an essential African spiritual practice. Not only is individual freedom connected to the communal; so is the freedom of those living on earth connected to those who have died and to those who will be born.

A second characteristic of African spirituality is continuity with the goodness and value of all facets of creation. For example, the sky, the sun and moon, mountains, forests and trees, rivers and water, plants and animals, all have implicit spiritual meaning beyond natural knowledge and often explicit significance for how human beings are to recognize the sacred and the profane. In African spirituality human personhood is interdependent with creation; one cannot be "spiritual" apart from being in harmony with creation. Crucial to an African spirituality of community is harmony and balance in the relationship among individuals, community, and creation. When good is done to any, it is good for the entire community; when evil is committed, the shame or victimization affects the whole. An African person discovers self through relationship to all creation in which spiritual norms and responsibilities then become intelligible.

An African person displays this essential spirituality of interdependence and relationality through the sacraments of various initiation rites that have been and, to a certain extent, still remain vital to the interpretation of what is African. Through these initiation rites, all of life is seen as sacramental, visible signs of invisible grace.

The rites of passage practiced among African communities integrate the person into the spiritual world so that she or he may find essential identity within community. This rite of passage continues beyond death, which becomes vital to the understanding of spiritual maturity in the African world. Since ancestors are regarded as intrinsically part of the community, able to influence events and guide the community, complete spiritual maturity is never reached among those living on earth. This emphasis upon maturity and passage into deeper stages flows from an African communal sense of personhood in which the individual becomes conscious of himself or herself through social interaction and is an important contribution to spiritual discourse with Western thought, which envisions spiritual maturation within the boundary of an individual's life in this world.

For further reading on African spirituality, see *Reconciliation: The Ubuntu Theology of Desmond Tutu* by Michael Jesse Battle. MB

AGAPE. See **LOVE.**

ALBIGENSIANISM. See **CATHARISM.**

ALLEN, RICHARD (1760–1831), founder of the African Methodist Episcopal Church. Richard Allen, born a slave in Pennsylvania, convinced his master, with the help of some traveling preachers, to let him buy his freedom at age twenty. In his autobiography (*The Life, Experience and Gospel Labors of the Rt. Rev. Richard Allen*) he concedes that his master was a good one, but that the condition of slavery must be abhorrent to any who suffer under it as well as distasteful in the eyes of God. An active abolitionist, he made his church a stop on the Underground Railroad, a ministry that continued even after his death.

Allen converted to Methodism as a young man because the frank and open language, spirit of love, and straightforward rules for living appealed to him. Further, early Methodism seemed to support a decidedly antislavery message. He began preaching in 1780, traveling throughout the mid-Atlantic states but refusing to go into the deep South. He eventually felt called to settle in Philadelphia, where he joined and helped construct St. George's Methodist Episcopal Church.

As Methodism in America became an organized denomination, desire for respectability began to outweigh evangelical fellowship, leading to increased marginalization of black members. In 1787, when the leaders of St. George's forced black members to sit in the balcony, Allen and other black members of the congregation left to form their own church, Bethel. In 1799 Allen was ordained and appointed to Bethel. Correspondence with black churches in other cities proved that Philadelphia was not alone, and in 1816 these scattered communities broke with the Methodist Episcopal Church and united as the African Methodist Episcopal Church. Allen was consecrated as the first bishop.

Not all of Allen's activities were religious. He helped found the Free African Society, which promoted self-reliance and education among the society of free blacks in Philadelphia. This organization provided aid to whites and blacks during the yellow fever epidemic of 1793, despite financial loss and great personal risk. LKB

AMBROSE (ca. 339–97), bishop of Milan. Son of the Praetorian Prefect of Gaul, Ambrose practiced law in Roman courts. Around 370 he was appointed governor of Aemilia-Liguria, which had its seat in Milan. When Auxentius, Arian bishop of Milan, died in 374, he presided over the disputed election of a successor. The Catholic laity demanded that Ambrose, a believer although not yet baptized, succeed him. After first trying to escape the call, he accepted and was baptized and ordained, studying theology under his former tutor Simplicianus. As bishop of Milan, he gained fame for his preaching, zealous support of orthodoxy, and mission endeavors. The importance of Milan in the West linked him closely to the emperors of the Roman Empire in the West—Gratian, Maximus, Justina, and Theodosius. He stoutly maintained the independence of the church against Justina's efforts to install an Arian bishop in Milan. He excommunicated Theodosius I for ordering the massacre of citizens at Thessalonica.

The Roman Catholic Church recognizes Ambrose as a **Doctor of the Church,** an authoritative teacher. His fluency in Greek enabled him to introduce much Eastern theology, especially that of the **Cappadocians**, into the West. He is now generally recognized as the author of a treatise *On the Sacraments*, which evidences Eastern influence. Although most of his surviving corpus consists of sermons and letters, his most noted writing is his treatise on Christian ethics, *On the Duties of Ministers*, an adaptation of Cicero's *On Duties*. He also wrote much on the ascetic life and strongly encouraged the development of monasticism in the West. He and Augustine deserve much credit for the West's reliance on a monastic model for the clergy.

For further reading see F. Homes Dudden, *The Life and Times of St. Ambrose*. EGH

*A*NCRENE *R*IWLE. (Middle English for *Anchoresses' Rule*), anonymous work written around 1215. While neither the author's name nor that of the audience to whom he was writing is known, it is assumed from the text itself that a cleric probably wrote this book of religious counsel (more guide than formal rule) for three English sisters who came from a well-to-do family. Anchoresses, laywomen who desired to live a life of solitude (for example, **Julian of Norwich**), made solemn vows to be "anchored" to the church building and attached to God in order to deepen their personal relationship with God through prayer, penance, and purity of heart. The *Ancrene Riwle* compares the anchoress's cell to a tomb. Anchoresses participated in a funeral or burial service as a ritual of enclosure to symbolize that they would never leave, that they were dead to the world and its temptations.

Anchoresses during medieval times felt called to lead hidden lives of extreme isolation. Like John the Baptist and Jesus, they withdrew into the desert of solitude where divine thoughts could freely occupy their soul. Purity of heart, the steadfast attention of the soul toward God, was the primary inner rule for an anchoress. The second, or outer, rule provides guidelines for proper conduct concerning fasting, sleeping, clothing to be worn, and keeping vigils. Besides these primary inner and outer rules, the *Ancrene Riwle* contains an additional eight sections offering guidance regarding prayers; devotions; the interior life; the regulation of emotions; the guarding of the five senses; the advantages of living the eremitical (hermit-like) life; the necessary virtues required; the temptations of body, mind and spirit; and the necessity for confession and penance. The anchoress embraced all these obligations and duties as her personal commitment to living the ascetic life, which she believed would keep her mind and will turned toward God.

For the *Ancrene Riwle* in modern English, see *The Ancrene Riwle*, translated by M. B. Salu and *Anchoritic Spirituality: Ancrene Wisse and Associated Works*, translated by Anne Savage and Nicholas Watson. EKM

ANDREWES, LANCELOT (1555–1626), prominent bishop, theologian, and apologist for the Church of England during the seventeenth century. Born at All Hallows parish in Barking, Andrewes was the oldest of thirteen children. He attended Merchant Taylors' School where he showed himself to be a serious and intelligent student. In 1571 Andrewes began his extensive academic career by entering Pembroke College, Cambridge. There he graduated with his B.A. in 1575, his M.A. in 1578, his B.D. in 1585, and his D.D. in 1589. Andrewes was ordained in 1580 and in 1589 made vicar of St. Giles and Master of Pembroke Hall where he served until 1605. Andrewes quickly became a royal favorite. During Queen Elizabeth's reign, he became her chaplain and the dean of Westminster Abbey. King James I also held him in high esteem and made him bishop of Chichester (1605), Ely (1609), and Winchester (1619). In turn, Andrewes saw the king as the Lord's anointed and believed in the "divine right of kings." He had the reputation for being an outstanding linguist who knew over fifteen languages. At the Hampton Court Conference, he was one of the first to be appointed as a principal translator of the Authorized

(King James) Version of the Bible (1611), chairing the committee responsible for Genesis through Second Kings. In opposition to Puritan Calvinism, Andrewes supported the Anglican "middle way" theology. Andrewes was known for his excellent sermons and lofty prayers. In 1629 a book of his sermons was published, but it was his *Private Devotions* (1648) that became a classic. Andrewes was an astute scholar and theologian, an eloquent preacher, a benevolent friend to the distressed, and a saintly man of austere piety and quiet meditation. ASJ

ANGELA OF FOLIGNO (ca. 1248–1309), member of the Third Order of Francis. Born in Foligno, Italy, into a wealthy family and married at a young age, Angela led a loose and unexamined life before her conversion. She began to question her self-indulgent, hedonistic ways after hearing Brother Arnold, a Franciscan friar, preach at the local church. After confessing to him and receiving counsel, she left with a desire to live a committed life in the Lord. Soon after (ca. 1290), Angela would be wholly transformed following the deaths of her mother, husband, and three sons. Angela joined the Third Order of **Francis**, lay followers of the Franciscan **rule** who seek to become mature followers of Christ by actively living out their faith in the world. On **pilgrimage** to Assisi, she had visionary experiences of God's trinitarian presence that transformed her sense of her calling. Like **Catherine of Siena**, Angela took on a public role and voice. She gave away most of her money, clothes, and property. Imitating Christ crucified and meditating on the **cross**, she pursued a life dedicated to **poverty** that she might remain mindful of others in need. Angela's writings about her mystical experiences (in her book *Memorial*) and her spiritual doctrine of poverty (in "Instructions," Part II of *Memorial*) were spoken and shared among her network of male and female disciples. Angela described her spiritual journey as a series of steps organized into three phases: imitation, **union** with God, and perfect union.

Angela's writings are collected in *Complete Works: Angela of Foligno*, translated by Paul Lachance. EKM

ANGELS. (From Greek *angelos*, "messenger"), representatives of God, spirits who have the ability to take on a form that appears human. Angels exist in nearly every culture. The Bible refers to three angels by name: Michael is called the angel of Israel in Daniel 10:21 and called an archangel in Jude 9. Revelation 12:7-12 describes him leading armies that battle Satan. Gabriel explains visions to Daniel (8:16; 9:21) and announces God's plan to Mary (Luke 1:19, 26, 30-33). Raphael is the heavenly healer and guide for Tobias in the book of Tobit. The idea of angels developed to include a hierarchy, as well as good and bad angels. By the time of Jesus, angels were considered spiritual beings allied with God against Satan. Fallen angels included Lucifer, now Satan or the **devil**, whose rebellion and fall are mentioned in 2 Peter 2:4 and Revelation 12:7, 9.

Writers have attempted to list orders of angels, drawing from Colossians 1:16; Romans 8:38; Ephesians 6:12. **Pseudo-Dionysius** lists nine orders hierarchically from highest to lowest: Seraphim, Cherubim, Thrones, Dominions, Virtues, Powers, Principalities, Archangels, Angels. In his book *Angels*, **Billy Graham** lists Archangels, Angels, Seraphim, Cherubim, Principalities, Authorities, Powers, Thrones, Might, and Dominion. Seraphim, described in Isaiah 6:1-6 as six-winged, minister at God's throne, praising God. In Ezekiel 10, the prophet describes cherubim as glorifying God and having wings and hands full of eyes.

As messengers of God, the angels have no importance in themselves. Rather, the focus is on their message, transmitted from God. In nearly three hundred references to angels in the Bible, these messengers carry out a variety of tasks: to instruct, to foretell the future, to guide, to feed, to destroy, to praise, to bless, to inspire, to proclaim judgment, to protect, to cause dreams. In the Gospels angels proclaim Christ's birth (in dreams in Matthew and directly in Luke), minister to him in the desert and in Gethsemane, and proclaim his resurrection. The author of Hebrews tells us we entertain angels unaware through our kindness to strangers (Heb. 13:2) and that one day we'll see the role of angels as ministering spirits in our lives (Heb. 1:14). This idea contributes to the belief in guardian angels: that one is assigned to each of us during our lives. They guide us, pray with and for us, protect us, reveal God's will, and receive our soul at the moment of death.

In Revelation 1–3 messages are given to the spiritual guardian angel of each church. John receives the message from an angel and writes to each angel of the seven churches. See *Breaking the Code* by Bruce Metzger.

In *Unmasking the Powers* Walter Wink looks in much greater detail at the various angelic (and demonic) powers mentioned in the Bible and offers suggestions for our understanding and recognition of these powers in our lives. Angels have been portrayed in our culture in a variety of ways in literature, music, film, television, and in many Christmas hymns. Awareness of the role of angels could promote attunement to God's message and encourage spiritual growth. KC

ANGELUS SILESIUS (1624–77), also known as Johann Scheffler, author of *The Cherubinic Wanderer* and *The Holy Joy of the Soul.* Johann Scheffler was born in Breslau (Poland), of Lutheran parents who fled religious intolerance in Cracow. The family lived an austere life despite the father's social rank as a wealthy burgher. Scheffler's parents died when he was a young teenager, but they provided educational opportunity for Johann through a trust. This money enabled Johann to study in Holland, where he was influenced by many different religious minorities, including Mennonites, Jews, and the mystical movements. This exposure made an impression on Johann. He transferred to study medicine at the University of Padua and graduated in 1648 with doctorates in medicine and philosophy. He had begun to write poetry and wanted to publish *The Cherubinic*

Wanderer but was censored and denied permission by a Lutheran court. Then, touched by the liturgy and devotion of Catholicism, he converted in 1653 and changed his name to Angelus, taking the region's name of Silesius to distinguish himself from another writer of the time. He returned to Silesius for his inheritance and worked briefly as a court physician. Reading *Spiritual Exercises* by **Ignatius of Loyola**, he kept a journal and continued to write poetry, publishing five volumes in 1657. In 1661 he was ordained a priest and committed himself to acts of charity, giving away his inheritance.

Scheffler's poetry is a rich resource of Germanic religious folk literature. He used brief two-line statements called epigrams to illustrate his mystical insight. These epigrams, a most difficult genre of composition, conveyed the experience of the mystical life in extremely succinct couplets. Enthusiastic about his experience of God, he attempted to verbalize in his poetry the indescribable. Not so endearing is the writing Scheffler did to protest the Reformation. These works pale beside the brilliant mystical poetry he left behind.

The Cherubinic Wanderer is available in English translation by Maria Shrady. NVV

ANSELM OF CANTERBURY (1033–1109), known as "the founder of Scholasticism" and the greatest Western Christian scholar between **Augustine** and **Thomas Aquinas**. Born in Piedmont of noble parents, Anselm entered the Abbey of Bec in Normandy in 1060 and was elected abbot in 1078. In 1093 he became archbishop of Canterbury. Canonized in 1163, he was proclaimed a **Doctor of the Church** (an authoritative teacher) in 1720.

Anselm wrote with precision and unusual clarity. As a pioneering theologian, he introduced analysis to theology and the use of reason alone to prove the truths of **faith**. However, when scripture clashed with reason, **scripture** was correct. He strove to press beyond faith to gain insight into faith, thus bringing us closer to the beatific **vision** and producing joy in the spiritual beauty of the truths of faith.

Anselm applied his arguments to the theological truths of the Trinity, **Incarnation**, and Redemption. Contrary to the prevailing custom of quoting supporting authorities, he demonstrated God's existence and attributes purely by reason. He developed the ontological argument (the very idea of an absolutely perfect being demonstrates its existence) for atheists who did not acknowledge the authority of scripture.

Many of Anselm's concepts reflect his feudal society, with God the absolute monarch, "beyond which nothing greater can be conceived." Being against God, **sin** is infinitely offensive. Pardon alone cannot reconcile it with God's justice. Only the God-Man could make atonement adequately, leaving the **devil** without a claim on humanity.

Anselm wrote systematic works, prayers, meditations, and letters. His *Cur Deus Homo* (*Why God Became Man*) focused on the virginal conception and original sin. In *De Concordia* he reconciles God's foreknowledge, predestination, and grace with human free will. His beautiful, artistic prayers are brief masterpieces, designed in six classical parts to move God or a saint to give aid. His meditation "On the Redemption of Mankind" summarizes ideas presented in *Cur Deus Homo*.

To learn more, see *St. Anselm and His Critics: A Reinterpretation of the Cur Deus Homo* by John McIntyre; *The Life of St. Anselm, Archbishop of Canterbury* by Eadmer, edited by Richard W. Southern; or *The Life and Times of St. Anselm* (two volumes) by Martin Rule. LSP

ANTONY OF EGYPT (251?–356), hermit, first of the **desert fathers**. Born into a family of some affluence, Antony, on the death of his parents around 269, experienced a radical "conversion." At about age eighteen or twenty, on hearing a sermon on Jesus' challenge to the rich youth, he gave up his possessions, arranged for a younger sister to live with nuns, and took up the life of an ascetic. After living for a time with a hermit, at about age thirty-five he sought solitude in the **desert** of Pispir. Fame soon disrupted his solitude, however.

So many desired his direction and counsel that around 305 he organized a community of solitaries and around 310 withdrew farther to the mountains near the shores of the Red Sea where he lived until his death. Occasionally he came out of retirement to support the Nicene party led by **Athanasius**, bishop of Alexandria, against the Arians. Athanasius's *Life of Antony* extended Antony's influence well beyond the monks of Egypt and his own lifetime. The story of his conversion, for instance, figured prominently in the conversion of **Augustine** and has served as a model for many youth up to the present time.

As depicted by Athanasius, Antony's spiritual life involved a battle with demons that inhabit the desert and put to extreme test those who pursue a life of devotion. Using contemporary psychological imagery, Athanasius helps us understand that Antony's struggle was not primarily external but internal, a battle to attain purity of heart in order that he might see God, in fulfillment of the **beatitude**, "Blessed are the pure in heart, for they will see God" (Matt. 5:8).

Antony's way to purity of heart focused on discipline, *askesis.* The discipline consisted primarily of **fasting** and **prayer**, two items often paired in the New Testament. Fasting strengthened the inner person by liberation from those habits of the head and the heart that stood in the way of complete devotion to God. Solitude intensified this inner struggle. Antony ascribed his victory to his participation in Christ's victory on the cross through fasting and prayer and the cultivation of virtues such as meekness, serenity, contempt for money, humility, love of the poor, almsgiving, and freedom from anger. He sought to pray without ceasing, and his basic form of prayer was **meditation** on scripture, which he memorized.

For further reading, see *St. Athanasius: The Life of Saint Antony* (Ancient Christian Writers, No. 10), translated by Robert T. Meyer. EGH

APATHEIA. A Greek word that literally means "not suffering" or "not feeling." In Christian spirituality, *apatheia* is a deep, unshakable calm; an inner freedom both from compulsion and obsession; and in a Christian context, a freedom from sin. Both the word *apatheia* and the concept behind it are Hellenistic rather than Hebrew in origin. *Apatheia* never appears in the Bible, though the idea of Christ setting us free from compulsion is pervasive, as in John 8:36, where Jesus says, "So if the Son makes you free, you will be free indeed."

Because it has a sense of detachment, the word itself has passed into English as "apathy." But in its Greek meaning, far from being apathetic, it describes an active consciousness, an inner freedom that allows one to feel and experience everything without giving in to emotionalism. There is no denial or repression. One remains conscious of fear or anger or desire, but these inner emotions and impulses have no power to control. With *apatheia* a person, while feeling everything, remains utterly free. One is conscious of everything but held by nothing.

As a Christian spiritual **disposition**, *apatheia* was first described by second-century writers. It came into common usage in the fourth and fifth centuries in the writings of the **desert fathers**. Many of these Christian mystics held *apatheia* as the supreme virtue to be sought above all others. They taught that living a true Christian life began with *apatheia*. Like any other Christian virtue, *apatheia* can be received only as a gift of **grace**. KS

APOPHATIC PATH. See **NEGATIVE WAY.**

ARNDT, JOHANN (1555–1621), Lutheran pastor and mystic. Arndt has been called the father of German Pietism and the second German reformer. Although an uncompromising Lutheran (he had to leave a troubled pastorate at Badeborn in 1590 because of Calvinist hostility to his strong views), he believed that acceptance of Lutheran dogma was not sufficient. He urged his followers to turn from confessions of faith to **faith** itself and to let the scriptures live in them. He felt that an overemphasis on **justification** by faith led to a denial of works and piety. For Arndt, justification by

faith must not hinder the moral betterment of life. His devotional writings, of which *True Christianity* is the most famous, call for an active faith that leads to **regeneration**. Arndt was a leader of the seventeenth-century revival of **mysticism** in the Lutheran Church, and his work *True Christianity* was second to **Thomas à Kempis**'s *Imitation of Christ* as the most widely circulated and read devotional book. In the foreword to *True Christianity*, Arndt says he wrote this book to "show simple readers wherein true Christianity consists, namely, in the exhibition of a true, living faith, active in genuine godliness and the fruits of righteousness." Later in the same foreword he writes, "True Christianity consists, not in words or in external show, but in living faith, from which arise righteous fruits, and all manner of Christian virtues, as from Christ himself." Arndt served pastorates in Badeborn, Quedlinburg, and Brunswick. Numerous editions of his work *True Christianity* are available today. DDW

ARNOLD, EBERHARD (1883–1935), German founder of the modern Bruderhof ("brotherhood") movement. At age sixteen Arnold became aware of an abiding and consuming love through Jesus Christ that changed his whole perspective and provided the purpose for the rest of his life. Although still in high school he divided his free time between community outreach and Bible study. At twenty-one he was already a popular public speaker. He entered college to study theology, but a break with the state church over his opinions on baptism meant that he would never be allowed to take his exams in theology. So he received his doctorate in philosophy instead. He read Christian philosophers avidly, as well as the writings of the early church and all subsequent societies that sought a life of **community** through Christ. His lectures and writing drew from these materials and thought, as well as from his knowledge of different sociopolitical trends in Germany and throughout Europe. He was active in many German youth movements, most prominently in the Student Christian movement.

The Sermon on the Mount became the focus of Arnold's drive for community, beginning with discussions at a 1919 conference. After several years a suitable location was found to form a community with a foster school and a printing house that would at once provide a means of spreading the message and fund-raising. Publications included everything from histories, to theological tracts, to songbooks, to collections of legends. The community, the Bruderhof, changed locations several times as it grew until finally settling on a farm near Rhön in 1927.

When the Nazis insisted on supplying teachers for the school, the Bruderhof moved the school and some members to Liechtenstein, though Arnold continued to speak in Germany. After Arnold's sudden death following surgery to repair a broken leg, the community moved to Paraguay and then to the United States. Today Bruderhof communities exist in England and Australia, New York and Pennsylvania. The American communities make school furniture, physical therapy equipment, and business signs. Plough Publishing (UK) publishes many of Arnold's books, including the anthologies *Salt and Light: Living the Sermon on the Mount* and *God's Revolution: Justice, Community and the Coming Kingdom.* Arnold's essays and sermons are available in English translation at www.eberhardarnold.com. Other writings are available as free e-books at www.bruderhof.com. LKB

ARS, CURÉ D'. See **Vianney, Jean-Baptiste Marie.**

ART AND SPIRITUALITY. The church has always had an ambivalent relationship with the visual arts. On the one hand, Hebrew tradition mistrusted all "graven images." On the other, Christ was God made visible, the ineffable incarnate. So perhaps visual representations of religious themes might be appropriate. Regardless, hostility to the arts in the church did not abate until the fourth century, when **Basil of Caesarea** and **Gregory of Nyssa** became the first major theologians to make positive statements about images.

However, the third century sees evidence of painting in buildings and burial places. Symbols in the catacombs include Christian interpretations of pagan images. The Orant, a man standing with his hands raised in prayer, was a Roman symbol of piety. The image of Christ as the Good Shepherd comes from a pagan symbol of philanthropy.

The **icon** is a painting intended as an instrument of prayer and a window into the Divine, executed according to specific rules. The earliest tradition of iconography is in fifth century Byzantium. By 537, when Emperor Justinian completed the church called Hagia Sophia (holy wisdom) in Constantinople, icons were accepted as servants of the church. The Iconoclast Controversy raged intermittently from 726 to 843. Icons were destroyed throughout the church. In fact, almost no icons from before 726 remain today. In 843 the Council in Constantinople reestablished the veneration of holy icons, though with a more self-conscious theological basis and a more profoundly understood spiritual function.

The Protestant Reformation, the Catholic counter-Reformation, and the Renaissance combined to change the rules of religious art. The arts blossomed from being simply illustrations for the illiterate to more sophisticated forms, though still biblically based.

All preindustrial art was designed to depict larger truths that revealed the sacred, often using an elaborate language of symbols. Today the spiritual in art continues to confront us with what we have forgotten. It shows us our deepest self and asks the deepest questions, inviting us to partake fully of the spiritual truths we often ignore or obscure with the veneer of the false self. WW

ASCETICISM. The term *asceticism* comes from the Greek root *askesis*, referring to **discipline**, training, or exercises. The New Testament uses two other Greek words in a similar way. One, *paideia* (from *paides*, "children") refers to *pedagogical* methods akin to what Plato meant by "the education of desire" (Heb. 12:8, 11; 2 Tim. 3:16). A second key word for discipline is related to the word *gymnasium*. Like a Greek athlete who would exercise naked (*gymnazo*), "training in godliness" requires a kind of spiritual stripping down (1 Tim. 4:7-8; Heb. 12:11). In **baptism** one dies with Christ as old practices are stripped away—then rises to put on the new clothing of **compassion** and **love** (Col. 3:9-12). In this sense every believer is called to divest attachments, to embrace vulnerabilities, and to become spiritually resilient.

Two forms of ascetic practice often appear in individuals seeking an eremitic life of **solitude** and small groups engaging in a **monastic** lifestyle of intentional **community**. The ascetic goal is not to demean the body, though it has been misapplied in this way. Rather it is to embrace a radical simplicity in order to enhance spiritual awareness and so to develop one's unique gifts, identity, and calling. As an athlete engages in self-discipline in order to cultivate inherent gifts or as a gifted musician commits to practice regularly, so the disciple engages in tried and true methods adapted from mentors of the past.

The relationship of physical disciplines to spiritual well-being emerges throughout human history. Thus ascetic experience predates any uniquely Christian expressions. In the Vedic period of Hinduism more than a thousand years B.C.E., monks gathered in small ashrams where **prayer**, **meditation**, and **poverty** became a way of life. In the fourth century B.C.E., the Buddha's disciples organized monastic communities to carry on his meditative practices.

In Jewish tradition, prophets like Jeremiah and Isaiah, along with a few followers, lived lives of prayer and radical simplicity. Later the Essene community (200 B.C.E. to 200 C.E.) advocated physical and spiritual purity and devotion.

John the Baptist, whose announced mission was to prepare the way for Jesus, followed the Jewish individual eremitic lifestyle yet also gathered a small community. In contrast to the settled Essenes, John roamed around the wilderness and villages, wearing clothing of camel's hair, eating locusts and wild honey.

Jesus is portrayed as more worldly and less ascetic than John: "For John the Baptist has come eating no bread and drinking no wine, and you say, 'He has a demon'; the Son of Man has come eating and drinking, and you say, 'Look, a glutton and a drunkard, a friend of tax collectors and sinners!'" (Luke 7:33-34). Actually Jesus' life reflects a balance of times for feasting on life's gifts (John 2:1-11; Mark 2:18-20) and **fasting** (Matt. 4:1-2).

After the Resurrection both feasting and fasting continued; but since Christian disciples, like other Jews, were a persecuted minority under Roman occupation, discipleship required a relatively ascetic life. With the assimilation of Gentiles some ascetic dietary and physical practices were altered (Acts 10; 11; 15), and charitable acts were emphasized (Gal. 2:10).

By the time the Roman emperor Constantine endorsed Christianity in 314, many Christians were acquiring wealth. Yet other individuals and small groups desired a simple life and so fled to wilderness areas of Egypt in the third and fourth centuries. Desert silence provided a spiritual gymnasium for the **desert fathers and mothers** to become true athletes of God. **Benedict of Nursia** wrote his Rule to establish healthy monastic communities. **Francis of Assisi** combined personal stripping of wealth with social concern for the poor.

Protestants have tended to devalue ascetic practices, believing that an individual is made right with God by grace alone, not by human efforts; and that inward practices like fasting and **contemplation** are less important than outward practices of loving one's neighbor. Nevertheless Church of England priest **John Wesley** in the eighteenth century reemphasized disciplines or methods so much that his followers were called "Methodists."

The late twentieth century witnessed a growing desire to reclaim the benefits and meaning of ascetic disciplines. The practice of **celibacy**, while sometimes abused as an ecclesiastical requirement, offers new insights into changing sexual mores and commitment for ordinary Christians. The Benedictine emphasis on *place* is being revalued as ancient sites like Iona in Scotland and "holy places" are sought out for retreat. The monastic value of *stability* is being reapplied to counter the fragmentation of family connectedness. **Obedience** is being reclaimed in its original Latin root, *ob-audire*: "Listen"—the first word in the Rule of St. Benedict. The practice of *fasting* is being applied not only to food, but also to fasting from materialism, which gives new meaning to the monastic vow of **poverty**. The Franciscan attitude of self-discipline is being interpreted as a way of enhancing one's **gifts** for the sake of community—caring for the environment and for marginalized people.

For further reading, see *Practicing Christianity: Critical Perspectives for an Embodied Spirituality* by Margaret R. Miles; *The Rule of Saint Benedict: Insights for the Ages* by **Joan D. Chittister**; and *The Cloister Walk* by Kathleen Norris. KIG

ASSURANCE. Understandings of assurance are often based on Romans 8:16, which speaks of the "Spirit bearing witness with our spirit that we are children of God." This verse might invite the reader to believe that assurance is most clearly realized in a strong feeling. But the Christian tradition has, in general, understood that while such a feeling may run deep, it will not be the constant companion of the believer. One thinker of the Christian tradition who reflected helpfully on this issue was the Anglican reformer **John Wesley**.

Wesley held that the witness itself was an ineffable and impossible-to-define set of sensations. The key for Wesley was that this deep and powerful witness was never truly found without the accompanying "**fruit of the Spirit**" (Gal. 5:22-24). He made this statement about the witness and the fruit: "What God hath joined together let no man put asunder" ("Witness of the Spirit II," IV.8), which echoes the scripture passage about marriage in Matthew 19:6.

When pushed on the question of assurance, Wesley resorted to a simple syllogism: A child of God is marked by **love**. I am marked by love. Therefore I am a child of God. (See his Sermon "Witness of the Spirit I" [I.11].) Since Christian love is best understood not in terms of strong feelings but as self-giving exercises of the will, to seek assurance does not necessarily mean "looking within." Others in the community are best situated to tell us if we are truly loving. Those who know us well can tell us if we are living a life of love and joy and peace, since these qualities are best perceived in relationship with others. We need not resort to endless introspective rummaging and internal quests to discover the right set of feelings that will tell us about our relationship with God. We simply need to discern in community if we are leading a life marked by the fruit of the Spirit.

For further reading, see Wesley's sermons and on discerning the fruit of the Spirit, see Philip D. Kenneson's *Life on the Vine: Cultivating the Fruit of the Spirit in Christian Community*. GSC

ATHANASIUS (ca. 296–373), bishop of Alexandria. A native of Alexandria, Athanasius was appointed a deacon and served as secretary to Alexander, bishop of Alexandria, whom he attended at the Council of Nicaea in 325. In 328 Athanasius succeeded Alexander. Because of his refusal to compromise on the decisions made at Nicaea, he earned the enmity of the Arianizing party that gained much power during the latter part of Constantine's and throughout Constantius II's reign. He was exiled five times.

Athanasius is remembered chiefly for his strong stand against Arianism. While in his twenties he wrote his famous work *On the Incarnation* in which he argued that restoration of human relationship with God necessitated the Incarnation. Between 339 and 359 he penned a series of treatises defending the decisions made at Nicaea. He even enlisted the venerable desert hermit **Antony** in the cause by writing Antony's biography in 356. After 361 he sought to win the large Semi-Arian party to the Nicene formula *homoousios* ("of the same essence") and to uphold the full divinity of the Holy Spirit. As a friend of Pachomius and Serapion and biographer of Antony, he gave a boost to the **ascetic** movement in Egypt. He also introduced **monasticism** to the West when he brought two Egyptian monks to Rome during his second exile in 339.

For further reading, see *St. Athanasius, The Life of Saint Antony* (Ancient Christian Writers, No. 10), translated by Robert T. Meyer; and David Brakke's *Athanasius and the Politics of Asceticism.* EGH

ATTACHMENT. See **Detachment.**

AUGUSTINE OF HIPPO (354–430), bishop, theologian, **Doctor of the Church** (an authoritative teacher). Born at Tagaste of a Christian mother, Monica, he was enrolled as a catechumen but not baptized. With some difficulty his parents managed to scrape up the resources to send him off to Carthage to study rhetoric with the object of becoming a lawyer, but he soon shifted to literary pursuits. At age eighteen, the year his father Patricius died, Augustine's reading of Cicero's *Hortensius* ignited an intense desire to seek God and to gain wisdom. His sexual needs and fascination with rhetoric, however, drew him away from the faith of his mother and into the **Manichaean** sect.

The dualist Manichaeans considered evil a corporeal reality poured into the soul and rejected entirely the Old Testament, a rejection that offended Augustine in many ways. He remained attached to that sect for nine years. However, unassuaged grief over the death of a dear friend provoked questions that even Faustus, the best Manichaean theologian, could not answer; before long Augustine launched a search that drew him back toward the Catholic Church of his youth.

In 385, slipping away so as to leave Monica behind, Augustine departed Carthage with his common-law wife and son and headed for Rome to teach. Although Roman students behaved better than those he had had in Carthage, they didn't pay their tuition. Therefore, he welcomed a professorship in Milan, where he came under the influence of **Ambrose**, bishop of Milan. Drawn initially to Ambrose because of his reputation as a rhetorician, Augustine found in his allegorical interpretation of scriptures an answer to the problem he had with the Old Testament. Meantime, surrounded by a cell group of friends, he went through an excruciating struggle that led finally to his conversion and baptism on Easter eve, 387. In **Neoplatonism** he found a more satisfactory answer to the problem of evil—that it is the absence or the perversion of good, which alone exists. Yet he knew that, like the apostle Paul, the good he would do he did not do when it came to his sex drive. The answer to that deficiency was the **grace** of God, which he placed at the center of his theology. Returning to Tagaste in 388, Augustine established with friends a contemplative community. On a visit to Hippo Regius in 391 the people seized him and demanded his ordination to the priesthood. In 395 he became coadjutor (assistant with right of succession) to Valerius, bishop of Hippo, and, on the death of Valerius about 396, bishop of Hippo. He held that position until his death on August 28, 430.

Few people did more than Augustine to shape Western Christianity or Christian spirituality. In the sixteenth century both Catholics and Protestants linked their theologies to his emphasis on the working of grace in Christian life. In his *Confessions*, composed in 397 partly as a reply to Manichaeism, he traced the operation of grace throughout his own life to the time of his conversion: through Monica, the death of his friend, the *Hortensius*, the circle of friends at Cassiacum. Controversy with **Pelagians** pushed him further to elucidate a scheme by which grace works to bring a rebellious will into harmony with the will of God. Whereas Pelagius believed that humans could obey God of their own volition, Augustine thought that they could do so only if aided supernaturally—that is, by grace. Prevenient grace confronts the will; operating grace evokes faith; cooperating grace makes the will work with God; and perfecting grace effects that perfect union of human and divine.

Augustine's preference for a monastic model and for Neoplatonism have assured the contemplative or mystical life an accepted place in Western Christianity. Popularized by Pope **Gregory I, the Great**, Augustine's thought supplied the framework within which contemplatives interpreted their experience of God, and that framework went virtually unchallenged until Scholastic theologians worked out a new one in the late Middle Ages.

The best introduction to Augustine's early life and inner life is his *Confessions*, available in a variety of editions. Much of his spiritual teaching comes through his sermons and homilies, which are harder to find. *The City of God* is heavy reading but forms a foundation for Christian understandings of the church and its role in society. Peter Brown's *Augustine of Hippo* is an excellent biography. EGH

AWE. One of the most foundational and personal of the spiritual **dispositions**; at its simplest level, the gasping of the body, mind, spirit, and soul in wonder and reverence at the mystery and greatness of God. It is a profoundly deep **experience** of God that leads us to unify all thought, emotion, and experience in rapt attention to God's presence, works, and wonders.

Most of us experience a sense of awe at particular times in our lives, even if we do not perceive our awe as God-directed. We have felt awe in the presence of a beautiful sunset or sunrise; at the birth of a child; on a mountaintop, while viewing a majestic scene; at the beach witnessing the vastness and power of the ocean; in church while grasping the beauty of a stained-glass window; while watching children play; or while gazing at the intricacies of a leaf. These experiences plunge us into awe because our souls recognize them as manifestations of God's **grace**, power, and presence.

Awe is also a disposition that can permeate our lives. It is nurtured by our continual awareness of God's omnipresence and omnipotence—of God's grace being everywhere at once so that in everything we do we sense God in awe. We nurture awe through prayerful attention to God's presence in our lives. It emerges as we become more and more aware of how God truly is "above all and through all and in all" (Eph. 4:6).

The formation of a deep spiritual life always entails a growing sense of awe as we increasingly experience God throughout our lives. Awe is closely related to a "fear of the LORD," which is the foundation of awe—an awe-filled fear in which we recognize with humility just how vast, wonderful, loving, and mysterious God is, and how small, insignificant, and powerless we are. This fear is also rooted in **faith**. Because we are rooted in God at our deepest levels, we recognize God's glory and power; and we tremble. John of Patmos recounts his vision of the four living creatures and the twenty-four elders gathered around the divine throne, worshiping and praising God for all of God's greatness (Rev. 4:8-11).

When caught in a state of awe, we feel a sense of mysterious unity with God, recognizing that we are a part of all God's creation but also that everything is in God's hands. God is in control of the cosmos; in giving ourselves over to God in awe and reverence, we share in God's grace and love.

The Idea of the Holy by **Rudolf Otto** is a classic book on the subject of awe. NGS

B

BAILLIE, DONALD M. (1887–1954), Scottish pastor, teacher, systematic theologian, and ecumenist; considered one of the most influential Presbyterian scholars of the twentieth century. Baillie was Professor of Systematic Theology at St. Andrews University from 1934 until the time of his death in 1954.

Baillie's most significant contribution to systematic theology came in his brilliant treatise *God Was in Christ* (1948), a Christology based in the foundational ideas of Incarnation and atonement. Key to his understanding of Jesus as the Christ was the human selfhood of Jesus being yielded totally to God in such a way that his whole life became a divine expression of God's love in human form. His interpretation of the Trinity began with the God of creation who was shared by the Christians with the Jews. However, he felt our understanding of God as Christians is completed by the Incarnation (God in the flesh) and Pentecost (the gift of the **Holy Spirit** to help us interpret the Incarnation).

Baillie believed that any Christian spiritual or devotional life needed a foundation based on a sense of the Trinity as a living reality. Beyond this, just as Jesus bore the essence of God through the incarnation in his life, he also bore the divine nature of atonement through his passion and death on the cross. For Baillie, the church truly becomes the **body of Christ** in the world to tell the sacred story of what God has done in Jesus Christ.

In *The Theology of the Sacraments* (1957) Baillie argued that the **sacraments** were concentrations of the much more widespread sacramental significance of everyday life. Why else, he posited, would Jesus incorporate the divine essence in something as mundane and commonplace as bread and wine? For him the sacraments were the vehicle through which the divine word broke into the wider world and sanctified it. Baillie also wrote a foreword to *A Dairy of Private Prayer* by his brother, **John Baillie**. SFP

BAILLIE, JOHN (1886–1960), distinguished Scottish scholar, teacher, author, and Presbyterian preacher. Baillie acquired his degrees at New College and the University of Edinburgh. After World War I, Baillie went to the United States and served on the faculty at Auburn Theological Seminary from 1920 to 1927. While there, he was ordained to the ministry. He taught briefly at Emmanuel College in Toronto, Canada, then from 1930 to 1935 at Union Theological Seminary. When Baillie finally returned to Scotland, he served as professor at the University of Edinburgh (1935–56) until his retirement.

Because of Baillie's contribution to systematic theology, Yale University conferred the honorary degree of Doctor of Divinity. Baillie, while recognized as a theologian, was involved in his own church affiliation. From 1943 to 1944 he served as the moderator for the General Assembly of the Church of Scotland and was the first person to hold this position without being ordained in Scotland.

Baillie was a prolific writer and had over fifteen books published during and after his lifetime. Some of his works include *Our Knowledge of God*, *A Reasoned Faith*, and *The Sense of the Presence of God*. The book that best reveals his spirituality is *A Diary of Private Prayer*, in which he emphasizes God's immanence in contrast to other twentieth-century theologians who emphasized God's **transcendence**.

Baillie excelled at balancing both mind and heart. Influenced by his Celtic roots, Baillie argued that all humans had some access to the knowledge of God and were not limited to biblical revelation alone. Humanity could be aware of God's presence through God's self-disclosure in the world. Baillie claimed that there was no time in his life when he did not sense God's presence. Baillie's writings demonstrated how his devotional life served as the center of his academic endeavors. ASJ

BAKER, DAVID AUGUSTINE (1575–1641), Benedictine spiritual director. Born into a Protestant family in Wales, Baker converted to Roman Catholicism after narrowly escaping death in London in 1603. The young lawyer joined the Benedictines in Padua, Italy. After his ordination, he served nine years as spiritual director to the English Benedictine Sisters in Cambrai, France, where he wrote about sixty treatises on ascetic and **mystical** theology.

Baker is considered the link between the fourteenth-century mystical tradition (represented by **Walter Hilton** and *The Cloud of Unknowing*, on which Baker wrote a commentary) and the modern period. As a spiritual director and teacher of prayer, he was much less structured and rigid than his contemporaries, which led to occasional conflicts. He expected people to begin the life of mental prayer by systematic **meditation**, using imagination and intellect. Eventually this experience would pall, signifying the time to move on to the contemplative way of life. Such a life would begin with active **contemplation**, consisting first of "forced acts" in which one short-circuits the preliminaries of meditation and goes directly to the desire for union with God and later of "aspirations" proceeding naturally from the **Holy Spirit**. Passive contemplation without forced acts or aspirations might follow active contemplation.

The monastic spirituality of the sixteenth century had become rigid and harsh. Baker abolished the daily **examens** of the sisters ; he felt they were being too hard on themselves, too plagued by scruples. He helped them distinguish between deliberate sin and the obscure, hidden tendencies to imperfection.

Baker taught no special method for prayer, only that one is free to follow the Holy Spirit, the one true director in the life of prayer. If one desires and seeks God, the Spirit will gladly lead in the way that is best for the individual. A wise spiritual director will also pay attention to the movement of the Spirit.

Baker's treatises were gathered and published posthumously as *Holy Wisdom: or, Directions for the Prayer of Contemplation.* WW

BAPTISM. Baptism is the unrepeatable ritual washing that signifies Christ's action in the church, which initiates persons into the life of the Christian **community**. Baptism is both a specific event in which persons are sprinkled, immersed, or have water poured over them in the name of the Trinity—Father, Son, and Holy Spirit—and a process of **conversion** and **formation** as persons learn what it means to profess their faith in Christ and to take on the life of discipleship.

Baptism is both God's act of **grace** in the world and the human community's response to that grace in **faith** and **obedience**. As God's gracious action, it is the means by which persons are initiated into Christ's church, incorporated into the story of God's saving action in the world, participate in Christ's death and resurrection, and given new birth or life in water and **Spirit**. As a response in faith, it is the means by which persons renounce and repent of the way of **sin**, confess faith in and commitment to Jesus Christ, and are joined to a community of Christian faith. Baptism is a **sacrament** in that it is a means by which we experience and receive God's gracious love. It is an ordinance in that the risen Christ commands the disciples to "go… and make disciples…, baptizing them in the name of the Father and of the Son and of the Holy Spirit" (Matt. 28:19).

Although the church often has minimized the diverse images of baptism present in the New Testament, these images reveal the richness of the meaning of Christian baptism. Christian baptism is the means by which we know the forgiveness of our sins and our adoption as God's children (Mark 1:4-11 and parallels); receive new birth (John 3:5); die and rise with Christ (Rom. 6:1-12; Col. 2:12); receive the washing away of sin and cleansing of the heart (1 Cor. 6:11); receive God's seal and guarantee (1 Cor. 1:21-22); are washed, sanctified, and justified (1 Cor. 6:9-11); participate in Israel's exodus from captivity (1 Cor. 10:1-2); are clothed with the new garment of Christ (Gal. 3:27); experience enlightenment or the healing of our blindness enabling us to see the light of Christ (Eph. 5:14); are renewed in the Spirit (Titus 3:5); and reexperience salvation from the Flood (1 Pet. 3:20-21).

The richness of these images invites the church to consider the many levels of meaning that inform the church's understanding of baptism. They also invite consideration of the ways in which baptism requires a commitment to ongoing growth, **conversion**, and transformation into the fullness of the image of Christ in the midst of a **community** of faith, regardless of the age at which a person receives baptism. These images also are reminders that baptism is an experience of a community of faith striving to live into **holiness** of heart and mind. Baptism calls the church both to personal and social holiness that seek **God's will** in all arenas of human life in the world.

Ecumenical conversations of the past generation press churches to reclaim baptism as a sign and seal of a common discipleship—a sign of the church's fundamental unity in Christ—and to live in the truth of the claim in Ephesians 4:4-6 that "there is one body and one Spirit...one Lord, one faith, one baptism, one God and Father of all, who is above all and through all and in all." This fundamental claim of baptismal unity as Christian people summons us to overcome the divisions throughout the church, whether these divisions are based in race, class, gender, sexual orientation, or doctrine.

For further information, read Maxwell E. Johnson's *The Rites of Christian Initiation: Their Evolution and Interpretation* or Laurence Hull Stookey's *Baptism: Christ's Act in the Church.* EBA

BARTH, KARL (1886–1968), Swiss Reformed pastor and theologian. Barth has been compared to **Augustine**, **Thomas Aquinas**, **Luther**, and **Calvin** in stature as a theologian. He was born in Basel, Switzerland, where he was baptized in the cathedral church. He later studied theology under the liberal theologian Adolf Harnack and from 1911 to 1921 pastored in Safenwil, a small town in Switzerland. During these years he wrote a commentary *The Epistle to the Romans* that dramatically impacted biblical and theological scholarship. He contended that the Bible was not a human word about God but a divine word about humanity. This work was well received, and Barth then assumed a series of teaching positions in Europe. He later came into conflict with the rising Nazi movement and returned to Basel, where he lived and taught at the university until his death.

From 1932 Barth worked on thirteen volumes of *Church Dogmatics*, which remain his most substantive contribution to modern Christian thought as the founder of the neo-orthodox movement in theology. In *Church Dogmatics* Barth offers a rich interpretation of scripture and the history of Christian thought, especially medieval, reformation, and liberal traditions. He insisted that the word of God stood in contrast to liberalism and conservatism, tradition and modernity. He began not with natural theology but instead with the revealed word of God in Jesus Christ. God's revelation is found first in Jesus Christ, then in scripture, and next in the preaching of the word. Human salvation is understood in the election of Jesus Christ for all. Barth's vast influence shaped the thinking of those who agreed with him and those who did not. The biblical God, according to Barth, could not be created in the image of humanity; instead, God was utterly free from human definition, sovereign over human affairs, and yet immersed in the human condition through Jesus Christ.

Many of Barth's shorter works are accessible to the lay reader. A collection of his sermons preached in the Basel prison, titled

Deliverance to the Captives summarizes his beliefs, particularly about incarnation and resurrection. His book of *Selected Prayers*, arranged according to the church year, reveals both his profound intellect and deep devotion. For those who want to delve more deeply into Barth's mature thought, *Church Dogmatics* III, IV include discussions of the **Sabbath**, **prayer**, family relationships, and vocation.

For further reading, see the above works. The best biography is *Karl Barth: His Life from Letters and Autobiographical Texts* by Eberhard Busch. KHC

BASIL OF CAESAREA (ca. 330–79), one of three theologians known as "the great **Cappadocians**." He came from a distinguished family that included **Gregory of Nyssa** and Macrina. After receiving the best classical and Christian education at Caesarea, Constantinople, and Athens, he took up the monastic life at the urging of his sister, Macrina. In 358, he visited monks in Syria and Egypt and then settled down as a hermit by the Iris River near Neo-Caesarea in Cappadocia.

Basil framed the monastic **rule** that bears his name between 358 and 364. Set out in a longer (313 items) and a shorter (55 items) form, the Rule avoided the extreme **asceticism** of the hermits. Basil preferred the model of Eustathius, bishop of Sebaste, to the Egyptian or Syrian models. As a means to the life of **perfection**, asceticism is best practiced in communal life under **obedience**. The main objective of the monk is to love God and neighbor, and that is best done in **community**. Unlike some hermits who devoted themselves exclusively to prayer, Basil required a combination of prayer and work. He believed monks should choose trades that would allow them to live tranquilly and should aim at simplicity and frugality. The monks should also perform services for the needy. By reducing the severity of some forms of monasticism and placing it in service of the church, Basil may have saved it.

In 364 Basil left his hermitage as his bishop, Eusebius of Neo-Caesarea, called on him to refute the Arianism of Emperor Valens. In 370 he was appointed to succeed Eusebius as bishop of Neo-Caesarea. He held this office for the rest of his life. His most important spiritual writings include many letters and a treatise *On the Holy Spirit.*

For additional reading, see *The Ascetic Works of Saint Basil*, translated with introduction and notes by W. K. L. Clarke; E. F. Morison's *St. Basil and His Rule: A Study in Early Monasticism;* or Philip Rousseau's *Basil of Caesarea.* EGH

BAXTER, RICHARD (1615–91), Puritan pastor and leader. Born at Rowton, England, he was educated at home by his father, Richard, a Puritan, and later at Wroxeter under Puritan leader John Owen and at Ludlow by Richard Wickstead, chaplain of the Council of Ludlow. The worldliness of Wickstead and then the court in London repulsed Baxter and pushed him toward the Nonconformists. When the Convocation of the Church of England passed the Et Cetera Oath in 1640 (an affirmation of episcopal polity against presbyterian or congregational church government), he refused to sign and welcomed an invitation to become pastor of Kidderminster. When the English Civil War began, Baxter sided with the Parliament and was twice driven out of town by Royalist sympathizers. He served as chaplain to the Parliamentary Army from 1642 to 1646 before taking a leave for rest and writing. Then he returned to Kidderminster for a long, happy period (1647–60).

In frail health throughout much of his life, Baxter preached "as a dying man to dying men." He also wrote voluminously and set a high standard for Protestant pastors. He composed his classic on Puritan **meditation**, *The Saints' Everlasting Rest*, following an extended illness in 1646. Baxter's method of meditation agrees in many respects with **Ignatius of Loyola**'s *Spiritual Exercises*, especially in encouraging imagination through the use of reason. Although his Nonconformist sentiments grew, Baxter remained critical of Oliver Cromwell's rigid Independent Church and the cause of

Parliament. Some scholars have classified him as a Presbyterian, but he fit no stereotype. At the restoration of the monarchy in 1660, he refused Charles II's offer of a bishopric. He took a leading role in the unsuccessful Savoy Conference in 1661 on behalf of the Puritans. When persecution of Nonconformists followed, the bishop of Worcester refused to let him return to Kidderminster. He spent much of the last thirty years of his life under virtual house arrest and in ill health. He died December 8, 1691, having lived just long enough to welcome the Toleration Act of 1689.

For further reading, see Richard Baxter's autobiography, *Reliquiae Baxterianae*; his books, *The Saints' Everlasting Rest* and *The Divine Life in Three Treatises*; and A. R. Ladell's biography, *Richard Baxter, Puritan and Mystic.* EGH

BEATITUDE. (From Latin *beatitudo*, "blessedness"), beatitude can refer either to the state of blessedness or to a literary form describing that state and those who will experience it. The literary form of a beatitude states the rewards of certain actions, attitudes, or life situations, typically in the form "Happy (or blessed) are those who… for…." The rewards though, as is clear in scripture, may not be evident to the secular world but only in relation to a cosmic divine order.

The Psalms contain several beatitudes where the writer claims, "Happy are those…" who do the work of the LORD or who receive God's favor. They may refer to experiencing forgiveness (32:1, 2), to caring for the oppressed (41:1), or to being drawn close to God (65:4). One disturbing beatitude reflects the happiness of attaining revenge (137:9). In the New Testament, beatitudes are most found in the Gospel passages as words from Jesus. They may be addressed to a general population (Matt. 11:6), to the disciples (John 20:29), or to an individual (John 16:17). Finally, beatitudes can also be exhortations, as in Revelation 1:3 and 22:14.

The most famous beatitudes are in Matthew 5:3-12, the beginning of the Sermon on the Mount. Scholars have debated whether the list is prescriptive (how Christians should be in order to be blessed) or descriptive (what kinds of people are blessed) and whether the order has a particular significance. **John Wesley**, in a series of sermons on the beatitudes, saw them as describing the progress of the spiritual life: knowing one's spiritual poverty produces mourning and humility leading to hunger for righteousness, which makes one increasingly merciful and pure. The state of blessedness these beatitudes describe includes the **assurance** that we are God's children; divine comfort, **justification**, and **mercy;** and the **vision of God**. A similar list in the Sermon on the Plain (Luke 6:20-26) adds a contrasting series of "woe to…" persons who act against God's reign.

Divine Guidance : Seeking to Find and Follow the Will of God by Susan Muto and Adrian van Kaam is a recent reflection on the Beatitudes. WBF

BEDE (ca. 672–735), English monk, biblical exegete, and historian. A product of the Northumbrian renaissance of learning, a skilled educator, and a creative writer, he was one of the most learned men of his age. Bede spent most of his life in the monastic communities of Wearmouth and Jarrow in northeast England, having been committed at the age of seven to the **rule** of life compiled by Benedict Biscop. Standing in the **Benedictine** tradition, his spirituality was also formed by the **Augustinian** influences that dominated the early medieval theological world. His writings, while fundamentally austere and erudite, reflect a profound pastoral concern and an emphasis on study in the service of the church and the explication of the Christian life.

While most famous today for his *Ecclesiastical History of the English People*, the first history of the church in England and the only source on the history of early mission in the British Isles, Bede was more esteemed by his contemporaries as a biblical commentator and a master of allegorical method. Other significant writings include both poetic and prose accounts of St. Cuthbert's missionary exploits and miracles, a history of Benedictine abbots, treatises related to the controversial dating of Easter, and scientific works. Particularly in his biographical and historical writings, he illustrates the church's unity and order through his vivid descriptions of moral Christian leaders. Bede was noted for his goodness and personal charm, and William of Malmesbury described him as one of the "most learned and least proud" monks of the English church. A later editor of his works described him as "the very model of the saintly scholar-priest." Less than a century after his death he was honored with the title *Venerable*, and in 1899 Leo XIII declared him a **Doctor of the Church** (an authoritative teacher).

In addition to Bede's own writings (the *Ecclesiastical History* is readily available in translation), consider reading George H. Brown's *Bede the Venerable*. PWC

BEGUINES. Laywomen who gathered in unofficial religious communities throughout the Low Countries and Germany, beginning in the late twelfth century. Their numbers peaked in the tens of thousands between 1220 and 1312. A smaller movement of men, the Beghards, also formed. The origin of the name *Beguine* may have referred to the ash gray (*bége* in French) clothing the Beguines typically wore. The early days of the movement are hard to trace, but it seems to have grown up in response to a religious revival that was sweeping Europe at the time. Among the burgeoning medieval cities and towns, traveling mendicants (such as **Dominicans** and **Franciscans**) preached in the streets to anyone who would listen. They called townspeople to return to the simple truth of the gospel, the "apostolic life." However, when women responded wholeheartedly to this call, they found that even progressive **monastic** orders had closed their doors to women. These laywomen began to form their own communities around urban centers, sometimes remaining with their families, but more often joining small communities of celibate women.

The Beguines served the sick and the poor—founding the first hospices for the dying. They supported themselves through weaving, embroidering, preparing the dead for burial, and undertaking manual labor. While there was no uniform **rule**, Beguines typically took simple, informal vows of devotion to the **Eucharist** and **prayer**, as well as gave their personal property to the **community** in the manner of the early church.

An important early supporter of the movement, Jacques of Vitry, admired the saintly life of Marie d'Oignies, a French Beguine. Jacques of Vitry wrote the story of Marie's life in 1215, revealing the Beguines as a pious alternative to the Albigenses, another communal group that existed outside the established tradition. In fact, not long after his publication, Jacques gained papal dispensation for these irregular Beguine communities. However, suspicions about these nonconformist communities of women grew as the century waned. William of St. Amour, the major detractor, appealed to ecclesiastical law to discredit them. *Beguine* gradually became a disparaging term for any woman who styled herself as religious. At the Council of Vienne (1312), the official status of the Beguines was condemned, although exceptions were made for some local groups to continue. In Belgium, for example, Beguinages (houses of Beguines) existed well into the modern day.

The tremendous mystical legacy of the Beguines, lost for centuries, has been recovered only recently. It includes the writings of the German Beguine **Mechthild of Magdeburg**; the Flemish mystic and poet, **Hadewijch**; and the martyred French Beguine, **Marguerite Porete**. Writing in the language of the people, the Beguines' texts testify to the rise of a compelling vernacular spirituality. In contrast to the formal Latin texts of monastics, the Beguine authors used familiar imagery, metaphor, paradox, and analogy—much like the popular imagery in the literature of courtly love. The writings testify to a spirituality that explored the paradox of **suffering** and **love** in the Christian life. Medieval theology viewed women as closer to the flesh than men; thus

Beguines readily identified with the human suffering of Jesus. Beguine mystics vividly depicted the internal suffering arising from the physical absence of Christ, the Beloved Bridegroom, in earthly life.

Saskia Murk-Jansen's *Brides in the Desert* is a readable, comprehensive book on the spirituality of the Beguines. SAF

BENEDICT OF NURSIA (ca. 480–547), monastic founder. At the time of Benedict's birth in the small town of Nursia about seventy miles northeast of Rome, the empire was crumbling. As a young man pursuing a liberal education in Rome, Benedict became disgusted by the debauchery and meaningless existence of many of his contemporaries. He abandoned his studies, became a solitary monk in a cave above Lake Subiaco, and soon attracted others on a serious quest for God. Under his guidance monasteries were founded to facilitate companionship and order. When Benedict and a group of his monks moved south to establish a new monastery at Monte Cassino, he composed his **rule**.

The Rule of Benedict incorporates material from earlier monastic sources and ecclesial documents. A wisdom text with numerous references to scripture, the rule offers practical directions for Christian life. Benedict clearly states that God is present at the heart of life, the "hub" of community, and also at its circumference. Balance is a core value. Each monastic day provides for **solitude** and **community**, work and rest, study and recreation, corporate worship and prayer alone. Benedict gives guidance on appropriate food consumption, discipline, service, and care for the sick and especially emphasizes hospitality. Each guest is to be received as Christ.

Many living outside the cloister are drawn to Benedictine spirituality because it is practical, biblically based, and capable of being interpreted in a variety of life situations. The three Benedictine vows of stability, conversion, and obedience are relevant for Christian disciples in every age. Stability means more than staying in place, i.e., in the cloister, and calls for a commitment to faithfulness where we are. Conversion provides a reminder that God is always inviting us to change and grow. The Latin root of the word *obedience* also means "to listen," indicating that our first obligation is to hear God address us through scripture, nature, and human experience and then do what God asks. The Benedictine model of biblical reflection known as *lectio divina* enables us to move from head to heart in our reading of scripture. Benedictine monasticism has continued to flourish since the sixth century and today includes both Roman Catholic and Anglican orders. Reform movements led to the foundation of new groups following a stricter observance of the Rule—the **Cistercians** in 1098 and the **Trappists** in 1893. **Thomas Merton** was perhaps the best-known twentieth-century American Trappist monk.

The Rule of Saint Benedict is available in many editions, including *St. Benedict's Rule: A New Translation for Today* by Patrick Barry. *Heart Whispers: Benedictine Wisdom for Today* by Elizabeth J. Canham is a recent reflection on the Rule as a guide for all Christians. EJC

BENEDICTION. A pronouncement of God's favor that often uses the trinitarian formula representing the Father, Son, and Holy Spirit. The formal **worship** service draws to a close, and the pastor dismisses the congregation with a blessing in the name of God.

Benedictions are found throughout the Hebrew Bible. God's promises to Sarah and Abraham in Genesis 17 include a special blessing for Sarah: "I will bless her, and moreover I will give you a son by her. I will bless her, and she shall give rise to nations; kings of peoples shall come from her" (v. 16). A blessing still used today comes from Numbers 6:24-26, where God gives Moses a priestly blessing for the use of Aaron and his descendants: "The LORD bless you and keep you; the LORD make his face to shine upon you, and be gracious to you; the LORD lift up his countenance upon you, and give you peace."

Many letters in the New Testament contain benedictions, particularly near their end.

Christians still use many of these, including Hebrews 13:20; 2 Timothy 4:22; Ephesians 6:23-24; and Romans 15:13. Best known of all is the trinitarian benediction in 2 Corinthians 13:13: "The grace of the Lord Jesus Christ, the love of God, and the communion of the Holy Spirit be with all of you." This and other trinitarian benedictions are often used simultaneously with the sign of the cross: the pastor motions with an outstretched hand from head to chest, and then left to right. PDB

BERNADETTE OF LOURDES (1844–79), French visionary. Born Marie Bernarde Soubirous, she was Francis and Louise's oldest child. When she was about fourteen years old, this uneducated French girl (along with two companions) was gathering firewood near the banks of the Gave de Pau river in Lourdes when her eye was caught by a bright light surrounding a lady in a cave. She continued to experience apparitions daily for eighteen days. Crowds drew near to witness Bernadette praying. Skeptical civil authorities were highly agitated by all the commotion that arose from her claims. When a previously nonexistent spring began to flow inside the grotto, it was taken as a "sign" from the Virgin Mary. Questioned unmercifully and under stiff scrutiny, Bernadette stuck to her message: The Lady said she is the "Immaculate Conception" and asked that a chapel be built where the apparitions took place. Today millions go on pilgrimage to Lourdes hoping to be healed in the miraculous waters. In 1866 Bernadette entered the Sisters of Notre Dame convent at Nevers, remaining there until her death on Easter Sunday, 1879. *The Song of Bernadette* by Franz Werfel is a novelization of her life that was made into a film. Bernadette was canonized in 1933. EKM

BERNARD OF CLAIRVAUX (1090–1153), French **Cistercian** abbot and preacher, and a principal promoter of the spirit of the New Monastery founded at Cîteaux in 1098 for stricter observance of the rule of **Benedict**. Bernard of Fontaines entered monastic life

there at twenty-two and was abbot of Clairvaux, one of the earliest foundations of Cîteaux, by his mid-twenties. Although his **disposition** was **contemplative**, he became the confidant of princes and prelates, traveling throughout Europe soliciting support for the causes he embraced. Arguably the most influential figure in Europe during his lifetime, Bernard led an active life of a sort that he discouraged in monks. Overly conscientious and sometimes blinded by his embrace of a cause, Bernard nonetheless had persuasive power.

Bernard was reticent in the face of the emerging approaches to theology in his day. He engaged in theological controversy only when told it was his duty to do so. While recognizing the distinction between the natural and supernatural, Bernard had no difficulty weaving through the boundary between them. Despite his influence on political and ecclesiastical affairs, Bernard's importance lies in his writing and teachings on the spiritual life.

Understanding Bernard's contribution necessitates recognizing that he was a product of monastic theology and the most distinguished writer representing the monastic experience. Monastic theology, in contrast to the theology of the medieval universities, is more symbolic and poetic, giving less attention to objective analysis and description. It is a discipline for educating the mind and heart to grow in **faith**, **hope**, and **love**. Its object is not the discovery of new corollaries or solutions to vexing problems but growth in **holiness**. It is an experientially based, relationally grounded traditional reformulation of the Christian teaching on the journey toward union with God. In this and more, the monastic way has wide appeal among many spiritual seekers today.

Monastic life gives priority to regular pondering of the Word through *lectio divina*, so Bernard's work is altogether scriptural. His writing is stunningly beautiful—prose poised at the brink of poetry. And perhaps because his work is grounded in the common life within the monastery, its governing concern is love more than knowledge.

Desire is the key to understanding Bernard's spiritual teaching. He traces the origin of desire for God to the human being's creation in the divine image. Humankind is endowed with a capacity for and compatibility with God. Any movement toward God is the result of this gift, and whatever love is experienced is God's gift. A human being is created with an emptiness that can only be filled through an intimate relationship with God.

Bernard's concern is with the *experience* of love in the interplay of presence and absence of what is desired. He explores this theme throughout his *Sermons on the Song of Songs*. What matters is not that one experience the presence of what one desires, but that one continuously live with, in, and from the desire for God amidst competing desires. Human desire thus becomes spiritual desire—the longing to be reunited in and through God's love known in the Incarnate Word, Jesus Christ, by the gift of the spirit of love.

This understanding gives rise to a spirituality in which the bodily, the earthly, the ordinary are central; and the beauty of God is beheld in fragile human flesh. As Bernard explains in *On Loving God*, love for God is expressed in and through loving self and others. Human relationships rooted in the gift of love are not a diversion but the way to God.

Bernard of Clairvaux: Essential Writings, edited by Dennis E. Tamburello, collects several works. MD

BÉRULLE, PIERRE DE (1575–1629), Cardinal, reformer, founder of the French Oratory (a spiritual community for diocesan priests) and chief figure in the French School of spirituality that came to dominate Roman Catholicism in the late seventeenth century. Bérulle's Christ-centered spirituality emphasized passive **mystical** participation in the inner "states" of Christ through cultivation of "adoration" and "servitude." Although his works are today little read, his stress on human "nothingness" and the grandeur of God greatly influenced later Catholic spirituality.

Other members of the French School were Jean-Jacques Olier (founder of the Society of Saint-Sulpice or Sulpicians) and Jean Eudes (founder of the Congregation of Jesus and Mary or Eudists). In the late eighteenth century the Sulpicians, fleeing the French revolution, carried the spirituality of the French School to the new American republic, where they established seminaries and trained the first generation of U.S. Catholic priests. Eudists have secondary schools and seminaries in Africa and Latin America and centers for individual and parish spiritual formation in the United States and Canada.

Treatises and letters by Bérulle, Olier, Eudes, and Madeleine de Saint-Joseph are collected in *Bérulle and the French School: Selected Writings,* edited by William M. Thompson and translated by Lowell M. Glendon. WMW

BIOGRAPHIES, SPIRITUAL. Spiritual biographies provide a glimpse into a life. As with any other biography of a historical figure, the best-known examples are of famous individuals or signature characters in an era. Spiritual biographies go beyond simply stating facts to dealing with the spiritual life of an individual. The spiritual nature of this literature answers on its most basic level what has happened in a life and how God has spoken at that time. Reflection on God's action in a life is what the writer longs to bring to the forefront of any spiritual biography.

For the Christian church, the first value of spiritual biographies is that the genre endures through the ages. For example, far more readers will encounter **Augustine**'s autobiographical *Confessions* than will read **Thomas Aquinas**'s doctrinal *Summa Theologica*. As treatises that will speak to new generations, they challenge future Christians to reexamine issues of salvation and Christian living and sometimes some of the most elemental Christian doctrines. On a personal plane, we get from these writings glimpses into personal evaluation, deep **confession**, and a keen sense of attentiveness to the personal journey of faith.

The second value of the biographies is

that they lift up the heroes of the faith. Some of the earliest Christian literature focused on the lives of the saints, stories of men and women who endured persecution and avoided the traps of the world. Tales of their miraculous powers, their faith amidst tragedy and persecution, and devotion to fundamental Christian doctrines were used to empower another generation to take Christianity to a new level of witness and discipleship. These lives used the scriptures as their model, for the Bible takes time to lift up heroes of the faith— most notably the life of Christ in the Gospels.

Spiritual biographies fall into four major genres. Biographies (or hagiographies, writings about saints) describe the spiritual life of another. Most likely the author is a close follower or disciple of the individual written about. *The Little Flowers of St. Francis of Assisi* is a classic example, along with the lives mentioned above. Biographies offer the perspective of somebody looking on a life, intertwining the best of the individual's journey with inner religious struggle. They may also embellish facts to augment the picture of sanctity.

Autobiography relates the subject's own account. **Augustine**'s *Confessions* fits this genre, although the book is written as a prayer to God. Its pages contain the inner thoughts and the intense spiritual quest of the bishop of Hippo, offering a deeper and more complex image of the journey to spiritual fulfillment than biography told secondhand. Typically, the autobiography is more in tune to one portion of the subject's life, and therefore more specific in its purpose.

Journals are much like autobiographies, but with a more personal immediacy that transports readers to life at a specific time or moment. The spiritual journey is looked at instantaneously without the help of hindsight. Famous journals include those of **John Woolman** and **John Wesley**.

Visions showcase images or words from God received in dreams, apparitions, and times of prayer by remarking on them and reflecting on their sacred importance. Many of this genre come from the lives of women: **Julian of Norwich**, **Teresa of Ávila**, **Hildegard of Bingen**, and **Catherine of Siena** all wrote reflections on visions. WBF

BIRGITTA OF SWEDEN (ca. 1303–73), visionary, mystic, and patron saint of Sweden. Born in Finsta, Sweden, Birgitta was the daughter of Ingborg Persson, governor of Upland. At seven she began having visions about the passion of Jesus, which influenced her deep devotion to Christ. Around the age of fourteen Birgitta married Ulf Gudmarsson, who became governor of Nericia. They were happily married for twenty-eight years, had eight children, and devoted themselves to God and their families. In 1335 Birgitta became the chief lady-in-waiting to the queen of Sweden. King Magnus II and his queen ignored Birgitta's counsel for many years, so finally Birgitta was granted permission to leave the royal court and accompany her husband on a pilgrimage to Compostela, Spain. After this trip in 1344, Birgitta's husband died, so she lived as a penitent outside a Cistercian monastery in Alvastra. The prior of this monastery recorded Birgitta's visions and translated her revelations into Latin.

In 1346 King Magnus endowed monasteries for men and women at Vadstena, where Birgitta began the Orders of the Most Holy Savior (Brigittines, one for men and another for women), confirmed by Pope Urban V in 1370. The monastery at Vadstena remained the intellectual center of Sweden until the sixteenth century. In 1350 Birgitta and her daughter Catherine (who later became Saint Catherine of Sweden) traveled to Rome, where Birgitta lived the rest of her life, devoted to prayer, providing shelter and aid to the poor and homeless, advising rulers on political matters, bringing about reform within the church, and warning the pope in Avignon to return to Rome. In 1372 Birgitta made a pilgrimage to the Holy Land, but upon her return died on July 23, 1373. She was canonized in 1391. Both her daughter Catherine and **Catherine of Siena** took up her causes of reform and restoration of the papacy to Rome.

Birgitta's revelations, first published in 1492, were widely read. *Birgitta of Sweden: Life and Selected Revelations,* edited by Marguerite Tjader Harris, offers an eyewitness biography and selections from her writings. ASJ

BLAKE, WILLIAM (1757–1827), English poet, engraver, composer, and artist, born in London. His parents, James and Catherine, had four other children, though all William's younger brothers died at an early age. From an early age, William exhibited unique mental and imaginative sensitivities. His parents sent him to drawing school. From 1772 to 1779 he apprenticed with James Basire, learning engraving, etching, stippling, and copying. While attending the Royal Academy, he studied the Bible, literature (especially Milton), theology, art history, and philosophy. Deeply concerned about the revolutionary events of his own day, Blake boldly addressed the cruelty and violence through political, moral, religious, and artistic themes. Blake focused his imaginative, spiritual, and artistic energy on helping people take responsibility for the brutal and oppressive ways of the world that left individuals and humanity feeling fragmented. His apocalyptic images in the *The Prophetic Writings of William Blake* offered new possibilities to improve the future. Using his prophetic, poetic, artistic voice he sought to inspire and rekindle the human spirit. He viewed the human capacity to imagine as a spiritual gift that keeps us in communion with God and one another.

In 1782 Blake married Catherine Boucher, who became his constant companion and who helped to engrave the copperplates used in "illuminated printing." While Blake enjoyed a seven-year creative burst, he lacked the recognition he deserved. Although known more for his carefully crafted designs and etchings than his poetry, this "social rebel" played a key role in advancing the revolt against rationalist philosophy.

For Blake's treatise on the importance of the imagination over sheer reason, read *There Is No Natural Religion* and *All Religions Are One.*

Blake's engraved illustrations of *The Book of Job* are considered his greatest artistic achievement. Other principal works include *Songs of Innocence and of Experience, The Marriage of Heaven and Hell,* and *Jerusalem,* his longest prophetic text. See Sheldon Cheney's *Men Who Have Walked with God* for a good general introduction to Blake's life and works. *Blake's Poetry and Designs: A Norton Critical Edition* by Mary Lynn Johnson and John Ernest Grant is a critical text containing illuminations in color, prose, and criticism. EKM

BLOOM, ANTHONY (b. 1914), Russian Orthodox bishop and teacher on prayer. Metropolitan Anthony of Sourozh, head of the Russian Orthodox Church in Great Britain, has gained an international audience through his books *Living Prayer* and *Beginning to Pray* and BBC radio and television broadcasts. His teaching stories and anecdotes are reminiscent of those of the **desert fathers and mothers** among whom the Orthodox tradition originated.

The son of a Russian diplomat, Bloom emigrated with his family to France because of the revolution. He attended the Sorbonne and finished medical school in 1939, just as the Second World War began. He served in the French army as a surgeon and in the French Resistance as well. In 1943 he secretly took monastic vows and in 1948 was ordained a priest. Soon afterward he was assigned to England, where in 1962 he became an archbishop and in 1966 a metropolitan (head of the Russian Orthodox church in Great Britain. RMH

BODY AND SPIRITUALITY. At the heart of Christianity is the **Incarnation**. God came to us in Jesus, in human form, in a human body. Throughout history many Christians have been unable to link the body of Jesus with the bodies of the rest of humanity.

Many attitudes toward the human body have been expressed throughout Christian history. At times attention to the body was absent from Christian writings. In these periods, the body was simply ignored. In others, the body was denied. At other times Christians were exhorted to control their bodies because bodily appetites and activities were viewed as a hindrance to spiritual development. Sometimes the followers of Jesus were taught to transcend their bodies in an attempt to live in the purely spiritual realm. Some Christians were taught to mortify the body, punishing themselves with whips, hair shirts, and beds of nails.

Some modern Christians have tried to compensate for centuries of misguided teachings about the body by embracing a *body-centered spirituality*. Although this term implies that we know the body is not excluded from the spiritual life, we are at risk of idolatry if we place the body, rather than God, at the center of our spiritual lives. Paul said, "Glorify God in your body" (1 Cor. 6:20). He did not say, "Glorify your body."

Jesus calls us into right relationship with God, with our sisters and brothers, and with all of creation. As Christians we are also called into right relationship with our bodies. We come into right relationship when we treat our bodies as friends rather than enemies, as gifts rather than chores, as temples of God rather than beasts of burden. In this friendship with our bodies we need to love them without becoming attached to them. We need to learn to accept changes in our bodies and to recognize the mystery of our bodies even as we seek to know, understand, and listen to them.

When we are in right relationship with our bodies, we can allow our bodies to teach us about God and the things of God. Instead of always praying with our heads bowed and our eyes closed, we might discover new ways of relating to God. We might pray as we stand with our arms flung wide or kneel with our hands clasped or lie on a warm beach gazing at the sky. Instead of only thinking about God we can open all our senses to the presence of God around us. Then we can know God in the song of a bird, the smile on a child's face, the smell of new-mown hay, the hug of a friend, or the taste of Communion bread and wine.

When we are in right relationship with our bodies we can also use our bodies in **worship**, praise, and the work of God. We can raise our voices in song, dance our joy before the altar, and learn the Lord's Prayer in sign language. We can write letters in support of low-income housing, serve the homeless at the local shelter, march against the death penalty. In the quiet of our homes we can bake bread for the Communion table, repair furniture for the Sunday school room, or call a friend in need of love and support. It has been said that we are God's hands and feet and eyes and ears and voices in the world. Through our embodiment God's love is expressed, service is rendered, justice is done, and peace is made known.

To explore further issues of the body and spirituality, see *Embodiment* by James B. Nelson, *Praying with Body and Soul* by Jane E. Vennard, and *Prayer and Our Bodies* by Flora Slosson Wuellner. JEV

BODY OF CHRIST. One of the images used to describe the Christian **community** in the New Testament. The image is prominent in the letters of Paul, especially 1 Corinthians 12–14 and Romans 12. A diversity of **spiritual gifts** is present in individuals, yet they have the same origin (the **Holy Spirit**). The corporate expression of these gifts is best understood through the **imagery** of the human body, which has different members that serve distinct purposes. Every gift within the body of Christ is necessary. The gifts are interdependent in that they strengthen one another, and those gifts that seem to be least important are sometimes the most critical to the body's functioning.

The apostle Paul's description of the body of Christ argues against a hierarchical understanding of ministry (although this appears later in the New Testament in the pastoral epistles: First and Second Timothy and Titus). The image of the church as the body of Christ is organic and dynamic—less structured than later definitions of the institutional church. Implied within Paul's discussion of the church as a body, however, is his own authority as an apostle to guide the mission of God's people.

The image of the body of Christ has much to offer modern Christian spirituality as a corrective to our heavily institutionalized forms of church practice and polity. It also stands against the excessively individualistic interpretations of spirituality present inside and outside the church. The image is strengthened by an understanding of the role of spiritual gifts in the lives of individuals, the way in which they are exercised, and their dangers to the community. Paul speaks at length about the latter subject in 1 Corinthians 14.

The body of Christ image gains further depth in the words of Jesus at the Last Supper: "This is my body that is for you" (1 Cor. 11:24). These words are set within a larger discussion of abuses of the Lord's Supper that were shaped by divisions and factions within the community (1 Cor. 11:17-34). The presence of the Holy Spirit brings unity to the body of Christ, and the sharing of **Holy Communion** signals that unity.

For further study, see Gordon D. Fee's *Paul, the Spirit, and the People of God* or David Bartlett's *Ministry in the New Testament*. KHC

BOEHME, JACOB (1575–1624), German Lutheran mystic. On the outside, the life of Jacob Boehme seems rather ordinary. Boehme was born into a Lutheran farming family near Görlitz, Germany, and received little more than an elementary school education before being apprenticed as a shoemaker. By 1599 Boehme had become a master shoemaker and moved into Görlitz proper, where he and his wife, Katharina, would have four sons. In 1600 a new Lutheran pastor, Martin Moller, came to town, calling believers to return to the renewal of orthodox Lutheran faith. Boehme became involved and later that year experienced a mystical revelation. This experience brought insights to Boehme about the spiritual life and the problem of evil. Sensing a prophetic call, Boehme recorded his insights and published *Aurora* in 1612. However, the book was promptly confiscated by Moller's

rigid successor, Gregor Richter, and Boehme was banned from further writing.

During the years of the enforced silence, Boehme continued to ponder his mystical intuitions and to integrate alchemy, **Neoplatonic** thought, and the Jewish mystical tradition of Kabbalah into his understanding. In 1619, in response to a mystical impulse, Boehme broke his silence with *Concerning the Three Principles of the Divine Essence* and continued to write prolifically (twenty-nine books in all) until his death in 1624.

Boehme's writings vary from esoteric philosophical theology to Christian discipleship. In fact, **John Wesley** required all of his preachers to study Boehme's writings. In Boehme's manual of the spiritual journey, *The Way to Christ*, the shoemaker reveals the path of the Christian life as a **pilgrimage** from self-knowledge to **conversion**, a path demanding active resignation of the soul to the burning love of God. Boehme believed that those illumined would return to the paradisiacal state of the first Adam, in whom characteristics of both genders were in perfect balance, reflecting God's true nature. Boehme personified God's female aspect in the heavenly Virgin Sophia. A central theme in Boehme's writings is the reconciliation of divine judgment with the merciful love revealed in Jesus Christ. Boehme is also known for his synthesis of mystical insight in a unique understanding of the solar system and alchemical knowledge. SAF

BONAVENTURE (ca. 1217–74), Italian professor, spiritual writer, and **Franciscan** friar. Bonaventure, born Giovanni Fidanza in Tuscany, taught and wrote at the University of Paris, served as the minister general of the Franciscan Order for seventeen years, and in 1273 was appointed cardinal bishop of Albano by Pope Gregory X. His writings filled nine folio volumes of approximately seven hundred pages each.

Bonaventure integrated the intellectual with the simplicity of **Francis of Assisi**. He wrote that knowledge of God is available to every soul and does not have to be derived by logic or reasoning. While the intellectual process is valid, it is not necessary for us to know God. We see the extensions of the spiritualities of Francis and Bonaventure in different expressions of the Franciscan order today.

Most of Bonaventure's spiritual works were written during his years as minister general of the Franciscan Order. His masterwork *The Soul's Journey into God* articulates a way toward **union** with God through contemplation of God in six stages: signs or traces of God in the universe as a whole, signs or traces of God in the world of the senses, the image of God in our natural powers, the image of God restored through **grace**, God as Being, and God as Goodness. It is possible to move toward God by reflecting on nature and soul since all of creation emanates from God and carries imperfect **images** of the Creator.

Francis's vision of the six-winged seraph on Mount La Verna (when he received the **stigmata**) inspired a treatise *The Six Wings of the Seraph*, in which Bonaventure described the qualities necessary for church leaders to "fly": zeal for justice, piety, patience, an exemplary life, circumspect discretion, and devotion to God.

Bonaventure held that the crucified Christ is both the gateway to the journey and the journey's goal. In his devotional work *The Tree of Life*, he celebrated the humanity of Jesus through contemplating Christ's birth, passion, and resurrection.

Ewert Cousins edited and translated *Bonaventure: The Soul's Journey into God; The Tree of Life; The Life of St. Francis.* SN

BONHOEFFER, DIETRICH (1906–45), German Lutheran pastor, theologian, professor, and martyr. Born in Breslau and raised in Berlin, Bonhoeffer studied theology at Tübingen and Berlin, where Harnack and **Barth** taught him. After a brief time at a German church in Barcelona and further study at Union Theological Seminary in New York, Bonhoeffer returned to Berlin to teach. In the early 1930s Bonhoeffer spoke out against Hitler and the growing accommodation between the German church and the Nazi party. He signed the Barmen Declaration (1934) that created a Confessing Church in protest. Bonhoeffer left Germany to pastor a German church in London but returned in 1935 when asked to head an underground seminary in Finkenwalde.

At Finkenwalde, Bonhoeffer completed two key books, *The Cost of Discipleship* and *Life Together*. These set forth a "religionless Christianity," in which God is not a philosophical abstraction once used to explain natural mysteries now explained by science, but rather a loving Guide who, through Jesus Christ, has taught us how to live responsible lives of discipleship individually and as the gathered **community** of the church. The call is not to be saved by Christ (salvation is a starting point, not a goal) but rather to live Christlike lives.

In 1937 the Gestapo closed the seminary, and Bonhoeffer was forbidden to teach in Germany. On a lecture tour in the United States when World War II began, Bonhoeffer chose to return to Germany. He became part of the German resistance while holding a job in the German government that enabled him to help Jews and others escape from Germany. He also became involved in a plot to assassinate Hitler. When his activities were exposed in 1943, Bonhoeffer was imprisoned, though never brought to trial. He continued to write letters and essays, later published as *Letters and Papers from Prison*. As Germany was falling, Bonhoeffer was moved to Büchenwald concentration camp. On Sunday, April 9, 1945, Bonhoeffer preached to other prisoners, then was led away to Flossenbürg prison, where he was hanged.

While *The Cost of Discipleship* is more famous, *Life Together* is a more readable introduction to Bonhoeffer's thought. KRB

BOOK OF COMMON PRAYER. The official service book within the Anglican Communion, which contains the daily offices of Morning and Evening Prayer, forms for the celebration of the **sacraments**, other public and private rites, a monthly cycle through the Psalter, and the Ordinal. **Thomas Cranmer** originally compiled this collection of prayers and services to simplify the highly complex patterns of **prayer** and **worship** inherited from medieval Catholic tradition and to make a program of daily prayer in English accessible to the priesthood and people of his day.

In 1549 Parliament approved the first edition of the Book of Common Prayer (BCP) and mandated its use throughout the land through the Act of Uniformity. Too conservative both in doctrine and ritual to please advocates of more radical reform, it was followed in 1552 by a second edition with a more Reformed recasting of the **liturgy** for **Holy Communion**. Following the brief return to Catholicism under Queen Mary, a new BCP was approved in 1559 reflecting Queen Elizabeth's *via media* (middle way). In 1662, following Civil War and Restoration, a revised version introduced the 1611 Authorized Version (KJV) in the readings of the Epistles and Gospels throughout. This edition of the BCP remained practically unchanged into the twentieth century, when supplemental alternatives were published in the 1960s and later. The BCP of the Episcopal Church in the United States was based closely on the English version and was revised in 1928 and 1979 to reflect the influence of the liturgical renewal movement and ecumenical conversations on worship. The history is similar in other Anglican bodies around the world.

The BCP bears witness to an essential Anglican principle of spirituality: *lex orandi legem statuat credendi* ("the law of prayer constitutes and shapes the law of belief"). Its purpose is to build lives of "fruitful communion," lives both eucharistic and corporate, lives reflective of a balanced understanding of the Christian life. This spirituality of comprehension, the large embrace that welcomes diversity while uniting in worship, reflects a commitment to being the church in the world. The BCP has exerted a profound influence upon Methodism and other denominations of British background.

For more on the BCP, see *A History of Anglican Liturgy* by G. J. Cuming. PWC

BOOTH, WILLIAM (1829–1912), evangelist, Christian activist, founder of The Salvation Army. Born in Nottingham, England, the son of a poor laborer, William Booth began his working life as an apprentice pawnbroker in London, where he was influenced by his daily contact with the poor and destitute. In 1850 he became a minister in the Methodist New Connexion. He met Catherine Mumford, who shared his commitment to social reform, in 1852. In 1855 they were married. Booth was appointed as pastor of Bethesda Chapel in 1858. Soon his fiery sermons were attracting crowds in the thousands. In 1861 he asked the church to appoint him as an evangelist. When the church refused he resigned from the Methodist ministry. On July 2, 1865, William and Catherine founded the Whitechapel Christian Mission in London's East End. In 1878 the mission was reorganized along military lines and called The Salvation Army. Two years later they began printing their magazine *The War Cry*, which is still published today. William Booth published his most important work *In Darkest England and The Way Out* in 1891. After his death, his eldest son, William Bramwell Booth, became the leader of The Salvation Army.

William Booth believed strongly that religion should alleviate the sufferings of the poor. A major task in the early days of the organization was the improvement of conditions for the working class in England. Catherine was instrumental in securing an equal role for women, who were even allowed to preach. These radical ideas caused the creation of a Skeleton Army responsible for attacks upon and arrests of many members of The Salvation Army. Their worship was filled with joyous singing and instrumental music, the Hallelujah Band being formed in 1864. In 1879 six young women, called the Hallelujah Lasses, were sent out to hold evangelistic meetings. Today, throughout the world, The Salvation Army supports hostels for homeless men and women, employment bureaus, hospitals, clinics, children's homes, and boarding schools.

For further information, in addition to Booth's book mentioned above, see Harry Edward Neal's *The Hallelujah Army.* DDW

BOSSUET, JACQUES BÉNIGNE (1627–1704), bishop, court orator called the "voice of France," advocate for the poor, and Louis XIV's tutor. Bossuet graduated from the College de Navarre, was ordained a deacon, and then began preaching at Metz. **Vincent de Paul** prepared Bossuet for the priesthood and remained his inspiration, along with **Francis de Sales**. Bossuet counseled King Louis against adultery, declaring God's law supreme. Bossuet thought universality, majesty, and unity important themes, attainable only through absolutism. His *Discours sur l'historie universelle* portrayed **Providence** as directing all history in relation to the Incarnation. He approved revoking the Edict of Nantes (which had allowed toleration of Protestants) and worked with Leibniz for world Christian unification, unsuccessfully. Although trying to understand mysticism, he condemned propositions drawn from Madame **Guyon**'s writings.

For further information, see Bossuet's *Panegyrics of the Saints: From the French of Bossuet and Bourdaloue* and William J. Sparrow-Simpson's *A Study of Bossuet.* LSP

BOUNDS, EDWARD McKENDREE (1835–1913), lawyer, minister, Confederate Army chaplain, author, and man of prayer. Born in Missouri into a political family, he practiced law until he felt a call to preach. Bounds began his ministry as a pastor in the Methodist Episcopal Church, South. He was twice held in a federal prison as a Confederate sympathizer. After release from prison, he returned to his pastoral duties. He became the associate editor of the *Christian Advocate*, the official weekly paper of his denomination. He wrote eleven books on prayer and expounded on the necessity of prayer—especially **intercessory** prayer—for a distinctive religious character and Christian conduct. He himself rose at four o'clock every morning to pray until seven o'clock.

The Complete Works of E. M. Bounds on Prayer collects eight of his short books. CIZ

BREATH PRAYER. A short prayer of petition or praise that develops our awareness of God's presence. The Hebrew word for breath is *ruach*, meaning also "wind" and "spirit." A breath prayer is a prayer of the **Spirit**. Romans 8:26 tells us that the Holy Spirit is praying for us. The name "breath prayer" was given to this form because prayer is to be as natural as breathing. In this way we have on our lips or in our consciousness what is always on our heart. The goal of this form, which

---

A METHOD FOR CREATING A PERSONAL BREATH PRAYER

Ron DelBene, author of *The Breath of Life: A Simple Way to Pray* and other books on breath prayer offers a simple method for creating a personal breath prayer.

Sit for a moment in silence and remember that God holds you in a loving presence. You may want to close your eyes and recall the words, "Be still, and know that I am God" (Ps. 46:10) or "Whenever you pray, go into your room and shut the door and pray to your Father who is in secret; and your Father who sees in secret will reward you" (Matt. 6:6).

Listen as God calls you by name and asks: "(*Your name*), what do you want?"

Answer the Lord simply, directly.

Write down your answer. You may write several responses if you have several answers.

Select a name of your choosing for the Divine.

Combine your desire and name into a six- to eight-syllable prayer such as "Jesus, teach me how to love" or "More of you, Lord, less of me."

can influence our entire life, is to integrate interior thoughts with exterior actions.

Breath prayers are usually personalized prayers that arise from our deepest needs. They clarify who we are and help us to understand our relationship with God. Examples are "Physician, lead me to wholeness" or "Shepherd, guide me to do your will." Such simple prayers can be used when illness, pain, or other distractions prevent lengthier prayers. Ron DelBene's *Into the Light* offers suggestions for using breath prayer with the terminally ill and their families.

Guidelines for breath prayer include the following: (1) Be honest and humble in your petition. (2) Pray a natural rhythm of six to eight syllables. (3) Search for several days to find the most comfortable and personal words; then pray them unchanged for at least a month. (4) Change your prayer as new insights come and your life situation changes. PDB

BREMOND, HENRI (1865–1933), French spiritual writer and literary critic whose masterwork, *A Literary History of Religious Feeling in France* (eleven volumes, 1916–31) was unfinished at the time of his death in 1933. The relationship between poetry and **mysticism** and the romanticism of religious experience intrigued Bremond. In *Prayer and Poetry* (1925) he argued that the conceptual intuition that led the poet to conceive a poem came in a naturally mystical state of consciousness and was linked to the psychological mechanism that gave rise to prayer through a state of **grace**. Bremond believed that poetry provided a stimulus to the mind of the reader that would lead him or her to the same deep mystical awareness as the source from which the poem had sprung. Bremond's second work concerning the relationship between poetry and spirituality, *Pure Poetry* (1926), influenced both theologians and poets, most notably **T. S. Eliot**. SFP

BROWNE, THOMAS (1605–82), British physician and writer. Unusually well-educated for his day, Browne completed studies in five European schools: Oxford, Leiden, Winchester, Montpellier, and Padua. After practicing medicine for a few years in Yorkshire and Oxfordshire, he finally settled in Norwich. While fully occupied as a doctor, he managed to explore his wide interests by experimenting in embryology, botany, physics, astronomy, and natural history.

His book *Religio Medici* (*A Doctor's Religion*) is a spiritually profound classic, though his heavy writing style makes for difficult reading. Paraphrasing him in the shorter sentences of modern English reveals the depth and charm present: "Acquaint yourself with the movement of the stars and the vast expanses beyond them. Let your brain perceive what cannot be seen through a telescope. Catch a glimpse of the incomprehensible. Think about the unthinkable. Ascend to the invisible. Fill your soul with the spiritual. Dig into the mysteries of faith, the huge concepts of religion. Then your life will honor God."

Religio Medici is available in various editions. For Browne's life, read *Approaches to Sir Thomas Browne*, edited by C. A. Patrides, and *Sir Thomas Browne: A Doctor's Life of Science and Faith* by Jeremiah S. Finch. BKB

BRUDERHOF. See **Arnold, Eberhard.**

BUBER, MARTIN (1878–1965), Jewish mystic, Zionist, educator. Born in Vienna, Buber studied philosophy and art at universities in Vienna, Zurich, and Berlin. After the Nazis removed him from his post teaching comparative religion in Frankfurt in 1938, he fled to Israel where he taught social philosophy at Hebrew University until 1951.

Buber, an ardent religious Zionist, believed in encountering a personal God. Besides Zionism, his primary interest was Hasidism, a mystical Jewish movement that began in Germany in the wake of the anti-Semitic violence following the Crusades. It was revived in Eastern Europe in the eighteenth century, then brought into the twentieth century by Buber's *Tales of the Hasidim* and other books. Hasidism has two main foci:

communion with God's presence in all things, and the necessity of the Zaddik or Hasidic master as spiritual guide for all Hasidim (as opposed to the spiritual elitism of Kabbalism). It is mysticism for the common people.

The Hasidic emphasis on the personal relationship with God led Buber to his Philosophy of Dialogue, a concept influential in Judaism and Christianity. Buber presented this philosophy in *I and Thou*, published in 1923 in Germany as *Ich und Du*. In German, *Sie* ("You") is the basic word for second person, whether singular or plural. *Du* ("Thou") implies great intimacy. It can be said only with one's whole being. This relationship is unmediated and has only a present, no past. The "I-Thou" relationship is the primary relationship, a genuine encounter and mutuality requiring openness, participation, and empathy. Such relationships cannot be coerced or sustained. They are rare, intense, fleeting revelations of new depths of meaning. The only way one can know God is in an "I-Thou" relationship. Most of life is spent in the "I-It" world of experiencing and using one another. While this is adequate for casual acquaintance, many of us seem to live exclusively as "I-It," avoiding all intimacy, denying full humanity to others, and creating a fatal remoteness from all who could be "Thou" and helping them grow into greater maturity. WW

BUECHNER, FREDERICK (b. 1926), American Presbyterian novelist and theologian. After military service and graduation from Princeton in 1947, Buechner became a high school English teacher. In 1954, inspired by the preaching of **George Buttrick**, he entered Union Theological Seminary in New York City. After his ordination as a Presbyterian pastor, he taught religion and led chapel services at Phillips Exeter Academy in New Hampshire. His chapel sermons were published in two books, *The Hungering Dark* and *The Magnificent Defeat*. In 1967 he moved to Vermont to write full-time. His 1977 Lyman Beecher lectures on preaching became *Telling the Truth: The Gospel as Comedy, Tragedy, and Fairy Tale*.

Buechner has written extensively as a novelist, an essayist, and a memoirist, often focusing on the struggle to understand and do the **will of God**. His novels include *Lion Country*, the first of four novels about Leo Bebb, *Godric* (nominated for the Pulitzer Prize), *The Son of Laughter* (about Jacob and his family), and *Brendan*. WW

BUNYAN, JOHN (1628–88), British nonconformist writer and preacher; author of *The Pilgrim's Progress*. Born at Elstow in Bedfordshire, England, Bunyan obtained a modest education in local schools and by reading the Bible. Living in the heyday of Puritanism and possessed of a hypersensitive religious conscience, he was frightened as a child by fearful dreams and visions. The death of his mother and when he was sixteen his father's hasty remarriage created a crisis that led him to enter the Parliamentary army in 1644. The New Model Army imprinted him deeply. After being mustered out July 21, 1647, he married a devout woman who brought to the marriage a concern for piety and two Puritan classics—Arthur Dent's *The Plain Man's Pathway to Heaven* and Lewis Bayly's *The Practice of Piety*—which spurred him forward in an outward reformation. Overhearing four village women discuss their spiritual experiences ignited in Bunyan a concern for his own inward transformation.

Caught up in the Puritan quest to determine if he were one of the "elect," Bunyan experienced severe depression. He recovered slowly and agonizingly with the help of the Bedford congregation. He began preaching in 1657 and became pastor in Bedford. His wife, the mother of his four children, died in 1658; he soon remarried. With the restoration of the monarchy in 1660, Bunyan went to prison for refusal to stop his unlicensed preaching. He left his children to the care of his young second wife, Elizabeth. Despite Elizabeth's efforts to have him freed, he remained in prison most of the next twelve years. The repeal of Charles II's Declaration of Indulgence with the Test Act in 1673 caused him to spend another six months in jail in 1675.

Bunyan's two most influential writings, the autobiographical *Grace Abounding to the Chief of Sinners*, written in 1660, and *The Pilgrim's Progress*, written during his second imprisonment, recount both his inward struggle of soul and his outward battle for freedom of religion. His courageous stand assured him of an exalted place in English history.

In addition to Bunyan's books, see *John Bunyan* by Richard L. Greaves or M. Esther Harding's *Journey into Self.* EGH

BUSHNELL, HORACE (1802–76), American Congregationalist pastor well known for his controversial writings. He was active in politics and community affairs as well as being a respected, if often criticized, preacher and theologian. In 1847 Bushnell published his most famous book *Christian Nurture* on the crucial role of parents and the family in the spiritual development of children. He wrote that children should grow up as Christians, never knowing themselves to be otherwise. He was a champion of children in the life of the church and wrote about the family being used by God as a means of grace.

In *Christian Nurture* Bushnell also argued for the practice of infant **baptism**. He emphasized the "law of organic connection" between parents and children that ensured the parents' influence on the child's character development. He believed that **regeneration** or new birth is a process, a developing relationship with God, more than one extraordinary event. He opposed revivalism and excessively emotional religious **experience**, though he did admit that religious experience could immediately transform one's character. Bushnell has been called the father of the Christian education movement in America and became a prominent figure in the nurture/**conversion** debate in Christian education.

Bushnell believed in religious intuition, the "sense of the heart" that led to a knowledge of God. He preached and wrote often about the need for "self clearing" to make room for God to fill the void. Bushnell called God an "agitating power."

Bushnell had a great appreciation for nature and believed that humans, God, and nature are tied together in an organic unity. He explained that God exists in nature and is present in all things, but that the supernatural is distinguishable from nature. Also among his many writings are *God in Christ* and *Nature and the Supernatural As Together Constituting the One System of God.*

For more information, see William R. Adamson's *Bushnell Rediscovered* or *Horace Bushnell and the Virtuous Republic* by Howard A. Barnes. SEW

BUTTRICK, GEORGE ARTHUR (1892–1980), British-American preacher, pastor, theologian, and editor. Born in Seaham Harbour, England, George Buttrick was the son of a Primitive Methodist pastor. During his youth he left the Primitive Methodist Church for the more liberal Congregational Church, where he came under the care of pastor John Gardner. He attended Victoria University in Manchester and Lancaster Independent Theological Seminary (England), graduating in 1915. Ordained that same year, he became pastor of the First Congregational Church, Quincy, Illinois, a position he obtained with the help of John Gardner, who had come to the United States. In 1916 he married Agnes Gardner, John's daughter. In 1927, after eight years of serving churches in Vermont and upstate New York, he became pastor of the First Congregational Church of Rutland, Vermont, and in 1921 he moved to the First Presbyterian Church of Buffalo, New York. In 1927, at age thirty-four, he succeeded Henry Sloane Coffin as pastor of Madison Avenue Presbyterian Church in New York City, where he remained for twenty-seven years. From 1954 to 1960 he was dean of Harvard's Memorial Church and Plummer Professor of Christian morals. After his retirement in 1960 he continued to serve as visiting professor at several seminaries until his death in 1980.

George Buttrick was "the preacher's preacher," having influenced three generations of seminarians. In his preaching he sought to lift up Christ, for he believed that only preaching based on the **cross** would impact life. *Preaching* magazine placed him as number three in the top ten preachers of the twentieth century. He had a detailed worksheet and a meticulous method of sermon preparation that he followed faithfully. He is also known as the editor of *The Interpreter's Bible* and *The Interpreter's Dictionary of the Bible*.

Buttrick's primary book on the spiritual life is *Prayer*, containing both a theological and experiential defense of prayer against a naturalistic worldview and basic directions on how to pray. For other aspects of his writing, try *Sermons Preached in a University Church* and *God, Pain, and Evil.* DDW

C

CALVIN, JOHN (1509–64), French-Swiss leader of the Protestant Reformation. Born Jean Cauvin in Noyon, France, Calvin has been called the intellectual backbone of the Protestant Reformation. Originally groomed by his father for the Catholic priesthood, Calvin in 1529 at his father's urging switched to the study of law, only to return to theology.

In his twenties, Calvin took the rudiments of earlier reformers like **John Hus**, John Wycliffe, and **Martin Luther** and gave their views orderly and systematic theological expression in the *Institutes of the Christian Religion* published in Latin in 1536, definitively revised in 1559.

Building on **Augustine** and **Luther**'s theology of salvation by **grace** through **faith** alone, Calvin insisted on the authority of Christ in the community to interpret scripture, to reform the church after its earliest roots. Calvin's unique gift was the form of representative democracy that would fundamentally alter Western church and political systems. Some of Calvin's followers, like Scotland's **John Knox**, adopted the name Presbyterian (from Greek *presbyter*, meaning "elder") based on church government, while others like Ulrich Zwingli maintained the name Reformed based on theology.

Calvin had many reasons to become melancholy: his mother's death when Calvin was four, being shunted to live with neighbors after his father's quick remarriage, lifelong sickliness, and the death of all three of his children early in his marriage. Yet Calvin relished life, enjoying good wine, playing skittles, and often referring ecstatically to nature as "the theatre of God's glory." He even approved of church drama in Geneva while others condemned it.

While detractors attack Calvin's belief in double predestination (divine election to salvation or damnation) and cruelty to heretics, both were at the time tenets of Catholic tradition. Others would argue that Calvin's reforms did not go far enough in not challenging two such major arenas of ecclesiastical faith and practice.

Later Calvinists would rigidify Calvin's ideas in *The Westminster Confession of Faith* of 1647, which became the doctrinal standard for Presbyterians through most of the following centuries. However, for Reformed and Presbyterian churches, the motto *reformata semper reformanda*, "reformed and always reforming," encourages believers to revise their faith and practice constantly in light of Christ, the Word behind scripture.

Calvin incorporated his **humanism** into Christianity. As others despaired during a plague, Calvin met with the magistrates to plan a sewer system to prevent future epidemics. Thus his favorite symbol—the flaming heart in the open hand—gives credence for present-day disciples to unite spiritual renewal and social involvement.

For further reading, see *Institutes of the Christian Religion* by John Calvin; *Calvin: The Origins and Development of His Religious Thought* by Francois Wendel, translated by Philip Mairet; *John Calvin: A Sixteenth-Century Portrait* by William J. Bouwsma; and *The Theatre of His Glory: Nature and the Natural Order in the Thought of John Calvin* by Susan Schreiner. KIG

CALVINIST SPIRITUALITY. See **Calvin, John.**

CÂMARA, HÉLDER (1909–99), Archbishop of Recife and Olinda in northeast Brazil, founder of CELAM (the council of Latin American bishops). The humble and simple-living archbishop of Brazil brought a preferential option for the poor to the center of Christian social thinking. When he was made archbishop of one of the poorest regions of Brazil in 1964, he refused to live in the customary mansion or wear the trappings of the office. Instead he wore a simple brown cassock with a plain wooden cross and lived in a house behind the cathedral.

Câmara spoke out for the poor, campaigned for agrarian reform, and sought to end torture of prisoners. He understood the paradoxes of the time. When he fed the poor, he was called a saint. When he asked why people were poor, he was called a communist. He believed in using Marxist tools for understanding the historical situation, but he was deeply committed to the gospel of Jesus. He called for "Abrahamic minorities," small groups of Christians who would band together to address the injustices in the local community. Hélder Câmara was nominated for the Nobel Peace Prize four times. Though he never won the peace prize, he was honored in many countries, held thirty honorary doctorates, and did receive the People's Peace Prize in Oslo, Norway, in 1974.

Câmara encouraged the leaders of the Roman Catholic Church in Rome to simplify their lifestyles and use the church's wealth for the poor. He pushed for change and prodded the church forward in the Second Vatican Council. Though he was often viewed as too strong a proponent of **liberation** theology, when he died, Pope John Paul II called him "the brother of the poor."

A good place to start reading Câmara's books is *The Desert Is Fertile*. LJP

CAPPADOCIANS. Three fourth-century theologians from Cappadocia (today eastern Turkey): **Basil of Caesarea**, his brother **Gregory of Nyssa**, and their friend **Gregory of Nazianzus**.

CARDENAL, ERNESTO (b. 1925), Nicaraguan poet and priest. In the 1970s Cardenal became known in the United States for his poetry and writing during the revolutionary movement to overthrow the oppressive Somozan regime. Cardenal founded a Christian community, Solentiname, on a small island in Lake Nicaragua where he developed a method of biblical reflection that invited people to analyze the historical situation and apply the ethical demands of the Bible to the creation of a new and just society. *The Gospel of Solentiname* was published in four volumes in the United States and contributed to the growing volume of literature on **liberation** theology. The vision and the commitment to justice in Solentiname and Cardenal's powerful writing increased people's awareness of this revolutionary poet so that when the Sandinistas overthrew the Somozan government, Father Cardenal was asked to be the Nicaraguan Minister of Culture. He served in that position from 1979 until 1988. He has continued to write poetry, and in his travels he is an articulate spokesperson for justice and self-determination in Latin America. Cardenal's poetry is a medium for his hopeful message of transforming the old order into a new and more just society. A little known fact is that part of his seminary training was done with **Thomas Merton** at Gethsemani, Kentucky. LJP

CARMELITES. Members of the **monastic** Order of Mount Carmel, both monks and nuns, and especially members of the reformed (Discalced) order begun by **Teresa of Ávila** and **John of the Cross**. Carmelite writers include **Lawrence of the Resurrection**, **Thérèse of Lisieux**, **Edith Stein**, and **Elizabeth of the Trinity**.

CARMICHAEL, AMY (1867–1951), missionary to India who wrote on the devotional life. The oldest child of an Irish Presbyterian family, Amy Carmichael served in India for fifty-five years. She established the Dohnavur Fellowship, a mission dedicated to rescuing and raising children at risk, including orphans and young girls given by their families as temple prostitutes. Her intense activism (such as befriending a notorious robber) was matched by her intense prayer life. In *Candles in the Dark*, the best-known of her thirty-five books, she wrote, "Keep close, keep close. If you are close, you will be keen. Your heart will be set on the things that abide. You will not be attracted by the world, but you will love the people in that world. You will live to share your joy. Nothing else will count for much."

You Are My Hiding Place (Rekindling the Inner Fire), edited by David Hazard, is a compilation of forty letters by Carmichael. *A Chance to Die: The Life and Legacy of Amy Carmichael* by **Elisabeth Elliot** is an excellent biography that describes Carmichael's prayer and work. JLJ

CARRETTO, CARLO (1910–88), Catholic activist, **ascetic**, author. Carretto was born in Alessandria, Italy, of poor, country stock. The family eventually moved to Turin, where the six children were raised in an atmosphere of traditional piety.

Carretto was a schoolteacher at eighteen. He eventually became a headmaster in Sardinia. After clashes with the fascist regime, he was removed from the register of headmasters and placed under surveillance. By the early 1930s, he had become active in the dynamic youth movement, Catholic Action. As director of Italian Youth for Catholic Action from 1946 to 1954, Carretto worked to bring the gospel message to bear on moral and social issues. Then, distressed by political conservatism and enforced busyness in the organization, he suddenly resigned and retreated to the Sahara.

While overwhelmed by the **desert**'s extreme elements, Carretto was glad to step out of the spotlight, as he explained in *Letters from the Desert*. Soon after his arrival, an improperly administered injection in his leg left him permanently crippled. Carretto struggled to find God's will in his tragedy. He found himself compassionately identifying with the **suffering** of others. He developed his understanding of the purpose of suffering in *Why, O Lord?*

Carretto learned in the Sahara that finding God in the ascetic life meant nothing if one could not find God among one's fellow human beings. In 1964 he returned to Europe, bringing the desert experience, which he recounted in *The Desert in the City*, with him. He joined the Little Brothers of the Gospel, an offshoot of the Little Brothers of Jesus, settling in Spello, Italy. There he gained great popularity for his retreats and his books. At the age of seventy-eight, Carretto died peacefully after a long illness.

Carretto represented a joyful asceticism available to all Christians. He showed through his life that prayer need not lead people away from social action in the name of Christ. Every Christian can have a deep, prayerful relationship with God through Christ and work among the least of Christ's brothers and sisters. WW

CARTHUSIANS. Members of the **monastic** order founded at La Grande Chartreuse in the French alps near Grenoble in 1084, known for strict **asceticism** and **contemplation**. **Guigo II** is a Carthusian writer.

CASSIAN, JOHN (ca. 360–435), monk. Born in either Provence or, more likely, Dobrudja, Scythia Minor of the Roman Empire. In 382 Cassian entered a monastery near the cave of the nativity at Bethlehem, accompanied by Germanus. In 385 he and Germanus went to Egypt in search of "perfection" and soon became enamored of the ideas of Egyptian hermits. They spent time in the salt marshes near Panephysis, the desert of Scete, and the region of Diolcos and Panephysis. At Scete they joined a community headed by Macarius (ca. 300–ca. 390), then nearly ninety. In 399 or 400, however, the controversy over **Origen** led to the expulsion from Egypt of many monastic leaders. Cassian and Germanus joined others in fleeing to Constantinople and the welcome of **John Chrysostom**. Around 405 Chrysostom dispatched him to Pope Innocent I, who ordained him as priest.

Some years later, Cassian founded two monasteries at Marseilles, one for women and one for men, dedicated to the martyr Victor. Around 415, under the apocalyptic stimulus of the Germanic invasions, St. Victor and other houses associated with it claimed five thousand monks. Cassian supplied the guidance this movement needed through the publication of his *Institutes* and *Conferences* between 425 and 430. In contrast to **Basil of Caesarea,** he thought that the *coenobium* (monastery) was for beginners, the hermitage for the mature. His special contribution lay in the development of the daily prayers of the **liturgy of the hours**. Whereas in Egypt monks observed only two times (nocturnes and vespers), he added prayers at the third, sixth, and ninth hours. He borrowed much from **Evagrius Ponticus**, whom he met at Nitria, but he also modified the latter's views. Cassian opposed excessive **asceticism** and emphasized scripture in **spiritual formation**. The goal is purity of heart, which one can attain by **unceasing prayer**. He is sometimes identified as the founder of semi-**Pelagianism** because he shared the Eastern concern for free **will**, but he depended to some extent on **Augustine**'s doctrine of grace. The Eastern but not the Western Churches have recognized him as a saint.

The many editions of Cassian's *Conferences* and *Institutes* include recent translations by Boniface Ramsey. See also Columba Stewart's study *John Cassian*. EGH

CATAPHATIC PATH. See Positive Way.

CATHARISM. From the Greek, meaning "pure ones," a designation for the various dualistic sects that flourished from the Balkans to Western Europe in the eleventh through thirteenth centuries. Catharism may have developed in Bulgaria as early as the tenth century with roots in earlier **Manichaeism** and **Gnosticism**. Bosnia was another early center of the movement. By the late Middle Ages, the principal Western Cathar stronghold was in southern France, where the adherents were known as the Albigenses.

The Cathari believed that matter was inherently evil and was created by an evil prin-

ciple. This evil principle was opposed by a good principle, who had created the invisible and spiritual universe. While absolute dualists within the movement may have espoused the equality of these two principles, it appears that the majority of Cathari claimed only the good principle to be eternal and the evil principle a mere creature. They believed that Christ had been an **angel** who had not suffered on earth because a shield of angels protected him, and that, since the material and spiritual realms did not intersect, he had no power over evil. They rejected the feudal hierarchy, both ecclesiastical and secular, and separated themselves into two classes: Believers (*Croyens*) and the Perfect (*Parfaits*). Cathari believed that those who died before becoming perfect would be reincarnated until they did so. They held that **perfection** was to be achieved through an **asceticism** that eschewed marriage and the eating of flesh. Those who were believed to have attained perfection would be given the *consolamentum*, which marked the joining of the **soul** and the **spirit** and consisted in the laying on of hands. Many received this "**sacrament**" only on their deathbeds.

The movement disappeared in the East after the conquest by the Turks in the late fifteenth century. Local secular and ecclesiastical attacks against the Albigenses led Pope Innocent III to proclaim a crusade in 1209. On March 16, 1244, the last stronghold, Montsegur Castle in the French Pyrenees, fell, extinguishing both the Cathar faith and its influence. RMH

CATHARSIS. See PURGATION.

CATHERINE OF GENOA (1447–1510), Italian mystic. Caterina Fieschi was a simple, quiet, intelligent girl and a person of deep piety and prayer. At thirteen she tried to enter the convent but was denied due to her young age. When she was sixteen, her parents prearranged her marriage to Giuliano (Julian) Adorno, a nobleman from the area. They were unsuited for each other, and the marriage was a disaster. Her husband proved to be a scoundrel, making Catherine's life miserable and leaving her feeling depressed and weary. She tried involving herself in high society, but this attempt left her feeling empty too. After ten years of marriage, while continuing to pray for divine guidance, she received an answer to her prayers: an inner experience of herself as overwhelmingly loved by God. From this moment on, she found new meaning and purpose for her life.

Having exhausted their financial resources through extravagant living, Catherine and Giuliano moved into a simple home. Giuliano underwent his own conversion, and the couple devoted themselves to caring for the sick and suffering, especially in the hospital that Catherine founded in Pammatone. She eventually became the hospital's director. While tending to the unwell, Catherine nearly died from the plague in 1493. She spent much time in prayer, where she "experienced the burning flame of God's presence in her heart." Balancing the rhythm of action and **contemplation**, this laywoman practiced a spirituality in the workplace that emanated from her devotion to the infinite God. During the years between 1499 and 1507 Catherine shared her mystical experiences with a group of friends and followers. As mentioned in her works, while most of her life was lived in **purgation**, the last few years of her life were lived being purified in the depths of her spirit.

For further reading, see *Catherine of Genoa: Purgation and Purgatory, The Spiritual Dialogue*, translated by Serge Hughes. EKM

CATHERINE OF SIENA (1347–80), Italian mystical writer. Born the twenty-fourth child (only twelve survived infancy) of Jacopo Benincasa and his wife Lapa di Puccio Piacenti in Siena, Catherine lived during dark times marked with social unrest, economic upheaval, bad government, and war. The greatest horror was the Black Death. Her father was politically savvy in a city-state racked by family feuds, class conflict, and revolution.

Around the age of six or seven, Catherine experienced what she later described as a vision of Christ. Radically impacted by this experience, Catherine took a vow of virginity (not uncommon for the spirituality of her day to show that one belonged entirely to God). Her mother's temper erupted when Catherine cut off her hair to protest the thought of marrying, but her father's calming presence fostered Catherine's call to **solitude**, **prayer**, and service. By age sixteen she was a Dominican tertiary, one of a group of laywomen (often older widows), bound by simple vows who lived in their own homes, prayed, and served the poor and sick. They wore a distinctive cloak or *mantella* for which reason they were called the *Mantellate*.

In 1366 Catherine's prayer experiences (**visions, ecstasies**, and inner struggles) culminated in her **spiritual marriage** with Christ. This profound personal relationship with her God compelled her to come out of solitude to serve the world and her neighbor for God's glory. Believing God was calling her to be a mediator between political and ecclesial factions, Catherine traveled to Avignon to convince Pope Gregory XI to return the papacy to Rome and wrote letters to bishops and monarchs reminding both to be faithful servants. Catherine taught that always, no matter what, God is "madly in love" with us. In her book, *The Dialogue*, she developed the image of Christ as the bridge from earth to heaven. Catherine died in Rome on April 29, 1380, and was canonized eighty-one years later. She and **Teresa of Ávila** were the first women declared **Doctors of the Church** (in 1970). Her writings still enkindle hearts to seek God, whom she called "Gentle Truth."

A good introduction to Catherine is Elizabeth A. Dreyer's *A Retreat with Catherine of Siena: Living the Truth in Love*. For those interested in going deeper, see *Catherine of Siena: The Dialogue*, translated by Suzanne Noffke. EKM

CAUSSADE, JEAN PIERRE DE (1675–1751), French **Jesuit** priest and spiritual writer. Caussade's name is associated with the classic spiritual text, *Abandonment to Divine Providence*.

The book was published posthumously as a synthesis of letters and conferences the Jesuit prepared for a community of French **Visitandine** nuns for whom he was spiritual guide, though some critics question how much of the form and content are due to the editor, H. Ramière. *Abandonment* teaches a radical acceptance of all experiences in life as expression of the **will of God** and stresses the embrace of the "sacrament of the **present moment**" as an ever-flowing source of **holiness**. Since its publication in the nineteenth century, the book has enjoyed a wide readership both in France and in the English-speaking world. WMW

CELIBACY. The state of both singleness and sexual abstinence. The tradition of celibacy within Roman Catholicism—and to a lesser extent Eastern Orthodoxy, where marriage is permissible prior to ordination or **monastic** vows. This tradition rests on the assumption that celibate clergy and religious (those bound—Latin *religatus*—by monastic vows) are an eschatological sign of the kingdom of God, where there will be no marriage, and persons more single-hearted in their devotion to Christ can give themselves more completely to religious duties.

Jesus recognized the celibate state as an expression of devotion in "eunuchs who have made themselves eunuchs for the sake of the kingdom of heaven" (Matt. 19:12), but this may be more a plea for tolerance of those who were different than an endorsement of the celibate state. The apostle Paul says, "I wish that all were as I myself am" (1 Cor. 7:7), but his concern is not about celibacy *per se* but about the end of the age, which he believed was at hand. Under those circumstances, marriage and raising children would represent an unnecessary complication for the faithful.

Augustine of Hippo, a man of great sexual appetite and one-time devotee of **Manichaeism** that regarded the soul as pure and the body as vile, became a strong advocate of celibacy after his conversion to Christianity. According to Augustine, **sexuality** is suspect, even in marriage, because the **sin** of Adam is passed on by intercourse and conception. Thus abstinence is a means of redemption from the taint of original sin.

After the Fifth Council of Carthage (401) suggested that priests separate from their wives and live as celibates, celibacy became the norm for priests and the religious in the Western church. At the Second Lateran Council (1139), Pope Innocent II declared marriages of priests invalid and the children of such unions bastards. The Council of Trent (1545–62) named marriage a **sacrament** while declaring virginity and celibacy nobler callings.

Martin Luther, in making celibacy optional for Protestant clergy, observed (from his own **monastic** experience) that there is never less **chastity** than in those who vow to be chaste. RMH

CELTIC SPIRITUALITY. By the first millennium B.C.E., the Celtic tribes ranged from Galatia to the British Isles. These invaders, whose descendants are found among the peoples of Ireland, Scotland, Wales, Cornwall, and Brittany, never thought of themselves as Celts; and the **monastic** artists who carved the high crosses and produced The Book of Kells were not expressing a Celtic identity. Although the consciousness of a Celtic Christianity or spirituality is a modern phenomenon, there does appear to be a uniquely Celtic Christian spirituality that fulfills all that was good and true in the pagan spirituality that preceded it.

Because the Celts and their descendants lived in close proximity to nature, they regarded the earth as their mother, the source of all fertility. Celtic Christians addressed God as "Lord of the Elements" and experienced communion with God in ancient trees, sacred groves, mountaintops, rivers, streams, and holy wells.

Irish monasticism had a strong mystical tendency informed by the theology of **Orthodox spirituality** in **Gregory of Nyssa**, **Maximus the Confessor**, **Pseudo-Dionysius**, and others.

Celtic Christians were devoted to **Mary**,

angels, and **saints**. They often referred to Jesus simply as "the Son of Mary." Indigenous Celtic saints appeared early in the Christian period, including Patrick, Bridget, Brendan, Columcille, and many more.

Celtic Christians believed that to make a journey for Christ, a **pilgrimage**, would bring blessings, increased intimacy with God, and the healing of body and soul. The early Irish missionaries inherited a love of learning from their Druid forebears and carried this love to France, Switzerland, Germany, and Italy. By the sixth century, many pilgrim scholars were coming from Ireland to Britain and Europe to study and learn.

Because the Celts lived close to the earth and to the cycles of the sun and moon, they understood time as a sacred reality blessed and redeemed by God's overflowing compassion. The monastic Daily Office pattern of worship was a natural one. For the Celts, the present contained past within itself and future events waiting to be revealed. They valued ordinary routine because of their belief that God was not so much to be found at the end of time, when the reign of Christ fully comes, but within the daily routine of work and ordinary chores. They did not believe that God—or the transcendent—spoke *outside* and beyond the natural environment. Celtic solitaries—like the **desert fathers and mothers**—attempted to enter an inner **solitude**, the cave of the heart.

Because the pagan Celts believed that everyone should have a "soul friend," or *anamchara*, who offered a compassionate ear and challenging word, the Christian Celts believed that God spoke heart to heart but also through soul friends. The emergence of the *anamchara* was an important contribution to the development of the practice of spiritual direction. It was a role confirmed by the practitioner's skills and exercised by men and women alike.

As in Orthodox spirituality, Celtic Christian spirituality includes a popular rejection of the doctrine of original **sin**. This rejection emerged out of a Celtic reverence for the natural world and became the background for **Pelagianism**. RMH

CENTERING PRAYER. A way of praying developed in the 1970s by **Trappist** monks William Meninger, **M. Basil Pennington**, and **Thomas Keating**, Centering Prayer is an adaptation of the contemplative practice of the early **desert fathers and mothers**, *The Cloud of Unknowing*, **John of the Cross**, and **Teresa of Ávila**. It is not contemplative prayer itself but a method of reducing obstacles to **contemplation**. It helps develop awareness of God's presence by withdrawing attention from the ordinary flow of thoughts.

For a thorough introduction to Centering Prayer, see Keating's *Open Mind, Open Heart: The Contemplative Dimension of the Gospel.* RMH

A METHOD FOR CENTERING PRAYER

Choose a short, "sacred word" of one or two syllables, such as *love, joy, peace, Lord, Jesus,* etc. This word symbolizes your intention to consent to God's presence and action within.

Sit in a comfortable position with your eyes closed.

Inwardly repeat the sacred word as a means of centering your thoughts on your yearning for God.

Whenever an emotion, image, memory, or even a spiritual communication appears, gently reintroduce the sacred word.

After twenty minutes have elapsed, return to ordinary thought by repeating the Lord's Prayer.

How do you know when twenty minutes have gone by? You could peek occasionally at a watch or clock. You could use a countdown timer, though these can be startling. Or you could use a recording with twenty minutes of silence followed by quiet music that fades in.

CHAMBERS, OSWALD (1874–1917), Bible teacher, military chaplain, and world-famous devotional writer; author of the classic *My Utmost for His Highest*. Born in Aberdeen, Scotland, he was converted upon hearing the preaching of **Charles Spurgeon**. He began his education with an eye toward art, but in 1897 he entered Dunoon College to train for the Baptist ministry. After traveling to America and Japan, he returned to London to serve as principal of the Bible Training College. With the advent of World War II, he felt a call to serve as a chaplain and superintendent of the YMCA for British troops in Egypt. He died there unexpectedly after an attack of appendicitis. Many of his Bible studies and lectures have been printed, and he has become one of the primary devotional writers of the twentieth century. SH

CHARISMATIC MOVEMENT. A manifestation of spiritual renewal in Protestant, Catholic, and even Orthodox churches with features similar to Pentecostalism. First called to public notice by Dennis Bennett, an Episcopal priest in Van Nuys, California, in 1960, reports of "baptisms of the Spirit," experiences of empowerment, fervent small-group meetings, **glossolalia**, healings, and other "charisms" (**gifts of the Spirit**) spread rapidly throughout the United States and beyond. Participants also claimed improved morality, cessation of alcoholism, integration of disturbed personalities, cure of various psychological and physiological disorders, restoration of marital harmony, and revitalization of Christian fellowship in churches. Although not directly connected to the **Pentecostal movement** that sprang up in the early twentieth century, the charismatic movement got a boost from the Full Gospel Businessmen's Fellowship founded in California by Pentecostals in 1953. Where the older Pentecostalism began as a blue-collar phenomenon, the charismatic movement appealed to white-collar types, including students in universities— Catholic charismatic renewal began at Notre Dame and Duquesne.

Churches have responded to the movement in a variety of ways. Because charismatics did not accentuate the phenomenon of speaking in tongues, many churches welcomed the vitality the movement infused into them. Pope **John XXIII** may have had some sense of the charismatic renewal when he spoke of a "new Pentecost." Beginning with Vatican Council II, the Roman Catholic Church made room for charismatics in its parishes and dioceses and looked to Cardinal Suenens of Belgium to give the movement worldwide support and direction. Many Protestant churches felt threatened from the outset by the religious fervor of members who were touched by the movement, and church leaders warned against divisiveness and disorderliness. Over the longer perspective, charismatic renewal has paralleled or been a part of the awakening that has been taking place in America since the 1960s and has been viewed more positively alongside specific renewal programs such as Cursillo and The Walk to Emmaus.

For further reading, see *Presence, Power, Praise: Documents on the Charismatic Renewal*, edited by Kilian McDonnell; Robert G. Gromacki, *The Modern Tongues Movement*; Edward D. O'Connor, *The Pentecostal Movement in the Catholic Church*. EGH

CHARITY. See **Love**.

CHASTITY. Like **poverty** and **obedience**, chastity has been a traditional vow taken upon entering a religious order. It has generally been understood as a lifelong commitment to **celibacy**. If this were the only aspect implied by chastity, however, it would simply be called the vow of celibacy.

Chastity, before it is an outward, behavioral practice of sexual abstinence, is an inward **disposition** of purity and moral excellence or virtue. The European words from which it derives have more to do with purity as the absence of temptation than with submission brought about by the harsh discipline of restraint. Rather than putting the emphasis on purity of action and behavior, the emphasis is on **love**—purity of thought and feeling. The real heart of this spiritual disposition, however, is neither intellectual (mental thoughts) nor affective (emotional) in nature. It is located, rather, in the volitional center, the human **will**.

Perhaps a good way to paraphrase the intent of this spiritual disposition is to call it "purity of heart," as **Søren Kierkegaard** does in his book, *Purity of Heart Is to Will One Thing,* where "one thing" is understood to mean "the Good"—the will of God. Kierkegaard, describing it as being "in but not of" the world, emphasizes how unattainable this paradoxical spiritual disposition would be without God's **grace**.

Being intimately involved in and totally committed to working in the world with and for others and yet simultaneously being free and detached from the world and others—both through God's grace in Christ—is at the heart of the spiritual meaning of chastity. JWK

CHESTERTON, GILBERT KEITH (1874–1936), British poet, journalist, novelist, and spiritual writer. He became most well known for his conversion from Anglicanism to Catholicism in his forties. Some fifteen years earlier, he had converted to Christianity from a troubled agnosticism during which he had dabbled in **spiritualism**. He wrote frequently and vigorously in defense of Christian orthodoxy (and later, Catholicism). Among his most famous books are *The Man Who Was Thursday, Orthodoxy, What's Wrong with the World,* his *Autobiography,* biographies of Saint **Francis of Assisi** and Charles Dickens, the Father Brown mystery stories, and numerous collections of essays and poetry. He was part of a circle of Christian writers that included his brother Cecil and Catholic apologist Hilaire Belloc, and he conducted debates in defense of Christianity with notables such as George Bernard Shaw. Chesterton married Frances Blogg in 1901; they had no children.

Chesterton, an imaginative and colorful writer, was attracted by what he called the wonder and romance of orthodoxy. His writings attacked skepticism, pessimism, and industrialization in modern society. Captivated by the simplicity and faith with which he characterized the Middle Ages, he advocated a spirituality that focused on enjoying life and appreciating the ordinary. His writings also show a keen awareness of humanity's possibility for evil without the **grace** of God. Chesterton's works greatly influenced the conversion and apologetic writings of **C. S. Lewis**.

In addition to Chesterton's works already mentioned, there are biographies by Maisie Ward and Dudley Barker. JLW

CHITTISTER, JOAN, American Benedictine sister, spiritual writer, peace and justice advocate. She is Executive Director of Benetvision: A Resource and Research Center for Contemporary Spirituality, former Benedictine prioress (Erie, Pennsylvania), and past president of the Leadership Conference of Women Religious. Author of some twenty books, including *Wisdom Distilled from the Daily, WomanStrength, Heart of Flesh: A Feminist Spirituality for Women and Men,* and *A Passion for Life,* she is a well-known international lecturer with special interest in justice, peace, and gender equality. She is an active member of the International Peace Council, an interfaith group of religious and spiritual leaders committed to applying the values of peace, love, and justice to situations of conflict and violence. Self-described as a "good Roman Catholic girl and a good obedient nun," she is a dynamic and challenging speaker who combines spirituality with radical commitment to social justice, prophetic vision, and pastoral concern. PWC

CHRYSOSTOM, JOHN (ca. 347–407), bishop of Constantinople. Born and reared in Antioch of Syria by his widowed mother, Anthusa, he studied rhetoric under Libanius, a distinguished non-Christian orator, and theology under Diodore of Tarsus, leader of the Antiochene school. Sensing a call to the **monastic** life, he lived under a **rule** at home. After his mother's death ca. 373 he lived until 381 as a hermit in the mountains south of Antioch following the Rule of Pachomius. His austerities damaged his health and required a return to Antioch, where he was made a deacon. In 386 Bishop Flavian ordained him as a presbyter. For the next twelve years he devoted himself to preaching. He earned the nickname "Golden Mouth" and gained a reputation as one of Christianity's greatest preachers. His homilies combined deep spiritual perception with practical application; but, like others in the Antiochene school, he opposed "allegorical" exegesis.

Against his wish Chrysostom was named Patriarch of Constantinople in 398. He immediately began the daunting task of reforming the court, the clergy, and the people—a task left untouched by his predecessor, Nectarius (381–97). His directness and lack of tact roused the ire of the Empress Eudoxia. With the aid of the Patriarch of Alexandria, Theophilus, she secured Chrysostom's condemnation at the Synod of the Oak in 403. Although an uprising of the people of Constantinople forced her to recall him, she rallied enough opposition to send him back into exile first to Nicaea and then to Cucusus in Lesser Armenia, where he died September 14, 407. In addition to his sermons, one will find spiritual food in his letters to Olympias, a deaconess of the church of Constantinople who defended him against attacks and ministered to him during his exile.

Chrysostom's sermons and other writings fill six volumes of *Nicene and Post-Nicene Fathers*. Helpful studies include Chrysostomus Baur's *John Chrysostom and His Times*, translated by M. Gonzaga, and J. N. D. Kelly's *Golden Mouth: The Story of John Chrysostom*. EGH

CISTERCIANS. Members of the **monastic** order founded at Cîteaux, France, in 1098 as a reform of the Order of Benedict. Cistercian writers include **Bernard of Clairvaux, Aelred of Rievaulx, Joachim of Fiore,** and **William of Saint-Thierry.** Further reforms led to the **Trappist** order.

CLARE OF ASSISI (ca. 1193–1253), founder of the Second Order of **Francis,** the Poor Clares. Clare was born during the time of the Crusades in the age of the Holy Roman Empire. Educated, attractive, and wealthy, she seemed destined to marry well and increase her family's power and prestige. But God led Clare in another direction. At age eighteen, Clare heard Francis (then about thirty) preach in San Giorgino Church in Assisi. Determined to follow Francis, Clare secretly left her parents' home. She donned coarse clothes; and Francis cut her long hair, symbolizing her total gift of self to Christ.

Being the only woman among Francis's followers, Clare was placed in a Benedictine convent where the sisters trained her in living the religious life. Within days, her fifteen-year-old sister, Agnes, joined her, along with others. Francis organized Clare and her associates into a separate order, wrote a basic **rule** for them, and housed them at San Damiano. Unlike their male counterparts, the Poor Clares lived within an enclosed convent. Devoted to a life of **poverty** and living only on alms, the Poor Clares remained firm in their rigorous conviction to bind themselves to Christ.

Clare's spiritual writings include her own rule for the order and some personal letters. From these we meet a woman for whom poverty was a privilege; that is, she saw all Poor Clares as "patterns and mirrors for those who live in the world." Therefore in imitation of her Lord neither she nor her cloistered sisters needed protection from **suffering** or from the harsh realities of their **penitential** life. Clare had to fight attempts to make her community less severe. Under Clare's spiritual leadership, additional Poor Clare communities developed throughout Europe. Clare died twenty-seven years after Francis, a few days after receiving word of approval for her rule.

Most studies of Francis also include information on Clare, who also figures prominently in Nikos **Kazantzakis**'s novel *God's Pauper: St. Francis of Assisi*. Recent studies of Clare include *Clare of Assisi* by Marco Bartoli and *The First Franciscan Woman: Clare of Assisi and Her*

Form of Life by Margaret Charney. Clare's writings are included in *Francis and Clare: The Complete Works,* translated by Regis J. Armstrong and Ignatius C. Brady. EKM

CLASS MEETING. See Covenant Groups.

CLEARNESS COMMITTEE. For over a hundred years **Quakers** (Society of Friends) have employed a form of spiritual **discernment** that makes use of the **community** of faith. Normally individuals facing difficult situations or decisions seek guidance from the larger congregation (referred to as the Friends Meeting in the context of the Quaker tradition); a couple, contemplating marriage, is offered such guidance from their Friends Meeting. Those who are seeking guidance are traditionally called focus persons.

Some important assumptions undergird this form of collegial discernment, and several practical guidelines are essential to its effectiveness. When these assumptions are understood and the guidelines followed or reasonably adhered to, this method can be adapted to a variety of settings and contexts of spiritual discernment, including a retreat setting or a local church context. It can be applied to individuals but also to couples or groups facing a common issue or dilemma.

The fundamental assumption behind this method is that each person or group already has all the resources needed for the discernment process. These resources simply need to be gently brought to the surface of awareness in order that the individual(s) might be able more freely and self-consciously to make use of them. Another assumption is that discernment can most effectively be achieved through the use of carefully worded questions rather than through advice, information, criticism, suggestions, or opinions from others.

A third assumption is that this prayerful and meditative process needs ample amounts of silence as the general background for any words that are spoken. After all, the **Holy**

PROCESS FOR A CLEARNESS COMMITTEE

(adapted for use within a retreat setting)

Early in the retreat at least a full day before the clearness committees are to meet, hand out a written explanation of the assumptions and guidelines for all retreat participants to read. Indicate that you will be asking for volunteers to be the "focus" people, and ask them to be praying about it.

Later, after people have read the material, ask for questions and for volunteers to be "focus" people or presenters. Give an overview of the process and how it will be conducted.

From those who volunteer, choose enough persons so that each presenter will have between four and six members on his or her Committee. Ask the focus persons to indicate names of ones at the retreat they would like to have on their Committee and names of ones they would prefer not to have. Instruct them to write out a description of their concern.

Choose the Committees and, before having them meet, go over the process with emphasis on what constitutes a valid question. Have members of the retreat suggest examples of appropriate and inappropriate questions. Emphasize the need for silence, confidentiality, a slow and unhurried pace, love, and prayer.

Before breaking into the individual Committees, make sure each Committee has a clerk to keep time and a recorder to write out the questions and responses to give to the focus person afterward.

Assign each Committee to a quiet and private space, giving them a suggested time frame, preferably from two and a half to four hours.

After the Committees have met, design a group reflection time where both the focus persons and the Committee members have a chance to reflect on the process.

Spirit is the active spiritual director, and the Holy Spirit likes to work in silence. Silence also helps those in the discernment process listen for the promptings of the Spirit. A fourth assumption is that each member of the Committee will hold both the focus person(s) and their concern in the light of God's **grace** and **love** at all times. Those presenting dilemmas or concerns are vulnerable and need to be held carefully and gently in a constant web of love and support.

A fifth assumption is that the group times together are only part of the actual discernment process. They help get it started, but the discernment continues long afterward and may even benefit from further Committee meetings if that is possible. A sixth assumption is that all that transpires within the clearness committee is totally confidential, to be discussed later only at the prompting of the focus person(s).

It helps all involved in the process to know some of the practical guidelines beforehand. First, the individual, couple, or group presenting the concern or dilemma should spend some time in prayer and reflection about it and put into writing the issues, where their unclarity lies, and how and where they are looking to the group for guidance. This written statement should be presented to the group of five or six before the formal gathering time if possible. Second, a clerk should be appointed for the Clearness Committee. The clerk opens and closes the meeting as well as sees that the guidelines are followed.

Third, the focus person, after an appropriate opening period of silence, presents his or her concern or dilemma verbally. Fourth, the only appropriate responses from the group take the form of silent prayer and spoken questions. The questions should be genuinely open-ended and not questions that offer a specific hidden or overt answer, opinion, judgment, or direction. Helpful information about and examples of what constitutes an open-ended question (as well as greater background and detail about clearness committees in general) can be found on several Web sites, such as that of the Friends General Conference (www.fgcquaker.org/library/fosteringmeetings/0208.html); Ability Now (www.abilitynow.com/Playground/Exercises/quaker.htm); the Center for Teacher Formation, sponsored by the Fetzer Institute (www.teacherformation.org); and the Chrysalis Group (www.thechrysalisgroup.com).

Fifth, the focus person(s) may choose to respond verbally to each question or not, a period of silence being an important interlude between questions and responses. Sixth, the clerk at some point in the process, which will last between two to four hours, gives the focus person(s) an opportunity to choose how to spend the remaining time together. Options include an open time of silence in which anyone may speak, as during a Quaker meeting for worship; a period of dialogue, where the focus person(s) responds to the process and asks the group for specific suggestions; or a period of focusing on one or more specific areas of concern. Finally, the focus person(s) thanks the Committee and may share with them any clarity or further unclarity that has surfaced. If an additional meeting is needed, arrangements for it can be made. JWK

CLEMENT OF ALEXANDRIA (ca. 150–ca. 215), theologian. Born of non-Christian parents, probably at Athens, Clement visited lower Italy, Syria, and Palestine before coming to Alexandria around 180 to study under Pantaenus, the head of the School of Alexandria. Ten years later, he succeeded Pantaenus. He fled Alexandria in 202 or 203 during the persecution under Septimius Severus. The date of his death is uncertain. The first Christian to attain some distinction as a scholar, he held Greek philosophy in high regard. He considered both the Hebrew prophets and the Greek philosophers precursors of Christ and inspired by the divine Logos. He agreed with certain **Gnostics** against those who insisted on "faith alone" that Christians should seek *gnosis* (mystical knowledge), but he disagreed with Gnostic views that matter is evil as well as their ethical attitudes that led to libertinism.

In typically Alexandrian fashion Clement employed allegorical interpretation. He found in scriptures three senses—literal, moral, and spiritual. But in practice he favored the moral sense. Several of his works have survived. In *Address to the Greeks* he defended Christianity against pagan charges and argued that it is the "true philosophy." In *The Instructor* he used the Stoic principle of moderation in all things as the guideline for Christian behavior. In *Stromateis* or *Miscellaneous Studies* he ruminated on the **contemplative** life, agreeing with the Gnostics that **mystical** experience is the chief goal of the life of perfection. That goal evidently eluded him, however. In *Who Is the Rich Man That Shall Be Saved?* he reassured the increasingly upscale people who knocked on church doors in his day that they should not interpret Jesus' warning in Mark 10:17-31 literally. Jesus meant that they should give up indulgent lifestyles and live temperately.

The works mentioned above are included in volume 2 of *The Ante-Nicene Fathers*. Studies of Clement include *The Christian Platonists of Alexandria* by Charles Bigg and *The Philosophy of Clement of Alexandria* by Eric F. Osborn. EGH

CLIMACUS, JOHN (ca. 579–649), Orthodox monk and spiritual writer. At age sixteen John Climacus joined the monks at Mount Sinai and pursued the common life. After taking final vows at age nineteen or twenty, John retired into solitude as a hermit at Tholos, near Mount Sinai, where he claimed to receive the gift of **tears** and the grace of **unceasing prayer**. After forty years at Tholus, he was elected abbot of Sinai, and while serving there he wrote his famous *The Ladder of Divine Ascent*. From then on he has been known as John of the Ladder, *Climacus* in Latin.

The Ladder was written by a monk for monks. John believed, however, that every Christian needed a personal encounter with God. In the book, he sought to evoke in the reader an experience similar to his own. Using the image of Jacob's ladder, John proceeded in thirty steps to guide the initiate into a process of **sanctification** and divine **union**. The work consists of three main sections. The first section (steps 1 to 3) begins a break with the world through renunciation, **detachment**, and exile. The second section (steps 4 to 26) deals with the practice of the **virtues** and the struggle with the vices of passion, which comprises the bulk of the work. The book concludes (steps 27 to 30) with the **disciplines** of the contemplative life that lead to union with God in the divine **fire** of love. John chose the number thirty to correspond to Jesus' hidden years prior to his baptism. The Orthodox Church so reveres the work that it is read in the monasteries and refectories every year during Lent.

John, a mystic of light rather than divine **darkness**, avoids **apophatic** language and does not intend that his "steps" be taken literally or dogmatically. His view of **spiritual formation** is dynamic and progressive: The goal of **perfection** is not arrival but a process of moving from glory to glory whose summit is Love.

A Spanish translation of Climacus was the first book printed in the New World (Mexico, 1532). *John Climacus: The Ladder of Divine Ascent* is translated by Colm Luibheid and Norman Russell. TCW

CLOUD OF UNKNOWING, THE. An anonymous guide to prayer. *The Cloud of Unknowing* was written around 1375 by an anonymous English spiritual director, presumably as a guidebook for a twenty-four-year-old novice. We know nothing about the author, although some scholars have speculated that the writer was a Cistercian monk. Others have noted the similarities of *The Cloud*'s prose to that of **Walter Hilton**. The author's thesis, presented in seventy-five chapters, is that God can be known by love but not by thought. Only **love** can pierce the "cloud of unknowing" that separates humankind from God. The novice is advised to try to penetrate the **darkness** above and to strike at that cloud of unknowing with the sharp dart of longing love and never think of giving up. The author's method is stated in chapter 3: One must lift up one's heart in love to God and have God alone as one's aim and none of God's goods, forgetting every creature that God has made and its works. In this effort, the soul will be helped by **grace** and feel the desire for God.

The Cloud offers a method by which even the uninitiated can approach contemplative prayer. Divesting the mind of all images and concepts may lead to an encounter with the unfathomable being of God. Although the intellect and the imagination initiate the ascent to God, these must be abandoned so that the soul may proceed by the **negative way** of imageless **contemplation**. The author's suggestion to repeat a simple word as the distillation of one's "naked yearning" for God serves as the foundation for **Centering Prayer**.

The Cloud of Unknowing is available in a variety of modern translations, often in combination with *The Book of Privy Counsel* and other works apparently by the same writer. RMH

COMENIUS, JOHN AMOS (1592–1670),
bishop of the Bohemian Brethren and educator. Born in Moravia (present Czech Republic), his life was marked by constant turmoil and personal loss both before and during the Thirty Years War (1618–48). He lived the majority of his life in exile, ending in the Netherlands.

Comenius is remembered as an educator, often called the "Father of Modern Education." His innovative pedagogical principles underscored the importance of teaching character through molding students into the image of Christ rather than through the mere accumulation of facts. He encouraged the education of women and stressed the importance of observation and drawing upon the insights of nature. While his efforts to create a "pansophic" college that integrated religion, science, and philosophy into an unified system failed in England, he was invited to reform the educational systems in Sweden and Hungary and to become president of Harvard University (which he declined).

Comenius was the last bishop of the Bohemian Brethren (*Unitas Fratrum*), spiritual descendants of **John Hus**, and the seed of the renewed Unity of Brethren associated with **Zinzendorf**. Amid his lifelong struggle, he remained an idealistic optimist, seeking to bring Christian unity and peace to the world through love and education. These educational reforms were theologically grounded in his life as a pastor. Three key components undergirded his spirituality: a personal relationship with Jesus Christ that emphasized Christ's lordship, ecumenical reformation, and a persistent belief in **hope**. According to Comenius, God provided humanity with three sources of knowledge: **scripture**, reason, and nature, all essential for growth in truth.

A recent translation of his devotional classic *The Labyrinth of the World and the Paradise of the Heart,* translated by Howard Louthan and Andrea Sterk, provides a good introduction to his life and spirituality. *The Labyrinth*, a precursor to **Bunyan's** better-known allegory *The Pilgrim's Progress*, traces the pilgrimage of a Christian who seeks to move from the false self to the true self. TS

COMMUNION, HOLY. See **Holy Communion.**

COMMUNION OF SAINTS. A term from the Greek *koinonia hagion*, meaning literally "fellowship or commonness of holy ones." The word *saints* simply means Christians in much of the New Testament. (For a more restricted use, see the article on **Saints**.) It is noteworthy that the early church's belief in the communion of saints, mentioned in the Apostles' Creed, has been relatively ignored and narrowly defined by Protestants, though it holds rich promise for spiritual growth and strength. The real existence of the communion of saints imparts pivotal support and a powerful fellowship otherwise missing.

The communion of saints means all Christians are united with one another in at least three ways. First, saints provide mutual care for one another and, more importantly, share everything in common. The Antioch church's offering for the church in Jerusalem was an expression of the communion of saints in the form of material resources (Acts 2:44-45). Second, saints share Christian fellowship when they receive the sacraments, especially the bread and wine of **Holy Communion**. This sharing at table is the primary Protestant understanding of the term and so predominates in Protestant churches that many of them simply call the Eucharist "Communion," as though it were the only communion among Christians. Third, saints have communion with—are in **community** with—all those saints who have passed through death. The *koinonia* shared by all Christians always comes through their *koinonia* with Jesus Christ, which is not dissolved by death. Orthodox Christians emphasize this community of saints regularly through the use of holy **icons** in churches and homes as physical reminders that the saints portrayed and all saints are truly present. Hymns often express faith in the communion of saints:

> One family we dwell in him, one Church, above, beneath,
> Though now divided by the stream, the narrow stream of death.
> —**Charles Wesley**

> O blest communion, fellowship divine!
> We feebly struggle; they in glory shine!
> Yet all are one in thee, for all are thine.
> —William H. Howe

JNE

COMMUNITY. Western Christians live in a culture that struggles with the idea of community. Since the Reformation, the rights, experiences, and significance of the individual have become increasingly important in politics, philosophy, theology, and religion. As a result, modern Western culture continually asserts the importance of individual experience and belief in spiritual life—evidenced most vividly in the growth of the New Age movement, which has attempted to create an individually focused spirituality that emphasizes personal growth, self-actualization, and self-awareness. Such individualism is the anti-

thesis of Christian **spirituality**, which at its core is a communal faith that emphasizes the individual in community, while emphasizing the importance of the individual.

First, it is communal because Christian spirituality has always been aware of how human sin can delude us as individuals. Sin can cause our spirituality to become ego-driven and self-focused, not God-driven and God-focused. When our spirituality remains primarily personal and private, it also can become selfish and self-focused. The community of faith, the church, helps us remain focused on God through communal worship, study, and service. Christian **worship** always focuses on God. Christian study always focuses on learning how to experience and serve God. Christian service always focuses on loving others for God.

Second, Christian spirituality is communal because it is built on the written, oral, and practical traditions that have been handed down from age to age. It is popular today for people to create their own personal spiritual approaches in an attempt to find God in their own way. Unfortunately, this leaves them open to both spiritually nourishing and malnourishing sources. Not everything labeled "spiritual" is necessarily spiritually healthy. Christian spirituality avoids malnourishment by feeding us from the ancient spiritual traditions that have taught people from age to age how to discover and experience God. By following, practicing, and learning the Christian spiritual traditions, we spiritually inoculate ourselves against the faddish spirituality of every age. This does not mean that the Christian spiritual tradition cannot be abused. In every age some Christians, churches, and denominations misinterpret the Christian tradition; but they are the exception not the rule. By being part of the Christian community, we are best able to discover and practice these traditions.

A third reason Christian spirituality is communal arises from scripture. The apostle Paul, in his first letter to the Corinthians, tells us that we are all part of the **body of Christ** (1

Cor. 12:12-31). We are not self-sufficient in ourselves but only discover our true **gifts** and purpose in the context of community. We were created to share in God's love and are called to share our God-given gifts with others. When we try to be self-sufficient spiritually, we end up being like an ear or a finger cut off from the rest of the body. True Christian spirituality and service are relational. They are meant to build up the body of Christ in the local church and throughout the world. Alone we can do nothing, but together in Christ the impossible becomes possible.

For further reading, see *A Testament of Devotion* by **Thomas R. Kelly**, *Discipleship: Living for Christ in the Daily Grind* by J. Heinrich Arnold, or *Forming Faith in a Hurricane: A Spiritual Primer for Daily Living* by N. Graham Standish. NGS

COMPASSION. One of the key transcendent **dispositions** needed for spiritual maturity, **discernment**, and social responsibility. Compassion's root meaning is "to suffer with," that is, literally to feel the suffering, pain, woundedness, or oppression of the other. It refers to a communal suffering or a unity in emotion. In the phenomenon of **stigmata**, for example, inner compassion for Christ can radiate outward to one's own body. Christ's Passion on the **cross** is the most perfect example of and the fullest expression of divine compassion. Participation in divine compassion is fundamental to the Christian life. It increases one's spiritual power to love God and fallen humanity. Taken in its most essential form, compassion is a graced disposition and a radical form of self-**poverty**. As such, it is formed by and is strengthened by faith, hope, and love.

Compassion is a critical disposition necessary for a healthy social presence and social responsibility. Without compassion, Christians cannot do justice, love **mercy**, and walk in the way of truth. It gives Christians the ability to embrace their own and others' limitations and takes into account the fallibility and vulnerability of the human condition or situation when responding to a social situation or so-cial evil. Compassion gives Christians the ability to embrace social reality as it is without becoming resentful, prideful, unjust, violent, or overwhelmed. Without compassion, reformation and social action can become another expression of oppression and the impoverishment of human dignity. Compassionate social presence directs us to creative means to reform deformative conditions and situations, both for specific people and for the good of all humanity. A modern exemplar of a well-developed disposition of compassion is **Teresa of Calcutta** (see *Something Beautiful for God* by Malcolm Muggeridge). CIZ

COMPUNCTION. Godly sorrow for **sin**, usually accompanied by spiritual **tears** welling up from the depths of our inmost being. Greek writers such as **John Climacus** and **Symeon the New Theologian** distinguished between a surface kind of tears and tears from the very depths of one's soul—tears of compunction. As followers of Jesus, we are on a journey to become more and more the unique persons God has called us to be in Christ. Compunction is an element of coming to know ourselves at a deeper level. This deep self-knowledge is often painful because we need to face up to the enslaved, unhealed, and darkened aspects of ourselves and the lives we are living. Compunction occurs as we open ourselves to God's light that illumines our own darkness.

Many Christians fear self-discovery. Recognizing, naming, attending to our shortcomings is a **cross** we must pick up and bear. Coming to grips with or facing up to how we often miss the mark as followers of Christ is a necessary first step in growing spiritually mature. As we confront our inner confusion, helplessness, frustration, and sense of sinfulness, we are flooded at the same time with an awareness of God's love.

The experience of tears or weeping is often how we can recognize that the Lord is calling us to a change of heart, or **conversion**, and setting us on the **purgative way**. This kind of weeping reminds us how much God loves us, and this reaffirmation of our transcendent dignity empowers us to be open to and accepting of the purification process that signals a growing and deepening relationship with the Lord. Being receptive to this spiritual gift takes courage. The immediate experience of our free-flowing tears blossoms into our becoming more and more convinced that without God we are nothing.

Thomas à Kempis wrote extensively on compunction in *Imitation of Christ*. A modern study is *Penthos: The Doctrine of Compunction in the Christian East* by Irénée Hausherr. EKM

CONE, JAMES HAL (b. 1938), American theologian, writer, professor. Author of *God of the Oppressed* and *A Black Theology of Liberation*, Cone says that we cannot separate our faith from our context: society, power structures, drives, issues, and everyday life. In the life and teachings of Jesus, we see God's identification with and desire to liberate particular oppressed people at particular moments in history. Today, especially in America, God is literally and symbolically present in black people. While Jesus' struggle in life and death parallels the struggle of oppressed people everywhere, Cone's theology is grounded in the religious significance of the black experience and the role of black Christianity in North America. God's response to the struggle, both for Jesus and for all oppressed people, is found in hope and resurrection. Oppressed people can and should take heart, for God is stronger than the evils of any person or system. SN

CONFESSION. A dimension of conversion, an ever-present dynamic of the Christian life made concrete either in public worship or private confession to God or to a spiritual **friend** or director. It is acknowledgment of individual and corporate responsibility for one's actions and for growth in likeness to Christ under the guidance of the Holy Spirit.

The Hebrew Bible frequently refers both to corporate and individual confession. The Law calls for individual confession upon realization of guilt (Lev. 5:5) and confession on behalf of all the people in the ceremony of the scapegoat (Lev. 16:21). Ezra and Nehemiah both lead times of national confession. In Psalm 32, the psalmist speaks of how refusal to confess his sins was physically debilitating, while confession brought relief and forgiveness. He calls on all the people to imitate his example. This psalm and Psalms 6; 38; 51; 102; 130; and 143 are known as the Seven Penitential Psalms and serve as models for personal and public confession.

In the Gospels and the early church, confession was generally treated individualistically in terms of hatred and atonement for sin. Peter's confession in Luke 5:8, where he admits he is a sinner, is related to his call to follow Jesus. In Acts 19:18 confession is associated with conversion. And the parable of the prodigal son in Luke 15:11-32 shows how confession is related to **penitence**, reconciliation, and celebration. James 5:16 urges Christians to confess their sins to one another.

By the second and third centuries persons who had fallen away went through a public, long, and arduous act of confession and repentance. The enrolled penitents were segregated from the congregation and kept from **Communion** for a period of time. Each Sunday they received a special laying on of hands by the pastor and were finally reinstated into the full assembly on Maundy Thursday. Since the process could only be undergone once in a lifetime, with a promise of lifelong continence, the system was replaced by the fifth century by private confession. By the Fourth Lateran Council in 1215, every Christian confessed his or her sin once a year by self-examination. Penance could consist of a dangerous **pilgrimage**, sustained **fasting**, and other inflicted discomforts.

In 1552 the **Book of Common Prayer** set confession of sin in the full context of **worship**. Liturgical confession is always corporate: "our sin," not "my sins." It is not a cry of the condemned begging to be saved from hell but rather a motivation for actively resisting sin and evil in one's own life and in society. Prayers of confession in worship are followed either by an act of pardon (a pastoral prayer for **forgiveness**) or by a scriptural assurance of God's love and forgiveness. The tone is one of **assurance**, acceptance, and **hope**.

Today there is a reemphasis on the spirit of baptismal conversion. Increasingly the community's spirituality of confession is correlated with the social teachings and social mission of the church. **Covenant groups** for accountability encourage this attitude of honesty to accept wholeheartedly one's responsibilities and call to holiness and also to recognize the difficulties that come with the effort to fulfill these responsibilities and this vocation. PDB

CONFORMITY TO THE WILL OF GOD.

The human response to God's **grace** takes a specific shape and form. The shape of our response is made possible by the **gifts of the Spirit**, especially the gifts of **faith**, **hope**, and **love** (1 Cor. 13). Our cooperation with God is defined by the Old Testament concept of **covenant**, by which we are called into relationship and sustained through steadfast love. The **will of God** is revealed through **scripture** and tradition, in law and gospel, in festival observance and sacramental liturgy. Our conformity to God's will is found in our adherence to law, our **receptivity** to gospel, our remembrance of God's actions in history, and our anticipation of God's fulfillment of promise in the future.

Conformity to God's will always requires vision and **discernment**. The will of God is revealed to those who resist cultural pressures to equate divine purpose with prevailing wisdom. An **obedience** marked by **humility**, relinquishment and **detachment** is often the setting for a clear perception of God's purpose. Vision gives the individual a sense of God's action across larger segments of history. Discernment helps us to act faithfully in the **present moment**, trusting that God is at work among us. Spiritual **disciplines** sharpen a person's vision and discernment, and these disciplines are best practiced in **community**.

Conformity to the will of God is the ex-

pression of human faithfulness, itself a **gift** of God but also a response to God, in the desire to live a **holy** and godly life. This can be misunderstood as confining or restraining; instead, conformity to the will of God guides us into the freedom offered in Jesus Christ, the narrow way that leads to life (Matt. 7:14).

For further study, see *Yearning to Know God's Will* by Danny E. Morris. KHC

CONSOLATION AND DESOLATION.

Feelings that reflect the movement of the **Holy Spirit** in our lives, often in response to a decision or a state of being. Consolation is related to a sense of freedom, **peace**, acceptance, and joy. Desolation is the experience of distress, **dryness**, heaviness, and **darkness**. The relation between consolation and desolation is prominent in the writings of **Teresa of Ávila**, **John of the Cross**, and **Ignatius of Loyola**. Ignatius discusses consolation and desolation in *Spiritual Exercises* within the context of "Rules for the Discernment of Spirits." The interior movement of consolation is an indication that the individual is growing closer to God; the time of desolation corresponds to the absence of God. Teresa and John discuss these spiritual feelings as aspects of the **illuminative way** and the beginnings of **union**. See, in particular, Teresa's *Interior Castle* and John's *Dark Night of the Soul*.

Both consolation and desolation present dangers. One who knows the former may become prideful or come to love God more for the good feelings than for God's self (what **Bernard of Clairvaux** calls mercenary love in *On Loving God*). The experience of desolation can discourage the individual, leading to a sense of **abandonment** by God. Reflection on these two terms can help Christians understand consolation and desolation, especially in conversation with a **spiritual director**, who can guide the individual through the varied experiences of life.

Jonathan Edwards looked at both the dangers and benefits of spiritual feelings in *A Treatise Concerning Religious Affections*. KHC

CONTEMPLATION. In Christian spirituality, contemplation refers to the focused attention of the soul toward the Divine. Contemplation is about the interior life of **prayer** that yearns to see and know God as God is, to experience a pure **union** with God, and to be absorbed by God's all-consuming infinite love. Ultimately this kind of union with God is a gift of **grace**.

From a historical perspective, we can see the evolutionary developments of contemplation. Initially two approaches to contemplation developed. One of the earliest church fathers to write about contemplation was **Origen** (ca. 185–255), who said that in the fall of Adam and Eve, humanity lost its divine likeness. Since the goal of redemption is to return to godlikeness, one must pass from **purgation** through **illumination** to **union**. Each stage brings movement toward greater light. The **positive way** approached this movement through **meditation** on God using metaphor and **imagery** and including contemplative use of **icons** and the **Jesus Prayer**. The **negative way** emphasized that no symbol or image could express who God is, only what God is not, transcending every analogy.

In this form of contemplation, **Gregory of Nyssa** said one begins in the light but moves toward the thick cloud of **darkness** symbolizing God's mystery. **Augustine** described contemplation as that special moment when the soul enters not by its own efforts but by God's grace into an intimate and loving union with God. In *The Ladder of Monks* **Guigo II** discussed contemplation as the fourth element of *lectio divina*. **Bonaventure** called contemplation "excessive knowledge" in which the mind is raised above itself and brought to perfection by the gifts of God's grace. **Thomas Aquinas** understood contemplation as "infused mystical prayer." The fourteenth-century work *The Cloud of Unknowing* emphasizes the inadequacy of cognition and says the only way to penetrate this "cloud of unknowing" between oneself and God is the "sharp dart of longing love." **Ignatius of Loyola** wrote about a different sort of contemplation in *Spiritual Exercises*, urging imaginative participation in

events of Christ's life as a means of growing toward union.

During the sixteenth century, **Teresa of Ávila** and **John of the Cross** wrote extensively about the difference between "acquired contemplation" and "infused contemplation." Acquired contemplation occurs when the heart, will, and mind are overwhelmed by the Divine but reasoning powers are not suspended. Infused contemplation occurs passively by entering a mystical transforming union with God in which the soul is completely surrendered to God.

Most of these writers considered infused contemplation a high form of prayer granted to only a few **saints**, but they considered acquired contemplation dangerous without clear signs of a divine call to such prayer. But in the twentieth century, **Thomas Merton** proposed that any Christian, not just a chosen few, can experience contemplation. Merton defined contemplation as resting in God by suspending activity, withdrawing into solitude, and allowing the intensity of Christ's love to work in the soul. In such contemplation the mystery of God is revealed in the center of the innermost self. Inspired by Merton's writings, **Thomas Keating** and others developed the method of **Centering Prayer** as a way of opening to acquired contemplation and making way for infused contemplation.

For further reading, see *New Seeds of Contemplation* by Thomas Merton or *Dark Night of the Soul* by John of the Cross. ASJ

CONVERSION. A radical changing of life so as to love God before all others. Conversion always involves repentance and **faith**. Several other words and concepts are related—*new birth, salvation, good* **works,** *forgiveness, grace, justification, sanctification, transformation, the kingdom of God,* **regeneration,** and **confession.** The essence of conversion is turning from darkness to light, from falsehood to truth, and from idols to God. It is not a momentary exertion of **will** but a continual effort of turning toward God. Such turning is necessary because of the powerful, pervasive human penchant for **sin** and for idolatry, giving to objects a priority that belongs to God alone. Idols commonly include oneself, others, physical beauty, fame, money, power, pleasure, and attention. The self seems by nature to crave these and other worldly prizes.

The most profound aspect of conversion occurs inside the self, a change of heart. In Jewish thought the heart was considered the seat of mind and will rather than the location of emotions. The true conversion of one's center, one's self, must involve the evidence of changing practices and behaviors that displease God. This need to alter behavior from self-centered to God-centered has created problems historically. Humans too easily fool themselves and others by imitating Christian behaviors while the heart remains relatively unchanged. Because such hypocrisy (role-playing) is often hidden from a person, conversion is one of God's deepest mysteries. In Jeremiah 4:4 the prophet addressed an acute problem of hypocrisy using the powerful metaphor of circumcision of the heart. He understood that conversion must be primarily an interior **disposition**; so obeying numerous commandments and sacrificial rites was not the same as loving and obeying God.

The interior processes of conversion have been much studied and written about. The early church discovered that preaching the good news of Jesus was a primary tool in bringing about conversion and that repentance and faith must always accompany conversion. Though conversion is an act of the soul itself, not something imposed from outside, a person cannot convert himself or herself. God alone can convert. Even though the power to repent and to have faith are ultimately gifts of God, we are required to exercise them by conscious decision and **penitence**. God will not force us or do them for us. Rather they are a matter of cooperation with God's grace.

In addition to the conversion of individuals, the Bible insists on the conversion of peoples and nations. The awareness of this expectation involves a greater challenge for the church. The interplay of human free will with the **will of God** is difficult to understand in the conversion of individuals and becomes even more problematic in understanding how families, groups, and nations are converted. Group conversions have often occurred, and in recent years they have been carefully studied. Some have been marred by mass emotionalism, while others have clearly been aspects of widespread authentic revival. JNE

COVENANT. In the Hebrew Bible, the word for covenant, *berit*, can mean different things: "promise," "pledge," "obligation," or "contract." It can stand for the bond of friendship between two people, as in the story of Jonathan and David (1 Sam. 18:1-4). Marriage is such a covenant. It may also stand for a political arrangement between two countries, two or more kings, or between a ruling class and its slaves. Most important, covenant is used to describe the divinely instituted relationship between God and God's people.

God's covenant, although the actual Hebrew term is not used, was implied when God created and gave humanity a special place in the created design. God put Adam ("the human") in the garden and provided for him a mate (Gen. 2:18). In return the human was to till and keep the garden (2:15). The first use of *berit* comes in the story of Noah. God's creation had been destroyed by the flood. When the waters subsided, God spoke, "I am establishing my covenant with you and your descendants after you, and with every living creature" (9:9-10). Through the sign of the rainbow, God made a pact with all living things, not just humanity.

Eventually God made an agreement with a particular people. Genesis 15 and following chapters outline God's covenant with Abraham and his descendants, the sign being circumcision. Abraham's duty was to follow God in all he did, evidenced by the test in chapter 22. God's promise was, "Look toward heaven and count the stars, if you are able to count them. So shall your descendants be" (15:5).

An important aspect of the divine

covenant is that it was ever changing. As it refers to the divine relationship between God and humanity, *berit* never occurs in the plural. Jeremiah 32:40 speaks of *berit olam*, an "everlasting covenant." God never breaks the covenant. One of God's key characteristics is *chesed*, usually translated as "steadfast love," though "grace" or "covenant commitment" would be accurate as well. The prophet Hosea's life provides a parable of such commitment. However, in God's dealing with a flawed humanity the covenant would need to be reworked and renewed. God made a reworked covenant with Moses and the children of Israel at Sinai, with a renewed promise of God's care and the more explicit instructions of Torah, the Law. Second Chronicles 15 and 34 and Nehemiah 8 through 10 describe times of national covenant renewal. Jeremiah promises a new covenant written directly on the heart (31:33).

In the New Testament, Paul proclaims that Christians are ministers of the new covenant "not of letter but of spirit" (2 Cor. 3:6). That is, through the death and resurrection of Christ, we can receive a new life characterized as Christ living in us through the Spirit rather than by the many specific demands of the Law. Again the covenant has been reworked as Christ completes the relationship begun with the promises in the Hebrew Bible.

Covenant is a term used widely in the scriptures but not often in modern Christian language except at Communion services. Early Puritan writers emphasized the covenantal nature of the Christian relationship with God and called for both personal and communal times of covenant renewal. These suggestions were taken up by **John Wesley** in services of covenant renewal, particularly on New Year's Day. Such services have been a regular (though by no means constant) part of Methodist worship since. One summary of these services is the **Covenant Prayer**.

For further reading, see the articles on covenant in *Long Ago God Spoke: How Christians May Hear the Old Testament Today* by William L.

Holladay and *Covenant: The History of a Biblical Idea* by Delbert R. Hillers. WBF

COVENANT GROUPS. The concept of a few people making a **covenant** with one another for mutual accountability has been part of Christian life in many different forms down through the centuries. **Pietists** and **Moravians** organized small "bands" of people according to gender and spiritual maturity. **John Wesley** and his followers put newly converted Methodists into special bands and had other groups for those mature in faith and for backsliders in need of special care. Most Methodists, however, were in "classes" that cut across gender and experience and were often geographical. At class meetings members answered the basic question, "How goes it with your soul?" and dealt together with problems that had arisen since the last meeting.

In the last half of the twentieth century, many churches have rediscovered the importance of small groups as centers for growth in knowledge, fellowship, and discipleship. Serendipity is an organization that has been producing small-group resources since the late 1950s. Megachurches have proclaimed the centrality of small groups for the assimilation and discipling of new Christians. Some groups place the primary emphasis on learning, others on community building. Covenant groups emphasize accountability in Christian living between group meetings.

One covenant group model is covenant discipleship, a renewal movement of The United Methodist Church rooted in John Wesley's organization of classes and bands for nurturing obedient accountable discipleship and ongoing Christian perfection. Covenant discipleship groups consist of five to seven people who seek to follow Christ and grow in faith by meeting weekly for **prayer**, support, and mutual accountability. Each group develops a specific covenant based on Wesley's "General Rules" for the Methodist societies. These Rules may be summarized as avoiding evil, doing good, and attending to the ordinances of the church (**disciplines** such as

---

SAMPLE GROUP COVENANT

(Note: this is the covenant of an actual group, not a general model.)

ACTS OF COMPASSION

　　I will spend two hours each month in service to one of our group's missions. (Prison Ministry office, Food Bank, Penelope House)

　　I will spend an additional two hours each month on a cause or project in my local community for the disadvantaged.

ACTS OF JUSTICE

　　I will speak out and write my legislative representatives on justice issues as they become apparent to me.

　　I will support local efforts to improve race relations in my community, business, and home.

ACTS OF WORSHIP

　　I will worship each Sunday unless prevented.

　　I will receive the sacrament of Holy Communion each week.

ACTS OF DEVOTION

　　I will pray each day.

　　I will read and study the scripture each day.

　　I will observe a "Quiet Day" on our group's selected theme each quarter.

---

worship, private and family prayer, reading **scripture**, **fasting**, etc.). The group's covenant is an agreement among members on how they will walk with Christ together. The covenant serves as the weekly agenda as each person in the group gives an account of what he or she has done or not done since the last meeting. The group leader (leadership may rotate) directs the questions and keeps the group focused on the covenant.

For more information on covenant discipleship the following are helpful resources: David Lowes Watson, *Covenant Discipleship: Christian Formation through Mutual Accountability*; Gayle Turner Watson, *Guide for Covenant Discipleship Groups*; or Steven W. Manskar, *Accountable Discipleship: Living in God's Household*. CIZ

COVENANT PRAYER. A brief prayer of self-**abandonment** and commitment.

　　I am no longer my own, but thine.
　　Put me to what thou wilt, rank me with
　　　　whom thou wilt;
　　put me to doing, put me to suffering;

　　let me be employed for thee or laid aside
　　　　for thee,
　　exalted for thee or brought low for thee;
　　let me be full, let me be empty;
　　let me have all things, let me have
　　　　nothing;
　　I freely and heartily yield all things
　　　　to thy pleasure and disposal.
　　And now, O glorious and blessed God,
　　　　Father, Son, and Holy Spirit,
　　thou art mine, and I am thine. So be it.
　　And the covenant which I have made
　　　　on earth,
　　let it be ratified in heaven. Amen.

The words are taken, with changes, from *Vindiciae Pietatis*, or *A Vindication of Godliness*, by Richard Alleine, a seventeenth-century Puritan. The body of the text is from Alleine's instructions on how to prepare to commit oneself to God in a solemn **covenant**. The concluding doxology is the end of a much longer covenant prayer that Alleine quoted from a pamphlet by his brother, Joseph. **John Wesley** printed selections from Alleine's book in his *Christian Library* and by 1755 began using the section on covenant renewal (eventually published as a separate pamphlet) as the basis for special renewal services. In its brief form, the Covenant Prayer is taken from a service of covenant renewal in a British Methodist worship book in 1932. The service is a thorough reworking of the older Wesleyan service. George B. Robson first suggested creating a short prayer as the climax of the service, but the final form is attributed only to the revision committee that he chaired.

Surrendering to God: Living the Covenant Prayer by Keith Beasley-Topliffe offers a more detailed history of the prayer. KRB

CRANMER, THOMAS (1489–1556), archbishop of Canterbury and liturgical theologian. Educated and appointed fellow of Jesus College, Cambridge, he was ordained in 1523. He counseled King Henry VIII with regard to the royal divorce proceedings, and Henry made him archbishop of Canterbury in 1532. In this office, which he accepted with great reluctance, he became one of the chief instruments in the overthrow of papal supremacy in England and one of the primary architects of the autonomous Church of England. The theological reformation of the English church advanced under his direction during the regency of Edward VI. During this period, Cranmer's ideas moved increasingly in a Protestant direction, most noticeably with regard to eucharistic theology. In order to push forward his plans for the union of the reforming traditions of Europe, he invited several of the prominent Continental theologians, including Peter Martyr and Martin Bucer, to England. In 1553 on the accession of Mary Tudor and the restoration of Roman Catholicism in the nation, he was accused of high treason, convicted, and imprisoned. He was eventually tried for heresy and recanted his Protestant beliefs, only to renounce his recantations later, dying at the stake in 1556. He is remembered primarily for his exquisite English style, expressed without parallel in the various editions of the **Book of Common Prayer** and the *Homilies* of the Church of England.

For more on his life, see Diarmaid MacCulloch's *Thomas Cranmer: A Life.* PWC

CREATION-CENTERED SPIRITUALITY. One of the most ancient of spiritual traditions. It presents the concept of original blessing from the creation story in Genesis as meaning we are created good and gifted with a life of continuing revelation. It is based on the current expanding understanding of creation as process rather than event. God created, is creating, and will create, with each person having a part in the continuing creation and participating in its sacredness.

Matthew Fox is the person most influential in the rediscovery of creation spirituality, which began in the Hebrew tradition with new insights throughout history. Fox's writings ignited an interest in the Rhineland mystics: **Meister Eckhart**, **Hildegard of Bingen**, and others. This interest broadened to include others whose **mysticism** grew out of a love of the natural world, from **Francis of Assisi** to William Wordsworth, and to consider the nature-based religions of many indigenous peoples.

Brian Swimme and Thomas Berry have helped in the understanding and experiencing of the "new" (old) cosmology with their book *The Universe Story: From the Primordial Flaring Forth to the Ecozoic Era, A Celebration of the Unfolding of the Cosmos.* They integrate the humanities with the sciences in helping us recognize our part in the universe story. In *The Dream of the Earth* Thomas Berry points out that our ecological concern should be driven by our understanding of the earth as a mode of the Divine Presence. We are within the Presence and participate in the great Mystery. EWF

CROSBY, FRANCES JANE (1820–1915), American Methodist hymn writer. Blinded by the treatment of a doctor at the age of six months, Fanny Crosby accepted her blindness as a blessing. As a young child she memorized major portions of the Bible, which she drew on later in life for imagery in her hymns. She wrote her first collection of poems at eight and enrolled in the New York School for the Blind at fourteen. After graduation she taught at the school and later married another teacher, the blind musician Alexander Van Alstyne. She championed the rights of the disabled and for many years lived as a servant among the poor in New York City. She wrote her first hymn at age forty-four and as many as nine thousand hymns, published under more than two hundred pseudonyms. Crosby became world famous by writing gospel hymns for Dwight L. Moody, the most important revivalist of the late nineteenth century and his song leader Ira D. Sankey.

Although Crosby's hymns are full of biblical imagery, her theology and poetry are often criticized as being trite and unsophisticated. However, she did not write to impress the intellect but to touch the hearts of those at late nineteenth-century revivals. Fanny Crosby's hymns are Christocentric—about Jesus Christ and a personal relationship with him. Very few texts are addressed to God or the **Holy Spirit**, and even those hymns are really about Jesus Christ. Her hymns are subjective, using "I" and "my" to personalize them for the singer. Because of her experience of human frailty and mortality, many of her hymns bring hope for a life that even death cannot destroy. Many of her hymns are still sung today, and her texts are useful for times of personal devotion.

For further information, see *Fanny Crosby* by Bernard Ruffin or *Fanny J. Crosby: An Autobiography.* DDW

CROSS. Christianity's most powerful and best-known symbol pointing to the death of Jesus. As a crucifix, with Jesus' body still shown on it, the cross symbolizes Jesus' ultimate sacrifice of his life for humankind. An empty cross expresses also his resurrection from the dead. In the Christian faith all crosses represent the centrality of Jesus Christ's death and resurrection.

As a symbol the cross has always been used for Christian worship and devotion. It has been the simplest and best emblem for conveying Christianity's countercultural truths, especially self-sacrifice. Jesus used the cross to illustrate a foremost characteristic of God's reign, the requirement for self-sacrifice, teaching that anyone who wished to be a disciple must deny self, take up his or her cross, and follow him. His disciples could understand his clear meaning, for they had seen condemned men carrying the cross-piece of a cross to the place of their own crucifixion. Jesus used the cross to dramatize humankind's primary obstacle to loving God wholly, namely self-love, self-interest. Even more powerful than the metaphor of carrying one's own cross was Jesus' example in carrying his cross to his own crucifixion. Because Jesus' crucifixion and resurrection actually happened in history, no symbol touches a Christian more profoundly than the cross in the spiritual work of being formed into Christ's likeness.

Saint Paul used the cross and crucifixion to explain God's gracious spiritual treasures. "The message of the cross" meant preaching the gospel (1 Cor 1:18). "Persecuted for the cross" (Gal. 6:12) meant confessing faith in Christ. Boasting "of the cross" (Gal. 6:14) meant celebrating Christ's saving work. "Making peace through the blood of his cross" (Col. 1:20) meant God used it as a chosen instrument for divine reconciliation with humankind and with all things. "I have been crucified with Christ; it is no longer I who live, but it is Christ who lives in me" (Gal. 2:19-20) meant that God uses the cross in a Christian's ultimate spiritual experience, mystical **union** with Christ. JNE

CYPRIAN OF CARTHAGE (d. 258), bishop. A rhetorician converted to Christianity around 246, Cyprian was elected bishop of Carthage two years later on the basis of his mastery of scriptures and **Tertullian's** writings. During the persecution under the Emperor Decius (249–51), he went into hiding, an act that complicated his policy regarding readmission of those who apostatized during the persecution. This act resulted in a schism led by Novatian. Cyprian nearly precipitated another schism in a controversy with Stephen of Rome over rebaptism of schismatics. Where Rome required only laying on of hands, Cyprian insisted on rebaptism. Persecution under the Emperor Valerian, however, claimed the lives of both Stephen and Cyprian. Cyprian was beheaded September 14, 258.

Although Cyprian is most widely recognized for his treatise *On the Unity of the Church*, in the aftermath of the Decian persecution he proved himself a caring pastor. He wrote many letters, sixty-five of which have survived, in which he addressed personal concerns. In a treatise titled *On the Lapsed* he stood firm against hasty reconciliation of those who offered sacrifices to Roman deities or secured certificates that showed they had done so on the basis of letters of "confessors," those who had not yielded. Subsequently, two councils that he led decided to reconcile such persons only after suitable manifestation of repentance. Novatian and opponents of Cyprian's own reinstatement adopted an inflexible view that forbade restoration of the lapsed. In a treatise titled *On the Lord's Prayer* (ca. 252) Cyprian instructed new converts to use only Jesus' own words, for God would hear best God's own words! Albeit not of equal ability as a theologian, he depicted a more compassionate God than his mentor, Tertullian. His treatise *On Works and Almsgiving* featured charitable giving as a means of grace.

For further reading, see Cyprian's works in *The Ante-Nicene Fathers*, vol. 5, and Edward White Benson's *Cyprian: His Life, His Times, His Work.* EGH

CYRIL OF JERUSALEM (ca. 315–86), bishop. Bishop of Jerusalem from around 349, Cyril did not please either Arians or Nicenes. Acacius, the Arian bishop of Caesarea, banished him in 357. Although the Council of Seleucia recalled him in 359, he underwent two more exiles. Because he disliked the term *homoousios* ("of the same essence") used in the Nicene Creed, the Council of Antioch sent **Gregory of Nyssa** in 379 to check on his orthodoxy. Gregory confirmed the soundness of faith of the Jerusalem church.

The chief surviving works of Cyril are twenty-four *Catecheses*, which he delivered to new converts during Lent and Eastertide around 350. These portray thoroughly the way the Jerusalem church prepared candidates for baptism and give much material for reconstructing the Palestinian liturgy in the fourth century. Cyril strongly affirmed the value and efficacy of **baptism**. Curiously, he did not mention the words of institution in **Holy Communion**, perhaps because they were so familiar or because he did not want the unbaptized to learn what they were.

For further reading, see *Cyril of Jerusalem* by Edward J. Yarnold, or read his works in volume 4 of *The Library of Christian Classics.* EGH

D

DANCE. Liturgical or sacred dance has been used in worship since biblical times. Miriam danced after the Red Sea crossing (Exod. 15:20-21), and David danced before the ark of the covenant (2 Sam. 6:14). Psalms 30; 149; and 150 speak of praising, worshiping, and celebrating the Lord through dance and movement. Religious festivals in particular were seen as an occasion for dancing and celebration. Sacred dance continued to be practiced in the early church, and early church writings used dance as an image for spiritual rejoicing and harmony. After Christianity became a state religion, dance was more restricted, but in the Middle Ages dancing became part of mystery and miracle plays, and characterized certain church festivals such as the "Feast of Fools." Emphasis on the intellect along with some distrust of secular entertainment led to dance as a form of worship that died out by 1700, although dance remained popular as a secular activity. Many Protestant sects founded around this time distrusted and prohibited all dancing, sacred or secular.

In the twentieth century sacred dance began to enjoy a resurgence, particularly after the **liturgical** renewal sparked in both Protestant and Catholic circles by Vatican II. Dance is used today in Protestant and Catholic churches in a variety of settings; it has diverse associations with **Pentecostal** worship styles, with an affirmation of the arts in worship, and with using the **body** in prayer. Dancing can be used in worship as **meditation**, proclamation, and celebration, and can be done alone, with a group, or as an act of the whole congregation. It has also been used as a component of personal prayer and devotion.

For more information, read Thomas Kane et al., *Introducing Dance in Christian Worship.* JLW

DARK NIGHT, DARKNESS. The concept of the dark night of the soul is echoed throughout the Hebrew and Christian Scriptures, which portray God as always present, though often seemingly absent: "Why do you hide your face?" (Ps. 44:24). Mysteriously, the believer may experience darkness all around, yet "even the darkness is not dark to you; the night is as bright as the day, for darkness is as light to you" (Ps. 139:12).

Biblically there is usually a difference between the soft sounding term *night* and the harsher sounding term *darkness. Darkness* (Hebrew *hoshek*; Greek *skotos*) connotes destruction, death, disease, and dread; whereas *night* (Hebrew *layil*; Greek *nux*) embodies newness, knowing, mystery, and transformation. Job experiences gloom and darkness (Job 10:21). But when Nicodemus comes to Jesus by *night* we hear the language of transformation: "You must be born from above" (John 3:7).

For the believer, God enters into the starkest suffering of humanity. Prophetic wisdom teaches, "I will give you the treasures of darkness and riches hidden in secret places" (Isa. 45:3). Thus Christ's mystery can transform destructive darkness into a night of beauty.

While many people associate "the dark night of the soul" with the Spanish mystic **John of the Cross**, its origins are found in ancient scriptures and its meaning in many early Christian writers. **Gregory of Nyssa** associates the "cloud" in Exodus 13 with the night of romance in the Song of Solomon. In his *Mystical Theology* **Pseudo-Dionysius** uses the language of light to speak of the self-communicating love of God as the **positive way** and of God's essential hidden nature in a "ray of darkness" as the **negative way**.

The anonymous late fourteenth-century English author of ***The Cloud of Unknowing*** describes how outward signs of God's presence will disappear, leaving a person barren. Gone will be the initial fervor of one's awakening, gone too the ability to meditate as one has long done before. The author speaks of two clouds: the cloud of forgetting below, separating the believer from lesser worldly loves; and the cloud of unknowing above, the darkness surrounding God, through which shines a ray of grace that kindles the believer's "dart of longing love."

John of the Cross, drawing on these metaphors and scriptures, especially Psalm 139 and the Song of Solomon, compares the traditional stages of spiritual growth to evening, deep night, and dawn. The night of the senses (sundown to midnight) is a time of *purgation*, when external verifications or inward feelings of God's presence seem to wane or disappear. The night of the spirit (midnight to dawn) becomes a time of *illumination*, of romance and deepening trust in the mystery of God who may seem absent, like a mountain hidden in mist. Then comes the dawn, the ultimate *union* of the lover with the beloved. One may glimpse this union in the present life, it is consummated in life eternal.

The nocturnal image of the dark night parallels other biblical images: the metallurgical image of purgation, the botanical image of pruning, the seasonal image of wintering of the soul, the ecological image of **desert** or wilderness, and the physical image of nakedness—a kind of stripping down or emptying (Greek, *kenosis*). Each has its counterpoint image: illumination, precious metal, fecundity, oasis, summering, and being clothed. Together they illustrate the paradox of transforming union where glory emerges in and through **suffering**.

For practical application, see *O Blessed Night!: Recovering from Addiction, Codependency, and Attachment Based on the Insights of St. John of the Cross and Pierre Teilhard de Chardin* by Francis Kelly Nemeck and Marie Theresa Coombs. Also see *John of the Cross for Today: The Ascent* or *John of the Cross for Today: The Dark Night* by **Susan Muto**. KIG

"DAY BY DAY." The prayer song popularized in the musical *Godspell*, based on a prayer of Richard of Chichester (1197–1253). The text, modernized, is:

> Thanks be to you, O Lord Jesus Christ,
> for all the benefits that you have given us;
> for all the pains and insults
> that you have borne for us.
> O most merciful redeemer,
> friend and brother,
> may we know you more clearly,
> love you more dearly,
> and follow you more nearly;
> for your own sake. Amen.

Richard knew about bearing pains and insults himself. When named bishop of Chichester by the archbishop of Canterbury, Richard's king, Henry III, refused to recognize the election and locked him out of the episcopal residence. Richard spent two years walking barefoot through his diocese, preaching in local churches and encouraging attendance at worship. Even after Henry relented, Richard continued to travel. In 1253 he began a **pilgrimage** to Jerusalem, but he died on the journey. KRB

DAY, DOROTHY (1897–1980), American Catholic social activist. Dorothy Day lived a life of radical commitment to the gospel. As a convert to Catholicism, she loved the church deeply but challenged the church to take its own message seriously. Her spirit of nonviolence and care for the poorest of the poor led her from involvement in socialism to the development of her own particular form of radical Catholicism. Her vision induced her to found the Catholic Worker movement, which survives to this day in over 120 communities across the United States.

Born in a journalist home, Day followed her father and became a journalist herself, working for several radical papers, especially *The Liberator*. After several affairs, an abortion, and a brief marriage, Dorothy found herself pregnant again and decided to keep the child, a daughter, Tamar, born in 1927. Motherhood caused Dorothy to think seriously about religion. Tamar was baptized over the objections of the child's atheist father. When Dorothy was baptized as a Roman Catholic later that year, the father left her. In 1933 she joined with Peter Maurin, a Christian Brother, and together they became a team for social change. Beginning with the newspaper *The Catholic Worker*, they moved on to found Houses of Hospitality where those who needed a place to stay were welcome. Although they began in the Hell's Kitchen area of New York City, these houses were established in many cities, nearly always in the poorest areas.

There are beginnings of a movement for Day's canonization. Faith was a constant struggle for her, and while she titled her autobiography *The Long Loneliness*, she was haunted by God from childhood until her death. Among her other books are *By Little and by Little*, *House of Hospitality*, *Loaves and Fishes*, and *On Pilgrimage*. HLR

DEATH OF GOD. A theological concept that presupposes the meaninglessness of God in modern society. In the mid-1960s the media in the United States named this concept the Death of God movement. In reality, there never was much of a movement. The four primary theologians who propounded the death of God were not in close contact and never tried to reach a consensus. Due to publicity that included a *Time* magazine cover story in 1966, the Death of God "movement" influenced many people who never read the original theologians' works.

In 1961 Gabriel Vahanian wrote *The Death of God*. Like Friedrich Nietzsche in the nineteenth century, he identified a cultural attitude but did not adhere to Nietzsche's hard line of rejecting the concept of God completely. Instead, he took **Karl Barth**'s softer line, rejecting the concept of God used to justify capitalism and war while seeking a new way to talk about God. This softer understanding of the death of God passed virtually unnoticed.

Thomas Altizer took the hard line when he wrote *The Gospel of Christian Atheism* in 1966. Influenced by Nietzsche, **Blake**, Hegel, and Eliade, Altizer claimed that the dignity and progress of humanity required the abolition of God. Although God as a transcendent Being had actually died at a particular moment in history, Jesus remains Lord, inspiration, and ethical guide. Altizer continued to expect Christ's Second Coming.

The two other founding thinkers, William Hamilton and Paul van Buren, were both influenced by **Dietrich Bonhoeffer**'s religionless interpretation of Christianity. Hamilton refused to advocate or argue his position. Van Buren declared "God language" dead, saying the term *God* probably never referred to anything actual.

Essentially the Death of God proponents argued that meaningful discussion about God is impossible because modern people need empirical evidence and because the idea of a benevolent ruler of the world lacks credibility after the Holocaust.

Aside from the lack of consensus among the founding theologians, the "movement" was doomed by their inability or unwillingness to offer a widely acceptable solution to the death of God. Nonetheless, the attention and responses created by the Death of God theology indicate the importance of the issues raised by the crisis of theism. WW

DEIFICATION. The divine activity of God's **grace** working through the process of **sanctification** with the assumption that this process has an end point or final stage of **union** with God. Some spiritual writers prefer the Greek equivalent *theosis* to avoid confusion with the secular meaning of deification as exalting some person or object to godlike status.

No single understanding of deification exists within the Christian tradition because it has been used, assumed, or referred to almost from the beginning of Christian spiritual writings. The term *perfection* is even more generally used, often in much the same way. In the works of **Maximus the Confessor**, while perfection seems to imply our human work through conscious use of our moral and spiritual freedom of will and toward our ultimate spiritual goal or purpose as humans, deification or *theosis* is God's grace at work within us, bringing us into that harmony or even union with God that was lost in the Fall. Maximus, perhaps more than any other single writer near his time, deeply influenced both Eastern and Western spirituality. He himself had been influenced by a wide variety of Christian writers such as **Origen**, **Augustine**, **Pseudo-Dionysius** and the **Cappadocians Basil of Caesarea**, **Gregory of Nyssa**, and **Gregory of Nazianzus** as well as Greek philosophy and even ancient Egyptian religion, all of which contained similar concepts. JWK

DESERT. The Bible consistently portrays the desert as the place of **conversion** and transformation. Many of the most significant figures of the Bible are led to a deeper, more tangible, and more vivid **experience** of God through their experiences in the desert.

For example, because of his nomadic wanderings in the desert, Abraham learned to surrender to God. Abraham's desert wanderings allowed his faith to become strong and resolute. Prior to their desert wanderings, the Israelites were an immature people with a weak faith and spirituality. Their forty-year desert pilgrimage transformed and prepared them to enter the Promised Land. David lived for years as an outlaw in the desert, eluding King Saul, who sought to kill him. The desert transformed him, strengthening and deepening his spirit, so that he could become king. Elijah, seeking to hide in the desert from the murderous intents of Jezebel, spent forty days in the desert; and in this desolate place he learned to listen for God in the **silence**. The **Holy Spirit** sent Jesus into the desert for forty days and nights so that he could be prepared for his ministry. He had been baptized, but he needed more time to unite his heart with God the Creator in order to fulfill his mission and ministry.

The desert was a real place for these biblical figures, and many Christians from **Antony of Egypt** and the **desert fathers and mothers** to **Carlo Carretto** have sought purity and simplicity by going into the desert to live. But any experience of prolonged **dryness**, confusion, waiting, uncertainty, **suffering**, and loss can be a metaphorical desert encounter for us. Desert times prepare us for a life of prayerful ministry to God. Without them, we remain immature and ill-prepared to do God's work and will. Desert experiences transform us because they are periods of uncertainty and confusion in which all we can do is rely upon God. Even though we rely on God, we do not necessarily experience God. God seems distant. It feels as though God has abandoned us. Our only choices seem to be to abandon God and walk out of the desert following our own guidance and direction or to give ourselves ever more deeply to God so that we begin to rely upon God for everything. **John of the Cross** discusses this call to greater **abandonment** to God in both *Ascent of Mount Carmel* and *Dark Night of the Soul*.

Temptations are real and powerful when we are in the midst of a desert experience. The temptation is to grab hold of anything that promises to make us feel stronger and in control in the midst of our weakness and powerlessness. Jesus was tempted to rely on his own power rather than the Father's; to seek tangible proof of the Father's presence rather than to trust that God the Father was already there; and to worship anything other than God the Father, anything that held the promise of releasing him from the desert. When we are in the midst of our own deserts we face many temptations that encourage us to give up our faith in God. If we maintain our **faith** throughout the desert, our weakness becomes a conduit for God's power (2 Cor. 12: 7-10); the power of the demonic to confuse us diminishes (Matt. 3:10); and we learn to trust in God no matter what (Gen. 22).

Ultimately deserts deepen our lives if we let them. The wounds of the desert can become a source of healing for us and others. The dryness of our deserts can empower us to lead others to the living springs of **water** Christ promised. The confusion and aimlessness of our deserts can help us to gain a sense of clarity and purpose throughout our lives. NGS

DESERT FATHERS AND MOTHERS. By the fourth century, Christianity was an accepted part of Roman society, and persecutions had ceased. Thousands of Christians, seeking to embrace a purer, more austere and less compromised practice of their faith, moved into the Egyptian desert and later to the deserts south of Palestine. This move involved more than flight from a declining civilization. The movement represented a choice of the absolute priority of the spiritual life lived in **solitude** and simplicity, an **abandonment** of everything in order to seek God. Those who grew in spiritual insight and Christian maturity became known as the desert fathers and mothers. They were sought out as spiritual guides by others desiring help with prayer and practical Christian living.

Antony of Egypt chose a cave in the rugged desert between the Nile and the Red Sea, now the site of the most ancient Christian **monastery**. Although many of these early Christians began desert life as solitaries, it became clear that some form of **community** life was necessary. **Athanasius** later described the monasticism of Antony's followers as consisting of "cells in the mountains… like tabernacles, filled with holy bands of men who sang **psalms**, loved **reading**, **fasted**, prayed, rejoiced in the hope of things to come, labored in almsgiving, and preserved love and harmony one with another."

Life in the desert was not idyllic, however. The daily struggle to survive in a terrain where water was at a premium challenged hermits and monastic communities to work long and hard at primitive forms of agriculture, repetitive labor, weaving of mats and baskets. Prayer was work and work was prayer. Dealing with boredom, frustration, isolation, depression, and doing battle with demonic forces demanded **vigilance** and **faith**. Out of this struggle was born a wisdom and profound

trust in God that would nurture others. Believers began to seek out these desert women and men of prayer in order to receive guidance for their own Christian discipleship, respectfully calling them Abba (Father) or Amma (Mother). The short, pithy sayings the desert mothers and fathers gave to individuals in response to specific questions seem to have been repeated from person to person. Many sayings have survived and are available today in various anthologies.

The origin of spiritual **direction**, or soul **friendship**, may be traced to the guidance given by desert abbas and ammas. Their teaching is characterized by repeated emphasis on **silence**, **solitude**, **prayer**, **penitence**, perseverance, and **obedience** to the gospel that calls upon us to renounce self, take up the cross, and follow Christ. Theirs was a radical response that inspired others and laid the foundations for later **monasticism**.

Benedicta Ward edited several collections of sayings and stories from the desert in modern translation, including *Sayings of the Desert Fathers*. EJC

DETACHMENT. Among all the **dispositions** of Christian **spirituality**, the practice of detachment is perhaps the most difficult. It is normal psychologically to form strong attachments to people, things, events, and experiences. Whether it is the extreme attachments of addiction to alcohol, drugs, gambling, work, sex, power, or food; the obsessions or compulsions of mental illness; or the less destructive attachments of regular life, such as the need to feel a sense of control over life, the passionate desire for another person, the need to achieve success, or the desire to have a sense of order and clarity in life, all of our lives are filled with attachments. From a spiritual point of view, attachments can slowly erode our faith and spirituality by directing our attention away from God and onto thoughts, passions, people, things, and events of temporary and diminishing value. The more we are attached to anything, the less receptive we are to God.

Detachment is the spiritual **disposition**, attitude, and practice of letting go of our attachments so that we can root ourselves in God. God becomes our guide and purpose. We no longer seek to satisfy the varying and temporary demands of the world, our culture, and our egos. Our detachment in life does not mean that we become unemotional robots—unmoved and unaffected by the people, things, events, and experiences of life. Instead, it means that we become involved in them but try to allow God to guide us in discerning what their impact is and should be. The greater our detachment, the more we incorporate the wisdom of Matthew 6:34 into our lives: "So do not worry about tomorrow, for tomorrow will bring worries of its own. Today's trouble is enough for today."

When we strive to become detached, we do not strive for objectivity and lack of passion in the way a scientist is expected to do while running an experiment or study. Rather, we detach from the thoughts, passions, people, things, and events of the world in order to "strive first for the kingdom of God" (Matt. 6:33). We try to detach from everything that consumes us so that we may align our minds, hearts, bodies, and souls with God in order to say with Christ, "Yet not my will but yours be done" (Luke 22:42).

To detach does not mean to cut off our emotions, thoughts, and perceptions. We do not cease to have feelings, opinions, or pain. Instead we form deeper, richer emotions, perceptions, and thoughts because the need to appease our egos, passions, or the constricting and repressing rules of our culture does not encumber us. In our marriages, we do not become distant and aloof. Instead we become more loving in the way God calls us to love (this does not mean our love becomes perfect, only that it grows deeper). We care more deeply for others without having to take their burdens onto our own shoulders. We give these burdens to God. We engage in projects without anxiety and fear about their outcomes. We do the best we can and give the results to God. In everything God is central.

Ultimately the ability to detach is intimately related to our ability to form other dispositions, attitudes, and practices in our lives. The more we are humble, able to live in the present moment, prayerful, faithful, hopeful, loving, compassionate, discerning, thankful, and peaceful, the more detached we will naturally become.

For further reading, see *New Seeds of Contemplation* by **Thomas Merton**. NGS

DEVIL. From Greek *diablos* ("slanderer"), the personified adversary of God, responsible for all evil. Christians who profess ultimate faith in God may find it awkward to believe in a personal power for **evil**. Numerous names and titles appear in scripture, including Satan, meaning "adversary" (Job 1–2); ruler of this world (John 14:30); prince of demons (Matt. 12:24); Beelzebul (Matt. 12:24); god of this world (2 Cor. 4:4); and tempter (1 Thess. 3:5). Biblical writers never argued about nor sought to prove the devil. Jesus clearly believed in the devil and thought of Satan in personal terms. The New Testament refers more to the devil than the Old, perhaps indicating that belief in the devil developed late in Jewish history. In spite of the many biblical references, no coherent, consistent depiction of the devil can embrace them all, so the Bible cannot be used to "prove" any single portrayal.

One aspect of Christian theology has remained constant: The devil is always under God's ultimate control, more powerful than humans but as nothing before God. In spite of this long-held theology, Christians today hold widely differing beliefs about the devil, some of which do not reflect historic Christian teaching. Some people perceive the devil in every problem, place, tragedy, and temptation. Others look at the same evidence but interpret it primarily as human **sin** or as **evil** embedded in culture and tradition.

The devil's nearly universal name recognition does not necessarily translate into firm belief. In fact Satan is largely ignored by many, even by those who fiercely oppose evil.

Relatively few people appear to speak of the devil in daily conversation. Some are troubled by the conundrum of having faith in God's omnipotence and yet at the same time believing the devil is powerful enough to contest with God. Since horrible tragedies and a ghastly holocaust involving millions of victims are clearly traceable to humans, there seems no need to posit an unseen devil.

The devil's clear connection to evil is less difficult to define and locate and is not as cloaked in mystery. Devastating evidence supports the fact that persons can do appalling evil by making choices, whether the choices are sinful, mistaken, or intended for good. It is not so clear how much responsibility the devil has for those choices. In individuals the interplay of sin, evil, and the devil is clouded. It is even more difficult to sort out when institutions, cultures, traditions, and nations make choices that result in evil. Wars, racism, sexism, economic injustice, and countless forms of human domination all oppose Jesus Christ, whether they are the work of the devil or can be ascribed to human sin or to impersonal evil. Such institutional evils help bring meaning to one of the Bible's phrases, "principalities and powers."

An interesting proposal for a contemporary understanding of the devil, as well as other spiritual beings named in the Bible, may be found in Walter Wink's *The Powers That Be*. Wink sees Satan as the inner spiritual reality of the external domination system that permeates human society. He also believes that system can be defeated in every place and time through the power of God's redeeming love. When Christ returns in glory, the defeat will be final and complete. JNE

DEVOTIO MODERNA. The "New Devotion," a movement of mystical **piety** that began in the Netherlands in the fourteenth century as a lay revival of traditional **monastic** spirituality with its emphases on constant inner devotion, frequent brief **meditations**, and keeping ritual alive through interior work. It spread throughout the Rhineland and into France, the rest of Germany, and Switzerland before emerging in Spain and Italy. As an independent movement, it died during the Protestant Reformation as Protestants and reform-minded Catholics absorbed many of its tenets.

The founder, **Gerhard Groote**, turned over his family home to a group of women who became the first Sisters of the Common Life. His first and principal disciple, Florent Radewijns (1350–1400), helped give structure to the Sisters and eventually to the Brothers of the Common Life. The guiding principles included surrender to God, spiritual **poverty**, manual labor, and the practice of **virtues**. The **contemplative** life and the active life held equal value. The members would read the Bible daily, in private and as a community, keeping notebooks of the most compelling passages they read.

The early Brothers and Sisters never took vows. Their participation was entirely voluntary. Although *devotio moderna* began as a lay movement and the Sisters remained laity, the Brothers eventually came to include priests and candidates. Both orders lived in cities and towns, attended local churches, and earned their own living. The Brothers served as copyists, the Sisters as seamstresses. Both groups were unique among church orders in their obedience to local civil law rather than to ecclesiastical rule.

In 1386 a group of Brothers organized a monastic community at Windesheim following the **Rule** of **Augustine**. A similar community for women followed in a few years. By 1460 eighty monasteries existed throughout Europe. Other devout communities joined the Third Order of Saint **Francis**.

The most famous proponent of *devotio moderna* was **Thomas à Kempis**, who wrote *Imitation of Christ*. This book's emphases on **affective** devotion and the contemplation of Christ's humanity mark the movement as a whole. Writings of Groote and other early Brothers and Sisters are included in *Devotio Moderna: Basic Writings*, translated by John Van Engen. WW

DIRECTION, SPIRITUAL. The practice of aiding another to mature and be formed in the Christian life. While spiritual direction involves the **formation** of the whole person in his or her relationship to all of life, its starting point is the God-experience of the person seeking direction. Spiritual direction in its broadest sense is the work of the gathered church where basic Christian teaching, proclamation, and worship are cultivated. Within the gathered church, intentional relationships may be cultivated that allow for more focused and individual formation. Usually spiritual direction appeals to mature Christians who experience the desire to respond more generously to God.

A classic form of spiritual direction is the one-on-one relationship. In this form of guidance a person qualified as a spiritual guide, the "director," listens to the "directee" and typically helps the directee recognize and respond to God's presence in his or her life. The director suggests disciplines that open the directee to the Spirit, encourages an examination of his or her life in view of God's love, and prays with and for the person.

Spiritual direction may also be practiced in a group. Variants on the group model include a small group with a trained director either with or without peer input, a small group that has been trained to practice peer direction, **covenant groups** (that hold members accountable for agreed-upon practices), and formation-focused scripture or prayer groups.

Spiritual **friendship** is a variant of these formative relationships. Friendship is typically more mutual and equal than other forms of guidance and has as its end shared encouragement in the love of God.

Spiritual direction may be distinguished from other helping relationships like pastoral counseling, counseling, psychotherapy, or Christian education in that it focuses on ongoing formation and not the resolution of specific problems. It also is generally seen as a contemplative rather than an analytic practice.

In the contemporary church, spiritual direction is practiced by a variety of persons of many Christian denominations, lay and ordained, men and women. Programs that provide training for persons who feel called to this ministry have developed around the United States since the middle of the twentieth century. Generally the call to spiritual direction is believed to be a gift of the Spirit, best honed by a training program. An umbrella organization, Spiritual Directors International (1329 Seventh Avenue, San Francisco, CA 94122-2507), has published a code of ethics for directors and provides a forum for ongoing direction issues.

In the course of the church's history, spiritual direction has taken many forms. The master-disciple relationship of the ancient ascetic **desert fathers and mothers** and their spiritual sons and daughters; the communal spiritual formation practiced in monastic life; the charismatic guidance offered by medieval holy women and men; the formal (Third Order or Associate Groups) or informal (the **Beguines**, the *devotio moderna* movement) formation groups of lay Christians; the Catholic priest-confessor model; the spiritual **retreat** model (**Ignatian** direction); Oratory communities for the spiritual nurture of priests; Calvinist mentoring by peers or elders; and Wesleyan class, band, and holiness groups exemplify spiritual guidance developed at various times in the church's history.

To learn more about spiritual direction, see Jeannette A. Bakke, *Holy Invitations: Exploring Spiritual Direction*; Margaret Guenther, *Holy Listening: The Art of Spiritual Direction*; Rose Mary Dougherty, *Group Spiritual Direction: Community for Discernment*; W. Paul Jones, *The Art of Spiritual Direction: Giving and Receiving Spiritual Guidance*, Howard Rice, *The Pastor as Spiritual Guide.* WMW

DISCERNMENT. The biblical concept of discernment is rooted primarily in the vision of the people of God living in a theocracy, where God guides the people in their daily and national lives and relationships. The whole nation knows and does the **will of God**. This was the vision of the early Hebrew experience.

This vision of a "kingdom of God" and a "people of God" needed spiritual leaders such as Moses and prophets to help the people come to know and experience the direct guidance of the **Holy Spirit**. Therefore, in the Old Testament, discernment was focused on rightly distinguishing between a true prophet and a false prophet. In this context of practical judgment Jesus and Paul gave instructions on *discerning of spirits* or *testing the spirits* (Matt 7:15 ff.; Acts 20:28 ff.; and 1 Thess. 5:19-22). The Greek word *diakrisis* most simply means the capacity to separate or distinguish. It is generally understood as the capacity to see, know, or understand the essence of a matter or inner nature of a person or object by immediate and direct insight.

In the early church, the people of God saw their struggles as an intense conflict between God and God's forces and Satan and the demonic forces. They understood that the strategies of the demonic forces did not always oppose God directly but used counterfeits, impediments, and deception (Eph. 6:12). Thus discernment was understood as the capacity to distinguish between the spirit of truth and the spirit of error, that which was of God and that which was not. In this context, what is being discerned is the spirit or energies at work that influence human motivations and actions. What was needed in the environment of the early church was an ability to distinguish among mere human illusion, demonic illusion, and the true prompting of the Holy Spirit. Because of the particular craftiness of the demonic, a special **grace** was needed. Paul speaks of this grace of discernment in 1 Corinthians 12 as a special **gift of the Spirit** given to individuals for the practical functioning, welfare, and effectiveness of the whole **body of Christ**.

From the Middle Ages until now, Christian discernment has come to be understood as a quest, both individually and communally,

---

A PROCESS FOR PERSONAL OR GROUP DISCERNMENT

(Based on *Discerning God's Will Together: A Spiritual Practice for the Church*, © 1997 by Danny E. Morris and Charles M. Olsen.)

Framing: Clearly state the question, the subject of the discernment.

Grounding: Select and state guiding principles, beliefs, and/or values that will be revisited at any point of the discernment process.

Shedding: Prejudices, false assumptions, predetermined desires or conclusions, and ego defenses or concerns may need to be brought to light and laid aside. This "letting-go" and "opening-up" process cultivates openness and humility in loving God's will more than your own will.

Rooting: Relate the subject in question to biblical images, texts, and stories of your own religious tradition.

Listening: Listening is everything from silent prayer, to conducting research, to asking others and sharing experiences. It is one of the central steps.

Exploring: Use the powers of imagination to identify all possible directions or options, and then examine these in light of the grounding principles.

Improving: Select the best possible options of the Exploring segment and improve or flesh out these options so that they are articulated as well as possible.

Weighing: Select options based on the preferences of the person or group. Test these preferences through practical judgments using reason, intuition, and traditional images (rooting).

Closing: Close the discussion and establish the decision or direction.

Resting: Allow the decision to rest to see whether it brings a sense of peace and movement toward God or a sense of distress and movement away from God.

for the will of God. In the context of this discipleship focus, discernment came to be understood as a process, a method or a technique by which one came to order one's life and bring all its details into harmony with God's will. A good study of discernment could start with some of the following spiritual classics: **Ignatius of Loyola**'s *Spiritual Exercises,* **John Cassian**'s *Conferences,* **John Climacus**'s *The Ladder of Divine Ascent,* **Thomas à Kempis**'s *Imitation of Christ,* **John Calvin**'s *Institutes of the Christian Religion,* and **Francis de Sales**'s *Finding God's Will for You.*

Modern writings on discernment techniques include both Old Testament and early church elements. These discernment processes have become more individualistic in practice. Often the overall concern is decision making in the context of personal discipleship. Many of these discernment techniques are rooted in practical judgment and are situationally specific—characteristics of the Old Testament use of discernment—but also have some elements of the spiritual grace of bringing to light spiritual energies, movements, or motivations. The Wesleyan quadrilateral, with its careful weighing of scripture, reason, tradition, and experience, is a discernment and interpretive process that relies heavily on practical judgment, characteristic of our Old Testament roots (see "Our Theological Task," ¶104 in *The Book of Discipline of The United Methodist Church—2000*). The Quaker **clearness committee**, with its emphasis on silence and prayer, demonstrates patristic spiritual elements of direct access to the Holy Spirit in the context of a group or community.

Some modern resources on discernment for individuals or small groups are *Yearning to Know God's Will : A Workbook for Discerning God's Guidance for Your Life* by Danny E. Morris and *A Guide to Spiritual Discernment* by Rueben P. Job, and *Discerning God's Will Together* by Danny E. Morris and Charles M. Olsen. CIZ

DISCERNMENT, GIFT OF. The **gift of the Spirit** for looking beyond certain behaviors and circumstances to determine if they are good or evil, right or wrong. Persons with this gift call others to accountability, as Jesus does in Matthew 7:5: "You hypocrite, first take the log out of your own eye, and then you will see clearly to take the speck out of your neighbor's eye." They look through apparent issues and see underlying truths. They make judgments concerning what is and what is not of God. In Acts 5:1-6, the apostle Peter brings to accountability two persons who have lied to the community.

Persons with the gift of discernment bring health and wholeness to the **community** of Christ. Because they are able to analyze what inclinations should be encouraged and what tendencies should be discouraged in brothers and sisters of the faith, they are valuable in personal counseling situations. In 1 John 4:1 we read, "Beloved, do not believe every spirit, but test the spirits to see whether they are from God." Some persons with the gift are able to perform this task better than others.

People with the gift of discernment have keen insight. Leaders appreciate having them attend their meetings or community gatherings because they call group dynamics into question and ask persons to be accountable for their actions. They "see through" surface actions and words to the spiritual needs within. They pick up subtle hints that tell them when words or actions are at odds with what may be in a person's heart. Having the ability to see through the facade, they differentiate between what is raised up by God and what pretends to be. They have the uncanny ability to unmask false teachings and ways. These people help others pinpoint and assess their own gifts and find their niche in the mission and ministry of the community. Men and women with the gift of discernment make excellent spiritual mentors and guides. PDB

DISCIPLINE. (Latin *disciplina,* "teaching" or "learning"). In a general sense, a discipline is a particular **rule**, a method, a set pattern of behavior or system of conduct that one adopts with the intended purpose to train, correct, mold, or perfect one's mental facilities or moral character. In a psychological sense, a discipline is related to **disposition** formation or personality formation. It is a particular technique or pattern of behavior used to facilitate the formation of a desirable disposition or to deactivate particular dispositions that make up a recurring pattern of undesirable behavior or thought.

In Christian spirituality, a discipline is a rule of life or a set pattern of living intended to facilitate spiritual growth and Christian community. Spiritual disciplines are concerned with our lifestyle or our practice of faith and faithful living. Among these patterns of living are some called the classical spiritual disciplines because they have biblical roots and because through the various ages and renewal movements of the church, Christians have tested them and found them central to experiential Christianity and growth toward spiritual maturity. **Richard J. Foster**'s *Celebration of Discipline*, **Dallas Willard**'s *The Spirit of the Disciplines*, and **Maxie Dunnam**'s *The Workbook on Spiritual Disciplines* are three good descriptive introductions to these classical spiritual disciplines. Foster divides them into three categories: (1) inward disciplines of **meditation**, **prayer**, **fasting**, and study or **spiritual reading**; (2) outward disciplines of social **mercy**, **solitude**, simplicity, submission to a rule or order; and (3) corporate disciplines of **worship**, guidance or **spiritual direction**, **confession**, and jubilee or celebration.

Spiritual disciplines involve more than just psychological change. Their concern is total and complete graced transformation and healing. The goal of the Christian disciple is to be completely conformed to the image and likeness of Christ or, as the apostle Paul describes it, having the mind of Christ within us (cf. Phil. 2:5). One of the chief dangers Christians face is forgetting that this change is a gift of God. People can easily fall into the trap of thinking that this transformation is attained through human effort and thus practice spiritual disciplines in terms of human effort. By themselves the spiritual disciplines cannot change us, but they offer a way to participate in the **grace** that is available for spiritual growth. That is why **John Wesley** called them the "means of grace." They are tools or conduits through which the grace is given that alone can transform the heart. In this sense, spiritual disciplines are relational expressions of our openness to God, of our longing for the life of God, of our commitment to the **covenant**, and our belief in the promise of complete transformation (or **sanctification**).

Monastic orders were formed around a common **rule** to facilitate life together, help

---

THE COVENANT AND COMMON DISCIPLINES OF RENOVARÉ

In utter dependence upon Jesus Christ as my ever-living Savior, Teacher, Lord, and Friend, I will seek continual renewal through: spiritual exercises, spiritual gifts, and acts of service. By God's grace:

I will set aside time regularly for prayer, meditation, and spiritual reading, and will seek to practice the presence of God.

I will strive mightily against sin and will do deeds of love and mercy that lead to righteousness.

I will seek the gifts of the Holy Spirit, nurturing the fruit of the Spirit and experiencing the joy and power of the Spirit.

I will seek to serve others everywhere I can and will work for justice in all human relationships and social structures.

I will study the Scriptures regularly and share my faith with others as God leads.

I will joyfully seek to show forth the presence of God in all that I am, in all that I do, in all that I say.

© 2001 RENOVARÉ, Inc. Used by permission.

in the administration of the community, and aid the community in developing a common spirituality. Less formal or enduring groups may agree on a common set of disciplines and so become a **covenant group**. Richard Foster's Renovaré groups follow The Covenant and Common Disciplines on page 84. CIZ

DISPOSITIONS. Any patterns or ways of thinking, feeling, and behaving that have become so embedded into the fabric of one's being that they seem to come naturally. Dispositions sink beneath the surface of awareness and therefore seem to come naturally. Found in early traditions of both Eastern and Western spirituality, disposition is only recently finding its way into more modern spiritual writings.

Some dispositions are truly natural or inborn. We can call these predispositions, as they predispose us to think, feel, or act in a certain way. We might speak of a musician, for example, as having a predisposition for enjoying or being able to play music. The actual disposition for playing the piano, however, would have to be learned or acquired through years of practice and hard work.

Other dispositions are learned, such as speaking, reading, walking, riding a bicycle, dressing, or eating with a knife and fork. We no longer need to think about how to do them. They seem to be a part of us. The same goes for spiritual dispositions or **virtues**. In the Bible, Paul calls some of these the **fruit of the Spirit**. They would traditionally include the Christian virtues of **faith**, **hope**, **love**, patience, kindness, **humility**, gratitude, forbearance, **mercy**, **compassion**, and joy. While they are gifts from God and require the power of the **Holy Spirit**, they also, for most people, need to be fostered consciously.

One way to understand the goal of the Christian walk or life of faith is to grow in our ability to be more like Jesus, in our **imitation of Christ**. In a practical way, this imitation involves growing in those dispositions or virtues that Christ exemplified. This spiritual growth is the purpose of spiritual exercises or spiritual **disciplines** such as **fasting**, **meditation**, morning or evening devotions, **prayer**, **spiritual reading**, **worship**, etc. They are not ends in themselves, but means to aid us in our journey toward being more Christlike in our "natural" ways of thinking, feeling, and acting.

At first, learning any new disposition requires hard work and a conscious effort. This is true with physical dispositions such as swimming, ice skating, knitting, or playing a musical instrument. We have to walk through the motions very slowly and self-consciously at first. Over time the movements become embedded beneath the surface of our awareness and seem to come naturally. The same is true with spiritual dispositions like gentleness, generosity, humility, **forgiveness**, and **peace**. At first, they may seem unnatural, especially when negative dispositions such as resentment, pride, selfishness, anger, and envy have been ingrained in us over many years. Like learning any skill or art, however, spiritual dispositions can become more and more a natural part of us, woven into the fabric of our mental, psychological, and spiritual patterns of thinking, feeling and acting. Thus they give shape and form to our life and world.

Many modern spiritual writers prefer the term *disposition* over the more traditional term *virtue* because of the moralistic and pietistic implications of being a virtuous person. No one wants to be called virtuous because it seems to imply being self-righteous. *Disposition* is preferred over the term *habit* because a habit implies a highly rigid pattern of behavior and is often associated with negative habits like smoking, drinking, and gambling that are difficult, if not impossible, to change or alter. So rigid are these habits that we often speak of needing to *break* them. The term *disposition*, while it refers to a distinct pattern of behavior, has a softness and gentleness to it that allows for flexibility.

No single definitive list of Christian spiritual or formative dispositions exists. However, in addition to the traditional biblical dispositions mentioned by Paul, we might add mercy, forgiveness, **detachment**, prudence, receptivity, honesty, courage, **community**, **solitude**, tolerance, confidence, commitment, sensitivity, flexibility, persistence, sincerity, fidelity, and balance. JWK

DISTRACTIONS IN PRAYER. Habitual difficulties in concentration, common to all people who try to pray. The human mind is busy most of the time, usually occupied with concerns of past or future, plans and responsibilities that are not happening in the present moment. In Eastern tradition this phenomenon is referred to as "monkey mind" because, like many monkeys chattering and swinging through trees, the mind is never still! When we seek to be focused and consciously prayerful, we become aware of these constant, busy thoughts and refer to them as distractions. They do not come only when we pray, but in prayer we are challenged to let them go.

Attempting to dismiss distractions or fight them is fruitless. One helpful method for dealing with their presence is to use imagination. Thoughts may be seen as boats on a river or clouds in the sky. We notice them and let them pass out of sight, returning to prayerful presence. Father **Thomas Keating**, who has developed **Centering Prayer**, advocates this process and suggests a simple word or phrase for repetition to refocus the mind.

Sometimes distractions occur in the form of "wrongful thoughts." Saint **Benedict** encourages Christians to "dash them against Christ," that is, to name such harmful distractions to God, remembering that in Christ forgiveness is offered. One could also seek help from a spiritual friend or guide if such distractions persist.

In some traditions the use of prayer beads or a **rosary** helps focus the mind. A natural object, such as a rock, feather, or pinecone may also be used to practice becoming attentive and increase awareness of God's presence in the moment. Paying attention to breath and progressive relaxation of the body also assists in the process of relinquishing distractions. A notebook in which to write "distractions" that require later attention is also a helpful device to relieve the mind of concern that the thought will not be forgotten.

We need not avoid all distractions. Sometimes the awareness of a need or person may come during prayer as an invitation to act. Jesus rose before daybreak to claim time alone with God, but when he was interrupted by disciples telling him that many were searching for him, he left the place of prayer to go and minister to the needs of others (Mark 1:35-59). When we become conscious of this kind of "distraction," it is appropriate to pause and recognize that the **Holy Spirit** may be inviting us to move into prayer that is also action.

For more on dealing with distractions, see *Invitation to Presence: A Guide to Spiritual Disciplines* by Wendy Miller. EJC

DOCTOR OF THE CHURCH. A spiritual writer, already canonized as a **saint** by the Roman Catholic Church, who is further commended as an authoritative teacher (Latin, *doctor*) of theology or spirituality. In the early Middle Ages, the original "four doctors" were **Gregory I**, **Ambrose**, **Augustine**, and **Jerome**. Others joined the list over the years. **Teresa of Ávila** and **Catherine of Siena** were the first women designated as Doctors, in 1970.

DODDRIDGE, PHILIP (1702–51), English Nonconformist minister and devotional writer. Born in London, Doddridge refused a university education because he could not conform to the requirements of the Church of England. Instead he entered the Dissenting Academy at Kibworth, later becoming its principal and moving it to Northampton, where he was pastor. He was known for his outstanding spiritual and pastoral sensitivity. In response to the heavy pastoral demands in his church, he advocated the restoration of elders to assist him. Doddridge took an active role in the blossoming evangelical revival of the eighteenth century. His moderate Calvinism was revealed in his passion for evangelism and mission; it often created strategic opportunities for ministry. He continuously sought reconciliation and unity among Christians, and his circle of friends included **John Wesley**, George Whitefield, the Countess of Huntingdon, **Count Zinzendorf**, and fellow hymn writer **Isaac Watts**.

In addition to his numerous concerns for outreach, Doddridge encouraged assorted works of charity and developed the means for distributing Bibles both at home and abroad. His soul was nourished through lengthy periods of **prayer** and **fasting**, expanded to the broader needs of his congregation and students at the training academy. Monthly celebration of **Holy Communion**, upon which he wrote meditative reflections, also refreshed his life. He stressed the importance of family spirituality for himself and others and encouraged the development of groups for young people to gather for the purpose of reading, spiritual discussion, and prayer. The American missionary David Brainerd, through his *Journal*, greatly inspired Doddridge's own zeal for advancing the gospel.

Malcolm Deacon's *Philip Doddridge of Northampton* is the best introduction to his life and ministry. Doddridge is best known today for his hymns, especially "Hark, the Glad Sound! The Savior Comes" and "O Happy Day That Fixed My Choice" and *The Rise and Progress of Religion in the Soul*, a classic on the Puritan **pilgrimage** of growing into spiritual maturity in Christ that was instrumental in the conversion of **William Wilberforce**. TS

DOMINIC (1170–1221), founder of the Order of Preachers (Dominicans). Dominic de Guzman was a Spanish priest and friar under the Rule of **Augustine**, who had been appointed prior of his community after only seven years of contemplative life. In his mid-thirties, he came into contact with the **Cistercian** mission to the Albigenses, a **Catharist** group in southern France. A papal legate en route to Denmark had just been killed. The Albigenses had formed churches and taken over dioceses, promoting their belief that the world and all created things were evil and should be shunned. Dominic knew how contrary this was to true Christian belief and realized the heresy was spreading because of poor religious education.

On his initial visit accompanying his bishop and a court army, Dominic realized a simpler arrival might do more good than a display of ecclesiastical ceremony and power. Dominic believed that conversion of lapsed Christians could best be accomplished through reasonable preaching and ascetic simplicity, not warlike force. Even though this approach had no immediate effect, he was convinced a peaceful approach with proper scholarship would be more persuasive. Supported by the pope, Dominic began to preach, a right reserved previously for bishops, and signed his name from this time on as "Brother Dominic, Preacher."

Dominic founded the Order of Preachers in 1214 to address through learning, scholarship, and preaching the need for **conversion** among the estranged Christians and non-Christians of his times. His spirituality was a blend of traditions that became distinctive, valuing the recitation of the Divine Office (or **Liturgy of the Hours**), study, penance, preaching, and the communal life. He left few writings except some letters, but he gave his followers a profound dedication to the apostolate of preaching. Dominic died of an illness at age fifty-two, having founded sixty friaries in eight provinces, extending from Poland, Scandinavia, and Palestine, to England, France, and Italy.

For further information, see *Early Dominicans: Selected Writings*, edited by Simon Tugwell. NVV

DOMINICANS. Members of the Order of Preachers founded by **Dominic** or one of the other groups for men and women inspired by him. Dominican writers include **Thomas Aquinas**, **Meister Johannes Eckhart**, **Johannes Tauler**, **Margaret Ebner**, **Henry Suso**, and **Catherine of Siena**.

DONNE, JOHN (1572–1631), the first and greatest metaphysical poet, possibly the most influential preacher in England in his time.

Born into a Catholic family during an age of religious strife, Donne was educated in theology and law. He converted to Anglicanism. His early poems reflect a profligate youth. At age thirty he secretly married Anne More. Impoverished, he turned to the church for advancement and began studying religion seriously. A spiritual crisis inspired his "Holy Sonnets," changing his focus from earthly to heavenly love, yearning for **union** with God. Six years after ordination, he became the dean of London's St. Paul's Cathedral.

Donne's writing encompasses love and religious poetry, elegies, epigrams, verse letters, and 160 surviving sermons. With powerful imagery he drew from Scholastic philosophy, science, trades, professions, and ordinary things. Reacting against ascetic ideals, Donne explored the interrelationship of **soul** and **body**. His intense, passionate poetry reflects a powerful intellect and great learning. His irregular and dramatic meter resembles the cadence and immediacy of ordinary speech.

Donne was plagued by poverty, ill health, personal tragedies, and bouts of depression. Much of his poetry was inspired by death, including the death of his patron's daughter, the deaths of his wife and five of his children, and anticipation of his own death. Thirty-two of his fifty-four songs and sonnets focus on death with hope. Two of his most famous phrases are "death be not proud" and "for whom the bell tolls." Death provided a springboard for meditations on all aspects of the Christian life. *Devotions upon Emergent Occasions*, a series of meditations composed while Donne recovered from a life-threatening fever, reflects the higher human aspirations and constant possibility of a relationship with God. Only days before dying from stomach cancer, Donne preached "Death's Duel," his final sermon.

Of special interest are Donne's collected sermons; *Essays in Divinity*; *An Anatomy of the World*; *Of the Progress of the Soul*; and *The Divine Poems*, particularly "Hymn to God My God, in My Sickness," "Batter My Heart, Three-Personed God," and "Death Be Not Proud."

A valuable companion to Donne's poetry is *Devotions upon Emergent Occasions and Death's Duel* (Vintage Spiritual Classics), which includes a helpful introduction, chronology, notes, and Izaak Walton's *The Life of Dr. John Donne*. LSP

DOROTHEOS OF GAZA (ca. 500–60), Palestinian monk. Dorotheos was born in Antioch. Dorotheos means "gift of God," and based on the meaning of his name, scholars assume Dorotheos was raised in a Christian home. He received an excellent education in philosophy and rhetoric under the philosopher Procopius. His enthusiasm for learning influenced his desire to become holy. He left school and entered the monastery of Seridos where he studied with Abba Barsanuphius and Abba John the Prophet. At first he served as the guest master of the monastery and later became the administrator of the infirmary. Much later his responsibilities included being spiritual director for the younger members. One of his novices, Dositheos, became well-known for living a consistent ascetic life. After the death of Abba John, sometime around 540, Dorotheos started his own monastery in Gaza. From this time until his death (ca. 560) Dorotheos developed a systematic examination of monastic life.

The writings of Dorotheos include a series of fourteen discourses that were lectures/sermons addressing problems of the spiritual life. His writing style is conversational, and his instructions are both theoretical and practical. He understands the powerful effects of sin and human psychology. The major themes in his discourses are the need for **obedience** in the struggle with human passions, the path of contentment found through **humility**, and the interdependence of monks in communal life. Dorotheos teaches that the root of all passions is self-love or one's own will. Only through Christ can one be freed from sin, forgiven, restored, and empowered to live a virtuous life. Humility is the key in overcoming the passions, and Dorotheos understands humility as the ability to know one's limits and to surrender oneself to the love and grace of God. Moreover, humility grows naturally within the soul by living a life of obedience. Dorotheos had a reputation for being a humble person and practicing what he preached.

Abba Dorotheos: Practical Teaching on the Christian Life and *Dorotheos of Gaza: Discourses and Sayings,* translated by Eric Wheeler, are recommended for further reading. ASJ

DRYNESS. The experience described as the feeling that "God has moved away and left no forwarding address." It is the feeling of God's distance, if not absence, with the attending sense of meaninglessness and emotional flatness in our faith. It is important to note that dryness is a feeling on our part, not an action on God's part. Dryness is described graphically in the Psalms (e.g., 6; 13; 22; 42; 55; 74; 77). In the New Testament, Jesus decried his abject dryness from the cross (Matt. 27:46), and Paul described an all-consuming dryness in his life (2 Cor. 1:8). A look at the lives of the saints reveals that it is a common experience, albeit an unpleasant one. Among those who have both experienced and written about spiritual dryness are **Teresa of Ávila**, **Martin Luther**, **George Fox**, **John Wesley**, **Charles Spurgeon**, F. B. Meyer, **E. Stanley Jones**, J. B. Phillips, **Susan Muto**, and **Henri Nouwen**.

Spiritual dryness technically differs from the "**dark night** of the soul" described by **John of the Cross** and others. The dark night is part of a larger mystical way in which God deliberately removes God's presence to see if we will persevere in our faith—a faith that relies on nothing for its existence. The dark night is a prelude to **union** with God. **Evelyn Underhill**'s book *Mysticism* provides a good understanding of the dark night.

Spiritual dryness, on the other hand, is a temporary condition (although it may last for a long time) brought on by such things as unconfessed sin, physical illness, anxiety during times of change, insufficient attention to our spiritual life, religious addiction, separating our spirituality from the rest of our life, claiming more of an experience of God than we actually have, and the vain attempt to imitate others. It is a condition that should be acknowledged rather than hidden. Spiritual direction and life together in **community** are two frequent means for restoring vitality.

During periods of spiritual dryness we should continue to practice the classic **disciplines** and the means of **grace**, for it is often through these actions that a sense of "God's return" and a general renewal in our spirituality vitality will emerge. SH

DUALISM. See **Platonism, Gnosticism, Neoplatonism, Manichaeism,** and **Catharism.**

DUNNAM, MAXIE (b. 1934), United Methodist pastor, writer, educator. As a pastor in Mississippi during the 1960s, Dunnam was a leader in the civil rights movement. Later he served as a pastor in California; world editor of The Upper Room; senior pastor of Christ United Methodist Church in Memphis, Tennessee; and president of Asbury Theological Seminary in Wilmore, Kentucky. He is a prolific author, best known for his many workbooks pertaining to prayer and the spiritual life, most especially *The Workbook of Living Prayer.* A leader in the World Methodist Council, with a particular passion for world evangelism, Dunnam is also a co-founder of the Confessing movement within The United Methodist Church. SH

Є

EBNER, MARGARET (ca. 1291–1351), German **Dominican** nun. Born to a leading family of Donauwörth (near Strassburg), Margaret followed several relatives in becoming a nun in the Dominican convent of Maria Medingen. In 1312 a lingering disease forced her to withdraw from many of the convent's normal activities. She devoted herself to prayer for souls in purgatory but soon developed a highly **affective spirituality** sometimes moving beyond her conscious control. At times she experienced "binding silence" and was unable to speak at all or even open her mouth to eat. Sometimes this binding included her body, so that she was unable to move. At other times, particularly when she heard references to the Passion story, she shouted out words like, "Oh, no, my dear Lord Jesus Christ!" These outcries were usually accompanied by great pain. During Lent, when readings focused on the Passion, her pain was constant and prevented her from attending worship with the community. Desiring even closer identification with Christ's passion, she prayed for, but never received, the **stigmata**, though she did feel the pain of nails and thorns on Good Friday. Release from outcries, pain, and binding silence often took the form of repeating the **name of Jesus** hundreds of times until she was exhausted. During Advent she had the gentler experience of identifying with Mary, wanting to bear and suckle the baby Jesus.

Henry of Nördlingen became her spiritual guide in 1332, though he became more friend and disciple in later years. He sent her books by **Mechthild of Magdeburg** and **Henry Suso** as well as the *Summa Theologica* of **Thomas Aquinas**. He corresponded with her when he could not see her in person and asked her to write about her spiritual experiences. These writings eventually became her book of *Reve-* *lations*, which describes her experience (through November 1348) in terms that echo Mechthild and Suso and, through them, **Meister Eckhart**. Through Suso she also began to correspond with **Johannes Tauler** and other "Friends of God."

Margaret Ebner: Major Works, translated and edited by Leonard P. Hindsley, contains the *Revelations* and has an excellent introduction to Margaret's life and writing. KRB

ECKHART, MEISTER JOHANNES (ca. 1260–1329), German **Dominican** preacher. Eckhart was born at Hocheim in Thuringia. He entered the Dominican Order of Preachers in Erfurt at age fifteen. He was named Chair of Theology at the University of Paris, the most distinguished university at that time. The honor of being called "Meister" ("Master") while teaching at the University of Paris has stuck with him throughout the centuries. Having achieved high academic recognition, he also succeeded in serving in various positions of leadership within his religious community.

Eckhart sided with the marginalized of his day: the ignorant, the peasants, and the lower-class women of the **Beguine** movement. A popular preacher, he kept his thinking rooted in the Bible and his own experience. He preferred to preach in German, though his formal and professional writings were written in Latin. Eckhart believed in the connectedness between reason and revelation in the scriptures. This Dominican preacher, teacher, theologian, philosopher, poet, and mystic (though he never wrote of his own mystical experiences) explored the eternal mysteries of the human soul and God. Following the **negative** (or apophatic) **way**, he sought to teach about a God who was intimately near yet also ineffably unknowable. He spoke of the calling of every Christian to incarnate the Son of God, that is, to give birth to Christ in their hearts. Many scholars found this unsettling and questioned if he was contradicting traditional Scholastic thought. Around 1326 formal challenges regarding what he preached and taught were brought by theological inquisitors.

For the last years of his life, Eckhart defended determinedly his faithfulness to the church and his orthodoxy. Even though Dominican leadership supported him, he appealed to the pope. He died before the matter was concluded, still under suspicion. Due to such controversies, his works were not read or consulted. About a generation later, Eckhart's influence would become obvious through two Dominican disciples: **Henry Suso** and **Johannes Tauler**. Indeed Eckhart's common appeal impacted **Martin Luther** (via the writings of Tauler), **Jacob Boehme**, and future monks, philosophers, psychologists, seekers, poets, novelists, and interfaith scholars.

Many of Eckhart's popular German sermons are translated in *Meister Eckhart: Teacher and Preacher*, edited by Bernard McGinn, and his Latin works in *Meister Eckhart: The Essential Sermons, Commentaries, Treatises, and Defense*, translated by Edmund Colledge and Bernard McGinn. EKM

ECSTASY. To speak of ecstasy is to walk on holy ground. It cannot be defined, only experienced. Each experience is unique to the person. A model for the experience is Paul's account in 2 Corinthians 12. Various translations suggest the following: swept in ecstasy to the highest heaven, caught up into paradise, had **visions** and revelations, heard unspeakable words inexpressible in language. Such experiences are not to be the cause of boasting.

One may gain a feeling for ecstasy by spending time with *The Ecstasy of St. Teresa*, a statue by Gian Lorenzo Bernini. Teresa appears to be overcome, bathed in light, and ministered to by an angel. Bernini captures the essence of what **Teresa of Ávila** writes of in her *Life*.

Hildegard of Bingen wrote of her visions or "illuminations" in her *Scivias*, as did **Julian of Norwich** in *Showings*. Teresa, Hildegard, and Julian all recorded their ecstasies under orders from their superiors. Most ecstatics are humble persons and hesitate to write of their experiences because ecstasies are so personal and because they might seem to elevate the ecstatic rather than give the glory to God.

Also, ecstatic experiences are difficult to put into words. Attempts at description include special grace, lifting of the veil of mystery, **union** with God, creative abiding, abiding power, profound joy, lifted out of self, raised to heaven, continued revelation, creative newness. Ecstasy is an unbidden gift from God, not an accomplishment. For some persons it seems to be a matter of degrees or powerful ways in which the soul is awakened by God and keeps enlarging.

Ecstatics tend to be persons who have a deep and profound prayer life and who are deeply aware of God's presence in their lives. **Prayer** and **humility** seem to be prerequisites. However wonderful and transcendent the individual experiences, the important aspect is how lives are subsequently carried out radiantly in love and service to others. EWF

EDWARDS, JONATHAN (1703–58), American **Calvinist** theologian and one of the most profound thinkers of the eighteenth century. Edwards served as a clergyman in New England (until his parish let him go) and later went on to serve as president of Princeton University. He was a faithful follower of Calvin and wrote many theological treatises emphasizing Calvinistic themes. While often noted as the preacher of the famous fire-and-brimstone sermon "Sinners in the Hands of an Angry God," he actually spent comparatively little theological effort on issues of hell and damnation. He wrote several influential philosophical works such as *The Nature of True Virtue* and *Freedom of the Will*. The works he aimed at the general public, such as his *The Life of David Brainerd*, *A History of the Work of Redemption*, and *The Great Awakening: A Faithful*

Narrative of the Surprising Work of God, painted an accessible and compelling vision of the gospel lived out in real life. These works inspired many people, including **John Wesley**.

One of the writings by Edwards most often read and referred to in the context of **spiritual formation** is *A Treatise Concerning Religious Affections* in which he asserts that "true religion consists, in great part, in Holy Affections." In this text Edwards discusses which signs or marks of religious affections (emotions) can or cannot be trusted when trying to determine if the affections are authentically religious, grounded in God. An affection is not necessarily trustworthy simply because it is very intense, has great effects on the body, or comes accompanied in the mind with texts of scripture. Among those signs that can be trusted are the affections accompanied by a sense of the truth of the gospel, tenderness of spirit, **humility**, and increased longing for spiritual attainments. Most important, truly religious affections show themselves in Christian practice—concrete and visible actions that form and express Christian love. Affections that lead to a life marked by such practice are indeed worthy of a Christian.

For further reading, see *The Theology of Jonathan Edwards: A Reappraisal* by Conrad Cherry, and Edwards's *Works*, especially his *Treatise Concerning Religious Affections*. GSC

EDWARDS, TILDEN (b. 1935), spiritual director, author. Edwards, a pioneer in the ministries of **spiritual formation** and **spiritual direction**, is a founder and senior fellow of the Shalem Institute for Spiritual Formation in Bethesda, Maryland. He was the executive director of Shalem for over twenty-six years. Under the guidance of Edwards, Shalem has become an effective training center for spiritual direction (group and individual), spiritual formation for Christians, and contemplative prayer. Programs are designed for clergy and laity of all backgrounds.

In addition to his ministry at Shalem, Edwards also writes books. In 1980 he wrote *Spiritual Friend: Reclaiming the Gift of Spiritual Direction*, one of the first modern books on the art of spiritual direction. His long-awaited follow-up was published in 2001, *Spiritual Director, Spiritual Companion: Guide to Tending the Soul*. His newly revised book *Sabbath Time* also offers direction. In addition, Edwards has written ten books about spiritual exercises and disciplines for everyday life. WW

ELIOT, THOMAS STEARNS (1888–1965), one of the greatest poets of the twentieth century. With the publication of "The Waste Land" (1922), Eliot became commonly understood as one of the primary spokespersons for his generation. This monumental work speaks of the ennui and spiritual bankruptcy of the modern era. Yet even in the midst of this spiritual decay, there are "hints and guesses" of another realm of being. Eliot would fully embrace this other realm when he became confirmed in the Church of England in 1927. In the next year, Eliot described himself as "a classicist in literature, a royalist in politics and an Anglo-Catholic in religion" (*For Lancelot Andrewes*, 1928). This important self-understanding reveals the core task of his **spiritual formation**: to find ways to live out the classic Christian faith in the modern age.

Eliot refused to turn his back on either classic Christianity or the modern context. He rejected both a conservative refusal to take seriously the contemporary world and a liberal denial of core Christian beliefs. This commitment was fundamentally based upon the doctrine of the Incarnation. In Jesus Christ, God has embraced the world, yet remains God. Eliot develops his remarkable vision in two primary works: "Ash Wednesday" and *Four Quartets*. In "Ash Wednesday" (1930) Eliot described the repentance of a modern person who must be taught how "to care and not to care" and how "to sit still." Eliot's Christian imagination comes to full maturity in the *Four Quartets* (1943). Written against the backdrop of World War II, these poems reflect upon the coming together of time and eternity as well as the place of **suffering** in Christian formation. Throughout his life, Eliot carefully observed the world in all its brokenness yet did not despair. For this is the world to which Christ has come, and the **Holy Spirit** remains present. PDJ

ELIZABETH OF THE TRINITY (1880–1906), French **Carmelite** nun. Marie Elizabeth Catez was born in Bourges, France, where her father was an officer in the French Army. Elizabeth first studied music, showing promise as a gifted pianist, but had early desires for a religious vocation. At the age of twenty-one, she was allowed to enter the Discalced Carmelite order. She was consumed with her love of the Trinity and search for a "divine inhabitation" of "heaven on earth," saying, "all three persons dwell in the soul that loves them in truth." From 1903 to 1906, she struggled through the pain of Addison's disease, which claimed her life on November 9, 1906. Elizabeth used the agony of the disease as a means of **union** with the Trinity by a continual offering of her **suffering** to God. She writes, "Only in God is everything pure, beautiful, and holy; fortunately we can dwell in Him even in our exile! But my Master's happiness is mine, and I surrender myself to Him so He can do whatever He wants in me."

Despite her short life, Elizabeth is known as a deep modern mystic and teacher of **mysticism** through her letters and reflections. Though never intended to be published, her writings have been compiled into a two-volume set, *Complete Works of Elizabeth of the Trinity*. The first volume introduces Elizabeth's life and writing style and contains what are considered her major writings or teachings. The second volume is a collection of her letters. These writings to friends and family record her quest for a deeper relationship with the "Divine Three."

For further information, see *God As Communion* by John Zizioulas and *Two Sisters in the Spirit: Thérèse of Lisieux and Elizabeth of the Trinity* by Hans Urs von Balthasar. CIZ

ELLIOT, ELISABETH (b. 1926), American missionary, teacher, and writer. Born in Belgium of missionary parents, Elisabeth Howard graduated from Wheaton College and married classmate Jim Elliot. She served as a missionary in Ecuador among the Auca Indians. She was an adjunct professor at Gordon-Conwell Theological Seminary (1974–80) and writer-in-residence there.

Elliot, an internationally popular and inspirational speaker, writes a bimonthly newsletter; produces "Daily Thoughts for Living" on devotions.org. Her recent books highlight biblical truths on the practical issues of life.

A prolific writer, Elliot recounts in her first book, *Through Gates of Splendor*, the stories of the five men martyred by the Auca Indians in Ecuador, including her husband. Her next several books relate her mission and translation work there. *These Strange Ashes* tells of her years in Ecuador. Among her recent books are *A Chance to Die* (biography of **Amy Carmichael**) and *The Music of His Promises*. LSP

ELLUL, JACQUES (1912–94), French theologian, philosopher, writer, and professor. Ellul wrote and taught about the intersection of technology and society (influenced by Marx) and **faith** (influenced by **John Calvin** and **Karl Barth**). In his philosophical and sociological work *The Technological Society* (1964), he argues that technology based on "technique" is a mechanical approach to life that subordinates the created and "natural" world. Technique, when strictly adhered to, leads to efficiency, not to the **will of God**. In *The Meaning of the City*, a theological work thematically related to *The Technological Society,* Ellul reflects on the cities in Hebrew and Christian Scriptures. To Ellul, while technology may try to make Earth our home, the Bible tells us that our home is found only in God. SN

EMERSON, RALPH WALDO (1803–82), essayist, poet, and philosopher, one of the primary architects of American transcendentalism. The son of a Unitarian minister, Emerson was educated at Harvard and after completing divinity school there, began a brief career as a pastor. Emerson resigned in 1832, when he realized he could not in good conscience offer Communion or pray publicly. He then began lecturing on natural history and later published perhaps his best critical work, *Nature*, in 1836. That same year he also joined the "Transcendental Club," a group of Unitarian ministers who had been deeply affected by German biblical scholarship and English romanticism.

Emerson expressed the heart of his transcendental views in his address at his alma mater, Harvard Divinity School, in 1838, a speech that dismayed most of his Protestant hearers. In sum, he declared that all things arose from one spirit and one will (monism), that biblical miracles were not outside of natural forces, that the person of Jesus had been exaggerated in the memory of the church, that dogma and preaching alienated the soul from its natural truth, and that scientific and religious realities would ultimately be discovered as one. While his speech fueled controversy, Emerson withdrew from the publicity and focused on writing. *Essays*, published in 1841, includes some of his best-known themes: "Self-Reliance," "Love," "Friendship," "Heroism," and "Art." Like other transcendentalists, Emerson believed in the concept of "over-soul," the idea of a harmonious union of divinity and matter. His vision was buoyant, and his enthusiasm fit this period of American optimism and progress. His essential virtue—self-reliance—was hugely popular. Thus, while he was out of step with important understandings in American Christian thought, he contributed to the ongoing spirituality of individualism, still a major theme in contemporary American spirituality. SAF

ENDO, SHUSAKU (1923–96), Japanese novelist, Roman Catholic, born in Tokyo. Feeling obligated to follow in the footsteps of his mother, Endo was baptized as a preteen. He experienced rejection and ridicule from within himself and from others after converting to Catholicism, becoming a misfit in his own country. As a young man, he visited a historical museum in Nagasaki (where Eu-

ropean missionaries first introduced Catholicism in Japan). He was drawn to notice the *fumie*, a bronze etching of the Madonna with the child Jesus, smudged with black marks caused by Catholics who had chosen to tread on it rather than be martyred during seventeenth-century persecution of Catholics. This painful history of his Japanese religious roots, as well as young Endo's immediate response to the *fumie* in the display case, would impact the rest of his life as a Christian, especially as a Catholic writer. Unwell for most of his life, Endo died from renal disease on September 29, 1996.

Endo struggled all his life to fit his Japanese heritage and culture into a seemingly foreign Catholic framework (less than 1 percent of the population was Catholic). He also struggled inwardly, doubting and questioning his own commitment to the Lord. While in Palestine researching the life of Jesus, Endo came to understand and appreciate that he and Jesus shared something in common: rejection. Like Jesus, Endo did not spurn disgrace, rejection, and **suffering**. Experiencing his own weakness, he claimed his deeper need for Christ and the church. Endo's haunting and fearful preoccupation with his own insincerity and cowardice, coupled with his longing to be faith-filled, were reconciled. With his faith intact, he returned to Japan renewed and determined to write about a God who is close to the people and who understands the sufferings of others. Endo developed Christlike characters in his stories. Surrounded by such themes as betrayal, rejection, and alienation, the one who imitates Christ develops and emerges as he or she realizes that self-sacrifice is required. Such **imitation** reveals the forgiving One who is always there in the midst of suffering.

In *Silence* (1966) and *The Samurai* (1982), his two great historical novels set in the seventeenth century, Endo treats moral and religious themes. Matters of conscience either form or deform a person's character. In his last novel, *Deep River*, he looks at the meaning of death and the possibility of reincarnation. In addition to his many novels, Endo also wrote short stories, one drama, articles, newspaper columns, comical essays, and a biography. EKM

ENGLISH MYSTICS. See **Rolle, Richard;** *The Cloud of Unknowing*; **Hilton, Walter; Julian of Norwich; Kempe, Margery.**

ENNEAGRAM. A Greek word meaning "nine points." It refers to an ancient form of identifying nine *types* of **personality**, often referred to as a spiritual psychology. The enneagram is portrayed as a circle with nine points around the rim of the circle. Lines and arrows within the circle connect each point to certain of the other eight points or types. These arrows depict the direction for movement toward balance and wholeness of each type or the movement toward imbalance and disintegration.

The origin of the enneagram remains somewhat mysterious. Traces of it can be seen in Pythagorean number theory. Russian mystic G. I. Gurdjieff used the enneagram in the late 1920s as a way of blending Sufi (the mystical sect of Islam) teaching and his own understanding of human psychology. Oscar Ishazo, a Chilean teacher of mystical traditions, and Claudio Naranjo, a psychiatrist, used the enneagram in their teachings in the early 1970s. Around this time some **Jesuit** priests began using the enneagram in teaching and in **spiritual direction**.

The theory of the enneagram states that each person's personality develops around one of nine types of imbalance. An individual must first recognize this imbalance, which produces a kind of *trance* in which the individual person becomes addicted to his or her own blind spots or worldviews. The enneagram shows definite directions on how to become aware of certain traps inherent in each personality type. It also offers specific directions on how a person can seek to balance the personality.

Spiritual growth comes by becoming *awake* to the given trance and seeking the di-

rection of integration for that particular personality type. One's type, known as the *compulsive type*, can be identified by either spiritual counseling with a trained person or by taking one of the enneagram inventories that have been developed by various enneagram teachers. Many counselors and spiritual directors use the enneagram as a way of helping individuals assess their spiritual type. Consultants are also using it in business and management much as the Myers-Briggs personality inventory is used.

Of the many books now available that offer enneagram instruction and personality inventories, *The Wisdom of the Enneagram* by Don Riso and Russ Hudson and *The Enneagram Made Easy* by Renee Baron and Elizabeth Wagele would be good starting points for further reading. JS

ENTHUSIASM. A religious term used from the beginning of the Reformation to the nineteenth century to connote a radical, spiritualist, or sectarian Christianity. An enthusiast was regarded as an impractical visionary with ill-regulated religious emotion. The term was also used to describe a self-deluded person who claimed to have received divine communication or private revelation. An enthusiast claimed the immediate inspiration of the **Holy Spirit** as the true source of religious authority above the scripture, creeds of the church, and civil or religious laws. Enthusiasm is synonymous with fanaticism—excessive religious zeal. **John Wesley**, who for much of his ministry was wrongly called an enthusiast, claimed that enthusiasm was a "species of madness" or a psychological disorder (see his sermon "The Nature of Enthusiasm").

Enthusiasts act out of a false subjective experience that they identify as spiritual or holy inspiration. In this isolated state they radically cut themselves off from the world and from the influence of **grace**. By willfully cutting themselves off from their own reason and from dialogue with the world, their subjective experiences cannot be examined or challenged. The enthusiast's abilities for rational discernment are refused, overwhelmed, cut off, or diminished by impulses rising from a distorted imagination. From the distorted imagination come false inspirations, from which flow behaviors or ambitions—sometimes obsessive in nature—attributed to divine directives but actually reflecting the power of human imagination under the influence of fallen human nature or the demonic. This religious psychological disorder is not limited to individuals. Whole faith communities and cultures can incorporate this religious mode of existence or orientation.

If you would like to learn more, see Ronald A. Knox, *Enthusiasm: A Chapter in the History of Religion*. CIZ

EPHREM SYRUS (ca. 306–73), Syrian biblical exegete and poet. Probably born at Nisibis of Christian parents, he was ordained a deacon, perhaps by Jacob of Nisibis, who attended the Council of Nicaea in 325. On his return from Nicaea, Jacob appointed Ephrem interpreter of the School of Nisibis. Ephrem began his writing there. After Rome ceded Nisibis to the Persians in 363, he settled in Edessa, where he wrote the bulk of his writings. He died on June 9, 373, while ministering to victims of a plague.

Ephrem composed most of his voluminous exegetical, theological, controversial, and ascetic works in verse. He wrote *Hymns on the Nativity* celebrating God's miraculous self-abasement out of love for humankind. He also composed hymns on paradise, on the feasts of the Lord, and on last things. He refuted heretics such as Marcion, Bardesanes, and Manes. He made a case against the apostate Emperor Julian in hymns. He urged devotion to the saints and especially the Virgin Mary in hymns. Although he wrote only in Syriac, his works were translated into Armenian and Greek at an early date, and from those tongues into Latin and Slavonic. His hymns exerted a great influence on liturgical poetry in Syriac and Greek.

Read Ephrem's writings in *Ephrem the Syrian: Hymns*, translated by Kathleen E. McVey

or *St. Ephrem the Syrian: Selected Prose Works*, edited by Kathleen E. McVey and translated by Edward G. Mathews Jr. and Joseph P. Amar. Read about him in Sebastian Brock's study, *The Luminous Eye: The Spiritual World Vision of Saint Ephrem the Syrian*. EGH

ERASMUS, DESIDERIUS (1466–1536), Dutch proponent of "Christian **humanism**," a literary movement interested in the ethical formation of the human being. Born near Rotterdam, Erasmus was the illegitimate son of a priest and a widow. Educated in Gouda, Utrecht, and Deventer, he was strongly influenced by the Brethren of the Common Life, a lay order that practiced a communal life of simplicity, **humility**, and piety, similar to the one described in *Imitation of Christ* by **Thomas à Kempis**. After his mother's death, Erasmus joined the Augustinian Regulars at Steyn and was ordained a priest. In 1495 he left the priory for the University of Paris, where he gained status as a man of letters. In 1516 he obtained a papal dispensation that allowed him to travel to England and throughout Europe, befriending many notable persons, one being **Thomas More**. His teaching reached the court of Prince Charles of Spain, who became Emperor Charles V.

Erasmus's literary scholarship brought Christianity's ancient texts into the sixteenth century as he restored and edited them for his Renaissance audience. In response to Scholasticism's emphasis on abstract reason, the humanism of Erasmus proposed a life of virtue, prayer, and study using the patristic sources. This way of life was more than an intellectual course of study: It restored Christ to the center of human life and practice. Erasmus encouraged the interior development of the person.

Erasmus's method involved recovering the "good learning" and culture of classical writers prior to the Dark Ages. He produced volumes of religious wisdom from the church fathers, including a Greek New Testament. He advocated the study of **scripture** for the formation of the good person. Equally noteworthy, his wit and creativity are illustrated in the *Ten Colloquies*, exercises for his students in Paris through which Erasmus expressed his views on the issues and customs of the day. In dramatic dialogue, ten scenes combine satire and humor to teach moral lessons effectively.

Ten Colloquies is available in translation by Craig R. Thompson. NVV

ERIUGENA, JOHN SCOTUS (ca. 810–77), Irish teacher and translator who advanced the **negative** (or apophatic) **way** as an approach to Christian spiritual formation. Eriugena's career centered in the Frankish (French) kingdom of Charles the Bald, where he served as court scholar. There he translated into Latin the works of such Greek Christian advocates of the negative way as **Gregory of Nyssa**, **Pseudo-Dionysius**, and **Maximus the Confessor**. These translations had an avid readership for many centuries due to Eriugena's reputation as a translator, as well as to the importance of the authors themselves. Christian teachers and mystics in later centuries, including **Bonaventure**, **Thomas Aquinas**, and **Meister Eckhart**, all read these works as translated by Eriugena.

Eriugena's most important original work advocating the negative way *Periphyseon (On the Division of Nature)* uses concepts from these same Greek writers. The book develops around a discussion between a student and his mentor about the structure of reality. Together they decide that nature, including the human soul, emanates downward from God as depicted by the biblical story of Creation and Fall. They understand biblical redemption as the upward return of the soul, together with all things, back to God.

According to this view, **spiritual formation** is the ascent of the human soul from the observable world along the negative way back to the immediate **vision of God**. This journey requires true philosophy, the pursuit of **wisdom** that seeks humbly to worship and rationally to understand God. We may begin this journey by making positive statements about God, e.g., "God is good," so long as we recognize

them as analogies. But since God stands beyond mere good, we approach the divine with more understanding when we deny that human concepts such as goodness strictly apply to God. Eriugena taught that such informed ignorance paved the way for the soul to enjoy mystical intimacy with God. Later Christians have criticized *Periphyseon* for its implicit pantheism and universalism, together with the limited place it gives to Jesus Christ. JB

ESCHATOLOGY. The theological study of "last things" or "end times" (from the Greek word *eschatos*, meaning "last"). Christian life and belief are shaped by our perspective about the future. The scriptures include teachings about the future that are *apocalyptic* (such as Daniel and Revelation) and *prophetic* (such as Isaiah and Jeremiah). The historical events associated with end times were often linked with military defeat, exile, or the destruction of the Temple. Apocalyptic eschatology perceived that present crises were the result of **evil**, while prophetic eschatology interpreted them as the judgment of God.

A Christian eschatology is rooted in the life, death, and resurrection of Jesus Christ. Throughout the Gospels, Jesus refers to the coming of God's kingdom (Mark 1:15, for example), and he calls his followers to repent in preparation. Many scholars speak of *realized* eschatology, in which many of the events to which Jesus refers occur in his lifetime, and *future* eschatology, the anticipation of future fulfillment of his teachings. In this respect the kingdom of God has both present and future meanings. The expected return of Christ after his ascension is also the occasion for readiness (Luke 21:25-28, 34-36), and the earliest Christians understood **Holy Communion** as a foretaste of the Great Banquet (Luke 14:15-24; Matt. 22:1-14) that would be a future gathering of the faithful around the table of the Lord. Many eucharistic liturgies summarize this dimension of the meal with the mystery of faith: "Christ has died. Christ is risen. Christ will come again."

A Christian perspective on eschatology is composed of many practical elements: our basis for **hope** in the future, our understanding of the meaning of final judgment, and our convictions about life after death. Our vision of the future greatly influences our life in the present. We live by hope, which is rooted in the confidence of what God has done in the past, is doing in the present, and will do in the future. We affirm resurrection life by which death is overcome, and darkness is cast out. We believe that our **works** will be judged; thus we seek to live faithfully. Ultimately, we trust that the future belongs to God, who is "the Alpha and the Omega" (Rev. 1:8). We live in the present with the hope that the purpose and **will of God** will be accomplished, on earth as it is in heaven.

For further reading, see Jürgen Moltmann, *The Coming of God: Christian Eschatology*, translated by Margaret Kohl. KHC

EUCHARIST. See **Holy Communion.**

EVAGRIUS PONTICUS (345–99), earliest **monastic** writer. Born in the small town of Ibora in Pontus (Asia Minor), Evagrius was the son of a pastoral bishop with limited ecclesial powers. As a boy, Evagrius was influenced by **Basil of Caesarea**, who ordained him a lector. **Gregory of Nazianzus** ordained Evagrius a deacon in 379, the year Basil died. Known for his theological acumen and virtue, he was invited to join in the Second Ecumenical Council in 381. Highly successful at preaching too, Evagrius made many friends in Constantinople, including **Gregory of Nyssa**, Basil's brother. Despite his natural penchant for prayer and quiet, Evagrius's world tumbled when he fell in love. He despaired over his struggle to control his passions. After dreaming that he swore to leave Constantinople, he set sail for Jerusalem. New friends led him to forget his intention to care for his inner life and spiritual nurture. He became very ill; the methods and remedies of the doctors proved fruitless. With the help of his dear friend, Melania, he discovered that his illness was tied to his inner conflict over his spiritual life. Evagrius recovered and left for the Egyptian desert to be with the monks, the **desert fathers**, and to learn from them. Evagrius died after living in the desert for fourteen years as a person of prayer, study, and **asceticism**, no longer tormented by unbalanced passions and thoughts.

Much of Evagrius's influence is attributed to his practical advice on living the spiritual life. For him the spiritual journey begins with **experience** and with reflection upon one's life experience. Analyzing the various passions with psychological insight, he accurately describes the struggles of the human heart seeking to live a life dedicated to God and in communion with others. In the *Praktikos* (the *practice* of the moral-ascetical journey in faith) and the *Chapters on Prayer*, he presents his map for growing in the spiritual life: First we struggle against temptation as we seek to grow in virtue, which leads to a deeper contemplative **prayer** life and the **experience** of God. EKM

EVIL. Anything opposed to the creative **will of God** and God's intention to redeem all of creation. Doing the will of God is good. Opposing the will of God is evil. What is good creates. What is evil destroys. For the Christian the most important question then becomes, "Why would a good God permit evil to exist at all?" This has come to be known in theological circles as "the problem of evil" (or *theodicy*) and forms the core of any spiritual response to God's intentions for creation.

Theologians divide evil into two distinct categories. The first is "natural evil" and the second "human (or moral) evil." Natural evil occurs in earthquakes, hurricanes, diseases, and birth defects. Why does this kind of evil exist? The most consistent answer is that the world we live in, in order to exist, must be subject to natural laws. The natural process of creation is not perfect, just as human beings are not perfect. When conditions are right in the atmosphere, a hurricane is created. The hurricane is not something God "intended" but is a by-product of the interaction between the dynamics of the natural order. The human body is frail and subject to decay. Death is inevitable. Diseases and birth defects are by-products of that human frailty. One cannot say that an earthquake or birth defect has any kind of intent or that God creates or causes these realities (or uses them to punish us); but because they destroy rather than create, they are viewed as evil. They could only be prevented if creation were subjected to some other kind of order. Our only true response to natural evil is to have **compassion** and relieve **suffering** by serving those in need.

Human evil, on the other hand, is the by-product of free human **will**. Spirituality and spiritual **discipline** are much more concerned with this kind of evil. Human beings have the freedom to choose to oppose God's will. Whenever they do, evil exists. For instance, we can choose to murder another person in order to accomplish our own selfish purposes. Even though we know that it is immoral, unjust, and contrary to the will of God to take another person's life, we remain free to act in a way of our own choosing. Human evil can transcend the individual and become corporate when communities, institutions, and nations choose to oppose the will of God. Christianity sees this kind of evil as responsible for much of the suffering human beings encounter in this life.

What spiritual response can we make to this kind of evil? The key to our response is found in the **Lord's Prayer** when we pray "deliver us from evil." God uses everything in God's power, short of taking away our free will and compelling us to do God's will, to save human beings and creation from the consequences of evil. An important element of spiritual discipline comes in resisting the power of evil in whatever form it presents itself. God does not expect us to resist evil by ourselves. When we pray "deliver us from evil," we pray to be liberated from the power of evil in creation and in ourselves, as well as to become liberators for others. We ask God to enter into our struggles with evil wherever we encounter it.

For further reading, see *When Bad Things Happen to Good People* by Harold S. Kushner or *Encountering Evil: Live Options in Theodicy*, edited by Stephen T. Davis. SFP

EXAMEN. A way of examining or assessing one's life before God on a regular basis. This way of prayer was first developed by **Ignatius of Loyola**, the founder of the **Jesuit** Order, and focuses our recollection on a narrow time span, perhaps the previous day or week. The purpose of this approach is to prevent our days and weeks from going by unexamined and to allow us to be increasingly in tune with the Spirit of God.

The examen prayer, also called the examination of consciousness, consists of two movements. The first moves us to pause and peruse how God has been present to us and at work among us throughout the day and our response. This examination is not so much a tallying of guilt or of failures and successes as an interior and exterior evaluation of the spiritual state of our **union** with God.

The examen of consciousness is one way we heed the call to remember the wonderful works of God, the means God uses to make us more aware of our surroundings. God wants us to be present where we are and to discern the footprints of the holy.

In the second movement of the examen prayer (sometimes called examination of conscience), we review our general spiritual health to uncover those areas that need cleansing, **holiness**, and healing. We invite God to search our hearts to the depths with the Divine's scrutiny of love. The words of the psalmist are in our mouths: "Search me, O God, and know my heart; test me and know my thoughts. See if there is any wicked way in me, and lead me in the way everlasting" (Ps. 139:23-24). Because God is alongside us in our search, we need no defense or apology. God comforts and protects, showing us what we need to see when we need to see it.

Christians hope this introspection leads to the priceless gift of self-knowledge, not as a way to personal peace but so that we can

---

An Examen Journal

Examen **journals** have been found to be an invaluable record of daily struggles and progress. Many people find that the **discipline** of journal keeping provides a means of spiritual growth. Angry words, a failed civility, a missed opportunity to express care are all put down on paper. But there is also the good: a word bravely spoken, a kind act, a quiet prayer. All are recorded.

At the end of this week stop, take up paper and pen, and ask the Spirit of God to guide your memory back over the week, step-by-step.

Locate activities and encounters for which you are grateful and give thanks.

Examine your days and pinpoint the moments when God's presence and reality were especially apparent.

Note any failings or **sins** that need your resolve and God's forgiveness. Write down each step.

As you review your written **confessions**, ask yourself if they brought you to feelings of **consolation**, that is, times when you felt drawn to God, or to feelings of desolation, times when you were drawn away from God and wrapped in selfish concerns. Give God thanks for whatever makes you grateful and ask God's forgiveness for failings and sins.

Once this writing is completed, enter into a determined time of prayerful repentance, which can be concluded by receiving **Holy Communion** in weekly worship.

---

resolve to be more fully Christian in our relationships and particular daily situations. It is not a journey into ourselves but a journey though ourselves so that we can emerge from the deepest level of the self into God. In this total, unvarnished self-knowledge we see our weaknesses and strengths, as well as our brokenness and gifts. As **John Chrysostom** wrote, "Find the door of your heart, you will discover it is the door of the kingdom of God."

For more examples of the use of examen, see *Inner Compass: An Invitation to Ignatian Spirituality* by Margaret Silf and *Eyes to See, Ears to Hear: An Introduction to Ignatian Spirituality* by David Lonsdale. PDB

Exodus. (Greek *exodos*, "way out"), departure, especially Israel's departure from Egypt; metaphorically, any journey from slavery though the **desert** to the Promised Land. The descendants of Jacob (Israel) were doomed to live and die in Egyptian bondage. God provided a way out. The blood of the innocent, unblemished lamb was the key to deliverance, causing the angel of death to pass over the houses of the Israelites. In Egypt the Israelites were oriented to a predictable existence with regular meals but no Sabbath, no individual identities, and no hope of freedom. The Exodus was a long journey required for reorientation to the risks and responsibilities of freedom, learning **obedience** to a caring but unmanageable God. The people needed to die to the old life of Egypt so they could begin new life in a different place, a promised land. Many nostalgic for Egypt never completed the Exodus but died in the desert. This core biblical story is told in the books of Exodus through Deuteronomy.

The Babylonian captivity inspired prophets and psalmists to long for a new Exodus. The great prophet of the exile speaks of making a highway through the desert for God to lead God's people home (Isa. 40:3-5; see also Ezek. 36:22-28). Psalms 66, 77, 78, 80, 81, 105, 106 and others all recall aspects of the exodus from Egypt in order to plead with God for renewal and restoration.

Matthew's account of the **Transfiguration** implies that, in keeping with long messianic tradition, Jesus is the new Moses (Matt. 17). Luke tells us that Jesus, Elijah, and Moses "appeared in glory and were speaking of his departure [literally, *exodus*], which he was about to accomplish at Jerusalem" (9:31). The pattern of slavery-desert-Promised Land is repeated and transformed in Christ's crucifixion-death-resurrection.

As *genesis* has become a pregnant noun embracing all beginnings—how things came to be the way they are—so *exodus* has become a pregnant noun referring to any event of deliverance and the process of reorientation. Both deliverance and reorientation are within the central messianic mission of *setting the captives free*. The exodus story has been important in the lives of many captive or oppressed people, from **African-American** slaves singing "Let My People Go" to the *campesinos* of Latin America and the **spirituality of liberation**. More broadly, it is an important reminder of the constant human need to be set free even from comfortable captivity so that God can lead us through the **desert** of confusion and the **dark night** and into the joy of God's presence. HWC

EXPERIENCE. In the common meaning of the term, the bread and butter of our everyday lives. In theological contexts, experience is one of the criteria for forming theological judgments, along with scripture, tradition, and reason. On this question, **John Wesley**, sometimes caricatured as regarding extreme experiences as normative in his Methodist revival movement, in fact held a very humble assessment of the theological significance of experience. Wesley, in his sermon "Witness of the Spirit," said that while experience cannot itself prove a doctrine, "Experience is sufficient to *confirm* a doctrine which is grounded on Scripture." On the whole, this has been the understanding of mainstream Christianity.

In the context of **spiritual formation**, though, discussions of experience tend to focus less on decisions about disputed doctrines than on understanding the role and relative place that religious experience should play in the whole of the Christian life.

One way of placing experience in the Christian life, which we might call the way of **mysticism**, emphasizes the direct experience of God as a way of initiating, deepening, and authorizing the Christian life. This kind of experience is especially manifested in intense feelings, visions, and revelations. On the whole, writers in the Christian spiritual tradition have seen that this dramatic and powerful way of the mystics should not have a normative claim on the lives of everyday believers. In any case, whether one pursues the mystical path or not, there are clear criteria by which to evaluate Christian religious experiences.

The majority of Christian spiritual writers have held that experiences of God, no matter how compelling, are important only to the extent that these experiences lead to a new quality of life. Even the most highly charged episodes of profundity do not bear much Christian weight if they do not lead to a changed life, a life of deeper **humility**, more committed **compassion** for the suffering and weak, and a greater desire to serve God. On this understanding, the primary question is not so much "What kind of experiences of God have you had?" but instead might be "How can you shape all of your future life experience to reflect more truly the God you have come to know?" This shaping, in a sense, is the whole agenda of spiritual formation.

For a helpful understanding of different ways that experience and theology can be conceived as interacting, see George A. Lindbeck's modern classic *The Nature of Doctrine: Religion and Theology in a Postliberal Age*. GSC

101

F

FAITH. A personal, positive, and dynamic relationship with God involving one's whole being and life. As the Bible predominantly sees it, faith is *trust*. Trust is lived, experienced as an assurance, a motivating force. It is not a theory or an idea. Luther called it "a confidence on which one stakes one's life," building on the claim in Hebrews 11:1 that "faith is the assurance of things hoped for, the conviction of things not seen." For Luther, such confidence and conviction lead to a radical devotion, the "losing"—or offering—of one's life (cf. Mark 8:35).

Faith as trust is complemented and explained by faith as belief: a set of theological propositions arrived at through the use of reason and logic. Theological belief is intentionally more impersonal, objective, and analytical. It explains the experience of trust.

The Jewish existentialist **Martin Buber** wrote in *Two Types of Faith* that belief is objectively "acknowledging a thing to be true," and the other type of faith is "a contact of my whole being with one I can trust."

Belief is knowledge about God. Trust is knowing God firsthand, made possible through prayerful **receptivity** and allowing God to live in us and work through us. Both knowledge and knowing are necessary, and each complements the other. Otherwise trust can be mindless and irrational, and belief can be empty and irrelevant.

Fideism is faith that not only states "God can do anything!" but limits God's work to the seemingly miraculous, outside the realm of human wisdom and aptitude, rather than through the guidance of the **Holy Spirit** in and through human sensitivity, training, and expertise. Fideism requires that God act upon nature from outside rather than from inside and through creation. Thus it expects God to move without human involvement or cooperation and misses the pervasively miraculous in ordinary life.

Rationalism is the opposite of fideism. It depends upon reason alone and says that nothing can be believed that cannot be logically proven. It appropriates the criteria of science in an unsuitable manner by demanding that the realm of the divine be measurable, definable, and even repeatable. Failing to deal with meaning and purpose, which are basic to faith, rationalism argues that God is only an idea created by the human brain: Human beings create God; there is no God whom reason can prove, who creates human beings.

Our faith may reside in an almighty and transcendent God who is wiser and greater than anything created. Therefore we can pray to and depend upon such a God. Our faith may also be in a God who, as Jesus said (John 4:24) is Spirit, the Holy Spirit present around us and received within us. Christian faith holds that both are true. However, if we emphasize only the first of these concepts, God may well be seen as acting without us or manipulating both history and us, causing everything that happens. This understanding of **providence** implicates God as the author of evil as well as good. On the other hand, if we recognize only an immanent God within, we may become our own god, self-sufficient, not needing the presence of anything greater in life. Yet in dependence upon both relationships, knowing and experiencing God in both ways, God's omnipotence and transcendence can be revealed within history by the Holy Spirit working in and through human beings.

In addition to Buber's book mentioned above, see *Faith, the Yes of the Heart* by Grace Adolphsen Brame. GAB

FAMILY SPIRITUALITY. The dynamics of **spiritual formation** within the family group. Because human babies are born without the instincts or strength of other animals, they depend on others, particularly family, for survival. To be human is to be both dependent and interdependent. We require healthy family dynamics throughout our long childhood to produce healthy adults. Initially when we think of family spirituality, we think of teaching children to say grace at meals, reading Bible stories to them at night, and going to church as a family. Books such as *Teaching Your Child How to Pray* (Rick Osborne), *Family, the Forming Center* (Marjorie J. Thompson), and *Raising Kids God's Way* (Kathi Hudson) are helpful resources, but family spirituality is more multifaceted than this. Family spirituality extends beyond the child-parent stage to the whole system of family relationships that spans generations (for an introduction to family systems theory, see John E. Bradshaw, *The Family*).

Family spirituality has both intentional and unintentional dynamics. The resources above focus on the intentional dynamics—what parents and the extended family choose to pass on to the child by reinforcing values, a sense of purpose, feelings of rootedness or a place in the world, a belief system, and identity formation. Parents express these by establishing a style of life and family rituals that reflect their core values. For example, the ritual of giving a weekly allowance is the opportunity to teach core values of tithing, saving, and spending that shape the child's and the family's relationship with material possessions and responsibility to others. Spiritual **dispositions** such as simplicity and justice could be reinforced each week in this simple, recurring ritual. See *Parents' Guide to the Spiritual Growth of Children* (J. Trent, Rick Osborne, Kurt Bruner) for practical ways to teach core values. Also see www.heritagebuilders.com for ideas and resources for intentional value-laden structures and observances for parent-child spiritual formation.

Christian family spirituality also has unintentional dynamics that shape its members. These flow from how family members respond to life situations, move through successive crises, and incarnate their relationship with God in a communal way. For example, a woman who is married to an alcoholic and has many children can face each successive crisis and abject poverty in a way that reinforces a sense of victimization in herself and the children. Or through her honesty, creativity, **humor**, and **faith** she can seek solutions for each crisis that pass on to her children a resilience, humor, and creative persistence that allow them, as individual persons and as a family, to transcend the particular pathology present in the family and their social situation. This aspect of spirituality is a way of being present to life that forms communal dispositions, character, and identity and that affirms the human spirit's possibility to become more than its particular dysfunction.

When this way of being present to life is distinctively Christian, the family's life together is patterned on the life of Jesus. Living in the light of Christ shapes how we interpret our lives, relate to one another, and engage the world in our everyday activities. The family lives out the reign of God in everyday routines and extraordinary times. This aspect of family spirituality continues long after the parent-childhood stage is over. The Greeks held that education of the young is the foundation on which *politike*—the art of enabling a shared life—rests. Family spirituality is actually the foundation of *politike*. When this spirituality is distinctively Christian, it is also a means of grace that fills ongoing relationships and enables the realization of human potential throughout life and from generation to generation. CIZ

FASTING. Abstinence from food or drink or both for a spiritual purpose and for a set period of time. Many religious groups and cultures practice fasting. For Christians fasting is a spiritual **discipline**. There are several different types of fasts: partial, total, and absolute. A partial fast is abstaining from selected food or drink as Daniel and his companions abstained from bread, meat, and wine to eat only vegetables and water for three weeks (Dan. 1:12 ff.). Many Christians practice partial fasts during the season of Lent (with the exception of Sundays). The **desert fathers and mothers** engaged in long partial fasts, eating bread and water only. Total fasts are abstinence from all food and drinking only water, as when Jesus fasted for forty days in the wilderness (Matt. 4:2). Absolute fasts are usually very short periods, such as Esther's three-day fast (Esther 4:16). Often a total fast may run from sunrise to sunset or for a full day (sunset to sunset), as on the Day of Atonement (Lev. 23:27-32).

Fasting is generally an individual spiritual discipline, but there are many scriptural accounts of communal fasts called in times of war, drought, sickness, national mourning, or commemoration of a calamity. Fasting as a sign of **penitence** is often connected in the scriptures with putting on sackcloth and ashes. This bodily form of prayer says, "I am penitent and humble myself. Do not afflict me, but restore me and forgive me." It may also confirm dependence upon God, affirming that God is the source of sustenance beyond food. Therefore, fasting is closely connected to the discipline of **mortification**. However, Jesus teaches (Matt. 6:16-18) that one should not make a show of being afflicted during the time of fasting. As a general rule, fasting is a spiritual discipline that requires regular, systematic practice to experience its spiritual benefits. Today practitioners usually combine it with **prayer** and service. Early Methodists connected fasting with a time of prayer and giving to the poor what would have been spent on food.

For more information, see the chapter on fasting in Richard J. Foster's *Celebration of Discipline: The Path to Spiritual Growth.* CIZ

FEMINIST SPIRITUALITY. Spirituality reflective of the diverse concerns of women worldwide while considering the unique spirituality of individual women. On one side of the definition are feminist concerns, which for many Christian women return the church to a table of gender equality that Jesus initiated. On the other side is an emphasis on Christian spirituality, the way that women experience communion with God. For Christian feminists, this means a reexamination of the church's use of exclusively male imagery for the divine and its heavy emphasis on male religious experience. In the 1960s women in general examined the societal impact of patriarchy. In the mid-1970s theologians like **Rosemary Radford Ruether** and others began to expose the detrimental aspects of centuries of male domination in Christianity. Biblical scholars like Phyllis Trible and Elisabeth Schüssler Fiorenza uncovered the male bias in scripture, such as the omission of female disciples and church leaders from the Gospel narratives.

Contemporary students of spirituality also explored the writings of medieval women mystics like **Julian of Norwich**, **Teresa of Ávila,** and **Mechthild of Magdeburg** to find feminine insights about God and religious experience. Although women's mission and prayer groups had long histories of significant influence in the church, new spirituality groups for women began to emerge in the 1980s, providing space for women to share as women their experiences of God's presence. Still active, these spirituality circles often include personal sharing, intentional group ritual, as well as prayer using feminine images for the divine. Christian feminists, both women and men, have also sought to empower women for their growing leadership in the church. Women's ordination to pastoral ministry, while still disallowed by the Roman Catholic Church, has finally been acknowledged in most Protestant denominations. Spiritual life resources like *The Feminine Face of God: The Unfolding of the Sacred in Women* by Sherry Ruth Anderson and Patricia Hopkins and *Swallow's Nest: A Feminine Reading of the Psalms* by Marciene Vroon Rienstra have now become available. A contemporary spiritual author like Sue Monk Kidd, in *The Dance of the Dissident*

Daughter: A Woman's Journey from Christian Tradition to the Sacred Feminine, has shared a personal struggle to find a wholeness of gender in the Christian experience.

As Christian feminist philosopher Grace Jantzen notes, the early Christian dichotomy of **spirit** and **body** placed women on the bottom of an unholy dualism, with Christian salvation understood as freeing the **soul** from the prison of the body, as well as from the burden of earthly existence. In contrast, contemporary feminists reaffirm the body as a location of spiritual formation, as well as the earth as being treasured by God. Refusing to be reduced to the either/or choice of a Greek-inspired dualism, Christian feminists have created new **imagery** to describe their sense of the interconnectedness of all things, using terms like *integration, bonding, weaving,* and *holism.* Some feminists are also concerned that Christian devotion has often been "over-spiritualized" to the neglect of biblical mandates for social justice. They point out that the majority of women throughout the world are abused, underpaid, and deprived of opportunity while affluent Christians seek inner fulfillment. To answer this concern, advocates of feminist spirituality respond that God's healing of individuals is crucial to Christ's transformative power at work in the world. Thus, the inner life of prayer and devotion must undergird the practical, outward journey toward a just and peaceful society for both genders.

Feminists contend that feminine images for God must be renewed for the church. For example, the Hebrew word for divine compassion, *rachum,* is related to *rechem,* the word for womb, and may be translated as "womb-love." The writings of **Julian of Norwich** contain images of Jesus as Mother, the second member of the Trinity, who shares her children's suffering from sin and physical deprivation. Scholars have also reminded us that Lady Wisdom, a metaphor in both testaments, offers a rich feminine image for the divine. SAF

FÉNELON, FRANÇOIS DE SALIGNAC DE LA MOTHE (1651–1715), French bishop and spiritual writer. Fénelon was prominent in the court of Louis XIV. He was appointed archbishop of Cambrai in 1695. He had become acquainted with Madame **Guyon** and her **Quietist** belief in the pure **contemplation** of God based on divine omnipresence and a mystical **union** with God, in whose hands the **soul** is entirely passive. At first apprehensive, Fénelon came to believe that the teachings were safely within the Catholic tradition. Rome, however, condemned them as dangerous; Fénelon was denounced and restricted to his diocese. Nevertheless he had wide personal influence through his vast correspondence.

Fénelon is best known for *Christian Perfection,* forty-one essays to be read devotionally. From them we get a deeper sense of God's presence, understanding that Christian perfection requires giving ourselves to God with our whole heart. God is loved for God's self alone, and no step is taken without God. Many of the chapters are taken from spiritual letters to prominent persons for whom Fénelon served as spiritual guide.

In his *Spiritual Letters to Women,* Fénelon's humanness and saintliness permeate all 138 letters. While a few apply only to his times, most contain truths for people of all ages to consider seriously. *Let Go* is also a series of letters of encouragement to struggling Christians. Fénelon addressed them to persons in the court of Louis XIV who sought to live spiritual lives amidst an immoral court life. He advises them to let go of selfish and sinful life in order to become the new creation God meant them to be. EWF

FERRÉ, NELS FREDERIK SOLOMON (1908–71), Swedish-American theologian, naturalized an American in 1931. Educated at Boston University and Harvard, Ferré was ordained a Congregational minister in 1934 and taught and lectured at many theological schools and colleges in the United States and beyond. He was a prolific writer, and his *Strengthening the Spiritual Life* was translated into Urdu, Hindi, Spanish, and Chinese. *The Universal Word: A Theology for a Universal Faith* culminated his lifework. Ferré emphasized **spirit**, **love**, and personal life as ultimate categories in Christian theology. God relates to the world through **nature**. Human and divine love are transcendent; God's word for humankind is universal. Love (God's self) is eternal, operative, ceaselessly creative, and integrative; reigning *with*, not *over*, the world. Each person or group best realizes selfhood in serving the larger whole, which is best done by becoming one's true (God-intended) self. Ferré saw Jesus as "normative," not God's *only* disclosure. LSP

FINNEY, CHARLES GRANDISON (1792–1875), American revival preacher. Finney was born in Warren, Connecticut, but his family moved to Oneida County, New York, when he was two. Growing up in Oneida County, he had little access to school, religion, or books. He interned in a law office and was admitted to the bar in 1818. On October 10, 1821, he experienced a dramatic religious **conversion** and soon after became a major revivalist in the Second Great Awakening. Finney challenged the Calvinist doctrine of passive salvation and believed that salvation came only through an active acceptance of God's invitation to **grace**. In 1835 he became a professor of theology at Oberlin College, where he also served as its second president (1851–65). He continued his evangelistic tours until his death, twice visiting England. His life and his revivals were steeped in prayer.

For more about Finney's revivals, see his *Memoirs*; for more about his life, see *The Conversion of Charles Grandison Finney* by Keith J. Hardman. DDW

FIRE. A key symbol in the lexicon of mystical spirituality. The Bible is filled with images of fire, symbolizing the presence of God. Perhaps the most famous is the angel who speaks to Moses from the burning bush, which is not consumed by the flames (Exod. 3:2). When Adam and Eve are expelled from the garden of Eden, God places a cherub with a flaming sword to bar their way from returning to the tree of life (Gen. 3:24). In Exodus 24:17 the appearance of God on Mount Sinai is described as a "devouring fire." Isaiah speaks of the seraphim (Hebrew for "burning ones"), angels of love, light, and fire who surround the throne of God unceasingly intoning "Holy, holy, holy" (6:2-3). Jeremiah compares the word of God to a fire in his bones that he cannot hold in (20:9). In the New Testament on the day of Pentecost, "divided tongues, as of fire, appeared among them" (Acts 2:3) to signify the presence of the **Holy Spirit**.

In the literature of **mysticism**, fire is both a source of refinement—the flames that burn away the baser elements of our being—and the source of a burning desire for oneness with Christ. **Bernard** gives us the famous metaphor of the self, purged in the flames like an iron pulled from the fire and glowing red-hot; it is neither the iron nor the fire, but a mystical combination of the two. **Catherine of Genoa** speaks of the purging fire of love burning away the rust of sin. The English mystic **Richard Rolle** writes of an elemental fire that burns in the soul and sets it aflame with a desire for Christ. **John of the Cross** gives us *The Living Flame of Love*, which embodies both anguish and delight. It purifies the soul to a state of perfect self-knowledge, then sets it aglow with an **ecstatic** spiritual fire and light. The fire and the light become two ways to experience the divine reality. SFP

FORGIVENESS. A gracious pardoning of transgression. "Forgive us our sins, as we forgive those who sin against us" is perhaps the clearest meaning of the **Lord's Prayer**. Jesus explains, "If you do not forgive others, neither will your Father forgive your trespasses" (Matt. 6:15). By choosing how we treat others, we choose how God will treat us. "Just as you did it to one of the least of these who are members of my family, you did it to me" (Matt. 25:40). Our words and actions toward others are words and actions toward God.

This reciprocity is not divine retribution,

but a natural result of the way relationships operate. Our relationships with God and others are intertwined. It is impossible, says 1 John 4:20-21, to say we love God if we hate someone. Why? Because our antagonism builds a wall around our heart, the same heart that we pray God will enter. God can't get through. The wall built to protect us from our neighbor shuts out God as well.

Being walled off from God is *hell*, a word whose roots mean "hidden, covered, or concealed." In an effort to protect ourselves, we build our own prisons. Life becomes small. When, for instance, we focus on the painful past, there is no hope for the future.

We do not want to forgive because our adversary has put us in touch with our own powerlessness, and a decision not to forgive gives us a feeling of power, of superiority. We would rather win an argument than transform a relationship. Winning seems to affirm us by confirming our strength.

We need a means to imagine a new way of feeling toward others, a way that will allow us to progress in the process of forgiveness. Christ forgave those who murdered him while they were killing him, because he loved and understood them so well. But we need to allow ourselves time to grow, to change, to understand, to see our adversary in new ways.

We can begin by being honest and venting anger in God's presence, offering to God our pain and helplessness, and praying for a desire to forgive. In meditative, **receptive** prayer, we can visualize ourselves with our adversary in the presence of Christ, asking to see with Christ's eyes the other's need, pain, and beauty. We can pray for the other's healing of spirit and for ours and affirm the transforming power of the One who created the world and recreates eternally. Drinking in God's grace that receives what we have asked for in prayer, we expect and look for results. We pray for the right time and place to approach the offender. Then we learn, as well as we can, to let go of what cannot be changed, as the **Serenity Prayer** suggests.

Self-forgiveness is the most difficult kind of all. It cannot happen until the inner judgment is recognized and released. Healing is a process that usually begins with repentance, a change of heart and of direction. It is accompanied by **confession** that unmasks and releases our hidden need. Healing services with the support of trusted others and healing of memories through guided visualization are enormous helps. In receptive prayer, we allow Christ to look into our hearts with us to show us patiently over time our treasure and our garbage, allowing Christ to wash us clean. There we can also learn to receive God's love through silence, through nature and music, and through the love of others. Without receiving, we cannot be healed. We can ask to be taught by our dreams, focusing not on loss but on what we have left and what we can do with it to bless others. We can be agents of forgiveness and hope and support others in seeing their own beauty. We forgive both ourselves and others by allowing God's love within our hearts, the love that says, "I know who you really are. I claim you as my own. And I affirm all that you can be."

For further reading, see *Receptive Prayer: A Christian Approach to Meditation* by Grace Adolphsen Brame and *Forgiveness, the Passionate Journey* by Flora Slosson Wuellner. GAB

FORMATION, SPIRITUAL. The dynamics of shaping the human **spirit** toward maturity and consonance. Spiritual formation can refer to two closely related processes. The first is a basic fact of life: as creatures we are constantly being formed by the world around us; and as creatures with a spirit capable of transcending our world, we can be aware of and take part in that formation. This process is studied in part by psychologists, sociologists, anthropologists, educators, and theologians. It is the primary focus of Formative Spirituality (more formally, the Science of Foundational Human Formation) as developed by **Adrian van Kaam**, whose basic assumptions guide the discussion below. The second process is the more deliberate attempt to form ourselves or allow ourselves to be formed within a particular spiritual tradition. We'll consider the second meaning after discussing the basic process.

At every moment of our lives we receive countless feelings, nudges, inspirations, suggestions, and commands that seek to direct our actions and attitudes. These *directives* can take many forms. Say you are in a bookstore and see a book about spiritual formation on the shelf. You want to learn more about **prayer** and think this book could help. You've read a review that recommended it. But as you reach for it, you remember an argument with your spouse about family finances. You hear the echo of your mother's voice: "Money doesn't grow on trees." Your stomach grumbles that it could use a hot pretzel more than a book. All of these directives play a part in deciding whether to buy the book. The weight you give to them may depend on your own past patterns of choosing, your **dispositions**. Some, probably most, of the weighing may not be fully conscious. But you must make a choice, and that choice will change you, even if only slightly, strengthening some directives and weakening others for the next time you must choose.

The ability to choose, not simply to be driven by external forces and internal feelings, is an essential part of what it means to be human. We can rise above the givens of our lives—that is, our human spirit makes us capable of **transcendence**. Even when our choices for action may be restricted by disease or captivity, we can choose our attitude toward these restrictions: fight them, resent them, accept them, or offer them to God as **suffering** on behalf of others. Furthermore, we can step back from the process, examine our choices, and reflect on both choice and process.

Looking at any one choice can tell us a lot about ourselves, our true priorities, and our strongest dispositions. In examining a choice, it helps to sort out directives by the various areas of our life from which they come. Van Kaam calls these the *spheres* of the *formation field*. One sphere is what we would usually call our selves—our body, mind, and spirit. These *intrapersonal* directives include our biological urges, our emotional impulses, our conscious plans and dreams, and the inspirations we may perceive as God's call to us. The *interpersonal* sphere includes all the directives we receive in one-on-one relationships, whether in person, through correspondence, or through books that seem to speak to us. The part of the world we know directly, our *situation*, is the third sphere, including directives we receive from groups we belong to, at our jobs, in our community. Beyond our situation is the *world* we know only indirectly, mediated through television, newspapers, etc. All of these spheres offer directives for every choice. And all of them are in turn grounded in the divine mystery that reaches out to us through our own deepest sense of who we are, through friends who speak God's word to us, through our churches and other groups, and even through the tragedies and triumphs we see on TV. As we become aware of these many sources of divine directives, we learn that all formation is spiritual formation.

Divine directives point to a goal, the re-forming and graced transforming of our lives to be more in tune with **the will of God**, God's call to us. Van Kaam calls this goal *consonance*, literally "sounding together," as when one string on a guitar vibrates because it is in tune with another that is being plucked. When our lives are consonant, we are in tune with ourselves, with God, with what is best in the world around us, what is **holy**. The Hebrew Bible's ideal of the kingdom of **peace** and the New Testament's call to unconditional **love** are other ways of describing the consonant life. Later Christian writers spoke of the **imitation of Christ** or of going on to **perfection**.

While it is possible to talk about directives separately or sorted by spheres, they are likely to be part of complex structures of interrelated directives that support one another and together create a more or less complete picture of ideal behavior. These structures are *formation traditions*. They offer a portrait of maturity that lifts up some dispositions as central **virtues** while belittling others as worthless. So, for example, Christianity emphasizes **faith**,

hope, love, **community**, and **compassion** while rejecting pride, individualism, greed, and vengefulness, labeling some of these as deadly **sins**. Some formation traditions, especially religious traditions, are vast and inclusive, offering guidance throughout life for many different types of people and situations. Other traditions—the Boy Scouts, the "company way," Alcoholics Anonymous, "how we've always done it in our family"—deal with limited areas of life and certain people.

Formation traditions teach their complex of directives, their way of life, through writings (sometimes regarded as sacred), indoctrination (whether through group teaching or personal mentoring), rituals, songs, paintings, stories, creedal or missional statements, and many other means. Large formation traditions may include subtraditions with their own special formation sources. Episcopalians, for instance, have the **Book of Common Prayer**, Methodists the hymns of **Charles Wesley**, and **Jesuits** the *Spiritual Exercises* of **Ignatius**. Monastic orders train novices in the particular dispositions of **poverty**, **chastity**, and **obedience**. All are part of the larger Christian formation tradition, although each holds up a different (or differently nuanced) ideal of the Christian life.

Most of us find ourselves aligned with several, often contradictory, formation traditions. Do we blast our enemies in accord with the rugged individualism exemplified by Dirty Harry, or do we love our enemies as Christ commands? When commitments conflict, do we go to a Lions Club meeting or to a church meeting or skip both to watch a football game? The answer shows that we have ranked our traditions, so that the directives of one tradition will outweigh those of another. Picture a pyramid of traditions, stacked according to the weight or priority we give them. Faced with a choice, we give greatest weight to our foundational tradition, turning to the next most cherished only if the first offers no clear guidance and so on up the pyramid. One way to view a **conversion** experience is to say that it reranks our traditions, giving us a new base.

For Christians, following Christ becomes more important than anything else. Other "converts" may see all of life in light of the **Twelve Step program** of Alcoholics Anonymous, analyze everything and everyone in light of Carl Jung's writings, or similarly exalt the directives of whatever tradition has gained their primary allegiance.

Formation happens by fits and starts, sometimes moving us for a while at least toward greater dissonance. Throughout our lives we can point to particular events that brought change. If we look closely, we'll find a consistent structure or plot to such events. We begin in stability with a basic pattern for our lives that represents a working compromise between conflicting directives that allows us to ignore the dissonance under the surface. (Van Kaam calls this working self a *current life form*—the shape our life takes for a while but not forever.) Then something happens to blow that compromise apart: a heart attack, for example, that causes us to reevaluate many priorities. Or it can be a tiny incident that highlights one small dissonance and causes the whole structure to collapse. As we look at ourselves, perhaps with the help of others, we come to new decisions, seek to form new habits, or cultivate other dispositions. Slowly we shape a new, slightly more consonant current life form. We can see this journey as a personal **exodus**, leaving the comfortable captivity of the old way to wander through a **desert** of confusion before reaching the land of promise.

The second, more limited, sense of spiritual formation can include all of the ways we seek either to grow toward greater consonance with a religious tradition or to form others within that tradition. Christian spiritual formation is the conscious effort to mold oneself or others in the traditions of Christian **spirituality**. Thus, Christian formation can begin with **family spirituality** and memorization of simple **verbal prayers**. Sunday school classes and **worship** services continue formation through reading and studying **scripture**; singing **hymns**; receiving the sacraments of baptism and **Holy Communion**; and joining or hearing prayers of **adoration, confession, thanksgiving, petition,** and **intercession**.

The classic spiritual **disciplines** are the means to promote such formation. Those who decide to deepen their spiritual life may join prayer groups or **covenant groups** where they can practice the disciplines with others. They may turn to spiritual **reading** of classic works on prayer and Christian living or to the more specialized prayerful reading called *lectio divina*. Spiritual formation can also include looking at our lives specifically to try to hear God's call and respond to it in obedience. **Examen** and keeping a spiritual **journal** are important helps in such self-examination. People can get help in processing this self-study by talking with a soul **friend** or entering into a more formal **spiritual direction** relationship.

The process of spiritual formation can differ widely from person to person, due to **personality**, personal history, and the particular formation tradition(s) embraced. The only certainties are that our spirits will continue to be formed (or de-formed) throughout our lives and that God will continue to call us into deeper, more consonant relationships with God, our truest selves, and the people and world around us. KRB

FOSDICK, HARRY EMERSON (1878–1969), American Baptist preacher. Born in Buffalo, New York, educated at Colgate University and Union Theological Seminary, and ordained into the Baptist ministry, he came to national prominence in 1922 when he preached the famous sermon "Shall the Fundamentalists Win?" The most prominent voice for the liberal theological position in the bitter fundamentalist/modernist debate, he was also an outspoken champion of **peace** in the midst of war, attempted to reconcile science and religion, and provided prophetic moral leadership in times of national crisis. In 1925 he was called to Park Avenue Baptist Church (New York) and later Riverside Church, where his person-centered ministry emphasized spiritual growth and social consciousness.

Fosdick articulated this Christian personalism most fully in the classic Meaning series on *Prayer* (1915), *Faith* (1917), and *Service* (1920), and in his autobiographical portrait, *The Living of These Days* (1956). See also the biography *Harry Emerson Fosdick: Preacher, Pastor, Prophet* by Robert M. Miller. PWC

FOSTER, RICHARD J. (b. 1942), Quaker pastor, teacher, author, and founder of Renovaré. Foster was born in Albuquerque, New Mexico, and began his ministry as a pastor in various church settings. He started his academic career at George Fox College, then earned a doctorate of pastoral theology at Fuller Theological Seminary with majors in biblical studies and social ethics. Foster taught biblical studies, theology, and **spiritual formation** at **George Fox** College, Friends University, and Azusa Pacific University.

Foster burst onto the American church scene in 1978 with *Celebration of Discipline*. This book became a significant part of adult religious education curriculum refocusing Christians on the classical spiritual disciplines of the church. His next book, *Freedom of Simplicity*, best reveals the heart of Foster's own spiritual experience and ethic. He uses a theme-tracing method to illustrate the principles and practice of the spiritual **discipline** of simplicity through biblical and historical examples and its implications for the transformation of society. Since the publication of these works, Foster has published dozens of books, tapes, films, and over sixty articles in the area of **spirituality** and spiritual formation. He is a modern-day prophet working to renew the church, a calling clearly seen in all his publications. To that end, he also founded Renovaré, a movement that seeks to use spiritual formation traditions and the historical disciplines of the church to bring about renewal. The heart of Renovaré is the formation of **covenant groups** for spiritual formation emphasizing common disciplines and **examen**. A more recent work *Prayer: Finding the Heart's True Home* shows Foster's belief that **prayer** is the most fundamental spiritual discipline. CIZ

FOUCAULD, CHARLES EUGÈNE DE
(1858–1916), active contemplative, ascetic. Born into an aristocratic family in Strasbourg, France, Charles was an indifferent student who was prone to getting into trouble. He tried to make the army his career but was discharged in 1881 for scandalous behavior. He had developed a fondness for North Africa during his stint in the military, and he returned to Morocco with the French Geographical Society. His observation of Muslim piety led him to a dramatic revival of his own Roman Catholic faith. A pilgrimage to the Holy Land had an additional powerful influence on his entire life.

Foucauld joined the **Trappists** and spent several years in a monastery in Syria. But the fit was not exactly right. He had received the insight that Christ had been a hard-working carpenter, a poor laborer. After several years in Nazareth, imitating Christ as a servant at the convent of Poor Clares, he realized that "Nazareth" could be anywhere and servanthood could mean many things.

Foucauld was ordained in 1901 and went back to North Africa, to the Algerian oasis Beni-Abbes. He intended to found a new order, the Little Brothers of Jesus, devoted to living among the poor in a spirit of service and solidarity. He spent fifteen years in the desert. He eventually moved from Beni-Abbes to a more remote village Tamanrasset, where Tuareg rebels killed him.

Foucauld's life might appear to have been a noble, or even foolish, failure. The community he prepared for, including composing his order's constitution, never materialized in his lifetime. He was murdered alone in a foreign, barely habitable land. However, in 1933 Rene Voillaume and four companions left France to live in the Sahara Desert. They became the core of the Little Brothers of Jesus and were joined a few years later by the Little Sisters of Jesus. Both groups have spread throughout the world, forming small communities in the midst of the poor and the outcast. The most famous member of this movement is the lay brother **Carlo Carretto**. ww

FOX, GEORGE
(1624–91), founder of the Society of Friends (**Quakers**). Born at Fenny Drayton in Leicestershire, England, Fox grew up as an unusually serious child. His parents, a weaver dubbed "righteous Christer" and Mary Lago, set a high standard of Puritan inward piety and outward good demeanor. Where the Puritans, like their mentor **John Calvin**, emphasized total depravity of human nature, Fox was what **William James** called "a once-born soul." Suffering bouts of severe depression as the Civil War raged, in 1643 he experienced a shock when a cousin and another nominal Christian taunted him at a fair to drink with them. Soon thereafter, he broke off all ties with family and friends and spent the next several years seeking enlightenment. Convinced that preaching in the Church of England could not speak to his condition, in 1646 he experienced a flash of revelation: "There is one, even Christ Jesus, that can speak to thy condition" (*Journal*, 11). Thereafter he emphasized dependence on the inner light, which to him meant both the living Christ and the **Holy Spirit**, to guide action.

Fox had unusual gifts as a leader and organizer. When he started preaching in 1647, his message based on inward personal piety and outward action drew a substantial following but also stern opposition from leaders of the Church of England. Between 1649 and 1660 he suffered eight imprisonments. In 1652 Fox's campaign got a boost when he won over the family of Judge Thomas Fell, Vice-Chancellor of the Duchy of Lancaster, and made Swarthmore Hall, their home, his headquarters. In 1669 Fox married Fell's widow, Mary. He undertook frequent missionary journeys—to Ireland (1669), the West Indies and North America (1671–72), and Holland (1677, 1684). He died January 13, 1691. Thomas Ellswood edited and published his *Journal* posthumously.

Influenced by earlier German and Dutch mystics, Fox believed strongly in human potential. The "seed of God" in human beings enables them actually to live righteous and holy lives. "That of God" is in everyone. Fox knew the Bible almost by heart, and it influenced him deeply; but he subordinated the written word to the living Word. He was convinced that his knowledge of God and Christ came not from scriptures "but by revelation." In his view salvation meant to live a victorious life, the life God intended for Adam. As a profound mystical "opening" in 1647 confirmed, God's infinite **love**, "an infinite ocean of light and love," far surpasses the "ocean of darkness and death" (*Journal*, 19). Fox saw the key to spiritual growth in attention to the "light within," which silent meetings could foster. Inspiration for this approach probably came from "seekers" in northern counties of Yorkshire, Lancashire, and Westmoreland drawn to Fox's preaching in 1651. They discounted preaching and public prayer and exalted silence over words. The silent meeting for worship became a central feature of the Society of Friends.

For further reading, see *The Journal of George Fox*, the biography *George Fox: Seeker and Friend* by Rufus M. Jones, and Douglas Gwyn's *Apocalypse of the Word.* EGH

FOX, MATTHEW (b. 1940). Christian mystic and educator. After a childhood that included a bout with polio, Fox joined the Dominicans, being ordained in 1967.

Fox's studies introduced him to a Christian tradition of creation-centered spirituality. Years later his interest in this field, combined with an unorthodox enthusiasm for interfaith dialogue, led the Vatican to have him silenced for a year, then dismissed from the Dominican Order. In 1994 he joined the Episcopal Church and was ordained a priest in what he called "a post-denominational move."

Calling creation spirituality "the oldest tradition in the Bible," Fox finds this field reaching its peak between the twelfth and fifteenth centuries, citing as exemplars **Hildegard of Bingen** (whom Fox was the first to translate into English), **Thomas Aquinas**, **Meister Eckhart**, and **Nicholas of Cusa**.

Fox's books include *Whee! We Wee All the Way Home, Original Blessing, Creation Spiritual-*

ity, The Coming of the Cosmic Christ, and *The Reinvention of Work.* WW

FRANCIS DE SALES (1567–1622), bishop of Geneva, leader of the Catholic Reformation, cofounder (with **Jane de Chantal**) of the Visitation Order, and influential spiritual writer. Francis was born of an aristocratic Savoyard family at a time of reform and spiritual renewal within the Catholic Church. His early education was in the Christian humanist tradition of the **Jesuits**. At the University of Padua he studied law at his father's request and theology on his own initiative. Ordained in 1593, he was shortly made associate to the bishop of Geneva and in 1602 succeeded to his predecessor's post. Since the Protestant city of Geneva did not allow Catholic presence, Bishop de Sales resided in the nearby town of Annecy. He actively evangelized his Calvinist opponents, especially through gentle persuasion. He engaged in vigorous reform of religious institutions and sought to revitalize faith among all in his diocese.

Francis de Sales believed that the "devout life" was open to all, not only monks and priests. God, he felt, raised up persons in all walks of life to be leaven in the loaf of a revitalized church. Thus he promoted many works of spiritual renewal, including **spiritual direction**, preaching (his sermons were said to speak "heart to heart") and writing. His best-known book *Introduction to the Devout Life* was based on the letters of direction he wrote to a woman who wished to live a Christian life in the midst of her husband's duties with the French court. A practical summary of the means by which one cultivates a living **faith** in the midst of the busy demands of family and work, the *Introduction* was an overnight success and has remained a staple of devotional literature to the present day.

Francis's other major work *Treatise on the Love of God* was written for those mature in the spiritual life and lays out the theological foundations of the "Salesian" spiritual vision. Optimistic about the **love** of God and the capacity of humans to respond to that love, Salesian spirituality can be summed up in the motto: "Live Jesus." Devout human hearts, joined together in true friendship and drawn by the love of God, encourage one another to live the little virtues of gentleness and **humility** that characterize the heart of Jesus (Matt. 11:28 ff.) and thus allow Jesus to live in their hearts. He cofounded The Congregation (later Order) of the Blessed Virgin Mary (Visitation Order or **Visitandines**) with Jane de Chantal in 1610 as a living expression of this motto practiced in community among women. Francis de Sales was canonized in 1665 and declared a **Doctor of the Church** (an authoritative teacher) in 1877.

The correspondence between the two is collected in *Francis de Sales, Jane de Chantal: Letters of Spiritual Direction*, translated by Peronne Marie Thibert and edited by Wendy M. Wright and Joseph F. Power. WMW

FRANCIS OF ASSISI (ca. 1181–1226). Arguably the most popular of all the Christian saints, Francis, founder of the Franciscan Order, is perhaps best known neither for his writings nor for his deeds but for his love of **nature**. His ability to see God's presence in all aspects of creation, including the sun and the moon as well as in plants and animals, has made it common to picture Saint Francis with a bird on his hand or shoulder.

Francis was born in Assisi in 1181 or 1182. Part of his mystique lay in the radical nature of his **conversion** experience. Born into a wealthy merchant family, Francis was a popular, fun-loving, and romantic youth. Upon returning to Assisi after spending time as a prisoner of war in the rival village of Perugia, Francis felt a strong but imprecise call to dedicate his life to God. This calling was confirmed by two experiences: hearing the voice of Christ coming from the cross in an abandoned sanctuary instructing him to rebuild the church, and encountering a leper whom he saw as Christ. These experiences prompted him to repudiate a military career and almost certain success in his father's business by publicly renouncing his father's worldly values.

Francis vowed to live in the simplicity of Christ's footsteps, begging for food, serving the poor, and dedicating his life to rebuilding Christ's church. Others soon joined him and after writing a short **rule** he was able to convince Pope Innocent III to recognize his group as a religious order. Their rule, based on scripture, emphasized **poverty**, simplicity, and service, with poverty at its center. A women's order, led by **Clare of Assisi**, and a Third Order as a renewal movement for laity soon followed. During a retreat at La Verna in 1224, Francis received **stigmata**, the first such case recorded. He swore his closest followers to secrecy until his death two years later. He was canonized in 1228, just two years after his death.

The best known of Francis's writings is probably his "Canticle of Brother Sun," which has been popularized in hymns such as "All Creatures of Our God and King." It is a classic example of kataphatic spirituality, which moves toward the created world and uses the five senses to discover and experience God (the **positive way**).

One powerful way Francis has affected Christian spirituality is not even associated with him by many. At Christmas in 1223 in the village of Greccio, he had the birth of Christ enacted in a barn, thus introducing the visual portrayal of the Nativity scene into the Christian tradition.

All known writings of Francis are contained in *Francis and Clare: The Complete Works*, translated by Regis J. Armstrong and Ignatius C. Brady. The story of his life has been told many times, including *The Little Flowers of St. Francis of Assisi*, as well as biographies by **G. K. Chesterton**, Omer Englebert, and Adrian House. **Nikos Kazantzakis** wrote a novel (*Saint Francis of Assisi*) about Francis and Clare. JWK

FRANCISCANS. Members of the Order of Friars Minor, founded by **Francis of Assisi**; the Poor Clares, founded by **Clare of Assisi**; or various Third Orders for laity. Franciscan writers include **Bonaventure**, **Jacopone da Todi**, **Angela of Foligno**, and **Francisco de Osuna**.

FRIENDSHIP. The relationship that results between persons who mentor, support, challenge, and correct each other. We do not live the Christian life alone. We are surrounded by a cloud of witnesses (Heb. 12) who strengthen and encourage us in the faith. We are a part of the **body of Christ**, the church (1 Cor. 12–14), which claims and uses our gifts. Yet the Christian life is often supported by companions who give us more individual attention and care.

The Bible records the friendship of David and Jonathan (1 Sam. 18); and in the Gospel of John, Jesus says, "I do not call you servants any longer…but I have called you friends" (15:15). Ecclesiastes 4:9-10 summarizes the importance of friendship: "Two are better than one, because they have a good reward for their toil. For if they fall, one will lift up the other; but woe to one who is alone and falls and does not have another to help."

Friendship is a complex topic both in Christian thought and practice. Friendship (*philia*) implies a relationship that is preferential and exclusive; **love** (*agape*) expresses a relationship that is without qualification and is inclusive. Friendships are mutual and reciprocal; love is sometimes given without response. Friendships can be rewarding and damaging, nurturing and frightening. Friendships lead us into relationships of intimacy with one another, and therein lie both promise and peril.

Christian friendship is an experience of support, accountability, acceptance, safety, and love. When these conditions are present, spiritual growth and transformation become possible. For this reason many use spiritual friendship as a more appropriate term for **spiritual direction**. The Irish term *anamchara* means "soul friend" and refers to the wisdom of a spiritual mentor.

In a culture of individualism, friendship can be an important corrective as we seek to grow in faith. Given the human temptation for self-deception, someone who befriends us with honesty can be a wonderful gift of God.

Gilbert Meilaender has argued that our culture has devalued friendship as it has elevated work as a means to fulfillment. He reminds us of the Greek tradition that saw work as a form of service to the common good and friendship as a means of self-fulfillment. As we invest the time and energy required to sustain friendships, we will discover them to be important instruments of spiritual growth.

For further reading, see C. S. Lewis, *The Four Loves*, and Gilbert C. Meilaender, *Friendship: A Study in Theological Ethics*. KHC

FRUIT OF THE SPIRIT. Described in Galatians 5:22-23 as **love**, joy, **peace**, patience, kindness, generosity, faithfulness, gentleness, and self-control. These **dispositions** are listed by the apostle Paul as an alternative to the "works of the flesh" (Gal. 5:19-21), within a larger passage about the obligation of the Christian to use freedom from the law as a means of service and love.

The fruit of the Spirit is not works or deeds that we accomplish. Instead, the fruit (*karpos*) is a collection of virtues that God cultivates within us as we mature in the Christian life. While some commentaries distinguish the fruit of the Spirit from the **gifts of the Spirit** (1 Cor. 12–14), they have many similarities: the greatest spiritual gift is **love** (1 Cor. 13:13), and the first fruit of the Spirit is love (Gal. 5:22).

The fruit of the Spirit is present in the life of a Christian, but it must always be understood as a gift to the community. God places the fruit of the Spirit within the Christian community. In the same way that the gifts of the Spirit help us to describe the body of Christ, the fruit of the Spirit assists us in understanding how God transforms the church apart from our human efforts. Ultimately, the individual and the community reflect the nature of God as these virtues are cultivated.

For further reading, see *Life on the Vine: Cultivating the Fruit of the Spirit in Christian Community* by Philip D. Kenneson. KHC

G

GERSON, JEAN CHARLIER DE (1363–1429), French theologian and chancellor of the University of Paris. Gerson was known as a church reformer, preacher, teacher, and writer on **contemplation**. He combined contemplation with action in his efforts at church reform during the Western schism, which forced his exile. His writings were popular during and after his lifetime.

Gerson's **mysticism** is distinguished by what he termed experiential knowledge of God through love, which does not require theoretical learning but is within everyone's grasp. His teaching on mystical theology was for the purpose of finding a better way to know God in this life. He praised the contemplative life and wrote *The Mountain of Contemplation* for his sisters to describe a method of contemplation that was accessible to anyone regardless of the level of education. He was determined to counter the false mysticism of his day, characterized by superstitious beliefs and practices. Gerson did not believe that the **negative way** of eliminating all positive descriptions of God was the only way to find God. Instead, he professed that there could be a positive **experience** of striving for and finding God. He wrote more than sixty works on the spiritual life.

Gerson had a special interest in the young and emphasized the importance of guiding them. He devoted the last years of his life to the pedagogy of children. He wrote *The ABCs for Ordinary Folk*, which contained lists of Christian beliefs, and *On Bringing Youth to Christ*. He emphasized the role of **confession** in leading young people to Christ and professed that confession has a prominent place in the spiritual life of the adult as well. **Penitence** and confession, in Gerson's thought, were ways to attain knowledge of God.

For more on Gerson's life and writings, see *Jean Gerson: Early Works*, translated by Brian Patrick McGuire. SEW

GERTRUDE OF HELFTA (1256–1301), also known as "Gertrude the Great," mystical writer. Gertrude entered the women's community of Helfta (near Saxony, Germany) as a five-year-old. The convent was governed by Abbess Gertrude of Hackeborn, who fostered devotion to God, learning, and the visionary life of the women under her care. Young Gertrude became well-versed in Latin, liturgy, and Cistercian theology. In 1281 she had a mystical experience concerning **Holy Communion** that overflowed into writing. Her account became a portion of *Legatus* (*Herald*), a writing that offers a classic expression of the devotion to the **Sacred Heart** of Jesus. Gertrude's images of Christ's heart are rich and varied: at times Gertrude describes the Sacred Heart as a furnace transforming her soul; at other times, a garden full of delight for the sincere seeker. She also connects Christ's heart to images of flowing water, honey, and blood—torrents of grace that bear the mystic into ecstatic **communion** with God. In one of her visions of **union**, Gertrude even sees herself as bodily held within Christ's heart.

Spiritual Exercises (available in translation by Gertrud Jaron Lewis and Jack Lewis) is Gertrude's other work, which describes the deepening of the spiritual life through the metaphors of **monastic** life: rebirth, **conversion**, dedication of the self, following Christ, mystical union, the gratitude and joy of that life, and the new life to be found after death. While the analogy describes the monastic journey, the book remains accessible to the lay reader, offering beautiful images for God and spiritual growth. Gertrude writes of the "earthquake of her heart" and God's living love as a spring day that never ends. Her writings express self-confidence in her feminine spirituality. In fact, she chooses the feminine ending to almost all of her Latin names for God. In some places she also transforms scriptural images to fit her gender, such as the "prodigal daughter." Gertrude's writings offer a wealth of spiritual **imagery** to contemporary women and men. SAF

GIFTS OF THE SPIRIT. Standing alongside the **fruit of the Spirit**, those qualities that comprise the basics of the Spirit-filled life. Two lists of gifts appear in the New Testament: Romans 12:6-8 and 1 Corinthians 12:8-10. Scholars differ as to whether these lists are comprehensive or illustrative. Most scholars tend toward a "comprehensive" view, given that the New Testament does not provide criteria for determining what else might be a gift of the Spirit. When we remember that a single gift may be exercised in different ways with a variety of results, the lists cover a wide range of ministry options. Furthermore, given that the gifts of the Spirit are the supernatural endowments for service, it is possible to go beyond them with an equal appreciation for the natural (given in creation) talents that further enhance a person's capacity for devotion to God.

Using the passage in First Corinthians as a guide, we learn that the gifts of the Spirit are given to Christians (12:7) according to the **will of God** (12:11) and for the benefit of the whole **body of Christ** (12:7). While some have attempted to classify the gifts of the Spirit (ending up with different ways of categorizing them), it is preferable to hold them in more or less equal regard, with **receptivity** on our part for whatever God gives us. This can save us from a "superior/inferior" mind-set that sometimes emerges when a gift or cluster of gifts is deemed better than others. We do well to keep the gifts in the same context as did the apostle Paul when he dealt with divisiveness in the Corinthian church because of the gifts. He placed 1 Corinthians 13 between chapters 12 and 14 (where gifts are mentioned) to show "a more excellent way"— the way of **love**. That particular fruit of the Spirit should attend any and all uses of the gifts, whether personal or corporate.

Kenneth C. Kinghorn's *Gifts of the Spirit* gives a good overview with an inventory to reflect upon one's own giftedness. SH

GILLET, LEV (1893–1980), monastery head and spiritual writer. Lev [Louis] Gillet writes in *The Jesus Prayer* that when we take up the invocation of the name of Jesus, we call him to mind until his name penetrates our hearts and becomes the center of our lives, holding everything together. He believes that the "way of the name," as he calls it, is followed by more Christians in this age of anxiety than ever before. *The Jesus Prayer* (also published as *On the Invocation of the Name of Jesus*) remains the best introduction to the practice of the invocation of the name.

Born in Grenoble, France, in 1893 to devout Roman Catholic parents, Gillet began his studies in philosophy in Grenoble and Paris shortly before the outbreak of World War I. He was wounded shortly after being mobilized, was captured by the Germans, and spent more than two years in a prisoner-of-war camp, where he began to learn Russian. After his release in 1917, he continued his education at Geneva, studying experimental psychology and mathematics. Between 1917 and 1919 he translated Freud's *The Interpretation of Dreams* into French.

In 1920 Gillet abandoned his academic career and entered the French Benedictine monastery at Farnborough, England, where he met the Uniate leader Andrew Szeptycky, Metropolitan of Lvov, who participated in his ordination as deacon and priest. His monastic name, Lev, is the Slavic equivalent of Leo. As the Metropolitan's private secretary he became convinced that reconciliation between the Orthodox East and the Roman Catholic West would not come about through proselytism, only through mutual respect and love. In 1928 he left Roman Catholicism and embraced the Orthodox Church.

In 1948 Father Lev was appointed chaplain to the Fellowship of St. Alban and St. Sergius, a post that he held until his death. His other books include *The Burning Bush* and *In Thy Presence.* RMH

GLORY. God's presence experienced as splendor, dignity, brightness, weight, or substance. There are many shades of meaning for the concept of *glory* as evidenced by the many different Hebrew words translated as *glory* in English Bibles. The scriptures speak of the glory of God in creation (including humanity), the glory of God in Christ, and eschatological glory. In these usages the concept is best associated with the Hebrew word *kabod*, literally "weightiness" but usually translated glory. A more theological translation would be "presentness," since the glory of God is the sign of God's presence. Spiritually this "presentness" brings one into the divine order of things, which is why the presence of God is a **sanctifying** presence (see Exod. 33:18-23; also John 1:14; 17:1, 4-5). Our divine calling and greatest joy as created creatures of God are to give praise and glory to God (Luke 17:18; Acts 12:23). The Westminster Shorter Catechism's first question and answer reflect this scriptural calling: "What is the chief end of [people]? [Our] chief end is to glorify God, and to enjoy [God] for ever." Most people can easily grasp the idea of giving praise to God but question what it means to give glory to God. If we allow the concept of presence/presentness to guide our understanding, then giving glory to God would be an attentive recognition of the divine order of all things and a participating in that glorious order. We glorify God by living out God's call to be sanctified, **holy** people who reflect God's order, intent, and presence in the world. CIZ

GLOSSOLALIA. Speaking in tongues. Glossolalia is sometimes interpreted as speaking foreign languages one has not learned, but it usually refers to unintelligible speech that would require interpretation. Modern studies have turned up evidence of such speech in the ancient world prior to the advent of Christianity, but glossolalia has left strongest traces in Christian history. In the book of Acts, Luke portrays the **Holy Spirit** as directing the mission of the church and glossolalia as one evidence of the Spirit's phenomenal guidance. In Acts 2 the Spirit reverses Babel as people from all corners of the earth gathered in Jerusalem understand and respond to the Christian message in their own language. In 1 Corinthians 12–14, Paul points to some problems in speaking in tongues, even though he claims to have spoken in tongues more than any of the Corinthians (14:18). He valued intelligible speech far more because it edified, and he believed that ethical behavior, especially **love**, proved inspiration by the Spirit more than speaking in tongues did.

Tongue speaking did not leave a wide trail until modern times. It appeared during the second century, notably among Montanists, a Pentecostal sect originating around 156 or 172 in Phrygia. Manifestations seem to have become extinct by the time of **John Chrysostom** (ca. 347–407) and **Augustine** (354–430). Speaking in tongues left no traces in the Middle Ages, but it began to bud again in the mid-seventeenth century among priests in southern France and dissenters in England, in the eighteenth century during the "Great Awakening" both in England and in the American colonies, and in the late nineteenth century among Irvingites in England. Consistent practice of speaking in tongues started at the beginning of the twentieth century with the emergence of **Pentecostal** churches. Since the 1950s, experiences of glossolalia and other **charismatic** phenomena have moved into non-Pentecostal churches as well.

For further reading, see *Glossolalia: Tongue Speaking in Biblical, Historical, and Psychological Perspective* by Frank Stagg, E. Glenn Hinson, and Wayne E. Oates. EGH

GNOSTICISM. (Greek *gnosis*, "knowledge"), a philosophical or religious movement whose roots are so shrouded in the mists of history that there is no broad consensus concerning its origins. It was either a pagan philosophy that preceded Christianity and influenced it from its earliest days; a heresy that emerged within Christianity in response to the delayed second coming of Christ (*parousia*); or a philosophy or religion that emerged alongside Christianity, influencing it from the outside by the second century.

Until 1945 most knowledge of Gnosticism came from its opponents' attacks on it. **Irenaeus**, **Tertullian**, and other church fathers wrote against Gnosticism. Even passages in the Gospel of John, First Peter, Second Peter, and First John address seemingly Gnostic heresies.

In 1945 a library was excavated at Nag Hammadi in Egypt. The codices (bound books as opposed to scrolls) include fifty-two mostly Gnostic treatises translated from Greek into Coptic in the fourth century. The book that has most thoroughly captured the imagination of modern readers is the Gospel of Thomas, a collection of 114 "secret" sayings of Jesus meant only for the apostles. These parables, proverbs, and exhortations contain no apocalyptic imagery, miracles, demons, or exorcisms. There is nothing about **sin** and **forgiveness**, and the kingdom of God focuses almost entirely inward.

According to the Gnostics, redemption came about through escape from the material world and reintegration into the spiritual world, becoming one with God, an idea that could be seen as a natural outgrowth of **Platonism**. The Gnostic God was entirely spirit and thus could have had nothing to do with the creation of the material world, which is inherently corrupt and evil. According to this view creation was performed by a demiurge (a lesser deity or a demon) or by a series of emanations that distanced God from the material world. The universe consisted of concentric spheres with the earth in the center, the lowliest sphere. When one died, the "divine spark," or the aspect of God that had been imprisoned in the physical body, was released and began its journey through the heavenly spheres back to the One. The key to completing this journey lay in knowing the secret names of the ruling powers of each sphere and the secret passwords to gain their permission to ascend.

In addition to the spirit/matter dualism, there were also dualisms between body and mind, good and evil. These fundamental Gnostic worldviews, combined with a complete disregard for social ethics, produced two completely opposite lifestyles. Rigorously ascetic Gnostics believed that the spirit needed to practice dominance over other material components (**body** and **soul**) to prepare for its release at death. These Gnostics practiced **fasting**, **celibacy**, and **poverty** among other **disciplines**. The libertine Gnostics believed that there was no point in disciplining the body and soul because the spirit would shed them anyway. This group indulged in sex, feasting, drinking, and wealth with impunity.

At the beginning of the second century, the two main Gnostic schools were the Basilideans and the Valentinians. By the middle of that century, the Christian heretic Marcion arrived as a critic of the creator God of the Old Testament. He made the first attempt to create a Christian canon, an authoritative collection of writings selected from the growing body of Christian literature. This forced the church to examine what sort of canon it should have. The church finally established its New Testament in the fourth century.

Although Gnosticism peaked between the second and fourth centuries, the school of thought founded by Mani in the third century, the **Manichean** sect, lasted a thousand years. One second-century sect survives today, the Mandeans of Iraq.

Today the Gnostic worldview pervades various aspects of the New Age movement. The belief in a changeless, universal, elusive, yet redemptive spiritual knowledge of reality that is pitted against an evil force is appealing in a society whose primary virtue is radical individualism. On the Internet, one can find sites promoting Christian Gnosticism, pagan Gnosticism, and a Gnosticism that complements any religion.

A good introduction to early Christian

Gnosticism is *The Gnostic Gospels* by Elaine Pagels. ww

GRACE. The essential nature of God (*agape*) and the fundamental intention of God (redemption), freely given and apart from any merit on the receiver's part. Grace is merciful **love**, aimed at nothing other than incorporating the recipient into the **body of Christ**.

For that reason the Greek word for grace, *charis*, has to do with rejoicing and has been variously used to describe beauty, charm, goodwill, favor, and the like. Grace is the divine atmosphere in which we live, move, and have our being.

As the Son of God, Jesus came to earth "full of grace and truth" (John 1:14), and from his fullness we received "grace upon grace" (John 1:16). The Gospel accounts do not use the word *grace* extensively but show us what the offer of grace looked like in the life and ministry of Christ. God's ultimate act of unmerited love took place on the **cross**, when Jesus died for our sins.

Paul puts *charis* into the vocabulary of the New Testament, making it virtually synonymous with the gospel itself—"the grace of our Lord Jesus Christ." Trained in the Hebrew Bible, Paul was able to link the earlier idea of God's **covenant** love with the **Incarnation** and culmination of that love in Jesus (Rom. 10:4). Thus to live in grace is to live "in Christ" and to allow Christ to live "in us." This, says Paul, is the secret of the ages now made known to us: "Christ in you, the hope of glory" (Col. 1:27). Or, in Jesus' analogy in John 15, we are to "abide in him" even as he "abides in us."

But grace is not merely a great truth about God; it is a transforming effect of the life of God in the human **soul**. To live in grace is to be changed "from one degree of glory to another" (2 Cor. 3:18). As we respond to God's ongoing offers of grace, we find ourselves becoming more like Christ in character and conduct. Such is the efficacious nature of grace.

In the Anglo-Catholic tradition (which includes the Wesleyan family), grace has been categorized according to how it operates in our lives. *Prevenient grace* (literally, "coming before") is our **experience** of grace prior to our profession of **faith** or the action of grace that precedes any conscious growth. It is sometimes associated with conviction of sin, but it can also describe the way grace awakens us to new challenges and opportunities.

Saving (or *justifying*) *grace* is properly the activity of grace in our lives at the time when we profess our faith in Jesus and begin to live the Christian life as new believers. Yet we also know that God's grace "saves" us again and again as time goes by from all sorts of things and for a variety of reasons.

Sanctifying grace is God's grace working in us as we deepen our faith and mature as disciples of Jesus. Again, it cannot be contained in any single experience, and it extends over all the years of our Christian journey.

Finally, *glorifying grace* is the presence of God's grace with us at the moment of death, enabling us to experience what many of the saints have called "holy dying." It is the grace that underlay Jesus' words in John 14, that in the Father's house there are "many mansions" (v. 2, KJV), and because of him a place has been prepared for us.

The experience of grace is the presence of God in us for a lifetime—before we were born and after we die. And for that reason, we use the term *grace* as a single-word description for so much of what it means to live the Christian life. SH

GRAHAM, WILLIAM FRANKLIN (BILLY)

(b. 1918), American Southern Baptist evangelist. Born in Charlotte, North Carolina, Graham was converted at age sixteen by the preaching of evangelist Mordecai Ham. While attending Florida Bible Institute, he joined the Southern Baptist Convention. He graduated from Wheaton College, where he met his wife, Ruth McCue Bell. Because of his desire to preach, Graham served a small church in Chicago instead of attending seminary. While there he was introduced to broadcast evangelism and also joined the staff of Youth for Christ. In 1947 he published his first of many books, *Calling Youth to Christ*, and was appointed president of Northwestern Schools in Minnesota, a post he held for four years. He became nationally famous in 1949 when his planned two-week revival in Los Angeles lasted two months. His call for a personal decision and a renewed national commitment to morality spoke to the uncertainties of postwar America. In 1950 he founded the Billy Graham Evangelistic Association, launched his radio show *Hour of Decision*, and first identified his revivals as *crusades*. In 1952 he began his newspaper column "My Answer." As a result of televising his 1957 New York City crusade, he emerged as America's leading evangelist. In 1960 he convened the first of many international conferences on evangelism.

Billy Graham adapted the revivalism of **Jonathan Edwards**, **Charles Grandison Finney**, Dwight Moody, and Billy Sunday to a new time and technology. He used radio, television, and film to bring people to a personal commitment to Jesus Christ. Mixing his evangelical conservatism with a political conservatism, he befriended many political leaders and presidents. He soon was speaking out against nuclear war and advocating a peace stance. He has long supported civil rights and social justice. His early crusades were noted for their policy to end segregated seating at revivals, and he has established numerous funds earmarked for social concerns.

The amount of literature available about Billy Graham is monumental. DDW

GREEK SPIRITUALITY. See **Orthodox Spirituality**.

GREEN, THOMAS H. (b. 1932), **Jesuit** spiritual writer. Born in Rochester, New York, Green received his philosophical and theological training at Bellarmine and Woodstock, with advanced degrees in education and physics from Fordham and a Ph.D. from Notre Dame. For more than twenty years he has served as the spiritual director of San Jose Seminary in Manila, Philippines, and teaches philosophy and pastoral theology at the Ate-

neo de Manila University. Green is one of today's most popular writers on the mystery of **prayer**. With his vast background in **retreat** work and **spiritual direction**, he offers clear and uncomplicated explanations regarding the life of prayer. Taking the reader by the hand, he leads beginners in the interior life from the **purgative** night of the senses through the illuminating **dark night** of the spirit. Two of Green's most helpful books are *When the Well Runs Dry: Prayer beyond the Beginnings* and *Darkness in the Marketplace*. EKM

GREENE, HENRY GRAHAM (1904–91), English novelist, short story writer, essayist, dramatist. Baptized in the Church of England, he was received as a communicant of the Roman Catholic Church in 1926. Greene is best known for his four early "Catholic novels": *Brighton Rock*, *The Power and the Glory*, *The Heart of the Matter*, and *The End of the Affair*. Among the spiritual subjects treated in these novels, respectively, are **evil**, priestly character, the real presence of Christ in **Holy Communion**, and baptismal **regeneration**. Later novels focusing on priestly resistance both to ecclesiastical and secular political power include *The Honorary Consul* and *Monsignor Quixote*. Many of Greene's short stories and novels that explore spiritual and moral themes have been adapted to film, including *A Visit to Morin* (**faith**), *This Gun for Hire* (betrayal), and *The Tenth Man* (substitutionary atonement). JCW

GREGORY I, THE GREAT (ca. 540–604), pope, **Doctor of the Church**. Gregory did much to shape Western Christianity. The son of a Roman senator, in 573 he became prefect of the city. Like many other noble people of his day, he sold his possessions, gave to the poor, and established six monasteries in Sicily and one in Rome, which he entered about 574. In 578, however, the pope compelled him to serve as papal emissary to the court of Constantinople. About 585 he returned to Rome and served as abbot of his former monastery until elected pope in 590. As pope he did much to stabilize Italy during the Lombard invasions, to secure the Western Church against capricious Byzantine emperors, to win England for Roman Christianity, and to strengthen the church in Spain, Gaul, and northern Italy. He set a high standard for himself as "servant of the servants of God." His most enduring contribution to spirituality, may have been his promotion of Benedictine **monasticism**. He idealized **Benedict** himself in his *Dialogues* (ca. 593). In theology he popularized the teaching of Augustine and the mystical theology of **Pseudo-Dionysius**. He made important changes in the liturgy and fostered the development of liturgical **music**. So attached is his name to plainsong that it came to be called "Gregorian Chant."

In addition to Gregory's life of Benedict, available in various translations, see the studies *Gregory the Great and His World* by Robert A. Markus and *Gregory the Great: His Place in History and Thought* by F. Homes Dudden. EGH

GREGORY OF NAZIANZUS (329–89), one of the "Great **Cappadocians**." The son of the bishop of Nazianzus in Cappadocia, also named Gregory, he studied at Athens as a contemporary of **Basil of Caesarea**. Soon afterward he became a monk. Against his will he was ordained a priest around 362 and consecrated bishop of Sasima around 372 but never visited his see. He remained in Nazianzus to assist his father until the latter's death in 374. He then retired to Seleucia in Isauria for several years. Summoned to Constantinople in 379, he helped to establish the Nicene faith through his preaching in the Church of the Resurrection and at the Council of Constantinople in 381. He was appointed bishop of Constantinople during the latter Council, but he resigned before the end of the year and retired to Nazianzus and then to his own estate. His major writings include an elaborate treatment of the doctrine of the **Holy Spirit**; *The Philokalia*, a selection of writings by Origen; a number of letters; and a large collection of poems.

For further reading, see *Select Orations and Letters* in *Nicene and Post-Nicene Fathers*, vol. 7, or Anthony Meredith's study, *The Cappadocians*. EGH

GREGORY OF NYSSA (ca. 330–ca. 395), bishop. Younger brother of Macrina and **Basil**, Gregory opted early on for an ecclesiastical career. He diverted for a time to rhetoric but returned to his original calling and entered a monastery founded by Basil. Consecrated bishop of Nyssa around 371, he strongly supported the Nicene Creed. Arians deposed him in 376, and he remained in exile until the death of the Emperor Valens in 378. Regaining his see, he refused election as bishop of Sebaste in 379. He eloquently championed the Nicene faith at Constantinople in 381.

A theologian of great originality and wide-ranging knowledge, Gregory had much to do with shaping the apophatic tradition or **negative way**. He also wrote important works on **spiritual formation**. In his *Catechetical Orations* he explained the doctrines of the Trinity, **Incarnation**, redemption, and the sacraments of **baptism** and **Holy Communion**. In *The Life of Moses* he outlined the mystical path as a journey from light to darkness, taking an allegorical approach to scripture. Like Moses, the higher we go, the more we enter into "**the cloud of unknowing**." When we reach the center, we find utter darkness, where God is. Gregory also gave homilies on the Song of Solomon, the **Lord's Prayer**, and the **Beatitudes**. His writings on **asceticism** included treatises on virginity, Christian perfection, and the life of his sister Macrina.

The Life of Moses, translated by Abraham J. Malherbe and Everett Ferguson, is a good starting place for Gregory, or see *Gregory of Nyssa* by Anthony Meredith. EGH

GRIFFITHS, BEDE (1907–93), a leading figure in cross-cultural dialogue, a scholar of world religion, a nominal Anglican who became a Roman Catholic monk after reading Cardinal **Newman**'s autobiography, *Apologia pro Vita Sua*, and a student of **C. S. Lewis**, whose friend he remained for forty years.

The spiritual journey of Griffiths convinced him that doctrinal diversity and sectarian division remain and will remain an unalterable fact at the intellectual level. But there is profound truth to be discovered and shared at the level of the heart. This unity is cosmic, enabled by a cosmic Christ. In his autobiography, *The Golden String*, Griffiths describes the sacrificial death of Christ as the central event in human history—the event that alone gives meaning to life. The resurrection of Christ shatters the illusions of this world and sets humankind free from bondage to space and time. Christianity does not attempt to explain this mystery but rather opens up the way of approaching it. RMH

GROOTE, GERHARD (OR GEERT) (1340–84), Dutch founder of *devotio moderna,* an ascetic movement that helped to reform religious life in the late Middle Ages. Groote began as a wealthy law and theology student, having spent time traveling and studying in Paris, Cologne, and Prague, but his experiences did not inspire him. Though he was a successful student on a slow but steady path to ecclesiastical accomplishment, ennui consumed him and he fell ill. During his illness Groote's life changed, and by 1374 he had signed away his ancestral home for charitable use and had withdrawn from academic life to live among the **Carthusians**. His writings from that time reflect a rejection of his former intellectual pursuits (though he never lost his love of books), demonstrate a conviction and passion for simplicity and practical piety, and formulate the beginnings of an ascetic lifestyle reminiscent of the early days of the mendicant (begging) orders.

Groote left the cloister after three years and became an itinerant preacher after being ordained as a deacon. His followers grew numerous as he preached and practiced a life of spiritual and practical devotion. Groote's stern criticism of the worldly living of the clergy led to the revocation of his license to preach in 1383. He died of the plague in 1384, but his followers, particularly Florent

Radewijns, organized devout clergymen and laywomen into the double communities of the Brothers and Sisters of the Common Life. They held all property in common, lived lives of sacrifice, **poverty**, **chastity**, and **obedience**, all without the restraints of formal orders.

Devotio moderna is so called because it was seen as a modern reform, a breaking from traditional ecclesiastical practice. It is, more accurately, a return to the best of traditional monastic devotion, which underscored an interior life of devotion and an outward demonstration of this love for God in service to others. The best example of the central thought of *devotio moderna* is *Imitation of Christ* by **Thomas à Kempis,** parts of which are sometimes attributed directly to Groote. SAW

GROU, JEAN-NICOLAS (1731–1803), **Jesuit** priest in exile who wrote about interior prayer. French-born Jean-Nicolas Grou gained a reputation for scholarly writing, especially his translations of volumes of Plato's dialogues. While working in Paris, he was advised to make a **retreat**, which he later referred to as his **conversion**. Afterward his life took on a spirit of prayer, a continual sense of God's presence, and complete **abandonment** to the holy **will of God**.

Underwritten with a pension from Louis XVI, Grou continued writing, including a commentary on **Augustine**'s *Confessions* and a book of spiritual maxims. At religious houses he gave addresses, which were published in the book called *Manual for Interior Souls.* (This is the basis of the book *The Hidden Life of the Soul* by H. L. Sidney Lear.) Forced to flee during the French Revolution, Father Grou spent the last eleven years of his life in a cell the size of a big cupboard. Under the protection of Thomas Weld of Lulworth Castle in England, Grou influenced the many Weld children as well as religious communities who considered him their founder or patron. He lived as a hermit, rising at 4:00 A.M. to pray and write all day. To maintain his vow of **poverty**, he asked his protector only for food, clothing, or books. He preferred **solitude** but participated in conversation only for the **glory** of God and the salvation of his neighbor.

During his last years, he wrote *The School of Jesus Christ,* a full treatment on the Christian life. One-fourth of the work focused on prayer and has been published separately as *How to Pray.* Grou insisted that because God teaches us to pray, we should focus on loving God, not on methods. He approached **unceasing prayer** in a commonsense way, saying that praying without ceasing occurs through our actions, **suffering**, and social duties. Rather than hinder those duties, such prayer makes us more energetic and more genial. JLJ

GUIDED IMAGERY. A structured form of **meditation** in which one follows instructions that guide one through a passage of scripture. These instructions may be either general (as with those in the box below) or specific to a particular passage. This is a good way to pray if you are beginning or if you have a busy schedule or harried nerves or are easily distracted. It takes seriously the power of the memory and imagination to influence thought patterns and to lend a serene alertness that is so helpful in prayer. It invites you to quiet yourself long enough for the Spirit to work within you and connect you to God.

Guided imagery meditations are particularly useful for group devotions. In this case a leader reads the instructions aloud and pauses often. Many authors have provided a variety of such instructions, notably Anthony

---

A METHOD FOR MEDITATION USING GUIDED IMAGERY

Choose a story of Jesus from the Gospels. In this process you will read the passage slowly, picturing the scenes in your own mind; pause as often as you feel appropriate. You may sit in a chair or get comfortable on the floor and accept the invitation to close your eyes and open your imagination.

In this prayer you will read the text slowly three times. After each reading, you will close your eyes and use your imagination to discover the text's meaning to you. When reading, remember that this is not a speed-reading course but a thought-filled time of listening. When you see the * symbol, remember to pause and close your eyes for at least 15 seconds. This is critical in order to get the most out of your prayer time.

Note that this method grows easier with practice. If you find nothing is happening or you cannot stay focused, try relaxing, taking a few deep breaths, and allowing yourself to grow quiet before trying again. If you feel trapped or upset during the meditation, ask God to send you whatever help or companionship you need to feel safe.

Read the sacred text slowly aloud. Close your eyes and use your imagination. Explore the scene fully. Enter into the action. * What is the setting? * What are the sounds, sights, and aromas? * Who else is there? * What do they look like? * What do their faces tell you? *

Open your eyes and read the text aloud a second time.

Close your eyes. * Where are you in the story? What is your role in this drama? * Let the story unfold. Does anyone speak to you? What does he or she say? What do you reply? * Is there other action of which you are a part? * What are you feeling? *

Open your eyes. Read the text aloud a third time.

Now the story is concluded. Close your eyes. Do you go elsewhere? * Whom do you tell about what you just witnessed? *

Bring your attention back to the present. Open your eyes and pause for one minute. Be open to any questions or insights that arise.

What is the story's meaning to you? *You may want to record your thoughts in writing.

Now put your thoughts into a sentence prayer. Write only a sentence. Pray the prayer aloud three times.

de Mello in *Sadhana: A Way to God* and Carolyn Stahl Bohler in *Opening to God: Guided Imagery Meditation on Scripture*. Bohler also offers advice on introducing and leading guided imagery meditation with groups and on practicing it individually.

Ignatius of Loyola believed that God invites us to enter a friendship closely linked to the life, death, and resurrection of our Lord and to everything he truly is. One way to allow this closer link is to enter imaginatively into scenes from the earthly life of Jesus in what is called imaginative meditation. PDB

GUIGO II (d. 1188), a **Carthusian** monk who became the ninth prior (1173–80) of the mother house La Grande Chartreuse. (Guigo I was the fifth prior.) *The Ladder of Monks, Twelve Meditations,* and *A Meditation on the Magnificat* are three works credited to Guigo. In *The Ladder of Monks,* Guigo writes to his elder mentor, Gervase. The image of a **ladder** is one of the oldest metaphors for the spiritual life. Spiritual **disciplines** or practices that lead one to **contemplation** or **union** with God are the real focus of *The Ladder of Monks,* which sets out simply and clearly the steps of *lectio divina*. Guigo explains the steps not only as a method but as life's work, as **reading**, **meditation**, **prayer**, and contemplation become, successively, the main focus of one's spiritual life.

In his *Meditations* (possibly written before *The Ladder*), we meet Guigo the scholar. With a keen understanding of the Bible, he conveyed his ideas couched in scriptural phrases and images. His experiential, inward writing was contrary to the more common literal and historical focuses of his day. In Meditation I, he elevates the solitary life and explores the interior hindrances to a life of **solitude**. In all twelve meditations, Guigo labors to share not only his profound reflections on the transforming powers we experience doing Bible study but also invites us to restore in ourselves God's image and likeness, the true essence of the contemplative life. In the *Magnificat,* he depicts **Mary**, known for her **humility** and ap-preciative **abandonment** to God, as the exemplary contemplative. For an easy introduction to Guigo, his times, his spiritual ladder, and his teaching on prayer, see Alfred C. Hughes, *Spiritual Masters: Living a Life of Prayer in the Catholic Tradition.* For Guigo's own writings, with an extensive introduction, read *The Ladder of Monks and Twelve Meditations,* translated by Edmund Colledge and James Walsh. EKM

GUTIÉRREZ, GUSTAVO (b. 1928), Peruvian priest, **liberation** theologian, author, educator. Gutiérrez serves in the slums of Rimac in his hometown of Lima, Peru. Ordained a Roman Catholic priest in 1959, he finds this to be his primary calling. His roles as a founder of liberation theology and as a professor of theology at Catholic University in Lima are secondary to his pastoral work among the poor.

In July of 1968, he delivered a speech titled "Toward a Theology of Liberation." This preceded by one month the groundbreaking Second General Conference of the Latin American Episcopate in Medellín, Colombia (which called the Roman Catholic Church to work for political reform and justice for the poor), and by more than three years the publication of his *A Theology of Liberation* in Spanish.

Gutiérrez defines theology as critical reflection on customary practice in light of scripture. Liberation is the aspiration of an oppressed people, the conscious responsibility for one's own destiny (self-creation). Christ liberates us from **sin**, the root of all injustice and oppression. Salvation, then, embraces all persons and each person wholly. Christian **conversion** is to be committed to the liberation of the poor and oppressed.

Despite the collapse of functioning Marxism in Eastern Europe and the New World Order economic situation, the core of liberation theology will not change because it starts with the poor. The model is one that begins with the reality of poverty and seeks its causes. Gutiérrez identifies the Christian virtue of **poverty** as a form of **love**. Involuntary poverty is not idealized. It is taken on as the evil it is. We voluntarily embrace poverty in order to protest against it and to struggle for its abolition. Identification with the poor is an authentic **imitation of Christ.**

Gutiérrez has continued to write and speak out concerning liberation theology. Among his books, *We Drink from Our Own Wells* is about the **spirituality of liberation.** *On Job* is a fresh study of that biblical book from the perspective of a developing country. *The Density of the Present* is a collection of essays about the church, theology, and spirituality in a world of suffering. ww

GUYON, JEANNE-MARIE BOUVIER DE LA MOTTE

(1648–1717), French writer on inward prayer. Born into a wealthy Catholic French family, Guyon grew up in convents and read works by **Thomas à Kempis** and **Francis de Sales**. At fifteen, she was married to a man twenty-two years her senior. Both he and his mother ridiculed her, driving her to wordless prayer. This was followed by years of a sense of losing God's graces and of spiritual **dryness.** Just before her husband's death (she was twenty-eight), she met Father François La-Combe and came under his direction.

By 1680 Madame Guyon moved out of her "**dark night** of the soul" and developed a keen sense of God's presence, using inward prayer constantly. She wrote of this mystical life in *A Short and Easy Method of Prayer* (now titled *Experiencing the Depths of Jesus Christ*). In this book, she describes praying the **scripture**, beholding the Lord, **meditation**, **unceasing prayer**, and active **contemplation**. Such prayer results in an ability to abandon one's whole existence to God. Madame Guyon saw **abandonment** as the key to approaching God and made it clear that people can actually live in **union** with God. Other books followed, including *Spiritual Torrents* and *Union with God*.

As a result of Madame Guyon's published books, seekers appeared at her door (scrub-women and ecclesiastical officials alike), asking her to teach them how to pray. But her guidance of souls displeased church officials, and King Louis XIV found too many similarities between her teaching and the **Quietism** of **Miguel de Molinos**. He imprisoned Father LaCombe and Madame Guyon.

Upon her release, Madame Guyon met **François Fénelon**, whom she influenced. After further examinations, she was imprisoned again at Vincennes, then in the Bastille. During this time, she was asked to defend herself by writing her autobiography. After seven years, she was released and lived quietly with her son. In 1704 her writings were published in Holland and became popular with Protestants. After her death, her works became classics, especially her autobiography and *Experiencing the Depths of Jesus Christ*. JLJ

H

HADEWIJCH, thirteenth-century **Beguine** mystical poet. Although we know little about Hadewijch's life, she has been called the finest Flemish poet of all time, and she has bequeathed to us a beautiful and sometimes complex text of love and **mysticism**. Hadewijch was a Beguine. Her writing—comprised of over sixty poems, over thirty letters, and fourteen visions—reveals that Hadewijch was well-versed not only in Latin, French, and the rules of rhetoric but also in scripture and the theology of mystics like **Augustine** and **Bernard of Clairvaux**. Like many of her Beguine sisters, Hadewijch made brilliant use of the courtly love tradition, a literature of knights who offer undying devotion to their lady love. Hadewijch describes her relationship to God as like that of a knight who experiences the suffering of love's absence but whose heart burns with longing for love's fulfillment. In the medieval mind, women were considered closer to the flesh and thus better able to understand Christ's human **suffering**. This closeness was a gift, for through emulating Christ in suffering love, women mystics achieved **union** with Christ. Hadewijch's poetry offers the hope that even in the darkest moments of life, Christ is intimately present. The union described by Hadewijch is so powerful in places that even the distinction between human and divine fades away, an idea seen in **Meister Eckhart**'s mysticism. Filled with biblical allusions, Hadewijch's writings also provide feminine metaphors such as pregnancy for spiritual growth. SAF

HAIL MARY. A brief petition addressed to **Mary** as intercessor for Christians.

Hail Mary, full of grace,
    the Lord is with you.
Blessed are you among women,
And blessed is the fruit of your womb,
    Jesus.
Holy Mary, Mother of God, pray for us
    sinners, now and at the hour of our
    death. Amen.

The first two sentences are based on scripture passages where Gabriel (Luke 1:28) and Elizabeth (Luke 1:42) salute Mary. As **Marian devotion** grew in the early church, these verses were often combined in prayers addressed to the Virgin, particularly in the Eastern Church. The final sentence was added in in the Western Church in the Middle Ages to make the address into a request for Mary's intercessory prayer.

While the Hail Mary may be prayed in many situations, its most significant use is as the primary prayer of the **rosary**. KRB

HAMMARSKJÖLD, DAG (1905–61), Secretary General of the United Nations from 1953 until his death in an airplane accident while on a peacekeeping mission in the Congo. Born into an aristocratic Swedish family, he was strongly influenced by **Albert Schweitzer**, whom he had planned to visit in Africa at the time of his death. Other influences include the writings of the medieval mystics and the book of **Psalms**. His journal was discovered and published after his death. (The English translation is called *Markings*.) This journal's mystical sense of God's presence surprised many of his friends. He believed that God is larger than any single religion or creed. A poet and scholar, he sought to deepen his relationship with God. Out of his struggle with faith, he developed a sense of God's providence and his own destiny, including premonitions of his premature death. HLR

HARKNESS, GEORGIA (1891–1974), Methodist personalist theologian, ecumenist, and theological educator. Born in Harkness, New York, she was educated at Cornell and Boston Universities. Despite her lifelong advocacy of women's rights in the church, she declined ordination, valuing her close association with the laity. The first woman named to a theological professorship and perhaps the most visible woman theologian of the mid-twentieth century, she taught at Garrett Biblical Institute and the Pacific School of Religion, where she distinguished herself as an articulate spokesperson of ecumenism and Christian pacifism. Her nearly forty books combine sound scholarship with concern for basic human needs. In devotional works such as *The **Dark Night** of the Soul*, she offers personal insight into the inner spiritual life. Her devotional autobiography, *Grace Abounding*, containing prayers and poetry of her own composition, reflects the "evangelical liberalism" she adopted and lived.

To learn more, read *Georgia Harkness: For Such a Time as This* by Rosemary Skinner Keller. PWC

HEILER, FRIEDRICH (1892–1967), German theologian and historian of religions. Heiler was raised in a Roman Catholic family and studied at Munich. His doctoral dissertation on the phenomenology of prayer from primitive petitions to mystical heights was published in 1918. It is available in English as *Prayer*. The next year he became a Lutheran but always sought to build bridges between denominations and faiths. He felt prayer was the key to unity, as all people seek to reach out to the God who seeks them. Focus on experience rather than on different ways of describing experience, he believed, could promote understanding and unity. He taught at Marburg from 1920 until he retired, serving as dean of the arts faculty from 1945. His phenomenological approach to comparative religions included studies of Hinduism and Buddhism.

Peter McKenzie adapted Heiler's phenomenological categories for his study *The Christians: Their Practices and Beliefs*. KRB

HERBERT, GEORGE (1593–1633), Anglican poet and priest. Born into a noble family, educated in the Cambridge tradition, and destined initially for worldly advancement, he turned his attention to serious spiritual concerns as a matter of personal response to the death of King James I in 1625. Following a period of profound soul searching, he was ordained to the priesthood in 1630. Gifted in both classical scholarship and musical ability, his prose and poetic writings reflect considerable skill in the handling of language, rhyme, and rhythm. He is considered one of the most authentic representatives of the Anglican *via media* (a "middle way" between Roman Catholicism and radical Protestantism) in both its spirit and teaching. *A Priest to the Temple; or the Country Parson*, published posthumously in 1652, is his most famous prose work. It portrays the model priest as sober, learned, temperate, and devout; ideals he sought to emulate in his own brief ministry at Bremerton, near Salisbury. The ideal parson acted as Christ's deputy, reduced human arrogance, and guided individuals to God. Herbert's collection of poems titled *The Temple* reveals his own personal struggles of faith, consisting primarily, as **Richard Baxter** once observed, of "heart-work and heaven-work." In these devotional writings he consistently emphasized the sense of intimacy with God, the priority of **prayer** to preaching, the integration of inward **grace** and outward expression, the exercise of Christian **virtue** in the supreme act of putting on Christ, and the resolution of life's contradictions in an abiding **faith** that leads to God.

Margaret Bottrall wrote a biography, *George Herbert*. PWC

HESYCHASM. (Greek, "stillness"), the state of inner stillness derived from practicing the **Jesus Prayer** or the practice itself (including specific posture and breathing). Hesychasm is a major theme of the spiritual tradition represented in *The Philokalia* and ***The Way of a Pilgrim.***

The tradition of seeking knowledge of God in a specific method of prayer goes back at least as far as **Evagrius Ponticus** (d. 399). He defined prayer as the shedding of thought, allowing the immediate experience of the Divine that transcends concepts and images of God. It is the intuitive apprehension of God, a sense of unity of all things, and loss of ego. In the fifth century, Bishop Diodochus of Photice discussed the Jesus Prayer as a way of achieving **deification** or union with God. **John Climacus** was instrumental in systemizing hesychasm in the sixth century. **Symeon the New Theologian** (949–1022) writes about the posture and controlled breathing of the hesychast while reciting the Jesus Prayer. He describes moving one's consciousness from mind to heart and the inner fire that hesychasm provides.

In the thirteenth and fourteenth centuries, hesychasm was practiced widely on Mount Athos, a promontory of the Halkidiki peninsula in northern Greece, that was home to about forty Eastern Orthodox monasteries with almost twenty thousand monks (today there are twenty large monasteries and a number of smaller monastic houses). Controversy boiled up when Barlaam of Calabria (1290–1350), a learned Greek from southern Italy, came to Mount Athos and ridiculed the postures of the hesychasts and accused them of Messalianism, a heresy condemned by the Byzantine Church in the fourth and fifth centuries. Messalianism states that one can have a material **vision of God.**

Gregory Palamas emerged from Mount Athos to defend the living experience of the hesychasts. He argued that the postures were not absolutely necessary to hesychasm, but that the **body** is beautiful because it is the image of God and should not be mocked regardless. The **experience** of hesychasm transforms the body and soul. Gregory's major contribution to the debate was his understanding of divine light. Using the **Transfiguration** of Christ on Mount Tabor as the source

of his argument, he refers to the divine light that shone forth from Christ at that moment. This light can be perceived (by **grace**) by the senses and the intellect even though it is above and beyond both. While human beings cannot know God's essence, we can experience God's energies. As an analogy, we cannot touch the sun, but we can see and feel its energy as light and heat.

The main characteristics of hesychasm involve entering into a state of mental quiet, followed by the loving recitation of the Jesus Prayer along with the regulation of one's breathing. One bends forward so that one's gaze is focused on the heart, the stomach, or the navel. One then feels the warmth of the fire within or sees the divine light of Tabor. Again, the ultimate goal of all this is deification, participation in the divine nature. ww

HILARY OF POITIERS (ca. 315–ca. 368), bishop and theologian. Born to a wealthy non-Christian family in Poitiers, France, Hilary was thoroughly educated in philosophy, especially **Neoplatonism**, but around 350 was converted to Christianity through a reading of the Hebrew and Christian Scriptures. Although married and with one daughter, he was elected bishop of Poitiers around 353. The church at this time was in the midst of renewed interest in Arianism, having strayed from the faith of the Council of Nicaea (325). During Hilary's time the emperor Constantius fully embraced Arianism. At the Arian-dominated council at Beziers in 356, Hilary refused to condemn **Athanasius** and was exiled to Phrygia.

During his four-year exile in the East, Hilary studied Greek theology and wrote his most famous work, *On the Trinity*, which not only condemned Arianism but also introduced Eastern theology to the Western Church. While in exile he also became familiar with Eastern **hymns**, several of which he translated into Latin. He also authored some hymns in defense of the Trinity and is credited with introducing the Latin hymn in the West. In 360 he returned to his see and in 364 traveled to Milan to debate, to no avail, its Arian bishop, Auxentius. Because of his defense of orthodoxy against Arianism, Hilary has been called the Athanasius of the West. In addition to his Latin hymns and his book *On the Trinity*, he wrote commentaries in the style of **Origen** on the **Psalms** and Matthew and a history of the Arian debates. In 1851 Pope Pius IX named him a **Doctor of the Church** (an authoritative teacher). DDW

HILDEGARD OF BINGEN (1098–1179), German Benedictine nun and mystical writer/composer. Hildegard was a woman of tremendous authority and influence within the Roman Catholic Church and the politics of her time. She was "rediscovered" in the late twentieth century after more than eight hundred years. She was an accomplished woman: mystic, visionary, prophet, poet, musician, preacher, reformer, administrator, and author of books and letters.

Hildegard was the tenth child of a noble family, given to the church at the age of eight. She was raised and educated by a Benedictine nun Jutta and made her vows as a teenager. At forty-three she had a prophetic call to write about her many **visions**. As a person she was courageous, independent, and divinely inspired. She developed an integrated and holistic approach to God and advocated for her nuns an orderly life of work, relaxation, sleep, and good food. Her health was never good, probably due to migraine headaches. Nevertheless she had a divine radiance about her and was ablaze with enthusiasm.

When Jutta died in 1136, Hildegard was elected abbess of St. Disabid monastery, a nunnery attached to a male monastery. In 1152 she and her nuns left that monastery, over the protests of the monks, to establish a women's monastery at Rupertsburg, near Bingen. With a deep desire for spiritual, judicial, and financial independence, she also established a daughter house in Ebingen that still thrives.

Hildegard left much material. The writing of *Scivias*, her major work, was officially endorsed by the pope. Her nine books include theology, natural history, and medical texts, all of which are valued today. Her morality play (still performed) and her seventy-two songs are available as audio recordings. She dictated her illuminations (paintings of her visions), which can be viewed in *Illuminations of Hildegard of Bingen with Commentary by Matthew Fox*, an excellent introduction to Hildegard. Many recent books discuss Hildegard and contain excerpts from her writings. Her one hundred letters, also still available, were addressed to kings, popes, bishops, nuns, and politically active men.

Hildegard was a respected voice, unusual for a woman of her time. She combined Christian doctrine with cosmology and identified the Creator with the Incarnate Word. She realized that creation has radiance and so united religion with science. Hers was a living cosmology, a concept of being a cocreator with God. Her experience of *veriditas*, or "greening power," was significant. The word combines the Latin *viriditas* (greenness as a symbol of life) and *veritas* (truth). This green/life/truth combination could apply either to the power of nature or to the Holy Spirit. Her illuminations manifest aspects of her concept of a living cosmology, in which we are to respect an earth that needs healing.

Some of Hildegard's books on health and medicine that evolved from her perception of Christ, Benedictine philosophy, and her visions, have implications for alternative medicine today, particularly the integration of physical healing with psychological and spiritual healing. She recognized **love** and **compassion** as being the healing energies of the body and the universe.

Hildegard appeals to spiritual seekers, scholars, artists, and others. As a preeminent woman theologian, she hints at what has been missed in a one-sided patriarchal culture that has dominated Christianity. Her teachings have implications for understanding and experiencing women's wisdom, for ecological concerns through the radiance of creation, for ecumenism and interfaith dialogue, and for individual mystical journeys. EWF

HILTON, WALTER (ca.1340–96), English mystic and author. Although we know little about Hilton's life, he obtained his doctor of theology degree from Cambridge University. Shortly after he attended Cambridge, he became a hermit. While Hilton saw the advantages of the solitary life, he was not completely satisfied. Sometime between 1375 and 1380 he joined the Augustinian Order at Thurgarton Priory in Nottingham. He lived there for the remainder of his life. Hilton is best known for his book *The Scale of Perfection*, the most comprehensive devotional guide on **contemplation** written during the Middle Ages. Although *The Scale* was written to an anchoress (a woman living a vowed life of **solitude**), it remained popular among the laity until the sixteenth century. One reason for this popularity was Hilton's insistence that the spiritual life was not restricted to a particular time, place, or set of circumstances such as the cloister.

The major thesis of *The Scale* is how a **soul**, originally formed in the image of God and then distorted by **sin**, could be "re-formed" to God's image. Hilton identifies two aspects of inner "re-formation." Reformation in faith is adherence to Christian beliefs and ethics. Reformation in feeling is a deeper level of **union** with God through the refashioning of one's soul. Another theme in *The Scale* involves three levels of knowing. The first is rational knowledge, in which insight comes through reason and study. The second is **affective** knowledge, in which devotion is directed by the heart, not the head. The third is contemplation, in which knowledge of God is a balance of cognitive and affective means. Hilton believed that contemplation comes through **reading** scripture, **meditation**, and **prayer** (defined as the withdrawal from earthly things in order to **experience** God's **grace** on a level that is beyond words).

Other writings by Hilton include *The Goad of Love, Of Angel's Song, On the Image of Sin,* and *The Mixed Life. The Scale of Perfection* remains his best and most popular work. ASJ

HOLINESS. An attribute of both God and God's people. Holiness is one of the most mysterious words in the Bible, especially as it relates to God. The holiness of God is announced and praised in scripture but never explained. This is our first clue that the idea of holiness is related to **transcendence**, majesty, and **awe**—that is, it is beyond human comprehension. The holiness of God is related to the biblical notion that nothing earthly can look on God directly. God is infinitely holy, as the ground of all righteousness. In fact, God's name is holy (Pss. 29:2; 30:4; 97:12; 103:1). When confronted with God's holiness, humans are overwhelmed with God's grandeur and cringe in God's presence. At the same time, God's holiness attracts because it is also an expression of covenant **love**. The psalmist glories in God's holiness and urges others to search for God and continually seek God's "presence" (105:1-5). As God's Son, Jesus is also holy and will draw others to his saving and hallowing life (Luke 1:35; John 6:69; Acts 3:14). The **Holy Spirit** is the Spirit of God among us, energizing and sanctifying dedicated believers, teaching us about God (Mark 13:11; John 14:26).

Isaiah 6:1-13 is a primary text when studying the holiness of God. God is present but not described; God is likely enveloped in clouds and darkness (Ps. 97:2) or in impenetrable light (Ps. 104:1-2). Heavenly beings praise and give witness to God's holiness. Isaiah is overcome with guilt (compare Peter's response to Jesus in Luke 5:8) yet he volunteers for a divine mission of delivering a message disobedient people do not want to hear: God will not compromise God's glorious majesty. Yet God's own self is not beyond reach; God is available. This is a key concept, that God's invitation to holiness of character is desirable and possible (compare Lev. 11:44 and 1 Pet. 1:13-25). Thus, majesty (kingship), justice, and **mercy**, as Isaiah teaches, reflect the holiness of God from which there is no court of appeal, though there is a welcome word of **grace**.

The church's witness to God's holiness is

virtually unanimous, except for a minor school of thought that the troubles we experience in the world are God's working out divine inner discord. The church generally, however, struggles to understand how it participates in God's holy character, not whether God's character is holy. It is obvious in the church's creeds that humans do not naturally share in the regal holiness of God but, as the scriptures bear witness, wrestle with unholiness or **sin**. In spite of our sin, God calls us to holiness, that is, to share in God's sanctity and manifest it in our values and work (Rom. 12:1).

The church is not unanimous in its view of holiness in human life. There are several schools of thought to consider. It is important to note that in the literature of Christian spirituality, "**perfection** in love" is often used interchangeably with "holiness of heart." The Roman Catholic Church and the **Orthodox** Church teach the possibility of perfection in love, or holiness of heart, in this life as a **gift** of God's grace. For the Romans this means a reconstitution of the "image of God" (*imago Dei*) in us; for the Orthodox it means living "in likeness" to God (**deification**).

Methodist holiness history also affirms, in agreement with **John Wesley**, that holiness and happiness are goals of spiritual grace now. This means that the Sermon on the Mount (Matt. 5–7) contains expectations for discipleship in this life, expectations actualized only by God's grace. Further, perfection does not mean "perfected" but "perfecting," or moving toward the goal of holiness in this life, with the fullness of holiness in the life to come. Notwithstanding its provisional nature, the grace of holiness constitutes a real change in one's heart and life. The result of holiness or perfection is love of God and love of others (which means active involvement for their benefit).

For the Reformed and Lutheran traditions, on the other hand, holiness is a state of being, incomplete in any sense until the time of death. Contrary to the Roman Catholic, Orthodox, and Methodist concept, holiness or perfection is thought of as a relative change. Christians are simultaneously sinners and saints, sanctity being a promise rather than a present reality. The Sermon on the Mount contains distant goals of discipleship that we always reach for but never achieve. The American Holiness Association teaches two works of grace, one superseding the other, **justification** and **sanctification** (or "the baptism of the Spirit"). In the **Pentecostal** tradition, baptism of the Spirit is related more to the power to do good works than to a purity of intention, though purity of intention is not excluded.

What, then, does it mean to be holy? Spiritual teachers in the traditions mentioned above, except the Reformation churches, have used terms like "purity of intention," "a clean heart," "beholding the **vision of God**," "being sanctified (made holy)," "complete integration of life," and "to will one (God's) **will**," among others. Holiness is a mind-set about life that has God at the center, considers God's will in how one lives, and has God as the desired end of life. Holiness is to reflect in one's life something of the character of Jesus. To be so focused is itself a grace that makes holiness, like justification, a sheer gift of God, not a reward for good works. The test of holiness or "perfection," as Jesus teaches in Matthew 5:38-48, is the love of our enemies. Holy living is a recipe for happiness in the way God intended in creation. God's profound happiness is not only a pure joy in being but also the delight in what is good and the anticipation of the triumph of righteousness. It is to this happiness that we are called in Christ.

For more information, see **John Wesley**, *A Plain Account of Christian Perfection*; **Thomas Merton**, *Life and Holiness*; and Vladimir Lossky, *The Vision of God*. For an interpretation of Wesley's views, see Jerry L. Mercer, *Living Deeply Our New Life in Christ: A Wesleyan Spirituality for Today*. JLM

HOLMES, URBAN TIGNER, III (1930–81), American Episcopal priest, theologian, seminary dean. Holmes was Episcopal chaplain at Louisiana State University (1956–66), professor of pastoral theology at Nashotah House (1966–73), and dean of the School of Theology at Sewanee (1973–81). He wrote or edited fifteen books, including *The Future Shape of Ministry* and *Spirituality for Ministry*. Holmes argued for a sacramental model of ordained ministry, as opposed to the modern professional model deriving authority from credentialed competence. In *Young Children and the Eucharist*, he wrote that the church should help children grow into an understanding of **Holy Communion** by allowing baptized children to participate at an early age. Holmes buttressed this argument with the theological proposition, in *Confirmation Issue: Celebrations of Maturity in Christ*, that baptism is the normative act of initiation into the Christian community. In *A History of Christian Spirituality*, Holmes introduced a typology of spirituality, denoted by tendencies to encratism (moralism), rationalism, **Pietism**, or **Quietism**.

For further reading, see *Discover Your Spiritual Type* by Corinne Ware. JCW

HOLY. See Holiness.

HOLY COMMUNION. A sacred ritual action, a holy meal through which the church remembers God's saving work in creation and **covenant**, in the life, death, and resurrection of Jesus Christ. The church invites and invokes the outpouring of the Holy Spirit, celebrating with **thanksgiving** Christ's continuing presence in the world through the **Holy Spirit**. We receive a foretaste of and anticipate the heavenly banquet.

Holy Communion is also often referred to as Eucharist or the Lord's Supper. Each of these names finds its roots in the witness of the New Testament and in the life of the early church. *Holy Communion* emphasizes the holy meal as a means by which we participate in a holy and loving relationship with God *and* our neighbors (1 Cor. 10:16-17). *Eucharist*, from the Greek word meaning "to give thanks," reminds us that when Jesus gathered his disciples for a meal, he gave thanks to God for God's creating and saving work in the world

(Luke 22:17-20; 1 Cor. 11:23-26). This understanding is reflected in the fact that many churches call the prayer at the holy meal the "Great Thanksgiving."

In *Eucharist* we continue Jesus' action of thanksgiving as we offer our own praise and thanks to God. The Great Thanksgiving typically includes remembrance of God's saving work in the history of Israel, in Christ, and in the church; a specific recalling (*anamnesis*) of the actions of Jesus at the Last Supper; and an invocation of the Holy Spirit (*epiclesis*) over the bread and cup that they may be, for God's people, the body and blood of Christ and that we may be Christ's body in the world.

The name *Lord's Supper* reminds us that this holy meal is neither one to which we invite ourselves nor at which we determine who will be at the table with us. As the Lord's Supper, Christ serves as host and issues the invitations (1 Cor. 11:17-22). Churches have debated exactly how Christ is present at the meal and in the elements. Perhaps it is best to follow **Charles Wesley**'s lead in his hymn "O the Depth of Love Divine" and admit that we cannot plumb the depths of God's mysteries.

Churches variously speak of Holy Communion as **sacrament** or ordinance. When we speak of the holy meal as sacrament, we emphasize God's action toward us. We see in the meal a sign and means of God's grace toward the world. In the sharing of bread and wine, God reaches out to persons and communities in **grace**, bringing life, strength, and confidence in the life of faith. In speaking of the holy meal as *ordinance*, we emphasize the way in which the meal is a command or law for the church. As such, the emphasis falls on our action of obedience to Christ's command that we "do this in remembrance of [him]" as recounted in the stories of the Last Supper (Luke 22:14-23 and parallels). These two understandings together enable us to see the holy meal as a means of God's gracious action toward us *and* a means by which we respond to God's grace with faith in **obedience**.

The basic ecumenical shape of Holy Communion reflects a fourfold shape of gathering, Word, table, and sending. The community of faith gathers with prayer and song. The Word is proclaimed through the reading of scripture and interpreted through preaching, music, and other arts. The community responds to the Word in intercessory prayer for the world and acts of commitment and baptism. We prepare the table with the offering of our gifts and with the gifts of bread and wine. Thanksgiving is offered, bread broken, wine poured; the bread and cup are shared with all who may receive. Depending on the rules of the community, these may be all who wish to receive, all who are baptized, all who are formal members of the community in good standing, or some other defined group. The action at the table reflects the biblical actions—take, bless, break, and give—that accompany all of the meals Jesus shares with his disciples. (See the feeding of the multitudes in Matthew 14:13-21 and parallels.) With concluding prayers, songs, and blessings, the community is sent into the world to continue its ministry of self-giving and worshipful service.

For further reading, see William R. Crockett's *Eucharist: Symbol of Transformation* or Laurence Hull Stookey's *Eucharist: Christ's Feast with the Church.* EBA

HOLY SPIRIT. The third Person of the Trinity, described in various creeds as "giver of life" and "the divine presence in our lives." The Bible gives two extraordinarily brief definitions of God. "God is spirit," says Jesus to the woman at the well (John 4:24). First John 4:8 adds, "God is **love**." In John 6:63, Jesus explains, "It is the spirit that gives life." These three quotations together say that God is the spirit of love that gives life to every living thing. God's very essence is spirit, life, being, and love. When Moses asks God to reveal God's self, Yahweh responds, "I AM WHO I AM" (Exod. 3:14). God is not a being alongside other beings, but Being itself. The Spirit of Love is the creative essence of God, the continual, faithful fountainhead of life.

Evelyn Underhill said that the third article of the Apostles' Creed is the "forgotten" article, referring to the fact that we emphasize theology and Christology (the understanding of God and Christ) but slight the study of the Holy Spirit: pneumatology (from *pneuma*, Greek "soul," "spirit," or "breath"). This slight seems strange in light of the second verse in the Bible: "And the Spirit of God was moving over the face of the waters" (Gen. 1:2, RSV). This Spirit turned unruly chaos into cosmos: order. Genesis 2 tells us that Adam came to life upon receiving the *ruach* (Hebrew for the breath or spirit of God). When God acts, it is by the Spirit.

Many people believe that the Holy Spirit did not exist among or within people until it was "given" at Pentecost. Yet, like God's love, it has been given since the beginning, although Hebrew Scriptures intimate that only the anointed—prophets, priests, and kings—could receive it. In contrast, Pentecost was a unique occurrence in which a body of people experienced the Spirit's power. Although the prophet Joel had prophesied "all flesh" would be so blessed (Joel 2:28), it was astounding when it happened. The simultaneous reception of the Spirit was so powerful an experience that the church was said to be born (created, given life) as a result.

The Bible speaks of "the Spirit of life" not only as the creative energy that formed the world but also as the power that sustains it. Scripture also makes clear that the Holy Spirit is the ground of God within our souls, calling to us from the core of our beings as inspiration; as the source of **wisdom**, vision, revelation; and as the magnificent **experience** of knowing God's reality. Jesus spoke of that inner presence as he prepared his disciples for his physical absence, explaining that the Paraclete would not only be with them, as he, Jesus, had been, but would be inside them (John 14:19, 20). The Greek word *paraclete* connotes comforter, exhorter, helper, and advocate, indicating the Spirit's role in leading, comforting, and strengthening us and in reminding us of Christ, his life, and his words. Paul writes of the Spirit within us, making our physical bodies temples where God's presence dwells. Thus we can truly become God's hands, eyes, and ears and together act for God as God's body. The Spirit will bind us in **community** with one another, in *koinonia*.

Martin Luther spoke of the Spirit's teaching us from inside as well. In *The Freedom of a Christian*, he wrote that everyone should wish to be among the *theodidacti*, those taught by God, by the Spirit. He also taught that we know scripture is true by the testimony of the Spirit within our hearts. He suggested that when we read the Bible prayerfully, as in *lectio divina*, the Spirit will speak to us. Then we should stop and wait to learn from the Spirit in silence.

Further reading could include Yves Congar's *I Believe in the Holy Spirit*, Jürgen Moltmann's *The Spirit of Life*, and the third volume of Paul Tillich's *Systematic Theology*. GAB

HOPE. A stance of confidence that just as God has been faithful in the past, God will also provide for the future. Christians live in the present with a distinct orientation toward the future. Hope figures prominently in the Hebrew Bible: Moses envisions a promised land (Exod. 6), and the prophets yearn for homecoming after the Exile (Jer. 29). Hope is also foundational in the New Testament: Paul speaks of a life beyond death in a resurrected body (1 Cor. 15:20 ff.), and the early believers pray for Jesus' return (Rev. 22:20).

Hope is a necessary dimension of Christian faith in this life and in the life to come. A portion of our hope must be in this life. We believe that God created a world worthy of redemption; thus hope motivates us to pray for the kingdom of God to come on earth as it is in heaven (Matt. 6:10), and to act upon our prayers. But a portion of our hope must be placed in the life to come, for justice, peace, and righteousness are not always realized in the human experience.

We claim God's gift of hope in many ways: in **reading** the **scriptures**, in praying for the kingdom, in receiving **Holy Communion** (a foretaste of the messianic banquet), and in singing **hymns** from different Christian tradi-

tions. Ultimately hope is grounded in the **experience** of Easter and in the presence of the risen Lord in the ongoing life of the church.

For further reading, see Walter Brueggemann, *Hopeful Imagination: Prophetic Voices in Exile*, and the following hymns: "Hymn of Promise," "Soon and Very Soon," "When We All Get to Heaven," "He Lives," and "Christ The Lord Is Risen Today." KHC

HOPKINS, GERARD MANLEY (1844–89), English **Jesuit** poet. Firstborn of Manley and Catherine's nine children, Hopkins entered a middle-class Anglican family of Stratford, Essex, England. Early on he studied music, sketching, art, and literature; but his unique, eccentric, and wild poetic artistry would be his greatest legacy. Beginning in 1863, Hopkins studied classic literature at Balliol College, Oxford, where he was drawn to the **Oxford movement** under the influential leadership of **John Henry Newman**. Like Newman, Hopkins converted to the Roman Catholic Church, left the university, and entered the Society of Jesus (Jesuits) in 1868 to become a priest. Believing his poetry was incompatible with religious life, he burned all his earlier verses. But seven years later, while studying in North Wales, he was asked to write about the widely publicized loss at sea of a German ship and produced "The Wreck of the Deutschland." This lengthy, religious poem demonstrates his original style with its abrupt intensity of language and poetic technique.

Hopkins is credited with originating the revolutionary "sprung rhythm." Through his keen sensitivity for detail and his ability to express religious feeling, he created striking images and descriptions that have become his unique poetic signature. Through intentional ambiguities with multiple meanings, irregular meter, and the use of peculiar compound words he developed the concepts of *inscape* and *instress*. *Inscape* is the unique essence and mystery of an object, be it a tree, breaking waves, or a distant hill. Through the *inscape* of natural phenomena, Hopkins knows the beauty of the Lord. *Instress* is the unifying energy that maintains something as itself, so that its outward reflection radiates a distinctive inner essence. *Instress* evokes in the perceiver a kind of quasi-mystical illumination, a seeing that enables deep joy and praise for the "grandeur of God" in all creation.

In 1884 Hopkins was appointed Chair of Classics at the Royal University of Dublin, Ireland. Severed from his home, struggling with depression, and under prolonged professorial stress—all evident in his last and unfinished poems—he suffered as his health deteriorated. He died from typhoid fever in June of 1889. Though few poems were published during his life, Hopkins is now considered one of the great religious poets. His works of "verbal music" are read, discussed, and critically taught in schools throughout the world. "Pied Beauty" and "The Grandeur of God" are widely anthologized.

Poems and Prose of Gerard Manley Hopkins, edited by W. H. Gardner, is a good basic collection. EKM

HOWE, JOHN (1630–1705), English Puritan pastor and writer. Having studied at Cambridge and Oxford, Howe preached at Winiwick and Great Torrington. In 1656 he was appointed domestic chaplain to Oliver Cromwell, returning to Torrington in 1659. Driven from his parish by the Act of Uniformity in 1662, Howe became a wandering preacher in hiding until 1671. He published *The Blessedness of the Righteous* in 1668. As domestic chaplain to Lord Massereene, of Antrim Castle, Ireland, he wrote *The Vanity of Man as Mortal* and began his greatest work *The Living Temple* while there. Howe began to pastor a dissenting congregation in Silver Street, London, in 1676. He traveled to Europe in 1685, settling at Utrecht until the Declaration of Indulgence allowed his return to England in 1687.

For more information, see *The Works of the Rev. John Howe with Memoirs of His Life* by Edmund Calamy. LSP

HÜGEL, FRIEDRICH VON (1852–1925), Roman Catholic layman, authority on **mysti**cism and religious philosophy. Hügel was born in Austria. His family moved to England in 1867, where he lived out the rest of his life. Typhoid left him deaf, nervous, and in delicate health. Educated by tutors, he received an honorary doctor of law degree from the University of St. Andrews in Scotland and was the first Roman Catholic since the Reformation to take an honorary doctor of divinity degree from Oxford University. Hügel founded the discussion group known as the London Society for the Study of Religion, which grew into a society of Catholic scholars. Known as an outstanding spiritual director, Hügel had a large influence on **Evelyn Underhill**.

In Hügel's extensive studies of the scripture and criticism, he championed the freedom of exegetes and their right to publish. He found three elements common to all religions: institutional, intellectual, and mystical. Beneath the desire for religion and mysticism lies a metaphysical base formed by a feeling of being trapped in the contingent. The otherness of reality arising from the transcendent God is the beginning of religion. There are two kinds of time: successive, or clock time, and duration, when a person is open to the infinite and experiences a taste of eternity. However, eternal life is part of people's present life, not restricted to the hereafter.

Other themes in Hügel's writings include the **transcendent** element in religion, the apocalyptic element in Jesus' teaching, institutional religion, church authority, and **suffering** in God. In *The Mystical Element of Religion as Studied in St. Catherine of Genoa and her Friends*, Hügel used **Catherine**'s biography as a core around which he developed his ideas of religion and mysticism. *Eternal Life* is Hügel's study of the eternal and the absolute in religion.

Learn more of Hügel's life by reading Michael de la Bedoyere's *The Life of Baron von Hügel*. Joseph P. Whelan's *The Spirituality of Baron Friedrich von Hügel* is a good introduction to Hügel's teachings on spirituality. LSP

HUGH OF ST. VICTOR (d. 1141), Augustinian monk at St. Victor in Paris and writer on philosophy, theology, biblical exegesis, and **contemplation**. His two treatises on Noah's ark, *On the Moral Ark of Noah* and *Mystical Ark of Noah*, detail his view of the spiritual journey. The treatises were based on a symbolic drawing of the ark representing the cosmos with Christ at the center and with the stages of the journey back to that center represented in the pyramidlike body of the ark. Hugh posits a four-part journey: awakening (with stages of fear, grief, and love), **purgation** (with stages of patience, **mercy**, and **compunction**), **illumination** (with stages of cognition, **meditation**, and contemplation), and **union** (with stages of temperance, prudence, and fortitude). The contemplative experience helps seekers to regain their original awareness of God's presence. **Love** is what compels a person to make the journey. Hugh describes love as the road to God. SN

HUMANISM. A philosophical perspective that underscores the importance of the human and therefore values human culture. In the Renaissance, humanism referred originally to a return to the study of Greek and Latin classics, mostly to recover a style of writing. In time this study shifted the Western outlook toward the Greek emphasis upon the human as "the measure of all things." The change manifested itself first in the writings of Dante, Petrarch, and Boccaccio; then in a return to classical sources; and finally in art that took nature and the human form as expressions of perfection. Michelangelo did not hesitate to depict even the Creator and Redeemer in human form.

Humanism originated, therefore, as a Christian recovery of its classical heritage wedded to Christianity in a new way. In the modern era, however, some have secularized humanism and thus created a conflict with Christianity. British humanist H. J. Blackham has ascribed to this form of humanism four presuppositions: that human beings are on their own; that this life is all there is; that

human beings are responsible for their own lives; and that they are responsible for the life of humankind. Christian humanists could agree with the last two but not the first two. **Hope** for humankind, they would insist, hangs on the recognition that human beings are not on their own and that this life is not all there is. Realistically, people must recognize their own frailty apart from God. God, however, has moved to help humans in their weakness by sharing the human lot. The Christian doctrine of **Incarnation** implies the highest doctrine of humankind possible—that God became human in order that humans might share God's life.

For further reading, see Martin D'Arcy, *Humanism and Christianity*; Jacques Maritain, *True Humanism*; and Carlyle Marney, *The Recovery of the Person: A Christian Humanism*. EGH

HUMILITY. A fundamental and deep-seated openness to God in daily life. In a Western culture that emphasizes individual ambition, achievement, and accomplishment, the idea of nurturing a humble approach to life can seem like a waste of time. Many confuse the idea of humbling ourselves with becoming insignificant, weak, spineless, and passive, which goes against our cultural tendency to glorify people who make an impact, who are strong, powerful people of action.

Too many modern Christians misunderstand the virtue or **disposition**. They think that being humble means having no opinion, emotion, or volition of their own; that it means being extremely self-critical to the point of having no sense of personal self-esteem. They think that it means walking about in some sort of spiritually blissful and passive state with hands folded at the waist, meekly smiling at all who pass as one contemplatively meanders through life. This is far from the humility of the mystics and the great spiritual masters of Christianity.

At its core, true humility means recognizing that God has created us out of nothing and that God has given us all of our abilities, aptitudes, and accomplishments as gifts of grace. In the Hebrew text of Genesis 2:7 the first human being, *Adam*, is created from the dirt, *adamah* (Hebrew). God breathes God's Spirit into the *adamah* to create *Adam*. The Latin word for dirt is *humus*. Many words spring from *humus*: **humor**, human, humus, homage, and humility. All connote a sense of groundedness—a recognition that we are nothing more or less than created matter. Thus to be human is to be "of the soil." Becoming humble means being grounded in an awareness that we have been created by God; only through the gift of God's breath or Spirit within us do we become anything special.

To be humble, then, means to become profoundly aware of our fragility, mortality, and dependence upon God. It is recognizing at our core that only by and through God's grace are we made special. Our true uniqueness arises only out of our ability to respond to God's call for us—to nurture the gifts God has given us so as to become who God calls us to be. So to be humble means to become profoundly open to God at all levels of our being. We root our action in prayerfully seeking the **will of God** in everything. As we become increasingly humble, we say to God, "Not my will but yours be done" (Luke 22:42), and then we act to the best of our abilities.

In the end, humility is not a condition in which we become weakly passive in life. We become actively engaged in life but seek God's will instead of our own **will** as far as we can ascertain it. We engage in mission, social action, evangelism, ministry, preaching, teaching, caring, healing, and service for God's sake. Becoming humble is the process of **abandonment**, of putting aside our own egos so that Christ can live in our hearts, the **Holy Spirit** can guide us, and we can respond to the call of our Creator to become the persons God created us to be.

For further reading, see *A Testament of Devotion* by **Thomas R. Kelly** or *Forming Faith in a Hurricane* by N. Graham Standish. NGS

HUMOR. A disposition or temperament that comes in many forms. Some varieties of humor destroy the spiritual life, while others offer positive evidence of a healthy spiritual life. Psalm 1:1 warns the reader not to sit in the seat of scoffers, a theme picked up by Paul when he says, "God is not mocked, for you reap whatever you sow" (Gal. 6:7). However, remember that, contrary to much of the humor in our popular culture, not all humor needs to be of the mocking variety. Proverbs 17:22 says, "A cheerful heart is a good medicine," and humor can certainly promote good cheer.

Humor, especially irony, and sometimes outright sarcasm, can be found in scripture (for example, 1 Kings 18:27; Gal. 5:12). Since irony is meant to jar the ear and the heart by pointing out the difference between an expectation and the actuality, ironic humor can foster **humility**. Because of its cauterizing effect, irony is less suited for promoting growth of the **fruit of the Spirit** than it is in clearing the ground for such growth to begin.

When it grows from a Christian disposition of joy, humor can be a positive expression of the Christian life. Humor can also serve the important purpose of reminding us of our freedom. The reality structures that seem to claim ultimacy in our lives can be shown to be much less than ultimate through humor. Humor allows us to unmask the "principalities and powers" for what they are. The violation of our reason that humor often signals can, in other words, make us question what is truly reasonable and invite us into an alternative perspective. Laughter can pull the curtain on worldly pretense, show us the futility of worry, and call us again to the simple **abandonment** of childlike trust and joy.

For further reading, see *Laughter at the Foot of the Cross* by M. A. Screech and *Redeeming Laughter: The Cosmic Dimension of Human Experience* by Peter L. Berger. GSC

HURNARD, HANNAH (1905–90), British and American writer most noted for her series of modern Christian allegories. The first, *Hinds' Feet on High Places*, draws on **holiness** doctrine and imagery from the Song of

Solomon to tell how Much-Afraid leaves her home in the Valley of Humiliation to follow the Shepherd to the High Places, a journey that involves increasing sacrifice and self-abandonment. Over the course of her works spanning thirty years (including *Mountains of Spices*, a sequel to *Hinds' Feet*) Hurnard shows a spiritual progression that becomes increasingly universalistic and esoteric to the point that many find her later views extreme. Hurnard also spent many years doing mission work in Israel through its tumultuous beginning as a nation in the middle of the twentieth century. Her work *Watchmen on the Walls* is a journal of those experiences. LKB

HUS, JOHN (ca. 1372–1415), Bohemian pastor and reformer. In 1402 Hus began a ten-year pastorate at Prague's Bethlehem Chapel, center of the growing reform movement and the symbol of expanding nationalism against the Roman Catholic Church and the Germans. His preaching in the vernacular explored the need for morality, especially in reforming the corruption of the church; the urgency for increased spiritual zeal; and a search of the scriptures for truth. Hus asserted that it was more important to follow Christ and the **scriptures** than the pope or tradition. Liturgically he introduced and expanded congregational participation, translating and writing **hymns** in Czech and a sung mass. The inscription on the Hus monument in Prague's Old Town Square bears these words from his *Exposition of Faith*: "Therefore, O faithful Christian, search for truth, hear truth, learn truth, love truth, speak the truth, hold the truth, defend the truth till death." Hus traveled to Germany in 1414 to defend himself but without a fair trial was convicted as a heretic and burned at the stake on July 6, 1415, singing praise to God. The reforming flame of his death immediately spread to the nascent Hussite movement as well as inspired the later *Unitas Fratrum* or **Moravian** Church.

For more insight into the spirituality of John Hus, read *The Letters of John Hus*, translated by Matthew Spinka, and Hus's classic *The Church*. Matthew Spinka's *John Hus* is a helpful introduction. TS

HUVELIN, HENRI (1838–1910), spiritual director. After graduating from École Normale Supérieure with a degree in history and being ordained in 1867, he refused a professorship at the Institut Catholique in Paris. Instead he chose service as a curate at the Church of Saint-Eugène in Paris for eight years and at Saint-Augustin for thirty-five years. Despite suffering from rheumatism, he spent long hours hearing confessions and giving counsel and direction. Huvelin was well-known for his conferences with young Parisians. Two of his penitents were **Charles de Foucauld**, whose vocation he encouraged, and **Friedrich von Hügel**. Although Huvelin did not write for publication, many of his conferences (including *Some Spiritual Guides of the 17th Century*) were taken down and later published with numerous letters of direction. See also Friedrich von Hügel's *Eternal Life*. LSP

HYMNS. Songs of praise and adoration of God, sacred poetry set to music. Perhaps the definition of the gospel hymn writer **Fanny Crosby** is best: "A hymn is a song of the heart to God."

Some of the earliest hymns are biblical. The Hebrew scriptures provide us with the Song of Moses (Exod. 15:1-18), the Song of Miriam (Exod. 15:21), the Song of Deborah (Judg. 5), and the Song of the Seraphim (Isa. 6:1-5). Hebrew religious poetry reached its zenith in the Psalms, which are still sung in many forms and settings. Luke included Christian hymns in the opening chapters of his Gospel. We also find hymn fragments in the Pauline and Pastoral Epistles and in the Revelation of John.

The first nonbiblical Christian hymn is thought to be "Shepherd of Eager Youth" by **Clement of Alexandria**. Many of the hymns written during the early church's struggle with numerous heresies are forgotten, but two major hymn writers did appear at that time.

Ambrose of Milan wrote hymns to combat the Arian heresy in the West. In the East, John of Damascus is noted for his Easter hymn texts "The Day of Resurrection" and "Come, Ye Faithful, Raise the Strain."

In his systematizing of church music, Pope Gregory I, the Great also caused the decline of congregational song and the rise of a liturgy sung by the trained priesthood. With the threat of heresies abating, the early Latin hymns fell out of favor in worship. In contrast to the early Latin hymns, the medieval Latin hymns were used to educate Christians and to win new converts to the faith. At first these hymns found a home in the corporate worship of the people. However, it was not long before they were used only in the monasteries. The later Latin hymns break out of the rigors of classical form and in simpler language and structure bring a rise in emotion and a movement from objective to subjective hymnody. A fine example of this new emotion and subjectivity is the powerful "Dies Irae" written during the time of the Black Death.

With Martin Luther and the Protestant Reformation came a renewed interest in congregational singing and the use of hymns to teach doctrine. During this time, hymn texts were written in the language of the people, and the musical form of the German chorale was developed, a form still used today. During the troubling times of the Thirty Years War (1618–1648) came hymns expressing a deep personal faith in the goodness of God, which were the beginnings of the great pietistic hymns of the late seventeenth century.

After 1800 we must look to England and America for developments in hymnody. Isaac Watts, the father of English hymnody, wrote many hymn texts that are widely used today. With Charles and John Wesley came a new way of using hymns as expressions of personal Christian experience. Their hymnal was arranged according to stages of the Christian life, not by doctrines or seasons of the liturgical year. Hymns became the framework and setting of worship. *Hymns, Ancient and Modern*, published in 1861 as a product of the Oxford movement, reintroduced many ancient hymns in English translation. America saw a tremendous growth in popular hymnody that climaxed in the gospel hymns of the Moody/Sankey revivals. The twentieth century saw increased use of hymns to address social concerns and a renewal of the basic use of hymns to praise God.

Although hymns are primarily used in corporate worship, they also speak to the hearts of individuals and thus are a vital resource for spiritual formation. They give people memorable words to express both their own deepest experiences and their love for God. DDW

I

ICONS. The word *icon* comes from the Greek *eikon*, meaning "image." Orthodox Christians believe that descriptions of the saints, first passed on by oral tradition, were later rendered into actual painted portraits or prototypes. Although these prototypes have been lost, they have been lovingly reproduced throughout the ages. Luke is believed to have painted a portrait of the *Theotokos* ("God-bearer," the usual Greek designation of **Mary**) and is thus regarded as the first iconographer.

In the painting—or writing—of an icon, we find a paradigm for the ascent of humankind toward the light of God. As the iconographer establishes the basic outline of the icon through tracing, so at our **baptism** the grace of God begins to trace in us the outline of the divine image. Then, as the iconographer fills in the darker colors and models the distinctive features of the subject through the use of lighteners, humankind through obedience moves toward the light—toward the likeness of God.

In the language of the icon, the traits of the face, hair, and wrinkles are reproduced faithfully but divested of all their sensuality. The sense organs are reproduced in a non-naturalistic manner. The eyes are large and wide and represent the spiritual eye that looks beyond the material world, for the light of the body is the eye (Matt. 6:22); the ears are large and convey attentiveness to the Word (Mark 4:23) and receptiveness to the invisible world of the Spirit. The face, which best expresses the spiritual life of the person, conveys the power of the Spirit over the body. The forehead, seat of **wisdom**, rises high above the arches of the eyes, strengthening the intensity of the gaze. The nose, which has its roots at the base of the forehead, is elongated to give an expression of nobility. The mouth, often the most sensual part of the face, is small and closed in **contemplation**. The "look" of the icon is devoid of all physical heaviness and indicates that the subject has purified his or her life through **fasting** and vigils. The face is peaceful and serene. An evil person or one who has not yet received the light of God must be portrayed in profile because it is deemed inappropriate to make eye contact with such a person or to meditate upon his or her image.

Simply to study an icon will not suffice. One must contemplate it by becoming gradually centered in its inner stillness, becoming collected and attentive. The icon challenges us to notice the visible element in our lives; to recognize its power over us; and to discover that it is the door to the invisible, which is the abode of God. The icon is a point of departure. It moves us, with our permission, beyond the image to an encounter with the divine reality the image represents. The icon becomes the place where we gather up all we know about the nature of God or of Christ or the particular saint the icon depicts. But we must move beyond this gathering up to an openheartedness and open-mindedness that lets God be God. We must stand before God without imprisoning God in images or concepts. When the icon assists us in doing this, it becomes a means of **grace**.

For further insight on praying with icons, try *Behold the Beauty of the Lord* by **Henri J. M. Nouwen**. For more on creating icons as a spiritual discipline, see *Communing with the Saints* by Russell M. Hart. RMH

IGNATIUS OF ANTIOCH (ca. 35–ca. 110), bishop and martyr. Probably born in Syria, Ignatius is virtually unknown apart from his letters and journey to **martyrdom** in Rome under a guard of ten soldiers. Received with honor at Smyrna by Polycarp, he visited neighboring communities and wrote letters of encouragement to churches at Ephesus, Magnesia, Tralles, and Rome. In the last he entreated that the Romans do nothing to interfere with his martyrdom. Taken to Troas, he wrote letters to the churches of Philadelphia and Smyrna and to Polycarp. From there he was escorted through Macedonia and Illyria to Dyrrhachium, where he boarded a ship to Italy.

The authenticity of Ignatius's letters remained heatedly debated from the late fifteenth until the nineteenth century because of interpolations and spurious letters bearing his name. The debate was put to rest with the publication of J. B. Lightfoot and J. R. Harmer's critical edition of *The Apostolic Fathers* in 1885. The genuine letters reveal a man passionately committed to Christ and intent on martyrdom, "ground by the teeth of wild beasts that I may be found pure bread of Christ" (Rom. 4:1). In the letters to churches he proposed as a solution to threats of division that they "do nothing without the bishop." The strength of insistence, however, indicates that the churches of Asia Minor did not accord their bishops such authority. Still more, the church at Antioch did not recognize Ignatius in that way. What lay behind the tension is a bit uncertain, but one facet was docetism, the belief that Jesus only *appeared* to be human. Ignatius emphatically underlined that Jesus was both truly human and truly divine. In connection with that affirmation, he also made much of **Holy Communion** as the symbol par excellence of the **Incarnation** and "the medicine of immortality."

For further reading, see *Ignatius of Antioch*, vol. 4 of *The Apostolic Fathers: A New Translation and Commentary*, edited by Robert M. Grant, or Virginia Corwin's study *St. Ignatius and Christianity in Antioch*. EGH

IGNATIUS OF LOYOLA (1491–1556),
Catholic reformer, mystic, founder of the Society of Jesus (**Jesuits**). Ignatius was born into the noble house of Loyola in the Basque area of Spain. In 1517 he did what was expected of one of his class and joined the army. In 1521, during a skirmish with the French, a cannonball shattered his right leg. After two surgeries he spent months convalescing. During this time, he began reading popular romance literature, which inspired daydreams about a chivalrous life of serving his king and his (imaginary) lady. Eventually he was given religious books, including *The Life of Christ* by Ludolph of Saxony; *The Golden Legend*, a collection of lives of the saints by Jacopo de Voragine; and *Imitation of Christ* by **Thomas à Kempis**. These books inspired more gratifying daydreams of serving Christ the King and emulating the **saints**.

In 1522 Ignatius made a pilgrimage to Manresa, a small town near the Benedictine monastery of Montserrat. There he spent months in a cave, facing temptations and desolation of spirit but also deep and refreshing mystical insights. It was here he composed much of his *Spiritual Exercises.*

Ignatius spent more than a decade traveling around Europe as an itinerant teacher and preacher. He lived and worked among the poor and outcast, even as he acted as **spiritual director** for people of all classes. By 1534 he had gathered ten men who were dedicated to following him in his ministry. They formed the Society of Jesus (**Jesuits**), taking vows of **chastity**, **poverty**, and **obedience** to one another and to the pope. Over the next two and a half years they were all ordained. Pope Paul III officially approved the order in 1540, and they elected a reluctant Ignatius their first secretary general. By the time Ignatius died in 1556, there were a thousand Jesuits. He left behind the constitutions of the order, seven thousand letters, and the *Spiritual Exercises* (which had received papal approval in 1548).

Before Ignatius, there were two forms of apostolic life: monastic (cloistered, with a rule of life, represented by the Benedictines and Cistercians) and mendicant (often in the world, preaching and practicing poverty, represented by the Franciscans, the Dominicans and the Carmelites). Ignatian spirituality was that of contemplatives in the midst of action. Prayer was integrated into daily life, and the world was a subject of prayer. This was a movement away from the world-hating spirituality of the Middle Ages and *devotio moderna* to more world-affirming piety. Ignatius represented an activist spirituality. Led by the discerned will of God, one performs **works of mercy** toward orphans, prostitutes, pensioners, prisoners, hospital patients, or those in Jesuit schools or inspired by the Society's preaching (instructing the ignorant, counseling the doubtful, and admonishing sinners are all works of mercy).

All of Ignatius's spirituality is found in *Spiritual Exercises*, his highly structured retreat method that includes meditation, contemplation, application of the senses, and examination of conscience (**examen**). Originally designed as a thirty-day retreat with a spiritual director, *Spiritual Exercises* is also available in the "Nineteenth Annotation" as a six- to nine-month long process involving one hour a day and weekly meetings with a spiritual director. By meditation Ignatius means placing one's self in God's presence using a passage from scripture or a specific meditative prayer. By contemplation he means placing one's self in the scene of a scripture passage, using all the senses to understand the passage's meaning. He also urges frequent repetition, returning to review a previous prayer experience that had resulted in consolation or desolation and uncovering a deeper sense of what was happening in that prayer.

Ignatius, like the Protestant reformers, emphasized the direct **experience** of God. He contributed to the Catholic counter-Reformation by encouraging *every* Christian, not just religious professionals, to practice an activist spirituality, beginning with an effort to grow closer to God through meditation and service. For further reading, see John O' Malley, *The First Jesuits*. WW

ILLUMINATION, ILLUMINATIVE WAY. The second formative shift in the threefold pattern mystical theologians have described for growing in **holiness**. Progressing along the **purgative** way, beginners have begun to know the experience of illumination. Beginners in the spiritual life have become proficient in purifying their senses and their minds by their active **detachment** and passive **receptivity** toward God's purifying **grace**. Passing from the prayer of simplicity that characterizes the summit of the purgative way, those faithful committed beginners move on to a deeper knowledge of God's presence. The illuminative way takes the proficient (the classical term for those in this stage) beyond the letting go and stripping away of worldly sensory perceptions and thoughts into a more transcendent awareness of the reality of God now-here-present. While still cooperating with God's grace as in the purgative way, the proficient learn to respond to God's new challenges, invitations, and appeals in a way that requires greater dependence on God alone. The purifying work accomplished in the "night of sense" has so formed the proficient that they desire to let go and **abandon** themselves to God with greater ease and deeper trust. The **Holy Spirit** enkindles deeper and deeper **conformity** in our mind and will to Christ. The desire to practice some form of **contemplative** prayer is evidenced as this middle stage of the spiritual journey continues. Though not contemplative prayer *per se*, **Centering Prayer** is a nondiscursive attention to the presence of God that instills a deep sense of stillness and peace.

Not all illumination comes in the form of spiritual insights and inner strength. There is a flip side to this reality: deeper, interior purification via the "**dark night** of the soul." Entering into the depths of personality via intellect, mind, will, memory, and imagination, the individual is freed by the Holy Spirit from the residue and vestiges of sinful behaviors, motivations, and attitudes. Those seeking spiritual maturity willingly accept the roller-coaster ride characteristic of the illuminative way that peaks with joyful moments of **consolations** and then dives deep into awful desolations. The purifying fire of God's love continues to pursue the soul as it increasingly yields with deeper **faith**, **hope**, and **love**. Encouraged by Jesus' words, "Zeal for my Father's house consumes me," one understands that growth and transformation in Christ are a reality with two interrelated contemplative experiences: stillness and **peace**, and the discomforting dark night of the soul. While not everyone will experience this dark night precisely as **John of the Cross** has described it, the Holy Spirit will refine and reshape all that is necessary according to the unique personality during the journey into illumination. This spiraling passage—cycling both higher and deeper—can eventually lead into the last stage of the threefold model, the **unitive** way. EKM

IMAGERY. Analogy and metaphor, especially as used in prayer and theological discourse. The use of analogy and metaphor is fundamental to the working of human minds. We learn by finding ways to connect new knowledge to things we already know. An iceberg is like a mountain of ice that floats in the ocean. A sofa is like an armchair, only wider, or like a bed with a back and armrests. Of course, any analogy has limitations, as the story of the blind men and the elephant reminds us. Even when a group of blind men who have felt an elephant put their partial perceptions together, an elephant is not at all like a wall mounted on tree trunks with a rope at one end and a snake at the other. Though we cannot avoid using analogy and metaphor, we need to remember that they can be deceptive

The problem becomes even greater when we try to deal with abstractions or mysteries. As soon as we begin to talk about God, we naturally try to draw connections with what we know. But when we say God is fatherlike, we bring into our portrait of God our own fathers, fathers we've seen on TV or read about in books, and cultural expectations of fatherhood. Even if we say God is the Almighty, we tap into images of power, whether of electricity, waterfalls, or powerful people. For this reason, some spiritual writers—the author of *The Cloud of Unknowing*, for instance—urge readers to follow the **negative way** of avoiding any use of imagery for God. Even that author speaks of God as dwelling in blinding light that we see only as the cloud of unknowing.

But without some sort of image, God remains a sort of indistinct smudge in our minds or a word with no meaning at all. Some writers concentrate on our relationship with Jesus as beloved or even bridegroom to our **soul** in a **spiritual marriage**. Others use a variety of images in the hope they will complement one another. Thus **Teresa of Ávila** speaks of union with God as a drop falling into the ocean or a candle flame added into an all-consuming **fire**, and of the **Holy Spirit** we receive in our prayer as **water** that helps the flowers of **virtue** grow in the gardens of our souls.

Imagery is more readily applied to the spiritual life itself. It can be pictured as a **ladder** by which we climb toward God, a **pilgrim's** progress, or our personal **exodus** out of captivity, through the **desert** of **purgation**, **dryness**, and **darkness**, and into the land of promise. **Francis de Sales** likens stages in spiritual growth to the ostrich (who never flies), the chicken (who makes a little progress for much flapping), and finally the soaring eagle. Teresa uses the life cycle from caterpillar to chrysalis to the moth that seeks the flame. **Jean Pierre de Caussade** compares our **abandonment** to God to a piece of marble, trusting that the sculptor knows what he is doing with hammer and chisel. Images like these can be an important part of our **meditation**, whether we simply reflect on an image in our reading or follow suggestions for more structured **guided imagery** meditation.

For a wealth of images suitable for deeper reflection, see *Interior Castle* by Teresa, *Introduction to the Devout Life* by Francis de Sales, or Caussade's *Abandonment to Divine Providence*. For a deeper look at Teresa's use of imagery (from a Jungian perspective), see *Spiritual Pilgrims* by John Welch. KRB

IMITATION OF CHRIST. Seeking to live a Christlike life. Since New Testament times, followers of Christ have always sought ways to make their lives more Christ-like. The *virgines sacrae*, beginning in the fourth century, were consecrated to their perpetual virginity in the imitation of Christ's. The Syriac tradition's original understanding of discipleship involved a literal imitation of the poor, homeless, celibate Jesus. In Ireland the Celts practiced the "green martyrdom," a voluntary exile, traveling in unknown areas in faith and trust, just as Jesus had done.

Francis of Assisi is considered by many the best imitation of Christ. He sought to conform to the life of Jesus through the practice of penance, **obedience**, and **humility**. Francis was also devoted to literal, contemplative imitation of events in the life of Jesus. He invented the "living nativity" in 1223. The following year he received the **stigmata**, which his followers interpreted as an outward sign of his interior relationship with Christ.

In the late twelfth century, the **Beguine** movement began in northern Europe. These women advocated the imitation of the primitive church through evangelization, service, gospel poverty, and manual labor in imitation of the poor Jesus. In the thirteenth century, a new devotion (called *devotio moderna*) to Christ's humanity spread throughout the church. The new emphasis on Jesus' historical life and imitating him was a response to the centuries-old devotion to Christ as eternal Logos or risen Lord and found its classical expression in *Imitation of Christ* by **Thomas à Kempis**. **Ignatius of Loyola** developed a spirituality that involved imitating Christ's **poverty** and **suffering** as a way to build the kingdom of God.

The **spirituality of liberation,** which emerged in Latin America in the 1960s, promotes solidarity with the poor and oppressed through voluntary poverty and service among the poor—not the idealization of poverty but a protest against the causes of poverty and an authentic imitation of Christ. WW

IMPASSIBILITY OF GOD. Literally, God's "incapability of **suffering**." Taking their cue from Greek philosophy, Christian theologians have denied God's "passibility" from three points of view: (1) being acted upon from without, (2) emotional changes from within, and (3) feelings of pain or pleasure as a result of action by another person. Accordingly, early Christian theologians such as **Tertullian** sharply distinguished between human and divine natures in Christ. Tertullian vigorously opposed those he called "Patripassians" ("Father-sufferers"), who believed Christ suffered in his human nature; but he could not experience pain and death in his divine nature. Such sharp distinction of natures, however, came under serious question in the early centuries, particularly because the Hebrew people did not hesitate to ascribe emotion to God, who is, above all, a God of **love**.

In the fourth and fifth centuries theologians debated heatedly the relationship between the two natures. Cyril of Alexandria charged that Nestorius and others in the Antiochene tradition distinguished the natures so sharply that they ended up with two *persons*. Cyril argued for a single divine/human nature in the Incarnation, a position known as monophysitism (one-nature-ism). In this view, the two natures were so integrally connected that God suffered in the Son. At Chalcedon in 451, however, the bishops underscored the distinctness of the two natures in such a way as to conserve the idea of impassibility.

Since the nineteenth century, theologians have questioned the concept more and more forcefully. Although it has had defenders, it has come under fire from such notable theologians as **William Temple**, H. Wheeler Robinson, **Dietrich Bonhoeffer**, and Jürgen Moltmann. The Hebrew Bible, especially Isaiah 40–55, depicts God as a God who suffers with and for the people of God. This portrait helped early Christians to make some sense of Jesus' death.

For further reading, see H. Wheeler Robinson, *The Cross in the Old Testament*; and Paul S. Fiddes, *The Creative Suffering of God*. EGH

INCARNATION. (From the Latin *incarnari*, "to be made flesh"), the "Word made flesh" in

Jesus Christ and, by analogy, the "fleshing out" of the presence of Christ in each believer and in the church as a whole. The doctrine of the Incarnation is central to the Christian faith, referring to the unique event in salvation history where God, the eternal Word, took on flesh, becoming Jesus Christ as stated in John 1:14. This teaching holds that the mystery of Jesus Christ is that he embodies both a fully divine and a fully human nature. Scholastic philosophy refers to this understanding as the hypostatic union: the union of two substances or natures so as to make one person. In this union, Jesus Christ is the perfect and complete revelation of God. In him God's very essence was made clear—God as self-communicating **love** and God's fundamental **will** to **sanctify** and redeem the world. Early church writers such as **Irenaeus** and **Athanasius** proposed that the purpose of the Incarnation was to demonstrate God's power to recreate the human world by doing so within that world and thus to impart **deification** or *theosis*. Therefore, this doctrine naturally flows into the Christian understanding of the nature of the church and its spirituality.

Roman Catholic, Anglican, and **Orthodox** traditions stress that the church of Jesus Christ is an extension of the Incarnation—a continued manifestation in time and space, embodied in the sacramental life and its spirituality. **Dietrich Bonhoeffer** extended this theme of the church as Christ in the world but in and through the fellowship of believers. The church passes on the divine indwelling life of **grace** that began in the life, death, resurrection, and glorification of Christ. The dynamics of the Incarnation intimately connect the doctrine of incarnation with the central theme of Christian piety and spirituality, the **imitation of Christ**. Through the formative and **sanctifying** work of the **Holy Spirit** (2 Pet. 1:4) human existence is transformed when Christ lives in (is incarnate in) the believer. **John Wesley's** doctrine of sanctification can be understood as the redemptive incarnation of Christ in each believer.

Modern theologians such as **Karl Rahner**

believe that the Incarnation reveals the intrinsic orientation of human nature to the divine life. Incarnational **spirituality** asserts that we, with **body** and spirit united to become a living **soul**, have an intrinsic openness toward God. Our authentic and true unfolding is a progressive realization of the image of God in which we were originally created (Gen. 1:26-27; 2:7). For Rahner self-transcendence is grounded in God's self-communication in the Incarnation. Our ultimate **experience** of grace moves and grounds our existence in the direct reality of the being of God. Incarnational spirituality, therefore, focuses on the process of gradually integrating or fleshing out all dimensions of the human personality in such a way as to conform human reality and human will to the will or image of God. CIZ

INDIFFERENCE. See Apatheia.

INGE, WILLIAM RALPH (1860–1954), Anglican priest and scholar, dean of St. Paul's Cathedral, London. Inge wrote a pioneering study, *Christian Mysticism*, in 1899, in which he sought to demonstrate the congruence of the Logos doctrine in John's Gospel with **Neoplatonic** mysticism: that the eternal was revealed in the temporal. He explained that **mysticism** arises as the soul, cleansed by faith, partakes of the divine life and contemplates a loving God. However, he erroneously questioned the place of apophatic, or **negative**, mysticism in the Christian tradition, believing it to be of Hindu origin. He also criticized the influence of the Song of Solomon on Christian mysticism, believing that erotic mysticism was not chaste. SAF

INTERCESSION. A form of prayer in which we ask not for ourselves but for another. We ask God to intercede in human affairs, making God's presence known on earth.

Intercessory prayers are found in the Bible. Many of the psalms were cries of intercession. The prophets offered prayers of intercession for the people of Israel. In the Gospel stories, Jesus instructed his disciples to intercede for the lost (Matt. 9:36-38), and he told his followers to pray for their enemies (Matt. 5:44). Jesus practiced intercessory prayer when he prayed for Peter (Luke 22:31-32), when he prayed for his disciples (John 17), and in his final hours when he prayed, "Father, forgive them; for they do not know what they are doing" (Luke 23:34).

We follow these biblical examples whenever we pray for others. Spontaneous intercessions are offered when we pray for a person who suddenly comes to mind or when we pray for victims of tragedies as we read the newspaper. Intercessory prayers can also become part of a regular prayer practice. Prayers of intercession may be very specific, asking God for exact outcomes in another's life. Others, more general in nature, ask God to be with another or to surround a situation with love. Some intercessions are wordless and use images or movement to call God's presence into the lives of others.

Some traditions understand Jesus to be the intercessor for all peoples. Believing this, people pray to Jesus to intercede with God on behalf of the world. **Mary** is also frequently understood to be a compassionate intercessor, and prayers may be offered to her on another's behalf. Sometimes **saints** are asked to intercede in human affairs.

We are invited into intercessory prayer whenever another asks for our prayers or when we request prayers from someone else. To deepen the practice of intercessory prayer, see *Praying for Friends and Enemies* by Jane E. Vennard. JEV

IONA. A tiny rocky island off the west coast of Scotland, chosen by Irish monk and missionary Columba in 563 as the site of his monastery. From Iona **Celtic** Christian missionaries reintroduced Christianity to Great Britain. In the Middle Ages, Iona was home to a **Benedictine** abbey. In 1938 **George MacLeod** founded the Iona Community, which began work on the reconstruction of the ancient abbey and became an ecumenical organization dedicated to the renewal of the Christian church through a **rule** of **prayer**, **worship**, and involvement in the structures of society to work for justice. At present the Iona Community has about 230 members and fifteen hundred associates, largely from England and Scotland. Pilgrims from around the world are attracted to this holy place because of its raw beauty and sacred connections that reach back into prehistory.

George McLeod called Iona a "thin place" where the veil between this world and the world beyond is almost gone. Among projects of the Iona Community is Wild Goose Publications, which produces new resources for worship and hymns often based upon ancient folk tunes from around the world. The journal *Coracle* is produced to inform members and associates of the Community's work. HLR

IRENAEUS (ca. 130–200), bishop of Lyons. Growing up in Smyrna under Polycarp, Irenaeus studied in Rome in the school of Justin Martyr (ca. 100–ca. 165). Sometime after 164 he moved to Lyons, where he was ordained a presbyter. He narrowly missed martyrdom in 177 when the aged bishop of Lyons, Pothinus, dispatched him to Rome with a letter for Pope Eleutherius (175–89). While he was away, Pothinus and other church leaders in Lyons were arrested and executed. When Irenaeus returned he succeeded Pothinus as bishop.

We know little of Irenaeus's activities as a bishop, but two of his major writings have survived—*Refutation and Overthrow of Knowledge Falsely So-Called* (usually referred to as *Against Heresies*) and *Proof of the Apostolic Preaching*, a manual for use by someone trying to win inquirers to the Christian faith. Unlike Justin, Irenaeus had few kind things to say about Greek and Roman philosophers or poets. He placed his confidence, rather, in the Old Testament and in writings being collected as the New Testament. Against Marcion and some of the Gnostics he argued that the same God inspired both testaments. The Logos or Word of John 1:1-18 is not a "Second God," as Justin said, but the One God self-disclosed. Drawing from Paul, Irenaeus developed a theory that

Christ "recapitulated" the whole human story, reversing the effects of Adam's fall. Whereas Adam disobeyed God and thus plunged humankind downward, Christ obeyed and pulled us back up. Irenaeus contended that Jesus lived to age fifty on the basis of John 8:57, passing through every stage of human life. He also laid a base for the Eastern Christian concept of **deification** with the remark that Jesus became human in order that we might become divine. His statement that all churches must agree with the Church of Rome on account of its greater antiquity or more powerful authority has occasioned much debate among Protestant, Catholic, and Orthodox scholars.

Irenaeus's writings include *Against Heresies* in *Ante-Nicene Fathers*, vol. 1, and *The Demonstration of the Apostolic Preaching*, edited by J. Armitage Robinson. Studies include John Lawson, *The Biblical Theology of St. Irenaeus*, and Robert M. Grant, *Irenaeus of Lyons*. EGH

J

JACOPONE DA TODI (ca. 1230–1306), **Franciscan** poet and mystic, considered perhaps the most gifted Italian writer prior to Dante. Born in the Umbrian town of Todi, Jacopone dei Benedetti became a well-to-do notary and, in his mid-thirties, married happily. His wife accidentally died after only one year. It is reported that the grieving Jacopone then learned that his wife had been practicing hidden self-mortification, wearing a hair shirt under her dress. This discovery triggered a spiritual crisis for the worldly Jacopone, who shed his possessions and became a wandering Franciscan tertiary for ten years. The renamed Jacopone da Todi formally entered the Order of Friars Minor in 1278 during a period of major disagreement between two divisions in the community: the Spirituals and the Conventuals. Jacopone sided immediately with the Franciscan Spirituals, who deplored the comfortable lifestyle adopted by the second-generation Franciscans. The Spirituals wished to return the Franciscan order to the founder's ideals of absolute **poverty**, simplicity, **penitence**, and charismatic **worship**—reforms that **Evelyn Underhill** observes would later be evident in the fire of early Methodism.

Jacopone was a passionate reformer, and the poetry emerging from his zealous heart reveals these pure Franciscan values. His poems, which he called *laude* ("lauds, praises"), include passionate love songs to God, ecstatic experiences of mystical closeness to God, satirical critiques on the worldliness of the church, and calls to repentance. Other hymns and treatises sometimes have been ascribed to Jacopone, but scholars agreed that the *laude* are genuine. A gifted orator, Jacopone was known to practice what he preached. In fact, he was excommunicated in 1298 and kept in solitary confinement for nearly five years when he spoke against the wayward Pope Boniface VIII. Jacopone was later restored to the church by Benedict XI, Boniface's successor.

Jacopone's poetry is available in English in *Jacopone da Todi: The Lauds*, translated by Serge and Elizabeth Hughes. For his life, see George T. Peck's *The Fool of God: Jacopone da Todi.* SAF

JAMES, WILLIAM (1842–1910), American professor, psychologist, and philosopher. Born in New York, William was the oldest of five children of Henry and Mary James. Because of his inherited wealth, Henry James saw that William received an excellent education. In 1861 William James entered Harvard to study chemistry and later physiology. In 1865 James had the opportunity to assist the biologist Louis Agassiz on a journey to the Amazon. During his travels, James contracted smallpox, which left him weak and in chronic pain. Finally James graduated with his medical degree in 1869. By 1872 James had become a professor of physiology at Harvard. Gradually James's lectures shifted toward psychology. In 1880 he was commissioned to write a textbook about the science of psychology. This definitive two-volume work, *The Principles of Psychology*, covered such topics as brain structure and function, habit, stream of consciousness, imagination, emotions, and **will**. James was also the first to establish a psychological laboratory.

One of James's greatest contributions was his ability to transform psychology from an abstract science into a useful discipline. His approach, known as pragmatism, evaluated ideas on their usefulness rather than on illusory truth. James also developed the philosophy of radical empiricism, in which ideas were centered on pure experience and judged by their outcomes. In 1902 William James was the Guifford lecturer at the University of Edinburgh. His address was later published as *The Varieties of Religious Experience.* James's spirituality was based not on institutional religion but on practical and experiential elements of religion. In his book, James analyzed **conversion**, distinguishing between "once-born" and "twice-born"; discussed healthy-mindedness versus the "sick soul"; explored **mysticism**; and reflected on saintliness and prayer. James wrote several other books, including *The Will to Believe, Pragmatism,* and *The Meaning of Truth.* At the time of his death in 1910 James was considered the most influential multidisciplinary thinker of his time. ASJ

JANE FRANCES DE CHANTAL (1572–1641), cofounder of the Order of the Visitation of the Blessed Virgin Mary (Visitation Order or **Visitandines**). Jane was born in Dijon, France, into a Catholic loyalist family in a period of Catholic reform and spiritual renewal. At the age of twenty she married the Baron de Chantal, produced four children, and enjoyed a happy union until his sudden death in a hunting accident. In her grief the young widow determined she would not marry again. She was introduced to the charismatic preacher, **Francis de Sales**, bishop of Geneva, and took him as her spiritual director. (Their correspondence is collected in *Francis de Sales, Jane de Chantal: Letters of Spiritual Direction,* translated by Peronne Marie Thibert and edited by Wendy M. Wright and Joseph F. Power.) The spiritual friendship that developed between the two bore fruit in the creation of the Congregation of the Visitation in 1610 in Annecy, in the duchy of Savoy. Carefully providing for her children, the widow became the first superior of this group designed for women drawn to a **contemplative** love of God but ineligible to join a traditional contemplative religious order because of age, health, handicap, or their widowed status. The original vision of the Visitation Congregation was of a simple congregation without lifelong binding vows. This allowed flexibility for its members to move in and out of enclosure to aid those in need and to attend to necessary family business. The Visitation also provided married women the opportunity for short **retreats**. The plan was modified when requests came for foundations outside of Savoy. In 1618 the Visitation Order was transformed into a formal religious order with lifelong vows and observing strict enclosure. At the heart of the life is the cultivation of Salesian spirituality. The popularity of the Visitation was immense. During her lifetime, Jane supervised the founding of over eighty new houses. She died in 1641 and was canonized in 1767. WMW

JANSENISM. A neo-Augustinian emphasis in Roman Catholic thought. What became known as Jansenism originated with Michael Baius, a professor of scriptures at the University of Louvain. Although his writings were condemned in 1567 and 1580, they appeared again in Cornelius Jansen's *Augustinus,* a work published posthumously by friends of Jansen (1585–1638) in 1639. Jansen, professor of scriptures at Louvain and then bishop of Ypres (1635–1638), stoutly opposed the Society of Jesus (**Jesuits**) and their methods of **spiritual formation**. Like **Augustine**, he insisted that human beings cannot obey God's commandments without the aid of divine **grace**, which is irresistible. Jansenists also attacked two other Roman practices: frequent Communion, and the sacrament of penance without emphasis on contrition. The result was a rigorist tendency. Jansen's chief work was condemned in 1641 and 1642, but his influence spread and gained considerable favor among French bishops. Jansenism's most eloquent protagonist was the brilliant mathematician and apologist **Blaise Pascal** (1623–62). From 1655 the movement centered at the convent of Port Royal, which Pascal's sister had entered earlier. Although Pope Clement XI condemned Jansenism, it continued to be vital, especially under the influence of Pasquier Quesnel (1634–1719) and the archbishop of Paris, Louis Antoine de Noailles (1651–1729). The Jansenist movement succumbed when de Noailles renounced some of its principles in 1728, but it survived in the thought of individuals.

To learn more about Jansenism, see Nigel Abercrombie, *The Origins of Jansenism* and Henri de Lubac, *Augustinianism and Modern Theology.* EGH

JEROME (ca. 342–420), biblical scholar. Born in Stridon in Dalmatia, Jerome studied in Rome. After traveling in Gaul, he took up the ascetic life with friends in Aquileia. About 374 he set out for Palestine but delayed at Antioch and settled down as a hermit near Chalcis in the desert of Syria. On his return to Antioch around 379 he was ordained by Paulinus and proceeded to Constantinople. In 382 he went to Rome, where the Aventine Circle led by Marcella prevailed on him to assist them in their Bible study. He began work on his Latin translation of the Bible (the Vulgate). Under sharp attack by critics of the **asceticism** he fostered, he left Rome in 385 accompanied by Marcella's daughter Paula and other members of the Aventine Circle. In 386 he settled in Bethlehem to head a new monastery for men, which Paula funded.

Jerome surpassed all except **Origen** as a biblical scholar. He translated most of the Bible into Latin, wrote many commentaries, and anticipated **Luther** in translating the Old Testament writings from the Hebrew text. He also translated and continued Eusebius's *Chronicle,* sketched 135 *Lives* of *Illustrious Men* (the last his own), translated writings of Origen and Didymus the Blind (ca. 313–98) into Latin, and left a significant corpus of letters. In numerous letters he detailed his perspectives on **spiritual formation.** Indicative of the severity of his outlook, he proposed that Paula's daughter Laeta insulate her daughter, also named Paula, from all things worldly and create for her a wholly Christian culture. Dress, food, literature, and as many other things as possible should distinguish her from others. If Laeta could not rear her by that standard in Rome, he advised that she send her to Bethlehem to be brought up in the monastery her grandmother founded. She did just that. In tracts *Against Jovinian* and *Against Helvidius* he set virginity as the highest **virtue** of Christians.

For further reading, see *The Principal Works of St. Jerome* in *Nicene and Post-Nicene Fathers,* vol. 6, and J. N. D. Kelly's study, *Jerome: His Life, Writings, and Controversies.* EGH

JESUITS. Members of the Society of Jesus founded by **Ignatius of Loyola.** Jesuit writers include **Jean Pierre de Caussade, Thomas H. Green, William Johnston,** and **Karl Rahner.**

JESUS, NAME OF. The origin of the name of Jesus is found in the Gospel of Matthew. The angel appears to Joseph in a dream and says, "You are to name him Jesus, for he will save his people from their sins" (Matt. 1:21). Rooted in the Hebrew name *Yehoshua* ("Yahweh saves"), the name of Jesus is linked to his core mission, to seek and save those who are lost (Luke 19:10).

In spiritual devotional practice, the name of Jesus is also linked to his core mission. As divine and human, Jesus unites God and humanity. He is the great high priest (see Hebrews), the mediator in whom we obtain access to God by faith. Thus Christians often conclude their prayers with phrases such as "through Jesus Christ our Lord" or "In the name of Jesus we pray." This practice acknowledges that his name is linked to his mission and purpose in our lives and in the world.

A number of **hymns,** both in traditional and gospel settings and in numerous praise choruses, speak of the name of Jesus. From "All Hail the Power of Jesus' Name" to "His Name Is Wonderful" to "There's Something about That Name," these hymns express an awareness of the power of salvation through Jesus Christ, a power that resides in the voicing of his name. The importance of the name of Jesus is present in hymns within scripture, such as Philippians 2:5-11, and liturgical formulas for **baptism** (Matt. 28:19). The name of Jesus expresses both **holiness** and humanity, our greatest longings, and our deepest need to know the salvation that is God's gift to us. KHC

JESUS PRAYER. A brief prayer that combines praise, **petition**, and **confession**. It is central to the **hesychast** tradition within **Orthodox spirituality**. The standard form of the prayer is, "Lord Jesus Christ, Son of God, have mercy on me." Often the words "a sinner" are added to the end.

The prayer is based in part on two prayers from the Gospels. One is the prayer of Bartimaeus, "Jesus, Son of David, have mercy on me!" (Luke 18:38). The other is the prayer of the tax collector or publican, "God, be merciful to me, a sinner!" (Luke 18:13). In its few words, it praises Jesus as Lord, Christ, Son of God, and source of **mercy**. It asks for mercy in light of self-identification as a sinner. Thus it says all that needs to be said to promote mindfulness of who Jesus is, who the one praying is, and what the relationship between them is.

The Jesus Prayer is recommended to be prayed constantly, repeated while meditating, while working, while walking. When used as a form of **meditation**, the prayer is sometimes taught with a physical method that calls for sitting with the back held straight and chin tucked in so that one can gaze upon the area of one's heart, then inhaling, reciting the prayer while holding the breath, and finally exhaling. This method, described in various parts of *The Philokalia*, is designed to focus the intellect on the prayer and to avoid distractions. In practice, though, the prayer is most commonly used as a **breath prayer**, prayed rhythmically over the course of one or two breaths. In *The Way of a Pilgrim*, a Russian peasant is told to pray the Jesus Prayer as many as twelve thousand times a day. KRB

JOACHIM OF FIORE (ca. 1135–1202), exegete and theologian. Joachim was the most influential and controversial exegete of prophecy in the latter Middle Ages. He was so famous that Dante placed him in the Circle of the Sun with **Francis** and **Bonaventure** in *The Divine Comedy*.

Joachim was born in Calabria, Italy. After visiting the Holy Land in about 1167, he had visionary experiences on the way home. This led him eventually to join a **Cistercian** monastery, where he became a monk and was elected prior, then abbot in only a few years. In 1186 he left the monastery for a private **retreat** and eventually founded St. John's monastery, where he had a stricter **rule** and more contemplative lifestyle. In 1196 he left the Cistercians to devote himself to his new order, which had sixty houses when he died.

Joachim's three most important works form a trilogy that explores all of the major themes of his life's work. *Liber de Concordia Novi ac Veteris Testamenti* (*Book of Harmony of the New and Old Testaments*), *Expositio in Apocalypsim* (*Exposition of the Apocalypse*), and *Psalterium decem chordarum* (*Psaltery of Ten Strings*) combine to explain Joachim's trinitarian theology of history and the coming apocalypse. He sees history as being divided into three epochs. The first epoch was before Christ. It was represented by the Law and the Old Testament, with laity ruling under God the Father. The second epoch—current for Joachim—is represented by **grace** and the New Testament, with clergy ruling under Christ the Son. The final epoch, due to begin in 1260, would be represented by liberty and love, with rule by monastics as the Holy Spirit gave to everyone a full, spiritual understanding of the entire Bible, the eternal gospel. The world would be converted, the church united, the Antichrist overthrown, and the Sabbath of God inaugurated. The church officially condemned Joachim's idea that a future historical age would censure and displace the Bible and the clergy. Nonetheless, the name of Joachim remained influential during the late Middle Ages, even though much of what was attributed to him was indirect, garbled, incorrect, or even the opposite of his intentions.

For further reading, see *Joachim of Fiore and the Prophetic Future: A Study in Medieval Millennialism* by Marjorie Reeves. WW

JOHN XXIII (1881–1963), pope from 1958. The oldest son of Giovanni and Marianna Roncalli's thirteen children, Angelo Giuseppe Roncalli was born near Bergamo, Italy. Drawn to Christ at an early age, he entered seminary at age fourteen. In 1896 he started keeping a **journal**, beginning a lifelong spiritual **discipline**. Ordained a priest in 1904, he was known for both his gregarious personality and his compassion for others. Sent to Bulgaria in 1925, Archbishop Roncalli helped heal anti-Roman attitudes among local church leaders. During World War II, he was stationed in Greece and Turkey, ministering to Greek and Turkish Catholics and helping to save thousands of Jews from concentration camps. As the Vatican observer for the United Nations Educational, Scientific, and Cultural Organization (UNESCO), Roncalli came to know that the church of the modern world needed its own reform and updating to meet the needs of the changing world.

In 1954, at the age of seventy-four, Cardinal Roncalli moved from France to Venice. For the next five years, he enjoyed his lifelong aspiration of pastoral work. In October 1958, Pius XII died and Roncalli was elected the new pope, taking the name John XXIII. Breaking with tradition, he often traveled outside the Vatican, visiting local parishes, hospitals, nursing homes, schools, and charitable institutions. Emphasizing his role as servant, John XXIII wanted all to know that first and foremost he was a pastor, not a sovereign.

The pope's greatest single achievement began in January 1959 when he called for the twenty-first Ecumenical Council, the first since Vatican I (1869–70). Convinced that the church needed updating (*aggiornamento*) if it were to be a viable presence in the world, John sought to air out the dusty cobwebs of a closed system by opening up the windows of the church to truth from the arts and sciences, as well as to social, political, and racial questions and concerns worldwide. His dream consisted of three elements: reform from within, the reuniting of the church, and world peace.

After four years of intense preparation,

John XXIII (already fighting stomach cancer) presided over the first session (of four) of the Second Vatican Council in the fall of 1962. Orthodox, Anglican, and Protestant religious leaders attended as observers. Eight hundred theologians and other experts were invited as active participants. His successor, Pope Paul VI, concluded the fourth and final session of Vatican II on December 8, 1965.

John spoke out loudly for world peace. His most notable encyclical, *Pacem in Terris* (*Peace on Earth*) was written to all humankind, not only Catholics. To him all faces, even those of nonbelievers, were the faces of brothers and sisters. EKM

JOHN OF THE CROSS (1542–92), Spanish **Carmelite** poet and mystic. He was born northwest of Ávila, Spain. Juan de Yepes (his name at birth) is most remembered for his life's theme of the soul's "**dark night**." Becoming a Carmelite brother around 1564, he studied philosophy and Scholastic theology at the Carmelite College in Salamanca, one of Europe's foremost universities. The year of his ordination in 1567 he met **Teresa of Ávila**, then in her fifties, who enlisted him in her reform work for the Carmelite nuns. He then embarked on the same reform work for Carmelite monks, who showed their lack of appreciation by arresting and imprisoning him early in his life and at the end abandoning him to a remote Andalusian monastery where he died in 1592.

John's childhood contained the seed for his intellectual genius and artistic expression and for his strange vocation of **suffering**. His father, Gonzalo, had been born of nobility but sacrificed his wealth by marrying his true love, Catalina Alvarez, the daughter of a poor weaver. The deaths of siblings, daily poverty, hunger, and rejection would develop young John's gift of caring for the sick. Financially assisted by means of a hospital job, while at the same time enrolled in a **Jesuit** school for poor children, he began to nurture his love of studying and reading by night. Thus John had already found the night to be his friend.

After his Carmelite brothers arrested John in December 1577, they imprisoned him in solitary confinement for eight months in the Carmelite monastery in Toledo. Literally one dark night, John escaped, taking with him many poems he had written. More poems followed. John's four major prose works are all presented as commentaries on poems. *Spiritual Canticle, Ascent of Mount Carmel,* and *Dark Night of the Soul* (the last two comment on the first stanzas of "The Dark Night") together could be considered a long treatise on **prayer** and the spiritual life, focusing on the deep love between the **soul** and Christ and both human and divine efforts to test and purify that love. *Living Flame of Love* emerged later.

The so-called radical monastic reforms that John of the Cross espoused often seem surprising to people who think of him only as a passive contemplative. In fact, he advocated that long periods of verbal prayer might better be spent in creative activities, including manual labor. John helped with construction of monasteries in Granada, or Segovia. After giving spiritual **retreats** or **direction** for communities of nuns, he might be found erecting partition walls, laying bricks, or gardening. And of course, at night he engaged in studies and poetry. Other times he would render architectural drawings for new monasteries, create short dramas or dances for liturgical holidays, or create sculptures.

John's poetic works are at once deeply intellectual yet self-reflective. The most famous of his symbols, the dark night of the soul, he drew from **Pseudo-Dionysius** and earlier theologians. But John extended and deepened the metaphor, interlacing his poem and commentary with images from the Song of Solomon; Psalm 139; and prolific references to other scriptures.

John of the Cross was canonized in 1726 and declared a **Doctor of the Church** two centuries later.

For further study, see *John of the Cross: Selected Writings,* edited by Kieran Kavanaugh; *John of the Cross for Today: The Ascent* and *John of the Cross for Today: The Dark Night* by Susan Muto. See also *O Blessed Night!: Recovering from Addiction, Codependency, and Attachment Based on the Insights of St. John of the Cross and Pierre Teilhard de Chardin* by Francis Kelly Nemeck and Marie Theresa Coombs. KIG

JOHNSON, JAMES WELDON (1871–1938), author, songwriter, poet. Johnson had a variety of careers in the course of his life: the first **African-American** admitted to the Florida bar, writer of "Lift Every Voice and Sing" (a hymn known as the "black national anthem"), American consul to Venezuela and Nicaragua, executive secretary of the NAACP, and professor of creative literature at Fisk University. But Johnson is best remembered for his literary achievements. Author of several popular novels and an autobiography, in 1927 he published *God's Trombones,* a collection of seven sermons in verse, preserving the style and rhythm of the old-time African-American folk-preachers he had heard in rural Georgia. He also pioneered in editing anthologies of African-American poetry and spirituals. In an age before the civil rights movement, Johnson explored what it meant to be black in a white culture as he moved among urban sophisticates and plain country folk. WW

JOHNSTON, WILLIAM (b. 1925), a **Jesuit** priest who places **mysticism** at the center of authentic religious experience and who dialogues with the great contemplative traditions of the East and West. Former director of the Institute of Oriental Religions and professor of religious studies at Sophia University in Tokyo, Johnston has translated a work by Japanese novelist **Shusaku Endo**, as well as the Christian classic *The Cloud of Unknowing.* Johnston encourages laity who feel called to develop their prayer life to enter the depths of mystical experience. Recognizing mysticism as the heart of theology and religion will bring healing to our hurting world. True prophets are "mystics in action" who are awakened by God to see God's glory and to know the suffering and sin of the world.

For more on mysticism as common

ground for dialogue between East and West, see *Christian Zen: A Way of Meditation* and *The Inner Eye of Love: Mysticism and Religion.* A good place to start would be Johnston's *The Mirror Mind: Spirituality and Transformation.* EKM

JONES, ELI STANLEY (1884–1973), American Methodist minister and world-renowned missionary to India and the world; founder of the Christian Ashram movement. Called to be a missionary evangelist while still at Asbury College in Kentucky, Jones used that call to direct his ministry, including his decision to decline his election as a bishop of The Methodist Church. His "round table" approach to evangelism through discussion about the importance of personal faith in life gave dignity to those with whom he worked and won him the admiration of leaders like Gandhi. He was the author of twenty-nine books, including *Christ at the Round Table*; among his readers' favorites were *The Way* and *Abundant Living.* SH

JONES, RUFUS MATTHEW (1863–1948), American **Quaker** philosopher. Born January 25, 1863, in South China, Maine, Rufus Jones grew up in the devout Quaker farm family of Edwin and Mary Jones. Educated initially in Friends schools in South China, he ventured into a larger world in 1879 by going to Friends School in Providence, Rhode Island, for two years. In the fall of 1882 he entered Haverford College as a sophomore and in 1885 attained an M.A. degree. Jones began his teaching career in the Friends Boarding School at Union Springs, New York (1885–86). After a year of traveling in Europe and study at Heidelberg, he served as a teacher at his alma mater in Providence (1887–89) and as principal of Oak Grove Seminary at Vassalboro, Maine (1889–93). The rest of his career (1893–1935) he spent at Haverford College. Although he did not fulfill his early desire to study philosophy at Harvard, his thinking was deeply influenced by **William James** and Josiah Royce. Definitely of a mystical bent, he interpreted the Quaker tradition in the lineage of the fourteenth-century German and Dutch mystics, particularly **Meister Eckhart**, **Johannes Tauler**, and **Henry Suso**. At Haverford, he did his best to convey four key truths: (1) the nearness of God, (2) the perfect union of the divine and human nature in Christ, (3) the belief that there is no conflict between physical and spiritual reality, and (4) the way of life that opens into vital contact and fellowship with God. He disseminated the same basic ideas through lectures and prolific writing. Beginning with a biography titled *Eli and Sybil Jones* (1889) shortly after having completed college, he published fifty-seven books. He put finishing touches to the last one, *A Call to What Is Vital*, moments before he died on June 16, 1948.

In addition to the books above, see *New Studies in Mystical Religion, The Flowering of Mysticism, The Inner Life, The Luminous Trail*, or *Rufus Jones Speaks to Our Time: An Anthology*, edited by Harry Emerson Fosdick. For his life, read Elizabeth Gray Vining, *Friend of Life: The Biography of Rufus M. Jones.* EGH

JORDAN, CLARENCE (1912–69), founder of Koinonia Farm in Americus, Georgia, and Bible translator. Jordan, believing his Southern Baptist upbringing had not shown the truth about the word of Christ, made the original language texts his focus in seminary. With a strong background in New Testament Greek and a developed social conscience, Jordan was a powerful public speaker. He often translated freely from a Greek New Testament that he carried with him, explaining that the words were written in the everyday language of their time so that they could be easily understood and that this was the form of language into which they should be translated. This emphasis led to his production of the "Cotton Patch" New Testament, where he not only translated the language into that of rural Georgia but the location as well. He often said that what upset the Jewish authorities was that Jesus spoke plainly so that anyone could understand and that most people would still be upset if they really understood.

Jordan felt that the "kingdom of God" was not something to look forward to passively but rather to strive for as the natural progression of the spirit of **faith**, **love**, and **community**—in Greek *koinonia*—that the early church experienced and that the Sermon on the Mount outlined. Koinonia Farm and ultimately the whole Koinonia movement were founded as a place for this community to be a way of life. An important part of the Koinonia mission is outreach. Jordan freely extended the injunction to love one's neighbor to include everyone, regardless of race, class, religion, or other designation. Jordan spoke against segregation and practiced what he preached, which often made him unpopular when traveling through the deep South.

Jordan also began an aid foundation that started as Koinonia Partners. It worked though the Fund for Humanity, supported in part by Koinonia Farm, to provide low-cost, no-interest housing for the rural disenfranchised. This organization has since been greatly expanded throughout the world as Habitat for Humanity. LKB

JOURNAL, SPIRITUAL. A written record of feelings, thoughts, and events as they relate to and affect the inner life. In the Christian tradition, journal keeping has a long history. The *Confessions* of **Augustine**, **Teresa of Ávila**'s autobiography, and, more recently, the journals of Pope **John XXIII**, **Thomas Merton**, and **Henri J. M. Nouwen** testify to the value of keeping a spiritual journal. Most writers did not have publication in mind as they recorded their **experiences**, clarifying them in the process and discerning the presence and **providence** of God. They learned about themselves in the writing, and as we read their journals we make connections with our own faith journey.

Keeping a spiritual journal helps us take the road inward to discover who and whose we are. As we write, the ambiguity of human experience with its hidden desires and impulses is revealed. Questions increase and require exploration, not so much to resolve them as to place them in the context of the Mystery at the heart of the universe.

Silence is an important preparation for journaling. Sometimes a way into silence may be through meditative music or through stretching and breathing exercises. Taking time to become centered and to be conscious of the messages our body is sending to us will help in the process of listening and awareness. It may be that our fatigue reminds us that yesterday was too busy and disorganized. This may be exactly the place to start journaling as we talk with God about our tendency to over-schedule and begin to explore some of the reasons. Prayer may then become a plea for wisdom in choosing healthier patterns of work and relationships and making a commitment to safeguard quality time for prayerful reflection.

There is no "right" way to keep a journal and no rules about what to include or when to write. It helps to have a book to write in because scraps of paper tend to get lost or forgotten. The book may be a beautiful leather-bound volume or an inexpensive spiral-bound notebook. A daily practice of writing helps establish a pattern, especially for beginners. Entries may be a few words or several pages long. Reflections may begin with thoughts that emerge after reading **scripture**. A prayer or **psalm** sometimes suggests itself. Observations in **nature** and daily **experience** are worthy of recording and frequently lead to further thought, prayer, and action.

A spiritual journal often comes to be regarded as a friend, rather like the diary named "Kitty" in which Anne Frank wrote while hiding from the Nazis. It is a place to observe God's grace and presence in our lives but also to record struggles, fears, and unanswered questions. Often **discernment** occurs in the action of writing, and choices become clear. In the Hebrew Bible those who wrote honestly of their anger, disorientation, and resistance to God's call found strength and new hope. Many of the psalms are born from feelings of being abandoned or oppressed. The book of Jeremiah is akin to a journal in which the reluctant prophet wrestles with God, himself, and his culture but remains faithful to his call.

Some people write more freely if they use a computer, which will work as long as each page is added regularly to a journal notebook. Anxiety about legibility, spelling, and grammar needs to be put aside, a difficult task for some of us conditioned by our education to expect bad grades if work is not "right." Confidentiality is also important. The journal is not open to others unless the writer chooses to share an entry with a **spiritual director** or **friend**. It should be kept in a safe place like a locked drawer. The knowledge that the content is entirely personal enables the writer to record freely without censorship.

Keeping a journal enables us to move into new stages on the journey toward wholeness, integration, and a deepening relationship with God. It is a deceptively simple means of **grace** and transformation.

In addition to the examples of journals listed above, you might read books about journaling: *Listening to Your Life* by Frederick Buechner, *Journaling: A Spiritual Journey* by Anne Broyles, or *Journaling with Jeremiah* by Elizabeth J. Canham. EJC

JULIAN OF NORWICH (1342–ca. 1423), English mystic and anchoress. On May 8, 1373, following a life-threatening illness, Julian experienced sixteen revelations of Divine Love, or "showings," which she later committed to writing. The revelations overwhelmed her with a deep understanding of Christ's passion and God's love. Julian became a solitary, devoting her life to prayer in an anchorhold (cell) adjoining the Church of St. Julian and St. Edward at Conisford (Norwich), England. Her real name forgotten, she was known simply as the anchoress at St. Julian's church and later, Julian the anchoress. Although the church was attached to the Benedictine community at Carrow, it is not known whether Julian was a nun.

From her anchorhold Julian dispensed spiritual counsel to all who came to her window, which opened to the street. She welcomed both rich and poor, especially those desperate for comfort following the period of turmoil that included the peasants' revolt and the Black Death (bubonic plague), which decimated the population of England. A second window in her cell opened toward the sanctuary so that Julian could participate in daily mass and receive the sacrament. She lived with a cat and had a servant who provided a link with the outside world.

Julian delighted in observing the natural world and is best remembered for her meditation on a hazelnut, in which she saw an image of God's unfathomable love. The nut in Julian's palm resembled the world in God's hand that continues its existence because God made it, loves it, and sustains it. In this assurance Julian declared that despite affliction and pain, "All shall be well."

Julian wrote two versions of her "showings"—one soon after her illness and then a substantial expansion after years of reflection. Both are available in modern translation by Edmund Colledge and James Walsh as *Revelations of Divine Love. Praying with Julian of Norwich* by Gloria Durka is a brief devotional book offering a simple introduction to Julian. EJC

JUSTIFICATION. A technical, theological term describing the results of the saving work of Jesus Christ. It has to do with setting right the relationship between God and humanity. As in word processing on a computer, where justifying text means aligning it according to a fixed standard, so theological justification has to do with setting the believer in proper relationship with God, specifically, by removing the impediment of human **sin** through the **forgiveness** that only God can offer.

Protestants typically understand justification as what happens when the believer trusts that his or her sins have been forgiven by the work of Christ. The Roman Catholic tradition, as formalized at the Council of Trent, uses justification in a wider, more inclusive sense to refer to the whole process of salvation, including the **works** performed by the believer in response to God's initiating **grace**. Protestants typically classify these works as belonging to a phase of salvation subsequent to justification that they term **sanctification**. In the late twentieth century, however, Lutherans and Roman Catholics spent many years revisiting this language, which so long had kept them apart, and determined that a nuanced understanding of what was at stake in their various formulations of justification should no longer be considered "church dividing." (See "The Joint Declaration on the Doctrine of Justification" at www.justification.org/ joint_eng.htm)

Ephesians 2:8 clearly states that believers are "saved through faith," yet several controversies have swirled around the question of just how the righteousness of Christ becomes real in the life of the believer. Theologians have used terms such as the *imputed* righteousness of Christ or the *imparted* righteousness of Christ to distinguish theories of what happens in justification. Those who speak of "imputation" see God as acting on a kind of legal fiction where sinful humanity is "pronounced" innocent because of what Christ has accomplished—his righteousness being "imputed" to the believer. Other thinkers have chosen to speak of justification as being about an actual,

realized change in those who trust in his action—Christ's righteousness actually being imparted to the believer through faith.

Conceiving of humanity's relationship with God in the term *justification*, borrowed, as it is, from the context of the law courts, invites such conceptual disputes. Alternative language to describe the restored relationship between God and humanity brought about by Christ's work, such as therapeutic or healing language, can also be found in the Bible (for example, 1 Pet. 2:24 and Rev. 22:2). Eastern **Orthodox** spirituality typically does not emphasize the juridical model of salvation implied in "justification" but usually favors the more therapeutic language that speaks of being restored to the image of God and growing in our likeness to God, or **deification**. Among Western thinkers, **John Wesley**'s language of salvation, though it employs the typical Western Christian terms of *justification* and *sanctification*, also tends to favor a more therapeutic emphasis.

For further reading, see Alister E. McGrath's two-part work, *Iustitui Dei: A History of the Christian Doctrine of Justification.* GSC

K

KAGAWA, TOYOHIKO (1888–1960), Japanese evangelist and writer. At the height of his fame in the 1930s, Kagawa's name evoked the kind of reverence we now give to Mother Teresa or Martin Luther King Jr. He was variously called Japan's **Albert Schweitzer**, the Japanese Gandhi, Saint **Francis** of Japan, the First Christian of the World, or simply Japan's saint. Among his roles were minister to those in the slums, novelist, trail-blazing sociologist, labor union leader, organizer of farmers' co-operatives, and pacifist. The last three all resulted in imprisonment.

The illegitimate son of a geisha, Kagawa was named after the god of a local Shinto shrine. His father adopted him into the Kagawa family; but after his father's death, he and his siblings were raised by their father's wife, who was bitter about being abandoned by her husband. Kagawa took to his books and learned English from American Presbyterian missionaries. In 1904 he was baptized. One of the first things he did as a new Christian was to declare himself a pacifist and refuse to carry a gun. While in seminary, he staged a protest against formalism and criticized Japanese Christianity for failing to bring faith into the world. He then moved into the slums of Kobe, preaching and ministering to the poorest people there, taking them into his tiny apartment, caring for the sick and feeding the hungry.

Kagawa became convinced that it was not enough to minister to those broken by society. Believing the structures themselves had to change, he became a socialist and labor union leader. Even as a union organizer he led the workers in singing Christian hymns. He met Gandhi and while much alike, they did not become friends. In 1940 Kagawa was arrested and charged by the Japanese military government with engaging in peace propaganda. Before and after World War II, he lectured to large audiences in the United States and Europe. Among his written works are his best-selling novel *Crossing the Death Line*, a book of poetry; *Songs from the Slums*; and *The Challenge of Redemptive Love.* HLR

KATAPHATIC WAY. See **Positive Way.**

KAZANTZAKIS, NIKOS (1885–1957), Greek philosopher and novelist. More popular in Europe than in the United States, Nikos Kazantzakis is perhaps best known for two of his novels *Zorba the Greek* and *The Last Temptation of Christ*, both of which won popularity as much from being made into Hollywood movies as from the books themselves. Born in Crete, Kazantzakis graduated from Athens School of Law in 1906, then studied in France under philosopher Henri Bergson. He received degrees in literature and art in both Germany and Italy. A truly global citizen, Kazantzakis lived and traveled in Russia, Israel, China, Japan, Egypt, England, and Spain as well as Greece. While writing was his passion and his vocation, he also served for brief intervals as the Greek minister of state and as the director of the Bureau of Translation from the Classics for the United Nations Educational, Scientific, and Cultural Organization (UNESCO).

In addition to his novels, Kazantzakis's writings include drama, poetry, and nonfiction of various kinds. While not an autobiography in the traditional sense, *The Report to Greco* is a powerful and personal testimony both to his own spiritual journey and to the places he lived and frequented. His writings are filled with passion, a deep thirst for God, and his own unique existential philosophical orientation. They also reveal his earthy and anti-pietistic spirituality. Perhaps the clearest statement of the philosophical basis behind his writings is his earliest book, *The Saviors of God: Spiritual Exercises.* This short work articulates his understanding of the interior spiritual life and journey. He sees the spiritual life as an upwardly spiraling struggle to engage fully in and then transcend (1) matter and the physical senses, (2) ideas and the intellect, (3) all emotions and desires of the heart, (4) one's own ego or self, (5) humankind and, finally, (6) spirit. One of his favorite phrases describing the task or call of each human being is, "to turn matter into spirit." JWK

KEATING, THOMAS (b. 1923), **Trappist** abbot and writer, one of the founders of the **Centering Prayer** movement. After attending Yale and graduating from Fordham University, he entered the Cistercian Order of the Strict Observance (Trappists) in Valley Falls, Rhode Island, in 1944. He was appointed superior of St. Benedict's Monastery, Snowmass, Colorado, in 1958, and was elected abbot of St. Joseph's Abbey, Spencer, Massachusetts, in 1961. After retiring as abbot of Spencer in 1981, he returned to Snowmass, where he established a program of ten-day intensive **retreats** in the practice of Centering Prayer and founded the Snowmass Interreligious Conference, a group of teachers from the world religions who meet yearly to share their experience of the spiritual journey in their respective traditions.

Keating is the author of many books and video/audiotape series. Perhaps the best place to start is with his trilogy of *Open Mind, Open Heart; Invitation to Love;* and *Intimacy with God.* EKM

KEBLE, JOHN (1792–1866), Anglican priest, theologian and poet, early leader of the **Oxford movement.** Educated at Oxford and ordained in 1816, Keble served as a tutor from 1817 to 1823 until he left to assist in his father's parish. He was professor of poetry at Oxford from 1831 to 1841 and served Hurs-

ley as a country vicar from 1836 until his death. In 1827 Keble published *The Christian Year,* poems for Sunday and the festivals of the church year, which portrayed the church as the visible channel of invisible **grace.** Widely circulated, it was the most effective means for spreading the ideals of the High Church movement in Anglicanism. Keble initiated the Oxford Movement with his sermon "National Apostasy" at University Chapel in 1833. A response to the government's efforts to appropriate church funds and property, the movement's activities expanded to a general theological and pastoral agenda. The movement's advocates became known as Tractarians because of their ninety *Tracts for the Times* designed to rouse Anglican clergy against the theory of a state-controlled church. Keble authored nine of the tracts. **John Henry Newman**'s conversion to Catholicism threatened the breakup of the movement in 1845. Keble and E. B. Pusey, however, kept it alive.

Keble's qualities as a humble pastor were his primary influence on the Oxford movement. He encouraged studying the early church fathers, edited their works, and arranged for their translation. Keble is remembered as well for his lyrics as his Tractarian role. Among his books of verse are *The Psalter, or Psalms of David* and *Lyra Innocentium,* children's poems. "O God of Mercy, God of Might" is one of his hymns. Oxford University named Keble College for him in 1869. LSP

KELLY, THOMAS R. (1893–1941), **Quaker** philosopher. Born on a farm near Chillecothe, Ohio, Kelly obtained a B.S. in chemistry from Wilmington College in 1913. A year spent in further study of chemistry at Haverford College in Pennsylvania brought him under the spell of **Rufus Jones**. After two years of teaching (1914–16) at Pickering College, a Quaker prep school in Canada, he entered Hartford Theological Seminary to prepare for religious work in the Far East, obtaining a B.D. degree in 1919. Newly married to Lael Macy, whom he met while at Hartford, he spent fifteen months working among German prisoners of war in England. He returned to Hartford in 1921 to obtain a Ph.D. in philosophy. In 1925 he began teaching at Earlham College in Richmond, Indiana.

Not content with teaching in the Midwest nor with his degree from Hartford, Kelly enrolled at Harvard in 1930 and found teaching positions in the East for two years. Reluctantly he returned to Earlham College to teach from 1932 to 1935. With some relief, he accepted a teaching position at the University of Hawaii (1935–36) and then welcomed a chance to return to Haverford College in 1936. Meanwhile he wrote and published a dissertation on *The Religious Philosophy of Emile Meyerson*. Unfortunately, during his oral he blacked out; although his committee had accepted his thesis, they failed him and would not permit him a second chance. In the midst of the depression that followed, Kelly had a profound mystical experience that gave new authority to his speaking and writing. Many have cherished the depth and power of his thought in *A Testament of Devotion*, a collection of five addresses given to Quaker audiences that Kelly was preparing for publication before his untimely death on January 17, 1941. Kelly's colleague, **Douglas Steere**, completed the editing and wrote a memoir in Kelly's honor.

Other Kelly essays and letters are collected in *The Eternal Promise* and *The Reality of the Spiritual World*. Studies include Richard M. Kelly, *Thomas R. Kelly, A Biography*, and T. Canby Jones, *Thomas R. Kelly as I Remember Him*. EGH

KELSEY, MORTON T. (b. 1917), American Episcopal priest, professor, author, Jungian therapist. Kelsey taught at the University of Notre Dame and San Francisco Theological Seminary. He studied with Carl G. Jung in Switzerland. He has written copiously on a wide variety of Christian spiritual topics including **journaling** (*Adventure Inward*), the Christian use of the imagination (*Myth, History and Faith*), **spiritual direction** (*Companions on the Inner Way*), the Christian interpretation of dreams (*Dreams; God, Dreams and Revelation; Dreamquest*), and psychotherapy for Christians

(*Christo–Psychology; Christianity as Psychology; Prophetic Ministry*).

Perhaps his most profound contribution is in the field of Christian **meditation**. *The Other Side of Silence: Meditation for the Twenty-first Century* is an updated revision of his 1970s classic. In this 1990s version, Kelsey has the luxury of referring to many of the books he wrote after the first edition, as so many fields of **spirituality** overlap and feed one another. Kelsey discusses the centrality of prayer to the Christian journey, preparation for meditation, the glories and dangers of the spiritual world, **silence** and imagination in meditation, and dreams. Of particular interest are Kelsey's diagrams and Jungian explanations of New Testament and postmodern worldviews, consciousness and the unconscious in relation to spiritual and physical reality, and the range of dreaming and meditation perception. In contrast to the **negative way** of **Centering Prayer**, Kelsey embraces the **positive way** of the imaginative creation of and interaction with images during meditation. The use of **guided imagery**, **imagery** from dreams, and images that come during stillness are all useful in listening to God through the prayerful opening of the barrier between the conscious mind and the realm of the unconscious, which dwells in the spiritual world.

The concluding section of the book titled "Windows Inward" includes nineteen guided meditations that range from the intimate retelling of biblical stories (allowing one to enter the story, as in the practice of **Ignatius of Loyola**) to eucharistic meditations to imaginative encounters with Christ and death. WW

KEMPE, MARGERY (ca. 1373–1440), English mystic, spiritual autobiographer. Some scholars call Kempe a mystic; others simply see her as a religious **enthusiast**. Whatever the appellation, she stands as one of the more interesting figures in English **mysticism**. Born into a wealthy family in Lynn, England (her father was the mayor), she married John Kempe at age twenty. After the birth of her first child, Kempe had a spiritual crisis that some would say verged on insanity. She was rescued from this state by a **vision** of Christ and spent the rest of her life dedicated to the relationship she had with the **holy**.

This spiritual relationship was recorded in *The Book of Margery Kempe,* the first known autobiography in the English language. Since she could neither read nor write, it is assumed that the book was dictated, transcribed, and then revised. In it she tells of her struggles as a wife. After bearing fourteen children, she was able to convince her husband to agree to vows of mutual **chastity**. She embarked on a life of **pilgrimage** and traveled as far as Jerusalem and Rome to meet with spiritual figures such as **Julian of Norwich** and Thomas Arundel, archbishop of Canterbury.

Kempe's intensely personal relationship with the holy included long conversations with Christ and God. When confronted with religious symbols and situations—seeing the host elevated during **Holy Communion** or hearing a particularly powerful sermon—she suffered from fits of hysterical **tears** and uncontrollable shrieks. These episodes, which she called her cryings, were the source of many of her problems. Fellow travelers wanted to avoid her. Church officials questioned her and accused her of heresy, though she was staunchly orthodox and handled her inquisitors with remarkable agility of mind. The open and honest way she lived is reflected in her *Book,* a vivid portrait of a remarkable woman. *The Book of Margery Kempe,* translated by B. A. Windeatt, includes a helpful introduction, chronology and suggestions for further reading. SN

KENOSIS. (Greek, "emptying.") The actual word *kenosis* as a noun means "emptying," although only the verb is used in the New Testament: Christ Jesus, even though in the form of God, "did not regard equality with God as something to be exploited, but emptied [*ekenosen*] himself"—being born as a human and dying on a cross (Phil. 2:1-11). In the context, however, the *kenosis* text is not simply a doctrinal statement about Jesus Christ as the incarnate expression of God dying and rising,

but it is first of all an invitation for believers to experience this transforming pattern in their lives. "Let the same mind be in you that was in Christ Jesus, who, though he was in the form of God... emptied himself...."

Yet in the Bible being emptied and being filled are complementary. The rhythm of emptiness (*kenosis* in Philippians) and fullness (*pleroma* in Colossians and Ephesians) represents the ongoing experience of baptism: continually dying with Christ to self-images and preconceived scripts that control our lives, and rising with Christ to claim the new life God offers. "Therefore God also highly exalted him..." (Phil. 2:9).

Thus *kenosis* does not need to convey deprecation of the self but rather a genuine emptying of others' imposed expectations or one's own false ideals that would inhibit spiritual affirmation of the genuine self. Genuine *kenosis,* like genuine humility, means that, like Jesus, one has the courage to place one's gifts before the world and endure the consequences. *Kenosis* is always an emptying of false images of the self, whether an emptying of self-deprecation or self-inflation, to claim as yet unrealized possibilities of resurrection life.

The concept of self-emptying represents the heart of the gospel: The experience of baptism is not a one-time act but a lifestyle embodying the **imitation of Christ**. It is not a mere outward copying of Jesus' acts in the first century but an inward patterning of the form of the living Christ in the life of the believer and the believing **community**.

Jesus' parables often create a "suspension" of the normal train of thinking in the hearer: The spoiled prodigal or the despised Samaritan becomes the hero; the first shall be last and the last shall be first. Thus the trancelike surprise in a dramatic story creates the empty space (*kenosis*) where grace can permeate the hearer. In Jesus' encounter with the Canaanite woman, he empties himself of the standard prophetic job description—"I was sent only to the lost sheep of the house of Israel"—then crosses the boundary into the (Gentile) territory of the marginalized (Matt. 15:21-28).

The experience of *kenosis* in a more prolonged form parallels the "void" of creation (Gen. 1:2), the concepts of the **dark night** of the soul, and the apophatic or **negative way** of emptying preconceived images of self and God—to rediscover the living God. Thus the final *kenosis* for Jesus is the cross. Yet even the dark "empty" tomb in the Gospel drama foreshadows meeting Jesus again for the first time in the world (the kataphatic or **positive way**): in the gardener (John 20:15) or in the stranger on the road, made known in breaking bread at Emmaus (Luke 24:13-35).

For further study, see *Jesus: God's Emptiness, God's Fullness* by Jennings B. Reid; *Spirituality and Emptiness* by Donald W. Mitchell; and *The Soul of Tomorrow's Church* by Kent Ira Groff. KIG

KIERKEGAARD, SØREN (1813–55), Danish theologian and philosopher of amazing depth and scope. While having the academic training of a philosopher, he also had the heart of a Christian spiritual writer. His failed romance with Regina, the love of his life, fueled an intensely reflective inner life. He had a profoundly dialectical way of writing and thinking (one idea was vigorously opposed by another), and his stark challenges called for the greatest honesty and humility in the reader. He did not want his readers to take his "results" as their own but rather to consider the evidence of their own lives and "judge for yourselves" (the title of one of his works.)

Kierkegaard's main philosophical works, including his *Concluding Unscientific Postscript* and the *Philosophical Fragments,* were expressions of his rebellion against Hegel and the Hegelian philosophy that dominated the intellectual life of Europe at the time. His incisive and often sarcastic criticisms showed both a subtle understanding of the intricacies of Hegel's thought as well as a vivid sense of its shortcomings as a model for life. The central point of the *Postscript* was that it is easy to know what Christianity is but exceedingly difficult to be a Christian. He lamented, "People had forgotten what it is to exist and what inwardness means." Disappointed in the promise of Hegel's totalizing system, he concluded in his *Postscript,* "A logical system is possible, but a system of existence is impossible." He is often characterized as a forerunner of postmodernism, in part because of this skepticism about large intellectual systems.

One of the most misunderstood features of the *Postscript* (a book that Kierkegaard saw as central to his overall authorship) was his famous statement that "truth is subjectivity." This phrase is sometimes cited to authorize an irrational and dangerous vision of the Christian spiritual life. It has to be seen, however, in its context. For Kierkegaard, truth is subjectivity only for a narrow range of areas of life, such as whether or not to get married or contemplating the incarnation and cross of Christ. He does not espouse a general irrationalism but instead calls his cultured listeners to engage the gospel story with all of their lives, not just in a superficially intellectual or rationalistic way.

Kierkegaard was not content simply to write philosophical critiques; he often alternated writing one of his philosophical books with writing "edifying discourses." He carefully avoided calling these discourses sermons, since he was not ordained by the church.

For **spiritual formation** purposes, such books as *Works of Love* (where Kierkegaard challenges the reader to consider what it means to be commanded to **love** neighbor) and *Fear and Trembling* (which vividly portrays the struggle of Abraham's sacrifice of Isaac) have found continuing audiences. Kierkegaard himself regarded the book *The Sickness unto Death,* with its themes of **sin** and **faith**, as the greatest of his religious works. The best biography of Kierkegaard remains the two-volume *Kierkegaard* by Walter Lowrie. A shorter sketch is available in Robert L. Perkins's *Søren Kierkegaard. The Essential Kierkegaard,* edited by Howard V. Hong and Edna H. Hong, provides an place to begin. GSC

KING JR., MARTIN LUTHER (1929–68), American Baptist minister and civil rights leader. Born in Atlanta January 15, 1929, Martin Luther King Jr. was educated at Morehouse College in Atlanta, Crozer Theological Seminary in Chester, Pennsylvania, and Boston University. In 1954 he became pastor of Dexter Avenue Baptist Church in Montgomery, Alabama, and quickly found himself thrust into the leadership of a bus boycott that lasted more than a year and ended in a U.S. Supreme Court order to desegregate buses and schools.

The experience in Montgomery inspired King to look more closely at Gandhi's nonviolent protest. In 1960 he resigned his pastorate to devote full-time leadership to the Southern Christian Leadership Conference, which he had helped to form in 1957. Already the most visible leader in the civil rights movement, his courageous conduct in the Birmingham march in 1963 in the face of bitter opposition further elevated his status and gained for the movement the backing of President John F. Kennedy. In the wake of Kennedy's assassination in 1963, the United States Congress passed civil rights legislation. In 1964 King was awarded the Nobel Prize. Adhering strictly to the principle of nonviolence, he organized further protests in Florida, Alabama, Mississippi, and other states. King was assassinated during a demonstration of support for striking sanitation workers in Memphis, Tennessee, April 4, 1968.

King and his work in civil rights depended heavily on the spirituality of **African-American** churches—the preaching, the spirituals, the communion. At Crozer Seminary he found kinship with **Walter Rauschenbusch**'s wedding of deep personal piety and social concern in the Social Gospel movement. At Boston University he came under the sway of **Howard Thurman**, a social mystic who espoused nonviolent social change. Being thrust onto center stage in the great ongoing drama forced King to draw from the deep well of piety that his own oppressed people knew.

King's books include *Stride Toward Freedom, Why We Can't Wait, Strength to Love,* and *The Autobiography of Martin Luther King, Jr.,* edited by

Clayborn Carson. See also David J. Garrow, *Bearing the Cross.* EGH

KNOX, JOHN (ca. 1513–72), Scottish preacher and Reformation leader. Knox expressed his spirituality in action and a determined pragmatism. He lived in times of ecclesiastical turmoil throughout Scotland, England, and Europe. Reformers were being burned at the stake for their beliefs. Nations became embroiled in religious wars as Catholics did battle with Protestant reformers.

In this environment came a man with a practical spirituality. Knox was ordained to the priesthood but became a disciple of **John Calvin** after visiting Geneva, where he contributed to the creation of the Geneva version of the English Bible. Unlike Calvin, Knox felt that it was necessary for common people to rise up against godless rulers. When he returned from Geneva, he entered the battle for Scottish independence and Protestant theology. The two were inextricably linked.

In December of 1560 the first Scottish General Assembly was held. Shortly thereafter the *First Book of Discipline* was presented to Parliament. The *Discipline,* a work of Knox and his followers, attempted to apply Calvin's thinking to political systems. While the names for the operating structures (or polity) developed over time, this document contained the basis for what became sessions, presbyteries, synods, and general assembly. Knox also created a *Book of Common Order* (also called "Knox Liturgy") that received general assembly approval in 1564. It provided for free prayer and, while it gave a generally accepted order of service, the order was understood to be a model rather than an absolute form to be followed.

Readers interested in John Knox may want to consider *From Gileskirk to Greyfriars: Mary Queen of Scots, John Knox and the Heroes of Scotland's Reformation* by Sir Walter Scott, or the more recent *For Kirk and Covenant: The Stalwart Courage of John Knox* by Douglas Wilson. SN

KOINONIA. A Greek word meaning fellowship, **community**, participation, **communion**, or sharing. The term has a rich history in biblical usage as well as in radical intentional communities in Christian history. Acts 2:42 describes believers who devoted themselves to "the apostles' teaching and fellowship, to the breaking of bread and the prayers."

Fellowship was a radical form of *koinonia*: "All who believed were together and had all things in common" and would sell all their possessions (Acts 2:44-45). The first-century Christian community appears to have been the first radical Christian "communistic" society, though many others would follow: single-sex **monastic** orders and **family** orders like the Hutterites, **Shakers**, **Bruderhof**, or **Clarence Jordan**'s Koinonia Farm.

Genuine *koinonia* connects believers in a web of solidarity with poor and marginalized people. Biblically it is impossible to experience the *koinonia* of warm Christian fellowship or Communion of the body and blood of Christ without also sharing one's material goods with the poor.

For further reading, see *A Call to Commitment* or *Journey Inward, Journey Outward* by **Elizabeth O'Connor**. KIG

LABYRINTH. A serpentine path used as a spiritual tool to help those who walk it grow in their relationship with God. While they walk it, pilgrims might offer the time to God or meditate on a pressing question, a **breath prayer**, or a passage of scripture.

Most labyrinths are constructed by interlinking a set of concentric circles. The seven-circuit Cretan labyrinth had its origins three thousand years ago. Many medieval cathedrals had labyrinths inlaid in their floors as a means whereby pilgrims could make a **pilgrimage** locally. The eleven-circuit labyrinth in Chartres Cathedral in France, built in the thirteenth century, is shown in the illustration.

The winding path leads toward the center, toward God, toward wholeness and integration. Many persons find it meaningful to remain a while in the center, praying and meditating. The journey out is a preparation toward offering one's gifts to others and to the larger world.

Walking the labyrinth is an individual imaginative experience that becomes more meaningful and profound the more it is

walked. It is a transforming tool, a mystery leading to wholeness of body, mind, and **soul**.

A good source for understanding the medieval labyrinth is *Walking a Sacred Path: Rediscovering the Labyrinth as a Sacred Tool* by Lauren Artress. She and Grace Cathedral in San Francisco have pioneered in bringing the message of the labyrinth to modern-day pilgrims. Also helpful are *Exploring the Labyrinth: A Guide for Healing and Spiritual Growth* by Melissa Gayle West and the video *Labyrinths: Their Mystery and Magic.* EWF

LADDER, SPIRITUAL. An image and metaphor that has been used in literature and art to describe the highlights and struggles along the mysterious **purgative**, **illuminative,** and **unitive** paths, commonly called the spiritual journey, into communion with God. Starting with the book of Genesis (28:10-22), where we read that Jacob dreamed of a stairway between heaven and earth, the image of a spiritual ladder has continued to be used. In the second century **Origen** likened the rungs of the ladder to a mystical journey that newly baptized Christians could seek. The ladder image continued in **Benedict**'s Rule (mid-fifth century), the sixth-century writings of **John Climacus**, through medieval times in **Guigo's** writing on the "four rungs," **Bernard of Clairvaux's** "twelve rungs," and **Walter Hilton's** "Ladder of Perfection."

Typically people ascend a ladder to move toward a desired object. The **monastic** tradition has always taught that **humility** is the **virtue** (**disposition** of the heart) *par excellence* that keeps a person of prayer "climbing" each rung to the highest truth: love of God. Equally true is that beginners and intermediates along the way up can and do tumble down when their self-centered **will** takes over, blocking them from their desire to live in harmony with God. The lower rungs of the spiritual ladder represent coming to an awareness and a deeper knowledge of self so that understanding of others might improve too. Often painful awareness of attitudes, behaviors, and motivations that need to change and be reformed accompanies new knowledge of self. One recognizes the need for ongoing **conversion** of heart and life as one "climbs." Self-giving love characterizes those who ascend to the heights. Purified of sinfulness, deformative interior appetites, vices and human weaknesses, the illumined one, further transformed, simply rests in God's all-embracing love. The forming, reforming, and transforming process inherent in climbing the spiritual ladder is seen as the fruit of the practice called *lectio divina.* EKM

LAUBACH, FRANK C. (1884–1970), American missionary, mystic. Born into a Methodist family in Pennsylvania, immersed in baptism by a Methodist pastor to satisfy the Baptists in the family, Laubach studied with the Schwenkfelders, worked for the Presbyterians in New York, and was sent by the Congregationalists to the Philippines where he answered the call of God to serve as a missionary. He became famous in two fields: world literacy and ecumenical mission. He developed the "Each One Teach One" method of teaching people to read, becoming a spokesperson for the world's illiterate masses. As a world leader among Christians, he was awarded The Upper Room Citation (given to a person of Christian faith who has made a significant contribution to the spiritual life of the church universal) and the Medal of Honor from the Theodore Roosevelt Association.

Among Laubach's thirty-five books are *Letters by a Modern Mystic, Channels of Spiritual Power, Prayer: The Mightiest Force in the World,* and *Wake Up or Blow Up.* HLR

LAVELLE, LOUIS (1883–1951), French philosopher of religion. Born in southwestern France in the town of Saint-Martin-de-Villereal, Lavelle sought to help people make connections between philosophy and religion. He was professor of philosophy at the Sorbonne (1932–34). From 1941 until his death, he taught at the College de France. Combining elements of French philosophy and existentialism, Lavelle wrote on subjects of importance in a way that everyone could understand. For Lavelle, philosophy deepened everyday pondering on topics such as freedom, human destiny, and **solitude**. Turning inward to reflect upon our life and our existence establishes spiritual identity and leads us to see the spiritual meaning in all of life. Freely recognizing God as the foundational mystery connecting the private interior self and the external world of daily **experience**, we discover God at work in our lives. While infinitely transcendent, God is immanently present in all creation, especially in each person, for all exist in God's presence.

Lavelle's books include *The Meaning of Holiness, Four Saints,* and *Evil and Suffering.* EKM

LAW, WILLIAM (1686–1761), English spiritual writer. Born at King's Cliffe, Law was educated at Emmanuel College, Cambridge, where he became a Fellow in 1711. His refusal to swear allegiance to King George I cost him his fellowship, however. From 1727 until 1737 he lived in the Gibbon household at Putney and tutored the father of future historian Edward Gibbon. In 1740 he took up residence at King's Cliffe as chaplain to Mrs. Elizabeth Hutcheson and Hester Gibbon. Together the three of them organized schools and houses for the poor and lived lives of admirable simplicity and devotion.

In 1728 Law published his influential classic *A Serious Call to a Devout and Holy Life.* In the midst of the Age of Enlightenment he framed a powerful rational argument for a life of devotion. Devotion, he argued, should entail the dedication of the whole and not just a part of one's life. Most Christians fall short of true devotion because they do not *intend* to please God in all they do. Scriptures amply prove that God will not look kindly on such careless commitment. We are obligated to order our everyday lives in such a way as to turn them to consistent service of God. Persons of leisure have a special obligation to devote themselves to God. Religious exercises such as prayer represent only a small part of devotion; unless life matches prayer, it is hypocrisy. True devotion, he assured, will bring peace and happiness. *A Serious Call* deeply influenced **John Wesley**, George Whitefield, and others who formed the "Holy Club" at Oxford. Around 1734 Law discovered the writings of **Jacob Boehme**, whose influence is noticeable in *The Spirit of Prayer* and *The Spirit of Love*. Both works emphasize the indwelling of Christ in the soul, very similar to the **Quaker** concept of the "Light Within." Unfortunately this shift in emphasis from devotional practice to **mysticism** alienated many former followers such as John Wesley.

For further reading, see William Law, *A Serious Call to a Devout and Holy Life* and Arthur Keith Walker, *William Law: His Life and Thought.* EGH

LAWRENCE OF THE RESURRECTION (ca. 1614–91), **Carmelite** lay brother and noted spiritual teacher. Born in Lorraine, France, Nicholas Herman at the age of eighteen underwent a conversion to the grandeur and presence of God when seeing a barren tree that would soon blossom. He first followed a military career, then lived as a hermit. In 1649 he became a lay brother in the Carmelite monastery in Paris and took the name of Lawrence of the Resurrection. His work in the monastery was mainly in the kitchen. His reputation as a spiritual guide grew, and people from all walks of life visited him.

After Brother Lawrence's death, his biographer who also frequently visited the monastery compiled his letters, maxims, and a summary of conversations under the title, *The Practice of the Presence of God.* At the heart of the book is the profound yet simple teaching of continual attentiveness to the divine presence realized in the midst of everyday activities in the **present moment**. The book was appreciated not only among Lawrence's French

Catholic contemporaries (he is frequently quoted by **Fénelon**) but was translated into German and English and widely circulated in Protestant circles. His reputation was diminished in France itself through the association of his writings with those of Madame **Guyon**, whose works fell under the suspicion of the heresy of **Quietism**. WMW

LECTIO DIVINA. Literally "divine reading," a particular way of encountering God in scripture that stands in contrast to the approach to scripture of disciplines of study, exegesis, hermeneutics, and theological reflection. Rather than the text being an object of the mind seeking understanding, in *lectio divina* the text is an **icon** of God that acts upon the heart. *Lectio divina* is an ancient spiritual practice rooted primarily in the Hebraic tradition of the "Shema." The Shema consists of repeated readings of Deuteronomy 6:4-9; 11:13-21; and Numbers 15:37-41, with exactness and built-in pauses between certain words. The last word of each verse is read with greater emphasis and mental concentration that facilitates a communal **meditation**.

In the Hebraic tradition, the holy and absolute transcendent God is present among the people in the Word (Torah, "instruction"). Jewish and patristic emphasis on the meditation on scripture is rooted in the command to hear; thus *lectio divina* is a dialogical hearing of scripture. It seeks to cultivate the ability to listen deeply to the God who speaks through the Word and then to allow that Word to shape an appropriate response in thought, prayer, and the conduct of daily life. This type of meditation on scripture in the Jewish and patristic context was a simple and spontaneous prayer movement. Traditionally four to seven people read at least three verses each of the Torah and Prophets, followed by a blessing; the text stimulated a "murmuring" (*haga* or *hagah*, often translated as "meditation") of the sacred Word, which took on the form of singing or chanting a verse. The repetition of the chanted verse facilitated a focus of attention that ultimately led beyond thought to a

---

A PROCESS FOR PERSONAL *Lectio Divina*

Preparation: Select a text for the session. Many use the lectionary readings or some thematic scheme. Take a moment to quiet the heart and mind in preparation to encounter God by using a deep breathing relaxation technique, **breath prayer**, or just two or three minutes of silence.

LECTIO – Hearing the Sacred Word

The emphasis here is on "hearing" God address you personally through the sacred text. The method suggests three slow readings.

First Reading: Read the entire passage slowly, allowing each word to speak to you. Pause often between words or verses. Sit silently for a minute or two.

Second Reading: Reread the passage, again slowly with pauses to allow a word or phrase or image in the text to call you to attention. This time make a mental note of the word, phrase, or image in the text that caught your attention. Again sit in silence.

Third Reading: Reread the passage up to the point you are touched by a word or verse. You have found the word or verse in the scripture that God desires to speak to you in a personal way. At this point you will flow naturally into the next step of meditation.

MEDITATIO – Pondering the Personal Word

 The emphasis in this step is on "pondering" the word or verse that touched you in the *lectio*. Pondering is like memorizing by repeating the word or verse gently to yourself. Allow the word to sink into your consciousness through a playful interaction with your thoughts, hopes, memories, imagination, desires, and fears. In this movement God can speak the individual personal word to your specific condition. In the fullness of this encounter you will flow naturally into the next step of vocal prayer.

ORATIO – Intimate Dialogue with God

Often the spontaneous vocal prayer that flows from the heart of meditation is an expression of love, praise, or thanksgiving. However, it is usually experienced as an intimate dialogue with God, a gentle movement between heartfelt expressions and responsiveness to the movements of the Spirit nurtured by deeper meditation.

CONTEMPLATIO – Heavenly Rest

Eventually a gradual simplification comes from the space created by vocal prayer, and your words begin to lack true expressive qualities. The heart and mind become still and silent. You simply rest and enjoy the experience of being in the presence of God. It is here you stop "doing" and learn to enjoy "being."

INCARNATIO – A Calling Forward

One cannot rest in the presence of God without being challenged and/or changed to some degree. In this movement, you are filled with a desire to love and obey God. This movement is experienced as a calling forward to some practical lived expression of loving God and neighbor. From contemplation, you move more confidently into the world as an agent of love and creative transformation.

---

wakeful presence to God. The combination of visualization and vocalization in the practice of "murmuring," or meditation on scripture sought to integrate body, mind, and heart.

During the **monastic** period, *lectio divina* maintained much of its spontaneous inspirational character in its movements of prayer from its Hebraic and patristic roots. However, in its practice by the **desert fathers and mothers** and later in monastic communities, it developed an emphasis on the individual interiorization of mental prayer. It became more and more a silent, reflective practice done by monks and nuns in **solitude**. This develop-

---

A PROCESS FOR GROUP *Lectio Divina*

During the Scholastic period (twelfth through sixteenth centuries), the practice of *lectio divina* became almost exclusively a solitary experience; however, there are contemporary movements toward recovering its more communal roots through *lectio divina* groups. Especially in developing countries where books and literacy are rare, Christians are experiencing the power of this practice in the context of small groups similar to the early Jewish and patristic context. The following are some suggested guidelines for *lectio divina* as a group experience (four to eight people works best):

Follow the general process as described for personal *lectio*.

Select three different readers for the three readings and, after each person reads, observe two minutes of silence.

After the first reading, simply let the passage soak in during the silence, without further comment.

After the second reading, ask participants to share without comment the word, phrase, image, or verse that "captured their attention." Allow 2 minutes of silence after the sharing and before the third reading.

After the third reading and silence, ask the participants to return to the word, phrase, or verse that they shared earlier. Encourage each participant to elaborate and explore the word or image evoked for him or her by this verse. Invite other group members also to explore this image before moving on to another member's word or image. Make sure that each person is allowed to speak. The group leader may facilitate "pondering" by a few questions. This is particularly helpful to novices in the practice.

Invite members to pray aloud or silently. (Some groups will allow **journal** keeping at this time.) Allow vocal prayers to move into 5 or 10 minutes of silence. (Some groups move into **Centering Prayer** here with a full 20 minutes of silence.)

After the silent prayer time open the group to some general sharing or reflection about the entire experience. Ask the question: "In all that you heard, both in the scripture and in the spiritual conversation of the group sharing, is there an invitation here to do something practical in the next few days to live this scripture?" Allow each person to respond to the question.

End the time together with a ritual of consecration or a sending-forth **benediction**.

For a more formally structured group process, see *Gathered in the Word* by Norvene Vest.

---

ment, now called discursive meditation, envisioned *lectio divina* as a praying of scriptures with identifiable movements of thought through a series of steps ending in contemplative prayer. During the monastic period the current four movements were identified: *lectio* (reading), *meditatio* (reflection), *oratio* (prayer), and *contemplatio* (**contemplation**). **Benedict of Nursia** (480–547) has long been credited for structuring the monk's life around a daily rhythm of worship, *lectio divina*, and communal work. However, not until **Guigo II** (d. 1188) did the Scholastic form of *lectio divina* harden into four distinct stages

or steps in a hierarchical pattern. We usually have this Scholastic form and understanding in mind when using the term *lectio divina* today. More recently practitioners and scholars in spirituality have added a fifth step, *incarnatio* (**incarnation**). This step is not a new step but a recovery of an emphasis found in the Hebraic, patristic, and early monastic roots of this spiritual **discipline**. Incarnation, putting into action what one has learned through meditation and contemplation and what one has resolved in prayer, was the ultimate goal. In the Shema, to listen means to obey. To hear and know God-truth is to love that Truth. Out of that love, Truth gives form and shape to life and the world. Monastic spiritual masters taught that *lectio divina* leads to a deeper **conversion** of heart and to obedience. Thus the incarnational aspect was always implicit in holy reading/hearing of scripture. CIZ

LEE, ANN (1736–84), the founder of the **Shaker** movement. Born to a poor and illiterate family in Manchester, England, at age twenty-two Ann Lee joined a small group, the so-called "Shaking Quakers" (who were in reality inspired more by the millennialist fervor of Protestant refugees from France than by **Quakers**). Expressive worship—often with frenzied body movements—and female preaching characterized the young group. The intensely devout Lee married Abraham Standerlin in 1762 and soon mourned the deaths in infancy of three children. When her fourth child died at the age of six, Lee became spiritually convinced that sexual relations were at the root of **sin** and that **celibacy** was needed for spiritual **perfection** on earth. More dramatically, Lee had visions that Christ's second coming would be in female form and that she was that one: the first among many to be wholly imbued by his spirit. Her **incarnation** of the Christ spirit would herald the millennium prophesied at the end of the world.

Through the sheer force of her charismatic personality and religious fervor, Lee became the acknowledged leader of the Shakers—as well as their principal confessor and prophet. Persecuted in England, a group of nine Shakers made the hard voyage to the United States in 1774, and after two years of being dispersed, the tiny band of followers was gathered by Lee in what would develop into a Christian **community** at Watervliet, near Albany, New York. Her husband left her, but by 1779 Lee had recovered her missionary zeal, gathering converts throughout New England and then the Eastern states. Numbers grew, but Lee suffered severe beatings and imprisonment by an unforgiving opposition. Having returned to Watervliet from her last trip, Lee died in 1784. Within a few years, Lee's position among Shakers as the female Messiah had become sacrosanct. While she never wrote a **rule**, Lee's ideas fueled the Shaker vision of a new kingdom realized on earth through a celibate community having an orderly governance, spirited dancing, and female participation in leadership.

For more on Mother Lee, read *The Shakers: Two Centuries of Spiritual Reflection*, edited by Robley Edward Whitson. SAF

LEE, JARENA (1783–?), first female preacher of the African Methodist Episcopal (AME) Church. Born a free black in New Jersey, Lee had religion come upon her as a teenager in what she described as a somewhat traumatic and powerful experience. Upon first hearing the preaching of **Richard Allen**, she came to the conclusion that the Methodists were "the people to which my heart unites." In 1809 she felt a strong call to preach the gospel, but upon application to the Methodists was told that there was no provision for women pastors in the discipline of the church. She was instead licensed to hold prayer meetings and exhort. She felt limited by this concession. Some years later she felt the call renewed; and upon hearing her speak, Allen, now Bishop Allen of the AME church, granted her request.

Lee presents a personal and mystical relationship with God. She states at the end of her autobiography that she cannot explain all of what she has witnessed but has nevertheless recorded it as it happened. She considered herself merely a vessel through which God spoke and worked.

Nearly all the information about Lee's life is contained in her autobiography, *The Life and Religious Experience of Jarena Lee*, first published in 1836, revised and expanded in 1849 as *Religious Experience and Journal of Mrs. Jarena Lee*. LKB

LEÓN, LUIS DE (1528–91), Spanish poet, theologian, biblical scholar. Born in Belmonte, Luis was a gifted writer, arguably

Spain's greatest poet. His father was a wealthy lawyer who became a judge. His mother's family included *conversos*, Spanish Jews who had converted to Catholicism several generations before (many *conversos* had been forced to convert). At fourteen he was sent to Salamanca to study law. Six months later, he entered the Augustinian monastery there and became a monk. After completing his studies, he was given a chair in theology at the University of Salamanca.

In spite of the decree of the Council of Trent (1545–63) that the Vulgate, or Latin translation of the Bible, was authentic, Luis continued to use Hebrew and Greek versions of the Old Testament in his teaching and writing. In 1572 the Inquisition arrested him on this and other charges. He was imprisoned as his trial went on for almost five years. His guilty verdict was overturned, and he was released. His second difficulty with the Inquisition came in 1582, because he differed with **Augustine** about predestination and received a warning to be more circumspect.

The Inquisition possibly targeted Luis because of Jewish ancestry on his mother's side. He was also a Christian Kabbalist, an adherent of a respected school of thought in the sixteenth and seventeenth centuries but one with Jewish undertones. The Kabbalah is a Jewish mystical system in which the names of God, the names of angels, and numerology merit importance.

In addition to his brilliant poetry and his version of thirty odes of Horace and forty Psalms, Luis's prose masterpiece was *Los nombres de Christo* (*The Names of Christ*). The names he lists are Bud, Face of God, the Way, Shepherd, Mountain, Everlasting Father, Arm of God, King of God, Prince of Peace, Husband, Son of God, Lamb, Beloved and Jesus. His contributions to the symbolic representations of Christ include Husband and Beloved, both images from the Song of Solomon. ww

LEWIS, CLIVE STAPLES (1893–1963), English scholar, novelist, and Christian apologist. C. S. Lewis was an Oxford scholar who became one of the world's most famous converts to Christianity. As a young man, Lewis rejected both the rigid, legalistic Christianity of his family and the liberal civil Christianity of the public schools in favor of an intellectual atheism. After becoming a tutor in English language and literature at Oxford, Lewis found more and more of his friends were faithful and practicing Christians; and he felt drawn to return to the church. He describes his **conversion** in his autobiography, *Surprised by Joy*: "In the Trinity Term of 1929 I gave in, and admitted that God was God, and knelt and prayed: perhaps, that night, the most dejected and reluctant convert in all England."

Lewis became an apologist for Christianity through his writings, both works of popular theology and fictional creations of imaginative power that continue to inspire his readers. Late in life he married an American divorcee, Joy Davidman Gresham, and lived through her process of dying of cancer. He wrote about this life-changing experience in *A Grief Observed*. Many of his early books, including *Mere Christianity*, began as radio broadcasts given from 1941 to 1944. Among his nonfiction works are *The Problem of Pain* and *Miracles*. *The Screwtape Letters* presents Christianity from the point of view of a senior demon giving advice to a nephew on how to corrupt his human "assignment." His works of fiction were inspired by the works of **George MacDonald**, to whom Lewis attributed the conversion of his imagination.

Lewis is best known for his children's books, the seven-volume *The Chronicles of Narnia* in which the Christian story is told through fantasy with the lion Aslan as the Christ figure. He also proclaimed his faith in his "space trilogy" consisting of *Out of the Silent Planet*, *Perelandra*, and *That Hideous Strength*. A group of his Oxford friends, including **Charles Williams**, Dorothy Sayers, and J. R. R. Tolkien, were known as "The Inklings" and gathered with him to share stories and the journey of faith together. Lewis remains one of the twentieth century's most published Christian writers. HLR

LIBERATION, SPIRITUALITY OF. A theological/spiritual movement developed in the 1960s in Latin America by Roman Catholic clergy and laity. Since then it has spread around the world. It addresses the liberation of women, Palestinians, Asians, Polish workers, gays, blacks, and hispanics in the United States, even animals and the environment. But whatever the focus, the core of genuine liberation theology is a spirituality of liberation enriched and deepened by each group's practice and reflection in the light of faith.

All Christian spirituality involves following Jesus. However, the spirituality of liberation differs from the forms of spirituality that ignore the workings of society and politics. It is practical and political, believing with Gandhi that people who say religion has nothing to do with politics have no idea what religion is.

The spirituality of liberation stresses the mystical and the prophetic, **contemplation** and action. Mystical language expresses the gratuitousness of God's **love**, while prophetic language expresses the demands this love makes. Both languages are necessary to feed and correct each other.

Gustavo Gutiérrez, one of the founders of liberation theology, says that all spirituality is a **community** enterprise. Within larger societies, there will be communities of the poor and the oppressed. The spirituality of liberation begins with them as it seeks to liberate all people, oppressed and oppressor, from the deadly cycle of discrimination and exploitation that denies everyone's humanity.

Wherever the spirituality of liberation is found, its first and foremost constant includes living with the **Holy Spirit**. The reign of God is the focus, mission, and hope of the spirituality of liberation, which affirms the essence and universality of Christianity, following Jesus and continuing his struggle for peace, justice, and freedom for all of God's children. This spirituality must be rooted in the real world, in history, in a particular place, in politics, and among the poor and oppressed, producing practical **holiness** that leads to commitment and action.

The enormity and depth of the causes of oppression and exploitation can lure us toward idolatry. We can clearly see the "other side" with its idolatry of money, power, luxury, and convenience. It is less obvious to those struggling against oppression that we can also make idols of the poor, the cause, or liberation theology itself.

Concern for the poor and oppressed did not begin with the twentieth-century spirituality of liberation. Hebrew Scriptures understand poverty primarily as the result of oppression. Jewish law included protection for the poor and marginalized (Exod. 22:21-24; Deut. 24:14-15). Later the prophets warned the rich and powerful that oppressing the less fortunate would incur Yahweh's anger (Isa. 3:14-15; Amos 5:11-13). Jesus Christ followed the Hebrew prophets in his love and concern for the poor and outcast, even to the point of identifying with them (Matt. 25:31-46). Everything Jesus said about wealth warned of its seduction toward idolatry (Luke 12:16-21) and away from generosity to the poor (Mark 10:17-22) and dependency on God (Luke 12:22-31). The earliest Christian community in Jerusalem took care of its poor members by sharing everyone's wealth (Acts 4:32-37). While this seems to be the only communal sharing experiment of the early church, generosity to the poor was encouraged among the fellowship (Heb. 13:16; James 2:14-17).

Throughout church history many movements have taken as their primary work the care of the physically and spiritually poor. But only in the liberation theology movement have systemic and institutional evils been addressed, along with the personal individual sinfulness that causes the oppression of the poor and other marginalized groups. ww

LITURGICAL SPIRITUALITY. Christian spirituality is a form of the personal interior life that develops in response to the presence of God revealed in Jesus Christ and sustained by the **Holy Spirit**. *Liturgy* refers to the "public work of worship" in which the Christian **community** engages. Christian *liturgical* spirituality, then, refers to those forms of this interior life in the presence of God that are formed, nurtured, and sustained in the public worship life of the church. A liturgical spirituality is communal rather than private, though no less personal. The public worship of the church and, therefore, liturgical spirituality, is grounded preeminently in the church's celebration of the Lord's Day (Sunday) and the **sacramental** life, especially **baptism** and **Holy Communion**, as well as in daily prayer and the observance of the Christian **year**. Each of these practices is inherently biblical, having their foundation in the story of the people of God as presented in the Old and New Testaments. Through these corporate practices the church remembers, proclaims, and enacts God's saving actions in the world and invites the community to make this story in its own time and place.

Liturgical practices and the spirituality that develops from them make use of and attend to the signs, symbols, and ritual actions that have characterized the Christian community throughout its history: book, font, table, water, and oil; bread blessed and broken, wine poured out, a community gathered and sent. Liturgical spirituality is therefore traditional, even as the particular styles and languages of these liturgical practices have changed in response to the changing world. By means of these traditions, persons not only express their faith but have modeled for them and are formed in particular understandings of themselves as a people joined to God and neighbor through Jesus Christ and in the Spirit.

For further reading, see Philip H. Pfatteicher, *Liturgical Spirituality*; Don E. Saliers, *Worship and Spirituality*; or Susan J. White, *The Spirit of Worship*. EBA

LITURGY OF THE HOURS. Divine Office, a daily cycle of nonsacramental, liturgical prayer consisting mainly of **psalms**, biblical canticles, **hymns**, readings, and historic forms of **prayer**. Based primarily upon the monastic *Opus Dei* (Latin for "work of God"), or Divine Office (Latin *Officium*, "duty"), and the pub-

lic prayer of local churches (the "cathedral office"), the present form of the liturgy, following ancient tradition, includes seven Hours, or specific times of prayer. The origins of this form of liturgical prayer reside in the Jewish synagogue with its pattern of Psalms, blessings, continuous reading of the Law and Prophets, rabbinic reflection, and **benedictions**. As early as the third century, Hippolytus described "hours of prayer" and ascribed particular christological significance to the third, sixth, and ninth hours of the day. In the **monastic** context of the medieval world, the prescribed offices evolved into exceedingly complex traditions of prayer.

The Hours have always been a major part of communal prayer in the **Benedictine**, **Trappist**, and **Cistercian** traditions, as well as in the **Dominican** and **Franciscan** traditions of mendicant monasticism. In the period of the sixteenth-century reformations of the church, both **Martin Luther** and **Thomas Cranmer** attempted to simplify the Divine Office so that laypeople as well as religious could pray it in their daily lives. Both conflated material from the various Hours into morning (matins) and evening prayer (vespers). Several efforts in this direction have been made in modern times, all of which culminate in the Liturgy of the Hours published in 1971 after Vatican II. The major elements in the present Roman rite include a hymn, psalm, and scriptural canticles (with appropriate accompanying antiphons), scripture reading, and response (and other readings in the Office of Readings), the Canticle of Zechariah, or Benedictus (Luke 1:68-79), at morning prayer and the Canticle of Mary or The Magnificat (Luke 1:46-55) at evening prayer, intercessions, the **Lord's Prayer**, a collect, and a final blessing and dismissal.

Primary among the seven times of prayer are morning prayer (lauds) and evening prayer (vespers), which the Second Vatican Council described as "the twofold hinge of the daily office." The Office of Readings (previously matins or vigil), which was prayed traditionally during the night, may now be prayed any time throughout the day. It consists of the normal pattern of prayer with three prescribed psalms or portions of psalms and two readings, one from the Bible and the other from the writings of the church fathers or about the life of a **saint**. The shorter offices of terce, sext, and none (Latin for "third," "sixth," and "ninth," i.e., hours) may now be used selectively as midday prayer or daytime prayer. Compline (or night prayer) concludes the day. The book used in the praying of these hours, which contains all of the prescribed readings and prayers, is called a Breviary (Latin *Breviarium*, "shortened version"). The Divine Office reflects Paul's exhortation about **unceasing prayer** in 1 Thessalonians 5:17. The purpose of this form of prayer is to offer perpetual praise and **thanksgiving** to God for creation and redemption. The Liturgy of the Hours is, therefore, a fundamentally incarnational approach to prayer and spirituality.

Orders for Morning and Evening Prayer can be found in the Episcopal **Book of Common Prayer**, *The United Methodist Hymnal*, and other worship resources. Breviaries are available at many religious bookstores. For more historical information, see A. M. Roguet, *The Liturgy of the Hours*. PWC

LORD, MAKE ME AN INSTRUMENT. A

prayer that seeks consonance, living in tune with the **will of God**. The most common form of the prayer is this:

> Lord, make me an instrument of thy
>   peace;
> where there is hatred, let me sow love;
> where there is injury, pardon;
> where there is doubt, faith;
> where there is despair, hope;
> where there is darkness, light;
> and where there is sadness, joy.
> O Divine Master,
> grant that I may not so much seek
> to be consoled, as to console;
> to be understood, as to understand;
> to be loved, as to love;

> for it is in giving that we receive,
> it is in pardoning that we are pardoned,
> and it is in dying that we are born to
>   eternal life.

Despite attribution to **Francis of Assisi** in recent popular literature and collections of prayers, the prayer cannot be traced back farther than the late nineteenth century, when it appeared in French as a summary of the **rule** of a Franciscan Third Order. An English translation misattributed it to Francis, and the mistake has flourished. The prayer does seem to be inspired by a short passage in "The Admonitions" of Francis, a collection of the saint's sayings written down during his lifetime. Here is that passage:

> Where there is love and wisdom, there is
>   neither fear nor ignorance.
> Where there is patience and humility,
>   there is neither anger nor vexation.
> Where there is poverty with joy, there is
>   neither greed nor avarice.
> Where there is peace and meditation,
>   there is neither anxiety nor doubt.
> Where the fear of the Lord stands
>   guard, there the enemy finds
>   no entry.
> Where there is mercy and moderation,
>   there is neither indulgence
>   nor harshness.

More of the text of "The Admonitions" may be found in *Riches of Simplicity: Selected Writings of Francis and Clare*, edited by Keith Beasley-Topliffe. KRB

LORD'S PRAYER. A prayer given by Jesus as

a model in Matthew 6:9-13 and (in simpler form) in Luke 11:2-4. The standard liturgical form follows Matthew, substituting *trespasses* for *debts* (some traditions retain *debts*) and adding a doxology. The traditional English translation is:

> Our Father, who art in heaven,
> hallowed be thy name.
> Thy kingdom come,

thy will be done on earth as it is in
    heaven.
Give us this day our daily bread.
And forgive us our trespasses,
as we forgive those who trespass against
    us.
And lead us not into temptation,
but deliver us from evil.
For thine is the kingdom, and the
    power, and the glory, forever. Amen.

An international and interdenominational commission on liturgical texts created a more modern translation:

Our Father in heaven,
hallowed be your name.
Your kingdom come,
your will be done, on earth as in heaven.
Give us today our daily bread.
Forgive us our sins
as we forgive those who sin against us.
Save us from the time of trial
and deliver us from evil.
For the kingdom, the power, and the
    glory are yours,
now and forever. Amen.

The most significant difference between the versions is in the object of **forgiveness**: debts, trespasses, or sins. Each offers a different picture of the problem separating us from God and from other people, of **sin**. *Debts* are owed, suggesting things we ought to have done but failed to do, sins of omission. *Trespasses* suggest stepping out of line or crossing boundaries, sins of commission. The Greek word for *sin* implies an image of missing the target, failing to do what we tried to do (or were expected to do).

Because of its centrality in Christian liturgy and devotions, the Lord's Prayer serves as the basis for many discussions of prayer, from **Origen**'s *On Prayer* through **Luther**'s *The Large Catechism* to **Evelyn Underhill**'s *Abba* and the recent *Catechism of the Catholic Church*. **Ignatius of Loyola** suggested contemplative dwelling on each word or phrase. **Teresa of Ávila** offered devotional reflections in *The Way of Perfection*. **Augustine**, **John Wesley**, and countless others have preached series of sermons on the prayer. *The Lord's Prayer* by Jan Milic Lochman offers a guide to this tradition of commentary and reflection. *Lord, Teach Us: The Lord's Prayer and the Christian Life* by William H. Willimon and Stanley Hauerwas is a recent devotional commentary. KRB

LORD'S SUPPER. See **Holy Communion**.

LOVE. Both the source and the goal of the Christian life. The steadfast love of God for humanity is a theme found throughout the Hebrew Scriptures, especially in the **Psalms**. Christians believe Jesus's death on the cross to be the ultimate expression of God's love for us, and that this act is the model for our own Christian life of love.

To define love, one must look to 1 Corinthians 13, which describes love manifested in concrete ways in relationship (e.g., patience, kindness, **humility**). The dual commandments of Matthew 22:34-40 (and parallels) state that the proper objects of such love are God and neighbor, while the parable of the good Samaritan (Luke 10:29-37) shows us that neighbor is anyone in need, regardless of racial, ethnic, or religious standing. This love is concisely defined in 1 John 3:16: "We know love by this, that he laid down his life for us— and we ought to lay down our lives for one another." Love is the laying down of our lives in the service of God and others, whether as **martyrs** or in small daily sacrifices that most ordinary Christians are called to make.

While love as a topic has been touched on by most of the great writers in the Christian spiritual tradition, two treatments are helpfully representative, those of **Bernard of Clairvaux** and **C. S. Lewis**. In his work *On Loving God*, Bernard of Clairvaux described four degrees of love, distinguished by their different objects and motivations. He started with self-love, a basic human, almost animal, state of self-regard in which we love ourselves for our own sake. The second degree of love finds us loving God, but for our own advantage—loving God for the consolations and benefits of the relationship. In the third degree of love we love God for God's sake. Instead of being obsessed with what we can obtain from our relationship with God, we appreciate God for God's self and acknowledge that God is worthy of praise, worship, and service simply because of who God is. Bernard shows great sensitivity to human nature and a profound sense of human wholeness when he names the fourth degree of love as loving ourselves for the sake of God. Bernard calls us to realize that as creatures we are not worthless but a precious creation in the image of God who exists for God's purposes. This fourth degree of love shows that self-love can, in the end, be refined when put in the context of God's love. This powerfully reminds us that true self-love is part of Jesus' summary of the law of the Hebrew Scriptures, namely, that we are to love our neighbors as we love ourselves (Mark 12:29-31 and parallels). We finally only make sense of our lives by relating to ourselves and others through the steadfast love of God.

C. S. Lewis, in his book *The Four Loves*, describes the four different Greek terms that are all, unfortunately, translated by the one English word *love*: *storge* (affection), *philia* (friendship), *eros* (romantic love), *agape* (self-sacrificial Christian love). Aware of the subtle interplay and mixture of these various loves in the average person's life, Lewis offers an analysis that helps us judge whether we in fact are living out the highest Christian love. CSC

LOVE FEAST. There seems to be little doubt that in the apostolic church, Christians observed a common meal generally known as the *agape* (Greek for "sacrificial love"), conjoined in some way with the **sacrament** of **Holy Communion**. Over the course of time these two observances were separated into

---

CONDUCTING A LOVE FEAST

Essential to the love feast is the balanced combination of three essential elements: a token meal, a measure of spontaneity in sharing spiritual matters with one another, and a liturgical pattern that links the participant to the past but adapts to the changing needs of the present. The elements of bread and water are generally used, but some traditions substitute coffee for water. The issue of spontaneous testimony is a matter of sensitive management. At the center of the feast is an appreciation for the movement of the **Holy Spirit** among God's people, but it is sometimes difficult to distinguish between the Holy Spirit and an individual's needs. The appointed leader needs to keep his or her finger on the pulse of the meeting, prompting speakers, directing times of prayer, and navigating the community through its conversation on the work of God.

SUGGESTED ORDER
- **Hymn** (or praise songs)
- Prayer
- Sung grace
- Blessing and distribution of bread
- Offering for the poor
- Blessing and circulation of the loving cup
- Address
- Testimonies interspersed with hymns
- Spontaneous **prayer** (and hymns)
- Closing exhortation
- Hymn
- **Benediction**

two distinct worship events in the life of the Christian community. While the sacrament celebrated the death and resurrection of Jesus, the *agape*, or love feast, developed into a less formalized fellowship meal centered in Christian witness and testimony. This meal became the occasion for the encouragement of growth in God-centered love. While unambiguous evidence for the love feast is scanty in the New Testament, the *Didache* (an early Christian book of instructions) preserves aspects of the meal as it was practiced as early as the second century. The love feast was a simple service with prayers before and after the meal, congregational responses, and various forms of the central refrain, "to Thee be the glory." *The Apostolic Tradition* of Hippolytus reveals the Roman practice of celebrating this meal in private homes. Various abuses and probable paganization eventually undermined this ancient fellowship meal to the extent that it seems to have become universally defunct by the eighth century.

The feast was revived, primarily through the efforts of the European **Pietists**, in the eighteenth century and found a special place among the **Moravians** and Methodists in particular. The love feasts conducted under the direction of **John** and **Charles Wesley** were originally monthly events but evolved into annual celebrations and momentous occasions within the Methodist Societies. While the original feasts were certainly full meals, the resurrected form often involved the simple use of water and bread. Sacramental in its feeling but lay (or clergy) in its administration, the meal involved a common loaf often passed hand to hand and a "loving cup" with two handles developed for passing the water in similar fashion. Testimony was the heart and core of the love feast in Methodist practice. The standard order for the service, followed throughout Wesley's lifetime, is replicated on the previous page. Charles Wesley wrote hymns specifically for use at the love feast that enunciate the central themes:

Come, and let us sweetly join,
Christ to praise in hymns divine;
Give we all with one accord
Glory to our common Lord.
Hands and hearts and voices raise,
Sing as in the ancient days;
Antedate the joys above,
Celebrate the feast of love.

For more information, read Frank Baker's *Methodism and the Love-Feast.* PWC

LUTHER, MARTIN (1483–1546), monk, professor, reformer, musician, biblical translator, theologian. His biblical rediscovery of God's grace in Jesus Christ inspired and ignited the sixteenth-century Reformation in the Western Church. His writings, translated into English, fill over fifty volumes.

Luther was born in Eisleben, Germany. His father was a copper miner. His mother took care of their home. At thirteen he was sent to a school in Magdeburg run by the Brethren of the Common Life, a religious order which advocated an interior piety based on introspection, **meditation**, and the use of the confessional. At eighteen Luther graduated from the University of Erfurt with a master of arts degree. In 1505 he was in the process of earning his law degree when he was caught in a thunderstorm. He promised Saint Anne, the patroness of miners, that if she would spare him, he would become a monk. In July 1505, Luther entered the Black Cloister of the Observant Augustinians at Erfurt.

Luther, an impeccable monk, prayed, fasted, flagellated himself, went without sleep. He pursued the **rule** earnestly, exceeding its requirements. He once said, "If anyone could have earned heaven by the life of a monk, it was I." With a doctorate in theology he became a professor. Yet the nagging question remained: "How can I find a gracious God?" What Luther called *anfechtung* would not go away. *Anfechtung* implies more than temptation, suggesting spiritual combat. Luther experienced being in the presence of God and experiencing God's wrath against his sins.

The phrase that bothered Luther the most was "the righteousness of God." Luther and the people of his time believed that God's righteousness was satisfied by a system of cooperation between God's **grace**, dispensed sacramentally, and human efforts and good works. But the system did not work for Luther. He could find no peace. As Luther dug deeper into holy scripture, he discovered Romans 1:17: "The one who is righteous will live by **faith**." Luther discovered that faith is a gift given by the Holy Spirit. We are made right with God by grace through faith in Christ alone, apart from the works of the law. The whole Bible took on a new meaning in light of the gracious God known in Christ. Luther said he felt born again.

Luther next turned to the teachers of the church: **Augustine**, **Bernard of Clairvaux**, **Hugh of St. Victor**, and **Bonaventure**. He found the theme of God's grace through their works and had especially high praise for the German mystic **Johannes Tauler**. Luther also published the anonymous mystical work titled ***Theologia Germanica***.

After this spiritual awakening to God's unconditional and unmerited grace in Jesus Christ, Luther publicly questioned the system of indulgences in ninety-five theses, followed by a variety of treatises promoting reform in the church. With the political support of the emperor, he was able to stand against the power of the papacy; and the Protestant Reformation began. Luther left the monastery, married, and had children.

Luther's discovery of God's grace deeply penetrated his heart and his **spirituality**. He not only discovered God's objective **love** in Christ, but he also discovered God's subjective love in Christ "in humankind." Christ became a loving presence, and the Word came alive for him. His day began with morning prayers between four and six o'clock. Then he gathered his family and house guests to pray and to recite the Apostles' Creed, the Ten Commandments, and the **Lord's Prayer**, and to chant the **Psalms**. He once said he had such a busy day that he needed to start with at least three hours of prayer. He also prayed using his Psalter after lunch and after dinner and had evening prayers before bed. In *A Simple Way to Pray*, Luther described prayer as a four-stranded garland: (1) instruction, what the Word teaches; (2) **thanksgiving**, what we appreciate from the Word; (3) **confession**, where we fall short of the Word; (4) and prayer to learn and to live by what the Word evokes in us. To Luther individual prayer was always an extension of the church, in heaven and on earth.

Luther wrote the *Small Catechism* to nurture Christians in the basics of faith, and he composed many hymns, including "A Mighty Fortress Is Our God." He translated the Latin mass into German. To Luther the church at worship, primarily through the preaching of the Word and receiving of the **sacraments**, was the main arena of **spiritual formation**. He taught the priesthood of all believers, believing that a scrubwoman, a farmer, and a prince performing their vocations to the glory of God are just as holy as a priest leading liturgy. The evangelical faith permeated and enlightened every area and aspect of the Christian's life. On February 16, 1546, just before he died, Luther wrote down his last words, "We are all beggars. That is true." Luther's life taught him that we are beggars and sinners; yet God loves us, accepts us, and saves us as we are, with no conditions.

James M. Kittelson's *Luther the Reformer* is a basic biography. In addition to works mentioned above, *Table Talk*, a collection of Luther's conversations, is an introduction to his thoughts on many topics. FPS

M

MACDONALD, GEORGE (1824–1905), lecturer, preacher, and writer. Born in Scotland and educated in London, MacDonald became a Congregational parish minister. In 1853 he was forced to resign when his theological ideas came into conflict with those of his parishioners. Rejecting the austere, judgmental view of God that was popular in his day, MacDonald forged a vision of a gracious God, a creative presence within each person.

After leaving the parish MacDonald began a long and fruitful, if difficult, life as a writer and lecturer. Among his literary friends were Carlyle, Tennyson, William Morris, and Lewis Carroll. In spite of a successful career in publishing (some fifty-two volumes of fantasy, sermons, prayers, and poems), he lived most of his life in poverty and suffered from tuberculosis, then asthma and eczema. In the face of adversity he was known for his lightness of heart. MacDonald wrote about and lived in a **present moment** he named as **holy**.

MacDonald is perhaps best known today for his fantasy works (e.g., *The Golden Key*), written for children but also for the childlike in people of all ages. His sermons, published under the title *Unspoken Sermons*, covered topics such as prayer, righteousness, and love of neighbor. In the poems found in *Diary of an Old Soul*, MacDonald speaks to God as would a child to a loving but hidden father veiled in the mystery of unexplainable and all encompassing love. Themes that run through these and other writings include the necessity of knowing God as the Christ within, the divine son-ship of humanity, and God as a **fire** of holy love rather than holy retribution.

C. S. Lewis wrote (in *Surprised by Joy*) that MacDonald was a major influence in his return to Christianity and a man who was close to the spirit of Christ himself. In Lewis's *The Great Divorce*, about a fictional trip to heaven, MacDonald serves as the narrator's guide.

The writings in *George MacDonald, Creation in Christ*, edited by Rolland Hein, introduce MacDonald's thinking. Many of MacDonald's books are in print, though often "edited for modern readers." One fantasy, *The Princess and the Goblin*, has been made into an animated movie. SN

MACLEOD, GEORGE FIELDEN (1895–1991), founder of the **Iona** Community. MacLeod was born the son of a conservative member of Parliament and educated at Winchester, Oxford, and Edinburgh. During his military service in World War I, for which he received the Military Cross and the Croix de Guerre, he was led to sense a call to the ministry rather than law as his vocation. As a pastor in Edinburgh's West End during the 1920s he earned a reputation as a great preacher. His years of ministry in the Glasgow parish of Govan during the Great Depression profoundly affected his politics, and he became a crusader for social justice and peace. In 1938 he organized a group of ministers and laypeople to begin the reconstruction of the Iona abbey to serve as a training place for those who wished to serve in the industrial slums. He also founded the Iona Community to renew the church. In 1957 he became the sixth member of his family to be elected moderator of the Church of Scotland. From 1968 to 1971 he served as Lord Rector of Glasgow University, and in 1989 he was awarded the Templeton Prize for Progress in Religion.

MacLeod had the wonderful ability to draw upon ancient **Celtic** traditions and to build an ecumenical organization that survived him and has had a deep impact upon thousands. His books include *Only One Way*

Left, Speaking the Truth in Love, Gowan Calling, and *We Shall Rebuild.* HLR

MALONEY, GEORGE (b. 1924), **Jesuit** priest, prominent spiritual writer of over sixty books; one of America's leading contemplative theologians. Ordained a priest in the Russian Byzantine Rite in 1957, he pursued a doctorate in Oriental theology from the Pontifical Oriental Institute and a licentiate from the Gregorian Pontifical University in Rome. After about seven years in Rome, Maloney returned to America in 1969 and taught graduate courses in **spirituality**, theology, and history at Fordham University. Gifted with the ability to weave together scripture, church teachings, Eastern fathers, **desert fathers and mothers**, and the writings of the great spiritual masters, he continued the dialogue he had begun between Roman Catholics and Orthodox Christians by founding the John XXIII Institute for Eastern Christian Studies at Fordham. In 1978 he left academia to lead **retreats** and missions for priests and to teach the laity about **prayer**, especially the indwelling healing presence of the Trinity. Father Maloney is currently director of Contemplative Ministries in Seal Beach, California, and devotes himself to full-time writing.

A good place to begin reading is *Jesus, Set Me Free!: Inner Freedom through Contemplation. Loving the Christ in You: A Spiritual Path to Self-Esteem* (coauthored with Barbara J. Rogers-Gardner) explores how one's whole existence can be a prayer. EKM

MANICHAEISM. An early Christian heretical movement, named after its Persian founder Mani, or Manichaeus. An ordained Christian priest, Mani longed to blend the Christian faith with ideas from the Persian and Eastern influences of Asia Minor and the ancient Middle East. Merging Christian teaching, including heretical views from both **Gnostic** and Judaizing sects, with such ancient religious traditions like Buddhism and Zoroastrianism, this sect reached its height in the third and fourth centuries. It was built around a radi-cally dualist theology, in which grave conflicts between good and evil, light and darkness, God and matter would later extend to New versus Old Testaments. The divine wars raging between these varying extremes led to strong ideas of the nature of Christ as liberator. The light and the powers of good would one day be rescued from the hands of the princes of darkness by such leaders as Jesus, the prophets, Buddha, and Mani himself.

Most of what we know of Manichaeism, as with most heretical sects, comes from the writings of their detractors, most notable among them **Augustine of Hippo**. At one time strongly attracted to Manichaeism, after his conversion Augustine diligently wrote in opposition to the doctrine. In a famous debate in 392 against a Manichaean elder named Fortunatus, Augustine dismissed the argument that Manichees did good works to focus on doctrine.

Manichaeism influenced later sects including **Catharism** in medieval France. To learn more, read *Manichaeism* by Samuel N. C. Lieu. WBF

MARIAN DEVOTION, practiced by both Catholic and Eastern Orthodox churches, develops a relationship with **Mary, the mother of Jesus**. It is viewed as completing devotion to Christ, not replacing it. A large place has been given to devotion to Mary in the lives of Catholic laypeople, leaders, and **saints** both East and West for two thousand years, developing a significant body of extrabiblical references and legends.

Occasional references were made to Mary in the first- and second-century writings of **Ignatius of Antioch**, Justin Martyr, **Irenaeus**, the Apocrypha, and Gnostic documents. According to the apocryphal second-century *Protevangelium* (also known as the Book of James), Mary remained a pure virgin during and after Jesus' birth. From this evolved the concept of the Immaculate Conception, her miraculous preservation from original **sin**. The debate over its acceptability, raging hotly for centuries, was resolved by recognizing

Mary's continued need for Christ's universal redemption to preserve her from contracting original sin and transmitting it to Jesus, which became Roman Catholic dogma in 1854. In parallel to stories of her early life, accounts arose of her bodily assumption into heaven, her sinless body not being subject to corruption. The Assumption became dogma in 1950. The fifth-century councils of Ephesus and Chalcedon proclaimed Mary *theotokos*, "God-bearer," bringing about an emphasis on Mary as *mater Dei*, "mother of God." Eventually Mary was recognized as the "mother of the church," for she brought forth Christ, its head. At the Second Council of Nicaea (787), "worship" was specified for God alone, "reverence" was proper for the saints, and "more than reverence" appropriate for Mary. Luther wrote of Mary as "the foremost example" of God's **grace** and human **humility**. Devotion to the Immaculate Heart of Mary developed in the seventeenth and eighteenth centuries. It focused on Mary's love, her entire sanctity and inner life. In 1942 Pius XII consecrated the world to the Immaculate Heart of Mary. A number of visions and appearances of Mary were reported in the nineteenth century. More restraint and balance in Roman Catholic theological writing about Mary and devotional life followed Vatican II.

Generally, three basic elements compose Roman Catholic devotion to Mary. First is reverent recognition of her dignity as the holy Virgin Mother of God. Mary's submission to God's will at the time of the Annunciation (Luke 1:38) became a model for all Christians. Entrusted with Jesus' care during his formative years, Mary has a unique position of lasting influence. When from the cross Jesus committed her to his beloved disciple (John 19:25-27), many Christians understand he committed her as mother to all Christians.

Second is calling upon our Lady (a term of reverent respect) for her motherly and queenly intercession on our behalf as she now reigns in heaven with her Son following her assumption. As Queen of Heaven, her dominion and concern are for her spiritual children. While Christ alone is Redeemer in the full, absolute sense, he willed to associate Mary with himself so that together they would form one total principle of human salvation. Some Catholic scholars speak of Mary's role as co-redemptive: While utterly dependent upon Christ's exclusive work of redemption, Mary, in her acceptance of God's plan, represented humanity and also participated in the redemptive process.

The third element of Marian devotion involves imitation, dedication, and consecration. These may be practiced by observing her many feasts that have developed over the centuries, as well as through litanies, repeating the **rosary**, wearing her medals and/or scapular, and in private prayers. Additional practices include **meditation** on her **virtues**, offering her acts of love, **fasting** in her honor, singing her praises, carrying little images of her, and consecrating oneself to her in a special and solemn manner.

St. Louis de Montfort's *True Devotion to Mary* is a Catholic classic on this subject. *Mary in the New Testament*, edited by Raymond E. Brown et al., surveys biblical origins for the purpose of Catholic-Protestant dialogue. *Mary through the Centuries* by Jaroslav Pelikan traces developments since biblical times. LSP

MARRIAGE, SPIRITUAL. The most profound **union** of the soul with God. *Spiritual marriage* is a mystical term used by many but fully formulated in the sixteenth century by **John of the Cross** in *The Spiritual Canticle* and *Living Flame of Love* and especially by **Teresa of Ávila** in *Interior Castle* (the seventh mansions). However, the term's roots are in the Old Testament, where marriage or sexual union describes the relationship between God and Israel (Hos. 2; Isa. 54:5-6; 62:4-5; Jer. 2:2; 3:20, and in the mystical interpretation of the Song of Solomon). New Testament writers similarly write of the church as the bride of Christ (Eph. 5:25-27; 2 Cor. 11:2; Rev. 19:7-9; 21:2; 22:17).

From these roots grew the understanding of **baptism** as the first step of participation in the marital relationship that is established between Christ and the church. Spiritual marriage is also connected to the idea of nuns becoming the brides of Christ and to the practice of **celibacy** for many of the religious orders. Those who have given themselves in marriage directly to Christ can marry no other. At other times, especially in the Middle Ages, laypeople felt moved to emulate this mystical marriage in their earthly marriages (see *Spiritual Marriage: Sexual Abstinence in Medieval Wedlock* by Dyan Elliott).

Spiritual marriage is more than just connection with God. It is an offering to God and God's wholehearted and complete acceptance. It is sharing a mutual soul with God. The "two becoming one flesh," which Genesis uses to describe marriage, reflects this bond; but with God the spiritual bonding is powerfully complete. ELS

MARTYRS. Those whose Christian witness led to death. In a time of severe religious persecution, martyrdom became a regular event in the lives of the earliest Christians. Legend tells of Christians thrown into the large Roman coliseums to be mauled by large animals and harassed by Roman sentries. Christians saw it as an act of Christlikeness to be slain in the same way as the Savior, whether through crucifixion or other forms of execution. Stephen was the first Christian martyr, as recounted in Acts 8. Luke tells us that Paul was on hand, and Paul refers frequently to his part in persecuting the church before his conversion.

Martyr comes from the Greek *martus*, "witness." So many Christians died bearing witness to Christ that the word came to mean "one who suffers execution, assassination, or murder for Christ." Martyrdom became an ideal for Christians to strive for, the ultimate example of **obedience** and **covenant** with God. Therefore, martyrs were the first to be honored as **saints**, the ones written most about in the accounts of the saints' lives. Martyrdom showed no preference toward male or female, for women were just as often martyred as men, though accounts of women martyrs

are scarce. The earliest known account of martyrdom, from eyewitness accounts by his disciples, is of Saint Polycarp. Many martyrs throughout Christian history have been missionaries. But others have been killed for standing up for their beliefs or for speaking out against oppression in supposedly Christian nations, including **Martin Luther King Jr.** and **Oscar Romero** in the mid- to late-twentieth century.

Several collections of early Christian documents, such as *The Martyrdom of St. Polycarp*, translated by Charles H. Hoole, and *The Martyrdom of Perpetua and Felicitas*, translated by Mark Reasoner, contain stories of martyrs. WBF

MARY AND MARTHA. The story of Jesus in the home of these two sisters (Luke 10:38-42) has been the subject of myriad sermons and theological debates. Simply put, it represents a dramatic commentary on the paradoxical union of **contemplation** and action. Most literature views Martha's service negatively while it eulogizes Mary's sitting at the feet of Jesus. The story invites the reader to a careful study of how an active spiritual life may be held in balance with one that is more contemplative.

These few powerful verses form the skeleton for understanding the contemplative life in the anonymous spiritual classic, *The Cloud of Unknowing*, which values the apophatic or **negative way** over the path of active service. Yet the reformers followed the Eastern Church's tradition where the two "sisters" are meant to live in a creative balance.

Meister Eckhart takes a friendly view of Martha: receiving Jesus into her home gave birth to Christ in her life, and her anxiety represents birth pangs. So Paul can say, "My little children, for whom I am again in the pain of childbirth until Christ is formed in you" (Gal. 4:19). It was Martha's *attachment* to her many good gifts that distracted her from her guest: too much *diakonia*, too much ministry.

Yet Mary quietly made the countercultural claim that nurturing the mind and heart for Jesus, for herself, and maybe for other disciples present was as important to the ultimate revolution of values as feeding the body. As a woman, Mary performed a bold act of claiming space to listen and learn that *was* her timeless service both for women *and* men. She discerned the need of their guest for spiritual companionship, for someone to appreciate the word he said because what he said expressed who he was.

Yet if Martha had not opened the door to the house, then Mary could not have extended her gift of hospitality to this homeless Galilean who had "nowhere to lay his head" (Luke 9:58). Martha made it possible for Mary to choose the better portion, the better helping: that the first service one owes consists of listening to the Christ in others.

Significantly the text of Mary and Martha is sandwiched between action (the Good Samaritan story, Luke 10:25-37) and contemplation (the **Lord's Prayer** and teaching on prayer, 11:1-13). "Mary has chosen the good *portion*" (10:42, RSV). "Portion" (*merida*) is a food word, as when one invites a dinner guest to take another "portion" or "serving." The better serving unites prayer and action; split apart they become anxiety (*merimna*, 10:41) instead.

Thus **Francis** could speak of meeting Christ in the leper he impulsively kissed. Brother **Lawrence** in *The Practice of the Presence of God* could tell how his most demanding work did not distract him from God, how he found ordinary tasks to be the best way of experiencing God, and how it was a delusion to think that intentional prayer times should differ from other times: working in the kitchen clumsily breaking dishes or keeping financial records for which he felt no business aptitude.

Those called to the contemplative life are as engaged in service as active Christians. **Thomas Merton** pointed out in *The Seven Storey Mountain* that the highest way is the union of the two. The story in Luke 10:38-42 may be read in this light: Martha's service was hospitality; Mary's was listening and learning. These two aspects of service are illustrated in synergy in the political life of **Martin Luther King Jr.** and the mystical life of **Howard Thur-** man. The spiritual art is to engage in either form of service as prayer without being distracted from the one thing necessary—the singleness of heart that is one's unique vocation.

In addition to the books listed above, see *The Spiritual Life* by Evelyn Underhill and *Life Together* by Dietrich Bonhoeffer. KIG

MARY, THE MOTHER OF JESUS. In the Christian (and Muslim) tradition, Mary is the virgin who gave birth to Jesus Christ of Nazareth in fulfillment of the ancient prophecies (Isa. 7:14).

Mary's story comes primarily from the New Testament Gospels. Luke tells of Gabriel's visit to Mary to announce God's plan and Mary's agreement: "Here am I, the servant of the Lord; let it be with me according to your word" (Luke 1:38). In this act of submission to God's will and her willingness to risk scandal and even death for God's sake, Mary becomes a model for all Christians. When she visits her cousin Elizabeth, who is pregnant with John the Baptist, the baby "leaps" in Elizabeth's womb and Elizabeth proclaims Mary blessed among women and blessed is Mary's child. Later Christians combined the greetings of Gabriel and Elizabeth as the opening of the **Hail Mary**. What follows in Luke's account is Mary's song, known as The Magnificat, significant as perhaps the first Christian prayer from a woman. Showing her devotion to the Lord, her willingness to be a part of the divine plan, and her roots in Jewish life with her acknowledgment of the descendants of Abraham, Mary in this song conjures images of the prayer of Hannah in 1 Samuel 2:1-10.

In the stories of Jesus' adult ministry, Mary appears infrequently. Jesus seems to rebuke her for trying to tell him what to do in the story of the wedding in Cana (John 2:1 ff.), then follows her wishes. Mark 3:31-35 and parallels seem to point to conflict or at least confusion between Jesus and his family. We finally see Mary at the cross, grieving the loss of her son because of a ministry she could not yet fully understand (John 19:25-27). When Jesus says to his beloved disciple, "Here is your mother," many Christians understand him to be offering her as mother to all Christians.

As Christianity spread, these few glimpses of Mary's life were expanded by legends about her birth and childhood (*Protevangelium*) and her later life and death ("The Assumption of the Virgin"). **Marian devotion** grew as Christians saw her not only as model and mother for believers but also worthy of veneration as Mother of God. She filled a need for a feminine face of God, as seen in the popularity of Mary in Ephesus, formerly a center of the cult of Diana, and in the similarity between depictions of Mary with the infant Jesus to depictions of the Egyptian goddess Isis and her infant Osiris. With Christ depicted increasingly as the all-powerful judge, Mary provided an approachable link to the divine presence.

For further reading on the biblical story, see Elisabeth Moltmann-Wendel, *The Women around Jesus.* For later developments, read *Mary Through the Centuries* by Jaroslav Pelikan. WBF and KRB

MAXIMUS THE CONFESSOR (ca. 580–662), Greek author and scholar whose difficult and obscure writings have formed foundations for better-known scholars such as **John Scotus Eriugena**. He is the author of the beautiful *Mystagogia* and other philosophical works in which he examines questions from the writings of others, including **Pseudo-Dionysius**. He is one of the earliest proponents of the doctrine of the absolute predestination of Christ: that Christ's incarnation was engendered by an independent God whose plans were not contingent upon humanity's need for salvation.

Maximus was born in Constantinople, was classically educated, and was well-acquainted with the spirituality of **Origen**, **Gregory of Nyssa**, **Basil of Caesarea**, and others, as well as with the philosophies of Aristotle and Plato. He was still quite young when appointed as first secretary to Emperor Heraclius, but later resigned the position to live in the monastery of Chrysopolis, adopting the ascetic life. He

later moved to the monastery of St. George at Cyzicus, and, when the Persians threatened Constantinople, fled to North Africa, where he lived for the next twenty-five years.

During this period, Maximus engaged in debates about the nature of Christ. The church had split over monophysitism, the doctrine that Christ had only a divine nature and so was fully God but not very human, as opposed to the Council of Chalcedon's declaration of two natures. An attempt at compromise called monotheletism accepted two natures but insisted that Christ had no human will, guided only by the divine will. To state otherwise was to compromise the omnipotence of the Godhead in Christ. For Maximus, Christ had to have a human will and human nature in order to redeem humanity's **sin**.

In 653 the emperor Constans II had Maximus and others arrested because of their continued insistence that Christ had two full and separate wills. Brought to Constantinople to stand trial for treason, Maximus was banished to Thrace; but he would not be silenced. Arrested again, Maximus was tried and ultimately condemned to mutilation. His tongue and right hand were cut off because he refused to sign the compromise statement of doctrine. He was banished to Lazica, where he died. He is called "confessor" because of his steadfastness in declaring his faith.

Maximus is most significant because of his writings regarding two important ideas. The first is the ineffability of God. Maximus cautioned against a spirituality so caught up in the idea of the **vision of God** and **union** that it loses the theology of **transcendence**. A proponent of the **negative way**, he fully believed that God is wholly other. Believers are brought into union with God only through Jesus Christ, who holds divine and human together.

Second, Maximus affirmed the idea of **deification**. He believed that ultimate union with God is possible after death, that salvation is a process of transformation, beginning in human existence by means of **faith** and the **grace** of God in the human/divine Christ and continuing after death into the world to come when believers then participate fully in the very nature of God.

For further reading, see *Maximus Confessor: Selected Writings,* translated by George C. Berthold. SAW

MAY, GERALD G. (b. 1940), psychiatrist and spiritual writer. May was active in private psychiatric practice for twenty-five years. He taught in the clinical medical facilities of Pennsylvania State University, Temple University, and the University of Maryland.

May was part of the original group that founded Shalem Institute under the leadership of **Tilden Edwards** in 1973. In 1983 he became a full-time associate at Shalem Institute for **Spiritual Formation** as Director for Spiritual Guidance and later became Senior Fellow in Contemplative Theology and Psychology. He has published many articles, tapes, and books and still writes and teaches. In his books, May explores the theory and experience of a contemplative spirituality that realizes God is everywhere and in all, creating aliveness. This spirituality waits with open hands to receive the gift of God, then acts upon God's presence and love—an integrated flow between being and doing.

May has been personally and professionally interested in the relationship between spirituality and psychology for many decades. *Care of Mind/Care of Spirit* is especially useful for persons interested in the psychological aspects of **spiritual direction**. Psychology can go only so far in healing; wholeness also requires the spiritual component. *Will and Spirit* is probably the book for which May is most known. He covers all aspects of human experience as a **pilgrimage**, linking willingness of mind to wholeness of heart. This linking helps to establish a meaningful relationship with God, realizing that God ultimately is Mystery. *Addiction and Grace* and *The Awakened Heart* address addiction as a social disease of the modern world. Addiction represents an attempt to assert complete control over our lives, rather than to allow God to gift us and lead us toward God. EWF

MCPHERSON, AIMEE SEMPLE (1890–1944), the most famous female evangelist of her day and founder of the Church of the Four Square Gospel, now with well over three million members in 107 countries. Her mother consecrated Aimee, a Canadian farmer's daughter, to **The Salvation Army** in infancy. By age thirteen McPherson won public speaking competitions. She was converted at seventeen. At nineteen, traveling to China with her first husband, missionary Robert Semple, Aimee Semple extemporaneously addressed fifteen thousand people in London for an hour. When her mother died, Aimee returned to New York. After a near-death experience, she left her second husband, Harold McPherson, to become an evangelist.

Charismatic preaching and thousands of healings characterized the tent revivals McPherson conducted across the nation with her theme "Jesus Christ, the same yesterday, today, and forever." In 1923 McPherson dedicated the fifty-three hundred-seat Angelus Temple in Los Angeles to interdenominational and worldwide evangelism. Temple prayer warriors handled requests twenty-four hours a day. The church's commissary provided food, clothes, jobs, and rent money to anyone on request, supporting thousands. McPherson started KFSG, the first religious broadcasting station, and founded L.I.F.E. Bible College. She delivered twenty-one sermons weekly and made evangelistic tours, seeking the lost even in nightclubs and speakeasies. Hounded by notoriety and scandal, she continued to be remarkably productive.

McPherson emphasized **conversions** over healings, kindness and sympathy over hellfire and damnation, leading by example rather than decree. Flamboyant and creative, she pioneered spectacular religious theater, writing and producing weekly illustrated sermons on contemporary topics, blending staged drama, music, and improvisational acting. A **Pentecostal** leader, she urged her students to keep in life's mainstream—be passionate but not excessive in celebrating the Spirit's gifts. McPherson influenced the Pentecostal/

charismatic movement with her theology that **perfection** is progressive; the Holy Spirit's **baptism** means empowerment, not sinlessness.

For years McPherson wrote her monthly newsletter, *The Bridal Call,* and later a magazine. She authored several books, including two autobiographies, *This Is That* and *In the Service of the King.* Daniel Mark Epstein's carefully researched biography, *Sister Aimee,* is an excellent resource. LSP

MECHTHILD OF MAGDEBURG (ca. 1207– after 1285), **Beguine** mystic. Mechthild grew up near Magdeburg, Germany. Her mystical account, *The Flowing Light of the Godhead,* reveals that Mechthild must have been born into a well-to-do family and so was well-educated and well-versed in courtly love literature. She writes that even as a young girl, she began to have daily visions but felt her comfortable family life was too easy. Leaving the small town of her birth, Mechthild journeyed to the city of Magdeburg, where she sought to live the devout life of a Beguine. There Mechthild began to receive **spiritual direction** from a Dominican, Heinrich of Halle. He encouraged Mechthild to record her visions, which she began to do in 1250. Early chapters of the manuscript were circulated, making Mechthild unpopular with the clergy whom she had criticized for hypocrisy and greed.

Perhaps weary of those battles or because of illness, Mechthild went in 1270 to spend her last years at the established convent at Helfta. There Mechthild, now a mentor to **Gertrude of Helfta** and other mystical writers, finished the last section of *The Flowing Light of the Godhead.* Comprised of visions, parables, allegories, prayers, teachings, criticism, and letters of advice, the book has a meandering but compelling style. Through romantic images, Mechthild depicts human desire for God and God's intense longing for union with us. She describes the joyful times of union, as well as the anguishing moments of absence. "When I may rest in you, Lord," Mechthild writes, "my joy is rich. You clothe yourself with my soul and you are her most in-

timate garment. That there must be a parting between them—never have I experienced greater heartache!" Mechthild depicts God in flowing images—milk, honey, blood, water, and light—for as life-giving blood flows within our bodies, so God's spirit flows through our spiritual lives. SAF

MEDITATION, MENTAL PRAYER. A method of prayer where reasoning predominates the pondering of God's activity and presence in human history and activity. Meditation is an expression of our response to God through silent or mental prayer—that is, conversation that fits the many circumstances of daily life. In mental prayer we attempt to say what we mean. Mental prayer, if it uses words, is not tied to any set formula but, as a spontaneous conversation, makes up the words as it goes along. Meditation provides the opportunity for receptivity to answers and for a deeper awakening to our union with God.

Meditation in this restricted sense of discursive or conversational mental prayer is the second stage in *lectio divina,* the time of reflecting on a passage of scripture, whether through thinking about the meaning, identifying with a character, or using **guided imagery**. Such meditation can also be practiced by moving slowly and reflectively through a **verbal prayer** such as the **Lord's Prayer** or reflecting on any **spiritual reading**. Sometimes it helps to write in a **journal** while one is meditating, perhaps writing out both sides of a conversation with God.

In a more general sense, meditation can refer to any spiritual practice and **discipline** that prepares one to enter into "pure prayer," also known as "**prayer of the heart**." It is a training process for **detachment** from earthly cares and centering on God. Meditation is a practice of all religions, though it employs different systems and can be explained in different terms. The primary elements of meditation are interior **silence**, stillness, simplicity, and an awakening to the silent presence of God within.

There are numerous ways to meditate, but

the essential elements are to still the constant movement of the mind and to open oneself to deeper **union** with Christ's indwelling and guiding presence. It is important to learn what works for you. Choose a daily time that is usually quiet and consistent. Early morning is best for most people. Decide on how much time is best for you. Thirty minutes is considered the optimal amount of time. Find a comfortable sitting position with your body balanced, your hands resting and your back straight. Using this position consistently will trigger the response of quieting yourself. Choose a point of focus to quiet your thoughts. Simply set aside thoughts that come barging into the mind.

There are four common ways to focus. (1) Follow the breath. Slow your breathing and notice how you inhale and exhale rhythmically. (2) Use a mantra. **John Cassian** taught that the continual recitation of a name for God or a word of the heart leads to a state of continuous prayer enjoined by Christ (Luke 18:1). The mantra may lead to complete silence and to being in the fullness of God. (3) Choose an image. Focus on a sacred object such as a cross, candle, or flowers. It will quiet the rumblings of your heart. (4) Employ sacred passage memorization. Benedictine monk John Main (1926–82) states that this does not mean thinking about the scripture or evaluating it—just enter it into your subconscious and keep your mind free during the process. This passage can help direct and inspire you. When you end your meditative time, sit quietly, and refocus on your surroundings. If you use verbal prayer, now is a good time to say a short prayer.

Meditation, as a foundation for spiritual life, leads not to escape but to a deeper knowledge of God (Ps. 46:10) and to involvement in God's presence in creation. It is an interior sacrifice that, through commitment and perseverance, allows the person to turn away from selfishness to cooperate with the transforming grace of the **Holy Spirit** to discover the true self in Christ (Gal. 2:20). Sustained meditation leads beyond all thought to the unfolding of consciousness from its habitual self-conscious and self-reflective state, including thoughts of oneself or one's experiences or progress. In meditation one's true self is inseparable from God in Christ. PDB

MENNINGER, KARL A. (1893–1990), American psychiatrist, author, and educator. Born in Topeka, Kansas, Menninger graduated from Harvard Medical School (1917). After several years of clinical psychiatric practice and formal psychoanalytic training at the Chicago Institute of Psychoanalysis, he established the Topeka Institute of Psychoanalysis (1938). The Menninger Foundation for research, training, and education (1941) became the world's largest psychiatric training center; Menninger served as chair of its board and chief of staff for nearly twenty-five years. Additionally, he founded the Winter Veterans Administration Hospital, the original training center for the Veteran's Administration (1946). Because of his contribution to society, he was awarded the Medal of Freedom, the nation's highest civilian honor (1981).

Menninger wrote numerous books, such as *The Human Mind* (the first psychiatric book to become a best-seller), *Theory of Psychoanalytic Technique, The Crime of Punishment.* In *Whatever Became of Sin?* Menninger critiques the increasing tendency of clergy in the second half of the twentieth century to use psychotherapeutic rather than moral or spiritual language in talking about **sin**. ASJ

MERCY. The Hebrew word for mercy (*racham*) is related to the word for the womb and so may be seen as nurturing, motherly love; the complement to the covenant-based *chesed,* steadfast **love**. Often partnered with **compassion** in describing God's ability to reach out to God's children, mercy is not simple clemency, excessive kindness, or sympathy. The psalm reminds us, "The LORD is gracious and merciful, slow to anger and abounding in steadfast love" (145:8). Israel pleads for mercy in **awe** of God's mighty power and trusts in God's ability to **forgive** beyond what humanity would forgive. Mercy is an indicator of the depth of the relationship between a broken people and an almighty God.

The New Testament describes how mercy (Greek *eleos* as the radical pity, compassion, and help of God) thrusts itself into humanity through God's Son. God's mercy now combines with empathy, healing, **peace**, justice, and faithfulness on a new level. Jesus, healer of sinners and stumbling block to those who would punish harshly, illustrates mercy through parables and by his own example.

Followers of Christ are to show mercy (to do **works of mercy**), as Christ has shown mercy. Rather than simply disregard a wrong or turn the other way when punishment is due, mercy pairs itself with compassion to offer grace and encouragement. Mercy is not a characteristic of the weak in spirit but of the strong in faith, the courageous in action, and those who reject evil but who, through God's love, recognize the flaws and sins of humanity in themselves as well as others. JHS

MERTON, THOMAS (1915–68), American **Trappist** monk whose writings have immeasurably influenced current **spirituality**. Merton's autobiography, *The Seven Storey Mountain* (1948), earned him a lasting reputation. Like a rare diamond, Merton was complex and multifaceted: lonely child, hedonistic teen, brilliant scholar, contemplative monk, prolific writer, social reformer, and ecumenical mystic.

Merton, born in Prades, France, on January 31, 1915, was the son of Ruth Jenkins (American) and Owen Merton (New Zealander), who were artists. Shortly after his birth, his parents moved to New York to escape World War I. Merton's mother, who was serious and demanding, taught Merton to read, write, and draw by the time he was five. At a young age, Merton expressed an interest in spiritual things, but unfortunately neither of his parents provided him with any religious formation. After his mother died when he was six, Merton, a lonely child, traveled with his father in the United States, Bermuda, France, and England. When Merton was fifteen, his father died, intensifying his loneliness, lack of continuity, and need for belonging. As a teen he lived an undisciplined, sensual, and restless life. Although he had received an academic scholarship to Cambridge, he did not apply himself. Due to poor grades and an "unfortunate incident" with a young woman, the uncle who served as his guardian sent him back to New York. When he entered Columbia University, his life began to change.

At Columbia, Merton read Etienne Gilson's *The Spirit of Medieval Philosophy,* which revolutionized his understanding of God. His professors Mark Van Doren and Dan Walsh recognized his brilliance and encouraged his writing. Also while at Columbia, Merton experienced conversion and was baptized into the Catholic Church. In 1939 he graduated with his M.A., accepted a teaching position at St. Bonaventure, and applied to the **Franciscan** Order of Friars Minor. By now the simplicity and spirituality of monastic life appealed to Merton. The Franciscans' rejection devastated him, yet his desire to pursue a contemplative vocation persisted. The turning point came during a retreat at a Trappist monastery outside Bardstown, Kentucky. This time he applied and was accepted by the Cistercian Order of the Strict Observance and entered Our Lady of Gethsemani in Kentucky on December 10, 1941.

At first Merton saw the monastery as a sanctuary where he could disappear from the world. However, he soon discovered that Merton the writer had followed him into the cloister. Fortunately the abbot recognized Merton's literary gifts, and by 1948 *The Seven Storey Mountain* was a best-seller. During his lifetime, Merton wrote eight volumes of poetry; six hundred articles; and over sixty books, several published posthumously. He wrote devotional meditations, theological essays, personal journals, social criticism, and studies of Eastern spirituality. His books include *Contemplative Prayer, New Seeds of Contemplation, The Ascent to Truth, The Wisdom of the Desert, The Sign of Jonas, Seeds of Destruction, Mystics and Zen Masters,* and *Conjectures of a Guilty Bystander.*

If a writing career was unconventional for a monk, Merton's involvement with social issues was even more unusual. From the monastery he wrote about the threat of nuclear war, opposition to American involvement in Vietnam, and civil rights. He corresponded with Boris Pasternak, **Martin Luther King**, **Rosemary Radford Ruether**, and D. T. Suzuki. His interest in Eastern spirituality, particularly Buddhism, influenced his decision to attend an East-West monastic conference in Bangkok, Thailand. During this trip Merton was accidentally electrocuted. He died on December 10, 1968, the twenty-seventh anniversary of his entry to Gethsemani. Thomas Merton was a prophetic voice who continues to guide the hearts of those pursuing the interior life, seeking the center of their "true selves," and discovering Christ's mysteriously transforming love.

Michael Mott's biography, *The Seven Mountains of Thomas Merton*, is excellent and makes extensive use of Merton's journals. ASJ

MOLINOS, MIGUEL DE (1628–96), Spanish theologian and priest. Molinos was steeped in the **mysticism** of **Teresa of Ávila** and **John of the Cross**. A scholar and spiritual director, he published *Spiritual Guide* in 1675, a book that combined mystical doctrine with practical forms of devotion. He taught that those who long for more than verbal prayer should seek God in a silence from words, desires, and thoughts and in total submission or **abandonment**. He maintained that inward prayer cleansed the soul and advanced one toward selflessness.

Molinos's followers were called **Quietists** and were characterized by silent, self-emptying prayer. Because his popularity fed into existing controversies, he was eventually imprisoned, becoming as despised as he had been admired. By some accounts, he admitted guilt to moral misconduct in 1687. He was sentenced to a life of penitential imprisonment and lived for nine more years. His writings influenced Madame **Guyon** and were reprinted (in part) by **John Wesley**. JLJ

MONASTICISM. (Greek *monachos*, "one who lives alone"), a specific expression of the Christian life that involves a serious response to God's call for **perfection** (Matt. 5:48) by giving oneself through vows to a life of common prayer and service, either alone or in **community**. While the degree of **asceticism** may vary from one monastic tradition to another, the concept of self-denial (or **discipline**) as a means of elevating the human spirit to God through Christ is central to all forms of monasticism. Monks and nuns are disciples of Christ who have separated themselves to find silence to pray and to live in communion with God.

Antony, first of the Egyptian **desert fathers** and founder of Christian monasticism in the third century, withdrew from social relationships and lived as a hermit in order to find God in a life devoted entirely to prayer. Three basic forms of monasticism are generally attributed to him. Eremitism (Greek *eremos*, "desert") refers to the life of complete **solitude** and withdrawal from the world. In the nascent stages of monastic development, however, monks and nuns who pursued the ascetic life frequently formed loose groupings, or *lavras*, around a spiritual leader known as an *abba* ("father") or *amma* ("mother"). Anchoritism (Greek *anachoreo*, "withdraw"), this second monastic form, is characterized by small groups of solitaries living near one another for mutual support. One of Antony's disciples, Pachomius, expanded this principle by organizing like-minded followers into communities (later known as monasteries) around a **rule** of life. He is thereby credited with founding Cenobitism (Greek *koinos bios*, "common life"), which remains the most widely practiced form of Christian monasticism today.

The writings of **Basil**, one of the great Cappadocian fathers, form the basis of Eastern monasticism. Influenced profoundly by **John Cassian**, Martin of Tours, **Augustine of Hippo**, and the anonymous author of *Regula Magistri* (*The Rule of the Master*), **Benedict of Nursia** through his *Rule* shaped the future of monasticism in the West. This *Rule*, compiled for monks at Monte Cassino in Italy, set out a moderate and flexible life of *ora et labora* ("prayer and work") in community that became the standard pattern for religious life in the West well into the Middle Ages. The only monastic tradition that stood outside its influence in the West was the **Celtic** tradition of the British Isles.

During the medieval period, through a series of monastic revivals, devout Christians attempted to rediscover the simplicity of the Benedictine tradition whenever it succumbed to the perennial temptations of success and prosperity. In the tenth century a reform movement began at Cluny, France, in an effort to refocus monastic life in the rich liturgical tradition of the community. The Camaldolese and the Carthusians, both products of the eleventh century, sought to combine an eremitic life with a shared, common liturgy, somewhat in the style of the ancient *lavras*. A reform based in Cîteaux (Latin *Cistercium*), which gave rise to the Cistercian tradition, notably represented by **Bernard of Clairvaux**, sought to restore a strict observance of the Benedictine Rule and was noted for its rediscovery of austerity, **poverty**, and contemplative practice. In the thirteenth century, the so-called Mendicant (or begging) Orders, and in particular, the Dominicans (Order of Preachers) and Franciscans (Order of Little Brothers), offered alternatives to the strictly contemplative lifestyle of the Benedictine orders. Both **Dominic** and **Francis** (and **Clare**) of Assisi, their respective founders, emphasized the importance of itinerant preaching and the proclamation of the gospel to the people wherever they were to be found.

While the Protestant reformers of the sixteenth century summarily rejected monasticism as a way of earning salvation through **works** rather than by **grace** through **faith**, a number of new monastic traditions sprang up in the life of the church at that same time, several of which are noteworthy. The Carmelites, a thirteenth-century tradition co-reformed by **Teresa of Ávila** and **John of the Cross** in the late fifteenth century, emphasized solitude, **silence**, and **unceasing prayer** in a life shaped by daily **Eucharist**. One of the most well-known of all Roman Catholic religious orders, the **Jesuits**, was founded by **Ignatius of Loyola** about the same time. Technically known as an order of "clerics regular," this Society of Jesus broke with traditional monasticism in not prescribing a common pattern of prayer, but it emphasized the conformity of life to the image of Christ through the means of **spiritual direction**. In the seventeenth century, an abbot of the Cistercian monastery at La Trappe spearheaded a new movement toward greater austerity, the followers of which, known as **Trappist** monks, became noted for their silent communities. Despite attempts such as this one to revive monasticism, many monasteries were repressed in the aftermath of the Protestant Reformations, only to be renewed in the twentieth century. This modern recovery is closely associated with Pope Leo XIII, who grouped formerly independent monastic communities into worldwide orders, with dominant renewal movements seeking to recapture the spirit of Cluny centered at Solemnes and Beuron. Monasticism continues to be an attractive alternative style of life in community for many, especially in the radically secularized contexts of the West.

There are a number of salient aspects of monastic spirituality. Monks and nuns profess *vows* that are distinctive to their way of life. Also known as the "evangelical counsels," the vows of **poverty**, **celibacy**, and **obedience** reflect the disciplined renunciation or asceticism that characterizes this form of spirituality. Profession of these vows dates from around the thirteenth century. The Benedictine tradition adds the vow of stability, or permanent association with a specific monastic community, to these three. The essential purpose of these vows is freely to center one's whole being and love in God and thereby pursue the fundamental baptismal vocation to love others as Christ has loved us.

In monastic spirituality, therefore, the entirety of one's life is oriented around the reign of God and the establishment of the life of Christ in the inner being. The means toward this spiritual end is a daily routine free from the distractions of life in the world. While the practical disciplines of simplicity, silence, and solitude, all in the context of poverty, characterize the monastic life, nothing is of greater significance than the centered life of **prayer**. The **Liturgy of the Hours** (or Daily Office), with its rich traditions of prayer, is the primary monastic pattern of continual **meditation** on scripture and the recitation of the **Psalms** in community. The Liturgy of the Hours, the liturgical expression of a life dedicated to continual doxology, constitutes the high point of the day for monks and nuns. In this school of prayer, sign and symbol, word and music combine to form heart and mind into the fullest possible image of Christ. One form of praying the Word that has flourished within the monastic tradition outside the daily rhythms of the Daily Office is *lectio divina*.

The contemplative nature of monastic life, rather than leading to isolationism, has often inspired the highest levels of service to others and has exerted tremendous influence on the social, economic, and political dimensions of the larger society. Today, perhaps more than ever before, there is an increasing awareness of the unity shared with all persons in Christ, both inside and beyond the walls of the monastic communities. New traditions birthed in the twentieth century, such as the uniquely ecumenical community of **Taizé** founded by Brother Roger in France during World War II, give renewed expression to the virtues of **humility**, **holiness**, and hospitality that stand at the center of the monastic vision of life in Christ.

For more information, see **M. Basil Pennington**, *Monastic Life.* PWC

MORAVIAN SPIRITUALITY. Founded by a group of followers of the Bohemian reformer **John Hus**, the Unitas Fratrum, better known as the Moravian Church, pioneered congregational singing and education that included a Czech-language translation of the Bible that enabled the members to read scripture and sing hymns as a family exercise. This ability was further developed and refined by the church during the eighteenth century under the influence of **Nicholas Ludwig von Zinzendorf**, who provided a refuge for the Moravians following the persecutions of the counter-Reformation, as well as spiritual leadership.

Scripture reading is emphasized and fostered by the use of the *Daily Text*, which provides both Old and New Testament verses for each day with amplifying hymn stanzas and a prayer. In continuous use since 1731, this devotional is printed annually in three times as many copies as the membership of the denomination. **Prayer** is emphasized by the daily practices connected with the *Daily Text* and the Unity Prayer Watch, an annual prayer discipline shared by the worldwide membership. Congregations arc assigned a day's intercessory responsibility for the work of the entire church's ministry. **Hymns** are seen as the vehicles of teaching and emphasize the doctrine of the denomination. Moravians have not engaged in creedal formulations of their own but use the ecumenical creeds. A *Lebenslauf,* or spiritual autobiography, is encouraged as a means of spiritual growth and is used as the basis for the development of a memoir at the time of death. Congregational worship includes preaching, the employment of the two sacraments of **baptism** and **Holy Communion**, and strongly emphasizes fellowship.

For further reading, see *The Moravian Church through the Ages* by John R. Weinlick and Albert H. Frank. AHF

MORE, HANNAH (1745–1833), Anglican evangelical and philanthropist. Drawn at an early age to drama and literature, she became well-known in the literary circles of her day. The first edition of her collected works extends to eleven volumes. Her native philanthropic interests, abolitionist sympathies, and close friendship with **William Wilberforce** drew her into the Clapham Sect, for which she became the preeminent propagandist, publishing hundreds of pamphlets. Among her primary concerns were the education of women and the elevation of women in evangelical Christianity. Her most important devotional writings include *Practical Piety, Christian Morals, Essay on the Character and Practical Writings of St. Paul,* and *Reflections on Prayer.* Her spirituality revolves around the themes of the religion of the heart, total dedication of life to Christ, and the discovery of God's claims in the everyday circumstances that surround people's lives.

For more information, see *The World of Hannah More* by Patricia Demers. PWC

MORE, THOMAS (1478–1535), English lawyer, philosopher, author. After meeting **Erasmus**, More entered the **humanist** movement, which championed the equality of classes and castigated rulers who worked for selfish interests rather than the good of the people. More's seminal work *Utopia* presents an ideal society where equality of work and wealth provides abundance for all. More promotes this spirit of democratic rule while attacking the evils of British society. The adversaries of his ideal are greed, poverty, violence, and self-service. More summarizes these as pride that will come between the human soul and its true destiny in both this life and the next. In 1529 Henry VIII appointed More Lord Chancellor. Asked to sanction the Act of Supremacy supporting Henry's right to break from the Roman Catholic Church, attain an annulment, and marry Anne Boleyn, More refused and was executed for treason on July 6, 1535. Pope Pius XI canonized him in 1935. More's story is told in the play and film *A Man for All Seasons* by Robert Bolt. SN

MORTIFICATION. The concept of mortification originates in Paul's instructions (Rom. 8:13; Gal. 5:24; Col. 3:5) to mortify (Latin *mortificare,* "put to death") deeds, passion, and acts of the "body of death" (Rom. 7:24) or sinful nature. **John Wesley**, commenting on Romans, said that Paul calls for the "killing" of our evil actions, desire, temperaments, and thought. This "killing" ends in a life of faith in this body and the glorified body to come. Mortification as a spiritual **discipline** involves a purposeful restraint, through the guidance of the **Holy Spirit**, of one's sinful impulses in order to diminish the power of these sinful impulses and actions and thereby make one increasingly open to greater **sanctification** or life in the Spirit. The resulting **fruit of the Spirit** is self-control. Paul's instructions to the early church connected this concept with the ideal of participation in the passion of Christ and the **incarnation** of a new life in Christ.

During the time of the great persecution, Christians could participate in the **suffering** of Christ through **martyrdom**. When persecution came to an end, **ascetic** practices of mortification began to take shape as a type of self-imposed martyrdom. Under the influence of **Gnosticism**'s spirit-body dichotomy, the concept gradually took on more extreme forms, such as self-flagellation, wearing of hair shirts, and excessive **fasting**. The general history of ascetic disciplines of mortification became connected to penitential symbols and rites, but the aim was for religious transformation of the individual through bodily disciplines that entailed some degree of actual physical pain or suffering.

Renewed emphasis on incarnational spirituality gives rise to reconnecting the concept of mortification with its biblical foundations as a call to put to death the sinful way of living so that one may experience fuller life in the Spirit. The goal is not suffering in itself but bringing the impulses that determine behaviors, thoughts, and desires under the Holy Spirit's influence. CIZ

MOTHER TERESA. See Teresa of Calcutta.

MUSIC AND SPIRITUALITY. Music has power. It has the ability to penetrate our minds and calm our souls. When King Saul was troubled in mind, body, and spirit, his aides summoned David to play the lyre and sing to calm the king. Music refreshed Saul's spirit and soothed his troubled being (1 Sam. 16).

Music touches the very depths of our lives. All cultures and civilizations have songs that tell their histories and give meaning to their lives. Today persons receive training in music therapy, which becomes a means of dealing with and treating major issues in our lives.

Music can also stir our souls and lead us to celebrate. When the Hebrews passed through the waters to safety, Moses led them in a song of celebration while his sister Miriam grabbed a tambourine and began to dance and sing. Everyone joined in the great celebration of God's victory (Exod. 15).

Throughout the Hebrew Scriptures, music accompanies all major events. Before the Israelites began a journey with the ark of the covenant, they sang. And at the journey's successful completion they sang again. The **Psalms** have set every human emotion in song, from our deepest despair—"Out of the depths I cry to you, O LORD. LORD, hear my voice!" (130:1-2)—to our greatest joy—"Clap your hands, all you peoples; shout to God with loud songs of joy" (47:1). The songs of ancient Israel capture all human emotions, all life experiences.

In the New Testament, the beginning of Luke's Gospel resembles a Broadway musical. With every event of importance, someone breaks into song. When Mary and her cousin Elizabeth, both of whom are expecting a child, greet each other, Mary breaks into song with The Magnificat. At John the Baptist's birth, his father Zechariah, who for months has been unable to speak, sings the Benedictus. When Jesus is born, the angels and heavenly hosts sing the Gloria in excelsis. And when the aged Simeon sees the baby Jesus, he sings the Nunc Dimittis.

After the Last Supper, Jesus and his disciples sang a hymn before they went to the Mount of Olives, where he was betrayed. The writer of Ephesians encouraged members of the young church to be "filled with the Spirit, as you sing psalms and hymns and spiritual songs among yourselves, singing and making melody to the Lord in your hearts" (5:18-19).

Many classical composers wrote religious works for the concert hall and/or expressed their faith in their music. Verdi's last musical works were his *Four Sacred Pieces*. Numerous commentators mention that it is not unusual for a person's thoughts to turn toward religion in the latter years of life. Stravinsky, who left the Orthodox Church at an early age, returned at age forty-four, and found both personal comfort and artistic inspiration. Today the music of John Tavener is thoroughly steeped in the liturgy of Russian Orthodoxy.

Music does not have to be religious to be spiritual. Classical, pop, country, jazz, and even rap can speak to the deepest needs of our human condition. Different forms and styles of music can be used to enhance meditation or aid us on our spiritual journey. Music speaks to the essence of our being, bringing tears to our eyes when it reminds us of cherished memories, making us smile, causing us to tap our feet, and sometimes making us dance. Music also helps us to reflect and quiet our spirits along our spiritual journeys, speaking to the entire range of our human emotions. DDW

MUTO, SUSAN ANNETTE (b. 1942), director of the Epiphany Association in Pittsburgh, Pennsylvania. Muto has lectured and written extensively in the field of **spiritual reading** and more recently in lay spirituality within the Roman Catholic tradition, particularly emphasizing women's issues.

Born and raised in Pittsburgh, Muto received her doctorate from the University of Pittsburgh in 1970 for her dissertation on the symbolism of **evil** in Dante's *Paradise Lost*. From 1966 until 1988 she served as an administrator and faculty member at the Institute of Formative Spirituality at Duquesne University. As professor she taught courses in formative reading of spiritual classics and wrote several books on the subject, including *Approaching the Sacred: An Introduction to Spiritual Reading, Steps Along the Way: The Path of Spiritual Reading, A Practical Guide to Spiritual Reading,* and *The Journey Homeward: On the Road of Spiritual Reading.* Together with her courses, these books helped to develop the concept of formative reading of spiritual classics into a recognized field within Christian **spirituality**. Muto is best known for her work in this field.

In 1988 she and **Adrian van Kaam**, founder of the Institute of Formative Spirituality, established the Epiphany Association, a lay institute for **spiritual formation**. In addition to her own books, which include *Womanspirit* and four books on **John of the Cross**, she has continued to coauthor books with van Kaam, from *The Emergent Self,* published in 1968, to *The Commandments: Ten Ways to a Happy Life and a Healthy Soul.* Dr. Muto continues to lecture and lead **retreats** and seminars in addition to writing and teaching courses for universities and seminaries. JWK

MYSTICISM. A spirituality grounded in radical openness to the divine mystery. In an age of spiritual consumerism fascinated with spiritual experience, the highest expression of which is thought to be mystical **experience**, it helps to consider mysticism, the mystical, and the mystic in view of the biblical category of mystery from which mysticism and related notions derive.

In view of the original biblical image, *mystery* is a plan that a king shares only with his closest advisors. The big picture of the mystery is known by the king and to some degree by those to whom he discloses it but not necessarily by all who are affected by it. From the perspective of Christian **faith**, God's plan has been disclosed in the Word through the presence and power of the **Holy Spirit**. Christian mysticism is simply the experiential participation in this mystery.

Mystery often conveys a sense of unintelligibility bordering on nonsense. Real mystery invites and allures us into fuller participation, all the while exceeding our want to grasp it, hold on to it, contain it. Indeed, in much the same way, human love is a mystery. We are invited, at times allured, by another. Something in us is touched, moved, drawn by the other. As we get closer and grow in love, it becomes clearer that the beloved cannot be tied down, grasped, defined once and for all.

The greatest mystery is the gracious pouring forth of God's life and **love** that is never emptied in giving. The incomprehensibility of God lies in the utter gratuity of life and love. Whatever may be known of this mystery is known in and through the gift of the indwelling Spirit of God that enables us to recognize the Word made flesh, whose life, passion, death, and resurrection are the very disclosure of God's mystery. These mysteries reveal who God is and how God is. But mystery is always more, always ahead of us, inviting us to greater life, light, and love. When we pray and engage in spiritual disciplines, most of us do not look *at* God but rather look *for* God, constantly seeking precisely because our lives are on the way to fuller participation in mystery. From this perspective, seeking and longing are as much a part of mystical experience as seeing and union.

Often understood as the fullest expression of Christian life and **prayer**, mysticism is usually spoken of in terms of an unmediated appropriation of the divine mystery. The individual soul encounters and is gradually, progressively united with God. From this perspective, the goal of the mystical journey is the immediate, experiential apprehension of the deepest recesses of divine life. Such a focus tends to emphasize subjective experience to such a point that the mystery itself is eclipsed.

The notion of an unusual experience of God can undercut the priority of earthly reality, of human life in its grandeur and vulnerability as the very locus where God discloses the mystery to be experienced. The mystery experienced is the providential plan of God for human beings and the whole world, mediated in and through the incarnate Word and in the specific, particular, earthly work of the Holy Spirit who brings about the reordering of all creation.

An approach to mysticism rooted in a clear consciousness of the trinitarian mystery requires attention to the whole range of human experiences in history, the world, culture, human relationships, and the church wherein God's presence and action are discerned. The experience of **union** with God is to be found in every form of communion: affective, sexual, familial, artistic; it is to be found in the intellectual pursuit of truth, the apprehension and pursuit of the good, and in the simple act of appreciating the beautiful. Every form of authentic communion is a potential avenue for union with God, known in the sending of the Son and in the gift of the Spirit, who enlightens, enlivens, guides, heals, and sends us forth to live in and from the mystery of God's love.

Some of the mystics' writings describe an experience of God clearly informed by the symbols and stories at the heart of the Christian tradition. Other cases exhibit little explicit trinitarian consciousness. But the communion of Father, Son, and Spirit is the reality that lies at the heart of Christian faith and life,

and therefore is the mystery formative of all Christian religious experience.

Whether or not a particular Christian's mystical experience is shaped by an awareness of the Trinity, all Christian mysticism is a path through the economy of redemption in which God is revealed through Jesus Christ in the Holy Spirit. Thus ordinarily Christian mystical experience, as an experiential participation in the mystery of God, must in some way or another reflect the particular symbols, stories, and events that are central to Christian faith and life.

Perhaps the best way to learn about mysticism is to read the writings of Christian mystics. Two excellent collections are *Light from Light: An Anthology of Christian Mysticism*, edited by Louis Dupré and James A. Wiseman; and *An Anthology of Christian Mysticism*, edited by Harvey Egan. MD

N

NATIVE AMERICAN SPIRITUALITY. This term can be misleading if taken to mean there is uniformity of religious practice and cosmology among Native American tribes and nations. In fact, wide diversity exists in the native peoples' customs, rituals, and beliefs. So varied are these people that an accurate study in native spirituality would need to be done group by group. For now, a general description is offered to begin such a study.

Typically indigenous peoples of the Americas had no concept of religion as a separate, identifiable entity. Thus inaccurate translations and understandings of their description of reality led early ethnologists to classify incorrectly these people as animist, polytheistic, or pantheistic.

The Native American's worldview is essentially a religious worldview—reality is spirit. Because there is no sense of division between the sacred and mundane, their mysticism understands and experiences life and the material world as total immersion in and revelation of the Divine Reality or Spirit. There is no dichotomy between human beings on one end and nature on the other, or spirit on one end and the material on the other.

Native American cosmology is multidimensional. The "Being" attributed to all creation gives rise to the expression "other-than-human-person" when referring to animals, plants, or the elements. The spirit-personhood of all creation is evident in the language structures as an absence of an objectifying pronoun "it." Thus the Native American does not act upon the world but meets the world. All things—earth, elements, animals, plants, and people—have a moral dynamic in their relationship, a mutuality of obligation for one another. The sacred *Wanka* (Sioux term for mysterious or spiritness) that the Native Americans recognized in all things is a gift of *Wanka-Tanka* (Sioux term for The Great Mystery or Great Spirit). Thus, greed and its corresponding dynamic of ungratefulness represent the greatest manifestation of evil.

The various tribes have different names for a sacred spirit-person or force, and some embrace the concept without naming it. Algonquian languages use *manitou* for spirit force and *Gitchi Manitou* as the Great Spirit. Hopi, Zuni, and Pueblo call this Being *Kachina*, and the Iroquoian term is *Orenda*. These terms describe a visible and invisible mysterious power or force that pervades the universe and shapes and directs all of life. It is the central spiritual reality for all that exists and can be shared with, incorporated into, or passed on to any created thing. When its power becomes focused on any object, animate or inanimate, it endows the object, place, or person for a time with powers. Thus all that exists is sacred in that it shares or participates in the Great Spirit's powers.

Sacred Center, or the circle, is a foundational symbol in Native American tradition and ritual practices. In ritual it becomes the "center of the universe" or the home of the Great Spirit. Since reality is multidimensional, any object or place can become the center of the universe for the ceremony's purpose, while its identity remains consistent. This centering is a gift of power to the participants of the ceremony. Thus prayer in native spirituality is primarily attentiveness not only in the ceremony but also to the multitude of the spirit voices present in the everyday natural world.

The natural response to the world both in its everydayness and in a special ceremony is attentiveness and prayers of thanksgiving. Prayer is a way of life that encompasses every activity. Without the help and cooperation of the "other-than-human-persons" and the Great Spirit, one cannot realize the fundamental goal of life. The Ojibwa expression of this goal is *pîmädäzîwin*, which can be translated "life in the fullest sense." *Pîmädäzîwin* is empowerment to meet successive changes or difficulties life may present and remain on the "right" path. This right path is uniquely individual but with overarching communal dynamics—balance and interrelational harmony with all of life.

These principles of mutual obligation and interpersonal harmony form the foundational values of the Ojibwa tradition and most North American tribal groups. The "vision quest," a rite that empowers or gives one the ability to live a life of balance or harmony, may be the single unifying religious phenomenon of North American native peoples. While the manner and frequency of its practice varies, it rises from a worldview that presupposes a powerful force that structures, animates, and directs all of life. The humble seeker performs this ritual to encounter and interact with this mysterious spiritual force. In this encounter a sharing of power occurs that empowers the seeker to obtain the ultimate goal of life or *pîmädäzîwin*.

For further reading, see Kathleen Dugan, *The Vision Quest of the Plains Indians*; or Black Elk, *Black Elk Speaks: Being the Life Story of a Holy Man of the Oglala Sioux as Told through John G. Neihardt*. CIZ

NATURE MYSTICISM. A religious phenomenon rooted in the doctrine of natural revelation. The nature mystic's basic vision is one of the interconnectedness of the world, God, others, and oneself. Natural revelation properly understood believes that God's self-disclosure is available to all by contemplation of nature. Christian nature mysticism holds that experiences of a sacred presence in the material world evoke a sense of interconnectedness or interrelational harmony, a "graced" unitive presence of the Ultimate Reality. The chief heretical hazards that the na-

ture mystic must seek to avoid are pantheism (all is God), monism (all is one), and **Quietism** (all action is God's).

Nature mysticism also stresses the mystery of God, holding that mystical experiences only provide a "taste" of God. Contemplation of nature helps us to grasp the Holy Presence within particular manifestations, but a sense of mystery and paradox remains because this world will never be large enough to provide a means of fully grasping God. Nature mystic writer **Pierre Teilhard de Chardin** devotes a great deal of attention in his book *The Divine Milieu* to what he calls "Omega Points," points of convergence and divine self-revelation in and through the natural phenomenal world. The contemplation of nature will carry us toward these points of convergence to ultimate truth, goodness, beauty, and unity.

One of the basic distinctions between nature mysticism and other more transcendently rooted mystical doctrines is the significance of matter. In other forms of mystical doctrine, the connection with the ultimate Mystery or God comes by moving beyond sensory experience or leaving behind matter. In nature mysticism, however, our sensing organs are critical to "ultra-sensing," the ability to perceive the spiritual power of matter or its ultimate center point, which connects it with all other created forms and thereby its specific meaningfulness. This ultra-sensing perceives the connections between the world, God, others, and oneself. It is a graced or spiritual mode of perceiving.

For further study, see Wolfhart Pannenberg, *Toward a Theology of Nature*, or Karl Rahner, *Hearers of the Word* and *Spirit in the World*. CIZ

NEE, WATCHMAN (1903–72), Chinese evangelist and writer. Rampant persecutions at the time of the Boxer Rebellion had the paradoxical effect of raising up many native Chinese evangelists who became excellent gospel preachers. One prominent Christian leader was Watchman Nee, a noted Bible teacher and preacher brought up in the Christian faith by both his well-educated pastor-grandfather and his second-generation Christian parents. Nee Shu-tsu changed his Chinese name to Tosheng, which means "God's watchman," sometime after his conversion at age seventeen.

Upon becoming a Christian, he also began writing about Christ and his church. Nee is known for his simple yet profound teachings. Being a "watchman for the Lord" in China, Nee set out through his writings to provide a balanced view regarding the Bible and living the spiritual life. Because of political, economic and spiritual unrest in China during that time, many Christians were forced to leave their own churches. Nee was there to offer sound biblical teaching as he gathered the lost sheep. Central to his thinking and ministry was his concept of "one church for one locality." His deep spiritual insights were not welcomed by all. When he was forty-nine years old, he was arrested and imprisoned for his initiation and leadership of the largest group of Chinese Christians called "Little Flocks." He died just three months after being released from twenty years of confinement. His plain sermons, uncomplicated teachings, and courageous leadership continue to inspire people around the world.

Angus Kinnear's 1973 biography of Watchman Nee, *Against the Tide,* is recommended reading. Books by Nee include *The Spiritual Man* (a three-volume work on sanctification, spiritual growth, and guidance for those lost in the darkness); *The Release of the Spirit; The Latent Power of the Soul; Not I, but Christ; The Song of Songs;* and *Changed into His Likeness.* EKM

NEGATIVE WAY. The *via negativa* (Latin) or apophatic (Greek "negating") path refers to the hidden aspect of God's nature and corresponds to the believer's **experiences** such as **desert**, **fasting**, and **silence**. It stands in contrast to the **positive way** (*via positiva* or kataphatic path), in which God is experienced through the creation, light and sound, colors and senses, words and images.

The negative or apophatic path emphasizes knowledge of God through unknowing—by way of subtraction. To use a metaphor from **Meister Eckhart**: God is "no thing" to be added onto one's life. The danger of words and concepts for God is that we may soon begin to focus on these human constructs that describe "God" rather than on the living God. We may be tempted, for our own selfish ends, to domesticate the Divine, who is beyond all human symbols or **imagery**.

Scripture speaks of the nature of God as beyond all knowing: "For as the heavens are higher than the earth, so are my ways higher than your ways and my thoughts than your thoughts" (Isa. 55:9). This tradition of God as being beyond all human thoughts is reflected in the Jewish practice of the unpronounceable name of YHWH, usually translated, "I am who I am" (Exod. 3:14). Still today when reading aloud from the Torah, Jews speak the word *Adonai* ("Lord") instead of YHWH

In the Christian New Testament, the apostle Paul, quoting Isaiah, says that "no eye has seen, nor ear heard, nor the human heart conceived, what God has prepared" for the beloved, and "no one comprehends what is truly God's except the Spirit of God" (1 Cor. 2:9-11). Christian hymns reflect the tradition as well: "Immortal, invisible, God only wise, in light inaccessible hid from our eyes."

Pseudo-Dionysius speaks about both paths in his *Mystical Theology.* While Protestant reformers did not use this precise terminology, **Luther** spoke of the *Deus absconditus,* the hidden God, the dark side of God's love—as well as God revealed in light and the Resurrection. In the twentieth century, apophatic-kataphatic terminology has been made more understandable through such writings as **Charles Williams**'s *The Descent of the Dove* and **Evelyn Underhill**'s *The Essentials of Mysticism.*

In Christian practice, the two paths in many ways correspond to the believer's experience of the **cross** (darkness, emptying, Greek **kenosis**) and Resurrection (light, fullness, Greek *pleroma*). In this way "the **dark night** of the soul" and **purgation** speak of living by **faith** and not by sight. Apophatic practices include silence, **retreat**, and **contemplative** prayer.

Fasting from food or material things can be a way of following the *via negativa* by identifying with the God who has been edged out of the world yet who is present in the marginalized and rejected (Matt. 25:31-42). Outward experiences of loss may serve to "empty" the believer of previously held images of God, setting in motion an inward purgation process and an openness to new perceptions.

Some disciples are called to an ascetic way of contemplation, others to a more active way of service (see **Mary and Martha**). All are called to appreciate both the negative way of God's mystery beyond all human thought *and* God's palpable intimacy in and through positive gifts of creation. KIG

NEOPLATONISM. Philosophical system of **Plotinus** (ca. 205–70) and successors. A later phase of **Platonic** thought that emerged in the third century, Neoplatonism linked itself more closely to religion than other philosophies. The acknowledged founder, Plotinus, expressed a special debt to Ammonius Saccas (ca. 175–242). The philosophy emerged first at Alexandria, then spread to Rome and other parts of the empire. Some of the more ardent Neoplatonists such as Porphyry vigorously assailed Christianity because of its doctrine of the **Incarnation** and its opposition to Greek philosophy. Nevertheless, Neoplatonism exerted a profound impact on Christian mystical thought through **Origen**, the great **Cappadocians**, **Augustine**, and **Pseudo-Dionysius**. Pope **Gregory I, the Great,** transmitted into medieval contemplative theology a popularized form of Augustine's Neoplatonism. It has continued to provide the basis for a variety of Christian philosophies, especially **mysticism**. While Neoplatonism influenced many Christian writers, it also provided a philosophical basis for dualistic heresies such as **Manichaeism** and **Catharism**.

The chief object of the Neoplatonists was to provide a foundation for religious and moral life. Like Plato, they started with the One, the World Soul. The One lies behind all experience and can be reached by human beings only by abstraction. The world came into being by way of a series of emanations from the One. Matter lies at the end of the emanation process and represents the greatest multiplicity. It does not really exist, however, for the Good alone exists. **Evil** is matter and therefore does not exist.

Because it possesses matter, the human body is the tomb of the **soul**, which has descended from above, stamped microcosmically with the imprint of the One. The soul's insatiable longing is to return to unity with the One. This may happen at death, but it may take place now by means of mystical **contemplation** because the Absolute "has its center everywhere, its circumference nowhere." The soul that has discarded all irrational impulses will attain the attributes of **virtue** and **wisdom** and possess a divine nature. It must free itself from all outward things and turn within, forgetting even itself. It may attain **union** with the One analogous to the union of lovers. It is a state of perfect stillness, not an annihilation of the self, as in Eastern religions, but of union with the perfect Self. The soul does not remain in this perfect state because it has not yet attained complete union. Ever after, though, it will long more ardently to escape the material world and return home.

For further reading, see John Gregory, *The Neoplatonists: A Reader,* 2nd edition; Thomas Whittaker, *The Neo-Platonists: A Study in the History of Hellenism,* 2nd edition. EGH

NERI, PHILIP (1515–95), Italian priest, founder of the Congregation of the Oratory. Born into a modest family in Florence, Neri refused a notable familial bequest following a conversion experience. Seeking to live a simpler life characterized by prayer and good works, he moved to Rome, a morally and spiritually corrupt city at that time. Neri's desire to serve God gradually disclosed his call: reinvigorating the hearts and minds of laity and clergy with a zeal to serve God. While the Council of Trent emphasized doctrinal reform, Neri focused on the **spiritual formation** of the laity. Ordained a priest in 1551, he busily arranged talks, faith-sharing, spiritual discussions, and prayer with groups attracted to his spirituality, which stressed the bond of love. As more of his followers became priests, Neri founded the Congregation of the Oratory. Today these priests staff the Newman Centers found on many college campuses across the U.S. and throughout the world. EKM

NEWBIGIN, JAMES EDWARD LESSLIE (1909–98), missionary bishop, Christian apologist, and ecumenist. Born in Newcastle upon Tyne and educated at Westminster College, Cambridge, he was ordained by the Church of Scotland in 1936 and appointed to missionary service in India. Having helped establish the Church of South India, he was appointed bishop in Madurai and Ramnad at its inauguration in 1947. In 1959 he left India to become secretary of the International Missionary Council, but he eventually returned to India as bishop of Madras until his retirement in 1974. In the last quarter of the twentieth century, his preeminence as a missiologist and ecumenical theologian remained unchallenged, but he devoted increasing energy to Christian apologetics and to his critique of classical liberalism. In *The Gospel in a Pluralist Society*, he articulates the central theme of God's call to bear witness to the saving grace of Christ, promoting a missionary encounter with contemporary culture.

For further reading, see Geoffrey Wainwright's biography, *Lesslie Newbigin: A Theological Life*. PWC

NEWMAN, JOHN HENRY (1801–90), Anglican priest and leader of the **Oxford movement**, later (after 1845) Roman Catholic priest and, from 1879, cardinal. "Heart speaks to heart," a quote from **Francis de Sales**, was Newman's motto as cardinal, pointing to his concept of spirituality. Newman believed in the importance of a personal religious **expe-**

rience that comes from both head and heart. Our hearts can and do speak with God through prayer, feelings, emotions, and experiences. Yet these experiences and our quest for holiness should be forever grounded within the boundaries of revelation found in scripture, tradition, the **sacraments**, and doctrine. These boundaries, which essentially define the church, provide the balance between heart and mind. *Parochial and Plain Sermons* (from his Anglican days) and *Essay on the Development of Christian Doctrine* (written following his change of allegiance) represent these two aspects of Newman's approach to the spiritual life. Perhaps his best-known writing today is the autobiographical *Apologia pro Vita Sua* (*In Defense of His Life*). SN

NEWTON, JOHN (1725–1807), Anglican pastor and hymn writer. Born in London, he spent his early years at sea and eventually became a slave trader. Reading **Thomas à Kempis**'s *Imitation of Christ* laid the foundation for his conversion in 1748. However, he continued to be involved in the slave trade for a number of years. In 1754 he was introduced to evangelicalism, and his spirituality was further nurtured and refined through the reading of Puritan and **Moravian** sources and individually shaped by George Whitefield and later **John Wesley**. Self-educated, Newton read broadly among Roman Catholic and Protestant devotional writings. He enjoyed those writings that encouraged an experiential spirituality that integrated head and heart. Newton gave significant leadership to the evangelical revival, and his moderate Calvinist spirituality influenced many notable Anglican evangelicals including **William Wilberforce**, Charles Simeon, and **Hannah More**.

Newton's regular personal spiritual practices consisted of devotional **reading**, **fasting**, mental **prayer**, contemplative walks through the country, self-examination (especially in preparation for celebrating **Holy Communion**), and recording his experiences in his diary. He also observed annual events such as New Year's Day, his and his wife's birthday, and the North Atlantic storm that awakened him to God as "memorial days" for devotional **meditation**. He was a popular and respected spiritual guide through his prolific correspondence, preaching, and visits to homes and other public settings. As a hymn writer many people associate Newton with "Amazing Grace." Other well-known hymns are "Glorious Things of Thee Are Spoken" and "How Sweet the Name of Jesus Sounds." During his pastorate at Olney (1764–79) he collaborated with William Cowper in producing the *Olney Hymns*. In 1779 he became pastor at St. Mary Woolnoth, London, where he served until his death.

A recent and excellent introduction to the life and spirituality of Newton is *John Newton and the English Evangelical Tradition* by D. Bruce Hindmarsh. Newton's *Cardiphonia* is a collection of letters revealing the depth and sensitivity of his spiritual life and illustrating the type of guidance he offered to others. TS

NICHOLAS OF CUSA (1401–64), German theologian and mystic. Nicholas's career was entirely within the church. He was made a cardinal in 1448; bishop of Brixen in 1450; and served as papal legate in Germany, where he worked to reform clerical and monastic life. He combined knowledge and theology with **contemplation** and **mysticism**. His thoughts led not to a simple logical truth but to a kind of truth or knowing found in ambiguity, which he called a coincidence of opposites.

Nicholas's use of ambiguity can be seen in *On Learned Ignorance* (1440) in which he outlined a cosmology wherein all things exist in or are enfolded in God. Creation is God's unfolding; and all is in union with God, which we cannot understand through reason. Instead we must use our intuition, or what Nicholas called learned ignorance. Even though union with God may only be intuited, yet the union is not pure affect, nor is it devoid of intellect. We must *learn* our way toward *ignorance*. We find God when we pass beyond the impasse of paradox and ambiguity and let go of worldly values and determinations made

by reason and logic. Though our minds tend to ignore or dismiss those things that are mutually contradictory, this is nevertheless where we find God. Christ, being both human and divine, is a coincidence of opposites—both the divine Word made visible and humanity at its highest potential and expression.

Nicholas challenges us to seek the undivided divine Trinity (unity-equality-connection) that we can deeply know only by experience but that requires our intellect to help us find our way toward knowing. In God all the ambiguities, distinctions, and differences we see from our totally human point of view are made one, united and enfolded in God.

For further study, consider *Nicholas of Cusa: Selected Spiritual Writings*, translated by H. Lawrence Bond. This volume contains *On Learned Ignorance*. SN

NICODEMUS OF THE HOLY MOUNTAIN (1749–1809), Greek Orthodox monk on Mount Athos and chief editor of *The Philokalia*, a collection of texts written between the fourth and fifteenth centuries by spiritual masters of the Eastern **Orthodox** tradition and compiled in the eighteenth century by Nicodemus and others. His own writings are entirely consistent with the whole Eastern Orthodox spiritual tradition. His choice of texts included in *The Philokalia* is consistent with the meaning of the term *philokalia* itself, "love of the beautiful."

These texts are guides to the practice of the contemplative life and constitute, as Nicodemus himself puts it, "a mystical school of inward prayer." Those who study these texts cultivate the divine seed implanted in their hearts at their baptism and grow in the Spirit until they become self-conscious children of God. Nicodemus was an advocate of the "inner work" whereby the inside of the vessel is cleansed so that the outside may also become clean (Matt. 23:26). He believed that many wear themselves out in "outer work" and thus make no real progress in the inner work. They fail to realize the purity of heart and illumination of consciousness that *The Philokalia* charts for us. Those who reach the advanced state of spirituality achieve *hesychia*—a state of tranquility, stillness, fixity, and concentration. One of the doors to this state of being, or "seeing," is the constant invocation of the name of Jesus (for example, the **Jesus Prayer**).

Among Nicodemus's other works are *Unseen Warfare*, an editing of *Spiritual Combat and the Path to Paradise* by Lorenzo Scupoli, first published in Italy in 1589, and a Greek translation of *Spiritual Exercises* of **Ignatius of Loyola**. Nicodemus was declared a saint by the Orthodox Church in 1955. RMH

NOUWEN, HENRI J. M. (1932–96), Dutch priest, theologian, and prolific writer on God's **incarnate love**, human woundedness, and healing. Born in Nijkerk, Netherlands, into a Catholic family, he heard his call to the priesthood at the early age of six. Educated by the **Jesuits** and interested in pastoral ministry, he was a pioneer in legitimizing the place of psychology in the field of pastoral care. His studies led him to a teaching career in the United States that included Notre Dame, Yale, and Harvard. Nouwen's seminal book on the subject of the clergy's own **suffering** in relation to their pastoral ministry, *The Wounded Healer: Ministry in Contemporary Society*, was written during his Yale years. Nouwen's deeply intimate yet challenging relationship with God, as well as his calling to love as Jesus loved, led to a variety of journeys of **faith** and exploration: from the **silence** and **solitude** of a **Trappist** monastery (*The Genesee Diary*) to the ecumenical nature of the church to the poverty of Central and South America (*Gracias: A Latin American Journal*).

A constant and open seeker of God's will for his life, in 1986 Nouwen left his academic career to become the priest and pastor of a L'Arche community in Canada (*The Road to Daybreak* and *Adam: God's Beloved*). In this community where people of able minds and bodies tend to the needs of and live among people with disabilities, the academician not only ministered to those around him but also allowed himself to be the recipient of care and ministry by people who had no interest in or understanding of his intellectual pursuits. After recovering from a severe depression, he embraced his role as mentor, writer, and counselor with a new fervor, touching hundreds of lives personally and many more through his writings. His own insecurities and struggles, in the midst of great popularity among and love of his parishioners, friends, and students, proved to be the fodder for many of his works, such as *The Return of the Prodigal Son* and *The Inner Voice of Love*. Ultimately it was the humanity of Nouwen that made him so accessible, his love for others that made him such a mentor for those who struggle to realize the full breadth of God's love for the individual.

For further reading, see *Seeds of Hope*, edited by Robert Durback, and *Wounded Prophet: A Portrait of Henri J. M. Nouwen* by Michael Ford. JHS

OBEDIENCE. Linguistically as well as theologically, right listening is the source of right behavior. *Shema* in the Hebrew Bible not only means "to hear, listen, or pay attention," but is also used as the primary word for "obey." In the New Testament, the Greek word for "obey" is *hyp-akouo* (root of *acoustics*), meaning "to listen beneath." Likewise the English word *obey* itself comes from the Latin *oboedio* (root of *audio*), meaning "to listen to or toward."

In technological culture where audio-video stimuli abound, a fresh definition of obedience might translate "listening beneath" the distractions of sounds and images to what life is really saying. Genuine obedience is to listen through the ancient words of scripture for the voice of the Lord down through the centuries as it has been interpreted and misinterpreted, and then to ask: What is God saying now?

The ethical issue of obedience is the spiritual issue of **discernment**: to discern what is the best (Phil. 1:10); to discern what is the will of God—"what is good and acceptable and perfect" (Rom. 12:2). "Listen carefully to the voice of the LORD your God, and *do* what is right in [God's] sight, and give heed to [God's] commandments...for I am the LORD who heals you" (Exod. 15:26, emphasis added). One is invited to listen through the words of scripture *to the voice* of the Lord for what God commands in each new day and age.

Blind obedience is condoned neither by Jesus in the Gospels nor the early church. "Neither will I tell you by what authority I am doing these things," Jesus retorts to bickering religious leaders (Matt. 21:27). "Whether it is right in God's sight to listen to you rather than to God, you must judge," early apostles answer boldly as they defy the authorities (Acts 4:19). Specific references to obedience need to be studied in the context of other scriptures, in the context of their historical situation, and in the context of one's life in the present time and place. Despite language about submission, even the writer of Ephesians counsels a mutual communal obedience: "Be subject *to one another* out of reverence for Christ" (Eph. 5:21, emphasis added).

The sixth-century **Rule** of Saint **Benedict** begins with the word *listen*. One is to listen carefully to the master's instructions and attend to them with the ear of one's heart. The reason for Benedict's more moderate rule was to correct abuses of monastic community life that had broken down either because of anarchy or authoritarianism.

The concept of obedience in the history of **spirituality** has a reputation of both freedom and abuse. There is the violence caused by unilateral obedience in the Crusades and the Holocaust. Women and dissenters have been silenced or executed, wars waged, and slavery condoned in the name of obeying "God's will." But there is also the tradition of spiritual disobedience and freedom from human tyranny: Sir **Thomas More** is executed vowing he is the king's loyal servant, but God's first; **Martin Luther** defies those who accuse him of heresy at the Diet (council) of Worms: "Here I stand; I can do no other"; Protestant reformers confess, "God alone is Lord of the conscience" (The Westminster Confession of Faith, 1647).

Martin Luther King Jr. and Archbishop **Oscar Romero** offer contemporary examples of civil disobedience on the grounds of spiritual obedience to the higher authority of divine preferential option for the oppressed. Intentional spiritual **communities** as well as established institutions of church and state have struggled to find appropriate ways of fostering personal obedience to conscience before God, coupled with commitment to the well-being of the community.

For further reading, see *The Cost of Discipleship* by **Dietrich Bonhoeffer**; *A Long Obedience in the Same Direction* by Eugene H. Peterson; *The Rule of St. Benedict;* or *Weeds among the Wheat: Discernment* by Thomas H. Green. KIG

OBLATION. See **Abandonment.**

O'CONNOR, ELIZABETH (1921–98), American spiritual writer. Born in Spring Lake, New Jersey, O'Connor attended Riverdale (New York) Country School for girls. She worked in public relations before 1953. She wrote extensively of the innovative work of the Church of the Saviour in Washington, D.C. Founded in 1946 by N. Gordon Cosby with nine members, the church proclaimed a revolutionary commitment to Christ and mission. It pioneered coffee shop ministry with the Potter's House and sought to address slum housing and the needs of inner-city children, the elderly, and adults with mentally handicapping conditions. O'Connor's book *A Call to Commitment* (1963) records the beginnings of this covenant ministry. As their "writer-in-residence," she had a profound effect on the church's members through her books, encouraging and spurring them to deeper levels of commitment. Her last publication, *Our Rag-bone Hearts*, emphasized that true Christianity must radically personify faith. O'Connor also wrote inspirational articles for *Faith at Work* magazine.

For more on the Church of the Saviour, read *By Grace Transformed*, a collection of Cosby's sermons. Other books by O'Connor include *Journey Inward, Journey Outward; Our Many Selves; The Eighth Day of Creation: Gifts and Creativity; Search for Silence; The New Community; Letters to Scattered Pilgrims;* and *Cry Pain, Cry Hope: Thresholds to Purpose.* LSP

ORIGEN (ca. 185–ca. 254), early Christian teacher and biblical scholar. Born in Egypt, probably at Alexandria, of Christian parents,

Origen received a thoroughly Christian education. When his father, Leonidas, was martyred in 202, his mother had to save the zealous youth by hiding his clothes to keep him from following. Shortly afterward, Bishop Demetrius made Origen head of the Alexandrian School to replace **Clement**, who fled to escape persecution. He adopted an **ascetic** regimen of **fasting**, **prayer**, and voluntary **poverty** and, in an excess of zeal, mutilated himself, interpreting Matthew 19:12 literally. His ordination as a presbyter by Palestinian bishops in 230 led to a breach with Demetrius, who removed him from his teaching position, deposed him from the priesthood, and sent him into exile. Origen spent the remainder of his life at Caesarea Maritima in Palestine. During the Decian persecution in 250, he was arrested, imprisoned, and subjected to prolonged torture. He survived only a few years.

One of the most prolific writers of his day, Origen focused especially on biblical interpretation. Of the three senses he found in **scriptures** (literal, moral, and spiritual), the spiritual sense fascinated him the most, for it enabled him to make something of passages that, interpreted literally, conflicted with the Rule of Faith, a collection of doctrinal statements that preceded the creation of formal creeds. Despite his conviction that truth is to be found above all in scriptures, Origen was saturated with **Platonism** and is credited by some as cofounder with Plotinus of **Neoplatonism**. Like other Platonists, he believed that God is in essence beyond knowing; but, as a Christian, he insisted that we can know God through the one he called "the Second God," the Logos of John's Gospel. His biblical studies and Platonism laid the groundwork for the contemplative movement in the fourth and fifth centuries. In *Homilies on the Song of Songs* he interpreted the whisperings of the lover to his beloved as Christ's words to the church or to the individual soul, and he laid out some of the lines of the mystical path—purgation, illumination, and union—that many contemplatives followed.

In the late fourth century, controversy

arose over various teachings derived from Origen. His interest in the spiritual sense of scripture caused some to ignore or reject the literal sense. His teaching on the pre-existence of souls was misinterpreted as implying reincarnation. As a result of these misunderstandings, some Egyptian bishops condemned all of Origen's writings.

Other works by Origen include *On Prayer* and *Commentary on the Gospel According to John.* See also Henri Crouzel's study, *Origen.* EGH

ORTHODOX SPIRITUALITY.
The Christian spirituality of the church of the East, often referred to as the Byzantine or the Eastern Church. The Eastern Orthodox Church is a family of self-governing churches held together not by an organization but by a bond of unity in faith and sacramental worship. "Orthodox" means "right believing"; therefore their piety seeks to maintain an uncluttered focus on the fundamentals of faith. They often refer to themselves as the Church of the Seven Councils, referring to the early church councils held between 325–787, which clearly defined Christian doctrine. This federation includes four centers or patriarchates, each headed by a patriarch: Constantinople, Alexandria, Antioch, and Jerusalem. Secondary centers are Russian, Romanian, Serbian, Greek, Albanian, Cypriot, Bulgarian, Georgian, Czechoslovakian, Polish, Sinaian. Normally Orthodox spirituality refers to the Christian church of Eastern Europe and Eastern Mediterranean.

Monasticism is an important part of Orthodox spirituality. Beginning with the hermitages and monasteries of the **desert fathers and mothers**, by the fifth century there were two great monastic centers: St. Catherine on Mt. Sinai and the many monasteries of Constantinople. By the tenth century, the monasteries of Mt. Athos in Greece had risen to prominence, and their teaching gave a fuller development to **hesychasm** and the **Jesus Prayer**.

Eastern monasticism gave the Christian world such significant spiritual masters as **John Climacus**, a teacher of **asceticism** who was responsible for shaping the doctrine of the **Incarnation**, and **Maximus the Confessor**, a teacher of **mysticism**. **Symeon the New Theologian**, whose mysticism gave full expression to **deification** as the goal of prayer, and later **Gregory Palamas**, defender of hesychasm, gave fuller development to the theme of prayer and illumination or light, which is a key theme in all Orthodox spirituality and liturgical forms. For further insight into these traditions and the early spiritual masters, see E. Kadloubovsky and G. E. H. Palmer's books, *Early Fathers from the Philokalia* and *Writings from the Philokalia on Prayer of the Heart.*

The Eastern Church also gives the Christian world the form of Christian art known as **icons**. Early in the eighth or ninth centuries a dispute over icons arose. Some saw the use of icons as a form of idolatry, while others claimed that icons were simply symbols. They explained that veneration of the icon was not directed toward the object itself, which would be idolatry, but toward the reality that is made visible or incarnated in and through the person depicted on the icon. The icon does not *re-present* a person but *presents* a redeemed, purified vision of holy reality that arouses adoration. Thus an icon is not an idol but a theophany, a revelation of God. The supporters of iconography won the dispute, resulting in some of Christendom's most magnificent sacred art and architecture.

Another aspect of Orthodox spirituality that comes out of this iconic tradition is the emphasis on illumination and mystery. The icon-covered screen (iconostasis) that separates and defines the worship space is understood not as a barrier but as a witness to the transcendent mystery. This points to another major feature of Orthodox spirituality, the emphasis on the concealment-illumination dichotomy. More than any other Christian spiritual tradition, Orthodox spirituality is apophatic, a spirituality of the "**negative way**," insisting that the hidden God is absolutely transcendent and that only negative language can describe God. This mysterious God can be mystically known and experienced through **detachment** and purification of the senses. Therefore one cannot grasp a knowledge of God through human intellect but instead is grasped by God in the **experience** of transcendent beauty or transcendent truth. Worship itself is seen as the icon of heaven—a transcendent mystery. For more study of icons, see Paul Evdokimov's *The Art of the Icon: A Theology of Beauty* and Daniel B. Clendenin's (editor) *Eastern Orthodox Theology*.

Orthodox spirituality's most visible feature is that it is a **liturgical spirituality**. **Worship** is the central and all-encompassing act, which involves perceiving the beauty of the spiritual dimension and expressing that celestial beauty. Worship is a foretaste of heaven designed to make us fit for heaven. For Orthodox Christians our primary purpose is to glorify God; therefore, we are most truly human in the act of worship. A strong incarnational theme also runs throughout Orthodox spirituality. **Spiritual formation** is the process of putting on Christ so that "It is no longer I who live, but it is Christ who lives in me" (Gal. 2:20). The "putting on of Christ" is created, fed, and renewed in the context of worship, so that spiritual formation in the Orthodox understanding begins and ends with worship.

Robert Taft's *Beyond East and West: Problems in Liturgical Understanding* is one of the most helpful resources to begin this study. Another good general study resource is George Fedotov's *The Russian Religious Mind*. CIZ

OSUNA, FRANCISCO DE (ca. 1492–1540), author of *The Third Spiritual Alphabet*, which significantly influenced the **spiritual formation** of **Teresa of Ávila** and **John of the Cross**. A Franciscan priest from southern Spain, Osuna coined the term *recollection* in the early sixteenth century to describe the fixing of the mind on God in **contemplative** prayer. His books provided practical instruction through carefully crafted maxims, organized alphabetically. Three lengthy treatises, organized around these ABCs, dealt in order with the passion of Jesus Christ, prayer and ascetic practices, and recollection. He provided solid

guidance for the development of the inner life when previously only external religious observance was understood as the means to **holiness**. His articulation of the nuances in mystical **experience** led to the Golden Age of Spanish **mysticism**.

For additional reading, see *Francisco de Osuna: The Third Spiritual Alphabet*, translated by Mary E. Giles. NVV

OTTO, RUDOLF (1869–1937), German Lutheran theologian. In Otto's first major work, *Spirit and Word according to Luther*, for which he was awarded a licentiate in theology from the University of Göttingen, he explored the non-rational "numinous" (the mysterious or supernatural) core of religion. This was the first of a series of books in which Otto explored the forms of religious consciousness shared by the world's great religions seeking a "true understanding of religion." His research led him to travel the world collecting cultural and aesthetic objects and to develop German translations of important texts of the world religions.

Otto's best-known work, which perhaps overshadowed his later work, is *Das Heilige* (published in English as *The Idea of the Holy*). In this book he explored the assumption that all religions derive from the natural spiritual capacity inherent in the human being. He gave particular attention to the paradoxical relationship between the *mysterium tremendum*—the tremendous mystery of the sense of awe and dread in the face of the Holy—and the *fascinans*—our fascination with the mystery experienced in our encounter with the Holy. In his later work, especially *Mysticism: East and West* and *India's Religion of Grace and Christianity Compared and Contrasted*, he began to challenge the idea of a common religious foundation in the **experience** of the Holy as peculiar to the West and especially to Judaism and Christianity. Although firmly committed to Christianity, Otto believed that Christianity's unique value could only be understood in the context of a comparative study of the history of religions. EBA

OXFORD MOVEMENT. Mid-nineteenth-century spiritual movement to renew the Church of England by introducing or renewing many early church and Catholic practices. The leaders and theologians of the movement were responding, with a strong emphasis on tradition, to both the eighteenth-century Evangelical revival (which had stressed personal **experience**) and to what they saw as growing liberalism in nineteenth-century society. Among the immediate causes for the Oxford movement were certain laws passed in the 1820s that loosened the ties of the Church of England with the British government, making some Anglicans look to other sources for authority. Centered at Oxford (hence the name), the movement was led by Anglican theologians and clergy including **John Keble**, **John Henry Newman** (who converted to Roman Catholicism in 1845), and Edward Pusey. Their ideas were first published in a famous series called *Tracts for the Times* (1833–41), edited by Newman; this group of theologians and clergy were often called "Tractarians." *Tracts for the Times* and other Oxford movement writings were widely read and controversial.

The Oxford movement stressed corporate **holiness** and **worship**, the divinely sustained nature of the church, the continuity of the Church of England with tradition through its liturgy and the apostolic succession of its bishops, the sacramental life of the church, liturgical worship and ceremonial, and an objective view of **faith** that was not based on feelings. The movement brought into Anglicanism a revival of Gothic architecture, a renewal of sacramental life and eucharistic practice, the incorporation of more Catholic ceremonies into worship, and the establishment of Anglican religious communities. Much of the aesthetic beauty and ceremony of Anglican and Episcopal worship today derives from changes introduced by the Oxford movement. JLW

P

PALAMAS, GREGORY (ca. 1296–1359), Byzantine theologian, spiritual guide, and exponent of **hesychasm**. Gregory was born in Constantinople of noble parents. When he was seven, his father died, and at age twenty he entered the community at Athos and became a monk. Driven from Athos by the Turks in 1325, he became a hermit on a mountain near Beroea, where he lived the life of a hesychast, practicing the **Jesus Prayer** five days a week. He returned to Athos in 1331. From there he took on the Calabrian philosopher Barlaam, who, trained in Western dialectics, denied the legitimacy of hesychasm and condemned the efficacy of its practice and theology. Palamas wrote a resounding defense of hesychasm that has come to be known as *The Triads*.

Gregory defended the idea that God can be **experienced** directly as "divine energy" and "uncreated light." Because God became human, humans can become divine and realize the "image of God" in which they have been created. Palamas agreed with Barlaam that both God's essence and energy are **transcendent**; but, while God's essence cannot be directly experienced, God's energy can be communicated through the **Holy Spirit** with sanctifying and purifying power. Gregory taught that not only is the soul transformed but the body as well. As proof of this, he refers to Jesus' **Transfiguration** and Stephen's and Moses' transformed faces. Through a process of **deification**, the believer achieves a **union** with God through **grace**. This experience denotes a mystery of an entirely different order, beyond reason and knowing in the Western sense, known only to those who have experienced it. Palamas was arrested for heresy in 1341, though the real reasons were more political than theological. In 1347 he was elected archbishop of Thessalonica, and new councils vindicated his theology. He achieved a great and lasting victory for hesychasm that has influenced Eastern Orthodoxy ever since. He died on Nov. 14, 1359. In 1368 the Synod of Constantinople declared him a saint.

Gregory Palamas: The Triads is a modern translation by Nicholas Gendle, with an introduction by John Meyendorff. TCW

PALMER, PHOEBE (1807–74), prolific American Methodist author and evangelist in the **holiness** movement. She was a poet, hymn writer, theologian, humanitarian, feminist advocate, and editor of *The Guide to Holiness*.

Recognized as the mother of the holiness movement, Palmer was a link between Wesleyan revivalism and modern **Pentecostalism**. She actively participated in camp meetings and other revival movements. She was most influential in the expansion of Methodism and was a driving force in beginning missions, launching one of the earliest inner-city missions and founding a mission to China. She serves as a model for advocates of women in ministry and of social causes such as women's rights, temperance, and serving the poor. Her deep grounding in classical Christianity made her spiritual writings of permanent significance. Her speaking, writing, and mentoring tremendously influenced many important leaders. She traveled and spoke widely, exemplifying her theology in the way she lived.

Palmer's writings include *The Way of Holiness* and *Entire Devotion to God*. To better understand and appreciate the person, theology, and writings of Phoebe Palmer, see *Phoebe Palmer: Selected Writings*, edited by Thomas C. Oden. EWF

PANIKKAR, RAIMON (b. 1918), philosopher and teacher, born in Barcelona, Spain, to a

Christian mother and Hindu father. He was heavily influenced by both his Christian and Hindu roots. Ordained a Catholic priest in 1946, he has also been described as a Hindu, a Buddhist, and a secularist. Panikkar has spent much of his life in India. He taught at the University of California in Santa Barbara until his retirement in 1987. He is a proponent of interreligious dialogue, not for the purpose of converting but of opening to the revelation of a truth that might otherwise be unknown. He wrote "The Sermon on the Mount of Intrareligious Dialogue," which gives guidelines for fruitful conversation that leads to happiness and wholeness. A theme of his writings is that truth is pluralistic.

Panikkar's theology, outlined in his more than thirty books, combines a trinitarian Christian understanding of God with Hindu and Buddhist understandings. For Panikkar, God, not a substance and beyond all naming, is best understood by the Indian term *advaita*. *Advaita* means that God is neither one nor many; thus monotheism and polytheism are equally false. Panikkar called himself a "monk without a monastery" and said that anyone is capable of a monastic spirituality. There is a monk in every one of us. The goal of **spirituality** is fullness of life, and to achieve it one must shun everything that is subordinate to it. Renunciation leads to a *Blessed Simplicity* (the title of one of his books).

To read selections from Panikkar's work, see *Invisible Harmony: Essays on Contemplation and Responsibility*, edited by Harry James Cargas. SEW

PARLIAMENT OF THE WORLD'S RELIGIONS.

The first interreligious dialogue of the Parliament of the World's Religions was held in Chicago in 1893. The centennial celebration of this important event in 1993 was also held in Chicago. It brought together 8,700 leaders, representing 125 religions, to discuss the role of religion and **spirituality** in the world. A third Parliament was held in Cape Town, South Africa, in l999. Another is planned for 2004.

Interspirituality (a word introduced by Brother Wayne Teasdale, one of the trustees for the Council of the PWR) describes the spiritual aspect of the world's religions. Persons of various religions experience a common spirituality above and beyond their individual beliefs. This mystical aspect is especially present during periods of silent **prayer** and **meditation** experienced by the **community** together. Teasdale's book *The Mystic Heart* develops this concept of interspirituality. EWF

PASCAL, BLAISE

(1623–62), French mathematician and philosopher. At the age of seventeen Pascal became known as a mathematical prodigy based on his first published works. By the time he experienced a religious conversion in 1654, he was already a respected scientist, having invented the first calculating machine and organized a public transportation system for Paris.

Although influenced by Cornelius Jansenius, late bishop of Ypres in France, Pascal never really identified himself as a member of the **Jansenists**, a lay renewal group later condemned by the Catholic Church. But the group's emphasis on **Augustine's** view of **grace** seems to have deeply affected Pascal's conversion, which he recorded on a scrap of paper pinned to his suit jacket and which was found after his death.

Pascal recorded nearly all of his religious reflections on such fragments of paper, seemingly in great haste, though he had begun to organize about half of them into a book, never to be completed before his death. These philosophical fragments are known as Pascal's *Pensées* and have been numerically codified. Many reflect Pascal's basic belief that nothing is more important for the human being than to know one's wretchedness and **humility** while also knowing one's greatness and dignity. He describes this wretchedness as that of a deposed king; thus humankind bears the traces of divinity.

Pascal is known for his "wise wager": that given what can be known about human

209

nature as both great and insignificant and about the facts of Jesus Christ's crucifixion and resurrection, Christian faith deserves respect and may be tested as a scientist would test a laboratory hypothesis. The personal experience of the inner fire of Jesus Christ is the foundation of Pascal's small book of private meditations, *The Mystery of Jesus*, never intended for publication.

For further reading, see the section on Pascal in *Three Outsiders* by Diogenes Allen and *Mind on Fire: A Faith for the Skeptical and Indifferent* by Blaise Pascal, edited by James M. Houston. KIG

PASCHAL MYSTERY. A central mystery of Christian redemption and salvation that in and through the person of Jesus Christ, we are invited to participate in Jesus' **suffering**, death, and resurrection. This is the meaning of the sacrament of **baptism** (Rom. 6:3-11). We are baptized into that same mysterious pattern; our own unique lives (both the ups and downs) become channels for Jesus' presence in our world.

Jesus' Last Supper with his disciples coincided with the annual celebration of Passover (*pesach* in Hebrew, *pascha* in Greek), commemorating God's powerful intervention in the lives of the Israelites in the **Exodus** from Egypt. Because they had marked their homes with the blood of a lamb, the Israelites were passed over by the angel of death, who struck down the firstborn of the Egyptians. Led out of Egypt via the Red Sea, the Israelites wandered in the desert for forty years until they reached the Promised Land.

In the New Testament, Jesus' blood and sacrifice on the **cross** set us free from the bondage of inner slavery, **darkness**, and **evil**. Through the blood of this lamb Jesus, death has been conquered. Jesus is the way out of all that enslaves us, the truth for which our hearts hunger, the life that leads ultimately to the Promised Land. In John's chronology of the crucifixion, Jesus hangs on the cross at the same time the Passover lambs are being slaughtered. The gift of life everlasting has

been accomplished through the new Paschal Lamb, Jesus, the Lamb of God. EKM

PATRICK (ca. 385–ca. 461), missionary to Ireland and bishop. The documented life and achievements of Patrick are as amazing as the legends that have been attributed to him over the centuries. When he was sixteen, young Patricius was kidnapped from his comfortable, middle-class life in Romanized (read "civilized") Britain and sold to King Miliucc, one of hundreds of kings in barbaric Ireland. For six years he was a shepherd-slave, alone in the hills of Antrim, hungry and naked. He developed a prayer life that eventually included hundreds of prayers each day and night. One night he heard a voice telling him he was going home. The next morning he began walking across two hundred miles of unfamiliar and dangerous territory to a southeastern inlet, where he boarded a ship that took him to continental Europe. A few years later he finally arrived home in Britain.

Although Patrick's family was thrilled to have him back, he soon heard a voice telling him to return to Ireland as a traveling missionary. To prepare he spent several years in Gaul receiving a theological education, followed by ordination as a deacon, priest, and bishop. At about forty-seven years of age, Patrick returned to Ireland. He was the first missionary bishop in history, as well as the first to travel among barbarians beyond the reach of Roman law. Irish Christianity was the first de-Romanized Christianity in western Europe.

Until his death, probably in 461, Patrick loved his Irish flock, offering them Christ without offering them "civilization." Because he did not judge their barbarous nation, he could reach directly into Irish hearts, sharing Christ as the answer to their deepest fears and needs and allowing the development of a distinctive **Celtic spirituality**. He helped them to understand nature as God's gift rather than as something threatening and offered them a loving God, not one who demanded human sacrifice. He was the first person to speak out unequivocally against slavery. Nobody else would speak out as strongly for almost thirteen hundred years. WW

PEACE. As a sign of Christian faith to the presence of God's kingdom on earth, peace is both an individual characteristic and a communal goal. The Hebrew Scriptures go beyond an understanding of peace as external good wishes, material blessings, and obvious absence of war. The Hebrew concept of *shalom*, as envisioned by the prophets (especially Isaiah 11:1-9), is a sign of God's reconciliation with and protection of God's people. God blessed the Israelites and, by God's presence, gave them peace. Well-being, absence of conflict both within the tribes of Israel and with other peoples, prosperity, and unity are markers of God's presence.

In God's continued effort to offer salvation, Jesus became the peace offering who brought about reconciliation. In Romans 5:1, Paul says, "Therefore, since we are justified by faith, we have peace with God through our Lord Jesus Christ." But Jesus served as more than a sacrifice for a people. He called on his followers to become peacemakers by resisting **evil** nonviolently and loving their enemies (Luke 6:27-36) and so to participate in God's **mercy**. Such peacemaking flows from internal peace, modeled by the "Prince of Peace," whose trust in his Father's plan shaped his treatment of detractors and led him to turn troubles over to God.

As an internal **disposition** and **fruit of the Spirit**, peace is a sign of **faith** and discipleship. Peace gives Christians the ability to have grace when facing enemies, an inward knowledge of and **conformity to the will of God**, a spiritual blessing, and a sense of security. Spiritual peace is often marked by a sense of calm and **assurance**, a trust that cannot be willed into existence but can only be felt when it is given. Peace found throughout the community and world is considered a sign of God's kingdom as envisioned by Jesus Christ.

For further reading on various communal and individual aspects of peace, see *Discovering God's Will Together* by Danny E. Morris and Charles M. Olsen, and *Prayer, Stress, and Our Inner Wounds* by Flora Slosson Wuellner. JHS

PEALE, NORMAN VINCENT (1898–1993), writer, pastor, motivational speaker. Peale was one of the most popular religious writers and speakers of the twentieth century. From his position as senior pastor at Marble Collegiate Church in New York City, he led what he called "the Movement," the pillars of which were his church, the American Foundation for Religion and Psychiatry, the Foundation for Christian Living, *Guideposts* magazine, and his more than forty books, the most famous of which is *The Power of Positive Thinking*.

The eldest son of a Methodist pastor, Peale grew up with what he later diagnosed as an inferiority complex. This complex continued to plague him in his college years and somewhat into his seminary experience, where he was intrigued by the inspirational healer Emile Coue, whose motto was, "Every day in every way I'm getting better and better." Upon graduation and ordination, Peale served two Methodist churches before being called in 1932 to Marble Collegiate, a congregation of the Reformed Church of America.

In 1944 Peale started up *Guideposts*, a small periodical originally designed for male industrialists, Peale's chosen mission field. Designed to emulate *The Reader's Digest*, it was modestly successful until 1952, when Peale published *The Power of Positive Thinking*, which changed everything for him and his ministry. Suddenly the letters he received were from middle-class, middle-aged women. *Guideposts* adjusted accordingly, and subscriptions rose to almost four million in 1990, declining to about three million by 2001. *The Power of Positive Thinking* was a best-seller and continues to sell around the world in a number of languages. Its message, the message of Peale's entire ministry, is a practical, politicized version of New Thought (a mental science movement from the turn of the century), with evangelical Protestantism, metaphysical spirituality, and the American dream mixed in. His "You can do anything with Jesus" message was perfect for Cold War

America and remains popular with evangelical Christians due to its conservative politics and with New Agers for its **mysticism** and human potential slant.

Peale retired as pastor of Marble Collegiate in 1984 after serving fifty-two years. He remained an active speaker and writer until his death in 1993. WW

PÉGUY, CHARLES PIERRE (1873–1914),
French poet and philosopher whose deep, personal **faith** carried Christianity, socialism, and patriotism into action. Born to a poor family in Orléans, Péguy attended secondary school on scholarship. After military service, he entered the École Normale Supérieure in Paris, intending to teach philosophy. He turned to socialism as a means to overcome modern poverty and destitution, choosing to live a poor life and dropping out of school to run a bookstore that became a center for pro-Dreyfus agitation (In 1894 Captain Alfred Dreyfus, the only Jew on the French army's general staff, was accused of espionage based on forged evidence. This incident exposed anti-Semitism in the French army, government, and church and polarized French society and politics for several years.) He edited an influential journal *Cahiers de la Quinzaine* that foretold the "city harmonious" replacing theoreticians with people of enthusiasm and faith. Viewing disembodied intellectualism as an evil fantasy, he held that liberty comes from daily struggle and rigid discipline. At times the mystic controls human actions, directing them with honor; at others the mystic is controlled by politics—unfeeling dogmatism replacing liberty of mind and heart. True history, Péguy felt, was reflected in the Gospels written by fishermen, boatmen, and tax collectors who actually encountered Christ. He was skeptical of the atheism of progress hiding under the protection of science.

Péguy wanted to advance a salvation that joined the spiritual with the temporal, intellectual, and vocational. To make God's loving **providence** real, Péguy in some of his poems has God speak like a French peasant. Péguy's play *Jeanne d'Arc* affirms his religious and socialist principles and proclaims the reality of the **Incarnation** and redemption. He enlarged upon its themes in his mystical poem *Le Mystère de la Charité de Jeanne d'Arc*. Written from the perspective of Christian revelation, Péguy's poem *Eve* presents the human condition since Adam's paradise. Péguy died as a lieutenant in the first Battle of the Marne in World War I.

Additional information is found in Marjorie Villier's *Charles Péguy, A Study in Integrity* and *Péguy* by Romain Rolland. LSP

PELAGIANISM. A fifth-century theory emphasizing human responsibility in salvation. Pelagianism derives its name from a British monk noted both for learning and piety. Pelagius appeared in Rome during the pontificate of Innocent I (399–401) and attracted followers among a group whom **Jerome** had headed in the 380s. Alarmed by the moral laxity he attributed to **Augustine**'s strongly predestinarian views, he emphasized natural **grace** and free will. His views attracted a considerable following among people of wealth and culture. About 409, as Gothic invaders approached Rome, he and his major supporter Caelestius fled to North Africa. Pelagius then proceeded to Palestine, where he found support for his views among Eastern theologians in the face of a growing critique by Augustine. Augustine insisted on the need for *super*natural grace. Two Palestinian synods cleared Pelagius of charges made by a Spanish bishop named Orosius.

A synod of bishops held in Carthage in from 411 to 412 condemned as erroneous six teachings of Caelestius: (1) Adam was created mortal and would have died whether he had sinned or not. (2) Adam's sin injured only Adam himself and not the whole human race. (3) Newborn infants are in the same state as Adam before he sinned. (4) Adam's sin and death did not cause the death of all humankind, nor does Christ's resurrection assure the resurrection of all. (5) The law brings people into the kingdom of God just as the gospel does. (6) Even before Christ came, there were those who did not sin.

Pelagius himself may have held less radical views, but he did not subscribe to key views of Augustine. In his treatise *Free Will,* he acknowledged the need for grace, but he defined it differently than did Augustine. Grace meant nature with free will, forgiveness of sins, law and teaching, inward illumination, baptismal adoption, and eternal life but not the **Holy Spirit**'s presence to empower, Augustine's definition. Pelagius and Caelestius gained a substantial following in Rome, especially among Christians of the upper classes, though African bishops, led by Augustine, secured their condemnation and exile from Rome by the Emperor Honorius in 418. What troubled many thoughtful laypersons as well as monks and clergy about Augustine's views was the evident arbitrariness of God's actions, and the emperor's action did not halt the movement.

Leader of the opposition to Augustine was Julian, bishop of Eclanum (417–54), whose family once had close ties to Augustine. Julian feared that Augustine's virtual determinism would result in human irresponsibility and would alienate cultured people by superficial piety. In 418 Julian and a group of nineteen Italian bishops set forth what has been called the Semi-Pelagian position: The grace of Christ cooperates with free will and "will not follow those who refuse it." Whether one person is good and another is bad is due to each person and not to God's will. Although there is need of both **baptism** and grace, that is not due to inheritance of **sin**. The Semi-Pelagians disagreed with Pelagius, however, in saying that the whole human race died in Adam and has been raised in Christ.

Augustine occupied himself with a reply to Julian until his death in 430. The debate, however, did not halt there. Pelagianism experienced a revival in Gaul and the British Isles. Monks at Lérins and Marseilles did not find Augustine's emphasis on prevenient grace convincing. The heatedly disputed issue was finally resolved at the Synod of Orange in 529 through the skillful guidance of Caesarius, archbishop of Arles (502–42). The synod upheld Augustine's doctrine of the Fall against Pelagius and insisted, against Semi-Pelagianism, on the need for prevenient grace. It did not, however, mention predestination or the irresistibility of grace. EGH

PENINGTON, ISAAC (1616–79), Quaker theologian. Penington grew up in a wealthy and prestigious family as the eldest son of Sir Isaac Penington, a Puritan statesman and Lord Mayor of London. Penington attended Cambridge and in 1654 married Lady Mary Springett, a young widow and mother. In 1658 the Peningtons met **George Fox,** who influenced them to become **Quakers.** They opened their home to the Quakers for worship. For spiritual convictions and theological writings, Penington was imprisoned six different times for a total of five years and lost both his home and his health. Penington was a prolific writer, the first true theologian in the Society of Friends. He defended Quaker spirituality without attacking his opponents. One of his better-known writings is *The Ancient Principle of Truth, or The Light within Asserted.* ASJ

PENITENCE. Penitence in the early church took place primarily in public worship, with corporate **confession**, absolution, and acceptance of some kind of penance. Only after the Constantine settlement ensured the imperial enfranchisement of the church did penitence become a private, personal spiritual **discipline.** By the early fifth century in the Latin West, various manuals were published in an attempt to bring uniformity to the practice.

Ambrose defined penitence as mourning for sin committed, coupled with the resolve to commit no more sin. Other post-Nicene theologians added the notion that true repentance also included some sort of punishment. The full flowering of medieval Scholastic theology eventually resulted in a detailed discipline to be followed by every believer who desired to turn from sin to salvation. **Sin** itself was described in seven general categories and in mortal and venial varieties. Venial sins cause one to love Jesus Christ less than one ought. Mortal sins are, according to **Augustine**, turning the heart from the unchangeable God to things that change and pass away.

This view of sin led to three kinds of penitence. In public penitence, a sinner was excommunicated from the church. In general penitence, the church directed groups of believers to go on **pilgrimages** or to practice certain disciplines during particular penitential seasons such as Advent or Lent. Individuals were required to perform private penitence regularly for their sins, through private confession and penance directed by a priest.

True penitence included three things: contrition of heart (**compunction**), oral confession, and restitution or acts of **humility**. Chaucer's Parson likens penitence to a tree: contrition is the root, confession is the trunk and branches, and restitution is the fruit. As John the Baptist said, "Bear fruit worthy of repentance" (Matt. 3:8).

Contrition is the real sorrow one feels in the heart for having sinned. There are six causes of contrition: (1) becoming conscious of one's own sin, not with pleasure but with shame in the knowledge it has offended God; (2) awareness that sin enslaves us; (3) fear of eternal damnation; (4) the unhappy memory of the good that is lost in sin; (5) remembering the passion of Jesus Christ for the forgiveness of our sins; and (6) **hope** for **forgiveness** of sin, the gift of **grace** to do good, and the **glory** of heaven. Confession is the sign of contrition. It must be full, hiding nothing from the priest. The prescribed penance must be completely fulfilled if forgiveness is to take effect.

This Scholastic scheme was utterly rejected by the Protestant Reformation as perhaps the primary example of a **works** righteousness that completely misunderstood the gospel of grace. The reformers held that we are saved from God's wrath against sin not by anything we can do or by anything that the church could offer through its sacramental ministry but solely by what God has done for us in Jesus Christ. We enter into forgiveness by repenting of our sins and putting our faith in Jesus. His death and resurrection alone are the ground of our salvation.

In the twentieth century theologians began to think about the nature of salvation in psychological and relational categories. Sin, or self-absorption, alienates us from God, from other human beings, and from creation itself. Sin is what causes most of our suffering, and we cannot keep from sinning. That is the human dilemma. The way out is repentance through confession and restitution. The literal meaning of *repentance* and its Greek equivalent *metanoia* is "turning around"—turning away from self to God and others with complete vulnerability and intimacy. Salvation still rests on what God has done for us in Jesus Christ, for his atoning death was the perfect act of vulnerability and unconditional love, destroying the power of sin forever. In seeking and receiving his forgiveness and that of those whom we have harmed, we overcome alienation and restore **community**. Often some sort of restitution is required to complete the healing. KS

PENN, WILLIAM (1644–1718), **Quaker** writer, preacher, statesman. Penn was born in London, the son of an admiral who first served the Commonwealth and later helped in the restoration of the monarchy. The well-educated young Penn had the promise of a bright political future, but his becoming a Quaker at age twenty-three took him in a different direction: to jail. Penn was imprisoned for his controversial writing on the Trinity, and while there the still youthful Penn wrote what is considered his best work *No Cross, No Crown*, a spiritual classic on Christian discipleship and commitment. In 1670 Penn was again arrested, this time for street preaching. His defense at the jury trial was a landmark case for the cause of religious freedom. That year he appropriately wrote *The Great Case of Liberty of Conscience*.

Yet Penn continued to dream of creating

a more just and peaceful society. This dream became reality when, in 1681, Penn was given a large tract of land in America in repayment of a debt the Duke of York owed Penn's father. The conscientious Penn governed the Pennsylvania colony according to Quaker principles. He negotiated a fair price with the Native Americans for the land, and Pennsylvania's constitution guaranteed freedom of religion, making it home to several religious groups persecuted for their convictions. But Penn never resided in the colony long, spending his last years in England.

Penn also composed a thoughtful book defending the Christian foundation of Quakerism, *Primitive Christianity Revived,* and a book of maxims on the spiritual life, *Some Fruits of Solitude.* The book of maxims offers ideas still relevant today, such as Penn's conviction that the inner core of all truly devout persons of different faith traditions is the same: "The humble, meek, merciful, just, pious and devout souls are every where of one religion; and when death has taken off the mask, they will know one another, though the diverse liveries they wear here, make them strangers" (no. 519). SAF

PENNINGTON, M. BASIL (b. 1931), **Trappist** abbot and author. Born in Brooklyn, New York, Pennington entered the Cistercian Order of the Strict Observance (Trappists) in 1951 at St. Joseph's Abbey in Spencer, Massachusetts. He assisted at the Second Vatican Council as a *peritus* (theological consultant) and in preparation of the new Code of Canon Law. In 2000 he was elected abbot of Our Lady of Holy Spirit Abbey in Conyers, Georgia. Pennington is known internationally as one of the founders, along with **Thomas Keating**, of the **Centering Prayer** movement. Pennington's book *Centering Prayer: Renewing an Ancient Christian Prayer Form* is an excellent introduction to the practice. More recent works include *Call to the Center, Centered Living: The Way of Centering Prayer,* and *Listening: God's Word for Today.* WW

PENTECOSTAL MOVEMENT. Pentecostalism as a concept dates to biblical times, where reports of divine healing, speaking in tongues (either unknown languages or existing languages not known to the speaker), and other "signs and wonders" are woven into the Gospels and Acts. However, in American history the term refers more specifically to a religious movement that originated in the ideas of Methodist founder **John Wesley** and grew out of the nineteenth-century **holiness** movement.

Wesley and the holiness movement emphasized the possibility in this life of receiving saving **faith** and knowledge of God as well as **sanctification**, to have one's will totally consecrated to God. This consecration was sometimes called the "second blessing" or the "second work of grace." In the late 1800s, some holiness people began to emphasize the "blessing" of speaking in tongues as a sign of sanctification. At the turn of the century this idea began gathering support through the work of Bethel Bible College professor Charles Parham. A tongue-speaking revival begun in 1906 on Asuza Street in Los Angeles, led by **African-American** preacher William Seymour, was a catalyst for the new Pentecostal movement. The Asuza Street revival lasted for three years and was noted by secular and religious observers alike.

Independent in temperament, Pentecostal groups weathered several controversies in the course of the twentieth century and split into a number of denominations. In the 1960s and '70s, Pentecostal ideas became popular in mainstream denominations, particularly Catholicism, resulting in what is now called the **Charismatic movement**. Charismatics generally remained within their own denominations and placed less emphasis on the "second blessing" and more on the exercise of spiritual gifts. Among the more famous Pentecostal denominations today are the Assemblies of God, the Churches of God, and the International Church of the Foursquare Gospel. Pentecostalism continues to thrive today with over 500 million members worldwide. Besides speaking in tongues, Pentecostals also emphasize divine healing and practice exuberant **worship** styles that involve much bodily movement. They have historically been particularly welcoming to the marginalized in society.

For more information, see *Heaven Below: Early Pentecostals and American Culture* by Grant Wacker. JLW

PERFECTION. A daunting concept grounded in a simple scriptural truth: "Be perfect, therefore, as your heavenly Father is perfect" (Matt. 5:48). Though many people have found it hard to see helpful spiritual guidance in this command, the context of this scripture passage makes clear the vision to which the author calls us, showing us just how it is possible to realize Jesus' command. The preceding verses in Matthew 5 contain a pithy discussion about loving our enemy. Thus, to be perfect as our heavenly Father is perfect means to love all, including our enemy. It is key, however, to understand that this does not mean love as warm feelings but the highest Christian understanding of **love** as *agape*.

Perhaps the most famous Western proponent of the doctrine of perfection was **John Wesley**, though the idea of perfection was certainly discussed and debated before his time, for instance, in the works of **Fénelon** and **William Law**. **Orthodox** writers had long discussed the closely related idea of **deification**. Wesley, though, brought the issue to a point of focused attention as few other Christians have been able to do. While many of the sixteenth-century reformers held that perfection was possible, they thought it was something only to be achieved in heaven. Wesley thought that such a qualification kept spiritual pilgrims from doing their utmost to achieve love of enemy and therefore thought that we should emphasize the attainability of perfection in this life.

Wesley wrote in his *Journal*, February 6, 1789, that the doctrine of Christian perfection was one that "God peculiarly entrusted to the Methodists" and one he needed to preach because it was a part of scriptural truth. Because leading a life of "perfection" can be so easily misinterpreted, he often ran into problems trying to proclaim this doctrine. He wrote several works related to the topic, many of them collected in *A Plain Account of Christian Perfection*. For his published sermon "Christian Perfection," Wesley took as his text "Not as though I had already attained, either were already perfect" (Phil. 3:12, KJV), apparently signaling that he never claimed perfection for himself. Wesley's use of this verse as a guiding theme might also express his understanding of perfection as dynamic, always capable of further growth. In any case, he did not rule out the possibility of the achievement of perfection on earth and sometimes pointed to specific individuals whom he thought had arrived at this level of Christian maturity.

In Wesley's mature view, being perfect does not mean never experiencing temptation, nor does it mean that one is somehow enabled with supernatural faculties of knowledge or reason. Wesley read in scripture, however, (e.g., Rom. 6:1-14) that the Holy Spirit does enable the believer to avoid **sin**, which Wesley understood as the willful violation of a known law of God. When we can trace our motives for every action, even those we take toward our enemies, to *agape* love, then we have achieved biblical perfection, since this humble, servant love is "the fulfilling of the law" (Rom. 13:10).

Wesley's followers often misunderstood his emphasis on perfection as humble love, which led to a misguided focus on intense internal sensations of love or to the claim that perfection should preclude negative fluctuations in feelings or even temptations. Arguments over these and related issues led to many splits in the **holiness** movement of the nineteenth and twentieth centuries. The mature Wesley, however, did not hold to such claims about the believer's internal life.

For further reading, see *Purity of Heart in Early Ascetic and Monastic Literature*, edited by Harriet A. Luckman and Linda Kulzer, and

The Idea of Perfection in Christian Theology by R. Newton Flew. GSC

PERSONALITY AND PRAYER. Studies of personality and prayer explore how people experience the spiritual dimension of life. Identifying personality preferences and developmental stages has proven to be influential in the area of Christian **spirituality**.

Three models of personality differences have particularly attracted the attention of those interested in the implications of personality type for ways of prayer and opportunities for growth. These are the Jungian-based Myers Briggs Type Indicator (MBTI), the Measures of Psychosocial Development Inventory (MPD) grounded in the theory of Erikson and Hawley, and the **enneagram**. These three theories are grounded in everyday experiences of normative functioning, not in human pathology. Presenting an optimistic view of personality and the opportunity for change and growth, each theory views human development and personality as a lifelong process in which central issues can be reworked. All have proven relevant and applicable in the study of spiritual formation and prayer.

All three models are highly nuanced instruments of spiritual and psychological growth that help people to understand themselves and those with whom they live and work. Each system uses an easy-to-administer inventory/indicator/questionnaire to help classify the individual. Classifications can then be interpreted to determine effective guidance and are helpful devices for guiding observations, generating information, and examining new possibilities in understanding **spiritual formation** and prayer.

MBTI: In his research Jung noticed that people could be classified into three pairs of personality characteristics relating to preference for a particular type of function in interactions. The three pairs are Extrovert/ Introvert (E/I); Sensing/Intuiting (S/N); and Thinking/Feeling (T/F). Every person has a preference toward one side of each of these pairs, and each preference has strengths as well as limitations. In the 1940s and '50s, an American mother-daughter team, Katherine Briggs and her daughter Isabel Briggs Myers, developed a self-reporting questionnaire to describe and delineate personality differences along the three Jungian scales and added a fourth scale (Judging/Perceiving), creating sixteen combinations of preferences or sixteen personality types. Because individuals actually show preferences from all of these types and because each type varies in degree, an infinite variety of combinations exists. Jung presented his theory in *Psychological Types*. Isabel Briggs Myers and her son Peter B. Myers wrote *Gifts Differing: Understanding Personality Type* to explain the preferences and the sixteen types. David Kiersey and Marilyn Bates offer a simplified scheme by sorting the types into four "temperament styles" in *Please Understand Me*, a scheme taken up with specific application to **spiritual direction** in *Prayer and Temperament: Different Prayer Forms for Different Personality Types* by Chester P. Michael and Marie C. Norrisey.

MPD: Using psychoanalytical, biographical, historical, and anthropological study methods, Erik Erikson (in *Childhood and Society*) identified eight developmental stages and the critical conflicts encountered at each stage. How a person resolves each crisis or conflict determines if there is a positive or negative attitude associated with that developmental stage. In each stage individuals must adequately find resolution. The awareness of "stages of development" and of the formative dynamics that accompany each stage is vital to holistic spiritual formation. These dynamics contribute to the characteristics of an individual's personality, and the degree of conflict resolution determines the overall health of the person.

Enneagram: The enneagram is a scheme of nine types modified from the teachings of George Ivanovich Gurdjieff (1877–1949) and has been developed over the years, most notably by Chilean psychiatrist Claudio Naranjo. For further information, see the separate article on the enneagram.

Despite precautionary warnings, these theories and their corresponding instruments are remarkable, self-revealing tools that can be used with individuals who seek clarity and depth in spiritual growth. The use of theology along with personality and stage-development theories provides an integrative orientation to faith development. PDB

PETITION. Prayers of request or pleas in which we ask God for various benefits, such as life, health, success, understanding, and deliverance for ourselves (in contrast to **intercession** for others). At the heart of petitionary prayer is our acknowledgment of complete dependence upon God's grace for all that we have and all that we are. Petitionary prayer is a chief spiritual **discipline** for facilitating growth in **humility**, one of the fundamental **dispositions** needed for spiritual maturity. Jesus instructed his followers to engage in petitionary prayer through parables and commands to "ask, seek, and knock" (Matt. 7:7-8, RSV). His sample pattern for our daily prayer, the **Lord's Prayer**, chiefly follows a petitionary pattern. Because petitionary prayers focus on personal concerns, they tend to be raw and intimate in nature.

In the Jewish prayer tradition, prayers of complaint also fall into the category of supplication or petition. Born out of human suffering, these prayers often are direct complaints to God about God's action or lack of action. The Old Testament book of Job includes many such prayers of complaint aimed directly or indirectly at God. Indirect criticism of God in this type of prayer speech is found in Abraham's words, "Far be it from you to do such a thing, to slay the righteous with the wicked.... Shall not the Judge of all the earth do what is just?" (Gen. 18:25). Petitionary prayer may also express questions and complaints as in Jeremiah 12:1, "You will be in the right, O LORD, when I lay charges against you; but let me put my case to you. Why does the way of the guilty prosper?" This type of prayer speech is bold and honest, even brash at times. However, it is authentic and profoundly spiritual, for it bares the heart before God. No emotion is left hidden from view, and no pretense can come between the "I" and the divine "Thou." CIZ

PIETISM. Pietism in the proper sense is connected with the names of **Philipp Jakob Spener** (1635–1705) and August Hermann Francke (1663–1727). While serving as a pastor, Spener felt a sense of call to revive the Lutheran Church. In 1675 he published *Pia Desideria*, a plan for the church's revitalization. The chief ingredients of his proposal included more diligent study of the scriptures in small cell groups, greater lay involvement in the life of the church, less theoretical and more practical application of Christian faith, loving rather than condemnatory treatment of nonbelievers, training of ministers in piety, and more preaching aimed at **spiritual formation**. Spener's thinking stirred a reaction among his fellow clergy. As he withdrew from public life, leadership fell more and more on the shoulders of Francke, who had come under Spener's influence while serving as a lecturer at Leipzig in 1685. Expounding the Bible devotionally, Francke was forced out of his position at Leipzig and moved to Berlin, where in 1692 he became professor of biblical languages at the newly founded University of Halle and pastor of the parish of Glauchau. In 1695 he launched the series of institutions that characterized the movement, opening a school for the poor in his home and a year later his *Paedagogium* and an orphanage. Other institutions followed.

Pietism's influence continued through the **Moravians** and the "Great Awakening" of the early eighteenth century. In 1722 **Count Nicholas Ludwig von Zinzendorf**, deeply influenced by Pietism, brought beleaguered followers of **John Hus** from Moravia to Herrnhut, his estate in Saxony. In 1732 the Moravians started their famous mission work. A group of Moravians bound for the American colonies in 1735 on the same ship with **John Wesley** opened the way for Pietism to shape the Wesleyan revival movement a few years later. Wesley joined a Moravian society and adapted some of Spener's basic ideas to his own movement.

For further reading, see Spener's *Pia Desideria* or Dale W. Brown's study, *Understanding Pietism.* EGH

PILGRIMAGE. Two paths converge in the making of a pilgrimage: the actual and the spiritual, a specific destination and a perpetual journey. Both require one to leave home, face discomfort, and sleep away from a familiar bed. Every pilgrimage begins with a call from God. It is always personal, an invitation to go deeper into the fullness of Christ. The word *pilgrimage* comes from the Latin *peregrinus,* meaning "stranger," denoting a person who travels to a foreign place. In a sense all people are pilgrims wandering here on earth, trying to find their way home: back to God.

Sacred sites have long been the objects of pilgrimage, but pilgrimage is more than religious tourism. Its dramatic simplicity invites us to root ourselves imaginatively in the past even as we search for the spiritual center of our being. **Origen**, in the middle of the third century, writes of travelers to Bethlehem being shown the cave where Christ was born. Fifth-century monks from Egypt journeyed to Jerusalem. Many stayed, planting themselves in the Judean wilderness outside the city and making the region a center of Christian monasticism. Pilgrimage was a striking phenomenon in the Middle Ages. Great European pilgrimage centers throughout the eleventh and twelfth centuries were established when Muslim occupation deprived Christians of access to the Holy Land. People took to the road willingly in self-imposed penance. Soon an entire industry grew up along pilgrimage routes: abbeys to give lodging and hospices to give aid and protection.

Santiago de Compostela in northwest Spain is the most famous of the pilgrimage destinations. The remains of St. James, the first martyred apostle, were believed to have been brought to Spain from the Holy Land during the ninth century. After James's death

he was thrown into the sea. When recovered, his body was covered with barnacles and shells. The scallop is the symbol worn by pilgrims even today.

If you want to learn more, read *On Pilgrimage* by Jennifer Lash; *Sacred Places, Pilgrim Paths: An Anthology of Pilgrimage* by Martin Robinson; and *Memoirs of a Medieval Woman: The Life and Times of Margery Kempe* by Louise Collis. PDB

PLATONISM. The doctrines of Plato (427–247 B.C.E.) and the philosophical tradition that flourished from late antiquity until the Renaissance. As a young man Plato met Socrates and stayed with him until the execution of Socrates in 399 B.C.E. at the hands of the Athenian democrats. Plato then fled to Italy, Sicily, and Egypt. Returning to Athens, he founded the Academy, where Aristotle became his most prominent student. After a disastrous experiment at Syracuse, where in 367 B.C.E. he had become tutor to Dionysius the Younger, Plato was imprisoned and enslaved. Ransomed by a friend, he returned to the Academy, where he remained until his death.

Socrates had taught that *concepts* represent the reality of *things,* and that the world of concepts exists above the world of *things,* which are reflections of these concepts. Plato posited that ideas are objectively real (the foundation of scientific knowledge), that an unchangeable world of ideas exists apart from the world of *phenomena* and that humankind lives in a shadowland of appearances, whereas it formerly lived in the *real* world of ideas. Consequently, when the mind contemplates phenomena, it remembers the actual idea it had contemplated in its previous existence. The task of philosophy, therefore, is to enable the mind to rise from the world of *phenomena* to the world of the *numina,* or reality.

In Book Seven of The *Republic,* Plato offers the allegory of a cave where some people have been chained in a fixed condition since birth, only able to look at the cave's rear wall. There they see shadows cast by models of people, animals, and other objects held in front of the light of a fire and imagine they see the real world. When some of the prisoners escape from the cave, at first they know only pain from the dazzling light of the sun. As their eyes adjust and they begin to see real objects in color and all three dimensions, they initially think that they have gone mad. But eventually they will learn the true nature of reality and understand that all they had known was a shadow of an image of the real world. Here Plato lays out his principle idea. Imprisoned in a world of sense-experience, humankind will not reach the *real* world except by **contemplation**. This idea is called *realism* because it holds that ideas are eternally real, while the material world is only temporary. (The contrasting, Aristotelian view, *nominalism*, holds that the material world is real, while ideas are merely human-created generalizations or names, *nomines*, derived from our observation of similarities or patterns.) Many people will choose not to pursue enlightenment because it can be painful and upsetting.

In later developments of Platonism, especially **Neoplatonism**, the contrast between eternal, real ideas and the passing world became a contrast between a good, spiritual realm of pure intellect and an evil world of matter. This dualism provided a philosophical underpinning for **Gnosticism**, **Manichaeism**, **Catharism**, and other heresies.

Of the thirty-six dialogues reputedly authored by Plato, *Phaedrus*, *Protogoras*, *Phaedo*, and *The Republic* are universally accepted as genuine. RMH

PLOTINUS (ca. 205–70), Greek **Neoplatonist** philosopher and mystic. A native of Lycopolis, Plotinus took an interest in philosophy at age twenty-eight and studied for eleven years under Ammonius Saccas. After accompanying the Emperor Gordian (d. 243) on an expedition to Persia to acquaint himself with Eastern thought, he established his own school in Rome in 244. He began writing at age fifty-one. After his death his disciple Porphyry (ca. 232–ca. 303) published his fifty-four treatises in six *Enneads* (groups of nine).

There is considerable debate about how to interpret Plotinus. He clearly rejected Gnostic dualism and the Christian concept of redemption within history. In place of these he argued for an intellectual **mysticism** whose main object is to explain the connection between unity and multiplicity and to assist the individual to attain mystical union. At the top of the hierarchy of being is the One or the Good, who is beyond comprehension. Next in order come the intelligible world of ideas and then the World Soul, which serves as intermediary between the intelligible world and the material world. This World Soul creates all material things and makes the universe function in an orderly way. Individual (human) **souls** separate from the World Soul by a mysterious process and are able to enjoy a spiritual life, for, in their highest point, they can contemplate the divine. **Contemplation** is the most perfect activity in which humans can engage, for it leads to union with God. To reach the goal, souls must prepare themselves by purity of heart and ascetic discipline. They must turn away from material things and devote themselves to recollection until they "feel" an ineffable Presence. Plotinus's "natural mysticism" differs from Christian mysticism chiefly in that the soul can attain the goal by its own efforts, whereas in the Christian view, it can achieve that only by God's **grace**. Despite this difference, Plotinus exerted a major influence on Christian contemplatives, especially **Augustine** and **Pseudo-Dionysius**.

The *Enneads* of Plotinus are translated in five volumes by Stephen Mackenna. See also John M. Rist, *Plotinus: The Road to Reality.* EGH

PORETE, MARGUERITE (d. 1310), French **Beguine** mystic and writer. Much of Marguerite Porete's life is unknown. She is referred to as a member of a mendicant group called the Beguines and, judging from her book *The Mirror of Simple Souls*, she appears to have had some theological education. What we do know about her stems as much from the church's reaction to her book as from the book itself. She was brought before an ecclesial hearing on several occasions and, based on the content of *Mirror*, was burned at the stake for heresy on June 1, 1310, in Paris. Many copies of the *Mirror* survived in monasteries throughout Europe, testifying to its popularity. It is probable that **Meister Eckhart** knew of Porete and her work.

The Mirror of Simple Souls is written in allegorical form. The speakers are **Love**, **Soul**, Reason, etc. (eleven characters in all); and through their conversation, Porete speaks to those who would follow the mystical path she sets out. *Mirror* is rather like a mystic's training manual. Porete follows Soul's journey from **humility** to a state of **glory** that comes only after the body dies. The journey, as she describes it, has seven states or beings. In the seventh state the perfected soul returns to the first Being (God). Porete writes that those who deeply love and live lives of charity are annihilated by Love. Such souls no longer live under rule of reason, **will**, **virtue**, or laws. Annihilated souls are so focused on God that they no longer have need of these things. Porete insists that souls need no intermediary between themselves and God. The relationship of love is direct. Porete's way of annihilation and her insistence that even virtues become meaningless render the church and all of its regulations and doctrine unnecessary. Her method of moving toward **holiness** proved to be more of a threat than the church could tolerate.

"The French Heretic Beguine: Marguerite Porete" by Gwendolyn Bryant, a chapter in *Medieval Women Writers* (edited by Katharina M. Wilson) provides a helpful introduction, bibliography, and selections from *The Mirror of Simple Souls*. You may also want to consider *Marguerite Porete: Mirror of Simple Souls*, translated by Ellen L. Babinsky. SN

POSITIVE WAY. The *via positiva* (Latin) or kataphatic (Greek, "affirming") path refers to the revealed aspect of God's nature, to how God can be seen and understood through the believer's **experience** of living in the world. It stands in contrast to the **negative way** (*via neg-* *ativa* or apophatic path), in which God is experienced *beyond* words, concepts, and **imagery**—through silence, **desert**, **fasting**, experiences of purgation, and the soul's **dark night**. The positive path emphasizes the experience of God through the palpable gifts of creation—light, sounds, colors and senses, words and actions, concepts and images.

In Christian history **Pseudo-Dionysius**, around the late fifth century, speaks in his *Mystical Theology* about both paths, using as his framework the threefold process of purgation (apophatic experience), illumination (kataphatic experience), and union (integration of the two). In *Divine Names* his goal is to develop perfect praise of God through various attributes of God—beginning with goodness and ending with unity. Thus kataphatic theology is knowledge of God through practicing affirmations about the divine. Yet Pseudo-Dionysius is clear that all human affirmations fall short of the living reality of God; thus in *Mystical Theology* he promotes the balancing of an apophatic theology—akin to the experience of the dark night of the soul, where instead of God present as light, one may experience God as a dark ray.

In terms of Christian practice, although the Protestant reformers did not use the precise terminology of the positive and negative ways, **John Calvin** spoke of creation as the theater of God's glory. And both **Martin Luther** and Calvin endorsed **sexuality** and marriage and worldly work in contrast to more **ascetic** practices as the norm for believers. On the other hand, in terms of devotional practices, Luther would have rejected practices such as scaling the sacred stairs in Rome as attempts to earn God's love by **works**. Yet he never ceased to use a crucifix as an outward aid to devotion, fondling in his hands the image of Christ on the cross. In terms of devotional practices, later followers of Calvin and Zwingli were more iconoclastic, opposing any outward art forms used for devotional practices.

In the twentieth century kataphatic-apophatic terminology has been made more understandable through such writings as

Charles Williams's *The Descent of the Dove* and **Evelyn Underhill**'s *Mysticism.* In one sense, the plain **Quaker** meeting, with neither stained glass nor scriptures nor sacraments but rather primarily silence, would represent the ultimate in apophatic spirituality. Yet the Quaker experience also promotes the ultimate in kataphatic spirituality, since every meal is viewed as **Holy Communion** and all creation is the word of God. In a similar paradox, Eastern **Orthodox** worship, filled with hearing music, kissing **icons**, and smelling incense, actually emphasizes the mystery and wholly otherness of the divine beyond human thinking.

Luke's Gospel brings together the "positive way" of Jesus with the more "negative way" of John the Baptist: "For John the Baptist has come eating no bread and drinking no wine, and you say, 'He has a demon'; the Son of Man has come eating and drinking, and you say, 'Look, a glutton and a drunkard, a friend of tax collectors and sinners!'" (Luke 7:33-35).

The positive way represents the Resurrection with its emphasis on light, eating, and conversing, like the highlights of a Rembrandt painting. But it is only meaningful because of the negative way with the dark background of silence, empty spaces, and night. The integrated life has a rhythm of emptiness and fullness, negation and affirmation. KIG

POULAIN, R. P. AUGUSTIN (1836–1919), **Jesuit** mystical theologian and writer. In 1858 Poulain entered the Society of Jesus. He completed his studies, then taught mathematics at Metz and Angers, where he also directed the schools. For five years he was director of the artists' guild in Paris. Since Poulain was not known as a **mystical** theologian, his publication of *The Graces of Interior Prayer* surprised his associates. An immediate success, the book went through nine editions and was translated into several languages. While not a strong theologian and having no direct personal **experience** with the mystical states, he wrote a clear, didactic treatise on **prayer**. Considerable controversy was raised concerning the way he kept **ascetical** and mystical states dis-

tinct. His work contributed to the revival of interest in mystical theology, which had been neglected since the seventeenth century. LSP

POVERTY. Historically poverty has been, along with **chastity** and **obedience**, one of the three traditional monastic vows taken upon acceptance into a religious order, made especially central by **Francis of Assisi**. A vow of poverty is a promise to maintain an interior stance or attitude of **detachment** and **humility**.

Spiritual poverty differs from social poverty (being poor financially) in two significant ways. First, spiritual poverty is voluntary, whereas social poverty is usually involuntary. And second, spiritual poverty focuses on the interior stance or attitude of detachment as opposed to the focus on external needs in physical poverty. It can, however, as in the monastic context, include some elements of physical poverty, symbolized by the monk's relinquishing of all personal possessions. This physical poverty is a constant reminder of the inner spiritual **disposition** of poverty or detachment.

Before Christianity, poverty was seen as strictly social or financial and had negative connotations. In the book of Proverbs, for example, poverty is a sign of God's disfavor and an individual's disgrace: "The wealth of the rich is their fortress; the poverty of the poor is their ruin" (Prov. 10:15). "Poverty and disgrace are for the one who ignores instruction, but one who heeds reproof is honored" (Prov. 13:18). Poverty is seen not only as external and physical but as involuntary, imposed by God as punishment for **sin**.

The change in emphasis from an external, socially imposed poverty to a spiritual notion of poverty as a Christian virtue can be traced to the New Testament. In Luke 6:20, Jesus says, "Blessed are you who are poor, for yours is the kingdom of God." While an external and involuntary state of poverty is implied, the social and religious stigma associated with it has been removed. Matthew 5:3 introduces a more explicitly spiritual context when Jesus says, "Blessed are the poor in spirit, for theirs is the kingdom of heaven." "Poor in spirit" here can be interpreted to include a chosen or voluntary spiritual disposition of poverty or interior detachment from all things.

To understand the purpose and role of poverty (detachment) in the spiritual life, seeing it in relation to our human condition and our natural rebellion from that condition can be helpful. When we are born into the world we become a separate entity or being, automatically and objectively separated or detached from all things (symbolized by the cutting of the umbilical cord). From this perspective, our natural tendency to become attached to things is precisely because ontologically we are detached—isolated and cut off—from them. We seek to fill the void or emptiness (loneliness and isolation) created by this detachment by clinging (attaching) to people and things, including our own ideas and feelings. We unknowingly become slaves to our attachments or possessions as they influence our thinking, feeling, and acting.

As **Augustine** in the opening sentences of *Confessions* writes, "My soul is restless until it rests in you, O God." Our clinging to things, in order to find fulfillment, keeps us from finding true fulfillment, which can be found only in our relationship to God. The spiritual virtue of poverty is thus an intentional decision to embrace our true condition of detachment from the world and everything in it. This intentional detachment provides us with the spiritual freedom to deepen our relationship with God, in whom we have our source and being. Spiritual poverty helps us let go of our dependence upon things and to trust instead in our dependence upon God's love, grace, and forgiveness in Jesus Christ.

While most spiritual masters, including **Benedict** and **Teresa of Ávila**, see **humility** as the foundational virtue of the spiritual life, some, including **Meister Eckhart**, give this priority to spiritual poverty or detachment. Today **fasting** and tithing can be seen as spiritual exercises of detachment or poverty. JWK

PRAYER. Communication with God through thoughts, words, and gestures whereby we express what we believe about God and our relationship to God and to one another. God intends and initiates this relationship and we accept it. In prayer we express God's activity in and presence to us. In faith we pray believing that God is concerned about and responsive to human need.

Prayer is found in all generations, cultures, and faith traditions. We pray because we long to feel joined to something greater than ourselves and our own limited perspective. We yearn to connect our everyday lives with a purpose and will greater than our own. We seek an answer that brings sense to the senselessness that life sometimes hands us.

Prayer was an integral part of Jesus' life and mission. His prayers form the core of our understanding of prayer. Jesus prayed at his baptism (Luke 3:21-22), before important decisions (Luke 6:12), and throughout his ministry. He spent entire nights in prayer (Mark 6:46; Matt. 14:22-23; John 6: 15) and in acceptance of the **will of God** (Matt. 11:25-26; Luke 10:21). At his death he prayed for his persecutors (Luke 23:34) and for himself (Mark 15:34; Matt. 27:46), finally surrendering himself to God in prayer (Luke 23:46). Jesus taught about prayer by word and example: how and to whom we pray—the Father (Matt. 6:6; John 14:12-14; 16:24); for what and for whom we are to pray—pray in everything (Matt. 18:19); and how we can pray to be heard—in faith (Mark 11:22-24). The best-known prayer of Jesus is the **Lord's Prayer** taught to the disciples. The disciples were assured that wherever they gathered to pray, Jesus would be present (Matt. 18:19-20). The apostle Paul and other New Testament writers say that Jesus now intercedes for us in glory (1 John 2:1; Rom. 8:34).

There are two basic kinds of prayer. (1) In **adoration** and **thanksgiving** we respond in **awe** to God's abundant **providence**. **Psalms** of praise acknowledge God's goodness and greatness in creation (Ps. 8) and guiding the events of history (Ps. 30). (2) In petition and

intercession we respond to human weakness and need by asking for God's help (Ps. 33).

No one style of prayer suits all people. Because cultures, individual **personality** types, and needs differ, prayers also differ. Even when we choose a certain method of prayer, we will often make it uniquely our own. In **verbal prayer**, whether spoken aloud or internally, we may use a preset formula to assure that we do not miss any important aspects of our relationship with God or spontaneously respond to the circumstances of daily life. **Meditation** or mental prayer may concentrate on our feeling (**affective**) or our thinking (discursive) as we address God. In discursive prayer, reason predominates as we discuss and reason with God. In affective prayer we express feelings of love, trust, surrender, etc. Discursive prayer can leave us stranded or caught up in **distractions**, missing the mystery of interaction with God. A common development is to move from a more discursive to more affective prayer. Examples of meditative prayer include **guided imagery**, **examen**, and **confession**. While our mind or intellect (including our imagination) predominates when we meditate, in **contemplation** the **will** predominates as we turn our hearts to God in simple **love**. The mind becomes quiet and we may even be caught up in **ecstasy**. Examples of contemplative prayer include adoration and forms of the **prayer of the heart** such as **Centering Prayer** and **breath prayer**. Again a common development of prayer is a move from meditation to contemplation.

In contemporary times we can easily grow cynical about the relevance of prayer. We often look to science and technology rather than God to solve problems of global **evil** such as war, massive genocide, famine, and disease. We fail to see how prayer can affect the real world. Perhaps God is a divine, immutable being utterly unaffected by anything we do. Prayer may simply be an emotional release in intolerable situations, a cry when we can no longer remain silent. Perhaps it is a way to adapt ourselves to what God has already determined or to express a dependency no longer needed in a culture of self-sufficiency. These understandings are important to many who desire an intense prayer life. Dealing with them—and therefore with the question of who God is—is a crucial area of theology.

Prayer is life with a living God, life wholly attentive to the sober truth and reality of God. Our mind and heart open to God so that we may grow in **holiness** and so give God **glory**. It is a face-to-face encounter with the God who loves us with the unflinching **mercy** and self-offering that is **grace**. We give ourselves to God in return. As our trust in and dependence on God as Father and Mother deepen and intensify, we pray for growth in our relationship as sons and daughters to God and as brothers and sisters to one another. Prayer teaches us patience, **compassion**, awareness, and simplicity, leading us to an understanding of ourselves as a part of the greater **community** and connected to all of life. PDB

PRAYER FOR THE DEAD. Death is one of the great realities of life to which the church must respond with the Word of God. The prayer for the dead celebrates the life and death of a person and helps the ordinary Christian cope with bereavement.

In spite of the pharisaic custom in Judaism of praying for the departed, the early church, expecting the imminent return of Christ, understandably gave little energy to such prayer. Only as more and more believers "fell asleep" did the church begin the slow process of articulating a theology of death as well as the relationship of the living to the dead. From the walls of the catacombs we know that early prayers confidently celebrated the journey of the dead through the gates of death.

By 160 to 220, the time of **Tertullian**, Christians prayed for the refreshment of the departed souls on the anniversary of their death. From the fourth century we have the writings of **Augustine**, who prayed for his deceased mother, eagerly reminding God of her sinless life since her baptism. Prayers for the dead came to include **petitions** for **forgiveness**, thus forming the seedbed of belief in purgatory. By the fourth century, it was common to pronounce regular prayers for the dead. Especially in the case of **martyrs**, churches maintained lists of the dead for the purpose of prayer.

Today the prayer for the dead continues to root itself in the anguish of bereavement. Prayers for the dead usually take place in a worship service, either at a general memorial occasion such as All Saints' Day or at a funeral or memorial service. This service of prayer offers a celebration of the promise of resurrection; thanksgiving for the person that affirms, without false glorification, the life that has been lived; ministry to the grieving family, friends, and community; and transition for the church to express farewell and adjust to the changes of life without the deceased.

For further reading, see Gregory Dix's *The Shape of the Liturgy* or reflect on the prayers in your church's funeral service. PDB

PRAYER MEETING. The prayer meeting, in its simplest form, is a gathering of like-minded believers who come together for a time of extemporaneous prayers offered at the leading of the **Holy Spirit**. Scripture readings, addresses, and instruction may also be added. Often times of prayer are interlaced with times of singing. Such meetings offer informal spontaneous devotion in fellowship with others. This form of open prayer began with the **Pietist** movement of the seventeenth century and the evangelical revival of the eighteenth century. These renewal movements, led by mission preachers and evangelists, brought together small groups of converts, new or revived Christians who found encouragement and spiritual growth in times of free witness and prayer.

Today, with the continuing institutionalization of much public worship, spontaneous times of prayer and praise are frequently used in addition to (and sometimes immediately following) more formal worship services. PDB

PRAYER OF THE HEART. A simple form of prayer in which a mantra or short phrase is repeated to keep one's attention focused in order to attend to the presence of God in the moment. Within the Christian tradition of the East comes the breath prayer called the **Jesus Prayer**: "Lord Jesus Christ, Son of God, have mercy upon me, a sinner." Other short prayers in times of need, stress, or joy can be used: "Jesus, help me"; "O Lord, hear my prayer"; or "Praise be to thee, O God!" The prayer of the heart includes more specific forms such as **breath prayer** and **Centering Prayer**.

To pray a prayer of the heart, sit alone and in silence; bow your head and close your eyes; relax your breathing and with your imagination direct your mind from the head into the heart. Regulate your breathing. Rhythmic breathing disperses distracting thoughts. With each breath repeat, "Lord Jesus Christ, have mercy on me," either softly with your lips or in your mind. Find the place of your heart and abide there. When thoughts come, whether good or bad, set them aside. Be patient and peaceful and repeat the process frequently. Beginners should know that they will experience discomfort, but if they persist they will attain increasing joy.

A primary source is *Writings from the Philokalia on Prayer of the Heart*, translated by E. Kadloubovsky and G. E. H. Palmer. *The Way of a Pilgrim* is a Russian spiritual classic that has been newly translated by Helen Bacovcin. PDB

PRESENT MOMENT. Most of us rarely live in the present moment. We think we are living in the present, but the truth is that we tend to live either in the future, the past, or a combination of the two. Our bodies may be in the present but not our minds.

For example, many of us live mostly in the future. We focus on what we will do today, tomorrow, next week, next month, next year, or even twenty years down the road. This is true whether we talk about our work or the way we manage our families and home life. We constantly make plans, juggle schedules, check our calendars, and look at our watches.

Yet many of us are also consumed with the

past. Wounded physically, emotionally, or mentally, we have spent much of our lives reliving a trauma, wondering what we could or should have done differently. We have learned that it is psychologically healthy to know ourselves, to know our motivations, and to examine our past. But on a spiritual level exploring our past differs from being trapped in the past. When trapped in the past, we relive events over and over in our minds, slowly eroding our faith and our spirit.

The true spiritual life is lived radically in the present moment according to Jesus' teachings: "Therefore I tell you, do not worry about your life, what you will eat or what you will drink, or about your body, what you will wear.... But strive first for the kingdom of God and his righteousness, and all these things will be given to you as well. So do not worry about tomorrow, for tomorrow will bring worries of its own. Today's trouble is enough for today" (Matt. 6:25, 33-34). Living in the present moment means living in an immediate openness to God in the *now*.

To live in the present moment requires an abandoning surrender and a trust that God will take care of us. This does not mean that we have to give up planning for the future or exploration of the past. We cannot live life without planning for the future. We have to be able to make plans about what we will do tomorrow, the next day, and next year. If it is our role to plan for a large conference several months from now or if we have to plan a family budget for the next year, we do what we can and then give the results to God. We let go of our worries and make our plans in the present in cooperation with God. Realizing God's presence in our moment-to-moment life, guiding us, celebrating with us, and cherishing life with us, we then listen to God in surrender. We can also explore the past with God in the present moment, examining our pains and struggles and then giving them to God.

Living in the present moment is simply the recognition that God is with us now in this moment and that we can share it with God. This is how we touch eternity, for God's eternal kingdom touches us whenever we live in complete openness to God.

Two classic writers on living in the present moment are **Jean Pierre de Caussade** and Brother **Lawrence of the Resurrection**. NGS

PROPHETIC PRAYER. A phrase used by German theologian **Friedrich Heiler** in his scientific study of religion to describe prayer addressed to God for "help in time of need" (Heb. 4:14), expecting God to take part in the world and in human life. He wanted to distinguish prophetic prayer from another popular form of prayer known as **mystical** prayer.

The differences between mystical prayer and prophetic prayer are apparent. Rather than being reflective, as is mystical prayer, prophetic prayer is straightforward; rather than being founded in **discipline** and self-denial, it arises spontaneously from crisis and need; and rather than coming out of refined meditative techniques, it is hostile to fixed forms and is a simple outpouring of the heart. According to Heiler, the truest test of prophetic prayer is that it culminates in the desire for the coming of the kingdom of God.

Perhaps the intent of Heiler's study, and thus his classification of prophetic prayer, was to assert that Christians do not need to have a mystical experience of God to validate their prayer. Common, spontaneous prophetic prayer is equally valuable and authentic.

Heiler's work is available in translation as *Prayer: A Study in the History and Psychology of Religion*. PDB

PROVIDENCE. God's continuous, parental care of the world. After creating the world, God did not leave it to run like some well-oiled machine or abandon it to be destroyed by evil. Instead God promises to sustain it through the abiding presence of the **Holy Spirit**, God's breath of life (Ps. 104:30), based on the reconciling work of Jesus Christ (Col. 1:17). God's wisdom and power constantly uphold, bless, and guide this world. Confidence in the providential hand of our heavenly Father enables us to live in the assurance that

God is present and actively works in our lives for good. Scripture celebrates many concrete situations in which God's providence expresses itself, but we can summarize the innumerable instances with three affirmations.

God faithfully preserves what God has created (Neh. 9:6; Heb. 1:3), protects it against any irrevocable harm and destruction (Gen. 8:21), and provides for the needs of creatures (Ps. 104:10-18, 27-28). Trusting this element of providence helps free us from anxiety in sickness or poverty (Matt. 6:25-34). It teaches us patience when things go against us (James 1:2-3), and gratitude when things go well (1 Thess. 5:18). God's providential goodness to evildoers defines our duty to love even enemies (Matt. 5:43-48).

God enables our actions as God's creatures, so that we live and move in God (Acts 17:28). God does not control our **wills**; rather God's power cooperates with our wills and actions. Thus our activity and divine activity are not mutually exclusive. We have no basis here for laxity, indifference, or resignation. The fact that God is at work calls for our faithful prayers and efforts as coworkers (1 Cor. 3:9).

God guides all things toward a purposeful end (Rom. 8:28). We do not always understand God's leading, but we find comfort in the knowledge that God shepherds us (Ps. 23). Christian traditions differ over the degree of God's activity in our care, particularly over the extent of God's involvement in free human actions and in the prevention of evil. Belief in providence raises such challenging riddles. (See G. C. Berkouwer, *The Providence of God.*) But the **cross** and resurrection of Jesus give us confidence that God overcomes evil with good, leading us to see in everyday life providential moments and gracious occasions for spiritual growth. These opportunities include times of **solitude** as well as our relationships with family and friends, our callings in work and service and leisure, the cultural and civic contexts in which we live, our experiences of gain and loss, success and disappointment. (See V. Raymond Edman, *The Disciplines of Life.*)

God's providence sustains our efforts in **spiritual formation** in much the same way that it sustains our labor in farming. Producing a crop demands hard work. We need to cultivate and fertilize the soil, plant seed and water fields, and perhaps remove weeds or tend vines. Then we wait patiently until it comes time to harvest the crop (James 5:7). But for all the effort we expend, the seed mysteriously germinates and grows according to its own intrinsic laws. God's providence functions both by governing the development of the plant and by empowering the efforts of the farmer.

Our growth in godliness also has an element of providential mystery to it. Wise, patient application of Christian **disciplines** can remove obstacles to growth and nurture it. But God gives the increase (1 Cor. 3:6-7). Even our fruitful practice of the disciplines can take place only because of God's providential care as God works in us both to will and to work for God's good pleasure (Phil. 2:13). JMB

PSALMS. The "songbook" of the Bible. These ancient poems, written over a period of several centuries and collected by unknown editors, were the hymnal of the second Temple in Jerusalem. Organized into five books, perhaps to model the five books of the Law, each book ends with a doxology and the last book with a doxological psalm. This pattern of organization suggests different collections. Although many Psalms are marked as "of David," Psalm 72 ends with the phrase, "The prayers of David son of Jesse are ended." Modern scholars believe that the Psalms come from many different authors over several centuries. These deeply personal poetic songs are unique among the sacred scriptures because they speak directly to the human situation. Beloved by Christians and Jews alike, the Psalms have been so important in Christian devotional life that the book of Psalms is often included with the New Testament in abbreviated pocket Bibles. Some **monastic** systems included daily recitation of the complete Psalter. The **Book of Common Prayer** has a schedule to read all 150 Psalms over a month.

Among the 150 Psalms, nearly half are songs of lament in which the author cries to God from a situation of great distress. These laments are never specific enough to identify the malady that causes the psalmist to cry out and are thus able to cross the great gulf of cultural difference between the time of their writing and our time. The hymns of praise and thanksgiving are also universal rather than specific. These ancient poems continue to speak for us and with us, enabling us to sense the presence of the **holy**. The Psalms have been called a "mirror of the human soul." Many contemporary hymnals contain fresh settings for singing the Psalms. HLR

PSEUDO-DIONYSIUS (late fifth century?), probably a Syrian monk who wrote as Dionysius the Areopagite, Paul's Athenian convert (Acts 17:34). The prefix "pseudo-" (false) is used by modern scholars to distinguish the anonymous monk from the biblical Dionysius. Since the latter had supposedly died in 96, it was commonly assumed that the works of Pseudo-Dionysius had been written in the first century and so were the teaching of the earliest church on mystical theology. Pseudo-Dionysius attempted to unite **Neoplatonic** philosophy with Christian mystical theology. The earliest known citation of his works is in 553 at the Second Council of Constantinople. The Eastern branches of Christendom, already sympathetic to Platonic thought, readily absorbed the Dionysian writings.

By the ninth century, Latin translations of these works by **John Scotus Eriugena** reached the West, profoundly affecting medieval Christian doctrine and **spirituality**. The writings of Pseudo-Dionysius consist of ten letters and four treatises: *On the Divine Names, On Mystical Theology, On the Celestial Hierarchy,* and *On the Ecclesiastical Hierarchy.* In the fourteenth century, the author of ***The Cloud of Unknowing*** (a book strongly influenced by Pseudo-Dionysius) produced an English translation of *The Mystical Theology* as *Dionise Hid Divinite.*

On the Divine Names, perhaps the most important of the Dionysian writings in scope and content, presents in thirteen chapters an explanation of the divine names. These names can only be learned from scripture and afford us an imperfect knowledge of God. God transcends all affirmation, negation, and intellectual conception. Only the force of God's **love** reveals God's true nature. Creatures absorb according to their nature more or less of God's radiated light, which grows weaker the farther it descends. Pseudo-Dionysius presents this procession of all created things from God as the result of the exuberance of being in the Godhead itself.

In *On the Celestial Hierarchy* Pseudo-Dionysius takes the names of his nine choirs of **angels** from the various lists of heavenly beings in scripture and arranges them in three triads: seraphim, cherubim, and thrones; virtues, dominations, and powers; and principalities, archangels, and angels. These choirs are less intense in their knowledge and love of God as they descend in the hierarchy, their sphere of activity farther from God's throne. Pseudo-Dionysius likens this diminishment to a ray of light that grows more indistinct the farther it travels from its source.

Perhaps the best known of the Eastern writers influenced by Pseudo-Dionysius is **Gregory Palamas**, the fourteenth-century mystic. A recent English translation by Colm Luibheid is *Pseudo-Dionysius: The Complete Works.* RMH

PSEUDO-MACARIUS (fourth century), monk. Purported author of *The Fifty Spiritual Homilies,* this Macarius carries the "Pseudo" title to distinguish him from the Coptic **desert father,** Macarius the Egyptian. The only thing to be said about the *Homilies* with certainty is that they originate from Syria or northern Mesopotamia and belong to a much larger corpus of material including *The Great Letter,* two other letters, some twenty dialogues, and thirty short collections of sayings.

The experiential, heart spirituality of Pseudo-Macarius is concerned primarily with **unceasing prayer** and an idea of progressive **perfection** similar to the vision of the Christian life in the Cappadocian fathers, **Gregory of Nyssa** in particular. As a more Semitic tradition it is often contrasted to the more intellectual or Hellenistic approach to matters of the spirit associated with **Evagrius** and **Pseudo-Dionysius**. Other recurrent themes include the internalization of the spiritual life, the importance and activity of the **Holy Spirit**, and the cosmic dimensions of a dualistic spiritual struggle. Prayer is understood primarily as a place of spiritual **discernment** in which love functions as the primary interpretive key. The spiritual life is essentially a synergistic process in which the believer cooperates with the **grace** of the Holy Spirit. **John Wesley** published extracts from the *Homilies* in the eighteenth century and was strongly influenced by the Macarian vision of Christian perfection.

George A. Maloney translated and edited *Pseudo-Macarius: The Fifty Spiritual Homilies and the Great Letter.* PWC

PURGATION, PURGATIVE WAY. Classically, writers on the spiritual life have described the way of purgation as the starting point for beginners who accept the call to follow Jesus. Continuing in the ways of **illumination** and **union**, this threefold process of unfolding, discovering, and reclaiming the image of Christ is the journey of a lifetime.

The first principal movement, the way of purgation, describes the **soul** embarking on the spiritual life. Often God's invitation to come closer is awakened in us through an experience while attending a church service, or upon hearing or reading something spiritual, or even through a simple conversation with someone. Nudged by the **Holy Spirit**, lured through everyday life experiences, beginners start desiring to cooperate actively with God's **grace**. Once awakened, beginners in the spiritual life seek to become more aware of God's presence in their lives. Drawn by God's inviting love (or prevenient grace), they yearn for the deeply spiritual. Through a process of purgation, or purifying the senses, the Holy Spirit continues to lead beginners into a deeper, though at times painful, self-knowledge and a more accurate understanding of and identification with the **Paschal mystery** of Christ's own **suffering**, death, and resurrection.

This is the main focus of the purgative way: becoming more aware and appreciative that God is God, not I. Coming to this realization requires interior and exterior **detachment** from attitudes, thoughts, and behaviors that bind and enslave the true self, the deepest-me-in-Christ. This purifying process is what leads beginners to stay focused on God and not self. Paul calls Christians to "lay aside the works of darkness and put on the armor of light," that is, "put on the Lord Jesus Christ, and make no provision for the flesh, to gratify its desires" (Rom. 13:12, 14). Answering that call involves a constant inward and outward struggle. So while enjoying the "honeymoon" of sensing God's presence, beginners are simultaneously drawn to let go of attachments, sinful inclinations, temptations, indeed anything that keeps them from the fullness of life in Christ.

Humility is a key **disposition** of the heart, a virtue that begins to form as one progresses along the purgative path. **Teresa of Ávila** describes humility as walking in the truth of who you are. Inspired to read the **scriptures** more, beginners feed and nurture their minds, imaginations, and memories with God's Word. Feeling supported, nurtured, and uplifted by the Word, they also feel challenged, invited, and confused. Classical spiritual writers like Teresa of Ávila and **John of the Cross** speak of the "active and passive nights of sense and spirit." During this journey of purification (and it never ends) into Christlikeness, we will experience the "active night of sense" and the "passive night of sense." As imperfect people of God, we can use our senses (knowingly and unknowingly) against ourselves. Active purgation of our senses involves working to overcome major obstacles that inhibit or block spiritual living and spiritual progress. It involves letting go of excessive or selfish desires and deliberately choosing what is life-giving over what feels awful, humiliating, or embarrassing.

In passive purgation God does something that we can only be open to and receive. God's grace can only be graciously received. It cannot be forced or hurried. Passive purgation of the senses is sometimes called the "winter of the soul." Things (even spiritual things) that once gave us joy now seem dull and tasteless. Unable to meditate, feeling an aversion to spiritual matters, we seem stuck in aridity or **dryness**. **Catherine of Siena** writes that we are being invited by God into this "night" (**darkness**) to let go of or be detached from the constant need for the sensible and spiritual experience of God's presence with us. Do we want just the **consolation** (good feelings) of God, or do we want God alone?

Classically, the "prayer of simplicity"— where we simply and humbly rest in Christ's presence, able only to say, "Your will be done"—is the apex of the active and passive nights of sense. This bittersweet time is normal and necessary as we progress into the next phase, illumination. EKM

Q

QUAKERS. Members of the Society of Friends founded by **George Fox**. Quaker **spirituality** is based on the conviction that God may be experienced today just as in the time of Moses or the prophets or the apostles. The key to this experience is steadfast attention to the "Light Within, the light referred to in the Gospel of John as "the true light, which enlightens everyone" (John 1:9). George Fox did not consider the Light a "spark of the Divine." It symbolized, rather, a stream that flows constantly from its divine source, something human beings can **experience**. Attending to the living Christ takes place *individually* among the Friends but, even more, *corporately* in the silent Meeting, the most distinctive characteristic of Quaker spirituality. Quaker **mysticism** has a corporate character. Meetings wrestle long and hard to discern the sense of the Spirit's guidance regarding critical issues. The aim is holy **obedience** that results from **discernment** of the **will of God** not only individually but also corporately.

From the very beginning, Quaker inward piety has resulted in pronounced prophetic and social concern. Many Quakers look to **John Woolman** as the model of Quaker spirituality. No other Christian group has surpassed the Friends in their activities on behalf of societal transformation. They have not shared with other Protestants the low view of human nature that causes some to throw up their hands in despair and avoid taking action. They have accentuated the goodness in nature; indeed, they consider all things **sacramental** and thus do not single out **baptism** or **Holy Communion** as sacraments. Although George Fox and most Quakers held **scripture** in high regard, they did not place it on the same level as the living Christ.

Quaker writers include **Isaac Penington**, **William Penn**, **Rufus Jones**, **Douglas V. Steere**, **Thomas Kelly**, **D. Elton Trueblood**, and **Richard Foster**. For further reading, see *Quaker Spirituality*, edited by Douglas V. Steere. EGH

QUIETISM. A spiritual movement located primarily in seventeenth-century France. In contrast to **Jansenism**, which suspected **contemplative** prayer and stressed moral uprightness and personal effort, Quietism distrusted human initiative and preached total **abandonment** to **grace**. Its roots go back to the **desert fathers and mothers**, the Rhineland mystics, and the Spanish **Carmelites**. A sort of proto-Quietism emerged in sixteenth-century Italy without stirring much controversy.

Miguel de Molinos (1628–96) developed Quietism as a movement by writing that only contemplative (purely passive) prayer leads to spiritual **perfection**. Practitioners avoid all strenuous **ascetic** efforts in order to concentrate entirely on inner quiet and abandon. He influenced German Protestants and Pietists. Madame **Guyon** (1648–1717) was a Catholic laywoman whose doctrine included the idea of the spiritual life as a process of disappropriation, a growing **detachment** that allows God to take gradual possession of the soul, and the concept that the spiritual life moves from lower to higher **stages**. Madame Guyon was influential among Protestants, including Englishmen such as **John Wesley**. Madame Guyon greatly influenced **François Fénelon** (1651–1715). His defense of Quietism in

Maxims of the Saints, translated into English, won a following in Great Britain that persisted throughout the eighteenth century. **Jean Pierre de Caussade** (1675–1751) promoted self-abandonment to divine **providence** (surrender to God's will) and humanity's duty to carry out the **will of God** in the **present moment**. Some consider his work the high point of the Quietist movement.

Quietism's influence is seen in the resurgence of interest in Christian contemplation, **meditation**, and **Centering Prayer**. WW

R

RAHNER, KARL (1904–84), German **Jesuit** theologian. One of the most influential Catholic theologians of the twentieth century, his theology may be called "a theological **spirituality**" because of its particular relevance for understanding **spiritual formation**. Not simply an academic, Rahner was a prolific writer of books on **prayer** and devotion and commentaries on the Ignatian *Spiritual Exercises*.

As a Jesuit, Rahner was influenced by Ignatian **mysticism**'s emphasis on finding God in all things. His theological anthropology (understanding of human nature) was that human beings are oriented toward and long for that Holy Mystery we call God. Rahner identified the human being as "spirit-in-world." All our human **experience** is a path whereby God may reach us. He believed in the intimate connection between the divine and the human and opposed a dichotomy between the sacred and the secular.

God's self-communication has occurred in human history and still occurs. The challenge, according to Rahner, is to be alert for signs and clues of God's presence in daily life. He believed God is in the ordinary, and our task is to find and serve God in daily existence.

Rahner's understanding of spirituality centered on the intellect, not as cognitive ability but as the attainment of knowledge of God that constitutes human fulfillment. Faith is our intimate knowing of God and cannot be proven by intellectual reasoning, only known by surrendering to the Holy Mystery. He wrote about "spiritual fortitude," or the need to pray faithfully even when God seems silent. He called prayer "a fundamental act of human existence" that brings us to God in total trust and **love**. To worry about the right way to pray may prevent prayer from happening. Prayer is not something we have to grasp for but is already within us. The history of prayer should prove to us that prayer is not magic and does not stop killing, disease, or evil. But prayer places us before God, revealing the sheer intensity of God's everlasting love.

Rahner recognized the spirituality of children and argued that they should not be treated as miniature adults who need to have beliefs and doctrines instilled in them. Rather children should be provided with opportunities to experience and know God as modeled by caring adults.

Rahner's writings include *Foundations of Christian Faith* (tough going but worth the effort), *Christian at the Crossroads*, and *Prayers for a Lifetime*. See also Geffrey B. Kelly, *Karl Rahner: Theologian of the Graced Search for Meaning.*
SEW

RAUSCHENBUSCH, WALTER (1861–1918), American Baptist preacher, professor, and proponent of the social gospel. Rauschenbusch saw himself standing in the tradition of the Old Testament prophets and Jesus. As a pastor in New York City, he had been deeply moved by the devastating effects of the 1893 depression. He opposed what he saw as the private, otherworldly piety of the churches, and came to believe that Jesus died as much for social as individual sins, for the kingdom of God and not the church. Since the church has never understood this, he argued, it has never really understood Jesus. He helped found the Society of Jesus (later the Brotherhood of the Kingdom) and published a periodical, *For the Right*, that called for the formation of a Christian socialist movement. He believed that God opposes capitalism in its method, spirit, and results, and that the social gospel calls for an expansion of the scope of salvation—that repentance be preached to the mighty who have "ridden humanity to the mouth of hell." In 1897 he joined the faculty of Rochester Theological Seminary and in 1902 became professor of church history.

His writings, *Christianity and the Social Crisis, Prayers of the Social Awakening, Christianizing the Social Order, The Social Principles of Jesus,* and *A Theology for the Social Gospel,* gained him recognition as the major spokesperson of the social gospel movement in the United States. The movement sought to apply Christian ethics to the social problems of industrialized society through fair wages, decent working hours, an end to child labor, and the nationalization of the coal and iron industries.

Rauschenbusch regarded himself as an evangelist seeking to win men and women to new birth in Christ and an agent of social as well as individual salvation. He died in 1917, a misunderstood and disappointed man, with "brother fighting brother" in World War I. RMH

READING, SPIRITUAL. A spiritual **discipline** aimed at the formation of conscience, so that we may live in **conformity to the will of God**. We read to be changed. A deliberate, unrushed, reflective reading of the **biography**, advice, poetry, and teaching of trusted authors, ancient and modern, can help us overcome the anxiety of self-discovery in the face of the reality of God. All people, including Christians, have self-serving justifications and defenses of attitudes and behaviors in conflict with God's self-revelation in Jesus. These need changing as we grow in likeness to God in Christ. A spiritual reading of and mature reflection on **scripture** can effectively help us adjust with joy and gratitude to God's saving and sanctifying **grace**.

Traditionally spiritual reading has been of two kinds. First, reading the Bible as God's revelation "from above" (beyond us) is the primary source of intellectual and **affective** spiritual life. The Bible, both Old and New Testaments, is the testimony of inspired writers who report and reflect, accurately and authoritatively, on God's saving acts in history.

As we read and meditate on the text, God's **Holy Spirit** opens us to prayer and praise. Our knowledge of and the depth of our commitment to God increase through such reading. The Bible is necessary reading for spiritual growth because, as the church witnesses in its creeds, biblical teaching is the basis for right belief, right worship, and right action. Such reading of the Bible has been referred to as *lectio divina* (divine reading). In the **monastic** tradition, the chanting of **psalms** is also regarded as *lectio divina.*

Second, reading respected Christian guides "from below" (among us) helps us sense the humanness of God's interaction with God's people. Others have walked the path before us, and we can profit from their **experience** and insight. This is especially true as we grow in prayer and the awareness of God in nature, the liturgy, and relationships with others. While desirable, this literature is optional, that is, it is not saving or sanctifying. It may lead to grace but it is not grace itself. In addition, the quality rather than quantity of the reading is more important. Though such reading helps us probe issues, raise questions, and learn **humility**, it cannot effect what it reveals. Only the Spirit of God imparts and cultivates the life hoped for by those moved to write for the church's benefit. Spiritual reading may be either a private or group exercise and is, for many, connected with the preaching and teaching of scripture.

As a term, *spiritual reading* is rather recent. Quite often histories, theologies, and theories of spiritual development do not mention spiritual reading, except as *lectio divina.* Yet clearly Christians began to read and rely on certain authors as defenders of the faith or as safe guides around the pitfalls of trial and temptation in this life. Though the type and tone of such literature shifted with changing times, customs, and needs across the centuries, three things remained central. First, all extra-biblical reading depended on scripture for its value, always returning to the "written Word." Second, all extra-biblical literature moved the faithful to **prayer** and praise. Generally spiritual literature assumes that all of life is to become prayer to God. Third, all extra-biblical reading cultivated humility and **obedience**. At first, these Christian **virtues** were private, but eventually they took on a social face. Who we are is not only important to God but to other people as well. Christian social values are intertwined with the **community**, both as church *and* as the world around us.

A review of spiritual reading as a Christian **discipline** reveals the following general trends from the early church to the present: movement from (1) separation from society to a tolerance or affirmation of society; (2) an almost exclusive interest in the knowledge of God to the **experience** of God; (3) avoidance of religious life outside one's group or church to a more ecumenical spirit; (4) little concern for the natural world to an emphasis on the environmental dimensions of spirituality; (5) male dominance to an inclusiveness with regard to female authors and guides; (6) mandating the shape of spiritual development to the creativity of structuring one's own approach; (7) self-denial to self-expression; (8) an exclusive emphasis on Jesus' divinity to stress on Jesus' humanity; (9) a consuming introspection to social concern; and (10) exclusive use of printed books to increasing use of audio books and film.

For a helpful overview of Christian **spirituality** with implications for spiritual reading, see *Exploring Christian Spirituality: An Ecumenical Reader*, edited by Kenneth J. Collins, or *A Practical Guide to Spiritual Reading* by **Susan A. Muto**. The following classics offer a good start in spiritual reading: *Imitation of Christ* by **Thomas à Kempis**; *The Cost of Discipleship* by **Dietrich Bonhoeffer**; and *New Seeds of Contemplation* by **Thomas Merton**. JLM

RECEPTIVITY. Openness to God's **love**, guidance, and power; a fundamental concept of critical importance to the divine-human relationship. It serves as the basis for all healing and, along with rest and trust, forms the heart of prayerful **contemplation**.

The Bible defines a human being as one

made "in the image of God." We are created enough like God to be in relationship and communication with each other, able to respond to God's outreaching **grace**. **Saints** and mystics have said we have been graced by "a capacity for God," a receptivity built into our very nature. Without that capacity, God could not ask or command us to follow or obey. Without it we would not pray and could not receive answers to our prayer. Without it we could not accept God's love, guidance, strength, or the **Holy Spirit**. Indeed, Christ asked his disciples to "receive the Holy Spirit" (John 20:22). Because we can receive that Spirit and its gifts, we can be instruments, channels, vessels, and temples of God's life and love. Paul puts it succinctly in 1 Corinthians 4:7: "What do you have that you did not receive? And if you received it, why do you boast as if it were not a gift?" In 2 Corinthians 4:7 he explains, "We have this treasure in clay jars, so that it may be made clear that this extraordinary power belongs to God and does not come from us."

Human beings receive automatically and unconsciously as they grow in the womb and later breathe in, see, hear, and are nourished by food and love. But we receive consciously, intentionally, and purposefully as well. We not only hear; we listen (a deeper level of consciousness). We do not just look, but we can perceive and understand. We not only talk to God; we can listen and drink in God's presence through **meditation** and **contemplation**. We can live consciously, in awareness. To learn more about conscious receptivity, read *Receptive Prayer: A Christian Approach to Meditation* by Grace Adolphsen Brame. GAB

REGENERATION. A theological term for rebirth or second birth. Regeneration is brought about by the action of the **Holy Spirit** to transform us so that we experience a new birth, also referred to as being "born again" or "born from above." Key biblical texts on regeneration or the new birth are John 3:5; Titus 3:5; and Matthew 19:28. According to John 3:3 Jesus told the Pharisee Nicodemus that no one can see the kingdom of God without being born from above. Jesus compared the new birth to the action of the wind in John 3:8: "The wind [spirit] blows where it wills" (RSV). We can be sure of its presence but cannot predict how or when it will work. Therefore the new birth is a mystery that is beyond our complete understanding and control. Paul spoke of death to the old state of sin and new life in the risen Christ.

Reformed theologians debated whether regeneration occurred in **baptism** or only as a result of an experience of repentance and **conversion** at the age of reason. Some held that the early church understood baptism to be a sacramental reenactment of Jesus' promise of new birth and taught that baptismal regeneration brought infants and children as well as adults into its fold. Evangelicals argued baptism could not be relied upon for assurance of salvation. Marks of the new birth, according to **John Wesley** are **faith**, **hope**, and **love**. Regeneration implies expanded access to God.

For further reading, see Peter Toon, *Born Again: A Biblical and Theological Study of Regeneration*, and John Wesley's sermon, "The New Birth." SEW

RETREATS. Intentional times alone with God to listen and respond to the **Holy**, possibly interspersed with individual or communal guidance or **spiritual direction**. In the history of Christian **spirituality** retreats have played a primary role for those who seek a deepening relationship with the Creator. Retreats may be individual or communal and will embody rest, renewal, and a reclamation of the awareness of our belovedness; space for reflection on **scripture**, creation, and our own lives, leading to deepening **prayer**; stillness, **silence**, and **solitude** received as gifts from a loving Creator; a necessary **discipline** in **spiritual formation**; and willingness to be challenged and redirected as we **discern** God's movement in our lives.

Following their highly successful mission (Mark 6:30-31) the disciples returned to Jesus and told him with great enthusiasm of lives healed and transformed through their ministry. Jesus' reply made clear to them their need for rest, quiet, and reflection—for a time of retreat from ministry. "Come away to a deserted place all by yourselves and rest a while," he invited, setting a pattern for them already established in his own life. Periods of withdrawal, often into a desert place, sustained Jesus and enabled him to keep focused on God's call. Today the word *retreat* is used widely and frequently even in the corporate world, often referring to a planning or development time apart for executives. The purpose of a spiritual retreat is to redirect our gaze on God, to listen to the Creator in order to find renewal and redirection in our lives.

Retreats take many forms and may vary in length from a few hours to a month or more. In a "guided retreat" the leader enables retreatants to experience reflection, silence, **worship**, and prayer through the offering of meditations on scripture. Music, art, movement, **journal** writing, and small-group discussion may be included. Some guided retreats may focus on a theme or book or be offered for specific groups, such as parents, youth, or older adults. A "quiet day" offers a brief time away from daily routines and includes silence and reflection, often conducted in a church setting. The content of a quiet day will be similar to that of a guided retreat, though it is important not to try to pack too much material into this shorter time.

A "preached retreat" is usually offered in a church or monastic setting in conjunction with regular worship times or "offices." The conductor gives addresses followed by silence for personal prayer. There is no group interaction, but individual conferences and/or **confession** are available.

A "directed retreat" provides regular meetings between the retreatant and her or his "director," whose role is to listen, guide, and support the retreatant's developing relationship with God. Ignatian retreats fall into this category and are usually eight or thirty days in duration. Distractions are minimized by limiting activities, conversation, and reading materials.

"Private retreats" may benefit those who have experienced retreats in the past and are ready to choose time alone in a context conducive to **contemplation**. This type of retreat has no director, but a rhythm of regular worship and simple accommodations, food, and lifestyle supports the retreatant's desire to place herself or himself simply in the presence of God. "At home retreats" are an important alternative for those unable to attend retreats due to infirmity or childcare responsibilities. Often a book will be used to offer an outline, and the retreat leader will meet in person or by telephone with the retreatant. Choosing an intentional time and creating sacred space are important constituents of the experience.

Clergy often provide leadership for retreats, but many laypersons are gifted in this ministry. Increased attendance at retreat centers and monasteries highlights the need for more leaders who are equipped to offer guidance through spiritual retreats, and the need for training is now being addressed through training centers such as Stillpoint Ministries. Retreats International offers an online directory of retreat centers.

For more information on leading retreats, you might read *All Ground Is Holy: A Guide to the Christian Retreat* by Jeanette L. Angell. EJC

RICHARD OF ST. VICTOR (d. 1173), mystical theologian. Born in Scotland, Richard entered the Abbey of Saint-Victor in Paris, becoming superior in 1159 and prior in 1162. Richard analyzed the abilities of the soul and forms of knowledge. He taught **contemplation** as a prime function of **faith**, searching after insight and **union** with God. Through a loving contemplation of God, divine gifts combine with the soul's desires gradually to raise the soul to a **vision** of the divine reality.

Benjamin Major and *Benjamin Minor*, Richard's primary works, outline six stages of contemplation moving from self-love to complete absorption into the Divine Beloved, supreme goodness, and perfect **love**. His

Latin writings influenced **Bonaventure** and the Franciscan mystics. *Selected Writings on Contemplation*, edited and translated by Clare Kirchberger, includes his work. LSP

ROLLE, RICHARD (ca. 1300–49), English mystic and author known as the Hermit of Hamphole. Rolle was born in Yorkshire, England. Although his parents had their own farm, they could not afford to send him to the university. Thomas de Neville, archdeacon of Durham, paid for Rolle's tuition at Oxford. Perhaps Rolle's contact with the Franciscan friars influenced him to leave Oxford before completing his degree. For whatever reason Rolle felt compelled to leave his home and follow his call to become a hermit, a life he followed for thirty-one years with the help of various patrons. Toward the end of his life Rolle moved to Hamphole and served as spiritual director to an anchoress, Margaret Kirkby, and to the nuns of a nearby Cistercian convent. He died on September 29, 1349.

Although Rolle was never canonized, his writings were highly regarded even two hundred years after his death. He was the first English mystic to write in both English and Latin. His best-known Latin works were *Incendium Amoris (The Fire of Love)* and *Emendatio Vitae (The Mending of Life)*. His English writings reached a broader audience, including lay men and women. These writings included *The Form of Living* and many translations of the **Psalms**. In fact, Rolle's translation of the Psalter was so good that John Wycliffe used it in the development of the English Bible. Rolle was an advocate of **affective** mysticism. He defined **contemplation** as knowing God truly, desiring God only, and loving God completely. He encouraged his readers to avoid worldly honor, to hate vainglory, to renounce materialism, and to fix their attention and love on Christ. Best known for his description of mystical union with God, he said that a spiritual flame kindled and ignited devotion so deep that his soul burned like **fire**.

To learn more about this mystical union, read Rolle's *The Fire of Love*. ASJ

ROMERO, OSCAR (1917–80), Salvadoran archbishop and **martyr**. When a conservative Catholic bishop was selected as archbishop of San Salvador on February 22, 1977, political activists were disappointed and El Salvador's elite oligarchy delighted. But soon after his consecration Romero became passionately aware of the political oppression of the poor. A major reason for so sudden a change was that on March 12, Romero officiated at the funeral of his close friend Rutilio Grande, who, as pastor of the rural parish in Aguilares, had been ambushed and murdered along with two parishioners.

Archbishop Romero put into practice the belief that Christ made his classroom of redemption among the poor. Romero spent time with the persecuted and families of "the disappeared" and spoke out to the powerful whose influence could ameliorate violence. Just weeks before his death in 1980, Romero wrote to American president Jimmy Carter, urging a halt to further military assistance to the military junta, thus averting greater bloodshed. The day before his assassination Romero appealed directly to the Salvadoran military to refuse illegal orders, saying the peasants they were killing were their own brothers and sisters.

Romero often stood before the altar and declared to his congregation that if the government should take away the church's radio station, close down its newspaper, and kill all the priests and the bishop too, then each one present must be "God's microphone." His words were prophetic as he said that if they killed him he would rise again in the hopes of the Salvadoran people. On March 24, 1980, he was shot and killed while celebrating Eucharist in the chapel of the Carmelite Sisters' cancer hospital where he lived.

Romero's writings were compiled and translated by James R. Brockman in *The Violence of Love* (foreword by **Henri J. M. Nouwen**). Brockman also wrote *Romero: A Life*. A biographical film, *Romero*, stars Raul Julia. KIG

ROSARY. A string of beads used to count prayers and/or the sets of prayers used with the beads. In the Middle Ages prayer beads became common in every part of Christian Europe. In the tenth century beads made of a string of knots were used to pray the **Lord's Prayer** and other repetitive prayers. Beads worn as a necklace or around the waist, wrist, or fingers were used to count sacred formulas or phrases. Taking seriously the mandate to pray always, clergy, monks, and nuns tucked a prayer cord into their belts or cinctures so that it was in easy reach whenever a hand was free, daily praying the 150 **Psalms**.

The three major ways to pray with the rosary are the Franciscan Crown; the Bridgettine; and the Rosary of the Joyful, Sorrowful, and Glorious Mysteries. This last is also called the Rosary of the Seven Sorrows and continues to be the most popular today as a major element in **Marian devotion**. Around 1250 the Western Church called this a *rosarium* (rose garland or garden), commemorating the white roses of joy, red roses of sorrow, and yellow roses of glory.

Protestants are only now gaining an understanding or appreciation of the use of beads in prayer. Fingering the beads often calms the spirit and helps the individual to concentrate as well as to integrate the senses of touch and sight into the prayer. With fingers busy, one's mind is open to ponder the deeper mysteries of God. Simply holding the string of beads can be an instrument of prayer, especially when one's mind is unable to formulate any helpful thoughts.

To learn more, try *Praying by Hand: Rediscovering the Rosary as a Way of Prayer* by **M. Basil Pennington** or *Praying the Rosary: The Joyful, Fruitful, Sorrowful, and Glorious Mysteries* by Warren F. Dicharry. PDB

RUETHER, ROSEMARY RADFORD (b. 1936), a leading Catholic feminist theologian, professor of applied theology at Garrett-Evangelical Seminary, and author or editor of over thirty-two books. Her early book, *New Woman New Earth*, remains current, since for

Praying the Rosary

- Begin at the cross or crucifix by making the sign of the cross and invoking the Trinity: "In the name of the Father, the Son, and the Holy Spirit, Amen." Recite the Apostles' Creed.

- At the first bead of the tail say the **Lord's Prayer**.

- For each of the remaining three beads of the tail say a **Hail Mary**.

- At the next bead "announce" the First Mystery, then say the Lord's Prayer.

- For each of the ten small beads (called a decade) recite the Hail Mary. At the end of each decade, pray the Gloria Patri ("Glory be to the Father, and to the Son, and to the Holy Spirit: as it was in the beginning, is now, and ever shall be, world without end. Amen.") and, optionally, the Fatima Prayer ("O Jesus, forgive us our sins, save us from the fires of hell. Lead all souls to heaven, especially those who are most in need of your mercy.")

- At the next large bead, repeat the last two steps, beginning with the next Mystery and repeat until you complete all five mysteries.

- After completing the rosary, end your prayer time with a general prayer or an address to Mary such as Hail, Holy Queen ("Hail, holy Queen, Mother of Mercy; hail our life, our sweetness, and our hope. To thee do we cry, poor banished children of Eve. To thee do we send up our sighs, mourning and weeping in this valley of tears. Turn, then, most gracious Advocate, thine eyes of mercy toward us. And after this our exile show unto us the blessed fruit of thy womb, Jesus. O clement, O loving, O sweet Virgin Mary. Pray for us, O Holy Mother of God, that we may be made worthy of the promises of Christ.")

- The four sets of mysteries in common use are the Sorrowful Mysteries (the agony of Christ in the garden of Gethsemane, Christ's scourging, his crowning with thorns, his carrying the cross, and his crucifixion), the Joyful Mysteries (the Annunciation to Mary, Mary's visit with Elizabeth, the birth of Jesus, his presentation in the Temple, and finding him in the Temple when he was a boy), the Glorious Mysteries (Christ's resurrection, his ascension, the coming of the Spirit at Pentecost, the assumption of Mary into heaven, and her coronation by Christ in heaven), and the Luminous Mysteries (Jesus' baptism, his first miracle at the wedding at Cana, his proclamation of the kingdom, his transfiguration, and his institution of Holy Communion at the Last Supper). As a rule the Joyful Mysteries are said on Monday and Saturday, the Luminous on Thursday, the Sorrowful on Tuesday and Friday, and the Glorious on Wednesday and Sunday.

thirty years she has been at the cutting edge of feminist and ecological concerns in theology, as well as of issues of racism and anti-Semitism. Ruether was born in St. Paul, Minnesota. Her **spiritual formation** was largely Catholic; but as she recalls, she was reared in an ecumenical and interfaith context. Her father's family was Protestant; a favorite uncle was Jewish; and family friends were Quakers and Unitarians. Thus, while Ruether's grounding was Christian, and Catholic in particular, she came to her study of religion with an appreciation of the strengths and limitations of various faith traditions. Building on that ecumenical foundation, she studied philosophy, ancient history, classics, and patristics, completing her doctorate in 1966 at Claremont Graduate School.

Ruether's comprehensive knowledge of religion enabled her to make insightful criticisms about the sexism that often hides under accepted truths within Christian thought, a critique clearly articulated in her best-known book, *Sexism and God-Talk*. In a recent book, *Women and Redemption: A Theological History*, Ruether points out that even though the early church wrestled with Jesus' vision of an egalitarian table realized in the present time, it accepted Paul's conclusion that such a vision could not be realized until the Second Coming. In *Women and Redemption*, Ruether seeks to reclaim women's historical spiritual contributions, from women mystics like **Hildegard of Bingen** and **Julian of Norwich** to Quaker women who worked for the abolition of slavery. Ruether's work opens up a wealth of new historical and theological perspectives as Christians try to understand women's significant contributions to Christian **spirituality**. SAF

RULE. A document drawn up by a **community** of faith for the purpose of describing that community's common life, the **disciplines** that bind the community together, and the purposes for which the community exists. In the history of the Christian church, four rules have been recognized as "canonical"—that is, considered to be normative patterns for the founding of religious orders: the rules of **Benedict**, **Basil**, **Augustine**, and **Francis**. New orders have taken one of these canonical rules as their standard. For example, the **Dominicans** chose the Rule of Augustine, and the Rule of Benedict has been used by Benedictines, Camaldolese, **Carthusians**, **Cistercians**, and **Trappists**. Subsequent orders were free to add constitutions—practical applications of a rule in a particular setting—and the constitutions could be changed, while the rule could not.

Rules first appeared when hermits (ca. fourth century) decided to live in proximity to one another and to seek the counsel of a more experienced monk. The leader came to be called the abbot, whom the other monks were obliged to obey and from whom the written rule evolved. It is thought that Pachomius (d. 346) wrote the first **monastic** rule. A study of the various rules in church history shows that they vary widely, but most set forth the community's pattern for the monastic synthesis of prayer and work.

By far the best-known rule is the Rule of Benedict. While following the basic pattern for previous rules, it was written as part of a larger reforming effort of the monastic movement put in motion by Louis the Pious during the Carolingian Renaissance. The Rule of Benedict has been published in both standard translations and contemporary paraphrases, so that Christians all over the world can both know the rule and use its insights in their own **spiritual formation**.

In the contemporary church, rules as such are no longer made, but the tendency for groups to make and keep **covenants** is widespread. Far less detailed than monastic rules, covenants create a sense of mutual accountability and life together for the **covenant group**. As spiritual formation has taken on new significance in the church, individuals likewise have framed "rules of life" for themselves as a means of recording their intentions and the means (spiritual disciplines) by which they will realize their commitments. Both group covenants and personal rules of life are dynamic documents, revised as the makers (or maker) deem the need to change or grow in particular attitudes and actions of the Christian life. SH

RUSSIAN SPIRITUALITY. See **Orthodox Spirituality**.

RUYSBROECK, JAN VAN (1293–1381), Flemish priest, writer, and mystic. Ruysbroeck was vicar and chaplain at St. Gudula in Brussels for twenty-five years until 1343, when he left parish life and moved into the forest in Groenendael. There he formed a contemplative community that eventually adopted the Augustinian **Rule**. When the forest hermitage became a priory, he became the first prior and served until his death. He was sometimes called the forest priest.

Ruysbroeck's **mysticism** is based on an introspective life described in *The Adornment of the Spiritual Marriage*, which speaks of three elements or ways of life and **union** with God: interior, active, and God-gazing. In the interior life we can meet and experience an essential unity with God, possible because of the essential unity that exists between God and all humanity. It is a **grace** given to all, regardless of their life or moral character. In the active life we experience an active unity with God, directed by the **Holy Spirit** through memory, intelligence, and **will**. This mystical way is not a simple opening to God but an **imitation of Christ** as well. Active works and intellect must coexist with passive enjoyment and affect.

Finally there is the God-gazing or God-seeing life that results from both essential and active unity. At this point we enter **contemplation**. While Ruysbroeck calls the contemplative level of his mystical way God-seeing or God-gazing, he tends to use more water metaphors than visual ones. We flow down into God who is the ground of our being, leaving behind our preconceived notions, ways of being, and false attachments. The eternal flowing down into God is balanced with an eternal flowing back to humanity through service and love.

Unlike some mystics of his time (such as the Brethren of the Free Spirit, a group that believed that mystical union freed them from all moral restraints and religious duties), Ruysbroeck maintains the importance of the church and the **sacraments**, especially **Holy Communion**, as means of grace.

John Ruusbroec: The Spiritual Espousals and Other Works, translated by James A. Wiseman provides an in-depth introduction. SN

S

SABBATH. Time set apart for rest and worship. From the beginning, God's people have been marked by the command and gift of sabbath, which is a Hebrew word meaning "to cease" or "to stop." Teaching about sabbath is rooted in the creation of the world, which culminates with the sabbath as the rest of God (Gen. 2:2) and is emphasized in both sets of the Ten Commandments. The two slightly different teachings about sabbath in the Ten Commandments point to complementary meanings: We are called to rest because God did so after the creation (Exod. 20), and we are commanded to rest in remembrance of God's liberating and saving action on behalf of Israel (Deut. 5). In the ministry of Jesus, there is at times conflict about the sabbath and its meaning; however, when Jesus heals on the sabbath day (as in Mark 3:1-6), he insists that he is reclaiming the true meaning of the day as one of restoration of life. The word *sabbath* is also related to the sabbatical year, the one year in seven when debts were forgiven; to the Jubilee year, the fiftieth year after seven cycles of seven years, when all slaves were freed; and to the concept of a sabbatical, in which one rests from ordinary labors.

The practice of sabbath is an essential spiritual **discipline** due to its origin as a command (God requires us to observe sabbath) and to its therapeutic value (we cannot continue to work or serve without rest). At its best the sabbath is an opportunity for prayer and play, self-denial and celebration. The practice of sabbath is also an act of trust and witness: God is able to act in the world apart from human effort or achievement. In this sense the sabbath can become a sign of God's **grace**.

For most Christians the primary day of worship is the Lord's Day (Sunday), which is the first day of the week and the day of Resurrection (John 20:1). In the Jewish tradition sabbath is the seventh day of the week and is observed from sundown Friday evening until sundown Saturday evening. Sabbath is also an experience of rest in the midst of work, **contemplation** in the midst of action, and **receptivity** in the midst of giving and serving. In a culture that affirms activity and busyness, the gift of sabbath is both a challenge to our lifestyles and a means of God's saving grace in our lives.

For further reading, see Dorothy C. Bass, *Receiving the Day*; Tilden Edwards, *Sabbath Time*; and Abraham Joshua Heschel, *The Sabbath: Its Meaning for Modern Man*. KHC

SACRAMENT. "An outward and visible sign of an inward and spiritual **grace**," according to the **Book of Common Prayer**. Sacraments combine physical actions, words, and objects to convey Christ's grace and presence to the believer. The word *sacrament* itself derives from the Latin word *sacramentum*, meaning "an oath or vow."

Sacraments have been practiced in the church since the time of the early Christians, whose view of religious practice came from the Jewish heritage in which the material world is an agency of God's revelation. Jesus is recorded as commanding the church to imitate him and to baptize in his name, and the New Testament makes numerous references to **baptism**, Eucharist or **Holy Communion**, healing, laying on of hands, and **forgiveness** of sins. The early church was rather indefinite about the number of sacraments and exactly how they work, but by the Middle Ages the number had been defined as seven: baptism, confirmation, Eucharist, penance (**confession** and forgiveness), extreme unction ("last rites," now called anointing of the sick), ordination, and marriage. This is still the view of the Roman Catholic Church. Luther and the other reformers argued that only two sacraments were clearly commanded and instituted by Jesus: baptism and the Eucharist. Protestant practice continues in this path, although some Protestant sects have elevated foot-washing to an almost sacramental place, since it too was commanded by Christ. The Enlightenment emphasis in the 1700s on the intellect and reason has tended in many cases (particularly in some Protestant denominations) to devalue the mysterious, numinous characteristics of the sacraments, placing the emphasis on human effort and understanding. However, developments in liturgy and sacramental theology since the 1960s, sparked by the liturgical renewal that came out of Vatican II, have helped counteract this intellectualizing emphasis.

Beyond and behind the specific sacraments practiced by Roman Catholics and Protestants, there is also the view that all of life can properly be considered *sacramental*, since God made the material world and works through it. Thus all objects and activities engaged in with the purpose of opening to God—the beauty of nature, the gathering of friends, the words of poetry, bread, oil, wine, water—can be seen as avenues where God brings invisible grace through visible signs. This *sacramentalism* is related to the Old Testament view of the world as a proper avenue of God's revelation and draws further strength from Christ's incarnation as part of this material world. This view opposes those who would limit knowledge of God only to verbal and intellectual means and distinguishes Christianity from other world religions that teach **detachment** from the material world.

Further reading might include James F. White's *The Sacraments in Protestant Practice and Faith* or *Outward Sign and Inward Grace* by Rob L. Staples. JLW

SACRED HEART. A devotional image, a defining symbol of Roman Catholicism from the late seventeenth to the mid-twentieth cen-turies. The modern form of the devotion is closely associated with the visions of a French **Visitandine** nun, Margaret Mary Alacoque (1647–90). From 1673 to 1675 she received a series of "great revelations" in which she reported Jesus' appearance to her, his designation of her as the "Apostle of his Sacred Heart," the mystical exchange of his heart and hers, and his request to establish a series of devotional practices in honor of his heart: Thursday night adorations of the Blessed Sacrament, **Holy Communion** on the first Friday of each month; and a yearly liturgical feast on the Friday following the Feast of the Body and Blood of Christ (*Corpus Christi*, the Thursday after Trinity Sunday). Margaret Mary's visions were promoted by Claude de Colombière and a series of other **Jesuit** priests.

The symbol did not originate with Margaret Mary but had evolved in varied visual and literary forms over the previous centuries. Private medieval devotion to the heart of Christ was associated with the Benedictine, Carthusian, Franciscan, and Dominican orders. In the modern period it was incorporated into the Jesuit, Salesian, and Eudist spiritual traditions. Jean Eudes (1601–80) developed its theological and liturgical foundations. The devotion in the form that Margaret Mary envisioned, with its emphasis on **adoration** and on reparation for the outrages committed against Divine **Love**, achieved widespread importance during the French Revolution where it became the standard of counter-revolutionary forces. It was established as a universal devotion for the Roman Catholic Church in 1856 by Pope Pius IX. In 1899 Leo XIII consecrated the entire human race to the Sacred Heart.

For further reading, see *Faith in Christ and the Worship of Christ: New Approaches to Devotion to Christ*, edited by Leo Scheffczyk. WMW

SAINTS. From the Latin *sanctus*, meaning "holy" or "consecrated." In the Hebrew Bible, **holiness** characterizes God, the "Holy One." Yahweh shares the divine holiness with the people of the **covenant** (Exod. 19). In the

New Testament, Paul calls "saints" those who are faithful to Christ. Followers of Jesus were typically referred to by this general term, though sometimes the term seems more restricted to community leaders or recognized models of Christian life and witness. The Apostles' Creed speaks of belief in "the **communion of saints**."

Saints were and are ordinary people. Though imperfect, doubt-filled, weak, lonely, and fearful at times, they chose to remain uncompromisingly faithful witnesses to the gospel. This great "cloud of witnesses" (Heb. 12:1) is the unity of all believers past, present, and future. There are no boundaries or barriers to its inclusiveness, not even between living and dead. As stained-glass windows and mosaics in churches around the world attest, during the persecutions of the early church and continuing until Constantine, many believers sacrificed their lives proclaiming their faith in Jesus Christ. Stephen in the Acts of the Apostles is called the first Christian martyr. To lay down one's life for Christ was the heroic witness of a **martyr**. Such martyrdom became a defining characteristic of a saint. These early martyrs of the church had "died in the Lord"; their saintly lives were commemorated on the anniversaries of their deaths. Honoring and venerating heroic and virtuous saints has been a tradition throughout Christian history.

Saints come from all walks of life and from every culture; the young, the old, the rich, the poor—all are illumined by the mystery of God's loving presence in their lives. These ordinary folks make loving God and neighbor their extraordinary choice day in and day out. Saints step out in faith, trusting and obeying the call of God. Their purity of heart awakens us to the realization that we too are called to be shining examples of God's spirit of love. These companions of God not only live in **imitation of Christ** but open up new possibilities for Christian living in new times.

Hagiographers have studied and written about the lives of the saints, including their stories of **conversion** and transformation.

Some nonbelievers (like **Edith Stein** reading the autobiography of **Teresa of Ávila**) have come into the church after reading about these friends of God whose lives proclaimed the mystery of Jesus' message. Saints (past and present) are not perfect humans, but they live authentic lives by surrendering themselves in **abandonment** to God, whom they love with their whole heart, mind, and strength.

Calendars listing saints deemed worthy of particular remembrance (typically on the anniversary of their deaths) existed by the late second century. Canonization is the process by which the Roman Catholic Church has added people to such lists after careful examination of their lives, with the final decision proclaimed by the pope. Permission to refer to a person as *Venerable* marks the beginning of the formal process, with a designation *Blessed* near the midpoint. Some canonized saints whose writings are as commendable as their lives may be further declared **Doctors of the Church**.

The Anglican Church and the Episcopal Church also maintain calendars of saints. In *All Saints*, Robert Ellsberg offers an interesting calendar—with brief biographies—of spiritual models for our time, including many Christians from the twentieth century and even some non-Christians (e.g., Gandhi). See also *The Oxford Dictionary of the Saints* (4th edition, 1998), edited by David H. Farmer. EKM

SALVATION ARMY, THE. An evangelical and socially active Christian organization founded in England in 1878 by **William** and Catherine **Booth**. Organized on a military basis, it is founded on eleven "Articles of War": (1) the Bible is inspired by God; (2) there is only one God; (3) there are three persons in the Godhead; (4) Jesus is both divine and human; (5) all persons are sinners because of the Fall; (6) Christ has made full atonement; (7) repentance toward God, faith in Christ, and **regeneration** by the **Holy Spirit** are necessary to salvation; (8) we are justified by **grace** through **faith** in Christ; (9) obedient faith is necessary to continue in salvation; (10) we can be wholly sanctified; and (11) we believe in immortality of the **soul**, resurrection of the body, and final judgment of all persons.

Although the Army is internationally known for its extensive social activities such as rescue work, soup kitchens, hostels and shelters, hospitals and schools, its primary purpose is converting individuals to belief in Christ and guiding them toward **sanctification**. They are noted for open-air meetings with brass bands and are identified by the bass drum and red kettle.

The Salvation Army came to the United States in 1880 and fit in with the theological ideas of the nineteenth-century **holiness** movement. An internal dispute among the children of William and Catherine Booth led to the formation of the Volunteers of America in 1896. Today the Army has around five hundred thousand members in eleven hundred congregations in the United States.

For further information, see Harry Edward Neal, *The Hallelujah Army*. DDW

SANCTIFICATION. The act and process of being made holy (from Latin *sanctus*, "holy" in imitation of and participation in God's own **holiness**). Biblical words for *holy* (Hebrew *qadosh*, Greek *hagios*) carry a basic sense of being *separated* or *set apart*. Throughout the scriptures, places and objects are sanctified, either becoming associated with God's presence or an instrument of awareness of God's presence and activity. Likewise, people are set apart for special duty or office. God's intent is clear: "For I am the LORD your God; sanctify yourselves, therefore, and be holy, for I am holy" (Lev. 11:44). That is, God's people share in the divine attribute of holiness and thus may be called **saints**, or sanctified (Exod. 19:6; Lev. 11:45; and 1 Pet. 1:13-16). With this call to holiness in mind, the New Testament emphasizes the believer's ongoing transformation to "Christlikeness" as the essential aspect of sanctification. In the New Testament, life in Christ is the foundation of **justification** and sanctification (1 Cor. 1:30; 2 Cor. 5:17; 2 Pet. 1:4). Thus, like places and objects, people are sanc-

tified by the presence of God through divine **grace**. However, as in all relationships, our response is required as we are called to an ongoing process of reformation and graced transformation. In both the Old and New Testaments, the sanctified person is filled with the **Holy Spirit** and dedicated to live a distinctive life as God's person. The historical theological emphasis is on the negative and positive dynamics of the concept: ethical prohibitions and the acts and virtues of love. The relationship of these dynamics to justification is at the heart of most theological debates on sanctification. See *Christian Spirituality: Five Views of Sanctification*, edited by Donald L. Alexander, for an accessible presentation of the debate issues.

While sanctification is an important doctrine in Christian **spirituality**, it became the key emphasis of the Methodist movement and of founder **John Wesley**. His teaching on Christian **perfection** became the distinctive contribution of the Wesleyan movement to Protestant thought and spirituality. John Wesley emphasized the relational dynamics of sanctification, defining it as a process of growing toward perfect love of God, or "entire sanctification." This process is the work of the Holy Spirit in the life of believers, shaping and transforming our inner reality to what is already ours in Christ through our new birth, or **regeneration**.

The Christian is always becoming, growing through various **stages of spiritual growth** and increasing in love of, knowledge of, and **obedience** to God through the *means of grace*: the classical spiritual **disciplines,** chiefly sacramental **worship**, **prayer**, accountability (e.g., through **spiritual direction** or **friendship** or **covenant groups**), **fasting**, and study of **scripture** and other **spiritual reading**. John Calvin's list of the means of grace also included the **providence** of God, emphasizing the opportunities in everyday life situations for continual **mortification** and union with Christ's life and suffering. On the human side of the relationship, the danger comes in works righteousness. Thus it is important to remember that God gives the increase or growth in holiness. Human activities are simply the ways we open ourselves to transforming grace. As Wesley emphasized, the motivation is not works righteousness but love. CIZ

SANFORD, AGNES WHITE (1897–1982), daughter of Presbyterian missionaries to China, lay minister, spiritual healer, and gifted spiritual writer. Her childhood and early adulthood were spent in China, where she met her husband, Ted, an Episcopal priest, and began rearing her children. After they returned to the United States, Sanford became deeply depressed but, through this experience, discovered the power of spiritual healing in her own life. Her healing ministry began to grow as she prayed for others and helped them to trust God for their recovery. Sanford's best-known writing *The Healing Light* was a pioneering book in which she outlined her experiences with the healing power of God, making the subject of divine healing accessible to modern Christians. Other books include *The Healing Gifts of the Spirit*, *The Healing Power of the Bible*, and her compelling autobiography, *Sealed Orders*. SAF

SANGSTER, WILLIAM EDWYN ROBERT (1900–60), English Methodist preacher. One of the greatest preachers in war-torn Britain during the mid-twentieth century, Sangster was converted in a Methodist mission, trained at Richmond College, and served congregations in northern England before appointment to Westminster Central Hall in 1939. He completed his London University doctorate by reading and writing in the bomb shelters of London during the German blitzkrieg and published his groundbreaking study of **John Wesley**'s doctrine of Christian **perfection**, *The Path to Perfection*, in 1943. Sangster was widely recognized for his saintly leadership in the Methodist Church, and his preaching regularly packed the large Central Hall during the height of the war. He was one of the most popular devotional writers of his day. Titles include *These Things Abide*, devotional meditations published at the onset of World War II;

Teach Us to Pray; and many collections of sermons. His biography, *Doctor Sangster*, is by Paul Sangster. PWC

SCHAFF, PHILIP (1819–93), America's greatest church historian. Born in Switzerland and educated in Germany (Tübingen and Berlin), in 1843 he became a professor at the German Reformed Seminary in Mercersburg, Pennsylvania, where, together with John Nevin, he founded the so-called Mercersburg theology. This theology combined personal piety with a Catholic outlook on the church. In the age of the great revivals, Schaff called for a more sacramental Protestant church. He proposed that the Reformation was not a return to the primitive church but a development of the best in Roman Catholicism that would eventually reunite Protestants and Catholics. These ideas twice led him to trial for heresy. From 1870 until his death, he was a professor at Union Theological Seminary in New York City. He published over eighty works of which the *Schaff-Herzog Encyclopedia of Religious Knowledge* and the seven-volume *History of the Christian Church* are his most famous. An excellent introduction to his works is *Philip Schaff: Historian and Ambassador of the Universal Church*, edited by Klaus Penzel. DDW

SCHWEITZER, ALBERT (1875–1985), biblical scholar, organist, biographer of J. S. Bach, and medical missionary in Africa, perhaps the single best-known Protestant figure of the twentieth century. He was born in Alsace, a part of France claimed by Germany, and was himself a German citizen. He became a leader in the nineteenth-century movement that sought to discover the historical Jesus behind the Gospel accounts. But he gave up the life of scholarship to follow his sense of call to serve the people of Africa. Although he had studied medicine, he gave organ concerts to pay for his missionary endeavors at Lambaréné in French Equatorial Africa (now Gabon). Caught up in the events of World War I, he was interned by the French government but returned to Africa in 1924. As a **nature**

mystic, Schweitzer developed the philosophy he called "reverence for life." As a doctor he fought against germs, but he was reluctant to destroy any life form. His writings include *The Quest of the Historical Jesus*; *On the Edge of the Primeval Forest*; *The Mystery of the Kingdom of God*; *The Mysticism of Paul the Apostle*; and his autobiography, *Out of My Life and Thought*. HLR

SCRIPTURE. The scriptures of the Old and New Testaments have always provided the chief means of **spiritual formation**. The Jewish people studied Torah, the first five books of the Old Testament, to learn the **will of God** for them in their **covenant** relationship. They put the rest of the books, divided into the Prophets and the Writings, on a slightly lower plane but expected to hear God speak through them too. They not only studied but also **meditated** on the scriptures, wanting the words to move from the head to the heart. After citing the Shema, the Deuteronomist commanded, "Keep these words that I am commanding you today in your heart. Recite them to your children and talk about them when you are at home and when you are away, when you lie down and when you rise. Bind them as a sign on your hand, fix them as an emblem on your forehead, and write them on the doorposts of your house and on your gates" (Deut 6:6-9). The **Psalms** were Judaism's prayerbook.

The first Christians continued Jewish reliance on the scriptures in the Greek version called the Septuagint and gradually added to them a set of Christian Scriptures. Second Timothy 3:16-17 indicates the role scriptures played in spiritual formation in the first century: "All scripture is inspired by God and is useful for teaching, for reproof, for correction, and for training in righteousness, so that everyone who belongs to God may be proficient, equipped for every good work."

Scriptures played a central role in **monastic** formation. Some desert monks tried to recite all 150 Psalms every day. The most basic form of prayer, however, was always meditation on scripture, especially the Gospels.

Clearly the monks drew support for their calling from selected texts such as Jesus' command to the rich youth or the **beatitude** "Blessed are the pure in heart, for they will see God" (Matt. 5:8). The **Rule** of **Benedict of Nursia** arranged for monks to divide their day among three endeavors—about six hours of manual labor, four hours in chanting the Psalms, four hours in *lectio divina*.

As the Protestant reformers placed scripture at the center of Christian faith and practice, they assured spiritual formation would revolve around reading and meditating on scripture. **Luther** outlined for his barber *A Simple Way to Pray* that relied chiefly on scripture but also such things as the Apostles' Creed. In the Reformed tradition Puritans emphasized memorization of texts and meditating on them. In *The Saints' Everlasting Rest*, Puritan **Richard Baxter** outlined a method of meditation on scripture remarkably close to the one **Ignatius of Loyola** featured in his *Spiritual Exercises*. Both stressed imagination controlled and directed by "consideration," that is, reason.

Unlike many other holy books, the Bible is not *one* writing but *many*, composed by different persons over many centuries. There are different types of writing—histories, prophecies, stories, songs, Gospels, and letters. What holds them together and draws us to them to sustain and direct faith is their witness to "the mighty acts of God" in human history. Entering into those acts in memory, we learn about God, God's purpose for creation, the covenant into which we have entered, and our own place in life.

For further reading, see *The Spiritual Formation Bible*, Timothy Jones, general editor; or Robert Mulholland's *Shaped by the Word: The Power of Scripture in Spiritual Formation*. EGH

SECOND JOURNEY. The movement in the spiritual life that begins with midlife **conversion** and crisis. The end of the first journey is characterized by loss of ideals and idols, a decrease in energy, a diminishing of power and self-control. The beginning of midlife or the second journey is marked by a disillusionment with external rewards and goals. The individual begins to feel the constraints of finitude; and as **detachment** occurs, there is a death of the old life and the formation of a new life. This process mirrors the mystery of Christ's passion, and can be likened to the **dark night** of the soul.

As the journey proceeds (note the beginning passages of Dante's *Divine Comedy*: "In the middle of life's journey I found myself in a dark wood... "), the individual experiences the transition from death to resurrection, from **darkness** to life. Preconceptions of success and achievement are relinquished, as new callings are perceived and new aspirations voiced. Less attention is given to external appearances, and more is focused on internal depth. Performance is placed in context: We are valued for our being rather than our doing, for who we are and not merely for what we accomplish. In this way the second journey is a gift of God's **grace**. Finally the second journey toward resurrection life is begun but never fully experienced in this life, a reminder that our **hopes** transcend human experience.

For further study, see *The Transcendent Self* by Adrian van Kaam. KHC

SEMI-PELAGIANISM. See Pelagianism.

SERENITY PRAYER. A simple prayer for divine guidance that has become a central prayer for Alcoholics Anonymous and other **Twelve Step Programs**. The prayer exists in a variety of forms, but the most common is this:

> God, grant me the serenity to accept the
>   things I cannot change,
> the courage to change the things I can,
> and the wisdom to know the difference.
> Amen.

The prayer is taken from the opening of a longer prayer offered by theologian Reinhold Niebuhr when he served as a guest preacher at a church near his summer home in Heath, Massachusetts, in 1934. A visitor at the service asked for a copy and reprinted it. Niebuhr said the prayer was his original composition, but the opening lines may have been inspired by a prayer of Friedrich Oetinger. In Niebuhr's original version, the prayer was communal rather than personal:

> God, give us grace to accept with
>   serenity the things that cannot
>   be changed,
> courage to change the things which
>   should be changed,
> and the wisdom to distinguish the one
>   from the other.

KRB

SETON, ELIZABETH ANN (1774–1821), patron of the American Catholic parochial school system and the founder of the American Sisters of Charity. The second child of Richard Bayley, prominent Episcopalian and New York physician, Elizabeth was married in 1794 to William Magee Seton. The couple had five children and enjoyed a prosperous life. Seton's spiritual life flourished during this time under the influence of Henry Hobart, assistant at Trinity Episcopal Church. By 1800 the family's mercantile business was failing, and William fell ill. In hopes of recovery, the couple and their eldest child traveled to Italy, but William died soon after their arrival. Under the care of her late husband's business associates, the Filicchis, the new widow was introduced to Italian Catholicism. The intense devotion of that people inspired her, as did their belief in the real presence of the Christ in **Holy Communion**. Returning home, she struggled with the conflicting claims of the two faiths. Despite Hobart's counsel and the threat of rejection by her extended family, in 1805 she and her children converted to the Roman Catholic faith.

Seton's new faith proved an obstacle to her employment in New York, so Elizabeth, financially strapped, moved to Maryland. There leaders in the Catholic community recognized her as essential in their plans for the mainly immigrant church. In Baltimore she started a school for girls, which then moved to Emmitsburg and became St. Joseph Academy. In 1809 she took vows as a Sister of Charity, modifying the **Rule** of the Daughters of Charity founded by **Vincent de Paul**. The community was assisted by the Sulpician fathers, leaders in the American Catholic educational enterprise. She suffered the death of two of her daughters and a number of the first Sisters of Charity, yet continued the administration of her growing religious community and the oversight of a school for paying boarders and day programs for the local poor. Elizabeth Seton died of tuberculosis in 1821. She wrote no extended treatises, but her collected letters and papers in *Elizabeth Ann Seton: Selected Writings*, edited by Ellin M. Kelly and Annabelle M. Melville, reveal a woman of immense and joyous faith cultivated in the midst of family, friendships, and community. Today there are six branches of "Mother Seton's Daughters" in North America. She was canonized in 1975.

For more information, see her biography, *Mrs. Seton: Foundress of the American Sisters of Charity* by Joseph I. Dirvin. WMW

SEXUALITY. Any definition of this major subject must take into account both the dimensions of *sexuality* as it relates to generativity in all of life and to genital and other physical sexual activity. The two cannot be split, yet Jewish and Christian history has focused more on regulating negative expressions of sex than on celebrating humans as sexual beings.

The Bible opens by affirming sexuality: God created humankind in God's image, "male and female," and blessed them and said, "Be fruitful and multiply," giving them dominion (responsibility) over every living thing. "And indeed, it was very good" (Gen. 1:26-28, 31). Only later does sin deface the gifts of sexuality and vocation. Sex degenerates into domination and exploitation (3:16), and work degenerates to drudgery (3:19).

Several things need to be noticed. First, the idea of the equality of male and female is an extension of God's own nature (1:27).

While on the whole the Bible reflects a male-dominated system, many essential texts of scripture teach that by virtue of creation and redemption in Christ, male and female, slave and free are equal (Gen. 1:27; Gal. 3:26). "Your sons and your daughters shall prophesy" (Acts 2:17-18; Joel 2:28-29). Thus Christian history has often seen egalitarian communities as well as strong individual women leaders, particularly in the present century.

Second, Jewish tradition taught that since God has both male and female qualities, so does each human being created in the divine image. Scriptures use not only masculine metaphors for divinity (such as father) but feminine ones as well: the Spirit (*ruach*, feminine in Hebrew) brooding over the waters of chaos, an eagle bearing her young on her wings, a rock that gives birth to God's people, a nursing mother, a woman searching for a treasured coin, a mother hen gathering her brood. Such androgynous qualities, emphasized by contemporary feminist theologians, have always been present in art, music, and such theological works as those of the fourteenth-century English mystic **Julian of Norwich** or of **Beguines** like **Mechthild of Magdeburg**. Jungian psychology speaks of male and female qualities in each human being and of the value of integrating the two. Some see this integration represented in the female and male characters in Jesus' parables.

Third, sex is a good gift: "God blessed them.... And indeed it was very good" (Gen. 1:28-31). Sexuality is to be celebrated, not looked on as an inherent hindrance to **holiness**. While monastics espoused the vows of **poverty**, **chastity**, and **obedience**, they often exemplified a creative vocational sublimation of their sexuality. Sixteenth-century reformers like **Martin Luther** and **John Calvin** broke with tradition and said that married life could be as holy as monastic life.

Fourth, "bearing fruit" means more than biological productivity. From Genesis to Revelation it means spiritual fecundity and vocational generativity in bearing the **fruit of the Spirit** in the world: love, joy, and peace, etc. (Gal. 5:22-24). The tree in the garden of Eden, linked with sexuality, is also the tree of life in the celestial city—its fruitfulness sublimated not only for healing of individuals but also for healing the nations (Gen. 1:9; Rev. 22:1-2).

Fifth is the ancient connection between sexual and spiritual knowing. The Song of Solomon celebrates sensual love, yet both Jewish and Christian traditions have also viewed it as a divine romance between the Lover and the beloved, so central to understanding the soul's dark night. Sexual longings, as in the case of Dante's failed love for Beatrice, often beckon us to joy beyond all sensual pleasures.

Sexuality then is our divinely given desire for loving, life-giving intimacy that nurtures all areas of life, physical expressions of sex, generativity in vocation, and a loving romance with God.

For further exploration, read *Praying with Body and Soul* by Jane Vennard; *Sexual Paradox* by Celia Alison Hahn; *Sacred Dwelling: A Spirituality of Family Life* by Wendy Wright; *Journeymen: A Spiritual Guide for Men (and for Women Who Want to Understand Them)* by Kent Ira Groff; and *The Dance of the Dissident Daughter* by Sue Monk Kidd. KIG

SHAKERS. A Christian commune movement most widespread in the United States during the 1800s. The United Society of Believers was better known as Shakers. The first so-called "Shaking Quakers" arose in Manchester, England, in 1747. Jane and James Wardley, the first leaders, while loyal to some **Quaker** ideas, were most inspired by the millennialist fervor of Protestant refugees from France. "Shaking" referred to the group's characteristic dancing and frenzied movements during worship. In 1758 the illiterate but high-spirited **Ann Lee** (1736–84) was drawn to the Shakers and revealed to the group her vision that Christ's Second Coming had been realized in her. The charismatic Lee declared that **celibacy** was necessary to remain free of sin. Persecuted in England, she led eight others to America in 1774 and formed a community at Watervliet,

New York, near Albany. Despite their pacifistic views and British origins, the Shakers gained converts during the American Revolution, many of them drawn by Lee's missionary efforts in the northeast.

After Lee's death, Joseph Meachum rose to leadership. His superb organizational skills were key to the eventual expansion of the Shakers into twenty-four communities from Maine to Kentucky. The frenzied dancing was gradually adapted into a stylized form. A common **rule** of life also developed, focused on an ethic of **perfection** of life and manners safeguarded by regular **confession**. The functional but beautiful Shaker dwellings, successful farming, and simply styled furnishings seemed idyllic, like the well-known Shaker saying, "Hands to work and hearts to God." Nevertheless their peaceable communities were strictly governed through authoritarian channels. By the turn of the twentieth century, the Shakers were shrinking in numbers. A single community endures at Sabbathday Lake, Maine, and continues to welcome visitors. Shaker life still centers around an understanding of Christian communal living in celibacy, a belief that the divine nature of Christ is both male and female, and a vision that the kingdom of God on earth is being realized through the Shakers.

For more about Shakers today, read *God among the Shakers: A Search for Stillness and Faith at Sabbathday Lake* by Suzanne Skees. SAF

SHELDON, CHARLES MONROE (1857–1946), American Congregational pastor and writer. Educated at Brown University and Andover Theological Seminary, Sheldon was ordained a Congregational minister in 1886. He ministered in Waterbury, Vermont, then in Topeka Kansas (1888–1919), and was editor-in-chief of *The Christian Herald* from 1920 to 1925. Sheldon defended the civil rights of African-Americans, Jews, women, and other groups and advocated prohibition, ecumenism, and world peace. In 1891, having lived in a black Topeka ghetto studying prejudice, poverty, and vice, he started a Christian social settlement to assist black residents and worship with them.

Sheldon wrote fifty books. His novel *In His Steps*, one of the all-time best-sellers, shows earnest, middle-class Christians trying to relate to working-class people by asking themselves, "What would Jesus do?" A 1990s revival of *In His Steps* led to the popular "WWJD" movement. Timothy Miller wrote Sheldon's biography, *Following in His Steps*. LSP

SILENCE. W. H. Auden observed that we are afraid of pain but more afraid of silence—for this void is the Abomination, the wrath of God. But Mark Slouka, writing in *Harper's Magazine* (April 1999) argues that silence is essentially neuter, neither balm nor curse. Like light or love, silence requires a medium to give it meaning, takes on the color of its host, and adapts easily to his or her fears and needs. There are many kinds of silence: the corrosive silence of anger; the suffocating silence of the morgue; the deafening silence of grief—silences that cry out to be broken. Silence is the imagination's habitat. It is also, according to Herman Melville, the voice of God.

God called the world into being through the Word—a Word that punctuates the silence but does not obliterate it. The divine word spoken to Jesus at his baptism drove him into the silence of the **desert**, where he could seek clarity that comes through a **discernment** process that depends upon silence. The clarity that is both human achievement and response to the Divine initiative is well-nigh impossible in a cacophony.

Our industrial, technological world depends upon machines, and machines make noise. While this background noise cannot be obliterated, it can be reduced if we have the will to do so. But the primary task for **spiritual formation** may not be to advocate for silence but to seek it and actively to engage it whenever and wherever it is found. God's first language *is* silence, and God is to be encountered primarily in that realm. RMH

SIN. Inner or outer actions or choices that reflect rebellion against God or apathy toward God. We refer to one such action as *a sin* (note the use of the article). The term can also refer to the constellation of inner attitudes, thoughts, feelings, or desires that leads to such action.

Before *a sin* is an action or even a thought, feeling, or desire, however, *sin* (absolute, no article) is an all-pervasive condition of our lives. Sometimes Christians make this distinction by calling this condition *original sin*, symbolized in the second chapter of Genesis by the story of the Fall. Intimately connected to our free **will**, the term *sin* points to a deep and mysterious aspect of who we are as human beings. It is a given that we are helpless to change or correct but also one that we choose to participate in and manifest actively (sins of commission) or passively (sins of omission).

To use a metaphor, sin can be seen as a deep chasm that represents our separation or alienation from God, from others, and from ourselves. This chasm does not belong there, of course (it was not present before the Fall, for example) but simply is there, and we cannot eliminate it. However, through **grace** God has in Christ forgiven our sin. When we experience the power of this loving grace of God, we are reconciled with that from which we have been separated or estranged but to which we ultimately belong—God, others, and ourselves. The chasm has not been removed but bridged. While the bridge itself is God's doing and not our own, we do have a responsibility to use it rather than choose to live out of our sin or separation. Our responsibility as Christians is to receive and accept God's gift of grace and to allow Christ to transform our thinking, feeling, willing, and acting so that they reflect our deep connection and intimacy with God, others, and ourselves.

Like its more common counterpart *sins*, *sin* has generally been applied to both the condition and choice of individuals. However, the concept of sin has also been applied to groups and institutions as well. We can speak of social sin as well as individual sin when addressing ourselves to social and cultural institutions and laws that seem to structure sin into the fabric of our lives. Racism, nationalism, sexism, and economic injustice are a few examples of social sin, which are, in fact, deeply connected to that condition of separation that exists within each of us.

In the context of Christian spirituality, spiritual exercises or **disciplines** are means to cooperate with God's sanctifying grace, though their purpose is not to save us from the power of sin. Only God can do that through the justifying grace of **forgiveness** in Christ. Once we respond in **faith** to God's saving, justifying grace, these exercises and disciplines allow the power of the **Holy Spirit** gradually to transform and reshape not only our external patterns of behavior but our internal patterns of thinking, feeling, and willing to reflect more accurately the love of Christ. Strengthening our spiritual **dispositions** or virtues, such as faith, **hope**, **love**, gratitude, patience, **mercy**, kindness, justice, **peace**, forgiveness, **humility**, **compassion**, and joy cannot eliminate our sinful nature, but we can learn as we mature spiritually to manifest an inner and outer life more open to the constant and abiding presence of God as Creator, Redeemer, and Sustainer. In spite of sin, in Christ God's "grace abounded all the more" (Rom. 5:20). JWK

SINGH, (SADHU) SUNDAR (1889–1929),

Indian Christian mystic. Born to a well-to-do family, Sundar Singh received the best education that India could provide. His parents were Sikhs, and he was given to a Hindu *pandit* (a teacher of Sanskrit and Hindu law, philosophy, and culture) for instruction. Following the death of his beloved mother, he contemplated suicide and demanded that God show him a sign. He saw a great light that filled his room; and, in the brightness, he saw the figure of Jesus. Before his conversion he had wanted to become a *sadhu*, a Hindu holy man. Now he resolved to become a Christian *sadhu*, adopting the traditional yellow robe

and turban and the **ascetic** lifestyle of Hindu holy men.

Singh traveled from place to place preaching Christ, accepting no money. If invited, he spent the night in the house but otherwise slept in a cave or under a tree. He was able to preach the Christian gospel in a form understandable to Hindus. A wealthy American became his companion and introduced him to the story of **Francis of Assisi**. In 1908, when he was just nineteen years old, Singh took his first missionary journey to Tibet and became convinced that God had set that country before him as a mission field. He went to study theology at the Anglican seminary in Lahore but did not fit in and after only eight months left school. Although he was given a license to preach by the Anglicans, he became persuaded that ordination in any denomination would limit his freedom. He often experienced mystical **ecstasy**, which he considered a gift to be accepted but not to be sought.

From 1917 Singh's fame began to spread, and he was invited to speak and preach in other countries. In 1920 he toured England and the United States. He always maintained that religion was not a matter of argument but of **experience**. Attracting attention because he refused to abandon his *sadhu's* clothing for Western dress, he also used concepts from Indian philosophy to express the inexpressible. During a mission to Tibet he disappeared and was assumed killed either by accident or by wild beasts. Among his books, the most famous is *At the Master's Feet.* HLR

SINS, SEVEN DEADLY. The seven deadly

sins have been traditionally regarded as those **dispositions** from which all other sins find their origin. Sometimes known as cardinal or capital sins, they were first listed by the **desert fathers**. The great spiritual athletes of the desert sought to name their greatest enemies in order to defeat them. The earliest list generated by **Evagrius** included eight sins: gluttony, lust, avarice, sadness, anger, spiritual lethargy or **accidie**, vainglory, and pride. **Gregory I, the Great,** would later modify this list.

Gregory added the sin of envy, merged vainglory into pride, and combined sadness and spiritual lethargy. This yielded the list used today: pride, envy, anger, sloth (the combination of sadness and spiritual lethargy), avarice, gluttony, and lust.

The lists are important not only because of what they include but also for the arrangement of the sins on the list. Dating back to at least **John Cassian**'s discussion in *The Institutes* was the belief that each sin had the power to generate the sin following it. Therefore pride was generally believed to be the foundation of all other sins. But during various periods of the church's history, other sins were believed to be more grievous. For instance, among some monastic societies, gluttony and lust were believed to be more harmful. And with the growth of the merchant class and its accompanying wealth toward the end of the medieval period, avarice came to be understood as the cardinal sin.

Thomas Aquinas was among the first to discuss the seven sins as disordered loves. Each sin was an excess, a deficiency or perversion of God's intention for the creation. Thus greed, lust, and gluttony are excessive loves. Sloth is insufficient love. And pride, envy, and anger are perverted loves. Dante in his *Divine Comedy* most colorfully illustrated the descent of the disordered loves in the *Inferno* and their proper reordering in the *Purgatorio*. This scheme of disordered loves helps succinctly define the various sins.

Pride is a placing of one's self before all others. Such self-satisfaction always implies a distancing from God and neighbor. Pride is the "nose in the air" that cannot properly take into account the needs of others.

Envy is manifested in one's inability to take joy in the accomplishments and possessions of others. Unlike the other sins, there is never any pleasure in envy. It alone is always wretched, characterized by constant looking to others.

Anger is a terrible outburst of emotion deeply connected to a thirst for vengeance. It is a fixation upon the enemy. The true sin of anger implies an ongoing wrath that consumes both the object and subject.

Sloth is far more than laziness. It is human unwillingness to respond to the good. When prompted by grace, sloth remains unmoved. In the end it despairs of any change.

Avarice not only is the disordered love of possessions but is primarily the love of possessing. It can be characterized not so much by what it desires as by its desire for more. Avarice can never be satisfied, for there is always something more to be acquired.

Gluttony, like avarice, is an appetite unto itself, a perversion of the proper love of food and drink. The glutton is unable to savor food and drink, only interested in devouring more.

Lust, closely related to avarice and gluttony, also desires more. **Sexuality**, like food and drink, is among God's great gifts to humanity, but lust devalues sex in its incessant desire for more. Unbridled lust destroys relationships.

An understanding of the seven deadly sins can be most helpful for **spiritual formation**. This typology can allow one to look beyond individual sins to the occasions for sin and the underlying attitudes from which they grow.

Lance Webb offered a readable look at the list in *How Bad Are Your Sins?* PJ

SMITH, HANNAH WHITALL (1832–1911), American evangelist and writer. Born in Philadelphia, Hannah was raised in a strict **Quaker** family but rebelled against the beliefs of the Quaker Meeting House and left the fellowship in 1859. This rebellion led to temporary estrangement from her parents. She exhibited an inquiring, independent mind and spirit. Hannah and her husband, Robert, led an evangelistic team ministry in England from 1874 to 1875; but Robert was prone to nervous breakdowns and wandering ways, so they returned to Philadelphia. His undependability was a distinct burden to Hannah, especially when he claimed he had become a Buddhist. Four of her children died in childhood, but the three who grew to adulthood did not embrace the Christian faith. The Smiths moved back to England in 1889, where Robert died in 1898. In 1903 Hannah published a spiritual autobiography, *The Unselfishness of God and How I Discovered It.* She suffered ill health the last years of her life.

Hannah Smith was ahead of her time in her theology. Her first book, *The Christian's Secret of a Happy Life*, was published in 1875. Her religious **experience** was not emotional; rather she thought it a matter of character, of recognizing God's presence within and living it without. She warned persons not to trust feelings about matters of faith, believing feelings are unreliable; faithfulness is the important thing. Her inner faith and relationship with God sustained her, and she taught that God is all—enough and all-sufficient. In addition to sharing a spiritual message, she was active in social causes, especially temperance and women's suffrage. *The God of All Comfort* was her last writing.

Smith's books are still available in various forms and editions. A biography, *The Secret Life of Hannah Whitall Smith*, by Marie Henry is based largely upon Smith's letters and journals. EWF

SOLITUDE. The experience of oneness with God that comes of taking the time and effort to be available to the One who is closer than our breathing, closer than our imagining. Solitude helps us find the answers to our own mystery and to the mystery of the God by whom we were created. Although both *monastery* and *monk* stem from the same Greek word, *monachos,* meaning "alone" or "single," it is not necessary to be alone to encounter solitude or to be in a definite place. Paradoxically, solitude actually enables us to connect to others in a far deeper way than does mere attachment to others. Solitude is a oneness of mind and heart.

True solitude cannot be entered without an attitude of **abandonment** or surrender—surrender of the ego and the affectations of the false self. We have entered into solitude when we no longer perceive God as judging parent but as friend. The essence of solitude

is to hear the voice of Christ, not only in mystical moments but also in and through the voice of every human—to see Christ's face in every human face. One who has received a oneness of mind and heart through solitude is a person through whom others experience **peace**—not only a peacemaker but also a peace-giver.

Solitude has been a major theme for spiritual writers from the **desert fathers and mothers** to **Carlo Carretto**. Recent writers exploring their own experience of solitude include Catherine de Hueck Doherty in *Poustinia* and Elizabeth J. Canham in *Heart Whispers*. RMH

SOUL. Theories about the nature of the soul, the soul's relationship to the body, and the soul's survival of physical death are numerous. Yet no clear and universally accepted understanding of the concept of soul has emerged. In common language the term is most often used as a synonym for **spirit**, denoting the mysterious, immaterial aspect, or "higher consciousness," of a human being. This common usage reflects the widespread assimilation of ancient Greek influence on language and thought. Platonists held that the soul was the immaterial substance or aspect of human beings that was most akin to the nature of the gods. Because of its temporary residency within the body, the soul was the rational or higher principle that accounted for human progress and becoming. It was this aspect of humanity that survived the death of the body. The ancient Greeks were not alone in developing a dualistic understanding of soul-body. The ancient Egyptians, the Chinese, and the Muslim and Hindu religions also conceived of a duality of the material and immaterial aspects of human nature.

Hebrew and early Christian tradition did not have a soul-body dichotomy. The founding understanding of human nature was of a unity—an indivisible being (Gen. 2:7, *nephesh*). The soul was not independent of the body. A soul did not possess a body nor a body a soul. Soul was synonymous with "being," so that a living person was understood as a "living soul." When the psalmist sings "my soul thirsts for God," his whole being desires God and needs God for existence: Just as one cannot exist without water, one cannot exist without God. This biblical use and understanding of the concept of soul is central to comprehending the emphasis placed on the bodily resurrection in early Christian doctrine.

The dichotomy current in Christian writings about the soul originates in the Greek philosophical influence on Christianity. Confusion in Christianity between the Judaic and Greek understanding of the word *soul* comes largely through a **Gnostic** and **Neoplatonic** misinterpretation of the apostle Paul's use of the Greek words *sarx* ("flesh"), *soma* ("body"), *pneuma* ("spirit"), and *psyche* ("mind" or "soul"). Paul uses *psyche* (1 Thess. 2:8), *pneuma* (2 Cor. 2:13), *soma* (Rom. 12:1), and *sarx* (2 Cor. 7:5) in similar ways to refer to the self, reflecting a Hebraic rather than a Greek-Hellenistic understanding. Christian theologians like **Gregory of Nyssa** and **Augustine** are largely responsible for the widespread misreading of Paul in Christian thought. Both represented the body as the seat of sin that imprisons the higher spiritual soul. This Greek-Hellenistic understanding is not congruent with Paul's preaching that the body is wholly redeemed and destined for the Lord (1 Cor. 15:35 ff). Yet the dualistic idea of the body and soul as distinct entities acting upon each other continued to gain strength from medieval Scholasticism (**Thomas Aquinas**) through modern philosophical schools (René Descartes, Benedict de Spinoza, and Immanuel Kant).

For various views of the soul in Judaism, Christianity, and other religions, see *Death and the Afterlife*, edited by Jacob Neusner. See also Wolfhart Pannenberg, *What Is Man?* and Hans Küng, *Eternal Life*. CIZ

SOUL OF CHRIST. A fourteenth-century prayer asking for Christ's help throughout life and beyond. Pope John II (d. 1334) commended it, and **Margaret Ebner** used it in her devotions in the 1340s. It became popu-

lar when **Ignatius of Loyola** gave it a prominent place in *Spiritual Exercises* alongside **Hail Mary** and the **Lord's Prayer**. The prayer was originally written in Latin (*"Anima Christi"*), and many different English translations exist. This rhyming one is by **John Henry Newman**.

> Soul of Christ, be my sanctification;
> Body of Christ, be my salvation;
> Blood of Christ, fill all my veins;
> Water of Christ's side, wash out my stains;
> Passion of Christ, my comfort be;
> O good Jesu, listen to me;
> In thy wounds I fain would hide,
> Ne'er to be parted from thy side;
> Guard me, should the foe assail me;
> Call me when my life shall fail me;
> Bid me come to thee above,
> With thy saints to sing thy love,
> World without end. Amen.

KRB

SPENER, PHILIPP JAKOB (1635–1705), German Lutheran pastor, writer, and religious reformer. Born in Rappoltsweiler and educated at Strassburg, Spener grew up in a church that emphasized dogmatic interpretation of scripture and rigid adherence to doctrine. His book *Pia Desideria* (*Pious Desires*) named what he saw as the problems of so exacting a faith system and proposed measures for reform.

Spener identified a number of problems with the religious system of his day: governmental interference, vice, the presumption that clergy were more holy or could be closer to God than laity, a general lack of piety, and a preoccupation with disputed theologies. He proposed concrete correctives that led to a type of religious life we now know as **Pietism**.

Two of his suggestions are of particular importance. Against the presumptuous position of clergy, Spener advocated the priesthood of all believers, a Lutheran doctrine that had lost prominence. He felt that laypersons had the same access to the Holy as did clergy, and with this access came responsibilities. Accordingly he organized the laity into small groups or circles (called *collegia pietatis*) so that they could study the scriptures or other devotional books and provide encouragement, accountability, and comfort to one another. For Spener, Christianity was not a matter of faith systems alone but of **faith** put to **work** in the diligent study of **scripture** and a life of Christian **love**. Faith involved the practice of **holiness** and an ongoing process of growth and rebirth. When people live into their faith through study and action, reformation of social injustice and help for the needy are natural outcomes. Some of the first charitable hospitals and orphanages in Europe were begun as Pietists acted out their faith in the world.

Against a preoccupation with theologies, Spener contended that Christian living was more than an intellectual endeavor and that arguments over points of doctrine only damaged the church and its people. He encouraged the subordination of scholarly study to **spiritual formation** in all religious training.

Pia Desideria is available translated, edited, and with an introduction by Theodore G. Tappert. SN

SPIRIT. Like **soul**, heart, mind, **will**, imagination, and intellect, the concept of a human spirit has been used to denote some aspect or power of a person's immaterial nature. These powers have sometimes been called "faculties of the soul." Unfortunately, such terms have been used both generally and specifically, formally and informally, without consistency of any kind. At first glance, the terms *heart* and *mind* may not seem as ambiguous as *spirit* and *soul*, which are often confused with each other and even used interchangeably by different writers. However, in the German language the same term—*geist*—has been used to refer both to the human mind and to the human spirit, implying that these terms are synonymous. In the history of Christian **spirituality** they are not.

The terms *spirit* and *soul* come to us with Hebrew roots in the Old Testament and Greek counterparts in the New Testament. The Greek terms are certainly influenced by

their Hebrew predecessors but are also heavily influenced by their use in Greek philosophy. To make matters worse, there is no consistency in the use of these terms in either the Old or New Testament, so their biblical roots are not a great source of help.

In its most general sense the term *spirit*, when used in a sentence like "Lucy's children were aware of her spirit whenever they entered the kitchen," can refer to a person's unique presence or individuality. This very general sense, while widely used, lacks the more specific uses of *spirit* within Christian spirituality to refer to one or more aspects of a person's spiritual nature.

Christian spirituality employs the term *human spirit* in two technical ways. Some of the ancient and esoteric traditions of Christian spirituality that trace their roots to the Dead Sea Scrolls and the Essenes of the New Testament times use *spirit* to refer to the deepest inner core or center of a human individual. The "image and likeness" of God is the deepest self of a person. Depending on the tradition, the eternal, divine, or uncreated part of the human being does not die but lives beyond death. These traditions, as well as their contemporary counterparts, tend to use the term *soul* or *ego* to refer to the temporary, created personality of the human individual, as opposed to the eternal spirit. While these traditions have always been present within Christian spirituality, they have normally been more prominent in Eastern Christian spirituality than in Western, taking a more peripheral, sometimes almost occult, role in the West.

Other more prominent traditions in Western Christian spirituality tend to use *soul* to refer to the deepest spiritual center of a person. For them, the term *spirit* is more dynamic, referring to the human capacity for **transcendence** or openness to God and the divine. Like the intellect and imagination, the spirit is assumed to be part of the larger, more general category of the human mind. The intellectual faculty of the human spiritual nature is the capacity to acquire and store knowledge and to think logically and systematically.

The imaginative faculty is the capacity to remember and to project into the future, perceiving what is not physically present. The spiritual faculty (spirit), while using both intellect and imagination, is the capacity to transcend the intellectual and imaginative faculties. It provides the human being with the ability to **meditate**, **contemplate**, **pray**, and be **receptive** to divine **grace** and inspiration from the **Holy Spirit**. JWK

SPIRITUALISM. Belief in a spirit world that coexists with and overlaps the material world, although some schools of thought deny material reality altogether. Known as spiritism in Europe, spiritualism combines elements of philosophy, science (or pseudoscience), and religion. Spiritualism reflects the notions of the surrounding culture, especially optimism about human nature, scientific progress, and social improvement.

The guiding principles of spiritualism include divine parenthood over the whole human family, the communion of spirits and ministry of angels, the continuous existence of the human soul, personal responsibility, compensation or retribution for all good and evil deeds done on earth, and the offer of eternal progress to every soul. These principles influence belief in extra sensory perception (ESP), psychics, clairvoyants, mediums, seances, hauntings, fairies, and other supernatural phenomena.

Some consider **Emanuel Swedenborg** (1688–1772) to be the godfather of spiritualism. He began his work in this field in 1744, claiming to communicate with spirits and travel through the spirit world. He touted himself as a clairvoyant, a psychic, able to see the future through dreams. He also wrote books that he said were directly inspired by spirits and angels. Modern spiritualism began in 1848 in Hydesville, New York, when sisters Margaretta and Catherine Fox moved with their parents into a haunted house. The girls developed a system of raps to communicate with the spirit. People, and evidently spirits, flocked to the house, and the sisters went on

tour to promote spiritualism. The most famous proponent of spiritualism was Sir Arthur Conan Doyle (1859–1930), who lectured extensively about the proof for life after death and life beyond our senses. He felt spiritualism rose above and beyond any one faith yet offered "a sound experiential basis for faith."

Spiritualism today offers immediate experience of the mysterious, a view of the afterlife that appeals to a sense of fairness, and a tradition of women in leadership, in contrast to and protest against the detached (often patriarchal) leadership, irrelevant theology, and boring worship of much mainstream Christianity. The success of movies, television series, and books about contact with ghosts and spirits testifies to the continuing popularity of spiritualism in our culture. WW

SPIRITUALITY. The Christian life lived in and through the presence and power of the **Holy Spirit**. In some earlier approaches to Christian life, spirituality was often associated with the interior life, the life of the **soul**, the life of the **virtues**, and the pursuit of **perfection** in and through their exercise. The soul was often viewed as the higher realm, and the spiritual life was aimed at keeping oneself unsullied by worldly concerns such as the tedium of family life and domestic concerns, the burdens of ill health, and the weight of too much work. While the view of Christian life in the Spirit in early Christian centuries included all dimensions of life, such an integrated and integrating view did not last. Spiritual concerns became more and more narrow over the course of Christian centuries until spirituality seemed restricted to the otherworldly **mysticism** of a spiritual elite, primarily religious professionals.

The Second Vatican Council (1962–65) affirmed that all the baptized are called to one and the same **holiness** through the perfection of charity. In the aftermath of this affirmation, it is more commonly recognized that the Spirit is present in a great variety of life forms, as well as in the wide range of Christian traditions. With this acknowledgment has come a measure of imprecision in the use of the term *spirituality*, even within a specifically Christian context.

Spirituality is a rich and multivalent reality with four strands or levels to which the term applies: (1) a fundamental dimension of human being; (2) the full range of human experience as it is brought to bear on the quest for integration through self-transcendence; (3) the expression of insights about this experience; (4) a disciplined study. Whether as lived experience or as a subject of study, the focus of Christian spirituality is Christian spiritual **experience** as such, that is as Christian, as spiritual, as experience. As a lived experience, Christian spirituality is a way of living for God through Christ, in the presence and by the power of the Spirit.

Contemporary approaches to Christian spirituality are greatly enriched by an appropriate understanding of the central Christian doctrine of the Trinity. Christian spirituality considered from this perspective entails being conformed to the person of Christ and brought into communion with God and others through the gift of the Spirit. Since the doctrine of the Trinity, with its insights on the three-in-one loving communion, expresses not just who and how we understand God to be but what we think a human is called to be and become, an approach to spirituality grounded in the Trinity emphasizes relationship, persons, and communion.

Since Christian spirituality *is* Christian living in the Spirit, it is concerned with every dimension of life: mind and body, intimacy and sexuality, work and leisure, economic accountability and political responsibility, domestic life and civic duty, the rising costs of health care, and the plight of the poor and wounded at home and abroad. All created reality is to be taken up in our quest to be conformed to the person of Christ and brought into communion though the Spirit to the **glory** of God the Father. The various dimensions of the Christian spiritual life—**prayer**, vocation, **discernment**, **asceticism**, the relationship of church and world, healing and

wholeness, action and **contemplation**, **mysticism** are thus understood to bring one into a deeper participation in the divine life, into fuller communion with the three-in-one Love, by living in right relationship with others and every living creature.

No single understanding of the Christian spiritual life has ever existed. From early Christian centuries there has been a variety of approaches, many different ways of following the Way. Various figures and movements have had different insights into the gospel message and have tried to give flesh to their insight, resulting in different traditions, teachings, writings, customs, forms of life, exemplary figures, and institutions. In due course, these come to be accepted as a gift to the whole church, a way for others to advance in the manner of the gospel. In an instance where a given way of living maintains its vitality over many years, thereby becoming a tradition within the church, it is referred to as a school of spirituality. Each school employs a distinctive understanding of such elements of the spiritual life as prayer, discernment of spirits, the place of **scripture**, the need for a **rule** of life, the function of **community**.

A school of spirituality may be understood in terms of a particular way of hearing and responding to the gospel. For example, **Francis** and **Dominic**, living at roughly the same time, listened to and heard the story of Christ very differently. Each appropriates a different image, a distinct understanding of Christ. For Dominic what is central is Christ the preacher and teacher; for Francis it is the crucified Christ as God's **compassion** for the world. These two ways of hearing the gospel then give rise to two distinct ways of living the gospel: the Franciscan and Dominican schools. In like fashion there emerge, from different ways of hearing and responding to the gospel, diverse schools of spirituality outside the Roman Catholic Church, for example, Lutheran or Wesleyan.

The diversity of Christian spiritualities is itself expressive of the magnitude of God's love in human life, history, the world, and the church, yet these spiritualities share common features. A Christian spirituality is rooted in the person of Christ, the **Paschal mystery**, and in the gift of the Holy Spirit, especially as disclosed in the scriptures and in the living body of believers, the church. Its hallmarks are **faith**, **hope**, and **love**.

For further reading, see *Christian Spirituality: Themes from the Tradition* by Lawrence S. Cunningham and Keith J. Egan or *Understanding Christian Spirituality* by Michael Downey. MD

SPURGEON, CHARLES HADDON (1834–92), English Baptist pastor and author. His early spiritual life was greatly shaped by his father and grandfather, who were Independent pastors. Following his conversion, he began ministry as a Baptist pastor at the tender age of seventeen. His growing popularity required larger and larger buildings to hold those who were attracted to his magnetic and convicting preaching. Before he was twenty, he was called to the New Park Street Chapel in London, later replaced by the six thousand-seat Metropolitan Tabernacle. His expository preaching, which blended humor and illustrations from contemporary life, was complemented by a sensitive compassion for others. Spurgeon demonstrated this balanced nature of the gospel through the establishment of an orphanage, an outreach institution, and other groups to distribute devotional literature and social services to those in need. He founded The Pastor's College (now Spurgeon's College) in London to train people for ministry. Spurgeon had a deep love for the Puritan writings of the seventeenth century, being particularly fond of Richard Sibbes and reportedly having read **John Bunyan**'s *The Pilgrim's Progress* more than a hundred times during his life. His theology recognized **sin**'s alienating effect and the saving **grace** of Jesus Christ to restore people to a proper relationship with God. His evangelical **Calvinist** spirituality emphasized the primacy of our union with Christ and often brought him into conflict with hyper-Calvinists on one side and Arminians

on the other. The punishing demands he placed upon himself led to periodic struggles with ill health.

Spurgeon authored more than 135 works and is best remembered today for his sermons, especially *The Treasury of David* (on the Psalms), his daily devotional classic *Morning and Evening*, and *Lectures to My Students* (condensed as *Encounter with Spurgeon*, with introduction and comments by Helmut Thielicke). The most prominent biographies are *The Forgotten Spurgeon* by Iain Murray and *Spurgeon* by Arnold Dallimore. TS

STAGES OF SPIRITUAL GROWTH. From the beginnings of Christianity, some have tried to describe the believer's progress and growth in the faith in terms of "stages." The various descriptions of faith stages seek to illuminate a steady and ongoing progression that leads to **holiness**, maturity, transformation, and Christian **perfection**, or Christlikeness. In 1 Corinthians 3:1-3, Paul describes the Corinthians as infants in Christ, unable to digest spiritual solid food; thus he offers teaching and instruction at that immature level. In Ephesians we read of helping one another to grow "until all of us come to the unity of the faith and of the knowledge of the Son of God, to maturity, to the measure of the full stature of Christ" (4:13). The fullness of redemption in Christ comes to us in the imperfect state of childhood and in the future state of maturity or being "grown-up" in Christ (1 Cor. 13:11). The perfection of maturity is not to be understood as an ethical or moral perfection but in the sense of an appropriation of the full salvation of Christ. "New life" experiences growth and an increase in faith, or advancement toward perfection. We seek to grow not in order to be saved but so that we can be more like the one who has already saved us.

Another ancient metaphor for stages of spiritual growth was the **ladder**, developed in the writings of **Origen**, **Evagrius**, and the sixth-century monk named **John Climacus**, whose handbook *The Ladder of Divine Ascent* became one of the most widely used in the

Greek Church and in the growing **monastic** movement.

During the time of the **desert fathers and mothers** and through the works of various mystical writers across the centuries, a three-stage schema was adopted to describe the degrees or stages of Christian perfection: the **purgative way**, the **illuminative way**, and the **unitive way**. Each of these "ways" had corresponding **disciplines** and prayers to aid the soul's advancement in the life of grace.

Søren Kierkegaard, a Danish pastor and philosopher, also asserted a three-stage format in his *Stages on Life's Way*. He called these three "existence-spheres" because each stage or sphere made an absolute claim upon the individual in such a way that everything was interpreted through the lens of that particular worldview. These stages are:

The Aesthetic: Living devoutly in the intellect or in the pursuit of pleasure. Devotion to the intellect is simply a sophisticated immediate pleasure, very much like the immediate common pleasure of the pursuits of money, power, reputation, or sex.

The Ethical: Seeking both self-understanding and self-mastery in conforming life to the standards of moral perfection. The ethical person's relationship with God is mediated by a sense of duty. Actions must always be measured against this criterion of moral perfection.

The Religious: Two ways of being that Kierkegaard calls religious A and religious B. The former is the universal religious, in that the individual relates to self in the light of eternal destiny. The latter is Christianity proper, or authentically Christian, because the individual relates the self to the absolute, eternal paradox of the God-Man Jesus.

Kierkegaard's stages allow for no gradual merging, development, or necessary transformation from one stage or sphere to another. Kierkegaard maintains that movement from one to the other requires a radical "leap" of faith and thus a totally new viewpoint.

The most recent use of the human maturation process to describe spiritual growth is James W. Fowler's *Stages of Faith: The Psychology of Human Development and the Quest for Meaning*. Fowler raises this biblical metaphor to the level of a comprehensive theoretical school within the discipline of religious psychology. The main assumptions of his stage theory are grounded in the theories of human development of Erik Erikson, Jean Piaget, and Lawrence Kohlberg. The key theoretical assumption Fowler takes from these theorists is that there is a normative progression that drives faith to maturity. Fowler's human moral development theory has tremendously influenced modern Christian education and the shaping of church curriculum. His stages are as follows:

Primal (infancy): A disposition of trust and mutuality in the context of one's relationship with primary caregivers.

Intuitive-Projective (early childhood): A sense of external dependability of the world and (through the experience of stories, moods, and actions) an imaginative sense of shared meaning.

Mythic-Literal (childhood and beyond): Binding personal experience into general meaning by adding one's story to the shared story, giving a sense of coherence to experience.

Synthetic-Conventional (adolescence and beyond): Stepping out of the self-narrative, or the flow of the shared story, to reflect on one's own ways of experiencing, allowing one to see patterns and structures of meaning.

Individuative-Reflective (young adulthood and beyond): Critical reflection upon shared beliefs and values and self-differentiation.

Conjunctive (midlife and beyond): The ability to embrace polarities, paradox, and multiple interpretations of reality; an integrative sense of self and self-exploration; and universalizing apprehensions.

Universalizing Faith (midlife and beyond): Overcoming the paradox of the previous stage to move toward "activist **incarnation**"— living out the imperatives of absolute love and justice.

See also such allegorical descriptions of Christian growth as *The Pilgrim's Progress* by **John Bunyan**, *Hinds' Feet on High Places* by **Hannah Hurnard**, or *The Pilgrim's Regress* by **C. S. Lewis**. CIZ

STEERE, DOUGLAS V. (1901–95), American **Quaker** philosopher and leader. Born in Harbor Beach, Michigan, he was educated in the Detroit public schools, at Michigan Agricultural College (now Michigan State University), and at Harvard University (Ph.D., 1931). A Rhodes scholar at Oxford (1926–29), he evidenced keen interest in Christian **mysticism** and wrote his dissertation on the religious philosophy of Baron **Friedrich von Hügel**. From 1928 to 1963 Steere served as professor of philosophy at Haverford College, first as a colleague of **Rufus Jones** and then as chair of the department. He and his wife, Dorothy, joined the Religious Society of Friends in 1932. An activist, Steere undertook numerous missions for the American Friends Service Committee, organizing a relief effort for war-torn Finland after World War II. From 1948 until 1984 he and Dorothy traveled in Europe, Asia, and Africa for six months every other year on behalf of the AFSC and/or the Friends World Committee for Consultation. He served as an Official Observer in three of the four sessions of the Second Vatican Council (1962–65).

Engaged in a deep religious search from his college years on, Steere contributed significantly to the deepening of **spirituality** among Protestants. Touched by a month-long **retreat** at a **Benedictine** monastery, he envisioned for himself the task of helping men and women become aware of the life of God in their own hearts and minds. Despite a crowded schedule, he conducted retreats patterned after the Benedictine model. Beginning with his popular book *Prayer and Worship*, he addressed most of his writings to living a life of devotion in a world that does much to inhibit it. In a treatise *On Beginning from Within*, written during World War II, he contended that **saints** are what the world needs

most. Some of his writings, especially his tribute to Baron von Hügel and *On Listening to Another*, directly focused on **spiritual direction**.

In addition to Steere's books, see *Love at the Heart of Things: A Biography of Douglas V. Steere* by E. Glenn Hinson. EGH

STEIN, EDITH (1891–1942), German **Carmelite** nun and **martyr**. Born into a devout Jewish family on Yom Kippur at Breslau, Germany, Stein died as a Carmelite nun at Auschwitz on August 9, 1942. At thirteen, she renounced Judaism and became an atheist. Showing exceptional intellectual capacities from early on, she sought to get to the root of things and understand them from their depths. Soon after she enrolled at the University of Breslau, Stein transferred to the University of Gottingen, where she studied under Edmund Husserl, the founder of phenomenology. Recognizing her intellectual acumen, Husserl invited Edith to assist him at his new assignment at the University of Freiburg. At twenty-five she completed her doctoral dissertation ("On the Problem of Empathy"), graduating *summa cum laude*.

Having been educated by some Christian professors, Stein sensed something different in them that attracted her. Her conversion occurred while reading the autobiography of **Teresa of Ávila**. Staying up all night to finish the book, she found the truth for which she longed. On January 1, 1922, Stein was baptized. She spent much time reading the New Testament, gradually reclaiming the faith in God she had earlier abandoned.

After teaching in a convent school, Stein became a leader in the German Catholic movement through her speaking, lecturing, teaching, and writing. Because of her Jewish background, she was not allowed to accept a lectureship at the University of Münster. In 1933 she entered the Carmelite monastery at Cologne as Sister Teresa Benedicta of the Cross, where she continued to work on her philosophical writings and translations. With the Nazi threat growing, she was transferred in 1938 to the Carmelite monastery at Echt in Holland. Her sister Rosa, also a convert, joined her at the monastery. On July 26, 1942, Hitler ordered all non-Aryan Roman Catholics arrested. Seven days later, the Gestapo arrested the two sisters. Just fifty years old, Edith died in the gas chambers of Auschwitz. Survivors have given eyewitness accounts of her unusual compassion and care as she ministered to those in need. Suffering for and with "her people" was a call from God that she willingly and lovingly accepted. On October 11, 1998, Sister Teresa Benedicta of the Cross was canonized.

For a biography, read Hilda C. Graef's *The Scholar and the Cross* (1955) or Waltraud Herbstrith's *Edith Stein* (1985). Many of Edith Stein's works have been translated into English. EKM

STIGMATA. A mystical phenomenon described as the appearance of the wounds of Christ on a Christian believer. The stigmata exist in two forms, visible and invisible. Visible wounds correspond with the marks of the Passion of Christ on the hands, feet, side, back, or brow, accompanied by intense suffering. Blood may flow from the openings for a time, then suddenly disappear and the wounds heal. A stigmatic may bear only one of the wounds of Christ or several simultaneously. In the invisible form, the stigmatic experiences intense pain corresponding with the marks of the Passion without any outward marks or blood flow. **Francis of Assisi** manifested visible stigmata. On the fortieth day of a **retreat** in 1224, while meditating on the Passion, he received a vision and stigmata of all five wounds. **Catherine of Siena** experienced the invisible form of stigmata. While she prayed on the fourth Sunday of Lent in 1375, the visible wounds of Christ's passion appeared on her hands and feet, but, concerned about the attention they drew, in **humility** she prayed that they might be made invisible. Though the intense pain remained, the visible marks disappeared. The grace of this psycho-spiritual-somatic phenomenon (the stigmata) is related to **compassion** for Christ in his **suffering** and sorrows. The psychosomatic

connection is the most scientifically accepted explanation for stigmata, while the Catholic Church and other Christian theorists hold to a supernatural cause or to some intermediate position.

Michael Freze discusses many cases of stigmata including that of Padre Pio (1887–1968), an Italian priest and well-documented modern stigmatic, in *They Bore the Wounds of Christ: The Mystery of the Sacred Stigmata.* CIZ

SUFFERING. Why does suffering exist, and where is God when we suffer? Does God speak to us through our suffering or in spite of it? Does suffering have any redemptive qualities at all? Can it strengthen us, open our eyes, and make us more compassionate? Can we suffer for another?

Two of the world's great religions Hinduism and Buddhism deal with this subject as a foundational concern. Hinduism speaks of *samsara*, the painful wheel of birth, death, and many reincarnations until one has satisfied *karma* (the law of retribution) and become one with Brahman through the *yogas.* Buddha states in his first two Great Truths: "All life is suffering. We suffer because we desire." That is, we suffer because we want too much, so our desires are never satisfied. **Augustine, Luther,** and others take up this theme, teaching that we are "curved in" upon ourselves, self-centered and greedy, never satisfied. That same theme flows through the story of Eden in Hebrew Scriptures. Islam's emphasis is more focused on Allah as sovereign, believing that history is the working out of Allah's will. Islam also insists that forgetting God, the greatest **sin**, will have dire consequences.

The **Psalms** in particular indicate that ancient Hebrews generally considered suffering the result of sin and righteousness the means to a happy life (see Psalms 1; 91 as examples). But Job was written to challenge this very assumption. And Jesus' life and teaching say the opposite is often true. Jesus suffered and died as the result of his goodness and **love.** He told his disciples in no uncertain terms that those who followed him would be persecuted, thrown out of religious institutions (synagogues), and killed. He warned that persecutors would even think they were serving God by their actions (John 16:2, 33).

E. Stanley Jones, in *Christ and Human Suffering*, lists three causes of suffering: inherited genetic tendencies, victimization by others, and our own tragic choices. Dorothee Soelle, in *Suffering*, includes the pain of those self-imprisoned by their inability to communicate or express their need.

Theodicy attempts to deal with God's relationship with and responsibility in human suffering. We frequently hear that God, who is supposed to be in control, sends suffering as a test or at least teaches us through suffering. But saying that God can bring good out of any circumstance differs greatly from insisting that God sends suffering for our good. Nevertheless, every major spiritual hero has suffered because of his or her witness and has been refined through **grace** within and in spite of tragedy. This surely is one of the meanings of Jesus' words: "Behold, I have conquered the world" (John16:33). That conquering will be clear in heaven. Suffering is not the last word. God's victory is.

Another major theme in both Hebrew and Christian scripture is God's presence in our suffering. Isaiah 43:2 says that God will go with us through the waters. Psalm 23:4 asserts confidently: "Even though I walk through the darkest valley, I fear no evil; for you are with me." God in Christ is Immanuel, "God with us." So Hebrews 13:5 states, "I will never leave you or forsake you."

Human beings suffer for one another in love; and in commitment and even **martyrdom**, some truly suffer for God. Christianity says that God has suffered and continues to suffer for us. Love involves suffering.

We suffer because of lack of knowledge and lack of sensitivity, because of accidents and random happenings. But suffering never has the final word. Grace touches us with insight and meaning, comfort and courage *now*. Grace also gives hope. Psalm 126:5 looks for a day when "those who sow in tears reap with shouts of joy!" And Jesus says, "Blessed are those who mourn, for they will be comforted.... Blessed are those who hunger... for they will be filled" (Matt. 5:4, 6). GAB

SUSO, HENRY (ca. 1295–1366), **Dominican** friar. An attractive and approachable German mystic, Suso was widely influential across many centuries. His books were extraordinarily popular in western Europe and were eagerly read by **Thomas à Kempis**. During his active life, Suso was in great demand as a spiritual director.

After beginning his education with the Dominicans in Constance, Suso studied for about four years with **Meister Eckhart** at Cologne. He absorbed the best of Eckhart's instruction but carefully expressed his own views and experiences in language that was less likely to result in misunderstanding and criticism. Suso had a **conversion** experience at the age of eighteen. Mystical visions and rapturous episodes often accompanied his life of **contemplation**. He spoke and wrote about these moments in the same terms used by Paul in 2 Corinthians 12:2-4 but with more elaboration and detail.

Suso's second book, *Little Book of Eternal Wisdom*, provides us with essential Suso in a straightforward, practical guide for the spiritual life. Six years later it was expanded and revised as *Horologium Sapientiae* (*The Clock of Wisdom*). Other books include a spiritual autobiography and collections of his sermons and letters. Suso's love for God and God's world radiates from his writing. In describing his personal prayer life, he speaks of assembling an orchestra of birds, animals, fish, plants, soil, moisture, and "specks of dust that dance in the sunbeams." Then, as a conductor, he leads all creation in praise to "our dear and gentle God."

Some of Suso's writings are available in *Henry Suso: The Exemplar, with Two German Sermons*, translated by Frank J. Tobin. BKB

SWEDENBORG, EMANUEL (1688–1772), theologian, scientist, philosopher, Sweden's foremost mathematician, and publisher of its first scientific journal. His followers formed the Church of the New Jerusalem, now numbering fifty thousand members worldwide. While searching for the "seat of the **soul**," Swedenborg studied philosophy, natural sciences, and mathematics at Uppsala University, learning most of the European languages, Greek, Hebrew, and Latin. He also studied physics, chemistry, optics, metallurgy, astronomy, several trades, and new concepts of mining. He was appointed to the Royal Board of Mines. Swedenborg envisioned complicated particle combinations developing into the planetary system and proposed the radical idea that matter was based on motion.

Following a spiritual crisis at fifty-five, Swedenborg concentrated on religious philosophy. Having studied science religiously, Swedenborg approached religion scientifically. He accepted the reality of the spiritual dimension and wrote accounts of going there. His human-centered theology postulated a spiritual world populated solely by dead humans grouped into heavenly or infernal societies. He taught that God is the infinite, indivisible power and life within all creation, unified in essence and being. The Trinity represents God's essential qualities: **love**, **wisdom**, activity. Since creation originates in divine love and wisdom, created things are forms and aspects of that love and wisdom. Material things "correspond" to spiritual realities. Humans brought **evil** into the world by diverting their love from God to their own ego. The Second Coming means God's revelation for a new age of religious truth and reason. Swedenborg's mystical visions influenced several writers, among them **Blake**, **Emerson**, Poe, Balzac, the Brownings, Coleridge, and Helen Keller. His most significant theological works are *Arcana Coelestia* (*Heavenly Secrets*), *Heaven and Hell*, *Divine Love and Wisdom*, and *The True Christian Religion*.

The Church of the New Jerusalem focuses on personal spiritual development illuminated by the divine presence within to bring in the New Age and the descent of the Holy City, New Jerusalem. Stephen Larsen's introduction in *Emanuel Swedenborg: The Universal Human and Soul-Body Interaction* (translated by George F. Dole) provides a helpful overview of Swedenborg's life and work. LSP

SYMEON THE NEW THEOLOGIAN (949–1022), Eastern Orthodox mystic and theologian. In the tenth century the Orthodox Church experienced a spiritual revival. At the apex of that revival was Symeon the New Theologian. For Symeon, God was a mystery beyond all reason and human understanding. Yet he insisted that true Christians can experience God directly and personally, contradicting those who held that the age of such connection to God had ended with the apostles. He even said that such an experience signals the authenticity of one's **faith**. He wrote that all people are capable of observing the commandments and becoming like the **saints** of the past. Those who deny that possibility are heretics.

Three things are important about Symeon's understanding of direct **experience** of God: First, the experience of God may come through the senses, such as visions of divine light. Second, it is paradoxical. Creation (even a blade of grass) is transformed by our **union** with God, yet remains unchanged. In union God is intimately known while remaining utter mystery. We humans are **deified** through union and can participate in the divine life here on earth, though we never lose our personal identity. What is more, we need not go to mountain caves or monastic cells to live a life of **holiness**. Such a life can be lived in the midst of everyday events. Third, the experience of God is not automatic. There is much work to be done if we are to live a sacred life. We must repent and show our great remorse.

For further study, you may want to consider *St. Symeon the New Theologian and Orthodox Tradition* by Hilarion Alfeyev or *Symeon the New Theologian: The Discourses*, translated by C. J. de Catanzaro. SN

T

TAIZÉ. A village in southern France where Swiss Reformed pastor Roger Schultz founded a unique **monastic** community in 1940. He originally intended to establish a bridge between French and German Christians that would become a source of reconciliation. The bridge-building later extended to the effort to reconcile East and West and Protestant and Catholic. The Taizé Community is ecumenical, one of the few places where Catholics and Protestants share in **Holy Communion** together with the blessing of the churches. It has always been a community that welcomes seekers. During the summer months, thousands of young people from all over Europe and beyond flock to the fields around the village to join in worship with the brothers and to study scripture together. The Taizé brothers are deeply committed to working with the poor and founded a mission in Calcutta alongside that of **Mother Teresa**. Perhaps Taizé is best known as the source of many meditative chants and songs used by Protestants and Catholics alike. This music, which is easily sung and frequently repeated, becomes sung prayer.

The community's history is told in *The Story of Taizé* by J. L. G. Balado. Its **spirituality** is described in *Living Today for God* by Brother Roger. HLR

TAKE, LORD, AND RECEIVE. This prayer of **abandonment** to Christ is found in paragraph 234 of *Spiritual Exercises* by **Ignatius of Loyola**. At the climax of the fourth week of exercises, after the retreatant has prayed through the birth, life, death, and resurrection of Christ, Ignatius offers a "Contemplation to Attain Love." The following prayer is part of that exercise of contemplation to attain love:

Take, Lord, and receive all my liberty, my memory, my understanding, and all my will, whatever I have and possess. You have given me all these things. To you, O Lord, I restore them. All are yours, dispose of them entirely according to your will. Give me your love and your grace, for these are enough for me.

Jesuit John Foley has written a beautiful musical setting for the prayer, "Take, Lord, Receive." KRB

TAULER, JOHANNES (ca. 1300–61), medieval German mystic, Dominican monk, and preacher. Johannes Tauler, like **Henry Suso**, was a disciple of **Meister Eckhart** and an important voice of German **mysticism**, sometimes referred to as *devotio moderna*, in the late medieval period. Known as a preacher and spiritual director in Strassburg and Basel, Tauler, like Eckhart, spoke and wrote about a spark or ground within the human **soul** that is both the image of God and God's perpetual dwelling place. Given to us as a result of **grace**, it is not an intrinsic part of the soul. God chooses to make a home in humans. In a related line of thinking, Tauler taught that the human soul goes back to God, its source. However, the return is accomplished by grace and the union of the human and divine wills, not through absorption into an infinite being.

Tauler valued the activities of everyday life, work, and labor, especially when entered into with an attitude of self-denial and sacrifice. He felt that the **contemplative** or **meditative** life must be balanced with the active life; the inward life must take into consideration the duties of living in **community**. His preaching, therefore, did not focus on carefully reasoned and intellectual approaches to faith but on moral issues and pious or religious living.

While he claimed that direct religious illumination was possible (because of the divine spark within each person), a sanctified life was one of love and service.

Tauler had a significant influence on **Martin Luther**, who said that Tauler's sermons were a source of pure theology. Luther was particularly drawn to Tauler's stress on the inward religion of **suffering**, self-denial, and corresponding reliance on grace that makes the inward religion possible. This emphasis, in part, moved Luther toward a theology holding that grace, not **works**, leads to salvation; yet works are of critical importance in our day-to-day living.

For further study, consider *Johannes Tauler: Sermons*, translated by Maria Shrady with an introduction by Josef Schmidt. SN

TAYLOR, JEREMY (1613–1667), Anglican bishop. Cambridge educated and associated with the Anglo-Catholic wing of the church during the reign of Charles I, he became chaplain to the king through the influence of Archbishop William Laud. He was imprisoned briefly by the Parliamentarians during the Cromwellian era, but after his release spent a decade under the patronage of the Earl of Carberry in Carmarthenshire. After the Restoration he was consecrated bishop of Down and Connor and appointed vicechancellor of Dublin University.

Taylor's devotional writings display great literary talents. *The Great Exemplar of Sanctity and Holy Life* was the first "life of Christ" in English but is also a book of devotional **meditation**, explication, and application. His twin works, *The Rule and Exercise of Holy Living* and *The Rule and Exercise of Holy Dying*, are handbooks for Christian living that draw on a wide range of both classical and Christian sources. They are characteristic expressions of Anglican **spirituality** in their balanced sobriety, disciplined piety, and emphasis on moderation in all things. Each chapter in these volumes concludes with prayers of his own composition that reflect his irenic outlook and spirit. Taylor's spirituality is both realistic and prac-

tical. His works combine thoughtful meditation on the most poignant aspects of life and death with astute advice and encouragement. The central theme of the Christian life, in his view, is God's requirement for believers to live holy lives. Such a life includes temperance and justice as well as godliness. The life of **holiness** demands a severe regimen and will include the ultimate crucible of **suffering** and death. Taylor exerted a profound influence upon the young **John Wesley**, who sought to exemplify his ideal of holy living and dying.

In addition to Taylor's books, see *The Piety of Jeremy Taylor* by Henry Trevor Hughes. PWC

TEARS. Christian spiritual tradition considers certain kinds of tears as a charism, a **gift of the Spirit**. Eastern churchmen like **Athanasius** and **John Climacus** in the early church and **Symeon the New Theologian** in the medieval era spoke of tears as such. Assuming that inner **dispositions** had corresponding outer expression, Eastern writers saw tears as the outward manifestation of the spiritual experience of *penthos* or **compunction**, the spiritual pain felt in recognition of sin and weakness and in an awakened longing for God. The ancient East understood there to be different types of tears, some of spiritual origin and import, others not. Spiritual tears were variously categorized and described. They could have purifying power and might function differently for those just beginning the spiritual journey and for those further along. They could be provoked by memory of sin as well as consideration of the goodness of God, the desire for heaven, the fear of hell, or the thought of judgment. Tears were a physical sign that a person's inner world was being transformed, manifesting the continuing power of the baptismal waters to redeem the created world.

The Western medieval church continued to explore the spiritual anatomy of tears. In the monastic **Rule** of Saint **Benedict**, tears are described as the natural accompaniment of true prayer. **Gregory I, the Great**, recounts the biblical story of Achsah, whose father Caleb gave her "the upper springs and the lower springs" near her home in the desert (Josh. 15:16-19). He interprets the upper springs as the tears we weep from desire for God and sadness at our separation in this life, while the lower springs are tears we shed for fear of punishment in hell. **Bernard of Clairvaux** spoke of tears of **penitence** as the bread from which one dare not fast and of tears of devotion, penitence, and neighborly love as the wine that grants spiritual inebriation. **Catherine of Siena** distinguished tears of death from tears of life and explicated four expressions of those living tears. She saw tears as the physical expression of a transforming inner process, reflective of the degree and direction of love at any given point in the spiritual journey. For Catherine, a disordered heart not yet fixed on God produces tears of death, referring more to the pain felt by the self than to any inner growth.

Tears of life, or spiritual tears proper, begin with the "puncturing" of the heart. At first such tears mainly purify: They come from sorrow for sins or fear of punishment. As love erodes fear and the **consolation** of a loving God is experienced, tears are prompted both by hunger for the **experience** of the divine in prayer or with others and by sorrow when these consoling experiences are withdrawn. As union with God occurs, tears spring from love of God in God's own self and from **compassion** for our neighbors. Finally, tears may be shed by a heart utterly identified with God's sorrowful, pierced, and loving heart. WMW

TEILHARD DE CHARDIN, PIERRE (1881–1955), French **Jesuit** priest, paleontologist, and philosopher.

Born into a pious French Catholic family, Pierre Teilhard de Chardin entered the Society of Jesus at the age of seventeen, was ordained a priest after thirteen years of training, and then served in World War I. He became recognized as a leading scientist and paleontologist of the twentieth century. Because his theological reflections pushed the seams of the institutional dogmas of the Catholic Church, he was forbidden to publish during much of his lifetime but was still allowed to do research, write, and teach. As an evolutionary scientist, Teilhard viewed the history of the human race within a framework both linear (Judeo-Christian tradition) and cyclical (Eastern forms of thought), substantiated by scientific research yet integrated into his Christian faith.

Teilhard was thoroughly committed to scientific progress yet equally committed as a Christian to Jesus Christ. His lifelong struggle with these two commitments became a gift to countless thinking believers. In *The Divine Milieu* he refers to this struggle as the double thread of inward spiritual development and outward success. The problem is how to reconcile love of God and **love** of the world, belief in the **cross** and belief in the fullest potential of human life. His resolution involved a new way of understanding the cross reflected in the diminishments of life, cosmically and personally, and in the Resurrection ultimately fulfilled by envisioning Christ as the "Omega Point" toward which all creation moves. Teilhard spoke of rhythms of "immersion" into the void and "emergence" into new life, simultaneously affecting the "within" of personal experience and the "without" of cosmic growth.

For further insight, read *The Phenomenon of Man* and *The Divine Milieu* by Teilhard de Chardin and *O Blessed Night!: Recovering from Addiction, Codependency and Attachment Based on the Insights of St. John of the Cross and Teilhard de Chardin* by Francis Kelly Nemeck and Marie Theresa Coombs. KIG

TEMPLE, WILLIAM (1881–1944), archbishop of Canterbury, theologian, and ecumenist.

One of the most prominent ecumenists of the twentieth century and arguably the most brilliant primate of the Church of England since Anselm and the most beloved archbishop of the modern era. Having received notable distinction in philosophy, classics, and ancient history at Oxford and possessing a rich variety of gifts, he was awarded a fellowship to teach philosophy, then became headmaster of Repton School, rector of St. James, Piccadilly, canon of Westminster, and after that successively bishop of Manchester, archbishop of York, and (like his father, Frederick Temple) archbishop of Canterbury, a critical wartime role cut short by his death in 1944. He combined a first-rate philosophical mind with theological acumen and a commitment to Christian social consciousness. His major theological writings—*Mens Creatrix, Christus Veritas,* and *Nature, Man, and God*—reveal an agile mind rooted in Platonic philosophical and Johannine theological traditions yet flexible and adaptable to changing currents of thought.

Temple came into prominence at the 1928 International Missionary Council meeting in Jerusalem, where he exhibited extraordinary gifts of mediation. He skillfully synthesized the divergent views of the participants, and the delegates unanimously approved his carefully crafted foundational document. Similarly in 1937, as chair of the Faith and Order Conference at Edinburgh, he was responsible for laying the groundwork for the World Council of Churches, though the Council's birth was delayed by the outbreak of World War II. In all of these activities he embodied the essential connection between **faith** and action, both rooted in his unshakable allegiance to Jesus Christ as Lord.

Temple's devotional writings were also widely read. The best introduction to his **spirituality** is his scriptural commentary, *Readings in St. John's Gospel.* Two of his most salient themes, the sacramental nature of the universe and the universal lordship of Christ, figure prominently in this volume, which introduced many to the Logos doctrine of the Fourth Gospel.

F. A. Iremonger wrote the biography, *William Temple, Archbishop of Canterbury.* PWC

TERESA OF ÁVILA (1515–82), Spanish **Carmelite** nun and reformer, mystic, and writer. Born in Ávila, Spain, Teresa took her surname from her mother, Beatriz de Ahumada, as her father, Alonso de Cepeda, had taken his stepmother's surname. These "old Christian" names helped hide the family's Jewish origins. Alonso's father, Juan Sanchez, was a *converso,* a Jewish convert to Christianity. In 1485, when Alonso was five, Juan and his two sons had been forced to perform penance for "secret Judaism" by visiting all seven churches in Toledo while the "faithful" jeered and spat. Juan moved to Ávila, remarried, bought a knighthood, and downplayed the family origins. Teresa's status as a descendent of *conversos* later contributed to the suspicions against her.

When Teresa was seven, she and her brother ran away to seek martyrdom and heaven at the hands of the Moors. An uncle found them at the outskirts of Ávila and brought them home. As a teenager she was steeped in romantic fantasies of knights and ladies, her mother's favorite literature. Yet her experiences in a convent school made her want to become a nun.

At twenty Teresa ran away from home to join the Carmelite Convent of the Incarnation in Ávila and made her final vows two years later, taking the name Teresa of Jesus. The young beauty found herself playing hostess to many visitors, male and female, who came to the convent for counsel or simply to enjoy the company of the nuns. Soon Teresa became gravely ill and was sent to the home of an uncle for a cure. The uncle loaned her *The Third Spiritual Alphabet* of **Francisco de Osuna**, which introduced her to deeper forms of prayer. The cure—strong purgatives and bleeding—nearly killed Teresa, and she was sent back to Incarnation to die. She recovered, though it was nearly three years before she could walk. Her sense of personal unworthiness crippled her prayer life until reading **Augustine's** *Confessions* convinced her that she could be forgiven.

At thirty-nine Teresa experienced a deep inner certainty of God's **love** while praying before a crucifix. She began to experience **ecstasy** and confounded many confessors who tried to advise her. They condemned her prayer as female emotionalism and somehow suspiciously Jewish. Her emphasis on inner prayer and experiences of God's presence seemed too close to Protestantism.

Teresa was ordered to write an account of her life and spiritual experiences for the Inquisition. She completed her *Life* in 1562. The central chapters are a treatise on prayer, in which she pictures the soul as a garden where **virtues** grow and blossom, and prayer waters the garden with **grace**. Teresa describes four ways of obtaining this water. Beginning prayer is like drawing water from a well with a bucket, requiring much work (discursive **meditation**) for little water. As the soul becomes more recollected, prayer is like turning a water wheel that gives more water for less effort. Eventually prayer is like having irrigation ditches coming from a stream. The soul needs only to open the floodgates and then rest in quiet as the water flows. Finally, sometimes it rains— God catching the soul up in **union** and ecstasy.

Meanwhile, Teresa urged reform of the lax practices in her convent and asked permission to found a reformed convent where nuns would live more enclosed lives of **poverty** and prayer. In late 1562 Teresa was allowed to found the convent of St. Joseph in Ávila, where she lived with four other nuns. During the next four years she served as prioress and wrote *The Way of Perfection* as a basic manual of mental prayer grounded in reflections on the **Lord's Prayer**. Teresa explains that mental prayer can begin by reflecting on the **verbal prayers** one is already saying, paying attention to the meaning of each word. In 1567 Teresa left St. Joseph to found a second reformed convent in Medina del Campo, the first of fifteen additional foundations in as many years, requiring constant travel and work by Teresa and involving her in both secular and ecclesiastical politics. Her reform spread to male Carmelites with the founding of a friary in 1568, with **John of the Cross** as one of three brothers. Her foundations were interrupted for two years when she returned to Incarnation in 1571 as prioress to bring at least partial reform. John soon joined her to be confessor to the nuns.

In 1577 Teresa began her most famous writing, *Interior Castle*, at the order of her confessor. In it she describes the soul as a crystal castle in which seven varieties of dwelling places grow increasingly interior. The first three correspond to the **purgative way** as the soul grows from nominal Christianity through a desire to grow spiritually to beginning in meditation and recollection (the first water). The fourth dwelling corresponds to the **illuminative way** of growing quiet and beginning **contemplation** (the second and third waters). The final three dwelling places are the **unitive way** as the soul moves closer to complete union, or **spiritual marriage**, corresponding to the fourth water. Teresa writes of spiritual courtship, betrothal (where union is promised and glimpsed), and marriage from her own experience. She experienced the first from 1554, the second in 1556 (both while still at Incarnation). Her spiritual marriage came in 1572 while she was prioress of Incarnation.

Teresa died in 1582 in the reformed Carmelite convent at Alba de Tormes and was canonized forty years later. In 1970 Teresa and **Catherine of Siena** became the first women designated **Doctors of the Church**, that is, authoritative teachers.

Teresa's writing is free-flowing and often repetitive because she had no time to revise. Since she knew that every word would be scrutinized by men firmly opposed to women teaching or writing theology, her works are full of self-abasement and are presented as stories about experience rather than as the sophisticated treatises on prayer they really are.

Teresa's major works were translated by E. Allison Peers. A more recent translation of her complete works is by Otilio Rodríguez and Kieran Kavanaugh, both Carmelite friars. Victoria Lincoln's *Teresa: A Woman* is an exhaustive biography, with numerous quotes from Teresa's books and letters. *Teresa of Ávila: The Progress of a Soul* by Cathleen Medwick is quite readable. KRB

TERESA OF CALCUTTA (1910–97), founder of the Missionaries of Charity and widely known in the late twentieth century for exemplifying humble dedication to Jesus Christ through service to the destitute. She received the 1979 Nobel Peace Prize and many university honors. Born Agnes Gonxha Bojaxhiu at Skopje, Macedonia, she was of tough, revolutionary, Albanian peasant stock. Called to missions in India, she joined the Sisters of Loretto when seventeen, arriving in Calcutta in 1929. Thirty-one years passed before she left Bengal.

Teresa taught geography and history in a girls' high school, becoming its headmistress. Her second call, in 1946, was to leave the convent and begin a new congregation ministering to the poorest of the poor. Adopting the lifestyle of the poor and surrendering herself to God's guidance, she went into the streets of Calcutta wearing a long-sleeved, blue-bordered white sari of cheapest cloth with a crucifix hanging from her left shoulder. A mud hut schoolroom in a Calcutta slum provided her first site. Roman approval for the Missionaries of Charity followed in October 1950, and their first big project, Kalighat Home for the Dying, opened in 1952. Expanding work included slum visits, establishing slum schools, dispensaries, homes for the dying, homes for abandoned and crippled children, care among tuberculosis and leprosy patients, teaching poor girls crafts, and adoption plans for orphaned children. Today 650 houses exist in 124 countries. The Missionary Brothers of Charity and several other related orders were also founded.

A tiny woman, active, and single-minded by temperament, Mother Teresa worked while others talked, rising regularly at 4:30 A.M. Her goal was making Jesus known and loved by the very poorest. "We do it for Jesus" was her motto. She saw Jesus in every sufferer and aimed at mirroring God's love to each one, being God's "pencil" and writing in people's hearts what God wants. Shunning political action to change structures, she urged going to the poor with Jesus' charity and open heart and hands, bringing a sense of respectability, decency, and self-respect to those unaware that they count in God's eyes.

In training new sisters, Mother Teresa stressed total **abandonment** to God, trust, and joy. Jesus, not the work, is first with the sisters. As Jesus did, they seek out those needing spiritual or material help. "I Thirst" is inscribed on a wall in each chapel. The sisters' function comes in quenching that thirst, supported by four hours of prayer daily. They seek God in **contemplation**, as well as in daily duties and in the brothers and sisters. Their spiritual life centers on **Holy Communion** and **Marian devotion**, providing a context that makes their life possible and meaningful.

Mother Teresa of Calcutta by Edward Le Joly, long a spiritual director for the congregation, provides special insights. LSP

TERTULLIAN (ca. 160–ca. 225), first Latin theologian. Reared in Carthage and well educated, Quintus Septimius Florens Tertullian converted to Christianity before 197. Despite **Jerome**'s claim that Tertullian was ordained a priest, he evidently remained a layman and established himself quickly as an apologist and theologian. Holding rigorist tendencies from the first, around 206 he joined the Montanists, who favored a sterner **discipline** than Catholics. Despite joining a sect later condemned as heretical, Tertullian himself was always highly regarded in the West.

Tertullian composed apologetic, theological, controversial, and **ascetic** works and may have edited *The Martyrdom of Saints Perpetua and Felicitas*, which contains the earliest Christian "diary" or "**journal**." In apologetic works he urged separation from non-Christians. Christians should distinguish themselves from pagans, even in the way they dress. They should not serve in the army or hold public office. Writing in a witty and highly polemical style, Tertullian rejected efforts of Marcion and certain **Gnostics** to distinguish the God of the Hebrew Bible from the God of Jesus. He had a gift for apt formulas and laid the foundation for the Western understanding of the Trinity. Strongly influenced by Stoicism, he represented a stern and unyielding type of Christianity that conversion to Montanism strengthened. He disputed the baptizing of infants in *Baptism*. In *Penitence*, written during his Catholic period, he considered all **sins** forgivable and agreed with Hermas that there could be one repentance after baptism. In Montanist works he hardened his rhetoric and his position. His treatise *Modesty* foreclosed on the church's right to forgive sins and limited **forgiveness** to God. *Fasting* lauded Montanists where Catholics faulted them because instead of marrying in order to engage in sexual activity, they fasted to help suppress sexual appetites. *Monogamy* forbade second marriages, even if a spouse died. Tertullian also tolerated no flight to avoid persecution.

Tertullian's works are in volumes 3 and 4 of *Ante-Nicene Fathers*. See also Eric F. Osborn, *Tertullian, First Theologian of the West*. EGH

THANKSGIVING. A personal, communal, or ritual acknowledgment of God's **grace** and **providence**. Personal expression of thanksgiving may include gratitude for all the good things in life (such as health, success for some venture, family); for transcendent values such as truth, goodness, unity, beauty; or for personal or private matters that were the subject of previous prayers of **petition**. Thanksgiving may spontaneously arise in moments of **awe**. The **dispositions** of joy, gratitude, and awe all lead us to give thanks.

In communal prayer, thanksgiving takes on a ceremonial grandeur. Its origin is Jewish Temple worship. The instrumental image in this type of prayer is that of standing before the sublime, the holy, as one who has been granted a royal audience. Every utterance must be weighed, counted, and measured in contrast to the more intimate and spontaneous speech of personal thanksgiving.

In the sacramental or ritual expression, thanksgiving prayer is the human response to God's self-revelation through God's action in history, especially in the life, death, and resurrection of Jesus. Therefore, this prayer speech is "creedal" or "doxological" in tone

and structure (such as a recitation of history as interpreted by faith). When the psalmist or the prophet proclaims, "Bless the LORD," he or she calls for the ritual of public thanksgiving prayer. The chief example of formal, ritual thanksgiving prayer in Christian worship is the Great Thanksgiving at **Holy Communion**. CIZ

THEOLOGIA GERMANICA. A fourteenth-century German treatise that centers on the question of **deification**, how the human **spirit** may become more nearly divine. The anonymous writing has characteristics of the **mysticism** of **Tauler** and **Eckhart** and attempts to delineate the delicate mystical/philosophical structure of experiencing the mystery and significance of loving God through and beyond the individual self to perfect **union** with God, particularly through the mediation of Christ. The treatise is most significant because of the individuals influenced by it, most notably **Martin Luther**, who edited portions of it, published it in its entirety in 1518, and gave it the title *German Theology*. According to the treatise, the **will** and conscious sense of individuals who strive for mystical union with God are to flow into one eternal and complete will so that nothing remains but the union of all. This mystical union is all-consuming, personal, almost deifying in its efficacy. Luther's Protestantism was deeply influenced by this notion of mystical union and by the necessity of Christ in making such divine/human contact achievable. *Theologia Germanica* is available in a translation by B. Hoffman. SAW

THÉRÈSE OF LISIEUX (1873–97), French **Carmelite**. Also called "Thérèse of the Child Jesus and the Holy Face" and the "Little Flower," Thérèse was born in Alençon, France. Her parents, having each had aspirations for **monastic** life, began married life in holy **celibacy** until a priest convinced them otherwise; thus, it is easy to imagine Thérèse's home life was one of intense Catholic piety. Her mother died when Thérèse was only four. She was left to the care of her eldest sister,

Pauline, who five years later left her to enter the Carmelite convent at Lisieux. When two other sisters entered monastic life, Thérèse desired to follow them to Lisieux, but she was still too young. Following a **conversion** experience on Christmas Day 1888, at the age of fifteen an idealistic Thérèse entered Lisieux.

Thérèse drank deeply from the well of **contemplative** writings of another Carmelite, **John of the Cross**. Thérèse also began to realize that though great deeds were not possible in cloistered life, she could offer small deeds of sacrificial **love** to Jesus. She sought to perform these acts of kindness in secret. In one case, she was falsely accused of breaking a vase—and instead of trying to clear her name, she knelt in contrition. In another case, Thérèse was so loving toward an irritable sister that the latter asked Thérèse why she liked her so much. Thérèse wrote, "I will look for some means of going to heaven by a little way which is very short and very straight, a little way that is quite new." It was this "little way" that would become Thérèse's spiritual legacy. Although she very much wanted to be a priest, when she asked God for the meaning of her vocation, Thérèse was given the answer that love was her vocation. Others saw this depth in Thérèse. Her sister, Pauline, now the prioress, directed Thérèse to write her spiritual autobiography.

In 1896 Thérèse continued to write her story in spite of serious illness. The last chapters reveal a maturing young woman struggling in the journey to her own death. She experienced the "**dark night**" of the soul, an impasse of doubt and emptiness. This she described as a bird flying toward the sun, who, encountering a terrible storm, sees only clouds around it and yet continues on in **hope**, "gazing at the Invisible Light which remains hidden from its **faith**." In her dying, she felt deeply Christ's prayer for his disciples in John 17, as she let go of the souls for whom she had regularly interceded. Thérèse died on September 30, 1897, leaving behind a stirring account hardly conceivable from one so young. *Story of a Soul* became popular among

Catholic laity and continues to be a standard, readable testimony to the life of faith. Within twenty years of her death, Thérèse was canonized. Her wisdom has been so esteemed that she was declared a **Doctor of the Church** (an authoritative teacher) in 1998. SAF

THOMAS À KEMPIS (ca. 1380–1471), Augustinian monk and writer. Thomas Hemerken was born in Kempen, near Düsseldorf, Germany. At thirteen he left his home to study in Deventer under Florent Radewijns, who had been an early disciple of **Gerhard Groote**, founder of the movement called *devotio moderna*, or New Devotion, and of the Brethren of the Common Life in Windesheim.

In 1399 Thomas entered the Augustinian monastery of Mount St. Agnes (Agnietenberg) where his brother Jan had just been elected prior. After making his religious vows in 1408, Thomas was ordained a priest in 1413. He was elected subprior of the community in 1425. His primary duty was teacher of novices. In this capacity he produced the four treatises that became *Imitation of Christ*. Except for a three-year period when the entire monastic community went into voluntary exile, Thomas spent the rest of his life at Mount St. Agnes.

Thomas is best known for *Imitation of Christ*, a book for which he does not always get authorial credit, since the earliest manuscripts are anonymous. While complete unanimity does not exist, most scholars today consider Thomas the author. *Imitation of Christ*, probably written between 1420 and 1427, is, next to the Bible, the most popular of Christian classics, appealing to Protestants as well as Catholics. Among those who found it invaluable were **Thomas More**, **Ignatius of Loyola**, German philosopher Gottfried Wilhelm Leibniz, **John Wesley**, and **Thomas Merton**. When **Dag Hammarskjöld**'s effects were removed from the wreckage of his plane crash, in his briefcase were his Bible and a copy of *Imitation of Christ*.

Since *Imitation of Christ* was originally written for novices, Thomas used simple, direct language to convey his practical advice. Showing a keen understanding of human nature and deep insight into psychology, he shares the spiritual truths he has gleaned from praying the scripture (there are almost seven hundred biblical citations and allusions), the *Devotio Moderna*, the writings of the church fathers, and the lives of the **saints** (especially **Augustine** and **Bernard**).

Thomas wisely connects Christian ideas with a Christian lifestyle, joining theory and practice. The book has become and remained a classic because of this practical interpretation of scripture and theology. Due to its richness and depth, it is best read slowly, repeatedly, and meditatively.

Book One, "Helpful Counsels for the Spiritual Life," encourages the reader to develop the interior life by renouncing vain and illusory things, including sensory delights. Through growing **humility**, one can seek what is true, interior, and eternal. Book Two, "Directives for the Interior Life," adds that the kingdom is interior and can be attained only by **union** with God through Christ. Book Three, "On Interior Consolation," emphasizes **love** and **grace**. Thomas imagines a dialogue between Jesus and a disciple that focuses on the disciple's desire to ascend to God and taste divine delights. Book Four, "On the Blessed Sacrament," continues the dialogue, discussing the fundamental importance of **Holy Communion** to a relationship with God through Christ. One is encouraged to dwell in the mystery of the sacrament rather than approach it analytically. ww

THOMAS AQUINAS (ca. 1225–74), **Dominican** theologian. Thomas was born near Naples into an aristocratic family. At fourteen he went to the University of Naples where he discovered Aristotelian philosophy, recently reintroduced into western Europe. When Thomas decided to join the Order of Preachers in 1244, his family had him kidnapped and kept him a prisoner for over a year as they tried to dissuade him. He escaped and became a Do-

minican. The order sent him to Cologne to study with Albertus Magnus. During his student days he was given the nickname "Dumb Ox" because he was large and said little. However, his brilliance was soon recognized, and he joined the faculty at the University of Paris. His theological/philosophical system, called Thomism, was controversial, but with strong support from the Dominican Order, by the sixteenth century it became the dominant philosophy of the Roman Catholic Church.

Thomas's magnum opus is *Summa Theologica* (available in various translations and abridgments), in which he attempts to link the God of philosophers and the God of the Bible by referring to God as "He Who Is." God is not the greatest of all beings but Being Itself. Though contemplative ascent to God is an intellectual process, the motivation has to be Christian love and must have an affective component. Thomas tried to retain the unity between loving **contemplation** and theological speculation in a time when spiritual life and theology were beginning to be considered separately. Convinced that philosophical arguments about the nature of God had nothing to do with the mystical God he experienced in prayer, Thomas believed religious **experience** was primary. In petitioning God, we sacrifice our planning intellect and learn that all good comes from God, that we have recourse in God at all times, and that we should be workers with God to execute God's purposes in our world. *Albert and Thomas: Selected Writings*, edited by Simon Tugwell, offers an introduction to the lives and works of Thomas and his teacher. ww

THURMAN, HOWARD (1900–81), **African-American** preacher and mystic. A leading voice for racial justice, Thurman struggled against prejudice all his life but refused to become bitter. He enrolled in Morehouse College, became active in the YMCA, and was exposed to a brilliant sampling of African-American leaders: Franklin Frazier, Benjamin Mays, and John Hope. His acceptance at Rochester Theological School was a special distinction since the school accepted only two black applicants in any given year. Rochester was his first experience in the white world and a difficult one. After seminary he became the pastor of a Baptist church in Oberlin, Ohio, and began graduate work at the Oberlin School of Theology. He was appointed by both Morehouse and Spelman Colleges to teach religion and be chaplain. A lecture series on the spiritual insights of the African-American spiritual became his book *Deep River*.

In 1935 Thurman was invited by the YMCA and YWCA to chair a delegation of African-Americans on a **pilgrimage** of friendship to India, Burma, and Ceylon. He accepted, though he was reluctant to be an apologist for segregated American Christianity. He became convinced of the distinction between the religion *of* Jesus and religion *about* Jesus. In India he met Gandhi and was quickly persuaded to imitate Gandhi's nonviolence. In 1948 he went to San Francisco, where he founded the Church for the Fellowship of All Peoples. His dreams for a congregation that was both racially integrated and ecumenical came true. After nine years he became dean of the chapel and professor of spiritual **disciplines** at Boston University. His ministry at the university and his preaching trips around the world had a wide influence.

Among Thurman's many books are *The Negro Speaks of Life and Death, The Centering Moment, Jesus and the Disinherited, Meditations of the Heart, Disciplines of the Spirit*, and his autobiography, *With Head and Heart*. HLR

TOURNIER, PAUL (1898–1986), Swiss physician, psychiatrist, and spiritual writer. A devout Christian, Tournier felt God calling him to spread the good news. Combining his knowledge of psychology and psychiatry with the Christian faith, he wrote about what it means to be a whole person in Christ and a moral person in a technological age. His harmonizing of medical science's wisdom with Christianity's profundity has led many to a deeper synthesis of body, mind, and spirit.

Tournier's books include *Escape from Lone-*

liness, The Healing of Persons, The Meaning of Persons, To Resist or to Surrender?, Guilt and Grace, The Whole Person in a Broken World, and *The Adventure of Living*. EKM

TOZER, AIDEN WILSON (1897–1963), American pastor and devotional writer. Although self-educated, Tozer became a prominent pastor in the Christian and Missionary Alliance. He is best known for his passionate, penetrating devotional writings— nearly forty books that challenge the contemporary church to awaken to a more vibrant love for and devotion to God. They focus on an intimate worship and **contemplation** of the triune God, dependence upon the **Holy Spirit**, **discipline**, prayer, personal **holiness**, and missions. Deeply rooted in the evangelical tradition, Tozer was a voracious reader of the early church fathers and **monastic** and **mystic** writings, as well as experiential Protestants such as Tersteegen, **Jonathan Edwards**, and **Charles** and **John Wesley,** enlarging his ability to address what he saw as a church fallen into spiritual lethargy. The most popular and best introductions to his writings are *The Pursuit of God* and *The Knowledge of the Holy* (exploring the attributes of God). TS

TRANSCENDENCE. Three related ideas of "going beyond." Divine transcendence describes the attribute of God's otherness, above and independent of the limits of the material universe and not to be identified with it. This doctrine is usually contrasted with divine immanence, since exclusive focus on transcendence suggests an absent and uninvolved God.

In philosophy, transcendence refers to the ability to go beyond the limits of sensory experience to nonempirical thought. **Thomas Aquinas** developed the argument that humans are transcendent beings in that our metaphysical questions reveal a drive to exceed the limits of empirical knowledge, a philosophy further developed and critiqued by thinkers such as Immanuel Kant, Joseph Maréchal, Bernard Lonergan, and Johann Baptist Lotz.

Spiritualities that primarily emphasize God's transcendence, such as Eastern spiritualities, stress the absolute mystery of God, who infinitely surpasses any category. These spiritualities focus on the **negative way**, in which ascent to God is achieved through moral and religious purification and through prayer or **contemplation** on unity, truth, goodness, and beauty. **Gregory of Nyssa**, known as the father of Christian **mysticism**, offers a good introduction to the negative way in his *Ascetical Works*, translated by Virginia W. Callahan. A good Byzantine source is **Gregory Palamas** in *Early Fathers from the Philokalia*, translated by E. Kadloubovsky and G. E. H. Palmer.

Modern sources for a study in transcendence as it relates both to spirituality and theology are **Karl Rahner** and **Adrian van Kaam** (e.g., *The Transcendent Self*). Both present God in terms of mystery, reality, holy mystery, or divine forming mystery, known only indirectly. We are capable of knowing God because we are "spirits in the world," that is, human beings are always moving toward or away from God. We can know or **experience** God by attending to the movements of our heart. CIZ

TRANSFIGURATION. The light of God's **glory**, seen in the appearance of Jesus or of a **saint**. Mark 9:2-8; Matthew 17:1-8; and Luke 9:28-36 record accounts of Jesus' transfiguration. On a mountaintop the disciples Peter, James, and John witness their master transformed, shining and his clothes remarkably white. They see Jesus, thus transfigured, speak to Moses and Elijah. Peter suggests building three shelters, one for each of them, but is interrupted by a voice coming out of a cloud that overshadows everything. The voice announces God's pleasure with Jesus and commands the disciples to pay attention to him. With these words, the voice, the cloud, Moses, and Elijah disappear, and Jesus returns to normal. This event is commemorated on August 6 in Orthodox and Roman Catholic Churches and on the Sunday before Ash Wednesday in many Protestant churches.

Gregory Palamas (ca. 1296–1359), an ex-ponent of **hesychasm**, proposed that the experience of the glory of God such as the disciples had at the Transfiguration is available to all. While God's essence is unknowable, God's energies can be made visible, experienced by the disciples in the radiance of Christ's nature shining upon them. The light of the Transfiguration is the light of the kingdom of heaven, communicated to all human beings through the **Holy Spirit**. In the Eastern tradition, the three shelters suggested by Peter represent three **stages** of salvation: virtue (represented by Elijah), spiritual knowledge (represented by Moses), and theology (represented by Christ). The shelters are temporary because the worthy will pass through higher stages of spirituality in the next life.

Christ's transfiguration leads to our transfiguration because it represents the coming of the kingdom of God into our world. The light reveals God's grace and promises renewal and re-creation for those who love God.

For more on transfiguration in Orthodox spirituality, see *Gregory Palamas: The Triads*, translated by Nicholas Gendle or *In the Light of Christ* (on **Symeon the New Theologian**) by Archbishop Basil Krivocheine. WW

TRAPPISTS. Members of the **monastic** Order of Cistercians of the Strict Observance, begun as a reform movement at the Cistercian Abbey of la Trappe in France in 1664 but only becoming a separate order in 1893. Trappist writers include **Thomas Merton**, **M. Basil Pennington**, and **Thomas Keating**.

TRUEBLOOD, DAVID ELTON (1900–94), American **Quaker** scholar and theologian. Born in Iowa and educated at Penn College, Harvard, and Johns Hopkins, Trueblood taught at Guilford College and Haverford College. From 1936 to 1945 he was chaplain and professor of philosophy of religion at Stanford University and from 1946 to 1966 professor of philosophy at Earlham College. He was regarded as an elder statesman in the fields of politics, education, and religion; he wrote over thirty books, each of distinct value. In 1954

Trueblood organized the Yokefellow Institute, a school of religion and a nonsectarian program for lay leaders involving retreats and training sessions. As an ecumenical movement, it led to renewal movements in various denominations such as Faith at Work, the Christophers, the Disciplined Order of Christ, and Lay Witness Mission.

Trueblood endeavored to make tradition alive and meaningful to the hearts and minds of modern persons, emphasizing that all—lay as well as clergy—are in ministry, living in commitment and participating in Christian **disciplines**. Individual commitment to Jesus Christ is essential, but **community** is also necessary. He promoted a way of life that included **compassion**, reverence, intellectual integrity, service, and fellowship. Considered a prophet, he changed many lives and communities through his vision. In one of his later books *The Essence of Spiritual Religion*, he continued his ecumenical emphasis on balancing tolerance of others with faithfulness to one's own convictions. According to Trueblood, God still speaks and continually offers relationship through scripture, spiritual giants of the past and present, groups of like-minded individuals, and experiences that lead us to be active in social concerns, particularly human rights.

Many of Trueblood's books are of great significance. Begin with *The Company of the Committed* or *The Incendiary Fellowship*. *The Meditations of Elton Trueblood*, edited by Stephen R. Sebert and W. Gordon Ross, gives a flavor of his message and a brief biography. EWF

TRUTH, SOJOURNER (ca. 1795–1883), **African-American** evangelist and abolitionist. Born a slave named Isabella in Ulster County, New York, she grew to womanhood working on the farms and in the homes of various slave owners. She and her slave husband, Thomas, had five children, also slaves. In her thirties she gained her freedom through New York's Anti-Slavery Law of 1827, left her husband, and found refuge with **Quaker** friends who lived nearby. Active abolitionists, they helped

Isabella fight those responsible for the illegal sale of her son Peter. She won her case and her son's return, becoming one of the first black women in America to win a court case.

During the late 1840s, Isabella became involved with antislavery movements. Converted during a time of prayer, she believed God had called her to become a traveling evangelist and wanted to change her name to reflect her new calling. Because Psalm 39:12 came to her mind, she chose Sojourner and from John 8:32, about the truth setting people free, she took her last name. At outdoor religious meetings Sojourner Truth spoke about the evils of slavery; and, though illiterate, she preached eloquently, effectively, and inspirationally. A fiery advocate for the women's suffrage movement, Sojourner passionately delivered her famous "Arn't I a Woman" speech at an Ohio convention in 1851. Through her powerful, booming, and prophetic voice, she raised awareness of racism and sexism, making it clear that such evils are unacceptable. Mixed in with her preaching and teaching, she sang moving renditions of church hymns. Her autobiography was printed in 1850. She continued to be an outspoken supporter of women's suffrage until she was in her eighties.

See Nell Irvin Painter's book, *Sojourner Truth: A Life, a Symbol*. Erlene Stetson and Linda David wrote *Glorying in Tribulation: The Lifework of Sojourner Truth*. EKM

TUTU, DESMOND (b. 1931), Anglican archbishop of the Church of South Africa, from 1986 to 1996, and Nobel Peace Prize winner in 1984. Born in the Transvaal and educated in Johannesburg and London, Tutu was ordained in 1961. He became bishop of Lesotho in 1976 and of Johannesburg in 1985 and the first black archbishop of Cape Town in 1986. As ecclesial head of a historically white church, Tutu had to negotiate effectively in a society so defined by race that Afrikaner and African each claimed God's election as the chosen race. From this context, Tutu's spirituality of Ubuntu was born. Tutu sought not simply to restore black people to a place where they could flourish but to practice a spirituality in which reconciliation of all human identities is possible. Such practices include hospitality to the stranger, political practices of inclusion, common prayer as practiced in the Anglican tradition, and a good sense of humor that often disarms the tension between enemies. Although Tutu is most widely known as a political actor, he understands himself primarily as an **African** Christian acting in the world. It is vital, however, to see Tutu's spirituality in order to understand the impetus for his political involvement. At the heart of Tutu's spirituality are practices to move people beyond the racial distinctions of apartheid.

Ubuntu operates from a distinctively theological model in which human identity depends on a trinitarian image of God, namely, the correct or healthy relation of persons. Tutu's more specific connotation of the term *Ubuntu* derives from the expression *Ubuntu ungamntu ngabanye abantu*: A person's identity is ideally expressed in relationship with others; and, in turn, personhood is truly expressed. Or simply put, Ubuntu means that a person depends on other persons to be a person. For example, to say that Mpho has Ubuntu means that Mpho is someone who cares about the deepest needs of others and abides faithfully in all social obligations. Mpho is conscious not only of her personal rights but also of her duties to her neighbor. Tutu's spirituality of Ubuntu shapes his political work to disallow false dichotomies of black and white persons and to make racial reconciliation intelligible on many racial and cultural levels. This African cultural conceptualization of recognizing one's identity in the other seeks to show that persons are more than either black or white. And Ubuntu, combined with the metaphor of the *imago dei*, becomes a concept that describes the divine life, i.e., just as the Father, Son, and the Holy Spirit are known through one another, so likewise human personhood is defined in the other.

Lastly, Tutu's spirituality assumes God's creation in which current conflicting racial identities are expressed and defined in the reconciling concept of the *imago dei* revealed through Jesus Christ, who manifests the proper meaning and relation of personhood. In short, Tutu's spirituality of Ubuntu demonstrates spiritual practices in a context of conflicting racial identities in a manner that makes their lives intelligible to one another as more than enemies. In fact, the goal is to flourish as neighbors.

For further reading, see Desmond Tutu and Michael Battle, *Reconciliation: The Ubuntu Theology of Desmond Tutu*, and Desmond Tutu, *No Future without Forgiveness*. MB

TWELVE STEP PROGRAMS. In 1935 two alcoholics met in Akron, Ohio: Bill W., a stockbroker from New York City, and Dr. Bob S., of Akron. Bill had become sober through his participation in the Oxford Group, a fellowship that stressed universal human values applied to one's daily life. He remained sober by working with other alcoholics. Bob, although he participated in the Akron chapter of the movement, had not yet achieved sobriety. Bill, who had been hospitalized many times for his disease, believed that alcoholism was a malady of body, mind, and spirit. After listening to Bill's ideas, Bob achieved sobriety and never drank again. Both men began to work with alcoholics at an Akron hospital, where one patient rapidly achieved sobriety. These three made up the nucleus of the first Alcoholics Anonymous group.

In 1939 Bill W.'s book *Alcoholics Anonymous* was published by the fellowship. It outlined the now famous twelve steps of recovery from addiction, which have become the founding principles of dozens of other self-help groups, including Gamblers Anonymous, Overeaters Anonymous, and groups struggling with a variety of sexual addictions. They can also be adapted for use by a **covenant group** seeking to deal with any sort of habitual sin. RMH

THE TWELVE STEPS OF ALCOHOLICS ANONYMOUS

1. We admitted we were powerless over alcohol—that our lives had become unmanageable.

2. Came to believe that a Power greater than ourselves could restore us to sanity.

3. Made a decision to turn our will and our lives over to the care of God, as we understood Him.

4. Made a searching and fearless moral inventory of ourselves.

5. Admitted to God, to ourselves, and to another human being the exact nature of our wrongs.

6. Were entirely ready to have God remove all these defects of character.

7. Humbly asked Him to remove our shortcomings.

8. Made a list of all the persons we had harmed, and became willing to make amends to them all.

9. Make direct amends to such people whenever possible, except when to do so would injure them or others.

10. Continued to take a personal inventory and when we were wrong promptly admitted it.

11. Sought through prayer and meditation to improve our conscious contact with God, as we understood Him, praying only for knowledge of His will for us and the power to carry that out.

12. Having had a spiritual awakening as the result of these Steps, we tried to carry this message to alcoholics, and to practice these principles in all our affairs.

U

UNAMUNO Y JUGO, MIGUEL DE (1864–1936), Spanish philosopher, poet, and novelist. His philosophy is existential, seeking life's purposes and deeper meanings through literal articulation. His language is evocative and emotional, his emphases the stuff of daily life: birth, death, suffering, and the eternal tensions between reason and faith.

Unamuno was born in Bilbao and studied philosophy and the classics at Madrid. In 1891 he was appointed to the faculty of the University of Salamanca as professor of Greek. His early novels, such as *Paz en la guerra, Amor y pedagogia* and *Del sentimiento tragico de la vida: en los hombres y en los pueblos*, explore the conflict and confusion inherent in life's dichotomies—war and peace, science and faith, the hope of salvation and eternal life in the face of death and destruction.

Unamuno's life took an activist turn as he protested the political machinations of dictator General Primo de Rivera. In 1924 he was deported to the Canary Islands but escaped to France, where he lived in exile until Rivera's overthrow in 1930. He returned to Salamanca and was reinstated to his university position. In 1933 his final and most famous novel appeared *San Manuel Bueno, Martir*, which describes the agony of a priest who does not believe. Unamuno ended his life under house arrest in Salamanca, unable to support either side in the growing conflicts that became the Spanish Civil War.

Unamuno's philosophy is not systematic but rather emotive and poetic. His exploration of the chasm between faith and reason led him to a vast skepticism tempered by the deep faith of a hopeful heart. Though he was deeply dissatisfied intellectually with the Catholic Church, spiritually he saw it as a necessity. He believed that humankind's existence found true meaning only in the context of its never-ending search to become God—or to seek for the realization of divinity within. Because Unamuno highly valued individualism, his philosophy and the characters in his novels reveal a courageous search for meaning, authenticity, and interior truth. For further reading, see *Unamuno* by José Mora Ferrater, translated by Philip Silver. Many of Unamuno's works are available in English, including *Tragic Sense of Life, Mist: A Tragicomic Novel*, and *Three Exemplary Novels*. SAW

UNCEASING PRAYER. The goal of many Christians through the centuries has been to fulfill 1 Thessalonians 5:17: "Pray without ceasing." Some desert monks, called *akoimitai* (nonsleepers), went without sleep in order to do just that, while others tried different forms of prayer. Some prayed all 150 **Psalms** every day. Others developed the **Prayer of the Heart** or the **Jesus Prayer**, trying to synchronize the words "Lord Jesus Christ, Son of God, have mercy upon me, a sinner" with their heartbeat. Today that prayer is the official prayer of Orthodox Christians.

More useful for modern Christians may be the approach of Brother **Lawrence** in *The Practice of the Presence of God*. Upon entering the monastery in midlife he had tried the **Carmelite** methods of prayer, but they merely frustrated him. Cooking and washing dishes in the monastery kitchen, he found he could maintain an attitude of attention to the presence of God. As he expressed it elsewhere, he could have a passionate regard for God in everything he was doing. "I turn my little omelet in the pan for love of God," he said.

Modern **Quaker Thomas Kelly** contended that we can live life on two levels. One is the level of activity, the only level on which some people live. But another level on which we may live is that of the interior life. Beginning may require forming some habits of inward attentiveness, saying little ejaculatory prayers such as "Be Thou my will." Longer prayers repeated often, like **George Herbert**'s "Teach me, my God and King, in all things Thee to see" may be required. **Teilhard de Chardin** remarked that our constant prayer should be the prayer of the blind man in Luke 18:41: "Lord, let me see again."

In a culture in which we get caught up in busyness and experience many distractions, recovery of inward attentiveness will almost certainly require times of **retreat**. Jesus withdrew at critical moments in his ministry— after his baptism as he sorted out his vocation, before choosing the Twelve, before asking the disciples to identify him at Caesarea Philippi, as people came to him asking for miracles, and then in Gethsemane. Withdrawal gives **solitude**, taking us away from the noise that overloads our senses and fragments our thinking. It permits us again to become collected, to be re-created, to center and become inwardly quiet.

As many of the **saints** have recognized, however, **silence** may not happen automatically. In fact, it may heighten the inner noises or **distractions** and make paying attention to God even more difficult. *Inner* noises do not stop because everything is quiet outside. Thus we may sometimes have to withdraw for longer periods and perhaps seek the others' help. The **desert fathers and mothers** frequently sought other abbas and ammas. Today many persons look for **spiritual direction** either individually or in groups. The object is not permanent withdrawal; some may have a contemplative vocation and temporarily retreat to gather the energies needed to be present to others and to sustain our attention to them.

To read further, see *Pray Always* (*Weavings: A Journal of the Christian Spiritual Life*, May/June 1998), *Time to Spare* by **Douglas V. Steere**, or *Be Still: Designing and Leading Contemplative Retreats* by Jane Vennard. EGH

UNDERHILL, EVELYN (1875–1941), English lay theologian and writer. Evelyn Underhill awakened the spiritual hearts of her contemporaries and—without realizing it— pioneered a path for women in ministry. Born in South Kensington the only child of nominally Anglican parents, Underhill described her early life as lacking religious nurture. But even as a teenager, Underhill showed spiritual sparks that would be fanned into flames in young adulthood. Underhill graduated from King's College, London, and in her twenties began writing novels about the spiritual quest. After her marriage to Hubert Stuart Moore, Underhill began writing her best-known work, *Mysticism* (1911), which continues to be a standard on the mystical life. After the devastation of World War I and years of struggling with a longing to become a Roman Catholic, Underhill renewed her membership in the Anglican Church. She turned her attention to the **spiritual formation** of the average Christian by offering **retreats** for clergy and laity, radio talks, and as a spiritual guide. Many of her talks were later published, including *The Spiritual Life* (a set of radio talks), *The House of the Soul* (on the **virtues**), and *Abba* (on the **Lord's Prayer**). Her own spiritual director, the renowned Catholic scholar **Friedrich von Hügel**, encouraged Underhill toward more self-compassion and a Christ-centered balance in her spiritual life.

Having a strong ecumenical vision, Underhill created important bridges to believers of the Eastern **Orthodox** tradition and to spiritual writers beyond the Christian tradition. She authored thirty-nine books and over 350 articles, almost all on spiritual themes. Her last book, *Worship* (1936), remains an ecumenical gem on the varieties of Christian corporate **spirituality**. Throughout a distinguished career the prolific author did not neglect her family or her many spiritual directees with whom she kept up a lively correspondence. By the time of World War II, Underhill was a committed pacifist, even when bombs were being dropped on London.

For more on her life and work, read *Evelyn Underhill: Artist of the Infinite Life*, a biography by Dana Greene. SAF

UNION, UNITIVE WAY. The third and final stage of the traditional understanding of spiritual growth as a threefold path. God leads the **soul** closer and closer to God's self through the states or ways called **purgation**, **illumination**, and union. Through this threefold ongoing process God calls us to begin, move through, and be united in mystical love. Having become proficient in faithful response to God's inward and outward promptings, enlightened and mature souls can be led into complete self-**abandonment** while still maintaining their uniqueness.

Augustine said that we are restless until our hearts rest in God. We long for union even if we do not recognize what the longing is. The unitive way is God bringing us to be able to rest in God on a daily basis so that "our **joy** may be complete" (1 John 1:4). Having consistently **detached** ourselves from what blocks this union in the purgative way and having become attentive to God's presence in the illuminative way, we are finally available for this deepest union of the unitive way. Ordinary consciousness is radically transformed as we live in a persistent awareness of God's presence. Fully engaged in life, those united in love with God often drink from the **waters** flowing deep within their united souls. This reservoir of **peace** within from which they draw strength and comfort is one of the fruits of the practice of **Centering Prayer** and other forms of or preludes to **contemplation**. Busy building God's reign of love, mystics such as

Teresa of Ávila and **Ignatius of Loyola** became more effective and productive in their ministries as their lives became more infused with God's unconditional **love**.

Transformation in Christ happens over time. **John of the Cross** (*The Living Flame of Love*) and Teresa of Ávila (*Interior Castle*) have written eloquently of the inflowing love of God shared with the soul in the unitive state. From them we learn that we cannot ourselves produce such depth of God's presence. All we can do is be **receptive** (John of the Cross's "passive night"). Only God can unite us with mystical understanding where we "pass beyond everything comprehensible to the incomprehensible." The faculties of the soul (mind, **will**, memory, imagination, and anticipation) continue to be purified (purgation and illuminative ways). With loving willingness, openness, and abandonment, the will is now freer to love as God created it to love. The lover in us has found our Beloved. We learn to walk by faith and not by sight. This is not necessarily pleasant. Spiritual **consolations** will dissipate or be withdrawn. This "night of spirit" is felt more intensely, for we have "tasted the goodness of the Lord"; we want to dwell and abide in that goodness always. Our spiritual powers of formation (mind, will, memory, imagination, and ability to anticipate the future) are still being shaped, formed, and fashioned by God. We understand and know by not knowing (**negative way**), and this is pleasing to the will that is already on **fire** with **affective** longing for God alone. This is God's way of making it clear to us that this union is all God's doing. EKM

V

VAN KAAM, ADRIAN L. (b. 1920), founder of formation science, an existential phenomenologist, psychologist, and Catholic priest in the Congregation of the Holy Ghost (a religious order also known as "Holy Ghost Fathers"). Born in the Hague, he started his academic life as a scholar of Thomistic philosophy (based on the writings of **Thomas Aquinas**) at the University of Nijmegen, where he was appointed professor. He earned a doctorate in psychology from Case Western Reserve University. During the Hunger Winter of 1944–45 in Nazi-occupied Holland, van Kaam participated in the Dutch underground to aid Jews and other refugees. This experience, van Kaam claims, is where he first began formulating a distinction between **faith** and **formation** traditions, which became the seeds of a new religio-psychological discourse and his psychological anthropology.

In 1954 van Kaam came to the United States to teach at Duquesne University and to inaugurate its existential phenomenological-anthropological approach to psychology. Van Kaam's early work focused on a critique of contemporary psychological theories and research methodologies. As a researcher of phenomenological alternatives for psychology, van Kaam contributed to the development, practice, and method of descriptive research, particularly through his writings and his work as editor of Duquesne's "Psychological Series." Van Kaam's later work focused on applying his phenomenological methodology and personality theory to psychospiritual experiences, opening the way for a scientific approach to the study of human formation and **spirituality**. From 1982 to 1999 van Kaam provided leadership for the discipline of formation science through Duquesne's Institute of Formative Spirituality.

Van Kaam's basic tenets of a science of spirituality can be found in his Formative Spirituality series. The specialized language makes this multivolume series daunting to most readers. In addition to his academic work, van Kaam has authored over twenty more accessible books that could be classified as Catholic devotional writings, including *The Woman at the Well.* Spiritual directors will find *The Transcendent Self* a good entry into his works. Now retired, van Kaam dedicates his time to finalizing his theoretical body of writings and to furthering the practice of spiritual formation among laity, clergy, and those in religious orders through the Epiphany Association, of which he is a cofounder with **Susan Muto**. CIZ

VERBAL PRAYER. The first prayers we learn are verbal ones: simple, spoken prayers for mealtimes and bedtime. Even the prayers that we pray silently are verbal prayers. While some people learn other ways of praying—such as image-based **meditation** (including the use of **guided imagery**), wordless **contemplation** or nearly wordless **Centering Prayer**, or prayer through body movement or dance—for many people prayer *is* verbal prayer.

Prayer is the center of the church's life, and verbal prayer is the most important form of communal prayer. In liturgical prayer church members gather as the body of Christ to express their common faith and worship through verbal prayers of invocation, **confession**, and **thanksgiving**. In verbal prayer the church most profoundly actualizes its reality as church, for prayer is also a confession of faith. It is a confession of who God is, of what God has done and can do, and of one's relationship to God. The central affirmation of the Christian faith is what God has done in and through Jesus Christ.

Verbal prayer can be extemporaneous or follow written and fixed formulas passed down from earlier centuries, such as the Great Thanksgiving in services of **Holy Communion**. The most familiar verbal prayer used in formal worship settings, informal gatherings, and private devotions continues to be the **Lord's Prayer**. Often the private use of verbal prayers involves repetition (the **Hail Mary**, the Lord's Prayer in praying the **rosary**, the **Jesus Prayer** and other **breath prayers**) or slow reflection on the prayer phrase by phrase or word by word (as taught for the Lord's Prayer in *Spiritual Exercises* of **Ignatius of Loyola** and *The Way of Perfection* by **Teresa of Ávila**).

For further guidance, see *Prayer: A Study in the History and Psychology of Religion* by **Friedrich Heiler**, or Philip Dunn's *Prayer: Language of the Soul*, which contains over three hundred prayers from around the world. PDB

VIA NEGATIVA, POSITIVA. See **Negative Way, Positive Way**.

VIANNEY, JEAN-BAPTISTE MARIE (1786–1859), French priest known as the Curé (parish priest) of Ars. Born in Dardilly northwest of Lyons, France, Vianney helped his peasant father with the small farm until he was about nineteen years old. Though he had desired to be a Catholic priest since his first Communion at age thirteen, due to little formal education and no training in Latin he was unable to keep up in the seminary. Because he was a model seminarian, the abbot personally chose to tutor Vianney in theology. He was finally ordained at age twenty-nine. Two years later he was sent to a remote village of about two hundred, called Ars, where religious neglect, spiritual indifference, and scandalous immorality were widespread. Vianney began his work of reform by setting a zealous example of holy living: praying and fasting for his parishioners, visiting families, teaching catechism classes, and preaching firmly but gently against their vices. Gradually their hearts were won over.

Vianney's gift of spiritual insight in the confessional was most remarkable, and soon many from far away were flocking to the little church in Ars. Word of his sanctity spread throughout Europe. By 1830 an average of three hundred visitors a day came to implore him for a blessing, a cure, or a word that would lead to their conversion. Along with getting little sleep, **fasting** often, and doing many penances and sacrifices for his people, Vianney performed constant pastoral duties that wore him out. Three times he asked to retire to a monastery where he would be free to live a life of **unceasing prayer** and to prepare for death. He was refused each time. At the age of seventy-three he died, completely worn out. He was canonized in 1925 and declared patron of parish priests. *The Curé D'Ars: St. Jean-Marie-Baptiste Vianney* by Francis Trochu is a biography based on accounts in the canonization proceedings. EKM

VIGILANCE. An alert watchfulness. Proverbs 4:23 admonishes the listener, "Keep your heart with all vigilance, for from it flow the springs of life." The centrality of vigilance to Christian **spirituality** begins with Jesus' teachings in Mark 13 (also known as the mini-apocalypse). Jesus tells his followers to keep awake, watchful, and alert, for no human being knows the time when the Son of Man will come again in the clouds. In 1 Thessalonians 5:2, Paul warns that the day of the Lord will come "like a thief in the night," echoed by 2 Peter 3:10. Revelation 3:3 calls for this kind of vigilance in regard to the second coming of Christ, and Revelation 16:15 warns, "See, I am coming like a thief! Blessed is the one who stays awake and is clothed, not going about naked and exposed to shame."

Spiritual vigilance is not only watching for the Lord but internal watchfulness against temptation and one's own tendencies to sin. Throughout the scriptures (most notably in the **Psalms**) the idea of spiritual vigilance is tied to the night watch. In Psalm 119:148 the psalmist pledges, "My eyes are awake before each watch of the night, that I may meditate on your promise." Christians should be alert and watchful when the rest of the world is asleep. This warning gave rise to the idea of the "vigil," a purposeful and watchful time of staying awake during the normal hours of sleep. The vigil was a time of devotion, prayer, and **contemplation** before **fasting** or on the eve of a Christian festival day. The contemporary idea of the "prayer vigil" finds its roots in this ancient form of spiritual **discipline**.

God also expresses vigilance in relation to human beings. Psalm 139:1-16 speaks of God keeping watch over us, and Proverbs 15:3 reminds us that God watches over both the evil and the good. Psalm 61 appeals to God's vigilance in regard to the king of Israel. While we wait and watch for God, God waits and watches over us as well. SFP

VINCENT DE PAUL (1581–1660), founder of the Congregation of the Mission (Lazarists or Vincentians), the Daughters of Charity, the Ladies of Charity, and a prominent spiritual leader in the French Catholic reform. Born to a peasant family in southern France, Vincent was encouraged to enter the priesthood. Seeking a lucrative church position, he came to Paris where he was affected by the stirring winds of spiritual renewal. He was made chaplain and tutor to a prominent family. Vincent's pastoral experience and the sad state of France's spiritual health led him to consecrate the rest of his life to serving the poor. He became engaged in preaching "internal missions" to the French people and encouraged the establishment of charitable groups. Chief among these were the Ladies of Charity, wealthy women organized to serve those in need. Appointed chaplain of the galleys by Louis XIII in 1617, he increased his efforts on behalf of the disenfranchised, in this case galley slaves. Contact with **Francis de Sales** and **Jane de Chantal** set his heart on fire. Over the next years he cultivated inner freedom to the point of full response to the call of the poor. With Louise de Marillac (ca. 1591–1660), he founded the Daughters of Charity, a community that served the homeless, sick, and hungry. In 1625 he founded the Congregation of

the Mission. The priests of the congregation engaged in internal missions and extended their work with the poor to Italy, Sardinia, Ireland, Scotland, Algiers, and Poland during Vincent's lifetime.

Vincent's evangelical witness, the communities he founded, and his solidarity with the poor were his lasting legacy. After his death in 1660, the extended family of Vincentian foundations spread worldwide. Vincent was canonized in 1737.

For further reading, see *Vincent de Paul and Louise de Marillac: Rules, Conferences and Writings*, edited by Frances Ryan and John E. Rybolt. WMW

VIRTUE. See **Dispositions**.

VIRTUES, THE SEVEN. The desirable qualities that characterize a Christian, the admirable **dispositions** reflected in the lives of saints. Four cardinal virtues are commonly recognized both in scripture and in other moral traditions: temperance, fortitude, prudence, and justice. Three higher theological virtues are distinctive to Christianity: **faith**, **hope**, and **love** (1 Cor. 13:13). Scripture teaches us to contemplate such virtues (Phil. 4:8) and to make them part of our lives (2 Pet. 1:5-7).

As a door swings on its hinges (in Latin, *cardines*), the moral life pivots on four cardinal virtues that sustain whatever other virtues we may need for our lives. Temperance or self-control (Gal. 5:23) is moderation in the pursuit of our aims and desires for our long-term good. Temperance requires that we know our limits and observe them, training us in sobriety, **chastity**, and **humility**. Justice (Mic. 6:8) is the habit of fairly assessing and acting on the claims that others hold on our lives, seeking to give each person his or her due (Rom. 13:7). A just person speaks truth to others, keeps promises, practices compassion for the weak and the poor, respects human life, and protects the property of others. Prudence, or **wisdom** (Eph. 5:15-17), is the habit of making wise and thoughtful choices that lead to effective action: showing kindness to those in need without embarrassing them and being generous without giving blindly. Fortitude (2 Tim. 1:7) is the disposition to act courageously as we boldly face the obstacles, fears, and disappointments of each day.

Our spiritual life hinges on the three theological virtues, portrayed in scripture as abiding **gifts of the Spirit** (1 Cor. 13:13). Faith, hope, and love direct the four cardinal virtues into the cause of devotion and service to God. Together they describe a life that finds its source, goal, and shape in God. Faith (Heb. 11:6) is a respectful and abiding trust that draws on God's resources and promises that give us hope (1 Pet. 1:3). Faith works itself out in a love (Gal. 5:6) distinguished by whole-hearted loyalty to God, just service to our neighbor, and faithful care of ourselves. Many Christian catechisms teach faith from the Apostles' Creed, hope from the **Lord's Prayer**, and love from the Ten Commandments (see **Augustine**'s *Enchiridion*).

For further reading, see James Stalker, *Seven Cardinal Virtues.* JMB

VISION OF GOD. An experience of the soul and the intellect, of faith and **contemplation**. For **Bernard of Clairvaux**, the vision of God (or beatific vision) is the process by which contemplatives apprehend supernatural realities. It is the ultimate purpose of human life according to classical Christian doctrine, often described by theologians and mystics as the highest pinnacle in a climb toward mystical **union**. It is often manifested in celestial light, all-encompassing peace and **ecstasy**, or by a sweeping sense of certainty and awareness of divine truth. Depending upon theological perspective, various mystics describe the beatific vision as an intellectual, a faith, an intuitive, or a contemplative experience. Most acknowledge it as a divine gift—not earned. **Augustine**, **Pseudo-Dionysius**, and others note that contemplation (the pathway to the vision of God) consists of three things: entrance into the divine mystery; suspension of physical capacities, producing a divine stillness; and finally, the vision of God and mystical union.

The vision of God is considered the culmination of all doctrine, all belief, all experience. Often it is described as the reward of a faithful life, the result of martyrdom, the achievement for which all the saints strive. In many classical writings, the vision of God is unobtainable in human existence because of the interruptions of **sins** of varying sorts and because of the limitations that mortality places upon the soul by virtue of its dwelling in and with a body. However, many mystics such as Bernard of Clairvaux, **Richard of St. Victor**, **Nicholas of Cusa**, and **Teresa of Ávila** describe in great detail the tiny moments of foretaste in which the tantalizing and elusive vision of God comes in some measure to human contemplatives. The mystics of the church are careful to describe their visions of God as "experience," as opposed to dogma or theological truth.

For further reading, see *Nicholas of Cusa: Selected Spiritual Writings*, translated by Hugh Lawrence Bond. SAW

VISITANDINES. Members of the Visitation Order (more fully, the Order of the Visitation of the Blessed Virgin Mary), founded by **Francis de Sales** and **Jane de Chantal**.

WARE, KALLISTOS (TIMOTHY RICHARD)
(b. 1934), Orthodox writer and bishop. Born
in Bath, England, Ware studied at Oxford,
then joined the **Orthodox** Church in 1958
and was ordained a priest in 1966. Ware became titular bishop of the Orthodox diocese
of Diokleia and assistant bishop in the archdiocese of Thyateira and Great Britain in
1982. He has also served as Spalding Lecturer
in Eastern Orthodox studies at Oxford University since 1966. Ware's writings include *The
Orthodox Church*, a standard introduction to
Orthodoxy *The Power of the Name* and *The Jesus
Prayer*. He served with G. E. H. Palmer and
Philip Sherrard as translator of the four volumes of *The Philokalia*. The first volume of his
collected writings, *The Inner Kingdom*, gives
particular attention to the spiritual life, with
essays on repentance, prayer, the theology of
worship, and the role of the spiritual guide in
Orthodox Christianity. EBA

WARFARE, SPIRITUAL. Prayer as combat
against evil. The author of Ephesians writes,
"For our struggle is not against enemies of
blood and flesh, but against the rulers, against
the authorities, against the cosmic powers of
this present darkness, against the spiritual
forces of evil in the heavenly places" (6:12).
This warfare can be an internal or external
struggle.

Spiritual warfare can signify the deep personal struggles of the faith that require intense conflict within oneself. This is known as
spiritual combat. The apostle Paul uses combat imagery in his epistle (2 Cor. 10:3-5), and
the writer of Revelation sees spiritual conflict
in the present and future in a vision filled with
vivid imagery of warfare. The sixteenth-century mystic **John of the Cross** reflected on the
struggle within one's heart in his *Dark Night*

of the Soul, which deals in part with the inner
conflict with the **seven deadly sins**. The remainder focuses on the encounter between
darkness and light in one's soul, striving for
righteousness but being tempted by the
world. **John Bunyan**'s allegory *The Holy War*
depicts the struggle of the city of Mansoul
against both external attacks of "Diabolus"
(especially at the "gates" of the senses) and internal rebellion, emphasizing the Christian's
helplessness against temptation until Christ
himself enters the battle.

Spiritual warfare can also refer to an external struggle of intense prayers of intercession. These prayers may be for an individual
facing physical danger, strong temptations, or
a difficult decision. Prayer warriors may also
address larger concerns, whether local or
global, such as justice, peace, or public morals.
Spiritual warfare of this sort may be conducted by an individual, a prayer group, or a
larger network of groups. For further information, see *Possessing the Gates of the Enemy: A
Training Manual for Militant Intercession* by
Cindy Jacobs. WBF

WATER. The symbolism of water figures
prominently in both the Old and New Testaments. In the Creation God's spirit moves
over the face of the dark waters and brings
forth light (Gen. 1). The great Flood (Gen.
6–8) reminds us of the cleansing judgment of
God. The deliverance of God's people from
slavery is accomplished as they pass through
the sea on the way to the Promised Land
(Exod. 14). The absence of water is also a recurring theme in the Old Testament, especially in the experience of wilderness. Psalm
63:1 voices the spiritual longing eloquently:
"My soul thirsts for you... as in a dry and
weary land where there is no water."

Water is particularly important in the writings of the New Testament in relation to baptism. John the Baptist offers a baptism for the repentance of sins, in preparation for the coming kingdom of God (Mark 1). Jesus experiences this baptism as identification with humanity, and as he rises from the waters of the Jordan River he is affirmed as the Son of God (Matt. 3). At the Last Supper, Jesus washes the feet of the disciples (John 13), and after his resurrection he instructs his followers to make disciples and to baptize them in the name of the Father, the Son, and the Holy Spirit (Matt. 28). The Bible concludes with an angelic vision of the river of the water of life flowing from the throne of God (Rev. 22).

Water is related to the process of birth, as the child lives in the mother's womb; it is also mysterious and is related psychologically to the unconscious. Water is both life-giving and life-threatening, a source of sustenance and danger. In agricultural settings water represents a sign of blessing, although Jesus speaks of the rain falling on the just and the unjust (Matt. 5:45). **Teresa of Ávila** compares watering a garden to the action of **grace** in helping virtues to grow in our souls. Water is sacramental in Christianity, pointing to the cleansing and renewing action of God in our life together. Many of these symbolic qualities of water are taken up in the prayers associated with **baptism**.

For further reading see your denomination's service of baptism and William H. Willimon's *Word, Water, Wine, and Bread*. KHC

WATTS, ISAAC (1674–1748), first great English hymn writer. Standing in the Puritan succession of dissent in England, Watts's **hymn** compositions (including "O God, Our Help in Ages Past," "Jesus Shall Reign," "Joy to the World," and "When I Survey the Wondrous Cross") have been sung throughout the churches of Western Christianity and beyond. He possessed an unusual poetic gift, producing hymns from childhood on. The **spirituality** of his hymns is characterized by a sense of divine **transcendence**, the glory and majesty of God, and the sweep of God's action in human history with particular focus on the gracious manifestation of God's love through the **cross** of Christ. Many of his hymns are essentially poetic paraphrases of the **Psalms** (compare "Joy to the World" and Psalm 98). In addition to his hymns, however, Watts devoted considerable energy to being a pastor and a "guide to godliness." His *Guide to Prayer* is a sober and rigorous examination of the classic parts of **prayer** and provides practical advice about the use and abuse of book prayers as well as addressing the issue of posture in prayer.

For more on his life, see Arthur Paul Davis, *Isaac Watts: His Life and Works*. PWC

WAY OF A PILGRIM, THE. This brief narrative, written by a nineteenth-century Russian peasant, tells of the author's longing to learn what the apostle Paul meant when he advised us to pray without ceasing. The tale begins with the peasant seeking help from the superior of a small monastery, who teaches him the **Jesus Prayer**: "Lord Jesus Christ, have mercy upon me." The peasant is instructed to repeat these words that summarize the gospel until the prayer moves from the mind to become the **prayer of the heart**.

The pilgrim takes this advice seriously and wanders across Russia practicing the prayer. He prays while sitting still and as he walks, both night and day; he learns to use his **breath** to support his prayer. At times he keeps track of the number of repetitions of the prayer by using a circle of one hundred beads. He reads from an abridgment of *The Philokalia*.

On his journey the pilgrim meets people who help him and others who hinder his progress. But through all his adventures he perseveres in the practice of the Jesus Prayer and eventually realizes that his heart is praying constantly. Filled with wonder, his heart overflowing with joy, the pilgrim continues his travels eager to share his experience with others so that they might also experience the glory of God's grace. JEV

WEATHERHEAD, LESLIE DIXON (1893–1976), English Methodist minister. Born in London, educated at Leicester, and prepared for the Methodist ministry at Cliff and Richmond Colleges, he returned to England in 1922 after serving as a chaplain in World War I in Mesopotamia and India. His reputation as a dynamic preacher took him to important city center churches and eventually secured the unique appointment as a Methodist minister to London's City Temple (Congregationalist), where he distinguished himself in a wartime pastorate that endeared him to the London populace and spread his fame. His doctoral studies at London in psychology, religion, and healing reflect his lifelong interest and pioneering work in interconnecting these disciplines. His pacifism, unpredictable theology, and unique pastoral techniques often placed him in the center of controversy.

Never fearful of the criticism he knew he would attract, Weatherhead published his thinking on subjects considered taboo by many in his day, reflected in titles such as *The Mastery of Sex through Psychology and Religion*, *Life Begins at Death*, and his highly controversial final work, *The Christian Agnostic*. His many volumes of published sermons reflect the wide scope of his interests and his concern to place the fullness of the gospel before as large an audience as possible in a language and form that was understandable and spoke to the need. He was also a teacher of **prayer**, both in public liturgical practice and through the means of his publications. His widely used prayer card, "Ten Minutes a Day," enabled busy people to experience a wide range of prayer in the midst of activity. His major devotional publication, *A Private House of Prayer*, introduced thousands of Protestant readers to a Catholic heritage of spiritual **discipline** and technique.

A. Kingsley Weatherhead wrote his father's biography, *Leslie Weatherhead: A Personal Portrait*. PWC

WEIL, SIMONE (1909–43), French mystic and philosopher. Born in Paris into a close,

nominally Jewish family, Weil empathized deeply even as a young child with the sufferings of others. She and her brother, Andre, donated some of their own rations to soldiers during World War I. Weil received an advanced degree in philosophy at the Sorbonne, but her concern always lay with the "least of these." When she became a teacher, she gave away most of her salary. Convinced that she needed to challenge her heart even further, she spent a year working in a factory. Weil's parents convinced their exhausted daughter to join them on a trip to Portugal, where she experienced a conversion to the "irresistible power" of Christ's humility at the crucifixion. At the **cross**, Weil believed, Christ went the "greatest possible distance" to offer a bridge for our return to God.

In spite of her Christian conversion, Weil hesitated to join the institutional church, feeling compelled to witness to her faith as an outsider. Though her meditations on **Holy Communion** were beautiful, her dissatisfied hunger before God was complicated by her identification with **suffering** to the point of anorexia nervosa. In 1941 Weil and her family left France because of their Jewish heritage, but Weil never felt at peace in the comfort of America. Instead she returned to England to work for the French Resistance. With her body now weakened from long hours of work and inadequate food, Weil contracted tuberculosis. She died at the age of thirty-four in a British sanitarium. Besides numerous philosophical writings such as *The Need for Roots*, Weil also wrote the arresting spiritual autobiography, *Waiting for God*. *Gravity and Grace*, a collection of spiritual sayings, was gathered after her death. Weil left a compelling, if complex, spiritual legacy of her mystical experience with the divine, her contemplation of suffering, and her sacrificial self-giving for others.

In addition to Weil's works mentioned above, you might read *Simone Weil: A Modern Pilgrimage* by Robert Coles. SAF

WESLEY, CHARLES (1707–88), cofounder of the Methodist movement and hymn writer.

Son of the Anglican clergyman Samuel Wesley and the incomparable Susanna, educated at Westminster School in London and at Christ Church, Oxford, and ordained to the priesthood in 1735, he developed an early love for the church. Though his older brother **John Wesley** was more prominent, Charles often led the way in many of the personal and institutional developments that helped begin the rising evangelical revival of the eighteenth century. It was Charles who founded the "Holy Club" while a student at Oxford and who first experienced God's unconditional love on May 21, 1738, preceding his brother's famous Aldersgate experience by three days. His greatest gift to the revival was the production of nine thousand **hymns** through which the vast majority of people called Methodists learned the theology of the movement. Methodism was born in the song of this amazing hymn writer. According to one scholar, in the early years of the revival, "he would preach in the open air to a spellbound crowd gathered by his rich voice singing one of his own hymns."

The blossoming of Wesley's evangelical hymns began in 1739 with *Hymns and Sacred Poems,* jointly published by Charles and John. Charles produced about 180 hymns per year for the next fifty years until his death in 1788. His most important publication was the 1780 *A Collection of Hymns for Use of the People Called Methodist.* For many years this hymnal shaped every dimension of Methodist spiritual life. Wesley's lyrical theology reflects the genius of Wesleyan spirituality that united Anglican **holiness** of intent with Puritan inward **assurance** within the larger context of the Catholic Christian heritage and worked out in structures of accountable discipleship. J. Ernest Rattenbury once observed that a carefully selected anthology of Charles Wesley's hymns would make a devotional manual second to none.

For more information, see S T Kimbrough Jr., *Charles Wesley: Poet and Theologian* or Charles Wesley's *Journal.* PWC

WESLEY, JOHN (1703–91), cofounder (with brother **Charles Wesley**) of the Methodist movement, Anglican priest, Oxford fellow, theologian, author, publisher, evangelist, and itinerant preacher. Wesley was the fifteenth child of Samuel and Susanna Wesley. At the age of five, John nearly perished in the Epworth rectory fire. From that moment, Susanna regarded John as a "brand plucked from the burning" and was convinced that God had some special purpose for his life. Wesley studied Greek, natural and moral philosophy, and logic at Oxford University. While at Oxford as a teaching fellow, he took over the leadership of the Oxford Holy Club, a group started by his brother Charles and a few close friends. The purpose of the group was to provide a mutual accountability structure for the **imitation of Christ**. Under John's leadership, they established a semimonastic lifestyle of extreme frugality (living on £28 a year), praying the Daily Office (**Liturgy of the Hours**), a form of daily self-examination (**examen**), twice weekly **Holy Communion**, serious Bible study, penance and **mortification** (especially **fasting**), and **works of mercy** among the poor. The methodical rigor of their pious practice caused much ridicule among the intellectuals of the university, who nicknamed them Methodists.

From the time of the Holy Club, Wesley kept a journal that he regularly edited for publication. The first volume recounts a disastrous trip as a missionary to Georgia, after which Wesley felt he was a failure as a priest, a Christian, and a human being. His search for a felt sense of **assurance** in his relationship with Christ culminated on May 24, 1738, when, at a **Moravian** meeting in Aldersgate Street, London, he felt his "heart strangely warmed." By 1739 Anglican pulpits were repeatedly closed to Wesley because of his strong preaching on salvation by **faith**. Reluctantly he began field preaching with his friend George Whitefield. While his association with Whitefield did not last, this did begin a wide range of preaching spreading from London throughout England, Wales, Ireland, and Scotland. From 1738 to

1765, Wesley built a strongly organized Methodist society as a renewal movement within the Church of England. Through his evangelistic preaching tours tens of thousands were converted to Christ and then organized into local *societies* and further divided into smaller **covenant groups**, known as *bands* and *classes*, for mutual support and accountability. (For more details, see D. Michael Henderson, *John Wesley's Class Meeting*.) In addition to preaching and organizing, Wesley also established schools, orphanages, and work cooperatives and published his own works and edited versions of many Christian classics. He said that his aim was "not to form any new sect; but to reform the nation, particularly the Church; and to spread scriptural **holiness** over the land." However, due to his pastoral concerns for the Methodists in America following the Revolutionary War, Wesley did set up the American Methodist Episcopal Church (1784) by ordaining and sending Francis Asbury and Thomas Coke to be its first bishops.

One of the most significant contributions of John Wesley to Christian **spirituality** was his presentation of the **stages** of the Christian life in terms of the action of God's **grace**: prevenient grace inviting repentance, justifying grace bringing new birth and assurance, sanctifying grace leading to Christian **perfection**, and glorifying grace at the time of death. His main concern was to lead men and women along the road of salvation by charting the way and assuring them that grace was available to empower them to walk in that way. For Wesley, Christian perfection, or **sanctification**, was a dynamic relational reality of perfect **love** and continual growth in **conformity** to God's perfect will. This emphasis was at the heart of a distinctively Methodist spirituality shaped by John and Charles Wesley that distinguished Methodism from the theologism of the Calvinistic debates and the rationalism of Anglicanism that raged during their time.

Wesley's *Journal*, letters, sermons, and treatises are available in many editions, including some available on-line. *A Plain Account of Christian Perfection* summarizes Wesley's teaching on that subject. Richard P. Heitzenrater's *Wesley and the People Called Methodists* offers a readable introduction to Wesley's life and the Methodist movement, along with many maps and illustrations and copious suggestions for further reading. CIZ

WILBERFORCE, WILLIAM (1759–1833), English evangelical Christian, member of Parliament, abolitionist, philanthropist. Born to a wealthy merchant family in Hull, he went to live with his uncle at the age of eight, when his father died. Under the influence of his staunch Methodist aunt, he came in contact with the great evangelist George Whitefield and the converted slave trader **John Newton**, author of "Amazing Grace." Upset by his religious enthusiasm, his mother soon brought him back home. At seventeen he entered St. John's College, Cambridge, where he met William Pitt, who would become England's youngest prime minister. In 1780, at the age of twenty-one, Wilberforce was elected to Parliament and served there until his retirement in 1825. In 1784 he was converted to evangelical Christianity and also began his career-long goal to abolish the British slave trade. He considered leaving politics and joining the clergy, but John Newton convinced him that God was calling him to a life in politics. Although Wilberforce presented his first bill to abolish the slave trade in 1791, such a ban was not passed until 1807. He then turned his energy to the abolition of slavery. Parliament passed the Slavery Abolition Act one month after his death in 1833.

Three years after his conversion Wilberforce founded the Proclamation Society, which aimed to suppress vice and reform public manners. Of the four books published during his lifetime, the most important is *A Practical View of the Prevailing Religious System of Professed Christians in the Higher and Middle Classes in this Country Contrasted with Real Christianity*, first published in 1797. A lengthy work not meant as a theological opus or as an attempt to convert the skeptic, it was an attack against the luxury and excesses of the rich.

Full of personal observations on "true" religion, it is a masterpiece of personal religion that was praised by both high Anglicans and dissenters. Little known today, the book appeared in fifteen editions by 1837 and sold in the hundreds of thousands. For more information see the 1958 abridgment published by SCM Press of *Wilberforce: A Narrative* by Reginald Coupland. DDW

WILL (HUMAN). Classical and medieval psychology conceived of the **soul** as having three primary faculties: memory, intellect, and will. **Augustine** saw these three different aspects of one soul as reflections of the three-in-one nature of the Trinity. But for Christian growth and **formation**, the will stood out above the other two human faculties in importance. Since the will both chooses and longs for what it chooses, the will is the human source of **love**, the greatest of Christian **virtues**. Spiritual writers, including **Teresa of Ávila**, **John of the Cross**, and the author of *The Cloud of Unknowing*, see memory and intellect as important in beginning prayer and discursive **meditation**. Ultimately, though, memory and intellect must be quieted as they become **distractions** from the **prayer of the heart**, the will's "naked yearning" for God in **contemplation**. In *Purity of Heart Is to Will One Thing*, **Kierkegaard** explains that the "one thing" is seeking the good in God.

While the will makes choices, theologians have debated how free those choices are. Augustine argued in *On Free Choice of the Will* that the will is bound by **sin**, so corrupted that it will always choose evil if not set free by divine **grace**. In this he set himself against the **Pelagian** view that people can choose the good on their own. During the Reformation, **Erasmus** supported a semi-Pelagian view of free will in *Diatribe on Free Will*, while **Luther** responded in support of Augustine with *On the Bondage of the Will*. More recent debates on the freedom of human choice have centered on psychological constraints, both conscious and unconscious, and on the role of **dispositions** in predicting many choices. Becoming aware of the bindings and blockages in the choices of our will is a central task in **spiritual direction**. Ultimately the goal of Christian spiritual formation is to bring our wills into **conformity to the will of God**, a process of learning to love God more completely, seeking **perfection** and self-**abandonment**.

For further reading, see *Will and Spirit* by **Gerald G. May**. KRB

WILL OF GOD. God's purpose, overarching time and space. The term carries an important added meaning that God constantly acts out that divine purpose; that is, God never wills something without at the same time acting to bring it about. God's will is an aspect of God's ongoing work of creation. The ultimate coherence of God's will with God's action is quite unlike that of humans, who often claim purposes that vary from their actions.

The interplay of God's sovereign will with human free will is a profound Christian mystery, since humans often freely oppose the designs of the omnipotent God. Even the thought that mortals could frustrate God's designs seems outlandish. The theological answer, considered unsatisfactory by some, is that God's will perpetually acts in sovereign ways that permit, and even use, human free will! Since humans cannot see the whole of creation and history as God does, our best visions are far too small to comprehend how God's will is eternally being enacted.

Faithful discipleship requires knowing the nature of God's will. Without such knowledge it would be impossible to obey God. Jesus knew God's will. In the **Lord's Prayer**, Jesus taught his followers to ask God to bring about God's purposes and to attune their wills to God's: "Your kingdom come. Your will be done, on earth as it is in heaven" (Matt. 6:10). His disciples became good examples of **discerning** God's will. The survival of the small early Christian community and its growth into a worldwide fellowship are powerful evidence of cooperation with God's will. However, the New Testament reports with candor the repeated failure of the twelve disciples to perceive God's will during Jesus' earthly life and even after his resurrection. Humanity's continued blindness in discerning God's will is manifest in wars (especially when opposing armies both believe God is on their side), racism, sexism, and unfair economic and political systems.

Christians experience God's will as daily guidance in things great and small, receiving both physical and spiritual gifts, strength and healing. Christian theology teaches that God's will is both sovereign and universal, sovereign because God's will is always God's decision and universal because it operates in and over every society and religion and throughout the universe. Yet many events, both victories and tragedies, seem not to be God's will at all, because human free will and nature often appear responsible.

Leslie D. Weatherhead's tiny book *The Will of God* is a helpful classic. Weatherhead outlines three aspects of God's will: intentional will, circumstantial will, and ultimate will. The original intentions of God's sovereign will are perfect, including human freedom to choose to love God. However, since human choices can produce tragic, even evil, consequences, God's circumstantial will seeks a restorative outcome (e.g., Christ's death on the cross brings reconciliation to a sinful world, though those who crucified him could not be said to have followed God's original intentions). Ultimately God's sovereign power uses even the most tragic outcomes of **sin**, **evil**, and error to bring results in which all the original intentions of God's will are completely fulfilled. JNE

WILLARD, DALLAS (b. 1935), American philosopher, educator, spiritual director. Willard is an ordained Southern Baptist minister, an expert on phenomenologist Edmund Husserl, **Richard J. Foster's** spiritual director, and professor of philosophy. He is best known to Christian readers for his trilogy of books about the human relationship with God. *In Search of Guidance* (reissued as *Hearing God*) leads the reader into communication, then companionship, with God. *The Spirit of the Dis-*

ciplines is a discussion of the role of God's grace and Spirit in developing the provisions and character intended for all people. *The Divine Conspiracy, Christianity Today's* Book of the Year for 1999, presents discipleship as the very heart of the gospel. Willard emphasizes the presence and availability of God's rule or kingdom to anyone who wants to recognize it. WW

WILLIAM OF SAINT-THIERRY (ca. 1085–ca. 1148), Benedictine monk, disciple of **Bernard of Clairvaux**, and spiritual writer. A **Benedictine** abbot when they met, William was greatly influenced by Bernard of Clairvaux and transferred to a **Cistercian** abbey in 1135. In his treatises *On Contemplating God, On the Nature and Dignity of Love,* and *The Enigma of Faith* and in his commentary on the *Song of Songs,* William explores a **contemplative** life based on **love**. For him strength of **will** toward God, balanced with a rational devotion, moves a person to love. With great **discipline** and **asceticism** a person can participate in the love between God and the Son through the Holy Spirit. This trinitarian **mysticism** is one of his most enduring contributions. SN

WILLIAMS, CHARLES WALTER STANSBY (1886–1945), British poet, novelist, critic, and theologian. Though he never completed his university education, Williams became known as a writer of poetry and "supernatural" thrillers and served as an editor at Oxford University Press (OUP) for most of his adult life. He also lectured on English literature at a London evening institute and later at Oxford. When the London branch of the OUP moved to Oxford in 1939, Williams became acquainted with **C. S. Lewis** and became a member of the Inklings, a group of Christian writers and thinkers that included Lewis and J. R. R. Tolkien. In 1943 Oxford granted Williams an honorary M.A.

Among Williams's most famous writings are *All Hallows' Eve* (1944, with an introduction by **T. S. Eliot**), *The Greater Trumps* (1932), *Descent into Hell* (1937), *The Descent of the Dove* (1939), *The Figure of Beatrice* (1943), and two volumes of poetry on the Arthurian legend. Williams's writings are dense but imaginative and packed with poetic language and symbolism. He attempted to reshape mythic and sometimes semi-occult legends, such as the Holy Grail and the Tarot, into a poetic and deeply Christian vision. His central theological idea, which he called variously "substitution," "exchange," and "coinherence," was that the Christian life involves a profound bearing of one another's burdens and relating to one another as part of the Divine flow of love. W. H. Auden once called Williams "the only writer... who has found out how to make poetry out of theology."

For further information, see *The Novels of Charles Williams* by Thomas Howard, *The Inklings* by Humphrey Carpenter, or *Charles Williams: An Exploration of His Life and Works* by Alice Mary Hadfield. JLW

WISDOM. Knowledge (especially knowing how to live well), judgment, and prudence are all aspects of wisdom, a fundamental attribute both of God and of people in scripture. In the Hebrew Scriptures, human wisdom is examined in its many forms in the so-called Wisdom Books, which include Job, Psalms, Proverbs, Ecclesiastes, and Song of Solomon. Two noncanonical writings that directly influenced the early church fathers are Ecclesiasticus (The Wisdom of Ben Sirach) and The Wisdom of Solomon (simply known as Wisdom). A meditation in the Wisdom of Solomon states that wisdom "is a breath of the power of God" and "a clear emanation... of the Almighty" (7:25), to make those who receive it "friends of God" (7:27). Sirach 1:9 claims that God has "poured" wisdom on all creation. Wisdom also encompasses fundamental principles of virtuous living as well as practical advice on how to succeed, live well, and be happy. All of these aspects are measured by the "fear of the Lord" (Prov. 9:10), the beginning of wisdom. Divine wisdom is seen in creation and in the destiny that guides nations and individuals. In Proverbs 8 wisdom is depicted at God's side during the creation of the world, foreshad-owing the Logos theology of Philo of Alexandria and the Gospel of John.

In the New Testament, wisdom is **incarnate** in Jesus of Nazareth, whom Paul calls the "wisdom of God" (1 Cor. 1:24), "in whom are hidden all the treasures of wisdom and knowledge" (Col. 2:3). Jesus is not only a Savior but also a teacher of wisdom whose parables about the wise and the foolish are intended to instruct the disciple along the wise path that leads to life (Matt. 7:24-27). John calls Jesus the Logos incarnate, the ordering principle of all creation. Wisdom is also considered one of the **gifts of the Holy Spirit** (1 Cor. 12:8), with whom it is associated. Many of the Greek fathers used *wisdom* as a synonym for the Word of God or Logos. The **Gnostics** treated wisdom as a divine emanation, the spouse of the Logos, or Word. More recently in theology, much is being made of the feminine gender of the word for wisdom in Hebrew and Greek. *Hochmah* in Hebrew and *Sophia* in Greek reflect a passive, **receptive**, and relational approach to reality that can help people align their lives in congruence with the **will of God**. Wisdom in effect is being in a relationship of **love** with the mysterious order of life we call God.

As one of the gifts of the Spirit, wisdom has the power to discriminate accurately, to enhance the capacity to **discern** the inner moral imperative of the concrete situation. Wisdom aligns us with inner logic of life and opens us to the *kairos* (ripening moment), knowing that "for everything there is a season and a time for every matter under heaven" (Eccles. 3:1). Wisdom always reminds us of the limits of our life and the necessity of placing our ultimate trust in God.

Gerhard von Rad's *Wisdom in Israel* is a classic study of biblical wisdom literature. Alyce M. McKenzie has written practical guides to biblical wisdom in *Preaching Proverbs* and *Preaching Biblical Wisdom in a Self-Help Society*. TCW

WOOLMAN, JOHN (1720–72), **Quaker** and abolitionist. Born in Northampton, Burlington

County, West Jersey (now New Jersey), of devout Quaker parents, Woolman became acquainted early with the operations of divine love. A serious youth, he developed a conviction that cruelty toward any living creature is inconsistent with the claiming of a love for God. Employed at age twenty-one by a merchant in Mount Holly, he quickly found his creed put to the test when he overrode his conscience to write a bill of sale for a black woman slave owned by his master. At twenty-six he began traveling the American colonies to strengthen various Meetings as a "minister" in the Religious Society of Friends. On the very first of these missions he witnessed the evils of slavery. From that time until his death from smallpox in England, he spent about one month a year traversing the colonies to plead with Quakers to free their slaves.

Woolman gave up a prosperous merchandising business to learn a tailor's trade lest daily demands encumber him and prevent him from doing God's leading. Little by little, he perceived that injustices such as slavery did not result from intentional hurt but from insensitivity to the impact of our desire for comfort and convenience on others' lives. The answer, therefore, begins with **love**. If we live by *agape* love, we cannot overlook the hurt we bring, however indirectly, to others. Woolman recognized that looking at such large problems as slavery may cause us to throw up our hands in despair and do nothing in response. Believing that small efforts matter, however, he acted out of the confidence that God would use any good effort. He did not live to see the end of slavery even among Quakers, but largely because of his efforts, by 1787 no American Quaker owned a slave.

Woolman's *Journal*, the primary source for his life and thought, is available in a variety of editions. See also Edwin Harrison Cady's *John Woolman: The Mind of the Quaker Saint.* EGH

WORKS. Christian works are acts, deeds, and conduct, the purpose of which is to love and obey Jesus Christ. In Christian **spiritual formation** works are actions to benefit others that reflect inward realities of **faith**, **hope**, and love. Works are not motivated by self-improvement or self-interest but rather by **love** of neighbor in obedience to God's desires and in response to God's love. Faith and works are bound together inseparably with love in Jesus' life and teaching. In Matthew 25:31-46 Jesus teaches that at the judgment of "the nations" those who have performed works of love and **mercy** for the poor and needy will be welcomed into God's kingdom. Such service to those in need is service to Jesus. Inward realities such as faith, hope, and love are connected to outward realities such as works, deeds, and conduct—the inward should always be expressed in outward manifestations, and the outward should always express the inward. When physical illness prevents a person from helping to prepare food, the physical disability is deeply felt in the heart that aches for the strength to be able to cook. When all one can do is pray, one yearns for the ability to engage in some help-giving activity. The bond is also seen in the negative. A person who grudgingly prepares food for a church supper often pretends to do the work joyfully in mute testimony of how heart and deed ought to be unified.

As the early church incorporated new Christians, it faced heresies concerning works. In response Paul condemned "works prescribed by the law" (Rom. 3:28), ritualistic actions offered to earn salvation, insisting that God's gift of salvation is based on faith alone, not on keeping strict rules based on the Jewish Torah. The author of James faced an opposite heresy, that inward faith in Christ is sufficient for salvation without deeds of love and mercy. The seeming contradiction between what Paul and James wrote created still another centuries-old heresy, that faith and works are opposed to each other. Such opposition is clearly not Jesus' teaching. Yet it is perpetuated generation after generation by Christians claiming that one or the other, faith or works, is being neglected. Christians and churches are labeled "mission-minded" or "contemplative," focused on the "outward" or the "inward" journey, community-minded or leaning to the mystical, seeking God or seeking to do God's will. Spiritual health requires both sides of the one coin of discipleship, faith and works. Even describing one without reference to the other reinforces the erroneous thought that either can stand alone.

Repairing a house as an act of charity differs from praying, of course. Yet both are works that, in God's plan, are to spring from the heart. Some works, like prayer, are inward in nature. The motive and intention may be inward, but an action is involved. Thus those who desire to become more prayerful are keenly aware that failing to pray is an undone deed. Similarly, loving is an action, whether it involves serving a person or cause or is an inward compassion. Even the planning and preparing for an action is a work. Reflection reveals how closely related are inward **dispositions** and the works that express them. This intimate relationship is expressed negatively in hypocrisy—contriving to do works that pretend to reveal an inward reality. A hypocrite does not want others to know the truth about inner dispositions. True works of love are often invisible to the person or group being served. The recipient of money often does not know who gave the dollars. The donor knows the gift was given but frequently does not know who was helped. Contemplative persons often sense their need to do good works, and activists often recognize weaknesses in their interior lives. Both experiences point to the crucial connectedness of faith and works. JNE

WORKS OF MERCY. While early Christians celebrated freedom from the obligations and prohibitions of the Law, they also made lists characterizing good and bad behavior. Paul gives a list of "works of the flesh" in Galatians 5:19-21, and a similar list appears in Revelation 22:15. Paul's list of the **fruit of the spirit** (Gal. 5:22-23) offers a positive portrait of a spirit-filled Christian. Perhaps the most obvious list of good actions is given by Jesus in Matthew 25:35-36 as the basis for the judgment of the nations: "For I was hungry and

you gave me food, I was thirsty and you gave me something to drink, I was a stranger and you welcomed me, I was naked and you gave me clothing, I was sick and you took care of me, I was in prison and you visited me."

By the Middle Ages, Christians had expanded these six actions to create a list of seven corporal (bodily) works of mercy: feeding the hungry, giving drink to the thirsty, clothing the naked, sheltering the homeless, visiting the sick, caring for prisoners (both by visiting and ransoming), and burying the dead. Concern that Christians should be at least as concerned with souls as bodies led to the creation of a second list, the seven spiritual works of mercy: instructing the ignorant, counseling the doubtful, admonishing sinners, bearing wrongs patiently, forgiving offenses, praying for the living, and praying for the dead. While these lists certainly do not define the limits of Christian charitable action, they form a good core. KRB

WORKS RIGHTEOUSNESS. See **Pelagianism**.

WORSHIP. The activities by which persons and communities direct themselves to God, the one who alone is worthy of worship, in acts of **adoration**, praise, **confession**, **petition**, lamentation, and **thanksgiving**. Worship is both a means to the spiritual life and an expression of that life. As such, worship is itself a spiritual **discipline**.

A decision to worship includes a decision to name what and whom we will worship. As a discipline, it requires both saying no as well as saying yes. Our decision to worship the God of Israel and the God of the church requires that we say no to the worship of other gods that vie for our attention and energy. We say *yes* when we remember and claim the first commandment that we are to have no other gods before us. We also say yes when we claim for ourselves the church's fundamental confession: "Jesus is Lord."

Like all spiritual disciplines, the discipline of worship requires that we learn how to worship. While humans seem to have an innate ability to respond to mystery and beauty with **awe** and wonder, such expressions do not in themselves develop the discipline of worshiping God with the whole of our lives. For some, a response to experiences of God with spontaneous expressions of delight, thanksgiving, or confession provides an invitation into a disciplined life of faithful worship. For others, the discipline or duty of turning to God faithfully in acts of thanksgiving and confession over time leads to such delight in God. (These varying starting points are frequently reflected in the **Psalms**.)

Worship is individual and corporate. *Individual worship* includes various forms of personal devotion—the **reading** and study of scripture or other sacred texts; **intercessory** and petitionary prayer; **Centering Prayer**; the use of various devotional guides; and prayerful **meditation** on **scripture** (such as *lectio divina*), on experiences in one's life, or on God's creation. Forms of *corporate worship* include reading the Daily Office or **Liturgy of the Hours**, the service of Word and Table (including preaching and the celebration of **Holy Communion**), the **baptism** of persons of all ages, and midweek **prayer services**. Special services are celebrated throughout the church **year**, such as services of foot-washing or Tenebrae during Holy Week, the Easter Vigil, the commemoration of the **saints** on All Saints' Day, and Christmas Eve services. These forms of worship often include the reading and interpretation of scripture, intercessory and petitionary prayer, confession, lamentation, thanksgiving, and congregational song. Many people also find these corporate forms helpful in shaping individual worship and prayer.

Worship is expressive and formative. *Expressive worship* emphasizes the ways in which we do something individually or communally. We bring ourselves and our lives before God, celebrate what God has done in our lives, and name who we are and what we have experienced. In response to God's saving work in our lives, we offer God our thanks, praise, and adoration. The brokenness of our lives and our world causes us to turn to God in confession and lamentation, seeking forgiveness and care. Alone or in community, we express these things through song, prayer, silence, self-dedication, and self-offering. In each of these practices, we are expressing an understanding of our lives with God.

Formative worship emphasizes the ways in which worship shapes us. When we sing a **hymn**, offer a **prayer**, recite a creed, gather around the Lord's Table, or sit in silence, the rhythms, words, images, and postures influence the way we think about and engage in life with God. Corporate and individual prayers draw on the resources of the greater Christian community that extends beyond time and place. When we read and hear scripture, share in baptism and Holy Communion, join a community in prayers of intercession and petition, confess our sins or cry out in lamentation individually and corporately, we are given a way of being Christian people. As we are drawn into the **community** of **faith**, we learn to share words and practices that may not be ours alone but give us a place and identity in the Christian community. Through the various worship practices, we are formed in particular ways of understanding ourselves as people of faith—as a **covenant** people whom God continues to seek out, as sinful yet **forgiven**, as one body in Christ Jesus, as a community with diverse gifts and ministries, all of which are required in worship. Even the rhythm of daily and weekly worship forms us into a people whose lives are turned to and centered on God.

For further reading, try *Worship and Spirituality* or *Worship Comes to Its Senses*, both by Don Saliers. EBA

WREN, BRIAN ARTHUR (b. 1936), Christian **hymn** writer and theologian. Born in Romford, Essex, England, Wren attended the Royal Liberty Grammar School and served for two years in the British Army. At age fifteen he became a Christian and joined the Congregational Church in England (now the United Reformed Church). He attended New

College, Oxford, graduating with a degree in modern languages, and Mansfield College, Oxford, earning a B.A. degree in theology (1962) and a Ph.D. (1968). Ordained in 1965, Wren served as minister of Hockley and Hawkwell Congregational Church, Essex, until taking a position with the British Council of Churches and later the role of coordinator of Third World First, a not-for-profit campaign on world poverty. He freelanced as a poet, theologian, and hymn writer from 1983 until he became the John and Miriam Conant professor of worship at Columbia Theological Seminary, Decatur, Georgia, in 2000.

Wren's hymn writing career began during his years at Mansfield College, as did his collaboration with hymn tune writer and musician Peter Cutts. At the center of his hymnody are the themes of social justice and inclusive language. For Wren, every naming of God is borrowed from human experience; he believes that for too long the church has used a limited, male-dominated, kingly imagery for God. His hymn texts, which include diverse metaphors for God, expand our language about God in support of a more just human society in tune with God's loving will.

For further information, see Wren's *What Language Shall I Borrow?* and *Praying Twice: The Music and Words of Congregational Song*. His hymn texts can be found in many hymnals and in his own *Piece Together Praise: A Theological Journey*. DDW

y

YEAR, LITURGICAL. The division of the calendar so as to draw the attention of the Christian **community** to the saving work of God in Jesus Christ through an annual cycle of remembrance. In the Western Church the year is essentially divided into two pairs of seasons around the major festivals of Christmas and Easter, a purple season of preparation and **penitence** before and a white season of celebration after. The time between these cycles is called Ordinary Time and counted simply as "Sundays after" the feast that ends the season of celebration. The liturgical color of Ordinary Time is green.

The liturgical year begins with the First Sunday of Advent (the fourth Sunday before Christmas). The preparatory season of Advent (Latin *adventus*, "coming") is a period in which the church anticipates the coming of Christ. Some churches use blue (associated with Mary) rather than traditional purple to distinguish this season from Lent. The observance of December 25, a date chosen undoubtedly to oppose the Roman pagan festival of the "Invincible Sun," as the date of Jesus' birth reflects the practice of the Roman church by the middle of the fourth century. White and gold are associated with the twelve days of Christmas, ending with Epiphany (Greek, *epiphaneia*, "manifestation") on January 6, still associated with the nativity in some Eastern traditions, but with the coming of the magi in the West. Lent (Old English, "spring") begins on Ash Wednesday (the Wednesday before the sixth Sunday before Easter) and ends on Maundy Thursday (the Thursday before Easter), when the Easter Triduum (Latin for "three days") begins.

As a preparatory season preceding the church's remembrance of Jesus' death and resurrection, Lent is also a reminder of Jesus' forty-day **fast** and temptation in the wilderness. By excluding the Sundays of the season, a forty-day fast can be observed from Ash Wednesday through Holy Saturday (the day before Easter). The penitential nature of the season is also reflected in the worship of the community through the use of the color purple, the omission of the *Alleluia* and the *Gloria in excelsis* in the eucharistic liturgy, and in practices of self-imposed abstinence.

The Easter Triduum, the three concluding days of Holy Week, commemorate particular events associated with the final days of Jesus' life. Maundy (Latin *mandatum*, "law") Thursday recalls Jesus' institution of the Lord's Supper in the upper room and his new law of love. Good Friday reminds the community of Jesus' crucifixion. Holy Saturday commemorates the resting of Jesus' body in the tomb.

Easter, or the Feast of the Resurrection of Christ (the first Sunday following the full moon after the spring equinox), is the greatest and oldest festival of the liturgical year. The derivation of the name "Easter" is uncertain but was most probably borrowed from an Anglo-Saxon spring equinox festival. The "Great Fifty Days" of Easter conclude with Pentecost (Greek *pentekoste*, "fiftieth"), the Greek name given to the Jewish Feast of Weeks, which fell on the fiftieth day after Passover. The descent of the **Holy Spirit** upon the apostles on this day transformed the Jewish feast for the Christian community into a festival celebrating the birth of the church and is remembered with the liturgical color red. The two green seasons each begin and end with feasts (liturgical color: white). The first Sunday after Epiphany commemorates the baptism of Jesus, and the last Sunday before Ash Wednesday is Transfiguration Sunday in some churches. The Sunday after Pentecost is Trinity Sunday, and the last Sunday before Advent is the Reign of Christ Sunday.

The liturgical year of the Orthodox tradition is based exclusively on Easter and divides the year into three basic parts: *triodion* (the ten weeks prior to Easter), *pentecostarion* (the paschal or Easter season), and *octoechos* (the rest of the year).

For a history of the liturgical year, see A. A. Allan McArthur, *The Evolution of the Christian Year*, or James F. White, *Introduction to Christian Worship*. PWC

Z

ZINZENDORF, NICHOLAS LUDWIG VON (1700–60), German aristocrat and leader of the **Moravian** Church. His early years were formed in **Pietism** under the influence of August Hermann Francke. Family pressures discouraged his desire for theological training and diverted him into government service. However, after inviting persecuted refugees of the Bohemian Brethren to his Herrnhut estate (1722), he became deeply involved in the revitalization of the *Unitas Fratrum* (Unity of Brethren), or Moravian Church. He organized members into small **covenant groups** or "bands" to study scripture, pray together, encourage and hold one another accountable as they sought to live under the guidance of Christ's love. Deeply anchored in his Lutheran roots, Zinzendorf appreciated Reformed and Roman Catholic theology.

This ecumenical background created a persistent desire to encourage Christian unity through love in Jesus Christ. Zinzendorf was known for his "heart religion," which focused upon the wounds of Christ. This deeply experiential spirituality was combined with a fervent zeal for witness and missionary efforts. Prayer was a significant component of community life, and the "100 Year Prayer Meeting" began to pray around the clock for advancing the reign of God in distant lands. A West Indian slave's visit to Herrnhut provided the impetus to send the first Moravian missionaries to the Caribbean. To promote the expansion of the Moravian communities Zinzendorf wrote a devotional book of meditations on scripture and hymns, *Daily Texts.* Theological and economic tensions from outside Herrnhut caused Zinzendorf's expulsion from his estate in 1736. During the next ten years he traveled widely throughout Europe, England, and America planting Moravian communities and developing missions. His influence upon evangelicals (**John Wesley** in particular) was considerable.

Zinzendorf wrote over two thousand hymns, many emphasizing Christ's atoning sacrifice ("Jesus, Thy Blood and Righteousness") and love among Christians ("Christian Hearts, in Love United"). His best-known book is *Nine Public Lectures on Important Subjects in Religion.* Among the numerous introductions to his life and spirituality, Arthur J. Freeman's *An Ecumenical Theology of the Heart* is most helpful. Older works by John R. Weinlick, *Count Zinzendorf,* and A. J. Lewis, *Zinzendorf the Ecumenical Pioneer,* are also valuable. TS

STREAMS OF CHRISTIAN SPIRITUALITY: *A Comparative Summary*

	Orthodox Spirituality/ Byzantine & Eastern	Celtic
Place/Time of Origin	Eastern Europe and Eastern Mediterranean, 325–787.	Ireland, Scotland and Wales, 4th century.
Influential Personalities	**Desert fathers and mothers; Evagrius Ponticus; Pseudo-Dionysius; John Climacus; Maximus the Confessor; Symeon the New Theologian; Gregory Palamas.**	**Patrick**; Bridget; Columba of **Iona.**
Image of Christ	Unity of the Godhead in a Trinity of persons. The **negative way**, i.e., a hidden transcendent God known only by who God is *not*; intimate communion (*parrhesia*) of the beloved; a sharer in the divine nature; mystery of the **Incarnation.**	Encircling presence of God; trinitarian; the leaping deer and the wild goose.
Ideals and Values	**Ascetic monasticism**; highly symbolic liturgical **sacramental** spirituality; primary purpose is to glorify God; ecclesiology rooted in **baptism** and membership as organic union in the **body of Christ**; **deification** and **transfiguration.**	The power of words, including scripture; hospitality; vow of **pilgrimage**; close-knit **community** and clan.
Prayer Disciplines	Veneration of the **icon** as a theophany; the **Jesus Prayer**; **deification** as the goal of prayer; **communion of the saints** with devotion to patron saints and guardian **angels.**	Poetry; **hymns** of the sacred in the domestic and natural; interweaving of everyday life concerns.
Ways of Knowing	Asceticism responsible for shaping the doctrine of the Incarnation of the word of Christ in the pilgrim; **illumination** and light in all spirituality and liturgical forms; veneration of Virgin Mary as *Theotokos* (God-bearer); **illumination** and transcendent mystery; **detachment** and purification of the senses.	Storytelling; blending of local spirituality with Christianity; visions; the Easter Vigil as key identifying liturgy.
Approach to Spiritual Direction	The "putting on of Christ" through sacramental worship, prayer, the Gospels, and the commandments; **confession** to a spiritual father or mother; individuals are created in the image of God and are summoned to be perfect, i.e., to love God with heart, soul, and mind; concentration on **sin** and repentance as a realistic acknowledgment of a factual situation. The holy traditions of the ecumenical councils speak to the inner life.	*Anamchara* or soul **friend**; life in loving relationship to all of creation; wisdom in playfulness.

Benedictine	Cistercian/Trappist
Italy, 6th century; Cluny, France, 9th century.	Cîteaux, Burgundy, France, late 11th century as Benedictine renewal; Order of Cistercians of the Strict Observance (Trappists) organized at La Trappe, France, late 19th century.
Benedict of Nursia 480–540; Scholastica, **Hildegard of Bingen**.	Robert of Molesmes, Stephen Harding, **Bernard of Clairvaux, Gertrude of Helfta, Thomas Merton, M. Basil Pennington**.
Highly exalted God and austere judge who tenderly protects; Christ met in all transactions; never used the name Jesus; divine presence in all; Christ encountered in hospitality and care of "the least."	See **Benedictine spirituality**; Intimate friend; lover and beloved; mystical marriage; mystery of the faith; incarnate Word who has already accomplished what is impossible to us.
Reverential **awe, humility**, and unworthiness underlies service; balance of work and prayer; **forgiveness, compassion**, and **asceticism** of common **celibate** life; vow of stability of residence; interpersonal virtues of mutual respect, patience, **obedience**, and renunciation of self-will and material possessions.	"Charter of Love" constitution; truth without compromise; unification and simplification of devotion leading to interior **conversion**; creativity in common life; respect for human freedom and diversity; strict rules on diet, **silence**, and manual labor; Mary as "spouse of the **Holy Spirit**"; humans have an orientation toward God; achievement not through merit but by grace.
Prayer is our response initiated by God; rhythm of prayer, work merged with learning (**meditation**) to form heart and mind through the formative practice of *lectio divina*; **liturgy of the hours** (Divine Office) as the "work of God" performed with reverent private prayer, **spiritual readings** and works of holiness; **tears** of compunction; memorization of the Psalter; prayer as inevitable consequence of God's presence; rituals of ordinary life made sacred.	Calm creates spaces; chanting psalms; Eucharist; spiritual scripture reading; silent prayer while working; desert **contemplation**; longing for **union** with God and a willingness to translate into practical movement in daily life.
Rule of **Benedict** as practical application of the gospel; observance and obedience to perfect following of Christ; attentive listening; God in the "least"; freedom of heart to obey the Holy Spirit.	Simplicity; space of interiority; academic; **vigilance** to Spirit; seeing inner mystery of all; poetic and artistic; symbolic theology; self-knowledge to discover spiritual energy within.
Abbot or Abbess is spiritual elder and believed to hold the place of Christ in parental relationship between master and disciple as the expression of Christ's sternness, gentleness, and love who reveals God's will and through whom one grows to perfection and obedience to carry out the **will of God**; importance of inner receptive attitudes of obedience, purity in heart, and loving response; hard effort will eventually make way to "delight in virtue."	Humble self-knowledge; intimately personal; relational; simplify one's life; *lectio* to arouse devotion and bring about behavior change; selflessness and dedication rather than subjectivity and techniques.

STREAMS OF CHRISTIAN SPIRITUALITY: *A Comparative Summary*

	Franciscan	*Dominican/ Order of Preachers*
Place/Time of Origin	Italy, 12th century, spreading in early 13th century to France and Germany.	Spain and France, late 12th century; a religious family of connected communities.
Influential Personalities	**Francis** and **Clare of Assisi**; **Bonaventure**; **Angela of Foligno**; Bernardine of Siena.	**Dominic**; Albert the Great; **Thomas Aquinas, Catherine of Siena; Meister Eckhart.**
Image of Christ	Francis became the face of Christ; highest good; transcendent mystery and holy love; Christ as mediator between God and humanity; poor crucified Christ; incarnate Word in creation; transcendent mystery; devotion to the Child Jesus in manger; the risen Lord present in the littleness and silence of the Eucharist.	Christ's depth of love; not suffering; in the highest intellect there is the ground of the soul that is equal to God.
Ideals and Values	To "follow the teachings and the footsteps of our Lord Jesus Christ"; simplicity and virtue of Lady **Poverty**: embracing radical material poverty in **detachment**, powerlessness and sharing is the highest wisdom demanding self-emptying to conform to Christ and allow the mind and heart to be filled with divine gifts; respect for individual uniqueness; eucharistic devotion to the **Sacred Heart**; balance of the feminine and masculine elements in human nature.	Rule of **Augustine**; combined common life, choral Office, study and **contemplation**, penance and the apostolate of preaching; "a grace of preaching" and teaching moral witness; love of God flowing to love of neighbor; pursuit of truth; customs of the order drafted by the community; "to be useful to the souls of our neighbors"; **obedience** and generosity of self-giving; intellectual work over manual labor.
Prayer Disciplines	Music and poetry; Office of the Passion of the Lord emphasizing the **suffering** of Christ; veneration of the **Eucharist**; the Crown Rosary (early 15th century); contemplative-active, fraternity and prayer.	Choral Mass celebration; simple chants; reciting psalms by heart; secret prayer following matins and compline; interior physical-emotional dialogue; choral office; contemplation means study of scripture; frequent brief prayer; oppose methodical approaches to private prayer.
Ways of Knowing	Francis as perfect exemplar of Christian action and contemplation; touched by God; know God through the poor and the suffering; study of scripture to reveal fallen and redeemed humanity; **nature mysticism** sees all creatures as revelations of God; wisdom, humility, and love.	Through baptism, worship, and Eucharist; universities established; identity as Order of Preachers; strongly intellectual rather than affective.
Approach to Spiritual Direction	Introspective self-knowledge; one is the mirror of Jesus to the world; penance as the decision to turn from **sin** to God; Scripture and liturgy guide the soul; primacy of **will** and primacy of **love**.	"Spiritual advisor;" Dominic wrote a book of guidance for preachers; teacher of the faith; mystical **union** by leaving all; trust in the individual and in God's **providence**.

Patricia D. Brown © Spiritworks, 2001

Beguines	Carmelite/Order of Our Lady of Mount Carmel
Belgium and France, late 12th century. No founder.	Legendary succession of monks from Elijah; N. Palestine, Mount Carmel, 12th century; "Discalced" reform, Spain, 16th century.
Beatrys of Nazareth, **Hadewijch** of Brussels, **Mechthild of Magdeburg**, **Marguerite Porete**, Marie d'Oignies.	Albert of Jerusalem, John Soreth; Mary Magdalen of Pazzi; **Teresa of Ávila; John of the Cross; Lawrence of the Resurrection; Thérèse of Lisieux, Edith Stein.**
Used imagination to envision Christ; noble, changeable, unattainable lady of courtly romance; lover imagery from the Song of Songs, Christ as lover; mystery; comforter and encourager.	Mystical love; daily Eucharist; imageless union with God; transcendence; bridegroom in **spiritual marriage**.
Sharing of wealth, atoning for past oppression; Bible as inspiration to life of service to others in order to draw near to God; use of vernacular language; soul as bride of Christ.	Tension between **solitude, silence, contemplation**, and pastoral oriented community; original eremitic asceticism (absolute poverty, pilgrimage, abstinence from flesh, and solitude) gave way to monastic community life and outside religious activity; owning neither personal or community property, committed to missionary work and pastoral ministry. Acts 2; mysticism of love; sacrament of **present moment**; individual cells around a common chapel.
God speaks directly to individuals, an easy intercourse reminiscent of a long-established marriage; journal writing to encourage other sisters to greater acts of sacrifice and love of God; prayer lived out in daily life; developed the stations of the cross; rosary is typical devotional practice.	Solitude, silence, and prayer; an intimate sharing between friends, praying the Bible: Song of Songs, prose and poetry using imaginative metaphor; intercession, penance and fasting; **liturgy of the hours**; daily Eucharist; continual prayer; the goal of mystical prayer, abandons all intermediary aids, is centered in God alone; pleasure in a "loving attention" to God.
Feeling the lover's presence; knowledge of one's inner self in order to understand one's relationship with God; meeting God in personal experiences.	Knowing Christ through love of neighbor; Marian devotion; "little way" of service in the present moment.
Balance of power between sisters; journal keeping; early 13th-century Beguines had the support from the church hierarchy, later 13th-century members met with male "spiritual advisors" to keep from the charge of heresy; perfection depends on charity, not on paranormal experiences.	Community-centered "way," passed on initial formation; study to experience the transcendence; reality of compassion as one stands naked before God; practice God-centered living away from self-deception; watchful of humility: pride is the gravest of all dangers.

STREAMS OF CHRISTIAN SPIRITUALITY: *A Comparative Summary*

	Ignatian/Jesuit	*Anglican*
Place/Time of Origin	Spain, 16th century.	England, 16th century.
Influential Personalities	**Ignatius of Loyola**, Francis Xavier, Peter Favre, James Lainez, Jerome Nadal.	**Thomas Cranmer**; Elizabeth I; Richard Hooker; **Jeremy Taylor; William Law; George Herbert**.
Image of Christ	Jesus Christ known in images that include the whole mystery of his humanity and divinity, Jesus of the synoptic Gospels, i.e., stories and pictures in scripture; king and "knight companion"; Lord of all the world; poor servant in mission; "Divine Majesty."	Christ is center of the community and found in the Eucharist, the "Real Presence"; young warrior who suffers the cross; the church as the continuation of the incarnate life of Christ.
Ideals and Values	Contemplation in action; focused ministry on the whole person, embodied, and not just to the **soul**; **affective** spirituality of **consolation**, in which one is moved to love and trust God's providential care for the whole world and for oneself in particular, and thus to hope; desolation as a lack of consolation, which paralyzes one's spirituality and action.	Devotion to the Passion; life centered on **worship** and liturgy with secondary piety in the home; "middle way" of moderation in all things; reason, tradition, and scripture as three-legged stool of authority; grace perfects the nature and restores the **image of God**; optimism of **grace**; inner **holiness** applied to practical works.
Prayer Disciplines	*Spiritual Exercises* by Ignatius. Periodic intensive **meditation** on Christ's life and ministry as it illumines personal call; seeing oneself in the narrative of scripture; seeking discernment through felt experience; **examen** and contemplation; *lectio divina*.	**Book of Common Prayer**; English lyrical poetry; corporate liturgical/sacramental acts and prayers within the congregation, respect for personal devotions.
Ways of Knowing	Through education and **discernment**; contemplation in action; finding God in all things; spiritual **journey** is in the community of those called "to labor in the vineyards of the Lord." Commitment to institutional church and its mission to be an instrument of consolation to the world.	Pragmatic: one participates in what the church does as church; liturgical acts as drama and means of grace; experiential through reason; mystical: God speaks directly to individuals.
Approach to Spiritual Direction	Frequent regular meetings between the one making the exercises and the spiritual director; **spiritual exercises** adapted and flexible to differences in person, need, and circumstances.	To encourage the examined life toward the goal of union with God; use of liturgical **year**, daily offices, readings; poetry and verse for meditation; artwork, fellowship, and communal covenant.

Quaker/Religious Society of Friends	Wesleyan/Methodist
Mid-17th-century England.	Early 18th-century England.
George Fox, Margaret Fell, **Isaac Penington, William Penn, John Woolman**.	**John** and **Charles Wesley**, Francis Asbury, **Richard Allen, Fanny Crosby, Phoebe Palmer**.
Inward immediacy of Christ's teachings, "Christ has come to teach his people himself." The light within: divine light of Christ in every person convicts of sin, enables reform, and holiness.	Pure universal love; the prodigal's father; love that welcomes the weary traveler home; Christ lived out in the "priesthood of all believers."
Moral character; simplicity, purity, truthfulness, personal integrity, and sobriety; refusal to take up arms; equality between men and women; social justice with equity in economic and social standings toward the transformation of society; refusal to swear oaths or to pay tithes; innate goodness of human nature.	Methodical spirituality; earnest approach to religious practice; synthesis of Anglican holiness and Puritan inward assurance; accountable discipleship; scriptural holiness; responsive to divine initiative through prevenient, justifying, and sanctifying grace; going on to **perfection**; faith and love in practice; "to reform the nation, particularly the church and to spread scriptural holiness over the land."
18th century: large public "threshing" meetings with vivid, impassioned missionary preaching designed to convert sinners. 19th century: corporately in meetings of worship "waiting on the Lord" in silence with exhortation for **discerning** prayer directly inspired by the Spirit of Christ; private or family meditative reading of scripture.	Personal private prayer and public worship; family devotions; prayer in scripture, songs, and hymns of adoration; both extemporaneous prayer and published prayer forms; balance avoiding both enthusiasm and formalism; attendance at **love feasts**, annual services of **covenant** renewal, and watch nights.
Inward light of Christ; spiritual baptism and spiritual; Christ works directly and inwardly in the soul, convicts of sin, empowers change of life, teaches and guides inwardly; spiritual baptism and spiritual communion; Christ leads/guides community into unity of action; community tests individual leadings.	A "felt" experience of being made holy lived out in acts of mercy; living the "means of grace": prayer, searching the scriptures, **Holy Communion, fasting**, and Christian conference; doctrinal standards including General Rules and forty-four of John Wesley's sermons; "scripture way of salvation."
Humble; relational and equitable; anguished search for truth, holiness, and the conviction of sin toward a new heart, new thoughts, and new obedience. Ministers gifted by God, but work with elders on discernment; **clearness committees**.	Classes and bands as **covenant groups** for community, advice, guidance, and mutual accountability under leadership of a class leader. Christian perfection sustained in disciplined obedience.

SPIRITUAL CLASSICS
Cross-reference from title to author

Abandonment to Divine Providence	Jean-Pierre de **Caussade**
Alive in Christ	Maxie **Dunnam**
Ascent of Mount Carmel, The	**John** of the Cross
Beginning to Pray	Anthony **Bloom**
Celebration of Discipline	Richard **Foster**
Centering Prayer	M. Basil **Pennington**
Christian Mysticism Today	William **Johnston**
Christian Perfection	François **Fenelon**
Christian's Secret of a Happy Life, The	Hannah Whitall **Smith**
Cloud of Unknowing, The	Anonymous
Confessions	**Augustine** of Hippo
Cost of Discipleship, The	Dietrich **Bonhoeffer**
Dark Night of the Soul, The	**John** of the Cross
Dimensions of Prayer	Douglas **Steere**
Divine Milieu, The	Pierre **Teilhard de Chardin**
Experiencing the Depths of Jesus Christ	Jeanne **Guyon**
Flowing Light of the Godhead, The	**Mechthild** of Magdeburg
Hind's Feet in High Places	Hannah **Hurnard**
Imitation of Christ	**Thomas** à Kempis
Interior Castle, The	**Teresa** of Ávila
Introduction to the Devout Life	**Francis** de Sales
Ladder of Divine Ascent, The	John **Climacus**
Ladder of Monks, The	**Guigo II**
Ladder of Perfection, The	Walter **Hilton**
Life Together	Dietrich **Bonhoeffer**
Markings	Dag **Hammarskjöld**
Meditations of the Heart	Howard **Thurman**
Mystical Theology	**Pseudo-Dionysius**
New Seeds of Contemplation	Thomas **Merton**
On Loving God	**Bernard** of Clairvaux
Open Mind, Open Heart	Thomas **Keating**
Other Side of Silence, The	Morton **Kelsey**
Philokalia, The	**Nicodemus** of the Holy Mountain
Pilgrim's Progress, The	John **Bunyan**
Pilgrim's Regress, The	C. S. **Lewis**

Plain Account of Christian Perfection, A	John **Wesley**
Practical Mysticism	Evelyn **Underhill**
Practical Piety	Hannah **More**
Practice of the Presence of God, The	Br. **Lawrence** of the Resurrection
Private House of Prayer, A	Leslie D. **Weatherhead**
Purity of Heart	Søren **Kierkegaard**
Pursuit of God, The	A. W. **Tozer**
Religious Affections, The	Jonathan **Edwards**
Rule and Exercises of Holy Dying, The	Jeremy **Taylor**
Saints' Everlasting Rest, The	Richard **Baxter**
Serious Call to a Devout and Holy Life, A	William **Law**
Seven Storey Mountain, The	Thomas **Merton**
Showings	**Julian** of Norwich
Spirit of the Disciplines	Dallas **Willard**
Spiritual Exercises	**Ignatius** of Loyola
Spiritual Friend	Tilden **Edwards**
Spiritual Friendship	**Aelred** of Rievaulx
Spiritual Life, The	Evelyn **Underhill**
Story of a Soul, The	**Thérèse** of Lisieux
Surprised by Joy	C. S. **Lewis**
Testament of Devotion, A	Thomas **Kelly**
Theologia Germanica	Anonymous
Transcendent Self, The	Adrian **van Kaam**
Way of a Pilgrim, The	Anonymous
Way of Holiness	Phoebe **Palmer**
Way of Perfection, The	**Teresa** of Ávila
Way to Christ, The	Jacob **Boehme**
Will of God, The	Leslie D. **Weatherhead**
Wounded Healer, The	Henri J. M. **Nouwen**

UPPER ROOM SPIRITUAL CLASSICS, SERIES 1

For those of us eager to deepen our spiritual lives through the great devotional writings of the church, Upper Room Books® presents reader-friendly translations of five writers — John Wesley, Thomas Kelly, John Cassian, Teresa of Avila, and Augustine. ISBN# 0-8358-0832-7 (5 titles in slipcase)

TITLES IN SERIES 1:

A Longing for Holiness • *Selected Writings of John Wesley*
John Wesley was the hugely influential eighteenth-century preacher, writer, and founder of Methodism. This booklet includes selections from Wesley's journals, sermons, and books, giving a clear picture of Wesley and the movement he helped create. ISBN# 0-8358-0827-0

The Soul's Passion for God • *Selected Writings of Teresa of Avila*
Teresa of Avila was a sixteenth-century Spanish nun, reformer, and celebrated spiritual writer. Included are excerpts from her three most influential works. ISBN# 0-8358-0828-9

The Sanctuary of the Soul • *Selected Writings of Thomas Kelly*
Thomas Kelly was a twentieth-century Quaker and philosopher whom Richard Foster calls "a giant soul." Kelly is best known for his *Testament of Devotion*. Included are excerpts from Kelly's other writings that have not been widely available until now. ISBN# 0-8358-0829-7

Hungering for God • *Selected Writings of Augustine*
Augustine was the fourth-century spiritual leader from North Africa who had a vast impact on the Christian church and whose *Confessions* has been noted as one of Western civilization's most influential books. This volume also contains other important writings of Augustine. ISBN# 0-8358-0830-0

Making Life a Prayer • *Selected Writings of John Cassian*
John Cassian was a monk from North Africa and a contemporary of Augustine, whose writings on prayer and spiritual living speak as practically and profoundly in today's age as they did in the fourth century when he wrote them. ISBN# 0-8358-0831-9

UPPER ROOM SPIRITUAL CLASSICS, SERIES 2

With this second set of devotional classics, Upper Room Books® offers selections from more great Christian writers—Francis and Clare of Assisi, Julian of Norwich, Evelyn Underhill, Toyohiko Kagawa, and Thomas à Kempis.   ISBN# 0-8358-0853-X   (5 titles in slipcase)

TITLES IN SERIES 2:

Encounter with God's Love • *Selected Writings of Julian of Norwich*
Revealing insights from a lifetime of prayer, the writings of this late fourteenth-century nun and mystic offer some of the most moving discussions of God's love in all of Christian literature. ISBN# 0-8358-0833-5

The Riches of Simplicity • *Selected Writings of Francis and Clare*
Perhaps no one has captivated the hearts of such a wide spectrum of Christians as Francis and Clare. These thirteenth-century saints are depicted through biographical vignettes as well as in prayers, letters, and other writings.   ISBN# 0-8358-0834-3

A Pattern for Life •
Selected Writings of Thomas à Kempis
From the time of its appearance around 1420, à Kempis' *The Imitation of Christ* has perhaps had more influence on Christian spirituality than any other book except the Bible.   ISBN# 0-8358-0835-1

The Soul's Delight •
Selected Writings of Evelyn Underhill
This twentieth-century British writer and retreat leader has been widely known for her compelling exploration of the spiritual life. Her work introduced many readers to the spiritual classics and offered profoundly simple advice on opening oneself to God.
ISBN# 0-8358-0837-8

Living Out Christ's Love •
Selected Writings of Toyohiko Kagawa
Often cited as a model of how to blend prayer, compassion, and social action, Kagawa worked in the period between the two world wars to establish settlement houses, labor unions, and peasant unions and carry on evangelistic campaigns. His writings include autobiographical reflections and thoughts about the Lord's Prayer.
ISBN# 0-8358-0836-X

UPPER ROOM SPIRITUAL CLASSICS, SERIES 3

This third set of devotional classics includes wisdom from spiritual leaders who strove to devote their lives totally to the will of God: John of the Cross, the Desert Mothers and Fathers, John Law, John Woolman, and Catherine of Siena.   ISBN# 0-8358-0905-6   (5 titles in slipcase)

TITLES IN SERIES 3:

Loving God Through the Darkness • *Selected Writings of John of the Cross*
Loving God alone requires detachment from other things, a process of moving through the "dark night of the soul." John of the Cross elegantly expresses this process of seeking divine union in his poems and books on the spiritual life. A Carmelite monk and a close associate of Teresa of Avila, John lived during the religious turmoil of sixteenth-century Spain. ISBN# 0-8358-0904-8

Seeking a Purer Christian Life • *The Desert Mothers and Fathers*
In the third, fourth, and fifth centuries, thousands of men and women moved into the deserts of Egypt and Syria to seek a simple way of living. Their sayings about prayer, spiritual disciplines, and living in community spread throughout the Christian world and became the foundation of monasticism. ISBN# 0-8358-0902-1

Total Devotion to God •
Selected Writings of William Law
In these selections from his book *A Serious Call to a Devout and Holy Life*, Law calls for a total devotion to God. Responding to the religious moderation of 18th-century England, Law writes that the truly devout must live their lives in utter accordance with the will of God. ISBN# 0-8358-0901-3

Walking Humbly with God •
Selected Writings of John Woolman
Woolman's journal reveals the development of a Christian soul seeking to know and do God's will in all things. A devout Quaker, Woolman lived simply, in solidarity with the poor and oppressed. He traveled throughout the American colonies in the mid-1700s, urging other Quakers to free their slaves and to stand with him against slavery.
ISBN# 0-8358-0900-5

A Life of Total Prayer •
Selected Writings of Catherine of Siena
In seeking to submit her will completely to God, Catherine of Siena practiced extreme self-sacrifice fueled by prayer so intense that she often lost awareness of the world around her. She expressed these experiences in letters and writings that address the turbulent times of fourteenth-century Italy in which she lived.   ISBN# 0-8358-0903-X